WAR BY CONTRACT

War by Contract

Human Rights, Humanitarian Law, and Private Contractors

Edited by
FRANCESCO FRANCIONI
AND NATALINO RONZITTI

OXFORD
UNIVERSITY PRESS

Great Clarendon Street, Oxford OX2 6DP

Oxford University Press is a department of the University of Oxford.
It furthers the University's objective of excellence in research, scholarship,
and education by publishing worldwide in

Oxford New York

Auckland Cape Town Dar es Salaam Hong Kong Karachi
Kuala Lumpur Madrid Melbourne Mexico City Nairobi
New Delhi Shanghai Taipei Toronto

With offices in

Argentina Austria Brazil Chile Czech Republic France Greece
Guatemala Hungary Italy Japan Poland Portugal Singapore
South Korea Switzerland Thailand Turkey Ukraine Vietnam

Oxford is a registered trade mark of Oxford University Press
in the UK and in certain other countries

Published in the United States
by Oxford University Press Inc., New York

© The several contributors

The moral rights of the author have been asserted
Database right Oxford University Press (maker)

First published 2011

All rights reserved. No part of this publication may be reproduced,
stored in a retrieval system, or transmitted, in any form or by any means,
without the prior permission in writing of Oxford University Press,
or as expressly permitted by law, or under terms agreed with the appropriate
reprographics rights organization. Enquiries concerning reproduction
outside the scope of the above should be sent to the Rights Department,
Oxford University Press, at the address above

You must not circulate this book in any other binding or cover
and you must impose the same condition on any acquirer

British Library Cataloguing in Publication Data
Data available

Library of Congress Control Number: 2010941694

Typeset by SPI Publisher Services, Pondicherry, India
Printed in Great Britain
on acid-free paper by
CPI Antony Rowe, Chippenham and Eastbourne

ISBN 978–0–19–960455–5

3 5 7 9 10 8 6 4 2

Acknowledgements

We are grateful to the many people who contributed with their ideas, time and support to bringing this volume into being.

First of all, we would like to thank the European Commission for funding the PRIV-WAR Project under the 7th Framework Programme (Socio-economics, Sciences and Humanities). The research undertaken in the context of this project forms the basis of this book. In particular, we thank Jean-Michel Baer and Peteris Zilgalvis in the Directorate General for Research for their valuable support. Our special thanks go to Angela Liberatore, also at the DG for Research, for her constructive guidance and her continual interest in the development of our work.

Our warmest thanks go to each of the authors who contributed to this volume. We are also grateful to our colleagues Nigel White, Ineta Ziemele, Thilo Marauhn and Eric Myjer for hosting workshops that greatly benefited our work and the preparation of this volume. Many thanks are also due to Carsten Hoppe for his valuable spport in the initial phase of the project and Mirko Sossai for his substantial contribution to the implementation of the research project and to the preparation of this volume. Ottavio Quirico deserves our thanks for preparing the bibliography, tables, and index of this volume.

We are especially grateful to Christine Bakker at the EUI for her invaluable contribution to the coordination of the PRIV-WAR project and to the editing process of this volume.

We thank the Academy of European Law of the EUI in Florence for hosting the PRIV-WAR project, and in particular Anny Bremner for her precious support to the project and its publications. Serena Scarselli at the EUI provided highly proficient administrative guidance and support.

Finally, we are grateful to Oxford University Press, in particular to John Louth for supporting the publication of this volume, and to Merel Alstein, Ela Kotkowska, Lucy Copp and Jeremy Langworthy for their efficient, professional and friendly approach to the entire publication process.

Contents

Table of Cases   x
Table of Treaties, Legislation, and Other International Instruments   xviii
Table of Reports and Other Documents   xxix
List of Abbreviations   xxxv
List of Contributors   xli

Introduction   1
Francesco Francioni and Natalino Ronzitti

I. SECURITY AND POLICY PERSPECTIVES

1. Policy Prospects for Regulating Private Military and Security Companies   11
Eugenio Cusumano

2. The Use of Private Contractors in the Fight against Piracy: Policy Options   37
Natalino Ronzitti

II. HUMAN RIGHTS

3. The Role of Human Rights in the Regulation of Private Military and Security Companies   55
Federico Lenzerini and Francesco Francioni

4. The Impact of the EU Human Rights System on Operations of Private Military and Security Companies   80
Ieva Kalnina and Ugis Zeltins

5. The Role of the Home State in Ensuring Compliance with Human Rights by Private Military Contractors   93
Francesco Francioni

6. Positive Human Rights Obligations of the Hiring State in Connection with the Provision of 'Coercive Services' by a Private Military or Security Company   111
Carsten Hoppe

7. Duties to Prevent, Investigate, and Redress Human Rights Violations by Private Military and Security Companies: The Role of the Host State   130
Christine Bakker

8. Adjudicating Human Rights Violations Committed by Private
   Contractors in Conflict Situations before the European Court
   of Human Rights 149
   Giulia Pinzauti

9. The Right to Life and Self-defence of Private Military and Security
   Contractors in Armed Conflict 171
   Guido den Dekker and Eric PJ Myjer

III. INTERNATIONAL HUMANITARIAN LAW

10. Status of Private Military and Security Company Personnel
    in the Law of International Armed Conflict 197
    Mirko Sossai

11. Private Military and Security Contractors as 'Persons who
    Accompany the Armed Forces' 218
    Giulio Bartolini

12. Private Military and Security Companies in Non-international
    Armed Conflicts: *Ius ad Bellum* and *Ius in Bello* Issues 235
    Luisa Vierucci

13. Children's Rights: The Potential Impact of Private Military
    and Security Companies 262
    Christine Bakker and Susanna Greijer

14. Women and Private Military and Security Companies 280
    Ana Filipa Vrdoljak

15. Private Military and Security Companies and the EU's Crisis
    Management: Perspectives under Human Rights and International
    Humanitarian Law 299
    Valentina Falco

16. Old Concepts and New Challenges: Are Private Contractors the
    Mercenaries of the Twenty-first Century? 321
    Marina Mancini, Faustin Z Ntoubandi, and Thilo Marauhn

IV. ACCOUNTABILITY AND RESPONSIBILITY OF PRIVATE CONTRACTORS

17. The Role of International Regulatory Initiatives on Business
    and Human Rights for Holding Private Military and Security
    Contractors to Account 343
    Sorcha MacLeod

18. Codes of Conduct for Private Military and Security Companies:
    The State of Self-regulation in the Industry 362
    Carsten Hoppe and Ottavio Quirico

19. Institutional Responsibility for Private Military and Security
    Companies   381
    Nigel D White

20. State Responsibility for Conduct of Private Military and Security
    Companies Violating *Ius ad Bellum*   396
    Charlotte Beaucillon, Julian Fernandez, and Hélène Raspail

V. CRIMINAL AND CIVIL LIABILITY OF PRIVATE MILITARY AND SECURITY COMPANIES AND THEIR EMPLOYEES

21. The Criminal Responsibility of Private Military and Security Company
    Personnel under International Humanitarian Law   423
    Ottavio Quirico

22. Immunity for Private Military Contractors: Legal Hurdles or
    Political Snags?   448
    Micaela Frulli

23. Liability in Tort of Private Military and Security Companies:
    Jurisdictional Issues and Applicable Law   470
    Andrea Atteritano

Bibliography   490
Index   507

Table of Cases

INTERNATIONAL

Permanent Court of Arbitration
Island of Palmas (United States of America v. Netherlands) 04/04/1928 409

Permanent Court of International Justice
Certain German Interests in Polish Upper Silesia (Germany v. Poland) (X:1) 25/06/1926 404
Exchange of Greek and Turkish Populations (VI:1) 21/02/1925 414
Factory at Chorzów (Germany v. Poland) (XIV:1) 26/07/1927 144–145
SS Lotus (France v. Turkey) (XII:2) 07/09/1927 386

International Court of Justice
*Application of the Convention on the Prevention and Punishment of the Crime of
    Genocide* (Bosnia and Herzegovina v. Serbia and Montenegro) 26/02/2007 .... 145, 389, 406
Armed Activities on the Territory of the Congo (Democratic Republic of the Congo v.
    Uganda) 19/12/2005 .... 147, 174, 185, 257, 406, 409
Arrest Warrant of 11 April 2000 (Democratic Republic of the Congo v. Belgium)
    14/02/2002 418
Barcelona Traction, Light and Power Co Ltd. (Belgium v. Spain) 05/02/1970 96
Case of the Monetary Gold Removed from Rome in 1943 (Italy v. France,
    United Kingdom and United States of America) 15/07/1954 168
Corfu Channel (United Kingdom of Great Britain and Northern Ireland v.
    Albania) 25/03/1948 and 09/04/1949 .... 104, 390, 409, 411-412
*Difference Relating to Immunity from Legal Process of a Special Rapporteur of the
    Commission on Human Rights* 29/04/1999 385
East Timor (Portugal v. Australia) 30/07/1995 .... 168, 243
Elettronica Sicula SpA (ELSI) (US v. Italy) 20/07/1989 174
*Interpretation of the Agreement of 25 March 1951 between the
    WHO and Egypt* 20/12/1980 .... 301, 384
Legal Consequences of the Construction of a Wall in the Occupied Palestinian Territory
    09/07/2004 .... 149, 158, 174, 242
Legality of the Threat or Use of Nuclear Weapons 08/07/1996 .... 149, 174, 214, 399
Military and Paramilitary Activities in and against Nicaragua (Nicaragua v.
    United States of America) 27/07/1986 .... 245, 389, 399, 402, 406, 426
Nottebohm (Liechtenstein v. Guatemala) 06/04/1955 96
Reparations for Injuries Suffered in the Service of the United Nations 11/04/1949 384
United States Diplomatic and Consular Staff in Tehran 24/05/1980 .... 404, 409

Arbitral Tribunals
Trail Smelter (USA v. Canada) 11/03/1941 .... 104, 409

Iran-United States Claims Tribunal
Ephanian V. Bank Tejarat (31-157-2) 29/03/1983 96

International Criminal Tribunal for the Former Yugoslavia
Aleksovski (IT-95-14/1) 433, 435
Blaškić (IT-95-14) 210, 436, 438-439, 449
Boskoški et al. (IT-04-82) 10/07/2008 175

Table of Cases

Delalić (IT-96-21) 291, 311, 427-428, 430, 433-434, 436
Erdemovic (IT-96-22) 17/10/1997 183
Furundžija (IT-95-17/1) 99, 291, 415, 428
Hadžihasanović and Kubura (IT-01-47-T) 15/03/2006 432
Halilović (IT-01-48-T) 16/11/2005 432
Kordic et al. (IT-95-14/2-A) 179-180, 204, 433, 435, 438
Krnojelac (IT-97-25-A) 17/09/2003 432
Krstić (IT-98-33) 02/08/2001 .... 291, 428, 439
Kunarac (IT-96-23) 279, 291, 428, 430, 431, 433-435
Kupreskić (IT-95-16-T) 14/01/2000 .... 291, 428
Kvočka et al. (IT-98-30/1) 291, 435
Orić (IT-03-68-T) 183, 432
Radislav Krstić (IT-98-33-T) 02/08/2001 .... 291, 428, 439
Strugar (IT-01-42) 31/01/2005 428
Tadić (IT-94-1) 102-103, 175, 199, 210, 235, 259, 291, 391, 406, 425-428, 430-431

International Criminal Tribunal for Rwanda
Akayesu (ICTR-IT-96-4) 291, 426, 428, 431-432, 438
Gacumbtsi (ICTR-2001-64-T) 291
Kayishema (ICTR-95-1-T) 21/05/1999 430-431
Musema (ICTR-96-13) 27/01/2000 .... 291, 428, 431, 436
Nahimana (ICTR-96-11) 28/11/2007 436
Rutaganda (ICTR-96-3) 06/12/1999 .... 426-428, 438
Semanza (ICTR-97-20-I) 15/06/2003 .... 291, 428

Special Court for Sierra Leone
Brima et al. (SCSL-2004-16-PT) 20/06/2007 268
Charles Taylor (SCSL-03-01-T) 267, 459
Fofana et al. *(Civil Defence Forces)* (SCSL-04-14-T) 02/08/2007 268
Issa Hassan Sesay et al. (SCSL-04-15-T) 25/02/2009 283
Sankoh et al. (SCSL-03-02) 267

International Criminal Court
Prosecutor v. Germain Katanga and Mathieu Ngudjolo Chui (ICC-01/04-01/07) 268
Prosecutor v. Thomas Lubanga Dylo (ICC-01/04-01/06) 29/01/2007 .... 208, 267

United Nations Human Rights Committee
Celeberti de Casariego v. Uruguay (Communication 56/1979) 134
Delgado Paez v. Colombia (Communication 195/1985) 112, 138
Lopez Burgos v. Uruguay (Communications R 12/52 and 52/1979) 121, 134, 158-159
Saldias de Lopez v. Uruguay (Communication 52/1979) 134

United Nations High Commissioner for Refugees
Abduali Ismatovich Kurbanov v. Tajikistan (Communication 1096/2002) 12/11/2003 122
Arhuaco v. Colombia (Communication 612/1995) 29/07/1997 120
Basilio Laureano Atachahua v. Peru (Communication 540/1993) 4/07/1994 .... 118, 120
Carlos Cabal et al. *v. Australia* (Communication 1020/2001) 07/08/2003 120-121
Dermit Barbato v. Uruguay (Communication 84/1981) 21/10/1982 144
José Vicente and Amado et al. *v. Colombia* (Communication 612/1995) 14/06/1994 .... 118, 121
Karina Arutyunyan v. Uzbekistan (Communication 917/2000) 29/03/2004 112-113
Moriana Hernandez Valentini de Bazzano et al. *v. Uruguay*
    (Communication 5/1977) 18/04/1979 144
Muteba v. Zaire (Communication 124/1982) 24/07/1984 144

Pedro Pablo Camargo v. Colombia (Communication 45/1979) 31/03/1982 118
Rodríguez v. Uruguay (Communication 322/1988) 19/07/1994 .... 121, 123-125
S. Jegatheeswara Sarma v. Sri Lanka (Communication 950/2000) 16/07/2003 120
Sergio Euben Lopez Burgos v. Uruguay (Communication R.12/52) 06/07/1979 121
William Eduardo Delgado Páez v. Colombia (Communication 195/1985) 12/07/1990 .... 112, 138

REGIONAL

African Commission on Human and Peoples' Rights

Amnesty International et al. v. Sudan (Communications 48/90, 50/91, 52/91, 89/93) 62
Article 19 v. the State of Eritrea (Communication 275/2003) 71
Civil Liberties Organisation v. Nigeria (Communication 151/96) 69
Democratic Republic of the Congo v. Burundi, Rwanda, and Uganda (Communication 227/99) 75, 152, 158
Forum of Conscience v. Sierra Leone (Communication 223/98) 62
Free Legal Assistance Group et al. v. Zaire (Communications 25/89, 47/90, 56/91, 100/93) 62
Huri-Laws v. Nigeria (Communication 225/98) 69
International Pen and Others (on behalf of Saro-Wiwa) v. Nigeria (Communications 137/94, 139/94, 154/96 and 161/97) 62, 69
Kazeem Aminu v. Nigeria (Communication 205/97) 63
Malawi African Association et al. v. Mauritania 2000
  (Communications 54/91, 61/91, 98/93, 164-196/97 and 210/98) 62, 65
Media Rights Agenda v. Nigeria (Communication 224/98) 69
The Social and Economic Rights Action Center and the Centre for Economic and Social Rights v. Nigeria (Communication 155/96) 59-60, 63, 66, 71–72, 75
Zimbabwean Human Rights NGO Forum v. Zimbabwe (Communication 245/02) 62, 141–142

Inter-American Commission on Human Rights

Armando Alejandro Jr. et al. v. Cuba 29/09/1999 .... 134, 156
Coard et al. v. the United States 29/09/1999 .... 134, 156, 158
Salas et al. v. the United States 14/10/1993 157
Victor Saldaño v. Argentina 11/03/1999 .... 134, 156

Inter-American Court on Human Rights

Bamaca Velasquez 25/11/2000 139
Barrios Altos 14/03/2001 143
Bulacio 18/09/2003 124-125
Caesar 11/03/2005 124-125
Cantoral Benavides 18/08/2000 124-125
Chitay Nech et al. 25/05/2010 .... 143, 145
Durand and Ugarte 16/08/2000 .... 139, 143
Godínez Cruz 20/01/1989 .... 114, 124-125, 139
Haiti 09/03/1982 143
Ituango Massacres 01/07/2006 124-125
Juan Humberto Sánchez 07/06/2003 .... 114, 124-125
La Rochela Massacre 11/05/2007 124
'Las Dos Erres' Massacre 04/11/2009 .... 143, 145
Las Palmeras 04/02/2000 151
Manuel Cepeda-Vargas 26/05/2010 .... 143, 145
Mapiripán Massacre 15/09/2005 123
Mayagna (Sumo) Awas Tingni Community 31/10/2001 73
Miguel Castro-Castro Prison 25/11/2006 143
Neira Alegría 19/01/1995 125

Paniagua Morales et al. 08/03/1998 .... 124, 139, 143, 164
Pueblo Bello Massacre 31/01/2006 .... 59, 114, 139, 146
Sawhoyamaxa Indigenous Community 29/03/2006 124–125
Servellón-García 21/09/2006 124
Suarez Rosero 12/11/1997 ....139, 143
Valle Jaramillo 27/11/2008 ....114, 139
Velasquez-Rodriguez 29/07/1988 ....58, 99, 113,-114, 139, 143, 145, 185
Villagran Morales et al. 19/11/1999 ....139, 143

EU Court of First Instance

Kadi v. Council of the European Union and Commission of the European Communities (T–315/01) 21/09/2005 87
Yusuf and Al Barakaat International Foundation v. Council of the European Union and Commission of the European Communities (T-306/01) 21/09/2005 87

European Court of Justice

A. Racke GmbH & Co. v. Hauptzollamt Mainz (C–162/96) 16/06/1998 301
Accession by the Communities to the Convention for the Protection of Human Rights and Fundamental Freedoms (Opinion 2/94) 28/03/1996 81
Anklagemyndigheden v. Peter Michael Poulsen and Diva Navigation Corp.
    (C-286/90) 24/11/1992 301
Carpenter v. Secretary of State for the Home Department (C-60/00) 11/07/2002 84
Comet v. Produktschap voor Siergewassen (45/76) 16/12/1976 91
Commission v. Council (C-176/03) 13/09/2005 91
Commission v. Council (C-440/05) 23/10/2007 91
Commission v. France (7/71) 14/12/1971 91
Criminal Proceedings against Maria Pupino (C-105/03) 16/06/2005 ....84, 301
Elliniki Radiophonia Tiléorassi et al. v. Dimotiki Etairia Pliroforissis et al.
    (C-260/89) 18/06/1991 83
Emesa Sugar (Free Zone) NV v. Aruba (C-17/98) 08/02/2000 89
Erich Stauder v. City of Ulm (29/69) 12/11/1969 81
Eugen Schmidberger, Internationale Transporte und Planzüge v. Republik Österreich
    (C-112/00) 12/06/2003 90
Fiona Shevill et al. *v. Presse Alliance SA* (C-68/93) 07/03/1995 473
Friedrich Kremzow v. Republik Österreich (C-299/95) 29/05/1997 83
International Fruit Company v. Produktschap voor Groenten en Fruit
    (Joined Cases 21-24/72) 12/12/1972 301
*International Transport Workers' Federation, Finnish Seamen's Union v. Viking Line
    ABP, OÜ Viking Laine Eesti* (C-438/05) 11/12/2007 83
*Internationale Handelsgesellschaft mbH v. Einfuhrund Vorratstelle für Getreide
    und Futtermittel* (11/70) 17/12/1970 81
J. Nold, Kohlen und Baustoffgroßhandlung v. Commission of the European Communities
    (4/73) 14/05/1974 ....81, 301
Kadi and Al Barakaat International Foundation v. Council and Commission
    (Joined cases C-402/05 P and C-415/05 P) 03/09/2008 ....302, 313, 394
Kamer van Koophandel en Fabrieken voor Amsterdam v. Inspire Art Ltd
    (C-167/01) 30/09/2003 91
Lechouritou et al. v. Dimosio tis Omospondiakis Dimokratias tis Germanias
    (C-292/05) 15/02/2007 473-475
Mangold v. Rüdiger Helm (C-144/04) 22/10/2005 84
Marinari v. Lloyds Bank plc and Zubaidi Trading Co. (C-364/93) 19/09/1995 473
Mrs Sirdar v. Army Board and SofS for Defence (C-273/97) 26/10/1999 286
Opel Austria v. Council (T-115/94) 22/01/1997 301

Roland Rutili v. Ministre de l'intérieur (36/75) 28/10/1975 83
Roquette Frères SA v. Directeur general de la concurrence, de la consommation et de la repression des frauds (C-94/00) 22/10/2002 302
Sonntag v. Waidmann (C-172/91) 21/04/1993 475
Sopropé – Organizações de Calçado Lda v. Fazenda Pública (C-349/07) 18/12/2008 313
The Queen on the Application of International Association of Independent Tanker Owners (Intertanko) et al. v. Secretary of State for Transport (C-308/06) 03/06/2008 .... 301, 309
Tokai Carbon et al. (joined cases T-236/01, T-239/01, T-244/01 to T-246/01, T-251/01 and T-252/01) 89
Unión de Pequeños Agricultores v. Council of the European Union (C-50/00 P) 25/07/2002 91
Von Colson and Kamann v. Land Nordrhein-Westfalen (14/83) 10/04/1984 91
Zuid-Chemie v. Philippo's Mineralenfabriek (C-189/08) 04/04/2008 473

European Commission of Human Rights
Freda v. Italy (dec.) (8916/80) 07/101980 158-161
Hess v. the United Kingdom (6231/73) 28/05/1975 133
Illich Sanchez Ramirez v. France (dec.) (28789/95) 24/06/1996 158-161
Loizidou v. Turkey (15318/89) 23/03/1995 133
W v. Denmark (17392/90) 14/10/1992 133
X v. Federal Republic of Germany (1611/62) 25/09/1965 133

European Court of Human Rights
A v. the United Kingdom (25599/94) 23/09/1998 64
A. et al. v. the United Kingdom (3455/05) 19/02/2009 136
Akkoç v. Turkey (22947/93 and 22948/93) 10/10/2000 .... 58, 85, 116
Akpinar and Altun v. Turkey (56760/00) 27/02/2007 126
Aksoy v. Turkey (21987/93) 18/12/1996 127
Al-Sadoon v. the United Kingdom (61498/ 08) 02/03/2010 105
Al-Skeini et al. v. the United Kingdom (55721/07) 134-135, 151, 156, 159, 161
Andreou v. Turkey (45653/99) 27/10/2009 157
Andronicou and Constantinou v. Cyprus (25052/94) 09/10/1997 .... 115-116, 140, 185
Angelova and Iliev v. Bulgaria (55523/00) 26/07/2007 126
Assenov et al. v. Bulgaria (24760/94) 28/10/1998 .... 115, 127, 143
Banković et al. v. Belgium and 16 Other Contracting States (52207/99) 58, 85-86, 133-134, 151, 156-162, 168, 170, 394
Bazorkina v. Russia (69481/01) 27/07/2006 126-128
Behrami and Behrami v. France (71412/01) 02/05/2007 .... 87-88, 151, 160, 168-169, 388, 391-392, 394
Ben el Mahi et al. v. Denmark (5853/06) 11/12/2006 133
Bosphorus Airways v. Ireland (45036/9) 07/07/2005 88
Budayeva et al. v. Russia (15339/02, 11673/02, 15343/02, 20058/02, 21166/02) 20/03/2008 ... 185
Buldan v. Turkey (28298/95) 20/04/2004 143
Chahal v. the United Kingdom (22414/93) 15/11/1996 143
Cooperatieve Producentenorganisatie Van de Nederlandse Kokkelvisserij U.A. v. the Netherlands (13645/05) 21/01/2009 89
Cyprus v. Turkey (25781/94) 10/05/2001 .... 127, 133, 158
Cyprus v. Turkey (6780/74, 6950/75) 26/05/1975 .... 86, 133
Demades v. Turkey (16219/90) 31/07/2003 133
Drozd and Janousek v. France and Spain (12747/87) 26/06/1992 86
Ergi v. Turkey (23818/94) 28/07/1998 62
Georgia v. the Russian Federation (38263/08) 151
Gezici v. Turkey (34594/97) 17/03/2005 117
Gillan and Quinton v. the United Kingdom (4158/05) 12/01/2010 72

Guerra et al. *v. Italy* (14967/89) 19/02/1998 71
Hasan Ilhan v. Turkey (22494/93) 09/10/2004 143
Ilascu et al. *v. Moldova and Russia* (48787/99) 08/07/2004 .... 103, 158, 163–164, 257
Ireland v. the United Kingdom (5310/71) 18/01/1987 88
Isaak et al. *v. Turkey* (44587/98) 133, 153
Isayeva, Yusupova and Bazayeva v. Russia (5747/00, 5748/00, 57949/00) 24/02/2004 143
Islamic Republic of Iran Shipping Lines v. Turkey (40998/98) 13/12/2007 164
Issa et al. *v. Turkey* (31821/96) 16/10/2004 .... 58, 86, 133, 159
Kalashnikov v. Russia (47095/99) 15/07/2002 117
Kallis and Androulla Panayi v. Turkey (45388/99) 29/10/2009 143
Kaya v. Turkey (22535/93) 28/03/2000 .... 85, 116, 142–143, 145, 412
Kaya v. Turkey (158/1996/777/978) 19/02/1998 126–127
K-H.W. v. Germany (37201/97) 22/03/2001 174
Khashiyev and Akayeva v. Russia (57942/00, 57945/00) 24/02/2005 143
Kiliç v. Turkey (22492/93) 28/03/2000 .... 58, 116
Klass et al. *v. Germany* (5029/71) 06/09/1978 143
Kontrová v. Slovakia (7510/04) 31/05/2007 .... 58, 85
Kress v. France (39594/98) 07/06/2001 89
Leander v. Sweden (9248/81) 26/03/1987 143
Loizidou v. Turkey (15318/89) 18/12/1996 158
M.C. v. Bulgaria (39272/98) 04/12/2003 72
Mastromatteo v. Italy (37703/97) 24/10/2002 116
McCann v. the United Kingdom (18984/91) 27/09/1995 .... 115–116, 126, 140, 183, 185–186, 214
McKerr v. the United Kingdom (28883/95) 04/05/2001 127
McShane v. the United Kingdom (43290/98) 28/05/2002 126
Mikheyev v. Russia (77617/01) 26/01/2006 .... 127-128, 143
Mubilanzila Mayeka and Kaniki Mitunga v. Belgium (13178/03) 12/10/2006 71
Üçalan v. Turkey (46221/99) 12/03/2003 158
Osman v. the United Kingdom (23452/94) 28/10/1998 .... 57-58, 85, 116, 141, 154, 185
Osmanoğlu v. Turkey (48804/99) 24/01/2008 .... 57, 63, 127
Pad et al. *v. Turkey* (60167/00) 28/06/2007 .... 133, 160
Papamichalopoulos et al. *v. Greece* (14556/89) 31/10/1995 145
Rantsev v. Cyprus and Russia (25965/04) 07/01/2010 .... 70, 77
Saramati v. France, Germany and Norway (78166/01) 02/05/2007 ... 87-88, 151, 160, 168-169, 388
Satabeyeva v. Russia (21486/06) 29/10/2009 143
Silver et al. *v. United Kingdom* (5947/72, 6205/73, 7052/75, 7061/75, 7107/75, 7113/75, 7136/75)
    25/03/1983 143
Solomou et al. *v. Turkey* (36832/97) 24/06/2008 .... 154, 157
Stephens v. Malta (no. 1) (11956/07) 14/09/2009 133
Tekin v. Turkey (52/1997/836/1042) 09/06/1998 .... 127, 143
Valašinas v. Lithuania (44558/98) 24/07/2001 117
Varnava et al. *v. Turkey* (16064/90, 16065/90, 16066/90, 16068/90, 16069/90, 16070/90, 16071/
    90, 16072/90, 16073/90) 18/09/ 2009 .... 57, 63, 65
W. v. United Kingdom (9348/81) 116
Women on Waves et al. *v. Portugal* (App. No. 31276/05) 03/02/2009 160
X and Y v. the Netherlands (8978/80) 26/03/1985 .... 115, 140
Xhavara et al. *v. Italy and Albania* (39473/98) 11/01/2001 161
Yasa v. Turkey (22495/93) 02/09/1998 86

NATIONAL

Post-World War II Military Tribunals

British Military Court for the Trial of War Criminals, Essen, *Erich Heyer and Six Others (The Essen Lynching Case)*, 18-19 and 21-22 December 1945 430

British Military Court, Hamburg, *Bruno Tesch and Two Others (Zyklon B Case)*,
1-8 March 1946...430
US Nuremberg Military Tribunal I, *Brandt*, 19-20 August 1947, Control Council Law No 10...433
US Nuremberg Military Tribunal II, *Pohl* et al., 03/11/1947, Control Council Law No 10 433
US Nuremberg Military Tribunal VI, *Farben*, 29-30 July 1948, Control Council Law No 10.....433
US Military Commission, *Alfons Klein and Six Others (The Hadamar Trial)*,
8-15 October 1945...430

Canada
Court of Appeal for Ontario, *Jaffe v. Miller*, 13 OR (3d) 745 450
Court Martial Appeal Court of Canada, *The Queen* v. *Private D.J. Brocklebank* (CMAC.383) 02/04/
1996..440

Germany
Federal Supreme Court of Germany (2008/23) 06/11/2007 473

Israel
High Court of Justice (Israel), *The Public Committee against Torture in Israel* et al. *v. the
Government of Israel* et al. (769/02) 13/12/2006..222

Italy
Corte di cassazione, *Rissmann* 29/02/1972 450
Corte di cassazione (Italy), Sez. Un., *Federal Republic of Germany v. Regional
Administration of Vojotia* (14199) 06-29 May 2000..476
Genoa Tribunal, *Rissmann* 06/05/1970..450

New Zealand
Supreme Court of New Zealand, *L. v. The Crown* 12/09/1977..450

Norway
OECD NCP, *Forum for Environment and Development v. Aker Kværner ASA* 2005......................357

UK
House of Lords, *Al-Skeini* et al. *v. Secretary of State for Defence*
(2007 UKL 26) 13/06/2007 134-135

USA
Court of Appeals (Ninth Circuit), *Chiudian v. the Philippine National Bank and Daza*
(912 F 2d 1095) 1990..450
— (Second Circuit), *Kyobel v. Royal Dutch Shell* 17/09/2010
— *Kadic v. Karadzic* (70 F.3d 232) 1995..479, 481
— *Abdullahi v. Pfizer* 77 (02-9223(L), 02-9303 (XAP)) 2003 478
— (Fourth Circuit), *Galustian v. Peter* (2010 WL 155456) 2010 482
— (Eleventh Circuit), *McMahon v. Presidential Airways, Inc.* (502 F.3d 1331) 2007 467
— (Columbia), *Saleh et al. v. Titan Corp.* (580 F.3d 1) 2009 ....469, 479, 481
— (Louisiana), *Alomang v. Freeport-McMoran* (811 So 2d 98) 2002..478
Court of Military Appeals, *Calley* (22 U.S.C.M.A. 534) 21/12/1973 ....437, 440
District Court (Pennsylvania Western), *Abu-Zeineh v. Federal Laboratories Inc.* (Civ 91-2148)
1994..478
— (California), *Doe v. Unocal Corp.* (963 F.Supp.880) 1997...478
— (Columbia), *Tel-Oren v. Lybia* (726 F.2d 774) 1984 480
— *Doe v. Exxon Mobil Corp.* (393 F. Supp. 2d 20) 2005..478
— *Ibrahim v. Titan Corp.* (391 F.Supp.2d 10) 2005 ....467, 479, 481
— *USA/Slaught* et al. (08-0360(RMU))..442, 444

Table of Cases

— (Eastern District of New York), *Abrams v. Société Nationale des Chemins de fer français* (175 F Supp 2d 423) 2001 478
— Ohio, *Al Shimari/Dugan, CACI International Inc., CACI Premier Technology Inc., L-3 Services Inc.* (08-cv-637) 30/06/2008 442
— (Southern District of New York), *Aguinda v. Texaco* (945 FSupp 625) 1996 (142 FSupp2d 534) 2001 (303 F 3d 470) 2002 478
— *Abdullahi v. Pfizer* (No 01 Civ 8118) 2002 478
District Court of Virginia, *Al Shimari et al./CACI International Inc., CACI Premier Technology Inc.* (08-cv-0827) 15/09/2008 and 18/03/2009 .... 442-443, 466
House of Representatives – Committee on Oversight and Government Reform, Hearing, *Blackwater* (110th Congress, 1st Session, 110-89) 02/10/2007 337
Supreme Court, *International Shoe Co. v. State of Washington* (326 US 310) 1945 .... 472, 479
— In re *Yamashita* (327 US 1) 04/02/1946 432
— *Reid v. Covert* (354 U.S. 1) 1957 458
— *Kinsella v. United States ex rel. Singleton* (361 U.S. 234) 1960 458
— *McElroy v. United States ex rel. Guagliardo* (361 U.S. 281) 1960 458
— *Grisham v. Hagan* (361 U.S. 278) 1960 458
— *Boyle v. United Technologies Corp.* (487 U.S. 500) 1988 .... 465, 483
— *Sosa v. Alvarez-Machain* (542 US 692) 2004 480
— *District of Columbia v. Heller* (128 S.Ct. 2783) 2008 184
— *McDonald v. City of Chicago* (08-1521) 28/06/2010 184

Table of Treaties, Legislation, and Other International Instruments

International Instruments
1856 Paris Declaration Respecting Maritime Law, 16 April 1865 41–42
1874 Project of an International Declaration concerning the Laws and Customs of War, 27 August 1874 219
1899 Hague Conventions, 29 July 1899 1
Convention (II) with Respect to the Laws and Customs of War on Land and its Annex: Regulations concerning the Laws and Customs of War on Land
   Art 13 219
1907 Hague Conventions, 18 October 1907
Convention (IV) Respecting the Laws and Customs of War on Land and its annex: Regulations concerning the Laws and Customs of War on Land
   Art 1 .... 176, 199, 248, 251
   Art 3 248
   Art 13 .... 219, 228
   Art 29(1) 210, 215
   Art 30 215
   Art 43 185
   Art 46 287–288
Convention (V) Respecting the Rights and Duties of Neutral Powers and Persons in Case of War on Land
   Art 4 .... 322, 418
   (1) 322, 418
   Art 5 .... 322, 410
   Art 16 322
   Art 17 322
Convention (VII) Relating to the Conversion of Merchant Ships into War-Ships. The Hague, 18 October 1907
   Art 1 41
1919 Treaty of Versailles, 28 June 1919 .. 287–288
1926 Slavery Convention, 25 September 1926
   Art 1 67
1930 ILO Convention No. 29 concerning Forced or Compulsory Labour, 28 June 1930 67
1945 Charter of the Nuremberg Tribunal, 8 August 1945

   Art 8 437
1945 Control Council Law No10, 20 December 1945
   Art 11(1)(c) 291
1946 Charter of the Tokyo Tribunal, 19 January 1946
   Art 6 437
1948 American Declaration of the Rights and Duties of Man, 2 May 1948 156
1948 Convention on the Prevention and Punishment of the Crime of Genocide 9 December 1948 .... 312, 409
1948 Universal Declaration of Human Rights, 10 December 1948 .... 30, 368
1949 Geneva Conventions, 12 August 1949...368, 425, 428–429, 440–441, 443, 445–447
Common Art 3 .... 175–176, 233, 425–429
Convention (I) for the Amelioration of the Condition of the Wounded and Sick in Armed Forces in the Field
   Art 12 289
   Art 13 175
   Art 49 .... 184, 425, 429
   Art 50 .... 425, 429
Convention (II) for the Amelioration of the Condition of Wounded, Sick and Shipwrecked Members of Armed Forces at Sea
   Art 2 288
   Art 50 .... 184, 425, 429
   Art 51 .... 425, 429
Convention (III) Relative to the Treatment of Prisoners of War
   Art 4 175
   (A) 176
   (A)(1) 221, 249
   (A)(2) 221, 249
   (A)(4) 219–220, 223, 228–230, 232
   Art 16 288
   Art 129 .... 184, 425, 429
   Art 130 .... 425, 429
Annex IV 232
Convention (IV) Relative to the Protection of Civilian Persons in Time of War

Table of Treaties, Legislation, and Other International Instruments xix

Art 4 233
Art 5 323
Art 14 264
Art 15 264
Art 17 264
Art 23(1) 264
Art 27 288
Art 146 .... 184, 425, 429
Art 147 .... 425, 429
1951 Agreement between the Parties to the North Atlantic Treaty Regarding the Status of their Forces, 19 June 1951 452
1951 Agreement on the Status of the North Atlantic Treaty Organization, National Representatives and International Staff, 20 September 1951
Art 18(a) 451
1951 Convention Relating to the Status of Refugees, 28 July 1951 .... 286, 312
1954 Hague Convention on the Protection of Cultural Property, 14 May 1954 314
1954 Agreement between the Government of the French Republic and the United Nations Educational, Scientific and Cultural Organization Regarding the Headquarters of UNESCO and the Privileges and Immunities of the Organization on French Territory, 20 August 1954
Art 22 450
1956 Supplementary Convention on the Abolition of Slavery, the Slave Trade, and Institutions and Practices Similar to Slavery, 30 April 1956
Art 7 67
1958 Convention on the High Seas, 29 April 1958
Art 29 42
1958 Convention on the Territorial Sea and the Contiguous Zone, 29 April 1958 .... 37, 40
Art 8 41
Art 15 39
Art 21 .... 41, 42
1961 Convention on Diplomatic Relations, 18 April 1961 452–453
Art 37(2) 452–453
1963 Convention on Consular Relations, 24 April 1963
Art 43 450
1965 International Convention on the Elimination of All Forms of Racial Discrimination
21 December 1965 67

Art 5 68
(e)(4) 65
1966 International Covenant on Civil and Political Rights, 16 December 1966 ... 112, 128, 130
Art 2(1) 56, 118
Art 2(3) 118
Art 6 .... 118, 173–174
(5) 290
Art 12 .... 64–65, 118
Art 24 263
1966 International Covenant on Economic, Social and Cultural Rights, 16 December 1966
Art 2(1) 56
1967 Protocol Relating to the Status of Refugees, 28 July 1951 286
1968 Brussels Convention on Jurisdiction and the Enforcement of Judgments in Civil and Commercial Matters, 27 September 1968
Art 2 263
1969 American Convention on Human Rights, 22 November 1969 471
1973 International Convention on the Suppression and Punishment of the Crime of Apartheid, 30 November 1973 67
1973 Convention on the Protection and Punishment of Crimes against Internationally Protected Persons, Including Diplomatic Agents, 14 December 1973
Art 3 410
1975 IDI Resolution – The Principle of Non-Intervention in Civil Wars 236, 240
1975 ILO Convention No. 105 concerning the Abolition of Forced Labour, 5 June 1957
1977 Convention for the Elimination of Mercenarism in Africa
3 July 1977 .... 243, 253, 324, 411, 415, 419
Additional Protocol I
Art 47 243
(2) 326
1977 Protocol Additional to the Geneva Conventions of 12 August 1949, and relating to the Protection of Victims of International Armed Conflicts
(Protocol I), 8 June 1977 .. 287–288, 309, 312–314, 328, 368, 425
Art 1
(2) 175
(4) 242, 251
Art 43(4) 232

Art 47 .... 31, 243
  (2) 324
Art 49(1) 177
Art 43 .... 175, 198, 200, 221, 249
  (2) 176
  (3) 248
Art 47 .... 175, 243
Art 50 175
Art 74 288
Art 85 .... 184, 425, 429
1977 Protocol Additional to the Geneva Conventions of 12 August 1949, and relating to the Protection of Victims of Non-International Armed Conflicts (Protocol II), 8 June 1977 .. 175–176, 233, 287–288, 309, 313–314, 328
Art 1
  (1) 248, 425
  (2) 248, 425
Art 3 .... 247, 426–427
Art 4 288
Art 13 175
Art 47 322
  (1) 323
1979 International Convention against the Taking of Hostages, 17 December 1979 40
1979 Convention on the Elimination of All Forms of Discrimination against Women 18 December 1979 .... 287, 294
1981 African Charter on Human and Peoples' Rights, 27 June 1981 .... 57, 130, 156, 174
Art 4 173
Art 20 75
Art 22(2) 76
1982 Convention on the Law of the Sea, 10 December 1982 49
Art 18(2) 48
Art 19(2)(a) 48
Art 21 48
Art 29 41–42
Art 60(2) 49
Art 80 49
Art 98 47
Art 107 41
Art 110 46
  (5) 42
1983 Protocol No 6 to the Convention for the Protection of Human Rights and Fundamental Freedoms concerning the Abolition of the Death Penalty, 28 April 1983 61
1984 Convention against Torture and Other Cruel, Inhuman or Degrading Treatment or Punishment, 10 December 1984 .... 130, 456
Art 2 99
Art 4 99
Art 5(2) 417
1985 Inter-American Convention to Prevent and Punish Torture, 9 December 1985
Art 1 125
Art 6 125
Art 8 125
1988 Convention for the Suppression of Unlawful Acts against the Safety of Maritime Navigation, 10 March 1988 40
1988 Protocol for the Suppression of Unlawful Acts against the Safety of Fixed Platforms on the Continental Shelf, 10 March 1988 .... 40, 49
1988 Lugano Convention on Jurisdiction and the Enforcement of Judgments in Civil and Commercial Matters, 16 September 1988 471
1989 Convention on the Rights of the Child, 20 November 1989 .... 263, 272, 274, 287
Art 1 262–263
Art 3 .... 75, 263
Art 6 263
Art 9 76
Art 11 76
Art 19 76
Art 24 65
Art 32 76
Art 33 76
Art 34 .... 76, 263
Art 35 263
Art 37
  (1) 263
  (1) 263
Art 38
  (2) 76, 263
  (3) 271
1989 International Convention against the Recruitment, Use, Financing and Training of Mercenaries, 4 December 1989 ...... 243, 253, 324, 326
1990 African Charter on the Rights and Welfare of the Child, 11 July 1990 270
Art 22(2) 76
1991 Torture Victim Protection Act .. 465, 481
1992 Petersberg Declaration of the Western European Union Council of Ministers 19 June 1992 299
1993 Chemical Weapons Convention, 13 January 1993 .... 368, 370

Table of Treaties, Legislation, and Other International Instruments

Art 1(B) 427
1993 Vienna Declaration and Programme of Action on Human Rights, 25 June 1993
  Art 38 294
1993 IDI Resolution on the Activities of National Judges and the International Relations of their State, 7 September 1993 468
1994 OAU Convention on the Prevention and Combating of Terrorism, 15 June 1994 64
1994 Statute of the International Criminal Tribunal for Rwanda, 8 November 1994 264
  Art 4 428
    (g) 289
  Art 6
    (3) 433
    (4) 437
  Art 23 325
1995 UNHCR, Sexual Violence against Refugees: Guidelines on Prevention and Response
  8 March 1995 286
  Section 3.9 284
1995 Beijing Declaration and Platform for Action on Women, 15 September 1995 294
1996 Agreement on Military Exchanges and Visits between the Government of the United States of America and the Government of Mongolia 453
1996 Final Declaration of the International Conference for the Protection of War Victims
1 September 1993 293
1997 Agreement for the Provision of Military Assistance between the Independent State of Papua New Guinea and Sandline International, January 1997 .... 237, 239, 241
1997 International Convention for the Suppression of Terrorist Bombings, 25 November 1997
  Art 15 410
1998 ILO Declaration on Fundamental Principles and Rights at Work, June 1998 368
1998 Rome Statute of the International Criminal Court
17 July 1998 131, 267, 269–271, 384, 427–429, 438, 446–447, 454–455, 461–464
  Art 5 415

    (g) 289
  Art 7 68
    (1)(g) 264, 289
    (3) 289
  Art 8 179
    (1) 429
  Art 8(2)
    (a) 415
      (i) 429
    (b) 415
      (iv) 180
      (xxii) 264
      (xxvi) 270
    (c) 415
      (i) 429
    (e) 415
      (vi) 264
      (vii) 270
    (f) 251
  Art 12 445
    (2) 429
    (3) 429
  Art 13
    (b) 429
    (vii) 438
  Art 16 .... 446, 461–462
  Art 17 .... 429, 445, 460
    (3) 132
  Art 25 (1) 429
  Art 21 179–180
  Art 27 .... 56, 445, 460
  Art 28 433
  Art 31
    (1)(c) 179, 181–182
    (1)(d) 183
  Art 33 437
    (1) 438
    (2) 438
  Art 36
    (8)(a)(iii) 292
  Art 42
    (9) 292
  Art 98 .... 445–446, 464
    (2) 463
1999 Convention No. 182 of the International Labour Organisation (ILO) on the Worst Forms of Child Labour, 1 June 1999 .... 268, 270
1999 Resolution on the Application of International Humanitarian Law and Fundamental Human Rights in Armed Conflicts in which Non-state Entities are Parties, 25 August 1999 .... 251, 256

xxii *Table of Treaties, Legislation, and Other International Instruments*

1999 Optional Protocol to the Convention on the Elimination of All Forms of Discrimination against Women, 6 October 1999... 287
2000 OECD Guidelines on Multinational Enterprises............6, 343, 345, 351–352, 355–360
2000 Optional Protocol to the Convention on the Rights of the Child on the Involvement of Children in Armed Conflict, 25 May 2000..76, 287
 Art 1 76
 Art 2 76
 Art 4 76
2000 Optional Protocol to the Convention on the Rights of the Child on the Sale of Children, Child Prostitution and Child Pornography, 25 May 2000.......76, 287
2000 Windhoek Declaration and Namibia Plan of Action on Mainstreaming Gender Perspective in Multidimensional Peace Support Operations, 31 May 2000...... 295
2002 Agreement regarding the status of United States Military and Civilian Personnel of the U.S. Department of Defense Present in Afghanistan in Connection with Cooperative Efforts in Response to Terrorism, Humanitarian and Civic Assistance, Military Training and Exercises and Other Activities 453
2002 SOFA Concluded between the USA and East Timor 452
2002 Statute of the Special Court for Sierra Leone, 16 January 2002 .... 264, 267
 Art 2(g) 289
 Art 3(e) 289
 Art 14(4) 292
 Art 19 325
2002 American Service-Members' Protection Act, August 2002 .... 445, 455, 461
2002 ICC Elements of Crimes, 9 September 2002
 (8)(2)
  (b)(xxvi) 270
  (e)(vii) 270
2003 Protocol to the African Charter on Human and Peoples' Rights on the Rights of Women in Africa, 11 July 2003 77
2003 Agreement between the European Union and the Republic of Turkey on the Participation of the Republic of Turkey in the European Union-led Forces in the Former Yugoslav Republic of Macedonia, 4 September 2003 313
2003 USA-Colombia Bi-national Agreement regarding the Surrender of Persons to the International Criminal Court, 17 September 2003 255
2003 Agreement between the Member States of the European Union Concerning the Status of Military and Civilian Staff Seconded to the Institutions of the European Union, of the Headquarters and Forces which May be Made Available to the European Union in the Context of the Preparation and Execution of the Tasks Referred to in Article 17(2) of the Treaty on European Union, Including Exercises, and of the Military and Civilian staff of the Member States Put at the Disposal of the European Union to Act in This Context (EU SOFA), 17 November 2003 306
 Art 5(b) 77
2003 USA-Afghanistan SOFA, 28 May 2003... 444
2004 Protocol to the OAU Convention on the Prevention and Combating of Terrorism 26 July 2004.. 64
2004 Protocol on the Improvement of the Humanitarian Situation in Darfur, 9 November 2004
 Art 2(1)... 258
2005 Agreement between the European Union and the Kingdom of Morocco on the Participation of the Kingdom of Morocco in the European Union Military Crisis Management Operation in Bosnia and Herzegovina, 24 January 2005 313
2005 Protocol Additional to the 1988 Convention for the Suppression of Unlawful Acts against the Safety of Maritime Navigation, 14 October 2005... 40
2006 Regional Cooperation Agreement on Combating Piracy and Armed Robbery in Asia 38
2007 Agreement on Accountability and Reconciliation between the Government of Uganda and the 1997 Lord's Resistance Army, as supplemented by the Annex of 19 February 2008 259
2006 Darfur Peace Agreement, 5 May 2006 259
2006 Convention on the Rights of Persons with Disabilities, 13 December 2006... 302

Table of Treaties, Legislation, and Other International Instruments xxiii

2007 Memorandum of Understanding – Addendum to the Lusaka Protocol for the Cessation of Hostilities and the Resolution of the Outstanding Military Issues under the Lusaka Protocol concluded between the Angolan government and UNITA 245
2007 Paris Commitments to Protect Children from Unlawful Recruitment or Use by Armed Forces or Armed Groups, 28 February 2007 272
2007 Lugano Convention on Jurisdiction and the Recognition and Enforcement of Judgments in Civil and Commercial Matters, 30 October 2007... 471–473, 483
2008 Agreement between the European Union and Georgia on the Status of the European Union Monitoring Mission in Georgia 306
2008 Agreement between the European Union and the Central African Republic on the Status of the European Union-led Forces in the Central African Republic 306
2008 Agreement between the European Union and the Republic of Chad on the Status of the European Union-led Forces in the Republic of Chad 306
2008 Agreement Between the United States of America and the Republic of Iraq on the Withdrawal of United States Forces from Iraq and the Organization of Their Activities during Their Temporary Presence in Iraq 445, 457
2008 Iraq-US SOFA 384
2008 International Convention on Private Military and Security Companies, Elaborated by the Experts for Regional Consultation for Eastern European Group and Central Asian Region 411
2009 IMO Code of Conduct Concerning the Repression of Piracy and Armed Robbery against Ships in the Western Indian Ocean and the Gulf of Aden 38
2009 IMO MSC 1/Circ. 1132, 1134, 1135, 1335 44
2009 Agreement between the European Union and the Somali Republic on the Status of the European Union-led Naval Force in the Somali Republic in the Framework of the EU Military Operation Atalanta 306
2009 Draft International Convention on the Regulation, Oversight and Monitoring of Private Military and Security Companies 51, 93, 411, 419
Art 3(2) 417
Art 21 417
2009 Montreux Document on Pertinent International Obligations and Good Practices for States Related to Operations of Private Military and Security Companies during Armed Conflict, August 2009 ...... 2, 30, 33, 50–51, 108, 137, 191, 220–221, 229, 282, 293–297, 335–336, 346, 351, 390, 396–397, 411, 413, 417–419, 436
2009 Harvard University Humanitarian Policy and Conflict Research Manual on International Law Applicable to Air and Missile Warfare, 11 August 2009 Rule 29 (xii) 213
2009 Declaration on Piracy – Institut de droit international, 10 September 2009 38
2010 Resolution RC/Res.6 'The Crime of Aggression', Assembly of the Parties to the Rome Statute 11 June 2010 1
(No date) NATO Standardization Agreement (STANAG) 2044, Procedures for Dealing with Prisoners of War, Edition n. 6 232

United Nations

1965 GA Res 2106 (XX), 21 December 1965 65
1966 SC Res 221, 9 April 1966 190
1974 GA Res 3314 (XXIX) 14 December 1974 .... 105, 241, 401–403, 415–416
1974 GA Res 3318 (XXIX) 14 December 1974 290
1979 UN Code of Conduct for Law Enforcement Officials, 17 December 1979 .... 182, 370, 379
1979 GA Res 34/180, 18 December 1979 294
1989 GA Res 44/25, 20 November 1989 65
1990 UN Principles on the Use of Force and Firearms by Law Enforcement Officials 7 September 1990 .... 182, 370, 379
1990 Model Status-of-Forces Agreement for Peacekeeping Operations (UN Doc A/45/594), 9 October 1990 453
1990 SC Res 678, 29 November 1990 190
1991 UN Compensation Commission Decision No. 3, Personal Injury and Mental Pain and Anguish 293
1992 SC Res 780, 6 October 1992 210
1993 GA Res 48/104, 20 December 1993 .... 290, 294

1993 GA Res A/48/157, 20 December 1993...... 273
1993 SC Res 827, 25 May 1993........ 289, 291
1996 ILC Draft Code of Crimes against the Peace and Security of Mankind 401
1996 ILC Draft Articles on State Responsibility, 26 July 1996 408
    Art 11 408
    Art 23 408
1997 SC Res. 1132, 8 October 1997......... 245
1998 UN Guiding Principles on Internal Displacement (UN DOC E/CN4/1998/53/ADD2), 11 February 1998 285
1999 SC Res 1261, 25 August 1999.. 272, 281
2000 SC Res 1314, 11 August 2000.......... 272
2000 SC Res 1325, 31 October 2000....... 281, 286–287, 292, 294–296
2000 SC Res 1332, 14 December 2000..... 271
2000 UNMIK Reg. 2000/47, 18 August 2000... 454, 476
2001 ILC Draft Articles on State Responsibility, 10 August 2001 .... 152, 163, 169, 256, 398–399, 403
    Art 1 397–398
    Art 2 397–398
        (c) 392
    Art 4 .... 153, 161
    Art 5 .... 100, 161, 391–392, 403–405, 407, 419
    Art 6 391–392
    Art 8 .... 161, 391, 405–407, 420
    Art 10 257
    Art 17 404
    Art 20 237
    Art 41(2) 243
2001 GA Res S-26/2, 27 June 2001 285
2001 SC Res 1341, 22 February 2001 272
2001 SC Res 1355, 15 June 2001 273
2002 SC Res 1422, 12 July 2002 ...... 446, 461
2002 UNHCR Guidelines on International Protection: Gender-related Persecution within the Context of Article 1A(2) of the 1951 Convention and/or 1967 Protocol relating to the Status of Refugees, 7 May 2002... 286
2003 SC Res 864, 15 September 2003 245
2003 SC Res 1460, 30 January 2003......... 272
2003 SC Res 1497, 1 August 2003............ 446, 461–463
2003 UN Norms on the Responsibilities of Transnational Corporations and Other Business Enterprises with regard to Human Rights, 26 August 2003................. 97, 346
2003 SC Res 864, 15 September 2003 245
2004 SC Res 1539, 22 April 2004............. 272
2004 SC Res 1546, 8 June 2004 238
2005 UN Inter-Agency Standing Committee's Guidelines for HIV/AIDS Intervention in Emergency Situations 284
2005 HCHR Res 2005/69, 20 April 2005... 346
2005 SC Res 1593, 31 March 2005 .... 429, 446, 461–463
2005 SC Res 1612, 26 July 2005 272
2005 GA Res 60/147, 16 December 2005... 147, 259
2006 SC Res 1674, 28 April 2006............. 258
2006 SC Res 1721, 1 November 2006 238
2007 SC Res 1772, 20 August 2007........... 38
2008 Human Rights Council Res 8/7, 18 June 2008.. 346–347, 356
2008 SC Res 1801, 20 February 2008......... 38
2008 SC Res 1814, 15 May 2008................ 38
2008 SC Res 1816, 2 June 2008 38
2008 SC Res 1820, 19 June 2008 292
2008 SC Res 1838, 7 October 2008............ 38
2008 SC Res 1846, 2 December 2008......... 38
2008 SC Res 1851, 16 December 2008....... 38
2009 Draft Articles on the Responsibility of International Organizations, 8 August 2008.. 168
    Art 6 390
2009 SC Res 1882, 4 August 2009............. 272
2009 SC Res 1897, 30 November 2009 38
2009 SC Res 1904, 17 December 2009..... 394
2010 SC Res 1918, 27 April 2010............... 38
2010 HRC Res A/HRC/15/L.22, 27 September 2010.. 2

European Union

1950 European Convention for the Protection of Human Rights and Fundamental Freedoms, 4 November 1950..5, 57, 64, 81, 83, 88–91, 112, 117, 128, 134–135, 151 154–155, 159–162, 165, 167, 169, 173 182–183, 274, 302, 313, 368, 391
    Art 1 .. 58, 85, 115, 155–156, 162, 166, 184
    Art 2 .... 85, 115, 127, 153, 157–158, 166, 173
        (2) 173
    Art 3 .... 115, 117, 127, 158, 160, 166
    Art 4 77
    Art 6 87
        (1) 89
    Art 13 .... 126–127, 160, 166
    Art 14 82

Table of Treaties, Legislation, and Other International Instruments

Art 15 .... 63, 136
  (2) 174
Art 34 160
1952 Protocol No 1 to the European
  Convention on Human Rights and
  Fundamental Freedoms 20 March 1952
  Art 1 87
1997 Treaty of Amsterdam Amending the
  Treaty on European Union, the Treaties
  Establishing the European Communities
  and Certain Related Acts, 2 October
  1997... 173
1998 EU Code of Conduct on Armaments
  Exports.. 34–35
1998 EU Guidelines on Death Penalty 303
1998 Joint Action 1999/34/CFSP, 17
  December 1998..................................... 34
1999 Council Regulation (EC) 975/1999, 29
  April 1999... 312
1999 Council Regulation (EC) 976/1999, 29
  April 1999... 312
2000 Council Regulation 337/2000, 14
  February 2000....................................... 87
2000 Council Decision 2000/354/CFSP, 22
  May 2000 316
2000 Council Joint Action 2000/401/CFSP, 22
  June 2000 34
2000 Council Directive 2000/43/EC, 29 June
  2000.. 82
2000 Council Directive 2000/78/EC, 27
  November 2000 82
2000 Council Decision 2000/803/CFSP, 14
  December 2000............................. 34, 308
2000 Council Regulation 44/2001, 22
  December 2000.................... 471–475, 478
2001 EU Guidelines on Human Rights
  Dialogues 303
2001 EU Guidelines on Torture and Other
  Cruel, Inhuman or Degrading Treatment
  or Punishment.................................... 303
2001 Council Common Position 2001/154/
  CFSP, 26 February 2001....................... 87
2001 Council Regulation 467/2001, 6 March
  2001.. 483–484
2001 European Commission Green Paper
  COM(2001) 366, 18 July 2001 362
2003 EU Draft Guidelines on Protection of
  Civilians in EU-Led Crisis Management
  Operations 316
2003 Concordia SOFA between the EU and
  the Former Yugoslav Republic of
  Macedonia......................... 306, 308–309,
  313–314

2003 Council Joint Action 2003/92/CFSP, 27
  January 2003...................................... 308
2003 Council Decision 2003/222/CFSP, 21
  March 2003 313
2003 Council Joint Action 2003/423/CFSP, 5
  June 2003 308
2003 Common Position 2003/468/CFSP, 23
  June 2003 34
2003 EU Guidelines on Children and Armed
  Conflict, September 2003 ... 275–276, 303
2004 EU Guidelines on Human Rights
  Defenders... 303
2004 EC Regulation 2004/805, 21 April
  2004... 474
2004 Protocol No 14 to the European
  Convention on Human Rights and
  Fundamental Freedoms, amending the
  Control System of the Convention, 13 May
  2004
  Art 17(1)..................................... 167, 303
2004 Council Joint Action 2004/570/CFSP, 12
  July 2004 308
2004 Council Decision 2004/803/CFSP, 25
  November 2004 .... 34, 308
2005 Council Joint Action 2005/190/CFSP, 7
  March 2005 319
2005 Council Secretariat's Generic Standards of
  Behaviour for the ESDP Operations 18
  May 2005 316–319
2005 EU Guidelines on Promoting Compliance
  with International Humanitarian Law 23
  December 2005................... 312, 314–315
2006 Council Joint Action 2006/319/CFSP, 27
  April 2006.. 308
2006 EC Regulation 2006/1896, 12 December
  2006... 475
2007 CONOPS for the EUPOL Afghanistan
  Police Mission, Council Doc. No. 8199/
  2007... 318
2007 EU Guidelines for the Promotion and
  Protection of the Rights of the Child .. 303
2007 OPLAN for the ESDP SSR Police Mission
  in the Democratic Republic of the
  Congo 318
2007 OPLAN for the EUPOL Afghanistan
  Police Mission 317
2007 Council Joint Action 2007/369/CFSP, 30
  May 2007 317
2007 Treaty of Lisbon amending the Treaty on
  European Union and the Treaty
  establishing the European Community,
  13 December 2007 .... 80–82, 92, 167,
  300–302, 310–311, 385

2007 Treaty on the European Union (as amended by the Lisbon Treaty) 13 December 2007............ 167, 300, 310–311
Art 3 311
(5).. 311
Art 6 87
(1)... 311–312
(2).................................... 274, 302, 313
(3).................................... 274, 302, 313
Art 11(1) 313
Art 21
(1).. 311
(2).. 311
Art 37 302
Art 42(1) 307
Art 43(1) 307
Art 249(2 311
2007 Charter of Fundamental Rights of the European Union, 13 December 2007 .... 4, 80–81, 83
Art 2 173
Art 24 274
2007 Treaty on the Functioning of the European Union (as amended by the Lisbon Treaty) 13 December 2007 311
Art 240(2) 316
2007 Regulation (EC) 864/2007 of the European Parliament and of the Council, 11 July 2007 483
2008 EU Guidelines on Human Rights Dialogues with Third Countries 303
2008 EU Guidelines on Violence against Women and Girls and Combating all Forms of Discrimination against Them 303
2008 Guidelines to EU Policy towards Third Countries on Torture and Other Cruel, Inhuman or Degrading Treatment or Punishment 303
2008 EU Guidelines on Children and Armed Conflict (Update) 275–276
2008 Council Decision 2008/101/CFSP, 28 January 2008 308
2008 Council Decision 2008/918/CFSP, 8 December 2008 308
2008 Council Joint Action 2008/736/CFSP, 15 September 2008 320
2008 Council Joint Action 2008/851/CFSP, 10 November 2008 .... 305, 308
2009 Technical Update of the EU Guidelines on Promoting Compliance with International Humanitarian Law, 23 December 2005 312

2010 Commission Recommendation 2010/159/EU, 11 March 2010 44
2010 Council Decision 2010/197/CFSP on the Launch of a EU Military Mission to Contribute to the Training of Somali Security Forces (EUTM Somalia), 31 March 2010 308

NATIONAL LEGISLATION

Canada

2001 Canadian Manual of Law of Armed Conflict at the Operational and Tactical Levels 13 August 2010 329

Democratic Kampuchea

2001 Law on the Establishment of Extraordinary Chambers in the Court of Cambodia for the Prosecution of Crimes Committed during the Period of Democratic Kampuchea (as Amended 2004) 289

France

2003 Criminal Code 328

Iraq

1969 Iraqi Penal Code 457
1971 Iraqi Law on Criminal Proceedings n. 23, 14 February 1971................................. 457
2004 Iraqi CPA, Order No 17: Status of the Coalition Provisional Authority, MNF-Iraq, Certain Missions and Personnel in Iraq, June 2004 ...... 26–27, 444–445, 454, 477, 547
2008 US Embassy in Baghdad – Iraq, Policy Directives for Armed Private Security Contractors in Iraq, Directive II 334
2009 Multi-National Force – Iraq Fragmentary Order 09–109, Applicable to Contractors Working for the US Department of Defence, MNF-I Frago 09–109, March 2009.. 334

Italy

1940 Italian Code of Civil Procedure 478
1995 Italian Law No. 218 on Conflict of Laws........................... 472, 476, 478, 485
2010 Disegno di Legge C 3321, 27 April 2010.. 45

Table of Treaties, Legislation, and Other International Instruments   xxvii

2010 Disegno di Legge S 2092, 31 March 2010 45–46

The Netherlands

1838 Dutch Civil Code 486
2001 The Netherlands Act on the Conflict of Laws Regarding Tort Claims (Wet Conflictenrecht Onrechtmatige Daad) 486

Russia

1996 Russian Criminal Code 329

Spain

1985 Spanish Organic Law of Judicial Power 472
2009 Spanish Decree No 1628 44

South Africa

1998 South African Foreign Military Assistance Act, 20 May 1998 28

UK

2001 UK Anti-terrorism, Crime and Security Act 136
2002 Green Paper on 'Private Military Companies: Options for Regulation', UK Foreign and Commonwealth Office, 12 February 2002 .... 2, 209, 329, 364, 381
2004 UK Manual of the Law of Armed Conflict 212, 222, 329
2008 UK Ministry of Defence, Defence Standard 05–129, Contractors on Deployed Operations 230

USA

1789 Alien Tort Statute 97, 465, 469, 477–483-488
1863 Instructions for the Government of Armies of the United States in the Field (Lieber Code) 219
1926 US Code 442–443
1948 Federal Tort Claims Act 465, 483
1950 Uniform Code of Military Justice 203, 293, 297, 441, 459
1974 US Department of Defence, Instruction 1000.1 228
1976 Arms Export Control Act 28
1980 US Air Force Commander's Handbook 212

1985 Army Regulation (AR) 700–137 – Logistics Civil Augmentation Program 439
1996 War Crimes Act 442–443
2000 Military Extraterritorial Jurisdiction Act, Public Law 106–523 459
2001 US PATRIOT Act 459
2002 US Army Field Manual 209
2002 Supplemental Appropriations Act for Further Recovery from and Response to Terrorist Attacks on the United States 455
2005 DoD, Instruction No 3020.41, Contractor Personnel Authorized to Accompany the U.S. Armed Forces, 3 October 2005 ..... 199–200, 207, 209, 218, 223–224, 230
2006 John Warner National Defence Authorization Act for Fiscal Year 2007 (Pub. L. 109–364) 211, 458
2006 US Department of Defence Instruction 1100.22, Guidance for Determining Workforce Mix 222, 231
2006 USA Directive 2311.01E on the Department of Defence Law of War Program 9 May 2006 .... 202, 427, 437
2007 Memorandum of Agreement between the USA Departments of State and Defense 203
2007 MEJA Expansion and Enforcement Act Adopted by the House of Representatives 4 October 2007 459
2007 Transparency and Accountability in Military and Security Contracting Act ... 29
2008 National Defence Authorization Act for Fiscal Year 2009 (Pub. L. 110–417) 29, 211
2008 Secretary of Defence, Memorandum for Secretaries of the Military Departments, Chairman of the Joint Chiefs of Staff, Undersecretaries of Defence, Commanders of the Combatants Commands 439
2008 DOD Directive 6495.01, Sexual Assault Prevention and Response (SAPR) Program 284
2008 DOD Instruction 6495.02, Sexual Assault Prevention and Response Program Procedures 284
2009 DoD, Defence Federal Acquisition Regulation Supplement – DoD Law of War Program (DFARS Case 2006–D035) .. 437
2009 Statement to Employees on the CIA's Interrogation Policy and Contracts by

Director of Central Intelligence Agency Leon E. Panetta.................................211
2009 US DoD Instruction 3020.50, 22 July 2009...203

Self-Regulatory Initiatives

2003 CoESS/Uni-Europa, Code of Conduct and Ethics for the Private Security Sector...................................365–368, 372
2006 PSCAI Charter for PMSCs 365, 370
2006 Sarajevo Code of Conduct for PSCs 363, 366–368, 370
2008 Dyncorp Code of Ethics and Business Conduct.......................................365–366
2008 Voluntary Principles on Security and Human Rights............362–363, 367–368, 370–371, 379
2009 IPOA Code of Conduct Version 12, 11 February 2009....346, 365–366–368, 370, 373–375, 379, 424
2010 BAPSC Charter................346, 364–367, 369–370, 373, 375, 379
2010 Ethical Code of Guardian Security Consultant 364, 367, 369, 372
2010 G4S Code of Ethics 364, 369
2010 Secopex Code of Ethics....364, 368–369, 371
2010 Sharp End International Code of Ethics...................364, 366–367, 369, 372
2010 Xe Code of Conduct..........364, 367–368
2010 Draft Code of Conduct for Private Military Companies and Private Security Companies, Swiss Federal Department of Foreign Affairs, 8 October 2010..........363

Table of Reports and Other Documents

Institut de droit international
Preliminary Report on the Extraterritorial Jurisdiction of States (1993) 468
Commission on Present Problems of the Use of Force in International Law – Sub-group on Intervention by Invitation, Draft Report on Intervention by Invitation (25/07/2007) 236, 238–239, 241

Inter-American Commission on Human Rights
Report on the Situation of Human Rights in the Peruvian State of Cayara, OEA/Ser.L/V/II.83, Doc. 32 rev. (1993) 123
Third Report on Human Rights in Colombia, Doc. OEA/Ser.L/V/II.102 Doc. 9 rev. 1 (1999) 204, 227
Report on Terrorism and Human Rights, OEA/Ser.L/V/II.116 (2002) 233

International Committee of the Red Cross
Statement, Interpretation of Art. 53 of the Fourth Geneva Convention of 12 August 1949 (25/11/1981) 226
Memoire – Update on Aide (03/12/1992) 293
Final Declaration of the International Conference for the Protection of War Victims (1993) 293
Women Facing War Report (2001) 281, 293
Report of the First Expert Meeting on the Notion of Direct Participation in Hostilities under IHL (02/06/2003) 212
Summary Report of Third Expert Meeting on the Notion of Direct Participation in Hostilities' (23/25 October 2005) 177, 198, 200, 230, 248
Support of the ICRC to the Implementation of the EU Guidelines on Promoting Compliance with International Humanitarian Law 1 (23/11/2006) 315
Summary Report of the Fourth Expert Meeting on the Notion of Direct Participation in Hostilities (27/28 November 2006) 205, 215, 231
Report Summary, International Humanitarian Law and Gender, International Expert Meeting 'Gender Perspectives of International Humanitarian Law', (4-5 October 2007) 293
Assembly, Interpretative Guidance on the Notion of Direct Participation in Hostilities under International Humanitarian Law (2009).......................206, 221-223, 226, 234, 250, 253-254

United Nations
CESCR, The Right to Adequate Housing (Art.11.1): Forced Evictions, General Comment No. 7, HRI/GEN/1/Rev.7 (1997)...66
——The Right to the Highest Attainable Standard of Health (Article 12 of the International Covenant on Economic, Social and Cultural Rights), General Comment No. 14, E/C.12/2000/4 (11/08/2000) 65
Commission on Human Rights, Report on the Question of the Use of Mercenaries as a Means of Violating Human Rights and Impeding the Exercise of the Right of Peoples to Self-Determination, E/CN.4/1997/24 (20/02/1997) 18
——Report on the Question of the Use of Mercenaries as a Means of Violating Human Rights and Impeding the Exercise of the Right of Peoples to Self-Determination, E/CN.4/1998/31 (27/01/1998) 244
Committee on the Rights of the Child, Consideration of Report Submitted by Costa Rica, Concluding Observations, CRC/C/OPAC/CRI/1 (15/01/2007) 271
——Consideration of Report Submitted by Bulgaria, Concluding observations, CRC/C/OPAC/BGR/CO/1 (05/10/2007) 271

Table of Reports and Other Documents

Department of Economic and Social Affairs, Statistics Division, The World's Women 2005: Progress in Statistics, ST/ESA/STAT/Ser.K/17 (2006) 283
GA, A World Fit for Children Document, A/S-27/2 (2002) 272
Global Compact, Communicating Progress (07/08/2009) 356
HRC, Consideration of Reports Submitted by States Parties under Article 40 of the Covenant, Concluding Observations – Comments on Sri Lanka, CCPR/C/79/Add.56 (27/07/1995) .. 121
—— Consideration of Reports Submitted by States Parties under Article 40 of the Covenant, Concluding Observations – Republic of the Congo, CCPR/C/79/Add.118 (25/04/2000) 120
—— Consideration of Reports Submitted by States Parties under Article 40 of the Covenant, Concluding Observations – Russian Federation, CCPR/CO/79/RUS (01/12/2003) 121
—— Consideration of Reports Submitted by States Parties under Article 40 of the Covenant, Concluding Observations – Philippines, CCPR/CO/79/PHL (2003) 118
—— Consideration of Reports Submitted by States Parties under Article 40 of the Covenant, Concluding Observations – Israel, UN Doc. CCPR/CO/78/ISR (2003) 134
—— Report, Systematic Rape, Sexual Slavery and Slavery-Like Practices during Armed Conflicts, A/HRC/Sub.1/58/23 (11/07/2006) 283
—— Report on the Situation in Colombia, A/HRC/7/39 (29/02/2008) 256
—— CCPR General Comment no. 6, Art. 6 (30/04/1982) 61, 112, 120, 173, 185
—— CCPR General Comment No. 7, Art. 11 (30/05/1982) 112-113, 138
—— CCPR General Comment No. 8, Article 9 (30/06/1982) 68
—— CCPR General Comment No. 9, Article 10 (30/06/1982) 69
—— CCPR General Comment No. 12, Article 1 (13/03/1984) 75
—— CCPR General Comment No. 14, Article 12 (13/03/1984) 65-66
—— CCPR General Comment No. 16, Article 17 (08/04/1988) 72
—— CCPR General Comment No. 17, Article 24 (07/04/1989) 76
—— CCPR General Comment No. 20, Article 7 (10/03/1992) 112-113, 118-121, 138
—— CCPR General Comment No. 21, Article 10 (10/04/1992) 69
—— CCPR General Comment No. 22, Art. 18 (30/06/1993) 70
—— CCPR General Comment No. 23, Article 27 (08/04/1994) 74
—— CCPR General Comment No. 25, Art. 25 (12/07/1996) 74
—— CCPR General Comment No. 27, Article 12 (02/11/1999) 71
—— CCPR General Comment No. 28, Article 3 (29/03/2000) 77
—— CCPR General Comment No. 29, Article 4 (31/08/2001) 78
—— CCPR General Comment No. 31, Nature of the General Legal Obligation on States Parties to the Covenant (26/05/2004) 56, 74, 112–113, 118-120, 137-138, 144–145, 156, 185
Human Rights Advocates, Written Statement on the Integration of the Human Rights of Women and the Gender Perspective, E/CN.4/2006/NGO/85 (28/02/2006) 283
ILC, Commentaries on the Draft Articles on State Responsibility (1975) 408
—— Report on the Work of its Forty-Eight Session, A/51/10 (1996) 408
—— Report on the Work of its Fifty-Third Session, A/56/10 (2001) 101, 145
—— Report on the Work of its Fifty-Fourth Session, A/57/10 (2002) 385
—— Report on the Work of its Fifty-Fifth Session, A/58/10 (2003) 385
—— Report on the Work of its Fifty-Seventh Session, A/60/10 (2005) 386
—— Report on the Work of its Sixty-First Session, A/64/10 (2009) 389-390, 392–394
Independent Expert on the Situation of Human Rights in the Democratic Republic of the Congo, Report, E/CN.4/2006/113 (2006) 283
International Commission of Inquiry on Darfur, Report to the UN Secretary-General (25/01/2005) 149, 250
Sotaniemi, A., Status of the Protocols Additional to the Geneva Conventions of 1949 and Relating to the Protection of Victims of Armed Conflicts, UN 61st Session, VI Committee, Agenda Item 75 (18/10/2006) 309
Secretary-General, Note on the Impact of Armed Conflicts upon Children, A/51/306 (26/08/1966) 284

Table of Reports and Other Documents xxxi

——Report, In-depth Study on All Forms of Violence against Women, A/61/122/Add.1 (06/06/2006) 282–283, 295
——Report, Women and Peace and Security, S/2008/622 (25/09/2008) 292
Special Rapporteur on Extrajudicial, Summary or Arbitrary Executions, Report – Preliminary Note on the Mission to Afghanistan, A/HRC/8/3/Add.6 (29/05/2008)..282
——Study on Targeted Killings, A/HRC/14/24/Add.6 (28/05/2010)..211
Special Rapporteur on the Prevention of Human Right Violations committed with Small Arms and Light Weapons, Final Report, A/HRC/Sub.1/58/27 (27/07/2006) 179
Special Rapporteur on the Responsibility of International Organizations, First Report on Responsibility of International Organizations, A/CN.4/532, (26/03/2003).........................385
——Second Report on Responsibility of International Organizations, A/CN.4/541 (02/04/2004) 387
——Third Report on Responsibility of International Organizations, A/CN.4/553 (13/05/2005) 385
——Fifth Report on Responsibility of International Organizations, A/CN.4/583 (02/05/2007) .393
Special Rapporteur on State Responsibility, Third Report – The Internationally Wrongful act of the State, Source of International Responsibility, A/CN.4/246 and Add.1-3 (1971) 403-404
Special Rapporteur on Torture and Other Cruel, Inhuman or Degrading Treatment or Punishment, Report – Promotion and Protection of All Human Rights, Civil, Political, Economic, Social and Cultural Rights, Including the Right to Development, A/HRC/7/3 (15/01/2008)...............286
Special Rapporteur on Violence against Women, Its Causes and Consequences — Preliminary Report, E/CN.4.1995/42 (22/11/21994)..283, 294
——Report, Alternative Approaches and Ways and Means within the United Nations System for Improving the Effective Enjoyment of Human Rights and Fundamental Freedoms, E/CN.4.1998/54 (26/01/1998)..282
——Report, Policies and Practices that Impact on Women's Reproductive Rights and Contribute to, Cause or Constitute Violence against Women, E/CN.4/1999/68/Add.4 (21/01/1999)........285
——Report, Economic and Social Policy and Its Impact on Violence against Women, E/CN.4/2000/68/Add.5 (24/02/2000)..287
——Report, Violence against Women Perpetrated and/or Condoned by the State during Times of Armed Conflict (1997-2000) E/CN.4/2001/73 (23/01/2001) 281, 283, 289, 295-297
——Report, Mission to the Democratic Republic of the Congo, A/HRC/7/6/Add.4 (28/02/2008)292
——Report, Political Economy and Violence against Women, A/HRC/11/6/Add.6 (23/07/2009)..285, 287
Special Representative of the Secretary-General on the Issue of Human Rights and Transnational Corporations and Other Business Enterprises, Interim Report E/CN.4/2006/97 (22/02/2006) 97
——Report, Business and Human Rights: Mapping International Standards of Responsibility and Accountability for Corporate Acts, A/HRC/4/35 (19/02/2007) 344
——Preliminary Work Plan Mandate 1 September 2008-30 June 2011 (2008)...................348-349
——Report, Protect, Respect and Remedy: a Framework for Business and Human Rights, A/HRC/8/5 (07/04/2008) 346
——Report, Corporations and Human Rights: a Survey of the Scope and Patterns of Alleged Corporate-related Human Rights Abuse, A/HRC/8/5/ADD.2 (23/05/2008)......................345
——Report, Business and Human Rights: towards Operationalizing the 'Protect, Respect and Remedy' Framework, A/HRC/11/13 (22/04/2009) 97, 352
——Report, Business and Human Rights: Further Steps toward the Operationalization of the 'Protect, Respect and Remedy' Framework, A/HRC/14/27 (09/04/2010)...........................348
——Letter to Daniel Bethlehem, UK Legal Adviser (14/07/2009) 351
Panel of Commissioners, Reports and Recommendations Concerning Part One of the Second Instalment of Claims for Serious Personal Injury or Death (Category 'B' Claims), S/AC.26/1994/4 (15/12/1994) 292
Secretary General, An Agenda for Peace Preventive Diplomacy, Peacemaking and Peace-keeping A/47/277 - S/24111 (17/06/1992)..400

xxxii *Table of Reports and Other Documents*

——Supplement to an Agenda for Peace: Position Paper of the Secretary General on the Occasion of the Fiftieth Anniversary of the United Nations, A/50/60 - S/1995/1 (03/01/1995) 400
——Report on the Protection of Civilians in Armed Conflict, S/PV5781 (20/11/2007) 243
——Note on the Use of Mercenaries as a Means of Violating Human Rights and Impeding the Exercise of the Right of Peoples to Self-determination, Report, UN Doc. A/62/301 (24/08/2007) 321
——Note on the Use of Mercenaries as a Means of Violating Human Rights and Impeding the Exercise of the Right of Peoples to Self-determination, A/63/325 (25/08/2008) 340
——Note on the Protection of Human Rights and Fundamental Freedoms when Countering Terrorism, A/64/211 (03/08/2009) 280
——Note on the Use of Mercenaries as a Means of Violating Human Rights and Impeding the Exercise of the Right of Peoples to Self-determination, A/64/311 (20/08/2009) 332
UNAIDS, Report on the Global AIDS Epidemic (2008) 285
WHO, Clinical Management of Rape Survivors: Developing Protocols for Use with Refugees and Internally Displaced Person (2005) 285
Working Group on the Use of Mercenaries as a Means of Violating Human Rights and Impeding the Exercise of the Right of Peoples to Self-determination, Report – Mission to Honduras, UN Doc. A/HRC/4/42/Add.1 (20/02/2007) 332, 336, 340
——Report – Promotion and Protection of All Human Rights, Civil, Political, Economic, Social and Cultural Rights, Including the Right to Development, A/HRC/7/7 (09/01/2008) 332, 336
——Report – Mission to Peru, A/HRC/7/7/Add.2 (04/02/2008) 332, 336, 340
——Report – Mission to Fiji, A/HRC/7/7/Add.3 (08/01/2008) 336-337, 340
——Report – Mission to Chile, A/HRC/7/7/Add.4 (04/02/2008) 332, 337
——Report – Latin American and Caribbean Regional Consultation on the Effects of the Activities of Private Military and Security Companies on the Enjoyment of Human Rights: Regulation and Monitoring, UN Doc. A/HRC/7/7/Add.5 (05/03/2008) 339
——Report – Promotion and Protection of All Human Rights, Civil, Political, Economic, Social and Cultural Rights, Including the Right to Development, A/HRC/10/14 (21/01/2009) 340
——Report – Promotion and Protection of All Human Rights, Civil, Political, Economic, Social and Cultural Rights, Including the Right to Development, A/HRC/15/25 (02/07/2010) 2, 336

European Union

Commission of the European Communities, Strategic Objectives 2005-2009, COM(2005) 12 final 274
——Communication to the European Parliament, the Council and the European Economic and Social Committee, Implementing the Partnership for Growth and Jobs: Making Europe a Pole of Excellence on Corporate Responsibility, COM(2006) 136 Final 345
——Towards an EU Strategy on the Rights of the Child, COM(2006) 367 final 274
Council, Conclusions on the European Union's Role in Promoting Human Rights and Democratisation in Third Countries (25/06/2001) 304
——EU Military C2 Concept, Doc. No. 11096/03 (03/06/2003) 320
——Conclusions on Human Rights and Democratisation in Third Countries (12/12/2005) 303-304
——Note regarding Checklist for the Integration of the Protection of Children Affected by Armed Conflict in ESDP Operations (26/05/2006) 276
——Note on the Promotion and Protection of the Rights of the Child in the EU's External Action (27/05/2008) 277
——Update of the EU Guidelines on Children and Armed Conflict (05/06/2008) 275-276, 303
——Conclusions on ESDP, Doc. No. 10087/09 (18/05/2009) 304
——Draft Comprehensive Annual Report on ESDP and ESDP-related Training (CART) 2010, Doc. No. 9472/10 (06/05/2010) 304
——Annual Report on Human Rights (2001) 304
——Annual Report on Human Rights (2002) 304
——Annual Report on Human Rights (2008) 304, 306

Council Presidency, Report on ESDP, Doc. No. 10748/09 (15/06/2009) 307
ECCJ, Corporate Social Responsibility at EU Level: Proposals and Recommendations to the European Commission and the European Parliament (2006) 356

Others

ActionAid, Letter to SGSR Ruggie (30/06/2008) 354
AMICC, Report on the Review Conference of the Rome Statute of the International Criminal Court, 31 May – 11 June 2010 (25/05/2010) 402-403
Amnesty International, Submission to the Special Representative of the Secretary-General on the Issue of Human Rights and Transnational Corporations and Other Business Enterprises, IOR 40/018/18/2008 (07/2008) 354
Bar Human Rights Committee, European Human Rights Advocacy Centre, Human Rights Watch, Interights, International Federation for Human Rights, Written Comments in Al-Skeini and Others v. the United Kingdom (without date) 156, 159
Council of Europe – Venice Commission Report on Private Military and Security Firms and Erosion of the State Monopoly on the Use of Force, CDL-AD (2009) 038, study No.531/2009 (29/06/2009) 191
Crawford, J. et al., Joint Opinion for the Lawyers Committee on Human Rights: In the Matter of the Statute of the International Criminal Court and in the Matter of Bilateral Agreements Sought by the United States Under Article 98(2) of the Statute (2003) 463
Elsea, J. K. et al., CSR Report for Congress – Order Code Private Security Contractors in Iraq: Background, Legal Status, and Other Issues', RL32419 (25/08/2008) 191
Human Rights First, Private Security Contractors at War: Ending the Culture of Impunity (2008) 207
ICC Assembly of States Parties, Report of the Special Working Group on the Crime of Aggression, ICC Doc. ICC-ASP/7/20/Add.1 (2009) 401
International Conference of the Red Cross and Red Crescent (26th), Resolution on Principles and Action in International Humanitarian Assistance and Protection (1996) 209
International Institute of Humanitarian Law, Declaration on the Rules of International Humanitarian Law Governing the Conduct of Hostilities in Non-International Armed Conflicts (1990) 427
Legg, T., Ibbs, R., Report of the Sierra Leone Arms Investigation, Return to an Address of the Honourable the House of Commons (17/07/1998) 29, 245
NATO Research Task Group HFM-107, Recruitment and Retention of Military Personnel (TR-HFM-107) (2007) 286
NGO Working Group on Women, Peace and Security, From the Local to the Global: Making Peace Work for Women (2005) 295
OECD Council, Decision on the Guidelines on Multinational Enterprises (2000) 356
—— Terms of Reference for an Update of the Guidelines for Multinational Enterprises (2010) .. 358
Political Affairs Committee, Parliamentary Assembly, Council of Europe, Report – Private Military and Security Firms and the Erosion of the State Monopoly on the Use of Force, Doc. No. 11787 (22/12/2008) 167
University Centre for IHL, Report on Expert Meeting on Private Military Contractors: Status and State Responsibility for Their Actions (2005) 101, 177, 198, 230, 248, 333, 426
UK Command of the Defence Council, Contractor Support to Operations, JSP 567 (2008) 230
UK House of Commons Foreign Affairs Committee, Second Report on Sierra Leone, Session 1998-1999 29
—— Ninth Report on Private Military Companies, Session 2001-2002 237
UK Legal Adviser Daniel Bethlehem, Letter to Professor John Ruggie (09/07/2009) 351
UK Ministry of Defence, Women in the Armed Forces Steering Group, Women in the Armed Forces, Report (2002) 286
UK NCP, Final Assessment on the OECD Guidelines for Multinational Enterprises: Das Air, 08/1161 (21/07/2008) 355
—— Final Statement on the OECD Guidelines for Multinational Enterprises: Afrimex (UK) Ltd, URN 08/1209 (28/08/2008) 355

xxxiv　　　*Table of Reports and Other Documents*

US Congress Budget Office, Contractors' Support of U.S. Operations in Iraq (2008)..........335, 337
US Congress House of Representatives – Committee on Government Oversight and Reform, Memorandum on Oversight and Government Reform, Additional Information about Blackwater USA (10/10/2007) 337
US Congress House Committee on Oversight and Government Reform – Subcommittee on National Security and Foreign Affairs, Commission on Wartime Contracting: Interim Findings and Path forward (10/06/2009) 204
US CRS, Report for Congress – The Department of Defense's Use of Private Security Contractors in Iraq and Afghanistan: Background, Analysis, and Options for Congress (19/01/2010).........331
US Department of State, Country Reports on Human Rights Practices 2006 Guatemala (06/03/2007) 265
US DoD, Office of Inspector General, Assessment of DOD Efforts to Combat Human Trafficking, Phase II – Bosnia-Herzegovina and Kosovo (H03188433128) (08/12/2003)......................284
——US General Accounting Office, Gender Issues, Trends in Occupational Distribution of Military Women, GAO/NSIAD-99-212 (1999) 286
——Office of Inspector General, Armed Forces 2002 Sexual Harassment Survey, Report No. 2003-026 (2003) 284
——Efforts to Prevent Sexual Assault/Harassment Involving DOD Contractors during Contingency Operations, Report No.D-2010-052 (2010) 280
US Secretary of Defense, Memorandum, UCMJ Jurisdiction over DoD Civilian Employees, DoD Contractor Personnel, and Other Persons Serving with or Accompanying the Armed Forces Overseas during Declared War and in Contingency Operations (10/03/2008)....................458
US Special Inspector General for Iraq Reconstruction, Oversight of Aegis's Performance on Security Services Contracts in Iraq with the Department of Defence, SIGIR-09-010 (14/01/2009) ..207
——Field Commanders See Improvements in Controlling and Coordinating Private Security Contractor Missions in Iraq, SIGIR 09-022 (28/07/2009)...203
——Ethical and Safety Recommendations for Researching, Documenting and Monitoring Sexual Violence in Emergencies (2007) 281

Priv-War Project
Abrisketa, J., Gómez, A., The Regulatory Context of Private Military and Security Services in Spain, Priv-War National Report Series 05/09 (02/2008) 471, 487
Atteritano, A., Italian Legislation on Private Military and Security Companies, Priv-War National Report Series 02/09 (01/2009) 471
Capdevielle, V., Cherief, H., The Regulation of Private Military and Security Services in France, Priv-War National Report Series 11/09 (05/2009) 329-330, 471
Creutz, K., Private Military and Security Services in the Regulatory Context of Finland, Priv-War National Report Series 08/09 (02/2009) 472
Den Dekker, G., The Regulatory Context of Private Military and Security Services in the Netherlands, Priv-War National Report Series 01/08 (12/2008) 460, 471
The Regulatory Context of Private Military and Security Services at the European Union Level, Priv-War National Report Series (04/2009)... 34-35, 171, 300
Everts, R., Regulation of Private Military, Security and Surveillance Services in Germany, Priv-War National Report Series 16/09 (06/2009) 471
Huskey, K., Sullivan, S., The American Way: Private Military Contractors & U.S. Law After 9/11, Priv-War, National Report Series 02/08 (12/2008)............................... 454, 465, 467, 471
Kowalski, M., The Regulatory Context of Private Security Services in Portugal, Priv-War National Report Series No. 09/09 (05/2009)..472
Novika, S., The Regulatory Context of Private Military and Security Services in the Russian Federation (Priv-War National Report Series 14/09 (05/2009) 471
White, N., Alexander, K., The Regulatory Context of Private Military and Security Services in the UK, Priv-War National Report Series 01/09 (06/2009) 26, 457, 460, 471
Ziemele, I., Zaharova, S., Miluna, I., The Regulatory Context of Private Military and Security Services in Estonia, Priv-War National Report Series No. 15/09 (06/2009) 416, 471

List of Abbreviations

ACDI	Annuaire canadien de droit international
ACHPR	African Charter on Human and Peoples' Rights
ACHR	American Convention on Human Rights
ACmHPR	African Commission on Human and Peoples' Rights
AfrJIntl&CompL	African Journal of International and Comparative Law
AID	Agency for International Development
Air Force LR	Air Force Law Review
AmUIntlLRev	American University International Law Review
AmUJIntlL&Pol	American University Journal of International Law and Policy
AP	Additional Protocol
ASPA	American Service-Members' Protection Act
ATCA	Alien Tort Claims Act
ATS	Alien Tort Statute
BAPSC	British Association of Private Security Companies
BCIntl&CompLRev	Boston College International and Comparative Law Review
BIAs	Bilateral Immunity Agreements
BIMCO	Baltic and International Maritime Council
BIS	Business, Innovation and Skills
BostonUIntlLJ	Boston University International Law Journal
BRA	Bougainville Revolutionary Army
BYU Journal of Public Law	Brigham Young University Journal of Public Law
CalWIntlLJ	California Western International Law Journal
Cambridge Review Intl Affairs	Cambridge Review of International Affairs
Cardozo L Rev	Cardozo Law Review
CART	Comprehensive Annual Report on ESDP and ESDP-related Training
CEDAW	Convention on the Elimination of all Forms of Discrimination Against Women
CESCR	Committee on Economic, Social and Cultural Rights
CFI	Court of First Instance
CFSP	Common Foreign and Security Policy
Chicago JIL	Chicago Journal of International Law
Chinese J Intl L	Chinese Journal of International Law
CIA	Central Intelligence Agency
CIVCOM	Committee for Civilian Crisis Management

CML Rev	Common Market Law Review
CNE	Computer Network Exploitation
CoC	Code(s) of Conduct
CoESS	Confederation of European Security Services
COJUR	Working Party on Public International Law
ColumJTransnatlL	Columbia Journal of Transnational Law
CONOPS	Concepts of Operations
CPA	Coalition Provisional Authority
CRC	Convention of the Rights of the Child
CrimLF	Criminal Law Forum
CSDP	EU Common Security and Defence Policy
CSR	Corporate Social Responsibility
DFARS	Defense Federal Acquisition Regulation Supplement
DoD	Department of Defence
DPKO	Department of Peacekeeping Operations
DRC	Democratic Republic of the Congo
EC	European Community
ECHO	European Community Humanitarian Aid Office
ECHR	European Convention on Human Rights
ECJ	European Court of Justice
ECtHR	European Court of Human Rights
EEZ	Exclusive Economic Zone
EIDHR	European Initiative for Democracy and Human Rights
ELR	European Law Review
EPL	European Public Law
ESDP	European Security and Defence Policy
EU	European Union
EUF	EU Forces
EUFOR	European Union Force
EUI	European University Institute
EULEX	European Union Rule of Law mission in Kosovo
EUPM	European Union Policy Mission
EUPOL	EU Police Mission
EUSRs	EU Special Representatives
EUTM	EU Training Mission
FDFA	Federal Department of Foreign Affairs
FinnishYBIL	Finnish Yearbook of International Law
FMAA	Foreign Military Assistance Act (South Africa)
Fordham Int'l LJ	Fordham International Law Journal
FPLC	Forces patriotiques pour la libération du Congo
FRY	Former Republic of Yugoslavia
FTCA	Federal Tort Claims Act
FYROM	Former Yugoslav Republic of Macedonia
GA	General Assembly
GCs	Geneva Conventions

Harv Int'l L J	Harvard International Law Journal
Harv L Rev	Harvard Law Review
Hous L Rev	Houston Law Review
HRC	Human Rights Committee
HRL	Human Rights Law
HRLRev	Human Rights Law Review
I Con	International Journal of Constitutional Law
IAC	International Armed Conflict
IACtHR	Inter-American Court of Human Rights
IAComHR	Inter-American Commission on Human Rights
ICC	International Criminal Court
ICCPR	International Covenant on Civil and Political Rights
ICESCR	International Covenant on Economic, Social and Cultural Rights
ICJ	International Court of Justice
ICLR	International Community Law Review
ICRC	International Committee of the Red Cross
ICTR	International Criminal Tribunal for Rwanda
ICTY	International Criminal Tribunal for the Former Yugoslavia
IHL	International Humanitarian Law
ILC	International Law Commission
ILO	International Labour Organization
IMO	International Maritime Organization
Ind L J	Indiana Law Journal
Int'l Peacekeeping	International Peacekeeping
IO	International Organization
IPOA	International Peace Operations Association
IRA	Irish Republican Army
IRIN	Integrated Regional Information Networks
IRRC	International Review of the Red Cross
IsLR	Israel Law Review
ITAR	International Traffic in Arms Regulation (United States)
ITF	International Transport Workers' Federation
IYIL	Italian Yearbook of International Law
J Int'l Affairs	Journal of International Affairs
J of Intl Peace Operations	Journal of International Peace Operations
JC&SL	Journal of Conflict and Security Law
JComMarSt	Journal of Common Market Studies
JPeaceRes	Journal of Peace Research
KBR	Kellogg, Brown, and Root Services Inc.
KFOR	NATO Kosovo Force
LOGCAP	Logistics Civil Augmentation Program
LPICT	Law and Practice of International Courts and Tribunals
MEJA	Military Extraterritorial Jurisdiction Act

Melb JIL	Melbourne Journal of International Law
MilLRev	Military Law Review
MRT	Moldovan Republic of Transdniestria
NATO	North Atlantic Treaty Organisation
NAVFOR	Naval Force
NCP	National Contact Point
NGO	Non-governmental Organisation
NIAC	Non-international Armed Conflict
NYUJIntlL&Pol	New York University Journal of International Law and Politics
OECD	Organisation for Economic Cooperation and Development
OPAC	Optional Protocol on the Involvement of Children in Armed Conflict
OPLANs	Operation Plans
OSCE	Organization for Security and Cooperation in Europe
OUA/OAU	Organisation de l'unité africaine/Organization of African Unity
PKO	Peace-keeping operation
PMSC	Private Military and Security Company
PMSI	Private Military and Security Industry
POW	Prisoner of War
PSCAI	Private Security Company Association of Iraq
PTSD	Post-traumatic Stress Disorder
RevDrMilDrGuerre	Revue de droit militaire et de droit de la guerre
RivDirInt	Rivista di diritto internazionale
ROE	Rules of Engagement
RUF	Revolutionary United Front
SAfrYIL	South African Yearbook of International Law
SC	Security Council
SCIPOA	Standards Committee of the International Peace Operations Association
SCSL	Special Court for Sierra Leone
SGSR	Secretary-General's Special Representative
SIP	Specific Instance Procedure
SMTJ	Special Maritime and Territorial Jurisdiction
SOFA	Status of Force Agreement
SOMAs	Status of Mission Agreements
SOPs	Standard Operating Procedures
STANAG	Standardization Agreement
StanJIntlL	Stanford Journal of International Law
TCN	Troops Contributing Nation
TEU	Treaty on the European Union
TFEU	Treaty on the Functioning of the European Union
TFG	Transitional Federal Government

The DISAM Journal	Defense Institute of Security and Assistance Management Journal
TNC	Transnational Corporation
Tul J Int'l & Comp L	Tulane Journal of International and Comparative Law
TVPA	Torture Victims Protection Act
TWQ	Third World Qarterly
U Kan L Rev	University of Kansas Law Review
UCMJ	Uniform Code of Military Justice
UDHR	Universal Declaration of Human Rights
UK	United Kingdom
UN	United Nations
UNCHR	United Nations High Commissioner for Refugees
UNCTC	UN Centre on Transnational Corporations
UNESCO	United Nations Educational, Scientific and Cultural Organization
UNGC	UN Global Compact
UNITA	União Nacional para a Independência Total de Angola
UNMIK	United Nations Interim Administration Mission in Kosovo
UPC	Union des Patriotes Congolais
USA	United States of America
Va J Int'l L	Vanderbilt Journal of International Law
VAW	Violence against Women
Virginia JIL	Virginia Journal of International Law
VPD	Vessel Protection Detachment
VPSHR	Voluntary Principles on Security and Human Rights
Yale LJ	Yale Law Journal
YIntlHL	Yearbook of International Humanitarian Law

List of Contributors

Andrea Atteritano is a Research Fellow in International Law at LUISS University and a Lawyer in Rome with Hogan Lovells–Arbitration/Dispute Resolution Department. He is the author of a number of publications on international and arbitration law including a recent book on the enforcement of international arbitral awads. He is a member of the Editorial Board of the Italian Arbitration Review. He assists multinational corporations in court, arbitration as well as on non-contentious issues.

Christine Bakker holds a PhD from the European University Institute in Florence, where she is currently a Research Fellow at the Academy of European Law (Priv-War Project). She has worked at the European Commission for several years and has carried out legal research on children in armed conflict as a consultant for the UNICEF Innocenti Research Centre.

Giulio Bartolini is an Assistant Professor of International Law in the Department of Law at University 'Roma Tre' and a Lecturer in International Humanitarian Law in the Department of Political Science at the University of Siena.

Charlotte Beaucillon holds a MPhil with honours in International Public Law, jointly from University Panthéon Sorbonne and the Institut d'Etudes Politiques de Paris. First a Lavoisier Fellow of the French Ministry of Foreign Affairs and then Allocataire de recherche in the European University Institute in Florence, her PhD research focuses on the restrictive measures of the European Union.

Eugenio Cusumano is a PhD candidate in Political Science at the European University Institute. His areas of research are international relations and security studies, and he is currently working on a comparative analysis of the privatization of military functions in different countries and its implication on civil–military relations and democratic control over the use of force.

Guido den Dekker is an attorney (specialized in supreme court litigation) with the law firm BarentsKrans N. V. in The Hague. Earlier, he worked as a researcher and lecturer at Utrecht University in the Department of International Law, and as an attorney in Amsterdam. He obtained his PhD in law (The Law of Arms Control, 2001) from the University of Amsterdam.

Valentina Falco is a PhD candidate in international humanitarian law and EU law at the European University Institute in Florence. She has been a consultant on human rights law for the European Commission, and has collaborated, inter alia, with the Legal Service of the Council of the EU and the UN Counter-Terrorism Committee Executive Directorate.

Julian Fernandez is Professor of public law at the University of Lille Nord de France (Lille 2). He is also a Research associate at the Centre Thucydide of the University Panthéon-Assas (Paris 2).

Francesco Francioni has a doctorate in law from the University of Florence and an LLM from Harvard and is professor of international law and human rights of the European University Institute in Florence, where he is also Co-Director of the Academy of European Law. He has been professor of international law at the University of Siena and visiting professor at the Universities of Oxford, Cornell, and Texas, and is a member (associate) of the Institut de droit international.

Micaela Frulli is currently Marie Curie Fellow at the Law Department of the European University Institute. She is Lecturer and Assistant Professor in International Law at the University of Florence, Italy. Her most recent publications include articles in Harvard International Law Journal, Journal of International Criminal Justice, and The Oxford Companion to International Criminal Justice (ed by A Cassese).

Susanna Greijer holds a Master's Degree in International Affairs from Sciences Po Paris and is currently a PhD candidate in International Law at the European University Institute, focusing her research on children's involvement in armed conflict. She has also done research for UNICEF and has lectured at the International Institute for Humanitarian Law and the NATO School.

Carsten Hoppe holds law degrees from the University of Michigan (JD, 2004) and the European University Institute (Doctor of Laws, 2009). He has published several articles on the subject of privatization of war and is especially interested in the issue of state responsibility in that context, to which he also devoted his doctoral thesis.

Ieva Kalnina (PhD candidate (EUI), LLM (Harvard), BA (University of Latvia)) is an attorney (New York) and a visiting lecturer at the Riga Graduate School of Law (Latvia). Her field of specialization is international public law and international arbitration. She is an associate at Lévy Kaufmann-Kohler law firm (Geneva) where she practices international investment and commercial arbitration.

Federico Lenzerini is Professor of International Law and EU Law at the University of Siena (Italy). He is rapporteur of the Committee on the Rights of Indigenous Peoples of the International Law Association and member of the Committee on Biotechnology of the same Association. He has occasionally provided consultancies to UNESCO in the field of cultural heritage.

Sorcha MacLeod is a Lecturer in Law at the University of Sheffield having studied at the Universities of Dundee and Glasgow. She researches and publishes widely on the topic of business and human rights and corporate social responsibility.

Marina Mancini is Lecturer in International Law at the Mediterranean University of Reggio Calabria. She also teaches International Criminal Law at the LUISS University in Rome. She holds a PhD in International Law from the University of Rome 'La Sapienza' (2003) and is author of a book on the concept of state of war and the consequences of the outbreak of armed conflicts in International Law (*Stato di guerra e conflitto armato nel diritto internazionale* (Giappichelli, 2009). She is a member of the Italian Bar.

Thilo Marauhn, Dr iur, MPhil, is Professor of Public Law, International Law and European Law at the Faculty of Law, University of Giessen, Germany. He has published widely in the fields of arms control law and international humanitarian law. He is a member of the German National Committee for Humanitarian Law and Chair of the Scientific Advisory Board of the Peace Research Institute Frankfurt, and also serves on the Advisory Board on United Nations Issues of the German Federal Foreign Office.

Eric PJ Myjer is Professor of Conflict and Security Law at Utrecht University (the Netherlands). Furthermore he is a member of the Dutch government Standing Advisory Committee on Issues of Public International Law and a member of the International Law

Association's Committee on the Use of Force. He is co-editor in chief of the Journal of Conflict & Security Law. He is also Judge (locum) at The Hague Court of Appeal.

Faustin Z Ntoubandi, Lic en Droit Public (Yaounde, Cameroon), LLB/LLM (Potchefstroom, South Africa), PhD magna cum laude in International Law (Giessen, Germany) and currently Assistant Professor in International Law and Researcher at the Franz von Liszt Institute of International Law, Justus-Liebig University of Giessen, Germany. He is author of the book *Amnesty for Crimes against Humanity under International Law* (Brill, 2007) and has published articles on various areas of international law.

Giulia Pinzauti is a PhD candidate in International Law at the European University Institute of Florence. She holds an MA in International Relations from the University of Florence, where she works as a teaching assistant. From 2009 she has been a member of the editorial committee of the Journal of International Criminal Justice.

Ottavio Quirico holds an LLM in International Relations and a PhD in Law from the University of Toulouse. He was a Visiting Fellow at the Lauterpacht Centre for International Law in Cambridge (2007–8); a Max Weber Fellow at the European University Institute (EUI, 2008–9) and a Lecturer in Law at the Academy of Lille (2009–10). Since September 2010 he has been a Marie Curie Fellow at the University Panthéon-Assas (Paris II) in collaboration with the EUI and the Max Planck Institute for Comparative Public Law and International Law.

Hélène Raspail is a PhD candidate in public international law and a Research Associate at the Institut des Hautes Etudes Internationales (IHEI) and the Centre Thucydide of the University Panthéon-Assas (Paris 2), where she is also a Teaching Fellow in public law.

Natalino Ronzitti is Professor of International Law at LUISS University, Rome, and Associate Member of the Institut de Droit International. Member of the Italian Bar (Corte di Cassazione), his professional experience includes the participation in several diplomatic conferences as a member of the Italian delegation. He has several times been heard as international expert before the Foreign Committee of the Italian Parliament.

Mirko Sossai is lecturer in international law at the University 'Roma Tre', Italy. Previously, he was research fellow at the LUISS Guido Carli University in Rome. He holds a PhD in international law from the University of Siena (2005) and a degree *cum laude* from the University of Padua (2001). He is member of the management team of the Priv-War Project.

Luisa Vierucci is a researcher and lecturer in international law at the University of Florence, specializing in international humanitarian law and human rights. Besides publishing extensively in international journals, she is the co-editor with Prof P-M Dupuy of the book entitled *NGOs in International Law: Efficiency in flexibility?* (2008).

Ana FilipaVrdoljak is Professor, Faculty of Law, University of Western Australia, Perth and Visiting Professor, Legal Studies Department, Central European University, Budapest. She has been a Marie Curie Fellow (2006–8) and Jean Monnet Fellow (2004–5), Law Department, European University Institute, Florence. She holds a PhD (in law), LLB (Hons), and BA (Hons) from the University of Sydney, Australia.

Nigel White is Professor of Public International Law at the University of Nottingham. He is author of several books including *Keeping the Peace: The United Nations and the maintenance of international peace and security*, 2nd edn (1997), *The Law of International Organisations*,

2nd edn (2005), *The UN System: Toward international justice* (2002), and *Democracy Goes to War: British military deployments under international law* (2009).

Ugis Zeltins (LLM (Bruges), BA (University of Latvia)) is an attorney (Latvia) and a researcher at the Riga Graduate School of Law (Latvia). His field of specialization is constitutional and competition law. He is an associate at Raidla Lejins and Norcous law firm (Riga).

Introduction

Francesco Francioni and Natalino Ronzitti

Armed forces have always represented, and continue to represent, the core function of the state as guarantor of external defence and security for citizens. Yet over the past decade the outsourcing of military and security services to commercially organized entities ('private military and security companies', henceforth PMSCs or private contractors) has grown in size and importance as part of a larger contemporary phenomenon of privatization of services which in the past were typical governmental functions.

For the purpose of this book, PMSCs can be defined as corporations offering security, defence and/or military services to states, international organizations, non-governmental organizations, and private companies and/or armed groups. These services include armed guarding and protection of persons and objects or buildings, maintenance and operation of weapons systems, prisoner detention and interrogation, intelligence, risk assessment and military research analysis, as well as advice to or training of local forces and security personnel.

Indeed, private contractors have replaced members of the armed forces in a number of situations ranging from actual participation in hostilities to support of armed forces in prolonged military occupation, security in peace-keeping/peace-enforcing operations, international administration in post-conflict institution building, and intelligence gathering. In addition, PMSCs have been used and continue to be used by non-state actors, such as NGOs and business corporations acting in conflict zones or in territories characterized by insecurity and weak institutional governance. Most recently, armed private contractors have been used to defend maritime commerce against the re-emerging plague of piracy.

In parallel with the expansion of this phenomenon, particularly in conjunction with the prolonged wars in Iraq and Afghanistan, there has been increasing concern about the adequacy of its regulation, both in domestic law and international law. At an academic level, this concern has generated an abundant literature, covering the historical and sociopolitical aspects of the phenomenon;[1]

---

[1] PW Singer, *Corporate Warriors: The Rise of the Privatised Military Industry* (2003); D Avant, *The Market for Force: The Consequences of Privatizing Security* (2005); D Isenberg, *Shadow Force: Private Security Contractors in Iraq* (2009); E Krahmann, *States, Citizens and the Privatization of Security* (2010).

its links with mercenarism;[2] constitutional law issues relating to the erosion of the traditional notions of 'inherently governmental functions', with consequent loss of democratic control over the use of force;[3] and the question of the uncertain legal status of private contractors in the context of the law of armed conflict.[4]

More recently, in the past two or three years, a number of policy initiatives have been launched aiming to improve the international regulation of the private military and security industry. Two of these initiatives are of special significance for the subject matter of this book. The first is the so-called 'Swiss initiative', from the name of the promoting government, which produced a soft normative document in November 2008 (the 'Montreux Document')[5] containing a set of guidelines of good practice for states and the industry.[6] The second initiative evolved in the United Nations Human Rights Council, and more precisely within the Working Group on the Use of Mercenaries. This led to the elaboration of a *Draft of a Possible Convention on Private Military and Security Companies,* which was presented to the Human Rights Council in July 2010.[7]

In Europe, where the phenomenon of private contractors remains limited as compared with the United States, regulatory approaches to PMSCs vary from country to country, ranging from outright criminalization of the activity of recruiting personnel and offering related services, to systems of prior licensing, to an attitude of *laissez-faire.*[8] This notwithstanding, the need for improvement of the regulation has emerged at the national and European Union (EU) level. In 2002 the British House of Commons published a Green Paper on the subject and opened up a public consultation on the role of the private sector in the provision of military and security services.[9] These consultations are still underway at the time of writing.

---

[2] S Chesterman and C Lehnardt (eds), *From Mercenaries to Market: The Rise and Regulation of Private Military Companies* (2007).

[3] S Chesterman and A Fisher (eds), *Private Security, Public Order: The Outsourcing of Public Services and its Limits* (2009).

[4] E-C Gillard, 'Business goes to War: Private Military/Security Companies and International Humanitarian Law', IRRC 88 (2006) 525; L Cameron, 'Private Military Companies: Their Status under International Humanitarian Law and its Impact on Their Regulation', (2006) 88 IRRC 573; L Doswald-Beck, 'Private Military Companies under International Humanitarian Law' in Chesterman and Lehnardt (eds) (n 2 above), 118.

[5] UN Doc A/63/467–S/2008/636, Montreux Document on Pertinent International Legal Obligations and Good Practices for States Related to Operations of Private Military and Security Companies during Armed Conflict (17 September 2008).

[6] A follow-up of this initiative is the recent finalisation of a Global Code of Conduct for Respect of Human Rights and International Humanitarian Law, specifically addressed to PMSCs.

[7] Working Group on the use of mercenaries as a means of violating human rights and impeding the exercise of the rights of peoples to self-determination, *Draft of a Possible Convention on Private Military and Security Companies (PMSCs),* attached to UN Doc A/HRC/15/25, 2 July 2010. The UN Human Rights Council decided to establish an intergovernmental open-ended working group with the mandate to elaborate a legally binding instrument on the basis of the principles, main elements, and draft text proposed by the WG on the use of mercenaries, Res A/HRC/15/L.22 of 27 Sept. 2010.

[8] For a collection of reports on national legislation and case law, see <http://www.priv-war.eu>, accessed 14 August 2010. For a comparative analysis see O Quirico, *National Regulatory Models for PMSCs and Implications for Future International Regulation,* MWP Working Paper, 2009.

[9] House of Commons Foreign Affairs Committee, *Private Military Companies,* 23 July 2002.

At the EU level, there is no common r...
conduct on the export of weapons d...
Yet, given the increasing need for r...
the EU security and defence po'...
of the phenomenon[10] with a...

The European Commi...
itiatives, has recognized t...
outsourcing of military and ...
financial support for study and r...
Framework Programme. A specific...
Programme was launched in 2008 unde...
'War': The role of the European Union in a...
humanitarian law and human rights (*PRIV-WAR*)...
participation of seven European universities[11] unde...
the European University Institute in Florence, has produ...
collecting data on the state of the security industry throu...
by publishing a series of national reports on the domestic legislat...
a wide range of relevant countries. At the same time, the project has ...
systematic, comprehensive analysis of the role of international law in prevent...
by private military contractors, in protecting them in situations of armed confli...
in providing a system of accountability of states and private actors in the event of har...
caused by such contractors. This book is a product of this research project.

Unlike other books on the subject, the main focus of this volume is the role of international human rights law (HRL) and international humanitarian law (IHL) in the governance of the transnational military and security industry. It examines the applicability *de lege lata* of principles and norms of HRL and IHL to states involved in the provision of private military and security services, to PMSCs and to their employees. Moreover, it addresses questions of state responsibility and of civil and criminal liability of private contractors, and examines issues of access to justice for victims of possible wrongful acts. At the same time, the book provides some policy perspectives, *de lege ferenda*, for improved regulation at the international level.

The volume is divided into five parts. Part I opens with a contribution by Eugenio Cusumano, which explores the nature and sociopolitical implications of the current outsourcing of security tasks and provides a theoretical framework for the analysis of different regulatory options. The chapter concludes with a proposal for a multilayered approach to future regulation. The second chapter, by Natalino Ronzitti, addresses the very timely topic of piracy, and provides an innovative examination of the policy implications of the use of PMSCs in the fight against this renewed plague affecting maritime commerce. The author argues that while

---

[10] See J Bailes and C Holmquist, *The Increasing Role of Private Military and Security Companies* (October 2007).
[11] European University institute (Florence), LUISS 'Guido Carli' (Rome), University of Utrecht, University of Sheffield, Justus Liebig Universitaet (Giessen), Riga Graduate School of Law, Univertsité Panthéon Assas, Centre Thucydide (Paris II).

Introduction

...ibits the arming of private vessels for pirate-hunting, there are ...ions against the use of security guards for protecting private ...e should be reconciled with the law of the sea.
...es the human rights dimension of the privatization of military and ... It opens with a comprehensive survey in Chapter 3, by Federico ... Francesco Francioni, of the applicable treaties and customary law, ...main obligations that derive therefrom, for states involved in the ...r use of private military and security services. The following chapter ...alnina and Ugis Zeltins focuses specifically on the role of the EU, ...y in light of the Charter of Fundamental Rights and in conjunction with ...man rights jurisprudence of the European Court of Human Rights in ...ourg. More incisive legal analysis follows in the three subsequent chapters ...sing on the specific legal obligations of the different states involved in the ...tsourcing of private military and security services. In Chapter 5, Francesco ...rancioni addresses the role of the PMSC's 'home state', ie the state where the company was constituted as a legal person or where it has its headquarters or its main place of business. The principal argument developed by the author is that the nature of human rights obligations permits the construction of a general duty of 'due diligence' in the constitution and licensing of the company and of its individual employees, as well as in the licensing of commercial exports of military and security services, as part of the general human rights obligation to prevent and protect against abuses. At the same time, Francioni provides a detailed analysis of the criteria of attribution of a wrongful act to the state, under the general principles of state responsibility, both in the case of private contractors who are integrated in the armed forces of the relevant state and in the (more frequent) case of private contractors who maintain a distinct position from the armed forces.

Chapter 6, by Carsten Hoppe, analyses the human rights obligations of the 'hiring state', ie the state that contractually engages the PMSC for the provision of services, most of the time abroad. The focus of this contribution is on the positive obligations of the hiring state in overseeing what the author calls 'coercive services' by a PMSC. By this expression Hoppe means those services that entail a certain measure of force either in the sense of military force or in connection with activities relating to the running of detention or interrogation centres. To grasp the relevance of this specific focus one need only think of the scandals surrounding the abuses committed by private guards at the Abu Ghraib prison in Iraq, the involvement of private contractors in the practice of secret 'rendition' of suspected terrorists to allow their torture in the receiving country, or the more recent Nisour Square 'incident' in Baghdad where many innocent civilians were killed as a consequence of reckless shooting by private guards escorting a convoy.

In Chapter 7, the issue of human rights obligations is examined by Christine Bakker from the perspective of the 'host state', ie the state in whose territory the private security or military services are performed. Without departing from the basic principle of territorial sovereignty and the international responsibility of the territorial state to ensure that its territory is not used to commit or allow the commission of international wrongful acts, the author cogently argues that the human rights obligations of the host state with regard to the conduct of PMSCs must be implemented within a perspective of substantive complementarity with the obligations of the hiring state and the home state. The argument is all the more convincing if one considers that the conditions in the host state that normally require the sending of private contractors are insecurity, weak institutional control, and often armed conflict. Thus, they are not conducive to the effective supervision of PMSCs.

In her chapter Giulia Pinzauti addresses the challenges posed by the increasing reliance on PMSCs for the supervision and adjudication of human rights violations committed in times of armed conflict, focusing on the potential role of the European Court of Human Rights (ECtHR). The author convincingly discusses the main challenges that the ECtHR will have to face if it is ever called upon to rule on the infringement of the European Convention on Human Rights (ECHR) by PMSCs acting in a situation of armed conflict, and suggests some possible solutions.

The second part of the book concludes with an innovative chapter by Guido Den Dekker and Eric Myjer, which analyses the relevance of the right to life for private contractors involved in armed conflict. The authors provide valuable insight into the interplay between human rights and IHL regarding the right to personal self-defence of individual employees of PMSCs.

The focus of attention in Part III is on the law of armed conflict. Chapter 10, by Mirko Sossai, offers an analytical framework to discuss the status of PMSC employees under the law of international armed conflict: in principle, they can fall within the category of legitimate combatants once the hiring state establishes a certain qualified factual link between them and its regular armed forces; if not, they are civilians. In this connection, Giulio Bartolini, in Chapter 11, discusses whether the category of 'civilians accompanying the armed forces', already present in the early codification of the laws of war, may be considered to cover the phenomenon of PMSCs. One of the main consequences thereof is that civilian contractors enjoy immunity from attack, unless they take direct part in hostilities. Thus, this book gives considerable attention to the ICRC's recently released *Interpretive Guidance on the Notion of Direct Participation in Hostilities under IHL* and the chapters in this part examine the approach taken by the ICRC in relation to tasks entrusted to PMSCs. Episodes of violence and abuse committed by PMSCs have shocked public opinion to such an extent that several academic commentators initially claimed that they should be banned under the existing norms on mercenaries. This radical view is challenged by Marina Mancini, Faustin Ntoubandi and Thilo Marauhn in Chapter 16. The authors assess the activities of the UN Working Group on the Use of Mercenaries and conclude that only a very limited number of PMSCs fall within the definitions of mercenary laid down in treaty law.

Chapter 12 by Luisa Vierucci aims to fill the gap in legal literature regarding the activities performed by PMSCs in non-international armed conflicts. First, it covers the *ius ad bellum* issues arising from this scenario, particularly the right of the constituted government to use foreign armed forces, including services provided by PMSCs. As for their legal status under IHL, one of the problematic aspects is whether PMSCs qualify per se as opposition armed groups. In this regard, the neglected question of the international liability of armed opposition groups is examined, with special emphasis being placed on the due diligence obligations accruing both to the group and the state.

Part III also addresses the impact of PMSCs on certain vulnerable groups, protected by both the law of armed conflict and by human rights. Chapter 13, by Christine Bakker and Susanna Greijer, considers whether PMSCs may be held accountable for recruiting children or for using them to participate actively in hostilities. Furthermore, it examines the measures PMSCs are required to take if they find themselves confronted with children participating in armed hostilities. The chapter by Ana Vrdoljak focuses on gender-related issues, with the crime of sexual violence at the core of her analysis. Women employees of PMSCs have recently brought actions against their employers for sexual assault; there have also been recent cases of female civilian victims of contractors operating forced prostitution rings. Both of these chapters emphasize that better recruitment processes, adequate training for PMSC personnel and effective accountability in the case of abuses are essential.

Also in Part III, the chapter by Valentina Falco considers the possible role and functions of PMSCs in the context of EU crisis-management operations and the challenges they pose for compliance with IHL and HR. Falco's analysis recognizes the lack of clarity in the legal framework of the Common Security and Defence Policy, particularly since recently adopted non-binding instruments in this context have, in the author's view, produced ambiguous legal effects.

The use of PMSCs by international and regional organizations is assessed by Nigel White, in his chapter in Part IV. The author discusses one of the most delicate issues of the law of international responsibility for wrongful acts: namely, whether the actions of PMSCs deployed as part of a peace support operation should be attributed to the international organization or to its member states. Issues of state responsibility arising from the acts of PMSCs are also covered in the chapter by Charlotte Beaucillon, Julian Fernandez, and Hélène Raspail, who investigate the conditions under which the hiring state could be held responsible for a violation of the prohibition of the threat or use of force committed by private contractors.

Part IV also contains two chapters which evaluate the state of self-regulation and corporate social responsibility initiatives within the PMSC industry. Ottavio Quirico and Carsten Hoppe examine a number of initiatives relating to the development of codes of conduct and offer a classification scheme of the different regulatory techniques and enforcement mechanisms. Sorcha MacLeod analyses the implications of the work of the UN Secretary General's Special Representative on business and human rights (SGSR), John Ruggie, particularly in relation to the due diligence requirement. MacLeod also examines the impact of the UN Global Compact and the Organisation for Economic Cooperation and Development's (OECD) Guidelines for Multinational Enterprises. Her chapter offers an important contribution to the debate on the viability of such initiatives, which are often voluntary in nature, lack individual redress, and often rely solely on the market to achieve compliance.

Part V concludes the book with an examination by Ottavio Quirico of the question of criminal responsibility of individual PMSC employees, a discussion of the role and limits of the international law on immunity as applicable to the conduct of PMSCs and their employees by Micaela Frulli, and on the prospect of adjudication of civil claims arising from torts committed by private contractors by Andrea Atteritano. These three contributions show that legal proceedings against PMSCs and their employees for violations of human rights or humanitarian law are comparatively rare and are mainly concentrated in the United States, where national legislation and jurisdictional provisions, including the well-known Alien Tort Claims Act, provide a legal basis for third-party claims. So far little success has been achieved at the level of judicial enforcement of state and PMSC obligations. On the contrary, obstacles remain, including immunity and political exceptions to justiciability. In addition, the human rights of the accused and due process considerations have been used, albeit correctly, to hinder the judicial enforcement of the responsibility of private contractors for serious breaches of human rights committed in the performance of their services (eg, the dismissal in the United States of the legal action against contractors accused of the killing of civilians in the Nisour Square shootings).

It is with an awareness of such limits and shortcomings, and with a view to overcoming them in the future, that the editors and authors of this volume have attempted to clarify the role of international law and of European law in preventing harm and in enhancing the legal accountability and remedies for violations of human rights and humanitarian law committed by, or against, private military contractors.

PART I

SECURITY AND POLICY PERSPECTIVES

1

Policy Prospects for Regulating Private Military and Security Companies

Eugenio Cusumano

> If our present doctrines of political economy be just, let us trust them to the utmost... Let us take the war business out of the government's hands and test therein the principles of supply and demand. Let our future sieges of Sebastopol be by contract—no capture no pay. Let us sell the commands of our respective battles to the lowest bidder so that we may have cheap victories.
>
> John Ruskin, 1863[1]

I. Introduction

Private military and security companies (PMSCs) do not operate in a complete regulatory void. Rather, they are embedded in a complex web of international and domestic legal norms, market pressures, contractual obligations, and self-regulatory measures that needs to be tightened so as to ensure a closer and more comprehensive control over the private provision of force. While it may be true that the private military and security industry (PMSI) is still 'less regulated than the cheese industry',[2] these two sectors are hardly comparable: the so-called market for force, where PMSCs operate, is a huge and fragmented sector with an inherently transnational nature that challenges traditional state regulation. Indeed, the rise of PMSCs forcefully shows that the provision and also the regulation of global security are now characterized by increasing fragmentation and denationalization, and thus by a shift from government to governance. Ensuring control over the PMSI is thus a complex endeavour requiring a broader approach to regulation based on both legal and informal tools, and involving a larger network of actors alongside states, such as international and non-governmental organizations (NGOs), private customers and the industry itself.

In order to unravel the challenges produced by the emergence of a PMSI, this chapter will focus on three questions. First, it will analyse *what* to regulate,

---

[1] Lecturing to the Woolwich Arsenal, 1863.
[2] PW Singer, *The Private Military Industry and Iraq: What Have We Learned and Where to Next*, Geneva Centre for the Democratic Control of Armed Forces Policy Paper, November 2004, 14.

exploring the nature and the activities of PMSCs. In addition, it will focus on *why* the market should be regulated by drawing on the literature on the control over military forces. Finally, it will concentrate on *how* to regulate the PMSI, addressing the issue from two different perspectives. On the one hand, it will focus on the main regulatory tools available to public actors, analysing the potential of a combined approach based on both legal and informal regulation grounded on market incentives and strengthened self-regulation. On the other, it will explore the challenges and opportunities of regulation at different levels. After looking at the role of home, contracting and territorial states, the final sections will explore different avenues for international regulation and focus on the need and the potential for EU action.

II. What to Regulate: Analyzing the Market for Force

According to Peter Singer, the emergence of private military and security firms stems from the 'tectonic change' in the international strategic landscape triggered by the end of the Cold War.[3] Although an embryonic private military industry already existed both in the United Kingdom and the United States, the transformations following the end of the cold war played a crucial role in the creation of a worldwide market for force for a number of reasons. First, the downsizing of major armies broadened the supply of military expertise enormously. At the same time, the transformations within Western armies increased the demand for external contractors in at least two respects. On the one hand, the strain on human and financial resources encouraged the increasing specialization of military personnel and the outsourcing of functions other than combat. In the 2001 Quadriennal Defense Review, for instance, the US Department of Defense (DoD) planned the gradual privatization of all activities not 'directly linked to warfighting'.[4] On the other, the increasing use of high-tech weaponry and equipment produced by the so-called 'Revolution in Military Affairs' has made Western militaries reliant on levels of technological expertise that can no longer be kept within the ranks.[5]

In addition, the end of the Cold War produced a disentanglement of major powers from many areas of the developing world. The increasing worldwide presence of transnational firms, as well as international organizations (IOs) and NGOs within the territories of weak and failed states has thus fuelled a demand for security and logistical support that neither local nor international public actors appear capable of satisfying. Finally, the increasing practice of outsourcing is driven by an ideological shift produced by the 'privatization revolution' following the rise of neo-liberalism, but also the growing awareness that an engagement with the private sector is crucial for world governance. In the United States as well as in other

---

[3] PW Singer, *Corporate Warriors: The Rise of the Privatized Military Industry* (2003), 49.
[4] US Department of Defense, Quadrennial Defense Review Report (30 September 2001) <http://www.defenselink.mil/pubs/pdfs/QDR2001.pdf>, at 53, accessed 10 July 2010.
[5] D Avant, 'The Marketization of Security' in J Kirshner (ed), *Globalization and National Security* (2006), 105–43.

states, not only military functions but also foreign aid and humanitarian relief are increasingly provided by business and non-governmental entities.[6] The new ideological environment appears to have triggered a trend towards the commodification of security: instead of a public good, security is increasingly conceived of as a commodity to be sold and purchased on the market rather than being exclusively supplied by public actors.[7]

As a result of these factors, the rise of PMSCs seems indeed to be the outcome of a systemic shift in both the international and domestic political landscapes, which cannot be easily reversed. Whilst the war in Iraq was famously defined as the first privatized conflict,[8] the tendency towards the privatization of a number of activities previously performed by uniformed military personnel long pre-existed the War on Terror. Indeed, logistics support firms were already involved in US peacekeeping missions in Kosovo and Haiti, as well as in the first Gulf War and in Vietnam.[9] Operations in Iraq and Afghanistan, however, have been a formidable source of growth for the industry: the British firm Control Risks Group, for instance, has since increased its revenues fifteenfold.[10] Recent figures forcefully show the current unprecedented reliance on PMSCs. As of September 2009, there were approximately 119,706 DoD contractors in Iraq, compared with about 134,571 uniformed personnel. In Afghanistan, the civilian workforce significantly outnumbered military personnel, with DoD contractors amounting to 104,100 units compared with only 63,950 troops.[11] Casualties among PMSCs personnel are also striking: as of June 2009, about 1,360 US government contractors have died in the two countries, and more than 29,000 have been wounded.[12]

Although the current Administration has taken steps to 'establish a balanced workforce that appropriately aligns functions to the public and private sector'[13] and gradually to reduce the number of support service contractors from 39 to 26 per cent,[14] PMSCs working for the US government remain an extremely significant presence in Afghanistan and Iraq.[15] Paradoxically, the withdrawal of US troops

---

[6] E Krahmann, *States, Citizens and the Privatization of Security* (2010); A Stanger, *One Nation under Contract* (2009).

[7] E Krahmann, 'Security: Collective Good or Commodity?' *European Journal of International Relations* 14 (2006) 3.

[8] *The Economist*, 'Mercenaries: The Baghdad Boom' (25 March 2004).

[9] D Isenberg, *Private Military Contractors and U.S. Grand Strategy*, Peace Research Institute of Oslo Report (2009), 12–19.

[10] M Hastings, 'We must Fight our Instinctive Distaste for Mercenaries', *The Guardian* (2 August 2006), <http://www.guardian.co.uk/commentisfree/2006/aug/02/comment.politics>, accessed 10 July 2010.

[11] M Schwartz, *Department of Defense Contractors in Iraq and Afghanistan: Background and Analysis*, Congressional Research Service Report for Congress (2009), <http://www.fas.org/sgp/crs/natsec/R40764.pdf>, 5, accessed 10 July 2010.

[12] Commission on Wartime Contracting in Iraq and Afghanistan, *At What Costs? Contingency contracting in Iraq and Afghanistan* (June 2009), iii, <http://www.wartimecontracting.gov/docs/CWC_Interim_Report_At_What_Cost_06-10-09.pdf>, iii, accessed 10 July 2010.

[13] US Department of Defense, Quadrennial Defense Review Report (12 February 2010), xiii, <http://www.defense.gov/qdr/images/QDR_as_of_12Feb10_1000.pdf>, accessed 10 July 2010.

[14] Ibid, 55.

[15] K Kinsey, *Contractors and War: The Transformation of United States, Military and Stabilization Operations* (2010).

from Iraq is producing an increase in State Department reliance on private security contractors.[16] Contractors are likely to keep playing a crucial role in other theatres too: in spite of the recent establishment of a US Army African Regional Command, the State Department is increasingly contracting out the provision of military assistance and Security Sector Reform to African armies.[17]

While the US DoD is the main customer of the PMSI, DoD contractors are far from being the only ones on the ground: PMSCs are also employed by other US governmental agencies such as the State Department and the Agency for International Development (USAID), other states, IOs, NGOs, and private firms.[18] Even now that the US government has planned to re-insource some previously privatized functions and commentators have observed the explosion of the Iraqi 'security bubble' underlying the recent abrupt growth of the market,[19] the overall demand for services provided by PMSCs is likely to keep growing, although less steadily, fuelled by the privatization of non-combat activities in Western armies and the increasing reliance of commercial and humanitarian operators working in high-risk environments on private security services. Indeed, while the Iraqi market is saturated, new business opportunities are now offered by the situation in Afghanistan and the insecurity of maritime routes off the coasts of Africa and East Asia.[20]

Different definitions have been used to break down the PMSI. Classifying the actors operating in the market for force is far from being a merely taxonomic issue: on the contrary, breaking down such a huge and fragmented sector is essential for any attempt to regulate the industry.[21] The very choice of a definition often reflects a precise regulatory position: while referring to military contractors as new mercenaries implies the need for a ban on their activities, talking about private security or a peace and stability industry suggests a more nuanced approach.

There is increasing consensus in the scholarly literature that PMSCs and their employees cannot be considered as mercenaries either on formal or substantial grounds.[22] As a number of authors have emphasized, existing international norms on mercenaries appear largely inapplicable to PMSCs.[23] In addition, there is also substantial agreement that even if they share some similarities, PMSCs represent a

---

[16] W Matthews, 'US Contractor Use in Iraq Expected to Rise' (12 July 2010), <http://www.defensenews.com/story.php?i=470826>, accessed on 15 September 2010.

[17] S McFate, 'Outsourcing the Making of Militaries: DynCorp International as Sovereign Agent', *Review of African Political Economy* 35(118) (2008), 646.

[18] Author's interviews with representatives of the industry.

[19] D Dominick, *After The Bubble: British Private Security Companies after Iraq* (Royal United Services Institute for Defence and Security Studies, Whitehall papers 2006).

[20] Author's interviews with representatives of the industry.

[21] Foreign and Commonwealth Office, *Private Military Companies: Options for Regulation* (26 February 2002) <http://www.fco.gov.uk/resources/en/pdf/pdf4/fco_pdf_privatemilitarycompanies>, accessed 10 July 2010.

[22] Singer (n 3 above); Avant (n 5 above).

[23] For a debate on the applicability of the definition of mercenary to PMSC see, for instance, L Doswald-Beck, 'Private Military Companies under IHL' in S Chesterman and C Lehnardt (eds), *The Rise and Regulation of Private Military Companies* (2007); I-I Drews, 'Private Military Companies: The New Mercenaries? An International Law Analysis' in T Jäger and G Kümmel (eds), *Private Military and Security Companies: Chances, Problems, Pitfalls and Prospects* (2007).

substantially new phenomenon, which differs from traditional mercenary ventures. The main difference lies precisely in their nature as legal entities based on permanent corporate structures with public rather than clandestine patterns of recruitment.[24] Such a distinction appears far from trivial from a regulatory perspective: given that they are corporate bodies with a long-standing existence on the market, PMSCs can be subject to a much broader set of both legal norms and informal constraints.

The most widespread distinction used in the literature, that between private military and private security companies, appears controversial for at least two reasons. First, most companies provide an array of different services, ranging from logistics, training, and intelligence to static, convoy, and personal security. Hence, most companies provide both private military and private security services rather than either one or the other. Moreover, the very distinction between security and military functions is often inherently blurred. What is crucial in assessing the military nature of an activity is not only the activity per se, but the theatre in which it is carried out: providing security for a site or a convoy in the theatre of an insurgency, under potential enemy fire, is a typically military function. While most of the scholarly and journalistic focus has been on private security contractors openly carrying arms, it is the provision of logistics that accounts for the largest part of the revenues of the PMSI. Security services, on the other hand, purportedly account for only 5 per cent of the industry represented by the International Peace Operations Association, the largest PMSI group.[25] Similarly, official estimates show that in 2008 only about 11 per cent of the contractors working for the US DoD were performing security functions.[26]

Other taxonomies, based on the offensive or defensive nature of the services provided,[27] or differentiating between military provider, military consultant, and military support firms[28] are similarly challenged by the low level of specialization of most companies, the increasingly technological nature of warfare and the complexities of asymmetric conflicts and operations other than war. Hence, existing classifications often little reflect the sensitivity and impact of PMSCs' activities. For instance, the training and strategic advice provided by the US firm MPRI in 1995 boosted enormously the offensive capacities of the Croatian army and therefore had a huge strategic impact despite not being directly operational.[29] Also, the outsourcing of intelligence and military weaponry operational support has given unarmed contractors working far from the frontline and carrying out activities that may ostensibly be classified as logistical support a significant

---

[24] Singer (n 3 above); Avant (n 5 above); S Percy, *Regulating the Private Security Industry*, International Institute for Strategic Studies (2006), C Kinsey, *Corporate Soldiers and International Security: The Rise of Private Military Companies* (2006).
[25] Author's interview with representatives of the industry.
[26] Schwartz (n 11 above), 7.
[27] S Makki et al, *Private Military Companies and the Proliferation of Small Arms: Regulating the Actors* (International Alert Briefing 10, 2001).
[28] Singer (n 3 above), 91–5.
[29] D Shearer, *Private Armies and Military Intervention* (1998); Singer (n 3 above).

responsibility in the use of lethal force. In Iraq, contracted personnel operated armed unmanned aerial vehicles until they reached the target of the bombing, being replaced by military personnel only at the moment of pushing the fire button.[30]

Classifying and regulating private military services are therefore complex operations that escape gross dichotomies and require a case-by-case analysis based on the provisions of each contract and the actual activities of the personnel on the ground. A company may thus be subject to different regulatory frameworks according to the differing levels of sensitivity of the activities it carries out.

III. Why Regulate: The PMSI and the Control over the Use of Force

As it has been argued, most of the current debate on the privatization of force has hitherto produced 'more heat than light'.[31] The need for regulation, however, seems now to have obtained widespread consensus, supplanting the call for a ban that long dominated a substantial part of the literature,[32] but is now generally considered unfeasible if not undesirable without solving the dramatic mismatch between the capacities of existing military forces and the global demand for security.

The impact of private military and security activities on the enjoyment of human rights and the need to prevent, prosecute, and punish international humanitarian law (IHL) infringements are crucial concerns which illustrate the need for further regulation. This section, however, will take a broader perspective, drawing on the insights offered by the literature on civil–military relations and the control over the use of military force in order to analyse extensively the challenges that the emergence of PMSCs pose not only to host countries, but also to home and contracting states.

Scholars working on globalization and the so-called 'new wars' have often associated the emergence of a market for military and security services with an end to the monopoly of legitimate violence long considered as the defining feature of state entities, and thus with a decline of sovereignty.[33] It is worth mentioning, however, that the public and the private provision of coercion are not necessarily antithetic phenomena: on the contrary, actors such as mercenaries and privateers

---

[30] D Avant, 'The Privatization of Security and Change in the Control of Force', *International Studies Perspectives* 5(2) (2004) 154. It was recently found out that unmanned aerial vehicles employed by the CIA against the Taliban in Afghanistan were maintained by civilian contractors working for Xe Services, previously known as Blackwater. See, for instance, J Risen and M Mazzetti, 'C.I.A. said to use Outsiders to put Bombs on Drones', *The New York Times* (20 August 2009), <http://www.nytimes.com/2009/08/21/us/21intel.html?_r=1&th&emc=th>, accessed 10 July 2010.

[31] JOC Jonah 'Foreword' in Chesterman and Lehnardt (n 23 above), v.

[32] See, for instance, D Francis, 'Mercenary Intervention in Sierra Leone: Providing National Security or International Exploitation?' *Third World Quarterly* 20 (1999) 2; A Musah and K. Fayemi, *Mercenaries: An African Security Dilemma* (2000).

[33] See M Creveld, *The Rise and Decline of The State* (1999); M Kaldor, *New and Old Wars*, 2nd edn (2006); H Münkler, *The New Wars* (2006).

played a crucial role in the development of the modern state system.[34] In addition, referring to a 'private challenge to state armed forces'[35] overlooks the fact that PMSCs have hitherto supported rather than threatened national armies, and the current process of outsourcing is a deliberate political strategy that allows Western states to pursue more flexible foreign policies and otherwise unfeasible military operations. Even weak and failed states, whose sovereignty may be endangered by the activities of PMSCs inside their territories, have often benefited from the PMSI as a last resort in order to curb enduring conflict and train more effective security forces.[36]

Although arguments based on the decline of the state ought to be taken with a grain of salt and fleshed out by a comprehensive case-by-case analysis, the outsourcing of military and security operations may indeed call into question public control over the use of force in a number of ways. The concept of control over the use of military force projected outside a state's borders can be broken down into three different notions: those of functional, political, and social control.[37] *Functional control* is based on the need to ensure that the military sector is capable of providing security effectively, protecting the polity from external threats. *Political control* refers to the importance of keeping the security sector under the rule of democratically elected leaders. Security operations have to be embedded in an institutional process establishing checks and constraints on the resort to force and ensuring democratic accountability over military activities. *Social control*, finally, implies that the military and security sector should be integrated in the wider social context and act according to established social values. Whilst Western military and security forces now respond, to a major or minor extent, to all of these forms of control, the surge of PMSCs may call each of them into question.

Some have suggested that PMSCs can enhance military capabilities by acting as force multipliers for national armies and providing new and more flexible tools of foreign policy. The emergence of private military companies may nevertheless pose a trade-off: whilst boosting functional control over the use of coercion, reliance on PMSCs diminishes social and political control.[38] A deeper look at the activities of the PMSI, however, provides a more complex picture, as private contractors may also engender problems for the functional effectiveness of military engagements. First, PMSCs have reportedly provided personnel not qualified to perform their contractual obligations.[39] Moreover, the presence in a theatre of operations of contracted personnel operating outside military chains of command may engender problems of C3—that is, communication, command, and control—and requires the

---

[34] J Thomson, *Mercenaries, Pirates and Sovereigns* (1996); Coker, 'Outsourcing War' *Cambridge Review of International Affairs* 13(1) (1999).
[35] R Mandel, *Armies without States: The Privatization of Security* (2002), 32.
[36] Shearer (n 29 above); O' Brien, 'PMCs, Myths and Mercenaries: The Debate on Private Military Companies' *Royal United Services Institute Journal* 145(1) (2000).
[37] D Avant, 'The Emerging Market for Private Military Service and the Problem of Regulation' in Chesterman and Lehnardt (n 23 above).
[38] Ibid.
[39] The firm CACI, involved in the scandals of Abu Ghraib, had for instance provided personnel without any previous experience in human intelligence. See S Chesterman, 'We Can't Spy...if We Can't Buy! The Privatization of Intelligence and the Limits of Outsourcing Inherently Governmental Functions' (2008) 19(5) EJIL 1063–4.

establishment of procedures ensuring the interaction between national armed forces and contractors, which to date appear to be absent or insufficient. In Iraq, this lack of coordination was epitomized by the frequent cases of blue-to-white fire, that is friendly fire between uniformed and contracted personnel. Between January and May 2005, twenty blue-to-white incidents were reported.[40] Also, relying on individuals with no obligations other than those stemming from their hiring contract can be problematic. Contracts are rigid legal tools that cannot be easily adapted to unexpected operational needs caused by the sudden changes of fluid, war-torn environments.[41] In addition, outsourcing places the success of military operations at the mercy of personnel outside the ranks, who may quit their jobs without being prosecuted for desertion. In Iraq, some logistics firms have suspended their activities because they found the local environment too dangerous.[42] Recent enquiries raise even more alarming concerns over the reliability of contractors: a US Senate Armed Services Committee, still partially classified, found ties between warlords involved in illegal activities and even Taliban insurgents and Afghan security guards, some of whom were reportedly using their access to coalition military bases to steal weapons and plan attacks against their employer.[43] Finally, the effectiveness of complex military operations like counter-insurgency requires a careful balance between the use of force against insurgents and the need to prevent collateral damage and the subsequent alienation of the local population that the presence of contractors operating outside the military chain of command may alter.[44] While enhancing the capacity of the US military to remain involved in Iraq and carry out the reconstruction of the country, some PMSCs may have hampered the success of the Coalition's counter-insurgency strategy because of their excess in the use of force, epitomized for instance by the infamous Nisour Square incident of September 2007.[45] As subsequently argued by then Senator Obama, the United States 'cannot win a fight for hearts and minds when we outsource critical missions to unaccountable contractors'.[46]

Although the warning that PMSCs 'have paved the way for the multinational neocolonialism of the twenty-first century'[47] seems at the least excessive, it is true

---

[40] US Government Accountability Office, *Actions Needed to Improve Use of Private Security Providers* (2005), 14, <http://www.gao.gov/new.items/d05737.pdf>, accessed 10 July 2010.

[41] J Stober, 'Contracting in the Fog of War' in Jäger and Kümmel (n 23 above).

[42] Singer (nn 2 and 3 above). See also Stober (n 41 above).

[43] United States Senate Armed Forces Committee. *Report of the Inquiry into the Role and Oversight of Private Security Contractors in Afghanistan*, (28 September 2010). <http://armed-services.senate.gov/Publications/SASC%20PSC%20Report%2010-07-10.pdf accessed 20 October 2010>, accessed 19 October 2010.

[44] S Percy, 'Private Security Companies and Civil Wars', *Civil Wars* 11(1) (2009) 64–5; PW Singer, *Can't Win With 'Em, Can't Go To War Without 'Em: Private Military Contractors and Counter-Insurgency*, Brooking Institute Policy Paper 4 (September 2007).

[45] On 16 September 2007, Blackwater contractors escorting a convoy of State Department and USAID shot and killed 17 Iraqi civilians in Baghdad. See, for instance, D Johnston and D Broder, 'F.B. I. Says Guards Killed 14 Iraqis without Cause', *The New York Times* (14 November 2007).

[46] C Hauser, 'New Rules for Contractors are Urged by 2 Democrats', *The New York Times* (4 October 2007).

[47] E Bernales Ballesteros, *Report on the Question of the Use of Mercenaries as a Means of Violating Human Rights and Impeding the Exercise of the Right of Peoples to Self-determination* (UNCHR Report E/CN.4/1997/24), para 109, <http://www.unhchr.ch/Huridocda/Huridoca.nsf/TestFrame/71e8763786cca82a8025666b004e1268?Opendocument>, accessed 10 July 2010.

that the provision of coercion by PMSCs on behalf of private firms is unaccountable to both territorial and home states' populations, and democratic oversight of the export of military services to foreign governments also appears insufficient. The direct use of PMSCs by contracting states poses further problems, affecting 'the institutional checks and balances and democratic practices that have been connected to restraint in military policy',[48] reducing governmental transparency and strengthening the executive vis-à-vis the legislature. Without adequate legal regulation, the use of PMSCs may offer 'alternative mechanisms for the executive body to conduct secret operations without other branches being involved',[49] providing ways to circumvent the political and legal obstacles associated with the deployment of uniformed military personnel.[50] Finally, with their intelligence, consultancy, training, and lobbying activities, PMSCs may play a role in shaping the security perceptions and strategic priorities of governmental agencies, thereby gaining excessive epistemic influence over the making of foreign policy.[51]

Social control over the use of force also involves democratic oversight and legal discipline of military and police professionals, aimed at establishing who is authorized to exert coercion, their training, and their hierarchies. This allows a 'sociological regulation' of security forces, ensuring that their organizational cultures reflect established social values.[52] Whilst this is the case in national armies, governments and parliaments lack any voice in recruiting procedures, vetting policies and career paths within the PMSI. Due to insufficient vetting procedures or the need for a cheaper workforce, PMSCs may employ individuals previously involved in human rights violations or other forms of criminal and socially unacceptable behaviour. There has been fierce criticism, for instance, of the use by some PMSCs of apartheid-era police, and officials of the Chilean army during Pinochet's dictatorship.[53] Given companies' huge reliance on local or third-country personnel, the assumption that because of their training in Western armed forces PMSCs personnel have 'inherited routines in which established military practice and international law and custom are already contained'[54] may not necessarily hold true.

Focusing on this threefold notion of control over the use of force shows the magnitude of the challenges posed by the rise of PMSCs. Although ensuring the prevention and prosecution of human rights abuses perpetrated in weak states is certainly a priority, this can only be part of a broader regulatory effort, which should ultimately be based on the subjection of the PMSI to the same control procedures already in place vis-à-vis public military and security forces.[55]

---

[48] Avant (n 5 above), 115–16.
[49] Singer (n 3 above), 214.
[50] J Michaels, 'Beyond Accountability: The Constitutional, Democratic and Strategic Problems with Privatizing War' (2004) 82 Washington University Law Quarterly 1039; see also D Avant, *The Market for Force: The Consequences of Privatizing Security* (2005), 62, 128–9.
[51] A Leander, 'Regulating the Role of Private Military Companies in Shaping Security and Politics' in Chesterman and Lehnardt (n 23 above).
[52] M Janowitz, *The Professional Soldier*, 1st edn (1960).
[53] Leander (n 50 above).
[54] C Ortiz, 'The Private Military Company: An Entity at the Centre of Overlapping Spheres of Commercial Activity and Responsibility' in Jäger and Kümmel (n 23 above), 61.
[55] Percy (n 24 above), 24.

IV. How to Regulate: A Multifaceted Approach

The previous two sections briefly analysed the nature of the PMSI and the number of problems it may pose to control over the use of force, not only in territorial states but also in home and contracting countries. Whilst a ban does not appear feasible, no single regulatory effort can offer a fully fledged solution to all these problems. Indeed, maximizing all dimensions of control may be impossible given the inherent trade-offs existing between them.[56] Regulation, as this section will try to show, may thus be grounded on a pragmatic approach based on three main kinds of instrument: legal regulation to be enacted at both the domestic and the international level, market incentives provided by the public demand for private military and security services, and strengthened self-regulation of the sector.

A. Legal Regulation

Although PMSCs do not operate in a complete legal vacuum, strengthening the existing regulatory regime at both the domestic and the international level appears crucial in order to hold the industry and its employees accountable for their misbehaviour and prevent an erosion of public control over the use of force.

Existing literature has hitherto focused on two major legal tools to be enacted or strengthened by home states where firms have their headquarters: a control on the export of armed services based on a licensing system and the establishment of extraterritorial jurisdiction on private military and security contractors.[57] The provision of extraterritoriality, however, may be appropriate only for the prosecution of major crimes, as it is hampered by a number of problems. Investigating a company's operation requires facilities, manpower, and financial resources that home countries' courts may lack, and is challenged by the difficulties of collecting evidence and witness statements in foreign, war-torn environments.[58] In addition, as already emphasized by the literature on transnational corporations, PMSCs may escape hostile domestic regulations by moving their headquarters into states with less stringent legislation. For these two reasons, most authors have emphasized the need for regulation at the international level, based on the drafting of a new international Convention addressing the PMSI and the establishment of international bodies monitoring and prosecuting companies' misbehaviour.[59]

All these measures will be further analysed below, in the sections dedicated to domestic and international legal regulation. The following sections will instead be dedicated to informal avenues for regulation, showing that market incentives and

---

[56] D Avant, 'Selling Security: Trade-offs in State Regulation of the Private Security Industry' in Jäger and Kümmel (n 23 above), 421.
[57] Percy (n 24 above); KA O' Brien, 'What Should and What Should Not be Regulated' in Chesterman and Lehnardt (n 23 above).
[58] Percy (n 24 above), 37.
[59] Ibid. See also Singer (n 2 above).

strengthened self-regulation may effectively strengthen and complement existing and forthcoming legal provisions.

B. Market Incentives: Public Demand as a Regulatory Tool

Whilst many have warned that PMSCs are business entities driven by corporate profit rather than public interest to emphasize the challenges posed by their emergence, fewer scholars have hitherto explored how their commercial *raison d'être* may also provide additional avenues for regulation, making them subject to a basic, extra-legal kind of pressure: consumer demand. It is widely held in the literature on industrial relations that public demand is a very effective tool in the regulation of a market. The PMSI is no exception: since home governments are often the major customers of their services, PMSCs may 'choose to abide by regulation to preserve their governmental contracts'.[60] The effectiveness of public demand as a regulatory tool, however, is deeply dependent on the structure, the number of players and the dynamics of each market. A brief overview of the PMSI appears therefore crucial. According to a set of interviews with representatives of the industry, three main processes appear clear.

First, while the PMSI is far from operating in a perfectly competitive market and some major contracts are still awarded non-competitively, it has developed increasing levels of competition. Following the abrupt surge in the demand stemming from the occupation and reconstruction of Iraq and Afghanistan, a huge number of new players have entered the market.[61] The supply of security services has thus quickly grown to match the demand, so that many firms have reported growing financial trouble.[62] This increased competitiveness appears ideal for enhancing the effectiveness of both consumer demand and self-regulation of the sector, which will be analysed below. Secondly, whilst the demand for commercial security and logistical support represents a valuable share of the revenues of the industry, public contracts awarded by governments and international organizations appear fundamental. In 2007, only about 15 per cent of firms responding to the annual International Peace Operations Association (IPOA) Survey were not providing services for some governmental actor.[63] Finally, although some niche for smaller specialized companies remain, the market appears also to be subject to a process of concentration characterized by mergers and acquisitions. Group4, for instance, to date the biggest private security company, purchased Wackenhut in 2002, Securicor in 2004, and took over the British PMSC ArmorGroup in 2008.[64] While the

---

[60] Avant (n 55 above), 421.
[61] JJ Messner and Y Gracielly, *State of the Peace and Stability Operation Industry*, POI second annual report 2007, <http://peaceops.org/poi/images/stories/poi_rp_industrysurvey2007.pdf>, 16, accessed 10 July 2010.
[62] Author's interviews with representatives of the industry.
[63] Messner and Gracielli (n 60 above), 21.
[64] H Power, 'Troubled ArmorGroup Secures Sale to G4S', *Daily Telegraph* (23 March 2008), <http://www.telegraph.co.uk/money/main.jhtml?xml=/money/2008/03/21/cnarmor121.xml>, accessed 10 July 2010.

creation of a small number of private security giants may reduce competition, bigger firms with an enduring existence on the market can be more easily subjected to both informal and legal regulation than smaller companies for at least two reasons. First, small companies with almost no assets or permanent personnel can more easily move offshore or underground, or dissolve and reopen under different names to circumvent regulation and escape prosecutions. In addition, smaller firms are more likely to act as 'single-shot players' whose aim is obtaining one single lucrative contract before closing their doors, and who are thus much less vulnerable to reputational pressures and market incentives promoting good behaviour.[65]

The evolution of the market underlying the three above-mentioned phenomena therefore offers new avenues for informal regulation, and appears to strengthen the importance of consumer demand as a valuable tool of control. Although it cannot replace the need for further legal regulation, the award, renewal, and termination of public contracts provide both incentives and deterrents for the industry, preventing some of the major problems associated with traditional domestic regulation. The prospect of losing lucrative state contracts clearly raises the costs of escaping regulation and provides crucial incentives to comply with major national and international legal norms as well as home states' foreign policy and values. Legal and financial tools of control are indeed mutually reinforcing, as without a public market of the services to be controlled regulation is likely to have a minor impact. Since 'the ability of individual states to regulate the market...is tied to their consumption',[66] a home state that is at the same time a contracting state like the United States or to a minor extent the United Kingdom, Canada, and Australia, seems to be in an ideal position to control PMSCs effectively through a synergy of legal regulation and market pressure. Although the increasing use of PMSCs by state actors allows for the exertion of stronger leverage on their behaviour, however, some kinds of activities ought not to be privatized. Services that are most likely to involve the discretionary provision of violence should be performed only by national military personnel subject to a chain of command, a system of military justice, and an institutional framework ensuring democratic oversight. The same applies to at least some intelligence services, which have instead been massively privatized in the United States.[67] Due to the sensitivity of the information collected and the high risk of abuses during human intelligence activities, this sector appears too controversial to be privatized, as clearly shown by the scandals involving employees of the firms CACI and TITAN operating in Abu Ghraib as translators and interrogators.[68] Outsourcing, therefore, should occur within the framework of a clearly stated and publicly debated governmental policy, establishing no-go areas and ensuring transparency and oversight.

---

[65] J Cockayne, 'Make or Buy? Principal–Agent Theory and the Regulation of Private Military Companies' in Chesterman and Lehnardt (n 23 above).
[66] Avant (n 55 above).
[67] On the US trend towards the privatization of intelligence see Chesterman (n 39 above).
[68] Investigation of the 800th Military Police Brigade (2004), 44, <http://www.npr.org/iraq/2004/prison_abuse_report.pdf>, accessed 10 July 2010.

In order for states' demand to develop its potential in shaping the behaviour of the industry, governments should use their procurements consistently, taking into account companies' good conduct as the major driver of contract awards and renewals. Strikingly, this does not always seem to be the case: despite the above-mentioned scandals and its provision of untrained personnel, for instance, CACI was awarded yet another contract for the supply of interrogation services in Iraq.[69] In the absence of clear governmental policies disciplining outsourcing, different agencies may award contracts solely according to a logic of cost-effectiveness, thereby triggering a race to the bottom in the quality of the services and personnel provided by PMSCs trying to offer lower and lower bids whilst keeping some margin of profit.[70] Relying on the purchase of military and security services as an informal regulatory tool requires the elaboration of instruments to monitor and assess firms' effectiveness and compliance with contractual provisions, their respect of domestic and international law, and their recruiting and operating policies.

Whilst further regulation still needs to be enacted, states have often failed to make the most of the legal tools already at their disposal. Contracts awarded in Iraq have often been 'strikingly vague', not incorporating crucial values including human rights, transparency and anti-corruptions norms, and possessing 'so few guidelines, requirements, or benchmarks that they effectively contain no meaningful evaluative criteria'.[71] Finally, governmental supervision, has also been stunningly insufficient: according to a 2004 DoD Inspector General Study, more than half of contracts were not adequately monitored.[72]

In order for governments to exert market as well as contractual pressures transparently and effectively, ensuring public scrutiny and parliamentary oversight, effective monitoring and assessment criteria need to be enhanced. It is clear, therefore, that the effectiveness of market pressure rests on a broader set of regulatory tools. Whilst it is correct that public demand can boost states' influence on firms and is crucial in ensuring compliance with regulation, the opposite also holds true: the use of public demand as a source of financial incentives and deterrents for the PMSI requires a degree of transparency and accountability that neither the industry nor its customers possess yet, and needs to be enforced by more effective monitoring policies, a strengthening of existing legal regulation, and more effective self-regulation of the sector.

---

[69] E McCarthy, 'CACI gets New Interrogation Contract', *The Washington Post* (5 August 2004), <http://www.washingtonpost.com/wp-dyn/articles/A41215-2004Aug4.html>, accessed 10 July 2010.
[70] Author's interview with representatives of the industry.
[71] L Dickinson, 'Contracts as a Tool for Regulating Private Military Companies' in Chesterman and Lehnardt (n 23 above), 218; See also Isenberg (n 9 above), 29–37.
[72] Office of the Inspector General, Us Department of Defense, *Acquisitions: Contracts Awarded for the Coalition Provisional Authority by the Defense Contracting Command* (18 March 2004), <http://www.dodig.mil/audit/reports/fy04/04-057.pdf>, accessed 10 July 2010.

C. Self-Regulation

The last part of this section will be dedicated to a brief analysis of the self-regulation of the industry and how it can be upheld by public actors' support. In recent years, both single firms and major industry associations have produced a number of codes of conduct, best practices, and ethics declarations. The two major industry associations, the British Association of Private Security Companies (BAPSC) and the International Peace Operations Association (IPOA), now rebranded International Stability Operations Association, mention 'compliance to the law of the countries in which members operate'[73] or 'high operational and ethical standards'[74] among their main statutory goals, and consider membership conditional to the respect of various norms and codes of conduct. Whilst self-regulation alone is insufficient and the substantial or merely declaratory nature of some efforts may be controversial, overlooking it would be a mistake. Indeed, given the nature and evolution of the market, meaningful efforts towards self-regulation can be taken seriously as they appear to be in the interest of the industry itself. The literature on industrial relations and corporate social responsibility shows that many markets are characterized by a strong business case for self-regulation.[75] Due to its legitimacy deficit, its increasing competitiveness and its strong reliance on public contracts, the PMSI is far from being an exception. Meaningful self-regulation is a way for companies to save the legal and reputational costs stemming from scandals and litigations, gain a competitive advantage vis-à-vis market rivals by pursuing a strategy of brand differentiation and, finally, discourage further legal regulation to be enacted by state actors.[76] The financial trouble suffered by Blackwater Worldwide, rebranded Xe in 2009 and now on sale,[77] forcefully show that the costs of misbehaviour are by no means trivial, and can at least in the long run jeopardize PMSCs' survival in a competitive market.

Whilst it remains clear that PMSI efforts per se are exposed to a number of problems that call into question their effectiveness, states can enact legislation that enables industry associations' regulation to develop teeth, providing meaningful supervision and credible sanctions against non-complying members. To date, the complaint procedure established by IPOA, based on a permanent committee that investigates stakeholders' complaints, has two major problems: first, members have no obligation to cooperate with the investigation by providing information and disclosing documents; secondly, the absence of independent monitors from outside

---

[73] British Association of Private Security Companies Charter, <http://bapsc.org.uk/key_documents-charter.asp>, accessed 10 July 2010.

[74] <http://www.ipoaworld.org/eng/aboutipoa.html>, accessed 10 July 2010.

[75] For instance, A Carroll and K Shabana, 'The Business Case for Corporate Social Responsibility: A Review of Concepts, Research and Practice' *International Journal of Management Reviews* 12(1) (2010).

[76] Cockayne (n 64 above), 215.

[77] K Roane. Wanted: A Buyer for Blackwater and its Baggage (9 June 2010), CNN Money.com. <http://money.cnn.com/2010/06/08/news/companies/blackwater_xe_sale.fortune/index.htm>, accessed 10 July 2010.

the industry hampers the credibility of the oversight mechanism. Legal provisions enacted at state level can, at least to some extent, overcome these limitations. Initiatives such as the creation of an independent ombudsman investigating complaints against PMSCs' activities, proposed by the BAPSC to the British government, are a valuable step in that direction.[78]

In addition, states as well as international organizations can enhance the effectiveness of collective self-regulation by making the award of major contracts conditional upon membership of the major industry associations, which would help to make the expulsion of non-complying members a costlier sanction. The fact that the British PMSC Aegis was awarded and renewed the major Coalition Provisional Authority (CPA) security contract in Iraq despite being rejected as a member of IPOA clearly damaged the effectiveness of the association's self-regulatory efforts.[79] It is true, however, that the credibility of industry associations is inherently stymied by the fact that membership is neither universal nor compulsory, and still excludes some major players on the market.[80] Since membership is now voluntary, a company may simply resign to avoid the reputational costs of industry investigations over its activities and exclusion from the association, as already done by Blackwater, which withdrew from IPOA after an enquiry over its behaviour in Iraq had started.[81] The most decisive contribution to the strengthening of self-regulation would therefore come from making membership compulsory in order for firms to operate on the market or at least to be awarded public contracts.

Finally, it is worth mentioning that when PMSCs provide commercial security for the private sector, self-regulation and corporate social responsibility can be promoted on both sides of the contractual relationship. The Voluntary Principles on Security and Human Rights, drafted by the governments of the United States, the United Kingdom, Norway, and the Netherlands, together with a few corporations operating in the extractive and energy sectors and some major NGOs, addresses the issues of transnational firms' use of the PMSI.[82] Whilst such principles have to date been signed by a limited number of firms and lack oversight and enforcement mechanisms, resulting in an impact which has to date been feeble,[83] they are a step forward to be further encouraged. The Voluntary Principles may, for instance, be included as a compulsory clause for private firms' contracts with PMSCs.[84] Whilst aware of the risk of associating themselves with PMSCs previously involved in misconduct or with insufficient ethical and professional standards,

---

[78] A Beapark and S Schulz, 'The Regulation of the Private Security Industry and the Future of the Market' in Chesterman and Lehnardt (n 23 above), 248.
[79] K Alexander and N White, *The Regulatory Context of Private Military and Security Services in the UK*, University of Sheffield: Priv-War Report 09 (2009), 21.
[80] Percy (n 24 above), 59.
[81] See Ch 18 by Hoppe and Quirico in this volume.
[82] *Voluntary Principles on Security and Human Rights*, <http://www.voluntaryprinciples.org/principles/private.php>, accessed 10 July 2010.
[83] C Holmqvist, *Private Security Companies: The Case for Regulation*, SIPRI Policy Paper no 9 (2005).
[84] J Spear, *Market Forces: The Political Economy of Private Military and Security*, Forskningsstiftelsen Fafo (2005), 17.

non-governmental customers of the industry often lack sufficient knowledge about the sector and its players. In order for firms and NGOs to choose responsibly among different security providers, state actors needs to disclose and share information about PMSCs' previous performance, so as to help create a more transparent and efficient market for security and logistical support in high-risk environments.

V. How to Regulate: A Multilayered Approach

As Alexander Wendt observes, 'since states are the dominant form of subjectivity in contemporary world politics, this means that they should be the primary unit of analysis for thinking about the global regulation of violence'.[85] While states' control remains the cornerstone of any regulatory effort, it is, however, no longer the only one: one of the crucial features of the emergence of a PMSI is precisely that it diffuses and redistributes the control over violence, engaging a broader network of public and private actors in the governance of global security.[86]

A number of factors erode the effectiveness of traditional single-state regulation. On the one hand, territorial states where PMSCs operate may lack the institutional capacity to hold PMSCs accountable under domestic and international law. On the other, due to the transnational nature of the industry, the possibility for firms to avoid hostile regulation by moving offshore and the difficulties of extraterritorial prosecution, home states' regulation alone is hardly a silver bullet.

There is indeed little doubt that an industry operating transnationally can be best regulated at the international level.[87] International regulation, however, is hampered by the well-known difficulties of collective action by states and the diverse role and interests that different states have vis-à-vis the market. The last section will explore the main avenues of regulation and the difficulties and potential of different regulatory options on the international stage.

A. Regulation at the Domestic Level

Given the transnational nature of the industry, the low institutional capacity of most territorial states and the problems related to extraterritorial monitoring and prosecution of PMSCs, domestic regulation alone cannot address all the challenges produced by the emergence of the PMSI. In the absence of relevant international action, single states' regulation remains, however, the most indispensable tool to regulate PMSCs. This section will focus largely on home and contracting states, which are often those with the highest regulatory capacities vis-à-vis the industry. A brief look at weak territorial states will however be provided below.

---

[85] A Wendt, *Social Theory of International Politics* (1999), 9.
[86] Avant (n 5 above); E Krahmann, 'Conceptualizing Security Governance' *Cooperation and Conflict* 38(1) (2003).
[87] Percy (n 24 above), 63.

1. Territorial States

Whilst it is not always the case, territorial states often lack the capacity to hold PMSCs and their personnel accountable for the violation of domestic as well as international law.[88] For a comprehensive analysis, see Ch 7 by Bakker. In some cases, territorial states' jurisdiction may be explicitly circumvented, as demonstrated by Order 17 of the Iraqi CPA, establishing that 'contractors shall be immune from Iraqi legal process with respect to acts performed by them pursuant to the terms and conditions of a Contract or any sub-contract thereto',[89] and later replaced by a Status of Forces Agreement (SOFA) between the US and the Iraqi governments. Although in most other cases contractors are no doubt subject to domestic legislation, the lack of monitoring and enforcement capabilities hampers host states' capacity to ensure their legal liability.

Due to their insufficient enforcement capabilities, strengthened regulation by territorial states is thus unlikely to make any substantial difference. Whilst territorial states may lack the capacity effectively to monitor, let alone prevent and prosecute, the activities of PMSCs within their territories, they can, however, find allies in transnational civil society actors operating within their territories. Media, non-governmental organizations, charities, and humanitarian operators can play a valuable role in the regulation of the PMSI by acting as fire alarms, signalling the misbehaviour of PMSCs. Civil-society actors may create transnational advocacy networks, that is networks of activists 'bound together by shared values, a common discourse and dense exchange of information and services' that have proved to be capable of promoting human rights across national frontiers thanks to their campaigns of shaming and blaming and their support for local civil society actors.[90] Such networks can help territorial states and their local population to denounce and punish PMSCs' misconduct by exerting pressure on home and contracting states, affecting the reputation of the company and providing the resources needed to access home countries' legal remedies. The support of the US Center for Constitutional Rights, for instance, allowed the families of the Iraqi civilians killed in Nisour Square to start a civil lawsuit against Blackwater.[91]

However, transnational civil society's support can only offer a limited response to the threat of PMSCs' misbehaviour in territorial states. As it has been correctly argued, the protection of weak states is indeed the most important reason to establish an international framework ensuring the monitoring and the prosecution of PMSCs.[92]

---

[88] For a comprehensive analysis, see Ch 7 by Bakker.
[89] Coalition Provisional Order 17, as amended 17 June 2004, at 5, <http://www.iraqcoalition.org/regulations/20040627_CPAORD_17_Status_of_Coalition_Rev_with_Annex_A.pdf>, accessed 10 July 2010.
[90] M Kekk and K Sikkink, *Activists Beyond Borders: Advocacy Networks in International Politics* (1998).
[91] R Ulam Weiner, *The Hidden Costs of Contracting: Private law, Commercial Imperatives and the Privatized Military Industry* (2008), 2, <http://belfercenter.ksg.harvard.edu/publication/18725/hidden_costs_of_contracting.html>, accessed 10 July 2010.
[92] Percy (n 24 above).

2. Home and Contracting States

Whilst home-state regulation is insufficient to regulate an inherently transnational industry, it appears so far to be the most effective instrument. Two major regulatory systems based on the licensing of the export of armed services are to date in place: the US International Traffic in Arms Regulation (ITAR) and the South African Foreign and Military Assistance Act (FMAA). Examining them in detail is beyond the scope of this chapter. Although these two acts are crucial benchmarks in today's regulatory landscape, they both suffer from some major shortcomings that need to be taken into account by forthcoming legislation.

The South African FMAA of 1998 is based on the distinction between mercenary activities, defined as direct participation as a combatant in armed conflicts for private gain and banned altogether, and foreign military assistance, which is conditional to the provision by the National Conventional Arms Control Committee of a licence which can be revoked at any time. Often mentioned with reference to the problems associated with stringent regulation, the FMAA has been doubtlessly unsuccessful. First, it suffers from major enforcement problems, and has so far led to very few prosecutions.[93] Moreover, such strict, unilateral regulation, unaccompanied by market incentives to comply with domestic legal provisions and by broader international regulations, appears only to have moved companies further away from governmental influence, pushing the South African industry across borders or underground.[94] Given the massive presence of South African contractors among PMSC personnel operating in Iraq, in 2008 the South African government enacted further legislation regulating the participation of its nationals in foreign conflicts.[95]

The US ITAR, part of the Broader Arms Export Control Act, regulates the export of military services as well as armaments abroad by making it conditional to the provision of a licence by the Office of Defense Trade Control within the Department of State. Whilst considered the most effective piece of legislation on the export of military assistance to date, the ITAR suffers from two major problems. First, the licensing process is described as idiosyncratic, inconsistent, lacking in transparency, and too exposed to firms' lobbying actions. Most importantly, the process suffers from insufficient democratic oversight, as Congress is notified only of contracts exceeding a threshold of US$50 million, and even major procurements can be easily unpacked into smaller contracts to escape Congressional control.[96]

Disciplining the export of armed services is a basic regulatory starting point, ensuring that governments have a degree of scrutiny on the activities of PMSCs and

---

[93] M Caparini, 'Regulating Private Military and Security Companies: The U.S. Approach' in D Alexander et al, *Private Military and Security Companies: Ethics, Policies and Civil–Military Relations* (2007).
[94] Avant in Jäger and Kümmel (n 23 above), 432. See also Caparini (n 91 above).
[95] *Republic of South Africa Government Gazette* (16 November 2007), <http://www.info.gov.za/view/DownloadFileAction?id=75729>, accessed 10 July 2010.
[96] Avant in Jäger and Kümmel (n 23 above), 432.

their compatibility with national foreign policies and international commitments. Whilst it is very likely that governments are aware of major PMSC activities even when official consent provided by the award of a licence is not required, established, bureaucratized procedures like those established by ITAR and FMAA are needed to avoid the ambiguities of an informal system of notification. A clear case in point showing the need for official authorization is the 1998 Arms to Africa Affair, when the British Foreign Office denied its awareness of the operations carried out by the PMSC Sandline in Sierra Leone after the firm had been found in violation of a UN arms embargo, in spite of substantial evidence of the contrary.[97] Established licensing mechanisms prevent home countries from keeping an attitude of plausible deniability on firms' activities, which hampers international and domestic accountability over foreign policy.

The shield of plausible deniability that governments may enjoy when using PMSCs as tools of foreign policy by proxy reflects a broader problem which forthcoming regulatory efforts need to take carefully into account: the abovementioned impact of the PMSI on democratic control over the use of force. Whilst escaping these constraints may allow states to pursue more flexible foreign policies, circumventing, for instance, the reluctance of Western public opinions towards deploying troops for humanitarian operations, it appears problematic on constitutional and moral grounds. Ensuring democratic control over the use of PMSCs thus requires enhancing transparency over states' use of PMSCs and strengthening both ex ante and ex post parliamentary powers vis-à-vis private military and security activities.[98] First, parliaments should be involved in the decision over what can be privatized and what should instead be considered as inherently governmental. In addition, all contracts between governmental agencies and PMSCs need to be notified to the relevant parliamentary commissions, specifying the numbers, the activities and the casualties of contracted personnel deployed abroad, as well as the disciplinary actions taken against them in the case of misbehaviour. Such provisions were foreseen by the Transparency and Accountability in Military and Security Contracting Act proposed by then Senator Obama in February 2007, but never passed into law.[99] With the National Defense Authorization Acts of 2007 and 2008, however, the US Congress has taken some valuable steps towards further regulation of PMSCs, explicitly extending military jurisdiction to contractors in situations of undeclared war, promoting official enquiries over the number and activities of PMSC personnel in Iraq and Afghanistan and establishing a Commission on Wartime Contracting.[100]

---

[97] T Legg and R Ibbs, *Report of the Sierra Leone Arms Investigation* (1998); House of Commons Foreign Affairs Committee, *Second Report: Sierra* (1999), <http://www.parliament.the-stationery-office.co.uk/pa/cm199899/cmselect/cmfaff/116/11602.htm>, accessed 10 July 2010.

[98] On parliamentary control over foreign and defence policy see, for instance, H Born and H Hänggi, *The Double Democratic Deficit: Parliamentary Accountability and the Use of Force under International Auspices* (2004).

[99] *Transparency and Accountability in Military and Security Contracting Act*, <http://www.opencongress.org/bill/110-s674/show>, accessed 10 July 2010.

[100] <http://www.wartimecontracting.gov>, accessed 10 July 2010.

B. Regulation at the International Level

Due to the transnational nature of the industry, the possibility for firms to avoid hostile regulation by moving offshore, and the difficulties of extraterritorial monitoring and supervision, domestic regulation alone cannot fully account for a tight control of the PMSI. A comprehensive regulatory strategy should therefore comprise regulation at both the domestic and the international level.

The prospects for international regulation, however, seem far from rosy. Intergovernmental cooperation is hampered by the different roles and interests that states have vis-à-vis the market, which make any agreement on the establishment of a regulatory scheme difficult too reach.[101] Collective action at the international level is further stymied by a range of practical problems, related to the nature and the costs of different international regulatory frameworks. Whilst such a problem no doubt exists, there seems to be an increasingly convergent approach towards the PMSI and its need for regulation. The Montreux Document on Private Military and Security Companies, drafted under the initiative of the Swiss government and the International Committee of the Red Cross in September 2008 and establishing recommendations and states' good practices, was finalized and supported by both the major home and contracting states and some of the territorial states most affected by PMSCs' activities.[102] The Montreux Document, however, is not legally binding, applies only to situations of armed conflict and has been criticized for the participation of a low number of states and the unbalanced representation of Western countries.[103]

This section will look at the different international regulatory options available, looking at the problems arising from the increasing use of PMSCs by international organizations and at the contribution that such entities can offer to regulation. A more comprehensive analysis will be dedicated to the European Union, which has an apparently huge potential to regulate the market which has to date been insufficiently exploited.

1. Avenues and Challenges for International Action

As it has been argued, 'if there is a regulatory vacuum regarding PSCs, it exists under international law'.[104] Such a claim may appear slightly misleading, since PMSCs and their employees are subject to IHL like all other actors. It is true, however, that international law lacks norms explicitly designed to regulate PMSCs

---

[101] Avant in Chesterman and Lehnardt (n 23 above), 194.
[102] J Cockayne et al, *Beyond Market Forces: Regulating the Global Security Industry* (2008), <http://www.ipacademy.org/media/pdf/publications/beyond_market_forces_final.pdf>, accessed 10 July 2010.
[103] Gómez Del Prado, 'Private Military and Security Companies and the UN Working Commission on the Use of Mercenaries' (2008) 13(1) JC&SL.
[104] Percy (n 24 above), 41.

and the application of IHL over the PMSI is plagued by legal ambiguities and enforcement problems.[105]

The long maintained claim that the PMSI operates in a legal vacuum, at least at the international level, arises from the substantial inapplicability of the international legal instruments directed against mercenaries. While these cannot be examined in detail here, it is sufficient to mention that Article 47 of the First Protocol additional to the Geneva Convention of 1977, the Convention for the Elimination of Mercenarism in Africa of 1985, and, finally, the United Nation International Convention Against the Recruitment, Use, Financing and Training of Mercenaries which entered into force in 2001 all make the status of mercenary conditional upon a number of requirements which PMSCs can easily escape, and often appear inapplicable even to mercenaries themselves.[106]

An answer to this problem may be the revision of the UN Convention long advocated by the UNCHR Rapporteur on Mercenaries, Enrique Bernales Ballesteros.[107] Such a solution, however, seems unsatisfactory for at least two reasons. First, the original Convention itself, only entered into force in 2001 due to the low number of ratifications, and has still only been ratified by 32 states. While an improved Convention may receive greater support and both PMSCs and mercenaries do need to be controlled, they are different actors requiring different levels of regulation and specifically tailored legal instruments. Treating mercenaries and PMSCs differently would therefore enhance the clarity and the effectiveness of the regulatory instruments designated to address each of them, and seems indispensable to obtain the support of both the industry and major home and contracting states.[108] The need for different legal instruments to address mercenaries and PMSCs has now been acknowledged by the UN Working Commission on Mercenaries, made up of five regional experts who supplanted the previously existing Special Rapporteur in 2005.[109] Indeed, the UN Working Commission has recently proposed the draft of a new international Convention aimed at regulating only PMSCs.[110]

Furthermore, effective international regulation and prosecution of PMSCs, often operating in weak states lacking the capacity to enforce their own domestic legislation, would require not only the drafting of an ad hoc international Convention supported by major state actors, but also the establishment of some international body monitoring and prosecuting PMSCs' activities. Two solutions may be foreseen.

---

[105] See F Francioni, 'Private Military Contractors and International Law: An Introduction' (2008) 19(1) EJIL.
[106] Doswald-Beck (n 23 above) and Drews (n 23 above). See also L Cameron, 'Private military companies: Their Status under International Humanitarian Law and its Impact on Their Regulation' (2006) 88 IRRC 863.
[107] Ballesteros (n 46 above).
[108] Percy (n 24 above).
[109] Del Prado (n 100 above).
[110] JC Haile, 'New U.N. Draft International Convention on the Regulation, Oversight and Monitoring of Private Military and Security Companies' *International Government Contractor* 6(9) (2009).

One option would be the monitoring of PMSCs' contracts and activities to be assigned to an already existing UN body. The UN Human Rights Council Working Commission on Mercenaries, in particular, is already involved in the oversight of the PMSI. Whilst it may appear a suitable monitoring body given its competency, some concerns can be raised given the intransigent approach long maintained within this body, grounded on the analogy between PMSCs and mercenaries and the scepticism of both major Western players as well as of the industry, as well as the doubts regarding its actual monitoring and sanctioning capacities. As mentioned above, however, the Commission has recently adopted a more pragmatic approach, and has taken some valuable initiatives such as the establishment of a complaint mechanism accessible to stakeholders and clients of PMSCs and the promotion of basic social rights for contracted personnel from developing countries.[111]

Alternatively, the oversight of the PMSI and its activities may be assigned to an ad hoc international body. Such an office may undertake a systematic contract review and monitor the activities of the industry on the ground by teams of independent observers.[112] Sanctions against the company as well as the prosecution of employees' crimes, may be ensured either by the International Criminal Court (ICC) or by an ad hoc body.[113] The latter solution ought to be preferred, due to the problems of the ICC's jurisdiction over firms and US contractors. Alternatively, the responsibility to enforce IHL vis-à-vis the PMSI may be left to state actors, assisted by a comprehensive international institutional framework based on a global watchdog monitoring PMSCs activities, an accreditation regime, an arbitral tribunal, a harmonization scheme, and a global security industry club.[114]

Such bodies may indeed have a potential in prosecuting and punishing PMSCs' misbehaviour and addressing the problems arising from extraterritoriality. Their creation, however, appears ambitious and costly. International relations theory shows that the establishment of new international regimes is an extremely difficult endeavour.[115] In this case, the problem is not only that of finding the international consent required for the drafting of a new international Convention, which appears complex given the different interests that states' have vis-à-vis the use and the regulation of PMSCs, but also that of collecting the financial and institutional resources needed to ensure the effective monitoring of their activities and the prosecution of their employees. According to representatives of the industry, 'no grouping of global powers will be willing to invest large amounts of money and manpower in the creation and maintenance of a major regulatory body'.[116]

---

[111] Del Prado (n 100 above).
[112] Cockayne et al (n 99 above), 3.
[113] PW Singer, 'War, Profits, and the Vacuum of law: Privatized Military Firms and International Law (2004) 42(2) Columbia Journal of Transnational Law 545–6.
[114] Cockayne et al (n 99 above), 3.
[115] Among many see A Hasenclever et al, *Theories of International Regimes* (1997); S Haggard and B Simmon, 'Theories of International Regimes' *International Organization* 41(3) (1997); O Young, *International Cooperation: Building regimes for Natural Resources and the Environment* (1989).
[116] Beapark and Schulz (n 76 above), 244.

A solution to the above-mentioned objection may lie precisely in a financial contribution from the PMSI, which could share the costs of this international regulatory body with its customers by the provision, for instance, of an additional charge to be applied to each contract.[117] The problems related to a fair division of the costs among the players or their excessive heaviness, which may alienate the willingness of the industry to cooperate, remain to be addressed.

The challenges briefly mentioned above authorize some degree of scepticism vis-à-vis the establishment of these systems in the near future. Even before more ambitious frameworks for the enhancement of international regulation can be drafted, there is however significant room for the action of existing international organizations. First, both existing IOs and ad hoc groupings of states as well as non-governmental actors, like the signatories of the Montreux Document, are crucial arenas for shaping the international discourse and building the agreement needed to undertake substantive action. A pragmatic approach based on the acknowledgement that PMSCs are legitimate actors whose activities require further regulation seems a better starting point than maintaining an analogy between PMSCs and mercenaries, which would polarize the debate and alienate both the industry and Western home and contracting states. The United Nations' long insistence on the mercenary nature of PMSCs, for instance, appears to have seriously hampered its role in the regulation of the PMSI.[118]

In addition, major international organizations such as various UN specialized agencies or the World Bank Group are meaningful consumers of PMSCs' services.[119] Hence, they also have the opportunity to use market incentives in order to drive the industry towards increased levels of self-regulation, transparency, and compliance with domestic and international law. The prospect for a greater involvement of PMSCs in peacekeeping operations, first raised by Kofi Annan in 1998,[120] can be used as a formidable incentive for the industry to develop higher standards in exchange for gradual access to a new, lucrative segment of the market. Like national governments, however, international organizations should be more transparent and consistent in their use of PMSCs. The example of the United Nations, condemning the activities of PMSCs through its Rapporteur for Mercenaries while some of its specialized agencies were already contracting out different services to these companies, is a paradoxical case in point.

A further degree of caution is required as the use of PMSCs contracted either directly by an international organization or by a member state like the United States, which has outsourced its provision of international police officers and border monitors,[121] raises additional problems related to the legal liability and democratic accountability of the use of force at the international level. The involvement of

---

[117] Singer (n 2 above).
[118] Percy (n 24 above); Holmqvist (n 80 above).
[119] Author's interviews with representatives of the industry.
[120] K Annan, *Ditchley Foundation Lecture* (26 June 1998), <http://www.ditchley.co.uk/page/173/lecture-xxxv.htm>, accessed 10 July 2010.
[121] M Caparini and F Schreier, *Privatising Security: Law, Practice and Governance of Private Military and Security Companies*, Geneva Democratic Control of Armed Forces Centre (2004).

34   *Security and Policy Perspectives*

Dyncorp employees in a child prostitution ring during their support for the North Atlantic Treaty Organization (NATO) operation IFOR in Bosnia provides a forceful example.[122] As the use of force by international organizations has already been considered as affected by a 'double democratic deficit',[123] reliance on private military personnel is in danger of creating a further layer of opacity and inaccountability. International organizations' use of PMSCs should therefore be as transparent as possible, envisaging mechanisms for the supervision of PMSCs activities and a role for the parliamentary assembly of the organization or for the national parliaments of the states that are party of it.

2. Regulation at the Regional Level: The European Union

Whilst many have called for a greater role of the European Union (EU) in the regulation of the PMSI, it is worth mentioning that the EU is already involved in the regulation of the industry to a limited extent in at least three respects. First, the EU has been a driver of harmonization of members' domestic regulation on private policing, recognized by the European Court of Justice as an economic activity subject to the rules of the Common Market.[124] Secondly, the EU Code of Conduct on Armaments Exports drafted in 1998 has produced greater transparency and encouraged increasing harmonization of national armed services as well as arms-exports legislation.[125] Finally, some Common Foreign and Security Policy (CFSP) Joint Actions and Common Positions have been used to restrict the supply of some kinds of military assistance as well as goods and to control the export of private military services to certain destinations.[126]

It is true, however, that a case can be made for the EU to take a much more direct role in regulating the PMSI, and that its greater involvement appears necessary for a number of reasons. First, the EU has an unprecedented regulatory capacity among regional organizations, and constitutes a huge pool of demand as well as supply for military services. In addition, regulation at the European level may find the support of both national governments, as it would be more cost-effective and easier to implement, and of the industry itself, as it would avoid the ambiguities of different regulatory frameworks and the risks of unfair competition and competitive

---

[122] Ibid. See also Singer (n 3 above).
[123] Born and Hänggi (n 95 above).
[124] E Krahmann, 'Regulating Private Military Companies: What Role for the EU *Contemporary Security Policy* 26(1) (2005) 117.
[125] Ibid, 115–16. See also H Born et al, *Regulating Private Security in Europe: Status and Prospects*, Geneva Democratic Control of Armed Forces Policy Paper 20 (2007).
[126] See, for instance, Council Joint Action 2000/401/CFSP concerning the control of technicalassistance related to certain military end-uses, OJ L159 (30 June 2000); Council Common Position 2003/468/CFSP of 23 June 2003 on the control of arms brokering, OJ L156 (25 June 2003); Council Decision 2000/803/CFSP of 14 December 2000 implementing Joint Action 1999/34/CFSP with a view to a EU contribution to combating the destabilizing accumulation and spread of small arms and light weapons in South Ossetia, OJ L326 (22 December 2000).

disadvantages across nations.[127] Moreover, given its capacity to act as a 'norm entrepreneur' on the international stage,[128] a direct role for the EU would greatly enhance prospects for further international regulation, encouraging other actors to address the issue. An explicit European policy vis-à-vis the use and the regulation of PMSCs appears particularly necessary since both the EU and the national military forces of its member states are growing increasingly reliant on contracted personnel. Indeed, the EU has already relied to a limited extent on PMSCs services for the guarding of its embassy in Baghdad[129] and during operations such as the European Union Police Mission (EUPM) in Bosnia.[130] Given the difficulties hitherto experienced by the EU in collecting the resources needed for its crisis-management activities, reliance on PMSCs may indeed appear a valuable option.[131] The current outsourcing of logistics for European crisis management operations was encouraged by Javier Solana as a way to 'release military personnel needed for operations in the field... save money while enhancing overall logistics performance... compensate for the absence of support assets of the Member States'.[132]

Finally, a reluctance of the EU directly to address the regulation of PMSCs would be at odds with the role of civilian[133] or normative[134] power that underlies the European foreign policy identity and its commitment to 'upholding and developing International Law'.[135]

As a priority, the EU may therefore pursue further actions through a twofold approach. On the one hand, it may regulate the activities of PMSCs abroad by specific CFSP Common Positions requiring members to implement certain standards of control, or by revising the above-mentioned EU code on the export of arms in order to cover the export of armed services more extensively.[136] On the other

---

[127] Krahmann (n 121 above). See also G Den Dekker, *The Regulatory Context of Private Military and Security Services at the European Union Level*, Priv-War National Report 04/09, <http://priv-war.eu/wordpress/wp-content/uploads/2009/05/nr-04-09-eu.pdf>, accessed 14 August 2010.

[128] On the role of the EU as a norm entrepreneur see C Hill and M Smith (eds), *International Relations and the European Union* (2005). A comprehensive catalogue of the influence of the EU on international law is provided by F Hoffmeister, 'The Contribution of EU Practice to International Law' in M Cremona (ed), *Developments in EU External Relations Law* (2008).

[129] den Dekker (n 124 above), 21.

[130] Holmqvist (n 81 above), 57.

[131] JK Wither, 'European Security and Private Military Companies: The Prospects for Privatized Battlegroups' *Connections* 4(2) (2004).

[132] J Solana, Opening Address, European Defence Agency Conference on 'Commercialising logistics', Brussels (27 February 2008), <http://www.eda.europa.eu/newsitem.aspx?id=327>, accessed 10 July 2010.

[133] F Duchêne, 'Europe in World Peace' in R Mayne (ed), *Europe Tomorrow* (1972); KE Smith, 'Beyond the Civilian Power EU Debate' *Politique européenne* 17(1) (2005).

[134] I Manners, 'Normative Power Europe: A Contradiction in Terms?' *The Journal of Common Market Studies* 40(2) (2002); H Sjursen, 'The EU as a "Normative" Power: How Can This Be?' *Journal of European Public Policy* 13(2) (2006).

[135] *A Secure Europe in a Better World. European Security Strategy* (Brussels, 12 December 2003), 9, <http://www.consilium.europa.eu/uedocs/cmsUpload/78367.pdf>, accessed 10 July 2010.

[136] A Bailes and C Holmqvist, *The Increasing Role of Private Military and Security Companies*, European Parliament Study EP/EXPO/B/SEDE/FWC/2006-10/Lot4/09 (October 2007), <http://www.isis-europe.org/pdf/2008_artrel_145_07-10-epstudy-pmc&psc.pdf>, accessed 10 July 2010.

hand, the EU may promote standardized rules for member states' use of private military companies, defining the limits of outsourcing and devising procedures for the supervision of contracts and the accountability of firms and their employees.

Furthermore, the EU should be clearer and more transparent in its current use of PMSCs and the role that these actors may play in the development of its military capabilities. Hence, it is crucial that the EU engagement with PMSCs responds to a clearly defined policy specifying the extent and the limits of outsourcing and the paths ensuring supervision, legal liability, and democratic accountability. Such a policy should be the outcome of a public debate involving specialized actors such as the European Defence Agency as well as the European Parliament, whose very limited role in European foreign and defence policy may be further called into question by the reliance on private military and security actors.

VI. Conclusions

Due to space constraints and the complexities of the issue, this chapter has provided only a short overview of the major problems posed by the surge of the PMSI, and an enumeration of a few pragmatic solutions, based on the awareness that international security governance is an increasingly fragmented domain involving a complex network of international, business, and transnational civil-society actors alongside states. For this reason legal regulation enacted at state level, whilst still crucial, is insufficient to ensure comprehensive control of an inherently transnational industry that raises a number of concerns related to possible infringements of human rights and democratic accountability over the provision of coercion. Whilst no single regulatory strategy appears capable of completely overcoming all these problems, a multifaceted and multilayered approach—based on both legal and informal instruments on the one hand and on national, regional, and international action on the other—can embed the PMSI in an increasingly tight regulatory web, which can shape the future evolution of the market and prevent a further erosion of public control over the use of force.

2

The Use of Private Contractors in the Fight against Piracy: Policy Options

Natalino Ronzitti

I. Introduction

Piracy is an old *crimen iuris gentium*, the repression of which is regulated by customary international law. The law was codified by the 1958 Geneva Convention on the Territorial Sea and the Contiguous Zone and restated by the 1982 UN Convention on the Law of the Sea.

Piracy has for years been a neglected issue and has recently been resurrected because of an exponential increase in the number of attacks on merchant shipping. The causes are manifold. The main cause lies in the fact that states are often unable to police their territorial waters due to the lack of a navy or coast guard vessels. As land dominates waters, insurgency and the absence of an effective government allow pirates to have their sanctuaries on land and to prepare criminal expeditions. A failed state cannot police its territorial waters. Small and speedy craft are easily available to carry out criminal activities and often pirates own a mother ship from which attacks with small craft are launched. Current technology renders weaponry easily available.

Modern piracy differs from that of old in that nowadays pirates do not usually capture a ship to take and sell the cargo. There is no more ships' plenty of bullion and gold coins. Instead pirates capture ships with a different but still valuable cargo, often oil and even tanks, as happened in the case of the Ukrainian ship MV *Faina*, and demand ransom for freeing the ship and the crew.[1] Piracy is a crime that by definition is committed on the high seas. If acts of violence aimed at taking the cargo are committed in territorial waters they are usually defined as armed robbery and their repression falls within the competence of the coastal state.

The International Maritime Bureau maintains shocking statistics on piratical attacks. In 2007, 263 attacks occurred worldwide (13 in the Gulf of Aden and 31 off the coast of Somalia). In 2008, 293 attacks worldwide were reported (92 in the Gulf of Aden and 19 off the coast of Somalia) and 406 worldwide in 2009 (116 in

---

[1] According to recent figures released ransom obtained by experienced pirates ranges between $600,000 and $5m: R de Wijk, 'The New Piracy: The Global Context' *Survival* 52 (2010) 39, 42.

the Gulf of Aden, 80 off the coast of Somalia and a few others in the Red Sea and off the coast of Oman). Thirty-five attacks occurred off the coast of Somalia in the first quarter of 2010. Hostage-taking is also a lucrative business, since insurers, shipping companies, and governments pay ransom. However, the US is considering prohibiting shipping companies from making any payments. Acts of piracy have also been carried out in a number of strategically important points such as the Malacca and Singapore Straits. Bandits operate in the Gulf of Guinea, including against oil platforms off the coast of Nigeria and robberies against trawlers have been reported.[2]

The UN Security Council has passed a number of resolutions allowing states to enter Somali territorial waters, the nominal consent of the Somali Transitional Federal Government (TFG) being insufficient due to its lack of effectiveness.[3] The International Maritime Organization (IMO) issued a code of conduct which has been signed by those African countries most affected and has collected 14 signatories.[4] On 11 November 2004, 16 Asian countries signed a cooperation agreement aimed at combating piracy and armed robbery in Asia.[5] The *Institut de droit international*, in its Naples session (2009), adopted a declaration on piracy.

The increase in criminal activities on the high seas or in territorial waters has immediately whetted the appetite of private military and private security companies (PMSCs)[6] that envisaged pirate hunting and shipping protection as a new lucrative business. Blackwater Maritime Security Services bought the *McArthur*, a ship equipped for coping with natural disasters, with the aim of outfitting it for pirate hunting. However, that adventure has not had any positive response.[7] More successful were the services provided by British companies, for instance, Hart Security, in helping the Puntland government to police its territorial waters and prevent illegal fishing in Puntland waters. Other companies are helping countries of the Gulf of Aden to train their coast guards. It seems that a number of small companies are based in ports of the region ready to offer their services on demand, where a vessel is attacked by pirates or is the victim of acts of banditry. Usually they are equipped with rigid-hull inflatable boats.

---

[2] For a complete list of incidents see SP Menefee, 'An Overview of Piracy in the First Decade of the 21st Century' in MH Nordquist et al (eds), *Legal Challenges in Maritime Security* (2008), 441.

[3] SC Res 1814 (2008); 1816 (2008); 1838 (2008); 1846 (2008); 1851 (2008); 1897 (2009). See also SC Res 1918 (2010). Before passing Res 1814, the Security Council had recommended states whose naval vessels operated in international waters off the coast of Somalia to be vigilant and to take appropriate steps to protect merchant shipping. Cf SC Res 1772 (2007) and 1801 (2008).

[4] Code of Conduct Concerning the Repression of Piracy and Armed Robbery against Ships in the Western Indian Ocean and the Gulf of Aden, 29 January 2009 (Djibouti), <http://www.fco.gov.uk/resources/en/pdf/pdf9/piracy-djibouti-meeting>, accessed 25 May 2010.

[5] Regional Cooperation Agreement on Combating Piracy and Armed Robbery in Asia (ReCAAP). The Agreement entered into force on 1 July 2006: see Kenyan Zou, 'New Developments in the International Law of Piracy' (2009) 8 Chinese J Intl L 323.

[6] PMCs and PSCs are here employed to indicate corporations or other business entities that provide military and security services. Fighting piracy is more a security than a military endeavour, since companies provide armed guards and/or training. However, we prefer to employ the acronym PMSCs for indicating both kinds of companies.

[7] Isenberg, 'The Right Way to Use Private contractors to fight pirates', 19 February 2010, <http://www.tinyurl.com/ybmdlqs>, accessed 25 May 2010.

Recent research has pointed out that services provided by PMSCs in the maritime domain range from training people to guard ports to providing services for coast-guard activities and fishery policing in the Exclusive Economic Zone (EEZ) of coastal states not having capability to do so. PMSCs are also providing services for oil rigs and supplying armed assistance for tugs and ships. More closely connected with piracy are those companies which provide intelligence and armed guards on board private ships. A service escorting merchant vessels is also supplied, namely in the Malacca Straits and in the Gulf of Aden.[8] Navies have been dispatched to waters where incidents most frequently occur, mainly in the Gulf of Aden and in the Indian Ocean off the coast of Somalia. In addition to navies of individual nations (China, India, Japan, Malaysia, the Russian Federation, and several other flags including South Korea), multinational operations have been set up, such as those under NATO (*Allied Protector and Ocean Shield*) and EU command (*EU Navfor- Atalanta*) and the Joint Task Force 151 under US command. They are equipped with helicopters and armed teams to be dispatched where necessary.

Even though navies are policing the seas, PMSCs have become a reality in protecting vessels and the use of their services has also been advocated by governmental authorities.[9]

II. Pirates, Insurgents, Bandits, and Terrorists

It is not the purpose of this chapter to define the perpetrators of criminal activities or violence at sea. This task has already been undertaken by the present author elsewhere.[10] However, a few lines are necessary since international law envisages different powers to combat violence at sea. The place where the criminal act occurs is also relevant.

Piracy, by definition, involves two ships (or two aircraft or an aircraft against a ship) and is motivated by private ends, for instance, robbery and/or ransom.[11] Piracy takes place on the high seas; otherwise, if committed on territorial waters, it is an act of banditry or armed robbery. The same is true if the two ships requirement is not fulfilled and persons on board mutiny or commit acts of banditry. If an act by a ship against another ship is motivated by political ends, this may be qualified according to circumstances as an act of insurgency or an act of terrorism, wherever it occurs.

---

[8] See C Liss, *Privatising Anti-Piracy Services in Strategically Important Waterways: Risks, Challenges and Benefits*, CrasSPP Working Paper Series, University of Tokyo (October 2009), 1–13, <http://www.pp.u-tokyo.ac.jp/research/dp/documents/GraSPP-DP-E-09-003OPU-DP-E-09-001.pdf>, accessed 25 May 2010.

[9] For instance by the US Vice Admiral (US) commanding the Combined Maritime Forces and his deputy (UK): see P Cullen, 'Private security head-to head against pirates: A practical answer to protecting commercial shipping' J Intl Peace Operations 4(3) (2008) 15.

[10] N Ronzitti, *Maritime Terrorism and International Law* (1990). For a more updated view see Nordquist et al (eds) (n 2 above); D Guilfoyle, *Shipping Interdiction and the Law of the Sea* (2009), 32–42.

[11] Art 15 of the 1958 Geneva Convention on the Territorial Sea and the Contiguous Zone; Art 101 of the 1982 UN Convention on the Law of the Sea.

Whilst states enjoy broad powers in combating piracy, the possibility of taking action against a foreign ship in the hands of terrorists is more limited, unless there is the consent of the flag state or a resolution by the Security Council (SC). The relevant Conventions generally impose a duty on coastal states to cooperate and to enact appropriate legislation to punish the wrongdoers and to free hostages.[12]

The traditional law of insurgency follows the same line. Third states are not allowed to enter foreign territorial waters to fight insurgents, unless the coastal state is asking for their aid. Usually if third states are not attacked, they do not take action against insurgents on the high seas.

The above distinction is a scholarly categorization and often the difference is not so sharp and the categorization becomes blurred. Cases in which defeated insurgents turn to piracy or where political motivation is only a fig leaf for committing depredation and robbery are not uncommon. For instance, one of the excuses raised by the Somali pirate community is that illegal fishing or dumping dangerous waste in Somali waters has sparked the local community to embrace the cause of piracy.

III. Pirate Hunting by PMSCs

As stated, one of the major PMSCs has offered services for hunting pirates and policing maritime routes. The offer has not been taken up by the shipping community which prefers to pay ransom or to rely on warships dispatched by major navies.

The question, however, is whether pirate hunting may be a service legally available to PMSCs.

Both the Geneva Convention on the Territorial Sea and the Contiguous Zone and the UN Convention on the Law of the Sea dictate strict rules for combating piracy since the law allows maritime powers to deviate from the ordinary rules on freedom of the high seas. A pirate ship may be seized and the pirates may be arrested. The tribunals of the state to which the ship operating the capture belongs may decide upon the penalties to be imposed and what should be done with the property which was seized. States are allowed to exercise the right to visit a foreign ship if there is a suspicion that it is engaged in piracy. The ship may be boarded and inspected. The law balances the exception to the freedom of the high seas with the responsibility of the capturing state. If the seizure is carried out without adequate grounds or the suspicions that a ship is engaged in piracy prove to be unfounded, the capturing state should pay proper compensation.

Because of the broad methods given to maritime powers and the liability incurred in carrying out an unlawful seizure, the law provides that only a limited

---

[12] Convention for the Suppression of Unlawful Acts Against the Safety of Maritime Navigation (1988); Protocol for the Suppression of Unlawful Acts Against the Safety of Fixed Platforms on the Continental Shelf (1988); Protocol additional to the 1988 Convention for the Suppression of Unlawful Acts against the Safety of Maritime Navigation (2005); International Convention against the Taking of Hostages (1979).

category of vessels is entitled to operate the capture. It may be carried out only by warships or military aircraft, or by other ships or aircraft clearly marked and identifiable as being on government service and authorized to that effect.

The definition of warships is set out in the above-mentioned law of the sea Conventions.[13] The main elements of the definition are the following. The ship should:

a) belong to the armed forces of the state;
b) bear the external marks distinguishing such ships of its nationality;
c) be under the command of an officer duly commissioned by the government and whose name appears in the appropriate service list; and
d) be manned by a crew under regular armed forces discipline.

The strict rules required by the law of the sea on warships exclude from the outset that PMSC ships could be defined as warships and thus entitled to engage in pirate hunting, unless contractors are incorporated in the armed forces of the state. A merchant ship may be converted into a warship according to the 1907 Hague Convention no VII. The Convention lays down requirements with which PMSCs would have difficulty in complying. In addition to bearing the external mark of warships, a requirement easy to comply with, the ship should be placed under the direct authority, immediate control, and responsibility of the flag state and the crew should be under military discipline. Moreover the ship should be under a commander in the service of the flag state and duly commissioned and whose name figures on the list of the officers of the fighting fleet.[14]

The law of the sea lists another category of ships entitled to fight piracy: 'ships . . . on government service authorized to that effect' (Article 21 of the Geneva Convention on the Territorial Sea and the Contiguous Zone) and 'ships . . . clearly marked and identifiable as being in government service and authorized to that effect' (Article 107 of the UN Convention on the Law of the Sea). The ownership of the ship by the state is not required nor is the presence of a commissioned officer demanded. According to some authorities 'no objection can be raised to the view that even private vessels may fall within this category'.[15] Is it thus possible that a PMSC could outfit a vessel for pirate hunting provided that it is commissioned to do so by a state and receives an authorization to hunt pirates? The ship should be clearly marked as being in government service and authorized to hunt pirates. The problem here is not the resurrection of privateering abolished by the 1856

---

[13] Art 8 of the Geneva Convention on the Territorial Sea and the Contiguous Zone and Art 29 of the UN Convention on the Law of the Sea. Here reference is made only to ships, but the definition applies, *mutatis mutandis*, also to aircraft.

[14] Recently Malaysia converted a containership into a naval auxiliary for escorting merchant vessels in the Gulf of Aden. The converted vessel has on board Navy Reservists as well as regular officers and men of the Malaysia navy for security related operations: *Marine Log*, 1 June 2009, <http://www.marinelog.com/DOCS/NEWSMMIX/2009jun00015.html>, accessed 25 May 2010. Naval auxiliary vessels are entitled to exercise the right of visit since they fall either under category of warships or under the category of ships duly authorized, clearly marked, and identifiable as being on government service.

[15] T Treves, 'Chapter 17 (Navigation)' in R-J Dupuy and D Vignes (eds), *A Handbook on the New Law of the Sea* (1991), II, 835, 899.

Paris Declaration: privateers were deemed to be employed to carry out acts of naval war, not to fight against piracy. Rather the problem is related to the exercise of functions which have elements of governmental authority. Arming vessels with contractors to fight piracy on the high seas has not yet passed the test of international practice. Take, for instance, the right of visit. Even though the flag state should bear international responsibility, it is difficult to conceive that third states are ready to have their ships stopped and visited by a ship manned by contractors. The right of visit is a state function and this is the reason why Article 45 of the project of the International Law Commission, subsequently Article 21 of the Geneva Convention on the Territorial Sea and the Contiguous Zone, listed only warships and military aircraft as vehicles entitled to fight pirates without mentioning government ships. The International Law Courmission (ILC), in its commentary, made clear that this choice was dictated by the wish to avoid abuses and friction between states. According to the ILC the use of other government ships did not provide the same safeguards against abuse.[16] During the Geneva Conference on the Law of the Sea the reference to ships on government service was added although those ships were only entitled to carry out a seizure, not to exercise the right of visit under Article 22.[17] This technical lacuna was filled by Article 110(5) of the UN Convention on the Law of the Sea. However, nowhere in the Geneva Convention on the High Seas or in the UN Convention on the Law of the Sea is there a definition of this class of vessels, unlike warships which are the object of a definition in both Conventions (Article 8 of the Geneva Convention and Article 29 of the UN Convention on the Law of the Sea). In the words of Panama, the reason for ships on government service being included was that some states do not possess any warship and the amendment made it possible to have the seizure carried out by a vessel on state service, which might be charged with that task 'either permanently or temporarily'.[18] In conclusion, arming vessels and hiring contractors for pirate hunting is in principle legally possible if the vessel is on government service, authorized to chase pirates, and the hiring government bears international responsibility. However, no practice of this kind exists to support such a finding.

IV. Self-Defence by Merchant Vessels against Pirate Attacks

The issue of self-defence by merchant vessels against pirates came under consideration when the ILC discussed draft Article 45 on piracy under which only warships were authorized to seize a pirate ship. In the ILC commentary it was stated that Article 45 'does not apply in the case of a merchant ship which has repulsed an

---

[16] Commentary to Art. 45 in (1956) II YILC 283.
[17] The addition was due to a proposal by Thailand which obtained 26 votes to 15 and 17 abstained: cf UN Doc A/CONF13/C2/L 10, reproduced in A/CONF13/40, UNCLOS I, Geneva, 24 February–27 April 1958, Official Records, vol IV: Second Committee (High Seas: General Régime), 117.
[18] Ibid, 12th meeting, 18 March 1958, 30, para 26.

attack by a pirate ship and, in exercising its right of self-defence, overpowers the pirate ship and subsequently hands it over to a warship or to the authority of a coastal State'.[19]

Obviously the reference by the ILC to the right of self-defence was not to the right of self-defence of states as embodied in Article 51 of the United Nations Charter. It was to the right of self-defence of human beings, a right which is recognized by all legal orders of the members of the international community. Usually domestic legal orders recognize not only the right of self-defence but also the consequential right to take into custody the aggressor for the short span of time necessary for handing him over to the police authority.

The ILC did not elaborate more on this scenario and in particular did not consider whether it was possible for an unarmed crew of a merchant vessel to repel an attack and capture a pirate ship or whether, on the contrary, the scenario devised implied that a ship should have arms on board. For our purposes it is sufficient to note that the right of self-defence by merchant vessels was recognized and duly pointed out.

V. Supplying Armed Guards on Board

Between the eighteenth and nineteenth centuries, shipowners used to equip their vessels with light armaments to counter piracy. Is that practice worth resurrecting? One of the services provided by PMSCs is supplying armed personnel on board vessels. If attacked by pirates armed guards may react and impede the capture. The legality of this service depends first of all on the flag state. Its legal order should say if the master or owner is entitled to bring armed personnel on board and whether the use of weapons is allowed. Sometimes the armed personnel make use of non-lethal weapons which may be employed without putting the lives of bandits at risk. The law of the port state also comes into consideration if the ship is making a call during its voyage and, as we shall see, the law of the coastal state may come into consideration if the ship is traversing foreign territorial waters and dangerous straits. It is reported that in 2005–6 a number of ships traversing the Malacca straits used armed contractors, notwithstanding the cooperation between Singapore, Malaysia, and Indonesia in patrolling the strait, even using air surveillance.[20] The US is advocating the presence of armed guards on merchant vessels in dangerous areas and on 18 November 2009 the US welcomed the armed repulsion of pirates by a private security team on board of the *Maersk Alabama* off Somalia.[21] In the autumn of 2009, Spain passed a law allowing private guards to serve on board Spanish-flag

---

[19] Commentary to Art. 45 (n 16 above).
[20] See Guilfoyle (n 10 above), 55–6. The practice of MALINDSO patrols curbed piracy attacks in the Strait.
[21] See 'US Welcomes Armed Repulsion of Pirate Attack', 19 November 2009, <http://www.america.gov/st/peacesec-english/2009/November/20091119112330ptellivremos0.5088922.html>, accessed 25 May 2010.

merchant and fishing vessels navigating waters where there is a risk to the security of persons and assets.[22] Armed teams are under a private contract stipulated with the shipowner and in this respect they differ from PMSCs, which normally serve armies under a public contract stipulated by government authorities, even though sometimes contracts are signed with private corporations. A number of countries, however, forbid the bearing of weapons on board, a possibility being to store them before entering a port of call. The IMO's policy is not to recommend armed guards on board, fearing an escalation of violence and pirates being pushed into employing ever heavier weapons for their attacks.[23]

Note that often ships fly a flag of convenience and are registered in countries where there is no legislation on the presence of security services on board. Several flag-of-convenience states support the policy of having armed personnel on board. For instance, on 29 May 2009 in New York, the Bahamas, Liberia, the Marshall Islands, and Panama signed a joint declaration advocating measures of self-protection by ships against pirates. It is reported that in March 2009 a private security team on board of the *Almezaan*, a Panama merchant vessel, reacted against pirates on the high seas off the Somalia coast, killing one of the assailants.[24] Since the incident happened on the high seas, the flag state criminal jurisdiction applies, even though the concurrent jurisdiction of other legal orders cannot be excluded.[25] Coastal states often have very poor legislation or no legislation at all to regulate the phenomenon of armed guards. In other instances, armed guards are permitted by the port state, as happens with fishing vessels stationed in the Seychelles hosting armed guards when they are fishing in the Seychelles's EEZ or in international waters. The trawlers belong to Spanish owners but fly a Seychelles flag.

VI. The Practice of Vessel Protection Detachment (VPD)

A similar but at the same time completely different phenomenon is having a detachment of armed soldiers on board. The French practice is to embark armed teams belonging to the French state (*Equipes de Protection Embarquée*) and made up

---

[22] Decree no 1628 of 30 October 2009, *Boletin Oficial del Estado*, 31 October 2009, no 263, Sec I, 90892.

[23] IMO, MSC 1/Circ 1335, 'Best Management Practices to Deter Piracy in the Gulf of Aden and off the Coast of Somalia Developed by the Industry', 29 September 2009. See also the following IMO circulars: MSC 1/Circ 1132, 16 June 2009; MSC 1/Circ 1134, 23 June 2009; MSC 1/Circ 1135, 29 September 2009. See also MSC, 86th session: 27 May–5 June 2009. Those measures have been endorsed by the EU: see the Commission Recommendation of 11 March 2010 on the measures for self-protection and prevention of piracy and armed robbery against ships (2010/159/EU), OJ 2010 L 67/13. The Recommendation indicates a number of best practices which do not include the use of firearms by the crew or by armed guards. Best practices also include a guidance for fishing vessels.

[24] A Cowell, 'Naval Force Frees Pirate Suspects after Firefight', *The New York Times* (25 March 2010). Usually private security teams fire warning shots and this is the first killing reported.

[25] Grounds of jurisdiction might be, for instance, the nationality of the victim, that of the shipping company and that of contractors. If the incident occurs in the territorial sea, the jurisdiction of the coastal state is paramount. The issue of criminal jurisdiction and the power to investigate the incident are not dealt with in this chapter.

of *Fusillers de Marine*. French teams are protecting ships traversing the Gulf of Aden and also on board trawlers with the French flag stationed in the Seychelles. To this end a Status of Force Agreement (SOFA) has been negotiated by France with the Seychelles for the protection of fishing vessels in sea areas plagued by pirates. The service is free of charge and it is provided only for French flagged ships. This service is working and practice shows instances of ships reflagging in order to enjoy French protection, as happened in the case of the Italian trawler *Torre Giulia*.[26]

Vessel protection detachments are covered within the framework of the Atalanta naval mission. They involve uniformed people under regular discipline and thus differ from PMSCs. Armed teams are stationed on land in the Gulf of Aden region. They are ready to board ships requesting the service and to disembark in another port of the region, after having escorted the ship through the most dangerous waters. The consent of the coastal states involved is necessary and appropriate. SOFAs should be concluded. Strictly speaking the presence of parent warships is not necessary, but the policy of some states, for instance, Italy, is to have a warship in the area in order to establish a link and operative control with the armed team on land ready to comply with directives and orders coming from the warship. The other possibility is for the armed team to be transported to the merchant ship on the high seas and thus the conclusion of a SOFA is not necessary. Until recently very few ships have used the VPD service; those which have are mainly ships belonging to the World Food Programme (WFP).

It seems that VPD teams are entitled not only to resist and defend ships from pirates, but also to deter and intervene in order to bring an end to acts of piracy, including powers of arrest and seizure of assets under pirate control. Pirate hunting should, however, be excluded since the merchant ship cannot qualify as a warship or a duly authorized vessel on government service, even though it has a VPD on board.

The presence of a VPD involves the stipulation of an agreement between the state to which the armed team belongs and the flag state of the merchant ship requesting the service.

The Chinese and Russian navies are offering VPD services that have been accepted by a number of ships.

The International Transport Workers' Federation (ITF) is supporting the idea of having armed military personnel on board ships in dangerous waters. The ship-owners' organization BIMCO is endorsing the idea of armed military teams but does not exclude proposals for utilizing the services of ship riders.

---

[26] The Italian Law regulating private security services is silent on the possibility of utilizing such services on board Italian ships. For this reason a draft was tabled on 3 March 2010 before the Italian Parliament to allow private security services on board of Italian flagged vessels (Senato della Repubblica, XVI Legislatura, Disegno di Legge d'iniziativa dei senatori Amato e Cantoni, no 2050. Adde drafts no 2092, submitted by Senatore Enrico Musso et al and no C 3321, submitted by MP Scandroglio). On 25 April 2009 the cruise ship *MSC Melody* was attacked by pirates off the Seychelles. The ship had on board an Israeli private security team which was successful in repelling the attack without the need for direct fire against the pirates (only warning shots into the air were fired) and making use only of hydrants and manoeuvring. The ship belongs to an Italian corporation but flies a Panamanian flag.

VII. Escorting Merchant Vessels

Experts say that the best way to avoid attacks by pirates is by convoying merchant ships and escorting them when navigating dangerous waters. During the seventeenth and eighteenth centuries the East India Company used to convoy its ships to protect them from pirates. Convoying is a measure which is almost impossible to implement, since it would be very expensive due to the amount of traffic and the long routes to monitor. Convoying is a measure admitted by the law of the sea. However, it is a measure taken by states in time of armed conflict and the convoy is carried out by warships and might be under the command of a belligerent or of a neutral power. For instance, towards the end of the Iran–Iraq War (1980–8) a number of maritime powers, including Italy, the United Kingdom, and the United States, placed their ships in the Persian Gulf under convoy. Whilst it is doubtful whether the territorial waters of belligerents may be traversed in innocent passage by a neutral convoy without the consent of the coastal state, it is generally admitted that a neutral convoy may enter an international strait and exercise its right of transit passage.

The navies present in the Indian Ocean since the resurgence of piracy, such as those under the aegis of NATO or the EU, do not convoy vessels. In addition to their deterrent function, they come to the defence of merchant ships if they are attacked by pirates, often making use of the helicopters they have on board. Escort is provided in Somali territorial waters for ships serving the WFP, as provided for by a number of UN SC resolutions. The EU anti-piracy task force has also organized a system of VPD for helping ships under piratical attack. Sometimes navies provide an escort but the service is not free. For instance, the Yemeni navy provides escort services in the Gulf of Aden and charges up to US$55,000 per ship.[27]

The issue is whether an armed escort service may be provided by PMSC ships.[28] The answer is yes, as long as they do not interfere with the freedom of the high seas and any lawful action taken by foreign warships. For instance, foreign warships may lawfully exercise the right of visit provided by Article 110 of the UN Convention on the Law of the Sea if there is a suspicion that the escorted vessel is carrying out an activity listed under para 1 of that provision. The escorting vessel may also be approached and visited since it cannot enjoy complete immunity, being neither a warship nor a ship used only on government service (Articles 95–6). It is assumed here that a PMSC's ship is not a commissioned vessel having the status of a ship on government service. Its role is merely defensive and it cannot be used for pirate hunting.

---

[27] S Bateman, 'Riding Shotgun: Armed Security Guards Onboard Merchant Ships', *RSIS Commentaries*, 5 March 2010, 1–2, <http://www.rsis.edu.sg/publications/commentaries.html>, accessed 25 May 2010.

[28] Merchant shipping has requested the services of private firms' vessels for protection against pirates in the Strait of Malacca: see *Oxford Analytica: Global Strategic Analysis*, 4 December 2008, <http://www.oxan.com/display.aspx?ItemID=DB147444>, accessed 25 May 2010. The draft legislation before the Italian Senate no 2092, quoted (n 26 above), proposes the presence of armed personnel on board ships and escorting vessels (Art 3). Rules on innocent passage should be abided by (Art 3, para 5).

The legal feasibility of arming a vessel for escorting merchant ships should be evaluated according to the legislation of the flag state, which should also allow escorting vessels to have a port of call on its territory. The reaction against a pirate attack will fall under the notion of self-defence as illustrated above. The notion of self-defence, as accepted by domestic legal orders, includes the right to intervene on behalf of a threatened individual.

VIII. Dispatching Security Teams from Land Bases

Often acts of piracy happen in international waters, but in proximity to the coast and a well-equipped security team may intervene on demand in a reasonable time span to counter the capture of the ship by pirates. The team may use helicopters or fast boats to reach the ship under attack or when navigating in dangerous waters. It is assumed that the territorial state has consented to host a PMSC with all necessary equipment. Another important condition is that the ship under assault by pirates is ready to accept the services offered or has addressed a specific request. Usually this may be done by the master of the ship under assault. It is assumed the ship is navigating on the high seas. If the attack occurs when it is traversing foreign territorial waters, the consent of the coastal state is also required.

If the above conditions are satisfied, the dispatch of the security team from land bases is in keeping with international law.

IX. Innocent/Transit Passage of Escorted Merchant Vessels

Are merchant vessels with security teams on board—whether PMSCs or VPDs—entitled to innocent passage through the territorial sea of foreign states and to transit passage through international straits? Does the same solution apply to merchant vessels escorted by PMSCs or are escorting vessels required to abandon the escort before entering the territorial sea or at the embouchure of an international strait? It must be noted that navigation through territorial seas and passage through straits is often very dangerous because waters are not properly policed by coastal states and episodes of armed robbery are frequent even though, strictly speaking, they cannot be defined as acts of piracy since they take place in territorial waters and not on the high seas.

Hunting pirates descending from the high seas or taking any police action against armed robbers is forbidden in foreign territorial seas unless authorized by the territorial sovereign.[29] Policing territorial waters is contrary to the very meaning

---

[29] There are authors who envisage a legal possibility of entering foreign territorial waters without the consent of the coastal state under the rationale of the disputed doctrine of humanitarian intervention or under Art 98 of the UN Law of the Sea Convention and the duty to render assistance to persons at sea in danger of being lost: see Wolfrum, 'Fighting Terrorism at Sea: Options and Limitations under International Law' in Nordquist et al (eds) (n 2 above), 79.

of passage, namely that traversing the sea and shall be continuous and expeditious. Maintaining law and order within territorial waters is an activity reserved for the coastal state and cannot be performed by foreign states unless the territorial sovereign consents.

Does carrying armed teams on board constitute a violation of the rules of innocent passage? The question may be answered in the negative as long as weapons are stored on board and the ship is not carrying out 'any exercise or practice with weapons of any kind', an activity which is forbidden under Article 19(2)(a) of the UN Convention on the Law of the Sea. Several coastal states prohibit ships from entering their ports with weapons on board. However, they cannot prohibit the presence of weapons on board during passage. Article 21 of the UN Convention on the Law of the Sea enables states to adopt laws and regulations relating to innocent passage. They should be in conformity with the provisions of the Convention and they cannot prohibit an activity which is not forbidden during passage.

What if a ship is assaulted by bandits during passage? In this case it is entitled to exercise the right of self-defence. The ship may also intervene on behalf of another ship assaulted by bandits. The rationale, in this case, is the concept of collective self-defence and stopping during passage may be justified under Article 18(2) of the UN Convention on the Law of the Sea, which allows for stopping to render assistance to a ship in danger.

Is the same finding applicable to a merchant ship where it is escorted by a PMSC vessel? In principle yes, even though this solution would not be easy to justify in the case of states which subject the innocent passage of warships to their consent. Escorting vessels are not warships but they may be considered similar to warships by the coastal state in order to deny passage. If the PMSC is equipped with small aircraft and helicopters, they cannot be used during the passage with the single exception of self-defence, since Article 19(2)(e) forbids any launching, landing, or taking on board of any aircraft.

The above finding may be applied, mutatis mutandis, also to transit passage. Over-flying international straits is permitted. It is a moot point, however, whether during passage escorting aircraft may land and take off from any vessel in transit.

X. Policing Territorial Waters

The main reason for contemporary piracy is disorder on land and the absence of enforcement of any law within the territorial waters. A jurisdictional void creates a favourable ground for illegal activities, such as dumping toxic waste, illegal fishing, and armed robbery. The case of Somalia shows areas of stability where the secessionist governments of Somaliland and Puntland have established their authority, even though as entities they are still unrecognized. Somaliland and Puntland have had recourse to the services of security companies for policing their waters. Mainly they have hired services for military advice and training, with special emphasis on coast-guard operations against illegal fishing, sea dumping, and armed robbery.[30] It is not clear whether the PMSCs have been contracted for training purposes only or whether they are directly carrying out coastguard activities through their own boats. Be that as it may, one cannot deny the lawfulness of such activity as long as it is carried out in conformity with the relevant provisions of the UN Convention on the Law of the Sea. The main problem with Somaliland and Puntland is that they are de facto authorities or unrecognized entities. But the PMSCs present in those territories, as can be deduced from current practice, are not helping a rebel government to combat the legally constituted government. They are only supplying services to help a de facto authority to fill a jurisdictional void. Therefore one cannot qualify their activity as a form of support to rebels and a new kind of mercenary system The main risk in a situation of poor governmental structures is that coast-guard personnel, once trained, might be converted into pirates!

XI. Protecting Oil Rigs and Fixed Platforms

Oil rigs and fixed platforms may be subject to acts of banditry or terrorism. Usually acts of violence against them do not amount to piracy since they are not ships and thus the two-ships requirement is lacking. This is true even when the oil rig or the fixed platform is on the continental shelf far from the coast and is surrounded by the high seas. In some countries, however, oil rigs are registered as ships and thus the question as to whether an act of violence against them may be defined as an act of piracy arises. This is particularly true for jack-up rigs or for dynamically positioned craft.

The 1988 Rome Protocol for the Suppression of Unlawful Acts against the Safety of Fixed Platforms Located on the Continental Shelf applies to structures permanently attached to the seabed. It covers criminal acts against platforms located on the continental shelf and thus in international waters. Since the structure is permanently attached it cannot be defined as a ship and a criminal act against it cannot, as previously stated, be considered an act of piracy. The Rome Protocol is not concerned with the power to intervene with an act of force against those who commit a wrongful act. It only regulates the obligation to enact proper legislation to bring to justice the wrongdoer and the principle *aut dedere aut iudicare*. The 2005 Additional Protocol the 1998 Rome Convention adds no further elements of regulation in this respect.

Fixed platforms on the continental shelf are under the jurisdiction of the coastal state[31] whose legislation will lay down whether or not armed personnel belonging to PMSCs are allowed to be stationed on board. Not all countries will allow the use of private contractors for protecting offshore installations.

---

[30] See CP Kinsey, SJ Hansen, and G Franklin, 'The Impact of Private Security Companies on Somalia's Governance Networks', *Cambridge Review of Intl Affairs* 22 (2009) 147.
[31] Arts 60(2) and 80 of the UN Law of the Sea Convention.

XII. Conclusion

From the point of view of shipping companies, the resort to armed guards may have the advantage of deterring pirates and impeding ships and their valuable cargo from being captured. The most preferable option is to have navies dispatched, since they offer more powerful protection and have a deterrent effect. However, according to some commentators and even naval commanders, navies cannot give complete protection. The fleets are too big to adapt to a variety of changing tasks and the role of small units and armed guards is gaining currency. Armed guards on board—whether private teams or military personnel—lower the insurance risk premium and thus are beneficial both to shipping companies and consumers. Moreover navies are costly compared with the advantages they yield. A cost–benefit analysis shows that with 50,000 ships employed in sea trade, losses from piracy are very modest and range between US$1 billion and 16 billion.[32]

Others take the opposing view. The main argument for refusing armed guards is that the presence of firearms risks increasing armed confrontations and escalating violence. The use of weapons on fragile cargoes such as oil tankers is extremely dangerous and may put the life of passengers on a cruise ship at risk. Therefore deadly force is rejected and non-lethal devices, such as acoustic instruments, high-pressure fire hoses and electrically charged barber winds, are recommended. Unarmed security officers are to be preferred to armed guards. Moreover there is a legal vacuum as to criminal jurisdiction and the use of arms. Which jurisdiction should prevail when a ship is in foreign territorial waters: that of the flag state or of the coastal state? What about the power to give the order to use weapons and employ lethal force? Does it belong to the master since he is responsible for the safety of life at sea and the security of the ship[33] or is it a matter to be regulated between the PMSC and the shipowner or user?

Piracy is not an armed conflict and this simple consideration should be of assistance in arriving at a solution for the regulation of armed guards on board commercial shipping. Armed guards cannot be compared to mercenaries and thus the negative judgement accompanying any discussion on contractors is here completely absent. There has also been a proposal to resurrect a form of 'defensive letters of marque' to show that armed personnel are acting under the licence of a government and under its supervision.[34]

As to the use of PMSCs during armed conflict, one may choose between regulating the phenomenon or creating an outright prohibition. The Montreux Document drafted under the auspices of the Swiss government is an example of the former,[35]

---

[32] A Scheffler, *Piracy-Threat or Nuisance*, Nato Research Paper no 56 (February 2010), <http://www.ndc.nato.int/research/series.php?icode=1>, accessed 25 May 2010.

[33] See Art 34-1 of SOLAS and the ISPS (International Ship Facility and Port Security) Code.

[34] Richard, 'Reconsidering the Letter of Marque: Utilizing Private Security Providers against Piracy' (2010) 39 *Public Contact Law Journal* 411.

[35] UN Doc A/63/467–S/2008/636, Montreux Document on Pertinent International Obligations and Good Practices for States Related to Operations of Private Military and Security Companies during Armed Conflict, Montreux, 17 September 2009.

whilst the current draft presented to the Human Right Council is an example of the latter, even if with some exceptions.[36] The Montreux Document does not cover the regulation of anti-piracy services by PMSCs, as it deals with armed conflict on land and hiring by state or non-state actors. Therefore if states choose to set out a soft-law document regulating PMSCs and piracy, they should elaborate it from scratch taking into account the specific context of the marine environment. Respect for human rights should be part of the regulation and this is an issue which is also emerging in the fight against piracy.[37] In recent documents, such as the Djibouti Code of Conduct drafted under the auspices of the IMO, there is no mention of PMSCs even though they have become a growing business in the maritime domain.

A third choice would be to leave things as they are without adding any new regulation either of hard law or soft law. Seafarers should adapt the current law to the new phenomenon. PMSCs should draft a code of conduct for self-regulation and establish clear rules of engagement, if resort to force becomes unavoidable.[38] This third choice is not recommended since it will encourage the present state of anarchy and conflicting regulations. Legislative or soft-law regulation is thus to be highly recommended.

---

[36] Draft of a Possible Convention on Private Military and Security Companies (PMSCs), attached to UN Doc A/HRC/15/25, 2 July 2010, Report of the Working Group on the Use of Mercenaries as a Means of Violating Human Rights and Impeding the Exercise of the Right of Peoples to Self-Determination

[37] See, for instance, Guilfoyle, 'Counter-piracy Law Enforcement and Human Rights', (2010) 59 ICLQ 59 141.

[38] This has, for instance, been done by the IPOA, which has enacted a code of conduct for PMSCs members. The Code does not specifically take into account the maritime domain: see 'Code of Conduct 12',<http://www.ipoaworld.org/eng/codeofconduct.html>, accessed 25 May 2010.

PART II
HUMAN RIGHTS

3

The Role of Human Rights in the Regulation of Private Military and Security Companies

Federico Lenzerini and Francesco Francioni

I. International Responsibility of PMSCs and Applicability of Human Rights Standards to PMSCs Operations

The activity of private military and security companies (PMSCs) potentially concerns five different levels of international responsibility, concerning respectively the PMSCs as single entities, their employees in their individual capacity, the state(s) which benefit(s) from their services, ie the hiring state, the territorial state—if different from the latter—as well as their 'home state' where the company is registered and based. With respect to the profile of 'direct responsibility' of PMSCs—which would be particularly useful when host states are unable in practice to control their activities—the main problem lies in ascertaining whether and to what extent these companies may be considered to hold legal obligations pursuant to international law. This issue is investigated in detail in another chapter in the present volume.[1] As for individual responsibility, there is no doubt that PMSC employees are to be considered responsible in their personal capacity for any act reaching the threshold of a war crime or a crime against humanity (including, for example, torture, rape, enslavement, etc), and may thus be subject, inter alia, to the application of the principle of universality of jurisdiction as well as—for the acts perpetrated in its personal and territorial scope of application—to the jurisdiction of the International Criminal Court (ICC).[2] With respect to the third profile of responsibility, when and to the extent that PMSCs operate in the service of a government, their activities are certainly suited to generating the responsibility of the state concerned, as they are 'empowered by the...state to exercise elements

---

[1] See Ch 17 by MacLeod in this volume.
[2] The problem of whether or not employees of PMSCs may be considered as acting in an official capacity is absolutely irrelevant with respect to the competence of the ICC, as—pursuant to Art 27 of the Statute of the Court—it 'shall apply equally to all persons without any distinction based on official capacity' (para 1) and '[i]mmunities or special procedural rules which may attach to the official capacity of a person, whether under national or international law, shall not bar the Court from exercising its jurisdiction over such a person' (para 2). On the issue of responsibility of PMSC personnel see Ch 21 by Quirico in this volume.

of the governmental authority'.[3] The fourth profile of responsibility concerns the national state governing the territory in which a PMSC operates when this is different from the hiring state; in this respect, a number of factors must be considered, which are carefully addressed in a separate chapter in this volume.[4] Finally, the responsibility of the state of origin of a PMSC may arise particularly because, in the real world, such a state might be the only one that is effectively capable of controlling the activity of its own national PMSCs.[5]

With respect to the applicability of human rights standards to PMSCs operations, there is no doubt that, in contemporary international law, human rights have a multilayered characterization. This characterization corresponds to a well-established principle of customary international law and is clearly expressed by pertinent treaties. For example, pursuant to Article 2(1) of the 1966 International Covenant on Civil and Political Rights (ICCPR),[6] states parties have the obligation 'to ensure [the rights granted by the Covenant] to all individuals in their territory and subject to their jurisdiction'.[7] As a consequence, individuals must be 'protected by the State, not just against violations of Covenant rights by its agents, but also against acts committed by private persons or entities'.[8] States parties are therefore bound to take 'appropriate measures or to exercise due diligence to prevent, punish, investigate or redress the harm caused by such acts by private persons or entities ... [as well as] to provide effective remedies in the event of breach'.[9] This characterization of the obligations set up by the Covenant make it irrelevant—under the ICCPR—whether PMSCs act as private companies or as entities exercising prerogatives of state sovereignty. Irrespective of the position of PMSCs as private or public entities, the ICCPR is in fact fully applicable to human rights breaches perpetrated by such companies. In the event that they operate as private actors, violations of human rights committed by PMSCs indeed fall within the scope of operation of the obligation to 'ensure' protection of

---

[3] See International Law Commission's (ILC) Articles on 'Responsibility of states for internationally wrongful acts' (ILC's Articles), 2001 ('noted' by the UN General Assembly in 2002; see Doc A/RES/56/83 of 28 January 2002), Art 5, <http://untreaty.un.org/ilc/texts/instruments/english/draft%20articles/9_6_2001.pdf>, accessed 21 February 2009. Pursuant to this Article, which reproduces customary international law, each action they perform is to 'be considered an act of the State under international law'. Even if one would not be in agreement with the characterization of PMSCs as entities exercising elements of the governmental authority, they should *at least* be considered entities acting 'on the instructions of, or under the direction or control of' the state at the service of which they operate, which would be in any case responsible in light of the rule of customary international law embodied by Art 8 of the ILC's Articles. See, on this subject, Ch 6 by Hoppe in this volume.

[4] See Ch 7 by Bakker in this volume.

[5] See, on this issue, Ch 5 by Francioni in this volume.

[6] 999 *UNTS* 171. Art 2 para 1 states that: 'Each State Party to the present Covenant undertakes to respect and to ensure to all individuals within its territory and subject to its jurisdiction the rights recognized in the present Covenant, without distinction of any kind, such as race, colour, sex, language, religion, political or other opinion, national or social origin, property, birth or other status.'

[7] See Human Rights Committee (HRC), General Comment no 31[80], 'The Nature of the General Legal Obligation Imposed on States Parties to the Covenant', UN Doc CCPR/C/21/Rev1/Add13, 26 May 2004, para 3.

[8] Ibid, para 8.   [9] Ibid.

individuals against non-state breaches of the rights affirmed by the Covenant; where they are exercising functions delegated to them by the state, the need to ensure compatibility of their operations with the standards set up by the ICCPR is dictated by the state obligation to respect those standards. In the second instance, the existence of the said obligation is made even clearer by para 3(a) of Article 2, which also requires states to ensure an effective remedy in favour of victims of human rights breaches when they are 'committed by persons acting in an official capacity'. As for the 'territorial extension' of the obligations arising from the ICCPR, the term state 'jurisdiction' included in Article 2 para 1 is to be intended as binding states parties to 'respect and ensure the rights laid down in the Covenant to anyone [regardless of his/her nationality or statelessness] within the power or effective control of that State Party, even if not situated within the territory of the State Party'.[10] This principle assumes special significance with respect to PMSC operations, as it also applies with respect to 'those within the power or effective control of the forces of a State Party acting outside its territory, regardless of the circumstances in which such power or effective control was obtained'.[11] In light of the main purpose of the ICCPR—ie to ensure the *effectiveness* of human rights—the term 'forces' is to be read as embracing not only the 'official' forces included within the context of the national army, but also PMSCs hired by the state in order to perform equivalent functions.

Equivalent observations can be developed with respect to the European Convention for the Protection of Human Rights and Fundamental Freedoms (ECHR),[12] the American Convention on Human Rights (ACHR)[13] and the African Charter on Human and Peoples' Rights (ACHPR).[14] The ECHR establishes in its very first article that '[t]he High Contracting Parties shall secure to everyone within their jurisdiction the rights and freedoms defined in Section I of this Convention'. Since the early 1980s the European Court of Human Rights (ECtHR) has correctly interpreted this provision as entailing the obligation of states parties to protect human rights against acts committed by private actors (therefore including PMSCs), ranging from the requirement to prevent the murder of a person by another person,[15] to that of preventing and/or investigating issues of disappearances of individuals effected by non-state actors.[16] However, in order for a state to be considered responsible for an act committed by a private actor, the ECtHR considers it necessary that:

---

[10] Ibid, para 10. [11] Ibid. [12] *CETS* no 5.
[13] OAS Treaty Series no 36.
[14] 21 *ILM* 58 (1982).
[15] See *Osman v UK*, Appl no 23452/94 (28 October 1998).
[16] See *Osmanoğlu v Turkey*, Appl no 48804/99 (24 January 2008); *Varnava and ors v Turkey*, Appl nos 16064/90, 16065/90, 16066/90, 16068/90, 16069/90, 16070/90, 16071/90, 16072/90, and 16073/90, Grand Chamber (18 September 2009). For a more comprehensive assessment of the relevant practice of the ECtHR see I Ziemele, 'Issues of Responsibility of Private Persons or Entities for Human Rights Violations: The Case-law of International Human Rights Courts and Monitoring Bodies', EUI AEL 2009/08, 12 ff, <http://cadmus.eui.eu/dspace/bitstream/1814/11409/1/AEL_2009_08.pdf>, accessed 14 May 2010.

the authorities knew or ought to have known at the time of the existence of a real and immediate risk to the life of an identified individual or individuals from the criminal acts of a third party and that they failed to take measures within the scope of their powers which, judged reasonably, might have been expected to avoid that risk.[17]

Interestingly, although the ECtHR approach is generally oriented towards considering the territorial extent of the applicability of Article 1 ECHR as limited to the territory of the state concerned,[18] the Court has affirmed that, in exceptional circumstances 'the acts of Contracting States performed outside their territory or which produce effects there ("extra-territorial act") may amount to exercise by them of their jurisdiction within the meaning of Article 1 of the Convention'.[19] This may happen not only in the event of military occupation;[20] in fact:

a State might also be held accountable for violation of the Convention rights and freedoms of persons who are in the territory of another State but who are found to be under the former State's authority and control through its agents operating—whether lawfully or unlawfully —in the latter State. Accountability in such situations stemmed from the fact that Article 1 of the Convention could not be interpreted so as to allow a state party to perpetrate violations of the Convention on the territory of another State, which it could not perpetrate on its own territory.[21]

This is particularly significant with respect to PMSCs when these companies are hired by—or are under the control of—a state and perform military or security services in the territory of countries other than that state.

As regards the ACHR, Article 1 commands states parties 'to respect the rights and freedoms recognized [by the Convention] and to ensure to all persons subject to their jurisdiction the free and full exercise of those rights and freedoms'. Therefore, in the event of human rights abuses committed by private entities, including PMSCs, the responsibility of the state may be triggered on the basis of an alleged failure to prevent, protect, or prosecute the private act that has caused the breach. This principle has been affirmed by the Inter-American Court of Human Rights (IACtHR) since its very first case, *Velasquez Rodriguez*,[22] in which the Court held that the question of whether state organs had directly engaged in a violation of the ACHR was not decisive; the decisive element for producing state responsibility was that the state concerned had failed to adequately protect the victims when faced with a widespread practice of human rights breaches which called for reasonable

---

[17] See *Osman v UK* (n 15 above), para 116. This approach has been confirmed in the subsequent jurisprudence of the ECtHR; see eg *Kilic v Turkey*, Appl no 22492/93 (28 March 2000); *Akkoç v Turkey*, Appl nos 22947/93 and 22948/93 (10 October 2000); *Kontrová v Slovakia*, Appl no 7510/04 (31 May 2007).
[18] See *Bankovic and ors v Belgium and 16 other States*, Appl no 52207/99, admissibility decision of 13 December 2001, para 61.
[19] See *Issa and ors v Turkey*, Appl no 31821/96 (16 November 2004), para 68; *Al-Saadoon and Mufdhi v UK*, Appl no 61498/08 (2 March 2010).
[20] See *Issa avd ors v Turkey* (n 19 above), para 69.
[21] See *Issa avd ors v Turkey* (n 19 above), para 71 (references omitted).
[22] See *Case of Velasquez-Rodriguez v Honduras*, IACtHR, Series C, no 4 (29 July 1988), particularly para 155.

measures of crime prevention and investigation and prosecution of the perpetrators. This principle has constantly been reiterated by the IACtHR in its subsequent jurisprudence. In particular, in case of the *Pueblo Bello Massacre*, concerning extrajudicial executions by armed paramilitary groups in Colombia, the Court held that 'it is true that in this case, it has not been proved that the state authorities had specific prior knowledge of the day and time of the attack on the population of Pueblo Bello and the way it would be carried out'. However, 'Colombia did not adopt sufficient prevention measures to avoid a paramilitary group . . . from entering the municipality of Pueblo Bello . . . [and from detaining] at least 43 alleged victims . . . , who were subsequently assassinated or disappeared'.[23] This construction of actual or required knowledge as a constitutive element of state responsibility for acts of private actors is very relevant to the operations of PMSCs. Although such companies cannot be likened to the criminal paramilitary organizations that were involved in the serious violations of human rights noted above, the approach developed by the IACtHR offers several elements that can be usefully applied to a PMSC scenario. First, if a relevant factor in establishing state responsibility is the knowledge of the risk posed by armed group to innocent civilians, greater knowledge must be deemed to exist when the state *itself* contracts certain coercive functions out to private military contractors. Then, full knowledge of the nature of these functions translates by necessity into an awareness of the risk that they entail, especially if this includes coercive services and use of weapons that might expose the civilian population to actual or potential danger to their life, security, or liberty. Secondly, although the criterion for establishing state responsibility is 'due diligence', rather than objective liability, the case law of the IACtHR shows that the standard of due diligence is not subjective but, on the contrary, must be objectively indexed to the human rights obligations as laid down in the Convention and as interpreted in the judicial practice of the Court. Thirdly, since in the PMSC scenario it is the hiring state that creates a contract for the services from which the risk of human rights violations arises, in the event of recurring or systematic violations the Court may even presume the breach of due diligence simply on the basis of a repetition of human right violations without any need for further inquiry into the knowledge or fault of the hiring state.

Concerning the ACHPR, the African Commission on Human and Peoples' Rights (AComHPR) has developed a construction of human rights that is particularly well suited to PMSCs' operations. According to the Commission: 'Internationally accepted ideas of the various obligations engendered by human rights indicate that all rights—both civil and political rights and social and economic— generate at least four levels of duties for a state that undertakes to adhere to a rights regime.'[24] This 'four-layer' categorization of human rights obviously entails, at 'a primary level', the obligation to *respect*, ie the requirement that states 'refrain from

---

[23] See *Case of the Pueblo Bello Massacre v Colombia*, judgment of 31 January 2006, Series C, no 140, paras 135–8.
[24] See Communication no 155/96, *The Social and Economic Rights Action Center and the Center for Economic and Social Rights v Nigeria*, 2001, 2001 AHRLR 60, para 44.

interfering [directly] in the enjoyment of all fundamental rights'.[25] The second layer is represented by the obligation to *protect* 'against other subjects by legislation and provision of effective remedies',[26] ie 'to take measures to protect beneficiaries of the protected rights against political, economic, and social interferences'.[27] This specific requirement clearly applies to activities carried out by private actors, with respect to which the state must interpose itself between potential perpetrators and victims, acting as a shield in order to prevent the human rights of the latter being prejudiced by the actions of the former. '[T]he tertiary obligation of the state' arising from human rights law is grounded on the same rationale; it consists in the requirement to *promote* 'the enjoyment of all human rights... [through] mak[ing] sure that individuals are able to exercise their rights and freedoms, for example, by promoting tolerance, raising awareness, and even building infrastructures.'[28] Finally, the fourth layer is represented by the obligation to *fulfil* human rights, ie 'to move [the state] machinery towards the actual realisation of the rights'.[29] In light of this four-layer construction, it is evident that when PMSC operations produce the objective result of generating a breach of a protected human right, international responsibility of the territorial state (or of the state which has—or should have—control over such activities) is triggered *irrespective* of whether or not the PMSC concerned may be considered part of the state apparatus. In fact, in the event that the PMSC is actually part of the governmental machinery, the state will be held responsible for breaching the obligation to *respect* human rights, while in the opposite situation the requirement of *protecting* (and, possibly, *fulfilling*) such rights is to be considered infringed.

II. Specific Human Rights Potentially Affected by PMSC Operations: Relevant Universal and Regional Practice

PMSCs are specialized companies providing high-tech intelligence, training and support of a military character as well as surveillance and protection to strategic installations, high-ranking officials, and economic plants of special importance (such as oil platforms). They often perform conflict activities, especially in particularly dangerous zones where it would not be possible for conventional armed forces to do so. Their activity has increased exponentially in recent years—especially in the context of military operations carried out by the United States—due to their growing specialization as well as to the contextual decrease of military support by Western allies. Therefore, the activity of PMSCs usually involves recourse to armed force, through the performance of typical conflict operations. It is thus self-evident how PMSC operations might affect the enjoyment of most human rights, the effectiveness of which is usually jeopardized in the course of armed conflicts. Not only human rights of individual character, but also collective rights are threatened

---

[25] See Communication no 155/96, *The Social and Economic Rights Action Center and the Center for Economic and Social Rights v Nigeria*, 2001, 2001 AHRLR 60, para 45.
[26] Ibid, para 46.   [27] Ibid.   [28] Ibid.   [29] Ibid, para 47.

by PMSCs operations. Those human rights most in danger of being affected by PMSCs are contemplated and protected by all the relevant international instruments at the universal and regional level, as well as, with respect to most of them, by customary international law.

The first right to be taken into account is the right to life, which, as emphasized by the HRC, 'is the supreme right from which no derogation is permitted even in time of public emergency which threatens the life of the nation'.[30] Whilst it was proclaimed in relation to the ICCPR, this principle also applies to any international regime dealing with human rights, including customary international law. At the same time, respect for the right to life obviously constitutes an essential prerequisite for making the enjoyment of all other human rights possible. Arbitrary deprivation of life is therefore prohibited under any circumstance, with no derogation possible. As a consequence, to ascertain the extent to which PMSCs and their employees are to be considered responsible for the breach of the right, it is necessary to investigate a contrarii the conditions that are to be satisfied in order for such an action to be considered non-arbitrary. First, deprivation of life is in principle to be considered non-arbitrary—thus legitimate—when is the result of the execution of capital punishment sentenced by a final judgment, rendered by a competent court, at the end of a trial in which all procedural rights of the accused have been granted, and only in those states that are not bound by any international treaty to abolish the death penalty.[31] This eventuality, however, is in principle not pertinent to PMSCs' operations, as they do not usually include the performance of judicial competences. Deprivation of life is also non-arbitrary when it is committed for reasons of self-defence, used by a person in order to prevent the loss of his/her/another's life. This situation is possible in the context of PMSC operations. However, self-defence may only be considered legal when the principle of proportionality is respected, ie when the only possible means for preventing a loss of life consists in taking the life of the offender. For this reason, a breach of the right to life will occur each time this condition is not met. A third situation in which taking of life cannot be considered arbitrary occurs in another context typically involved in the exercise of PMSC operations, ie in the event of armed conflict, although the conditions to be met in this respect are controversial. In sum, the taking of someone's life by a PMSC employee constitutes a breach of the right to life in all circumstances except when it is justified on grounds of self-defence or when—in the event of armed conflict—such an employee may be considered a lawful combatant using lethal force within the limits allowed by applicable international human rights and humanitarian law. However, when a PMSC operates as a state agent, it is not sufficient to demonstrate

---

[30] See General Comment no 06, 'The Right to Life' (Art 6), 1982, para 1, <http://www.unhchr.ch/tbs/doc.nsf/(Symbol)/84ab9690ccd81fc7c12563ed0046fae3?Opendocument>, accessed 21 February 2009.

[31] Eg, the death penalty is today prohibited by Protocol no 6 to the Convention for the Protection of Human Rights and Fundamental Freedoms concerning the abolition of the death penalty, 1983, CETS no 114, which has been ratified by all members of the Council of Europe, with the only exception of Russia (see <http://conventions.coe.int/Treaty/Commun/ChercheSig.asp?NT=114&CM=8&DF=6/1/2009&CL=ENG>, accessed 19 October 2010).

that it has acted in the context of the legitimate exercise of its competences in order to exclude state responsibility; in fact, as stressed by the ECtHR, not only is a state responsible when 'misdirect fire from agents has killed a civilian', but also in the event that such agents:

> fail to take all feasible precautions in the choice of means and methods of a security operation mounted against an opposing group with a view to avoiding and, in any event, to minimizing, incidental loss of civilian life. Thus, even though it has not been established beyond reasonable doubt that the bullet which killed [the victim] had been fired by the security forces, the Court must consider whether the security forces' operation had been planned and conducted in such a way as to avoid or minimise, to the greatest extent possible, any risk to the lives of [civilians], including from the fire-power of the [rebel faction].[32]

In practice, most cases of unlawful deprivation of life by PMSCs take place in the form of extrajudicial executions, particularly when they are perpetrated in the framework of the performance of military operations (which represent one of the typical mandates of PMSCs). Instances of extrajudicial executions have been considered—as violations of the right to life—in many communications released by the AComHPR.[33] However, the Commission has held that 'extra-judicial executions and torture are caused by the state or through its agents or acquiescence'.[34] For this reason, killings committed by non-state actors do not entail state liability for extrajudicial executions, on the condition that state authorities undertake investigations on such killings, which 'must be carried out by entirely independent individuals, provided with the necessary resources, and their findings must be made public and prosecutions initiated in accordance with the information uncovered'.[35] This means that, according to the AComHPR, when extrajudicial executions are committed by persons operating as PMSCs' agents, state responsibility is only generated when the PMSC concerned is acting within the framework of the governmental organization or when—the company being a private entity—the state fails to carry out an investigation into the killings.

Other actions committed in the framework of military or paramilitary activities can actually translate into violations of the right to life. This can be the result, for example, of massive action resulting in the destruction of the environment and living resources of a community, as was found by the AComHPR in the renowned case of the Ogoni people in Nigeria, decided in 2001. This concerned a number of

---

[32] See *Ergi v Turkey*, Appl no 23818/94 (28 July 1998), para 79.

[33] See eg Communications nos 25/89, 47/90, 56/91, 100/93, *Free Legal Assistance Group and ors v Zaire*, 1995, 2000 AHLRL 74; Communication no 245/2002, *Zimbabwean Human Rights NGO Forum v Zimbabwe*, 2006, 2006 AHRLR 128; Communications nos 137/94, 139/94, 154/96 and 161/97, *International Pen and ors (on behalf of Saro-Wiwa) v Nigeria*, 1998, 2000 AHRLR 212; Communications nos 54/91, 61/91, 98/93, 164–96/97 and 210/98, *Malawi African Association and ors v Mauritania*, 2000, 2000 AHRLR 149; Communication nos 223/98, *Forum of Conscience v Sierra Leone*, 2000, 2000 AHRLR 293.

[34] See *Zimbabwean Human Rights NGO Forum v Zimbabwe* (n 33 above), para 181.

[35] See Communications nos 48/90, 50/91, 52/91, 89/93, *Amnesty International and ors v Sudan*, 1999, para 51, <http://www1.umn.edu/humanrts/africa/comcases/48-90_50-91_52-91_89-93.html>, accessed 12 March 2009. See also *Zimbabwean Human Rights NGO Forum v Zimbabwe* (n 33 above), para 181.

abuses perpetrated by Nigerian military forces in the ancestral lands of the Ogoni indigenous community with the purpose of facilitating oil exploitation in those lands by a consortium involving the National Petroleum Company and the multinational company Shell Petroleum. According to the Commission, a breach of the right to life occurred on account of the fact that:

> Given the wide spread violations perpetrated by the Government of Nigeria and by private actors (be it following its clear blessing or not), the most fundamental of all human rights, the right to life has been violated. The Security forces were given the green light to decisively deal with the Ogonis, which was illustrated by the wide spread terrorisations and killings. The pollution and environmental degradation to a level humanly unacceptable has made it living in the Ogoni land a nightmare. The survival of the Ogonis depended on their land and farms that were destroyed by the direct involvement of the Government. These and similar brutalities not only persecuted individuals in Ogoniland but also the whole of the Ogoni Community as a whole.[36]

Another interesting position taken by the AComHPR is that according to which a breach of the right to life may take place not only when actual loss of life occurs, since 'It would be a narrow interpretation to [the] right [to life] to think that it can only be violated when one is deprived of it'. 'It cannot be said', the Commission continues, 'that the right to respect for one's life and the dignity of his person ... would be protected in a state of constant fear and/or threats', as, although the victim 'is still alive[, he is constantly] hiding for fear of his life'.[37] A similar approach is followed by the ECtHR, which has developed jurisprudence according to which, in the event of the disappearance of a person in life-threatening circumstances, the lack of appropriate investigation by the state entails a violation of the right to life—irrespective of whether state agents or private entities were responsible for the disappearance of the victim—as long as the state has failed to protect the latter.[38] The fact that these kinds of situation may arise at the hands of a PMSC is clearly evident.

The right to be free from torture and cruel, inhuman, and degrading treatment is also of particular significance for the present enquiry. In principle, myriad acts might be perpetrated by PMSCs that reach the threshold of cruel, inhuman, or degrading treatment or even torture. When this happens, a breach of the right in point inevitably occurs, as the prohibition of torture and cruel, inhuman, or degrading treatment or punishment corresponds to a rule of jus cogens, and no derogation from it is possible in time of emergency—even in the event of armed conflict—pursuant to relevant international instruments.[39] As emphasized by the ECtHR, states are responsible for acts of torture or degrading treatment or

---

[36] See *The Social and Economic Rights Action Center and the Center for Economic and Social Rights v Nigeria* (n 24 above), para 67.
[37] See Communication no 205/97, *Kazeem Aminu v Nigeria*, 2000, <http://www1.umn.edu/humanrts/africa/comcases/205-97.html>, para 18, accessed 14 March 2009.
[38] See eg *Osmanoğlu v Turkey*; *Varnava and ors v Turkey*, Appl nos 16064/90, 16065/90, 16066/90, 16068/90, 16069/90, 16070/90, 16071/90, 16072/90, and 16073/90 (18 September 2009) (Grand Chamber).
[39] See eg Art 4 ICCPR; Art 15 ECHR; Art 27 ACHR.

punishment even when such acts are 'administered by private individuals'[40] (thus including PMSCs). This also applies in the context of the fight against terrorism, a situation that is especially relevant to PMSCs, particularly when they provide security services in less developed countries, which sometimes have to face terrorist groups that in many cases possess military technology far more advanced than that available to national security forces. In fact, PMSCs can be equipped with highly sophisticated intelligence and equipment, adequate to face the said terrorist groups efficiently. However, in performing their counterterrorism operations PMSCs must refrain from (ab)using their powers to the extent of perpetrating systematic human rights breaches, particularly absolutely intolerable ones such as torture or cruel, inhuman, or degrading treatment. This conclusion is explicitly or implicitly confirmed by a number of human rights treaties, including the 1999 OAU Convention on the Prevention and Combating of Terrorism[41] and its 2004 Protocol,[42] which, at Article 3(1)(k), affirms the commitment of states parties to outlawing 'torture and other degrading and inhumane treatment, including discriminatory and racist treatment of terrorist suspects, which are inconsistent with international law'.

A typical situation of inhuman or degrading treatment that may arise from PMSC operations is the disappearance of persons in life-threatening circumstances; in such an event, lack of investigation by the state authorities, besides giving rise to a breach of the right to life, results in the said treatment to the prejudice of the relatives of the disappeared person, due to the 'length of time over which the ordeal of the relatives has been dragged out and the attitude of official indifference in face of their acute anxiety to know the fate of their close family members'.[43]

The prohibition of torture and cruel, inhuman, or degrading treatment partially overlaps with the right to physical and mental health, as torture and similar treatments inevitably jeopardize the physical and/or mental health of the victim. A distinctive right to health is not in fact expressly contemplated either by the ICCPR or by the ECHR, whilst the ACHR, at Article 5, subsumes the right to 'physical, mental, and moral integrity'—together with the prohibition of torture or cruel, inhuman, or degrading punishment or treatment—within the provision concerning the 'right to humane treatment'; this right may not be suspended or derogated from even in 'time of war, public danger, or other emergency that threatens the independence or security of a state Party', pursuant to Article 27 para 2. The right to the enjoyment of the highest attainable standard of physical and mental health is instead expressly contemplated—as a social right—by Article 12 of the International Covenant on Economic, Social and Cultural Rights

---

[40] See *A v UK*, Appl no 25599/94 (23 September 1998), para 22.
[41] The full text of the Convention is available at <http://www.africa-union.org/root/au/Documents/Treaties/treaties.htm>, accessed 31 May 2009.
[42] See Protocol to the OAU Convention on the Prevention and Combating of Terrorism, 2004, <http://www.africa-union.org/root/au/Documents/Treaties/Text/The%20Protocol%20on%20Terrorism%2026July2004.pdf>, accessed 29 March 2009.
[43] See ECtHR, *Varnava and ors v Turkey* (n 16 above), para 202.

(ICESCR),⁴⁴ Article 5(e)(iv) of the 1965 International Convention on the Elimination of All Forms of Racial Discrimination (Racial Discrimination Convention),⁴⁵ Article 12 of the 1979 Convention on the Elimination of All Forms of Racial Discrimination against Women (CEDAW),⁴⁶ Article 24 of the 1989 Convention of the Rights of the Child (CRC),⁴⁷ and by Article 16 ACHPR. In general terms, however, these provisions consider the right in question in terms of a right of access to healthcare, particularly through national sanitary services, in order that all sectors of civil society (including the most vulnerable and disadvantaged groups) are granted this access on an equitable basis. In this respect, PMSC operations are apparently unlikely to interfere with the realization of this right. This conclusion, however, is to be revisited in consideration of the broad meaning accorded to the right to health by the 'quasi-judicial' bodies entrusted with controlling the implementation of the relevant international instruments, particularly the Committee on Economic, Social and Cultural Rights (CESCR) and the AComHPR. So, this right could potentially be breached by PMSCs, for instance, when their actions result in the limitation of 'access to health services as a punitive measure, e.g., during armed conflicts in violation of international humanitarian law'.⁴⁸ The same can be asserted, mutatis mutandis, with respect to the situation of arrested persons who are kept in inadequate conditions of detention. For example, the AComHPR has found a violation of the right to enjoy the best attainable state of physical and mental health, contemplated by Article 16 ACHPR, in light of the fact that some detainees had died 'as a result of the lack of medical attention'; in addition, the 'general state of health of the prisoners deteriorated due to the lack of sufficient food; they had neither blankets nor adequate hygiene'.⁴⁹

Furthermore, in its General Comment no 14 (2000) on Article 12 ICESCR, the CESCR considered that proper realization of the right to health requires states to:

> refrain from unlawfully polluting air, water and soil, e.g., through industrial waste from state-owned facilities, from using or testing nuclear, biological or chemical weapons if such testing results in the release of substances harmful to human health, and from limiting access to health services as a punitive measure, e.g., during armed conflicts in violation of international humanitarian law.⁵⁰

From this perspective, PMSC operations might well interfere with the enjoyment of the right to health, given that the types of interferences to this right listed by the CESCR—or at least some of them—can certainly be committed by these companies in carrying out their usual mandate. An example of the situation just described is that of 'development-related activities that lead to the displacement of indigenous

---

⁴⁴ 993 *UNTS* 3.
⁴⁵ UN GA res 2106 (XX) of 21 December 1965.
⁴⁶ 660 *UNTS* 195.
⁴⁷ UN GA res 44/25 of 20 November 1989.
⁴⁸ See General Comment no 14, 'The Right to the Highest Attainable Standard of Health (Article 12 of the International Covenant on Economic, Social and Cultural Rights)', UN Doc E/C12/2000/4, 11 August 2000, para 34.
⁴⁹ See *Malawi African Association and ors v Mauritania* (n 33 above), para 122.
⁵⁰ See General Comment no 14 (n 48 above), para 34.

peoples against their will from their traditional territories and environment, denying them their sources of nutrition and breaking their symbiotic relationship with their lands',[51] in which PMSCs may well be involved, through providing either military intelligence or security services. This is even clearer if one takes a look at the practice of the AComHPR. In particular, in the above-cited Ogoni case, serious environmental degradation and health problems for the members of the group resulted from contamination in the Ogoni's land. As the operation of the oil exploitation project was (peacefully) opposed by the Ogoni people, the Nigerian government ended the protests through military force, including (but not limited to) destruction and burning of several Ogoni villages. The Commission found that, due to this behaviour, Nigeria had breached, inter alia, Article 16 ACHPR.[52] In this respect, it is easy to note that a decisive role in producing this violation was played by the Nigerian security forces, which in the specific case carried out operations (ie 'protection' of state investments against possible interference or 'boycott') that may be part of the usual mandate of PMSCs.

Another interesting point to be emphasized is that the right to physical and mental health implies that states 'have to respect the enjoyment of the right to health in other countries, and to prevent third parties from violating the right in other countries, if they are able to influence these third parties by way of legal or political means';[53] these 'third parties' might well be PMSCs, with respect to which a profile of responsibility of their 'home' state may arise. This form of responsibility might be accompanied by that of the host country, which may arise from its 'failure to regulate the activities of individuals, groups or corporations [including PMSCs] so as to prevent them from violating the right to health of others'.[54]

A related right is that of an adequate standard of living for the person and his/her family, including adequate food, clothing, and housing, as well as to the continuous improvement of living conditions, protected by Article 11 ICESCR. This provision may be breached in a number of cases occurring in the context of PMSC operations, particularly in the event of forced evictions. This practice, which is often connected with forced relocations taking place in wartime, may easily be perpetrated by PMSCs not only in the event of armed conflict, but also in peacetime, when security services are provided in order to help realize 'development and infrastructure projects, such as the construction of dams or other large-scale energy projects, with land acquisition measures associated with urban renewal, housing renovation, city beautification programmes, the clearing of land for agricultural purposes, unbridled speculation in land', etc.[55]

---

[51] See General Comment no 14 (n 48 above), para 27.
[52] See *The Social and Economic Rights Action Center and the Center for Economic and Social Rights v Nigeria* (n 24 above).
[53] See CESCR, General Comment no 14 (n 48 above), para 39.
[54] Ibid, para 51.
[55] See CESCR, General Comment no 7, 'The Right to Adequate Housing (Article 11.1): Forced Evictions', 1997, para 7, <http://www.unhchr.ch/tbs/doc.nsf/(symbol)/CESCR+General+Comment+7.En?OpenDocument>, accessed 28 February 2009.

The exercise of an element of state sovereignty by PMSCs may also result in the imposition on persons external to the company of forcible conditions of work which may reach the threshold of forced or bonded labour or even, in the most serious cases, of enslavement. This practice is prohibited by most international instruments generally dealing with human rights, as well as by two specific International Labour Organization (ILO) Conventions on the subject.[56] Ordinarily, the subjection of a person by a PMSC to work amounting to forced labour is therefore to be considered a violation of internationally recognized human rights. However, exceptions are possible in which the imposition of forcible conditions of work does not amount to a breach of international law, ie when forced labour is imposed—by the competent governmental authority (which may be represented by a PMSC when authority has been delegated by the state)—during an armed conflict or in other situations of emergency, pursuant to the relevant international instruments.[57] In any case, any authority representing a state party to the ILO Convention no 29 (1930) that is competent to exact forced or compulsory labour must ensure that 'the work to be done or the service to be rendered is of important direct interest for the community called upon to do work or render the service', is of 'imminent necessity', that it is impossible 'to obtain voluntary labour for carrying out' the work needed, as well as that 'the work or service will not lay too heavy a burden' upon the population.[58] The applicability of the exemptions to the prohibition of forced labour is in any case excluded when forced labour deteriorates into conditions analogous to slavery. Enslavement, servitude, and other institutions and practices analogous to slavery—to be intended as the exercise of 'any or all of the powers attaching to the right of ownership' over the victim, pursuant to the definition of slavery proclaimed by relevant treaties[59] and also accepted by customary international law[60]—are in fact prohibited by a provision of customary international law of peremptory character, and the possibility of any derogation from this prohibition is categorically excluded by relevant treaties.

Other human rights law breaches that can potentially be perpetrated by PMSCs are behaviours resulting in racial discrimination or apartheid. In addition to the cases in which racial discrimination or apartheid are practiced *deliberately*,[61] the

---

[56] See Convention no 29 concerning Forced or Compulsory Labour (1930) and Convention no 105 concerning the Abolition of Forced Labour (1957), <http://www.ilo.org/ilolex/english/convdisp1.htm>, accessed 22 February 2009.

[57] See eg Art 2(d) ILO Convention no 29 (1930).

[58] See Art 9.

[59] See Art 1 of the 1926 Slavery Convention (60 *LNTS* 253); Art 7 of the 1956 Supplementary Convention on the Abolition of Slavery, the Slave Trade, and Institutions and Practices Similar to Slavery (226 *UNTS* 3); Art 7 of the 1998 Rome Statute of the International Criminal Court (2187 *UNTS* 90).

[60] See F Lenzerini, 'La Definizione Internazionale di Schiavitù Secondo il Tribunale per la Ex-Iugoslavia: Un Caso di Osmosi tra Consuetudine e Norme Convenzionali' (2001) 84 Rivista di Diritto Internazionale 1026 ff.

[61] Racial discrimination and apartheid are specifically addressed by, respectively, the 1965 International Convention on the Elimination of All Forms of Racial Discrimination (660 *UNTS* 195) and the 1973 International Convention on the Suppression and Punishment of the Crime of Apartheid (1015 *UNTS* 243).

right to be treated without discrimination is infringed each time that the majority of internationally recognized human rights are *applied in a discriminatory manner*, ie distinctly among different groups on grounds of 'race, colour, sex, language, religion, political or other opinion, national or social origin, property, birth or other status'.[62] In concrete terms, pursuant to Article 5 of the Racial Discrimination Convention, the prohibition of racial discrimination implies that the right of everyone to equality before the law—'without distinction as to race, colour, or national or ethnic origin'—is guaranteed with respect to a huge list of rights, including: the right to security of person and protection by the state against violence or bodily harm; the right to freedom of movement and residence; the right to leave any country and to return to one's own country; the right to property; the right to freedom of thought, conscience, and religion; the right to freedom of opinion and expression; the right to freedom of peaceful assembly and association; the right to housing; the right to equal participation in cultural activities; and the right of access to any place or service intended for use by the general public (such as transport hotels, restaurants, cafés, theatres, and parks). In this respect, each time that a PMSC restricts one of these rights on one of the grounds listed above—for example, to the prejudice of a racial or political group hostile to the national government—a breach of the prohibition of racial discrimination occurs.

The right to liberty and to security of the person is also particularly relevant to PMSCs' activities. International human rights instruments usually refer the right to the security of the person to situations of arrest and detention, in conjunction with the right to liberty.[63] Violations of this right may well be committed by PMSCs, especially when they are entrusted with the duty of providing police services. One may reasonably assert that, when a measure of deprivation of liberty is carried out by a PMSC, its possible arbitrariness is even more likely than when it is executed by a 'regular' state officer, as the presence of all the necessary guarantees in order for this measure to be lawful are not necessarily granted by a private operator which—whilst authorized to exercise such power—is usually disconnected with the ordinary state authorities entrusted by law to ensure respect for these guarantees. So, for instance, PMSC operators may lack the necessary legal expertise in order to ensure that deprivation of liberty takes place 'in accordance with such procedure[s] as are established by law';[64] also, the modalities of PMSC operations may prevent the arrested person from being brought 'promptly before a judge or other officer authorized by law to exercise judicial power'.[65] The same can be said with respect to the right of the arrested person that the lawfulness of his/her deprivation of liberty is scrutinized by a court with the competence to 'order his[/her] release if the detention is not lawful',[66] or with respect to the requirement that '[p]re-trial detention should be an exception and as short as possible'.[67] In addition, even in

---

[62] See Art. 2 para 1 ICCPR. [63] See eg Art 9 ICCPR.
[64] See eg Art 9 para 1 ICCPR. [65] Ibid. [66] See eg Art 9 para 4 ICCPR.
[67] See HRC, General Comment no 8, 'Right to Liberty and Security of Persons' (Art 9), 1982, para 3, <http://www.unhchr.ch/tbs/doc.nsf/(Symbol)/f4253f9572cd4700c12563ed00483bec?Opendocument>, accessed 22 February 2009.

the cases where arrest and/or detention carried out by a PMSC could be considered lawful per se from a 'procedural' perspective, the human rights of the arrested or detained person are breached when the person is treated without humanity,[68] eg when an arrested person—irrespective of whether or not his/her arrest is lawful in itself—is not separated from convicted persons and/or is not granted separate treatment appropriate to his/her status as an unconvicted person,[69] as well as when accused juvenile persons are not separated from adults or granted prompt access to justice in order to be tried without delay. In this respect, the AComHPR has considered many cases of detention as tantamount to violations—in addition to the right to liberty and to security of the person—of the right 'to the respect of the dignity inherent in a human being' as well as to freedom from all 'forms of exploitation and degradation of man' granted by Article 5 ACHPR. For example, in 1999, in a case concerning Nigeria, the Commission held that '[d]eprivation of light, insufficient food and lack of access to medicine or medical care . . . constitute violations of article 5'.[70] Also, cruel, inhuman or degrading treatment has been found in another case on detention where the victim was kept 'in leg irons and handcuffs'—with 'no evidence of any violent action on his part or escape attempts that would justify holding him in irons'—as well as 'in cells which were airless and dirty, then denied medical attention, during the first days of his arrest'.[71] In a later case, a similar finding was based on the fact that the prisoner was detained with 'his legs and hands chained to the floor day and night. From the day he was arrested and detained, until the day he was sentenced by the tribunal, a total period of 147 days, he was not allowed to take a bath . . . he was kept in solitary confinement in a cell meant for criminals'.[72] The very fact of 'being detained arbitrarily, not knowing the reason or duration of detention, is itself a mental trauma. Moreover, this deprivation of contact with the outside world and the health-threatening conditions amount to cruel, inhuman and degrading treatment'.[73] A very similar approach has been adopted by the ECtHR; in a very recent case, the Court considered the detention of one person at a police station as being arbitrary even though it only lasted for two hours, on account of the modalities of the detention (the person concerned was not informed of the reason for her detention) and of the serious consequences resulting from it (the victim died after falling from a balcony of the police station in an apparent attempt to escape induced by the frustration of being

---

[68] See eg Art 10 ICCPR, according to which '[a]ll persons deprived of their liberty shall be treated with humanity and with respect for the inherent dignity of the human person. 2. (a) Accused persons shall, save in exceptional circumstances, be segregated from convicted persons and shall be subject to separate treatment appropriate to their status as unconvicted persons; (b) Accused juvenile persons shall be separated from adults and brought as speedily as possible for adjudication'.
[69] See HRC, General Comment no 21, 'Replaces General Comment 9 Concerning Human Treatment of Persons Deprived of Liberty' (Art 10), 1992, para 9, <http://www.unhchr.ch/tbs/doc.nsf/(Symbol)/3327552b9511fb98c12563ed004cbe59?Opendocument>, accessed 22 February 2009.
[70] See Communication no 151/96, *Civil Liberties Organisation v Nigeria*, 2000, 2000 *AHRLR* 243, para 27.
[71] See *International Pen and ors (on behalf of Saro-Wiwa) v Nigeria* (n 33 above), para 80.
[72] See Communication no 224/98, *Media Rights Agenda v Nigeria*, 2000, 2000 *AHRLR* 262, para 70.
[73] See Communication no 225/98, *Huri-Laws v Nigeria*, 2000, 2000 *AHRLR* 273, para 40.

detained without knowing the reason of her detention) in the concrete case.[74] A situation of this kind may very easily occur in the context of the exercise of security functions by PMSCs.

In the same situations in which a breach of the right to liberty and security of the person might occur in the context of PMSC operations, it is also possible that the right to freedom of expression may be breached. Unlawful arrest and/or detention of a person may in fact be undertaken in order to prevent him/her from expressing his/her opinions, in the event that they are perceived by the authorities as fomenters of anti-governmental feelings.

With respect to the related right to freedom of thought and religion, there are at least two prerogatives arising from such a right that can be affected by PMSCs. First, the right in point may be infringed by these companies to the same extent of freedom of expression, when a person (including an individual belonging to a religious minority) is arrested or detained for a religious reason; in these cases, religion-based persecution adds to unlawful arrest and/or detention. The other case is where a person is prevented—through coercive powers—from the opportunity of exercising or manifesting his/her beliefs individually and/or in the community. Relevant treaties generally allow restrictions on this freedom, on the condition that such restrictions are prescribed by law and are necessary to protect public values like national safety, public order, public health, or morals, or the rights and freedoms of others. However, as affirmed by the HRC, 'Limitations may be applied only for those purposes for which they were prescribed and must be directly related and proportionate to the specific need for which they are predicated'.[75] In addition, 'Restrictions may not be imposed for discriminatory purposes or applied in a discriminatory manner'.[76]

In performing their usual military and police activities, PMSCs may also easily interfere with the enjoyment of the right to freedom of movement. This may happen not only in the form of restrictions to the most apparent prerogative attached to this right, ie to move freely in the territory of the country, but it may be breached in other ways, for exemple, when a PMSC performs a border control activity, and arbitrarily prevents a person from exercising the right of leaving the country or even the inherent right of a citizen who is abroad to re-enter his/her country. However, when and to the extent that PMSCs act under state authority—thus taking the position of governmental officials—they may benefit from exemptions of responsibility when the restrictions contemplated by the pertinent treaties with respect to this right are applied, provided that the conditions are met for these restrictions to be lawful. In particular, any restriction must be provided by law and based on the necessity of protecting collective values like national security, *ordre*

---

[74] See *Rantsev v Cyprus and Russia*, Appl no 25965/04 (7 January 2010), para 314 et seq.
[75] See General Comment no 22, 'The Right to Freedom of Thought, Conscience and Religion' (Art 18), 1993, para 8, <http://www.unhchr.ch/tbs/doc.nsf/(Symbol)/9a30112c27d1167cc12563ed 004d8f15?Opendocument>, accessed 22 February 2009.
[76] Ibid.

public, public health, public morality, or the rights and freedoms of others.[77] In addition, restrictions 'must not impair the essence of the right... [and] conform to the principle of proportionality', in the sense that 'they must be the least intrusive instrument amongst those which might achieve the desired result... [and] proportionate to the interest to be protected'.[78]

In addition, PMSCs' coercive functions might well interfere with the enjoyment of the right to freedom of association, as it is usually exercised by people in a democratic society. Like freedom of movement, this right is also subject to restrictions, which, however, must be justified by the need to safeguard national security or public safety, public order, public health or morals, or the rights and freedoms of others. In this respect, the same restrictive criteria that are necessary in order to ensure lawfulness of restrictions to freedom of movement can be considered applicable to freedom of association as well.

The next right of interest to the present enquiry is the right to private and family life. International jurisprudence and 'para-jurisprudential' practice has recognized a broad scope of operation for the right to private and family life, which has been translated into a wide range of specific prerogatives, the respect for which is essential in order to ensure proper enjoyment of this right. These include, inter alia, the right not to be separated from the members of one's family,[79] the right to shelter,[80] the right of detained persons to communicate with their relatives,[81] as well as the right that living conditions in the area where the family house is located are not deteriorated by polluting emissions originating from industrial activities.[82] Given this broad range of ways in which the right to private and family life may be breached, this right is particularly threatened by PMSC operations, particularly because they often operate in situations in which—due to war or political instability —legal guarantees are weaker than usual. So, for instance, in a number of cases characterized by frequent arbitrary arrest and detention performed by military authorities—justified by the state concerned through relying on the situation of emergency faced by the country—the AComHPR has found violations of the state obligation to protect the family[83] arising from the lack of communication between detained persons and their families. For example, the Commission has held that:

---

[77] See Art 12 para 3 ICCPR; Art 22 ACHR; Art 12 ACHPR; Art 2 para 3 of Protocol no 4 to the Convention for the Protection of Human Rights and Fundamental Freedoms, securing certain rights and freedoms other than those already included in the Convention and in the first Protocol thereto, *CETS* no 46.

[78] See HRC, General Comment no 27, 'Freedom of Movement' (Art 12), UN Doc CCPR/C/21/Rev1/Add9, 2 November 1999, para 13 f.

[79] See, among the innumerable relevant decisions, ECTHR, *Case of Mubilanzila Mayeka and Kaniki Mitunga v Belgium*, Appl no 13178/03 (12 October 2006).

[80] See eg AComHPR, *The Social and Economic Rights Action Center and the Center for Economic and Social Rights v Nigeria* (n 24 above), para 60 et seq.

[81] See eg AComHPR, *Article 19 v The State of Eritrea*, 2007, 2007 AHRLR 73, para 102.

[82] See eg ECTHR, *Case of Guerra and ors v Italy*, Appl no 14967/89 (19 February 1998).

[83] See Art 18 ACHPR.

[the] State's obligation to respect housing rights [resulting from the obligation to ensure family protection] requires it, and thereby all of its organs and agents, to abstain from carrying out, sponsoring or tolerating any practice, policy or legal measure violating the integrity of the individual or infringing on his or her freedom to use those material or other resources available to them in a way they find most appropriate to satisfy individual, family, household or community housing needs.[84]

The right to private life in particular may be easily breached by a number of activities typically carried out by PMSCs. For instance, according to the HRC, '[s]urveillance, whether electronic or otherwise, interceptions of telephonic, telegraphic and other forms of communication, wire-tapping and recording of conversations should be prohibited';[85] also, 'gathering and holding of personal information on computers, data banks and other devices, whether by public authorities or private individuals or bodies, must be regulated by law'.[86] A different situation, also resulting in a breach of the right to private life, is that occurring when 'grave acts such as rape [are perpetrated], where fundamental values and essential aspects of private life are at stake'; cases like this, according to the ECtHR, impose upon states an obligation to proceed to effective investigation and prosecution even when the relevant conduct is committed by a private person.[87] The ECtHR has also held that in the exercise of security operations, the carrying out of stop and search powers granted to the competent authorities (which can certainly be officials of PMSCs, to the extent that they act on behalf of the state) may result in a breach of the right to private life of the stopped persons, when such powers are neither appropriately circumscribed nor subject to adequate legal safeguards against abuse.[88] The kinds of violations just described are highly likely to occur in the context of PMSC operations. Similarly to the other rights previously examined, the right to private and family life might be the object of restrictions, in accordance with the law, when limitations are necessary for national security, for public order, for the protection of health and morals, and for the protection of the rights and freedoms of others. As usual, the lawfulness of these restrictions is to be evaluated according to the same restrictive approach, mutatis mutandis,[89] already described above.

The right to the use and enjoyment of one's own property may also be easily negatively affected by PMSC operations. This may happen, for example, when

---

[84] See *The Social and Economic Rights Action Center and the Center for Economic and Social Rights v Nigeria* (n 24 above), para 61.

[85] See HRC, General Comment no 16, 'The right to respect of privacy, family, home and correspondence, and protection of honour and reputation' (Art 17), 1988, para 8, <http://www.unhchr.ch/tbs/doc.nsf/(Symbol)/23378a8724595410c12563ed004aeecd?Opendocument>, accessed 22 February 2009.

[86] Ibid, para 10.

[87] See *MC v Bulgaria*, Appl no 39272/98 (4 December 2003), para 150 ff.

[88] See *Gillan and Quinton v UK*, Appl no 4158/05 (12 January 2010).

[89] With particular respect to the right in point, as interference to private and family life must not be 'arbitrary', 'even interference provided for by law should be in accordance with the provisions, aims and objectives of the Covenant and should be, in any event, reasonable in the particular circumstances'; see ibid, para 4.

private property is seized by one such company for military or security reasons, or in any other case when—for whatever reason—a person is prevented by a PMSC from enjoying his/her possessions. However, restrictions of private property rights arising from PMSCs' activities may be lawful when the company concerned acts on behalf of the state and the possibility of applying these restrictions is provided by law for the general interest of the society. On the other hand, the scope of the right to property is not confined to private property rights as conceived in Western legal orders. Certain forms of collective possession are also to be considered included within that scope, although—being the right to property of an individual nature—they have to be separated into a number of individual rights corresponding to the sum of persons sharing the collective prerogative at issue. This applies in particular to possession of ancestral lands by indigenous peoples; consistently, the IACtHR has held that:

> Through an evolutionary interpretation of international instruments for the protection of human rights . . . the right to property [is protected] in a sense which includes, among others, the rights of members of the indigenous communities within the framework of communal property . . . the close ties of indigenous people with the land must be recognized and understood as the fundamental basis of their cultures, their spiritual life, their integrity, and their economic survival. For indigenous communities, relations to the land are not merely a matter of possession and production but a material and spiritual element which they must fully enjoy, even to preserve their cultural legacy and transmit it to future generations.[90]

The nature of PMSCs' interferences with the enjoyment of this communal characterization of the right to property is evident; a typical example is given by the situations in which PMSCs provide safety services—on behalf of the territorial government—in favour of foreign companies intending to exploit traditional indigenous lands economically against the will of the indigenous communities concerned.

In performing their usual activities, PMSCs can also infringe rights of a collective character. The range of collective rights that can be breached by PMSC operations is quite broad. There are basically two 'categories' of internationally recognized 'collective' rights. The first is represented by those collective prerogatives which are the necessary result of the need to enjoy certain individual rights in a community with the others in order to make them effective, as in some cases their effectiveness may not be ensured without translating them into communal prerogatives. This happens, for example, with respect to the right of manifesting one's own religion or culture, which is made void if it cannot be exercised in common with other people sharing the same religious convictions or belonging to the same culture. This has been made clear by the HRC, which has emphasized that 'many of the rights recognized by the Covenant, such as the freedom to manifest one's religion or belief (article 18), the freedom of association (article 22) or the rights of members of

---

[90] See *Case of the Mayagna (Sumo) Awas Tingni Community v Nicaragua*, IACtHR, Series C, no 79 (31 August 2001), para 148 f.

minorities (article 27), may be enjoyed in community with others'.[91] These principles were previously expressed by the committee in clearer terms with specific respect to the right of persons belonging to minorities to enjoy their culture with other members of their group, provided for by Article 27 of the Covenant. In the words of the HRC, '[a]lthough the rights protected under article 27 are individual rights, they depend in turn on the ability of the minority group to maintain its culture, language or religion'. Consequently, 'positive measures by States may also be necessary to protect the identity of a minority and the rights of its members to enjoy and develop their culture and language and to practise their religion, in community with the other members of the group'.[92]

The second category of collective rights is composed of those prerogatives which are recognized by human rights treaties *directly* in favour of peoples. In addition to the right of self-determination of peoples, provided for by common Article 1 ICCPR and the ICESCR (as well as by Article 20 ACHPR), a number of peoples' rights are contemplated by the ACHPR, including the rights to existence; to economic, social and cultural development; freely to dispose of their wealth and natural resources; to peace and security; to a safe environment; and to preserve and enjoy their own culture. All these rights—which apply indistinctly to *national* peoples and to *minority groups* living within a state—may be breached by PMSC operations to a variable extent. For instance, with respect to the right of self-determination of peoples, this could be breached by a PMSC through supporting a *coup d'état* by a political group which is not supported by the people; through helping such a group to preserve its political power and repelling the attacks of revolutionary forces enjoying popular support; or through performing vigilance activities at elections in a way which threatens people to the extent of preventing them from freely manifesting their voting choice.[93] In this respect, it is interesting to note that the HRC has expressed the position that the right under discussion

---

[91] See General Comment no 31[80], 'The Nature of the General Legal Obligation Imposed on States Parties to the Covenant', UN Doc CCPR/C/21/Rev1/Add13, 26 May 2004, para 9.

[92] See General Comment no 23, 'The Rights of Minorities' (Art 27), 1994, para 6.2, <http://www.unhchr.ch/tbs/doc.nsf/(Symbol)/fb7fb12c2fb8bb21c12563ed004df111?Opendocument>, accessed 22 February 2009.

[93] With respect to the latter situation, it is to be noted that it also entails a violation of the individual right to take part in the conduct of public affairs, directly or through freely chosen representatives, as well as to vote and to be elected at elections that guarantee the free expression of the will of the electors, protected by Art 25 ICCPR. In fact, as emphasized by the HRC, '[that right is] related to, but distinct from, the right of peoples to self-determination. By virtue of [that right] . . . peoples have the right to freely determine their political status and to enjoy the right to choose the form of their constitution or government' (See General Comment no 25, 'The Right to Participate in Public Affairs, Voting Rights and the Right of Equal Access to Public Service' (Art 25), 1996, para 2, <http://www.unhchr.ch/tbs/doc.nsf/(Symbol)/d0b7f023e8d6d9898025651e004bc0eb?Opendocument>, accessed 22 February 2009. Therefore, when a PMSC carrying out vigilance activities at elections prevents national citizens from freely manifesting their voting choice, or in any way intimidates people in order to 'persuade' them to support a particular political candidate, in addition to violating the collective right to self-determination breaches the individual right in point as well (and, possibly, the right to freedom of expression). This is made clear by the HRC in affirming that a necessary requirement arising from the right in question demands that 'voters should be protected from any form of coercion or compulsion to disclose how they intend to vote or how they voted, and from any unlawful or arbitrary interference with the voting process' (ibid, para 20).

'imposes specific obligations on states parties, not only in relation to their own peoples but vis-à-vis all peoples which have not been able to exercise or have been deprived of the possibility of exercising their right to self-determination';[94] this could support the idea that—in the event that a foreign PMSC is hired by a non-democratic government with the purpose of creating or preserving a situation of sovereignty contrary to the will of the local people—the national government of the PMSC concerned may be considered internationally responsible vis-à-vis the said people to the extent that it is capable of exercising its control over such a company.

Another collective right that can be breached in the context of military and security operations—and is therefore particularly pertinent to PMSCs—is the right of peoples freely to dispose of their wealth and natural resources contemplated by Article 21 ACHPR. In the Ogoni case the AComHPR found that such a breach had been committed in view of the fact that the Nigerian government had facilitated the destruction of the Ogoniland through giving 'the green light to private actors, and the oil Companies in particular, to devastatingly affect the well-being of the Ogonis'.[95]

In a different case, concerning military activities carried out by the armed forces of Burundi, Rwanda, and Uganda in the territory of the Democratic Republic of Congo from August 1998 to January 1999 resulting in a large number of dreadful and massive human rights breaches, the AComHPR found a violation by the three respondent states of, inter alia, a number of collective rights, ie: the peoples' rights to national and international peace and security contemplated by Article 23 ACHPR;[96] 'the rights of the peoples of the Democratic Republic of Congo to their unquestionable and inalienable right to self-determination provided for by article 20 of the African Charter', in consequence of the occupation of territories in Congo;[97] the right granted by Article 21 ACHPR, in light of the 'illegal exploitation/looting of the natural resources of the complainant State';[98] and the right to development guaranteed by Article 22 ACHPR, as result of 'the indiscriminate dumping of, and/or mass burial of victims of the series of massacres and killings perpetrated against the peoples of the eastern province of the complainant State'.[99]

A particularly vulnerable category of persons is represented by children. As emphasized by Article 3 CRC, 'In all actions concerning children...the best interests of the child shall be a primary consideration'; this principle presupposes that in each material circumstance involving a child the usual efforts to ensure respect for human rights may be inadequate, as a specially tailored action is required in light of the special condition of the specific child involved. With respect to PMSC operations, this means that companies must always act paying special

---

[94] See General Comment no 12, 'The Right to Self-Determination of Peoples' (Art 1), 1984, para 6, <http://www.unhchr.ch/tbs/doc.nsf/(Symbol)/f3c99406d528f37fc12563ed004960b4?Opendocument>, accessed 22 February 2009.
[95] See *The Social and Economic Rights Action Center and the Center for Economic and Social Rights v Nigeria* (n 24 above), para 58.
[96] See Communication no 227/99, *DR Congo v Burundi, Rwanda and Uganda*, 2003, 2004 *AHRLR* 19, para 68 ff.
[97] Ibid, para 77.   [98] Ibid, para 94.   [99] Ibid, para 87.

attention to the necessary specific measures appropriate to ensure actual protection for the best interests of children in all circumstances in which their activity could affect a juvenile. In order to give effect to this principle, specially construed measures—different to those that are usually sufficient for adults—are required to ensure that children properly enjoy human rights in the light of their situation of special vulnerability.[100] As emphasized by the HRC, 'The right to special measures of protection belongs to every child because of his status as a minor';[101] these measures include, inter alia: protection from economic exploitation and from performing any work that is likely to be harmful to his/her health or physical, mental, spiritual, moral or social development;[102] prevention of children being 'subjected to acts of violence and cruel and inhuman treatment or from being exploited by means of forced labour or prostitution,[[103]] or by their use in the illicit trafficking of narcotic drugs';[104] prevention of the danger of abduction, sale, or trafficking in children;[105] the right of the child not to be separated from his/her parents against their will;[106] the right not to be illicitly transferred or not returned abroad;[107] the right to be protected from all forms of physical or mental violence, injury, abuse, neglect or negligent treatment, maltreatment, or exploitation, including sexual abuse;[108] and the right of children not to take a direct part in hostilities[109] as well as not to be 'compulsorily recruited into . . . armed forces'.[110] In this respect, of special significance for PMSCs is Article 4 of the Optional Protocol to the Convention on the Rights of the Child on the Involvement of Children in Armed Conflict, according to which '[a]rmed groups that are distinct from the armed forces of a State should not, under any circumstances, recruit or use in hostilities persons under the age of 18 years'; in providing this rule, the Optional Protocol followed the example of Article 22(2) of the African Charter on the Rights and Welfare of the Child,[111] which, through prohibiting *tout court* that a 'child shall take a direct part in hostilities' or be simply recruited, is the first international

---

[100] See, inter alia, Art 24 ICCPR.
[101] See General Comment no 17, 'Rights of the Child' (Art 24), 1989, para 4, <http://www.unhchr.ch/tbs/doc.nsf/(Symbol)/cc0f1f8c391478b7c12563ed004b35e3?Opendocument>, accessed 22 February 2009); see also Art 19 ACHR.
[102] See Art 32 CRC; see also HRC, General Comment no 17 (n 101 above), para 4.
[103] See also Art 34 CRC.
[104] See HRC, General Comment no 17 (n 101 above), para 3; see also Art 33 CRC.
[105] See HRC, General Comment no 17 (n 101 above), para 7. See also Art 35 CRC and the Optional Protocol to the Convention on the Rights of the Child on the Sale of CHILDREN, Child Prostitution and Child Pornography, 2000, UN Doc A/RES/54/263, 25 May 2000.
[106] See Art 9 CRC.
[107] See Art 11 CRC.
[108] See Art 19 CRC.
[109] According to Art 38 para 2 CRC this right applies to the persons who have not reached the age of 15 years. This provision is improved by Art 1 of the Optional Protocol to the Convention on the Rights of the Child on the Involvement of Children in Armed Conflict, 2000, UN Doc A/RES/54/263, 25 May 2000, according to which states parties are bound to ensure that 'members of their armed forces who have not attained the age of 18 years do not take a direct part in hostilities'.
[110] See Art 2 of the Optional Protocol to the Convention on the Rights of the Child on the Involvement of Children in Armed Conflict.
[111] Adopted in July 1990, <http://www.africa-union.org/root/au/Documents/Treaties/treaties.htm>, accessed 31 May 2009.

instrument to exclude the participation of persons of less than 18 years old in armed conflicts in any situation. Like all other actors in society, PMSCs must abide by the obligation to prevent children from being involved in all such practices.

Another vulnerable category is that of women, with respect to which several international human rights instruments and provisions prohibit any gender-based discrimination.[112] According to Article 1 CEDAW, the term 'discrimination against women' means 'any distinction, exclusion or restriction made on the basis of sex which has the effect or purpose of impairing or nullifying the recognition, enjoyment or exercise by women, irrespective of their marital status, on a basis of equality of men and women, of human rights and fundamental freedoms in the political, economic, social, cultural, civil or any other field'. From this definition it is evident that a number of profiles of responsibility—resulting from PMSC operations—may arise in terms of discrimination against women, especially in light of the fact that, as noted by the HRC, 'Women are particularly vulnerable in times of internal or international armed conflicts'[113]—ie in one of the typical contexts in which PMSC operations usually take place—when rape, abduction, and other forms of gender-based violence are particularly exacerbated. Among the intolerable offences that can be perpetrated by PMSCs to the prejudice of women are the following: trafficking in women and forced prostitution;[114] deprivation of liberty on an arbitrary or unequal basis;[115] unequal protection of the rights of women and men deprived of their liberty (particularly when they are not separated in prisons and when women are guarded by male guards);[116] and differential treatment of women and men with respect to certain rights such as freedom of movement,[117] access to justice,[118] privacy,[119] freedom of thought, conscience and religion[120] and female genital mutilation, scarification, medicalization and para-medicalization of female genital mutilation and other harmful practices.[121]

A final point is to be raised before concluding the present section. It concerns the fundamental importance of access to justice in order to guarantee the effectiveness of all human rights. These rights may in fact be considered 'effectively enjoyable'

---

[112] See eg the whole CEDAW or Art 3 ICCPR (according to which 'The States Parties to the present Covenant undertake to ensure the equal right of men and women to the enjoyment of all civil and political rights set forth in the present Covenant').

[113] See General Comment no 28, 'Equality of Rights between Men and Women' (Art 3), UN Doc CCPR/C/21/Rev1/Add10, 29 March 2000, para 8.

[114] Ibid, para 12.

[115] Ibid, para 14. It is to be noted that, in *Rantsev v Cyprus and Russia* (n 74 above), the ECtHR held that trafficking in human beings 'falls within the scope of Article 4' ECHR, prohibiting slavery, servitude, and forced or compulsory labour (see para 282).

[116] See General Comment no 28 (n 113 above), para 15.

[117] Ibid, para 16.

[118] Ibid, para 18.

[119] Ibid, para 20.

[120] Ibid, para 21.

[121] See Art 5(b) of the Protocol to the African Charter on Human and Peoples' Rights on the Rights of Women in Africa, adopted in July 2003, <http://www.africa-union.org/root/au/Documents/Treaties/treaties.htm>, accessed 31 May 2009.

only when and to the extent that the right to judicial protection is effective, so that an efficient remedy is available allowing victims to obtain redress in the event of them being breached. The key role of judicial protection in the architecture of human rights is confirmed by Article 27 para 2 ACHR, according to which not only certain basic 'primary rights' (including, inter alia, right to life, humane treatment, and freedom from slavery) are to be considered absolutely non-derogable even in 'time of war, public danger, or other emergency that threatens the independence or security of a State',[122] but the same applies to 'the *judicial guarantees essential for the protection of such rights*'[123] as well. This position has also been shared by the HRC in its General Comment on states of emergency, in which it stressed that:

> the Covenant requires a State Party... to provide remedies for any violation of the provisions of the Covenant. This clause is not mentioned in the list of non-derogable provisions in article 4, paragraph 2, but it constitutes a treaty obligation inherent in the Covenant as a whole. Even if a state party, during a state of emergency, and to the extent that such measures are strictly required by the exigencies of the situation, may introduce adjustments to the practical functioning of its procedures governing judicial or other remedies, the State Party must comply with the fundamental obligation... to provide a remedy that is effective.[124]

The right to judicial protection includes, inter alia, the right of victims to have access to an effective remedy to vindicate breaches of recognized human rights as well as the right of any person imprisoned, detained, or charged with a criminal offence to be informed in a language which he/she understands of the charge against him/her and to be tried without delay before an impartial judge. It is evident that these requirements may easily be infringed by PMSCs. This might happen in the event that these companies exercise coercive functions where persons are arrested and/or detained for military or security reasons without being provided with adequate information and/or without being promptly brought before an impartial judge. At the same time, unlawful arrest and detention of a person by a PMSC—leading in itself to a violation of the right to personal liberty—may also imply the 'additional' breach of the right to judicial protection, when prolonged detention prevents the victim from the opportunity of having access to a remedy against his/her arbitrary arrest.

III. Conclusion

The foregoing analysis demonstrates that PMSC operations come within the scope of international human rights obligations, as well as that the inherent nature of such

---

[122] See Art 27 para 1 ACHR.
[123] Emphasis added.
[124] See HRC, General Comment no 29, 'States of Emergency' (Art 4), 1982, UN Doc, 31 August 2001, para 14, <http://www.unhchr.ch/tbs/doc.nsf/0/71eba4be3974b4f7c1256ae200517361/$FILE/G0144470.pdf>, accessed 15 August 2010.

operations entails a certain potential for human rights breaches, of both an occasional and a systemic nature. This potential danger is increased in light of the fact that PMSCs are often in possession of and make use of highly sophisticated military and security technology and operational systems, which sometimes cannot be taken under control by the authorities of the territorial state in which they operate. It is therefore essential to keep the activities of such companies under strict control and to develop alternative profiles of international liability to the classical construction of state responsibility,[125] in order to ensure efficient prevention of human rights abuses and to ensure the effectiveness of human rights in favour of all individuals and communities affected by PMSC operations.

---

[125] See, in this respect, Part IV of this volume.

4

The Impact of the EU Human Rights System on Operations of Private Military and Security Companies

Ieva Kalnina and Ugis Zeltins

I. Introduction

The commitment of the European Union (EU) to human rights has been gradually increasing over time. Even though the EU was not founded as a human rights organization, there is no longer any doubt that human rights form an integral part of its legal order. The entry into force of the Lisbon Treaty on 1 December 2009 is expected to impact further the EU human rights regime, although the scope and benefit of such impact still remains to be seen.

The purpose of this chapter is to provide a brief overview of the main features of the EU human rights regime, its sources and addressees, with a particular emphasis on the jurisprudence of the European Court of Justice (ECJ) and the European Court of Human Rights (ECtHR) insofar as the latter is relevant for assessing the impact of EU human rights law in the context of operations carried out by private military and security companies (PMSCs). Finally, judicial remedies are also discussed.

II. The Main Features of the EU Human Rights Regime: Primary Law, General Principles and the EU Charter of Fundamental Rights

The need for the protection of human rights in the EU's legal order was first explicitly recognized in the Amsterdam Treaty of 1997, which recalled that a 'serious and persistent' violation of human rights by a Member State may result in a suspension of its rights under the treaty. Today, Article 6 EU Treaty is the basic primary law provision that establishes the EU's commitment to human rights.[1] In

---

[1] In accordance with Art 6(2) of the treaty: 'The Union shall respect fundamental rights, as guaranteed by the European Convention for the Protection of Human Rights and Fundamental Freedoms signed in Rome on 4 November 1950 and as they result from the constitutional traditions

addition, there are pillar-specific primary law provisions which oblige the EU to respect human rights.² The relevant treaty provisions on the ECJ's jurisdiction also arguably recall the Court's duty to pay due regard to the general principles of law.³ Other, more specific, provisions also contain language implying the existence of certain rules of law that are superior to the EC Treaty.⁴

However, the treaties alone do not reflect the particular 'brand' of rights that bind the EU. Explicit reference to the European Convention on Human Rights (ECHR) is made in Article 6(2) EU Treaty, alongside the reference to 'general principles of Community law', which are 'inspired' by the constitutional traditions of the Member States⁵ as construed by the ECJ's jurisprudence.⁶ In other words, 'international treaties for the protection of human rights on which the Member States have collaborated or of which they are signatories, can supply guidelines which should be followed within the framework of Community law',⁷ and 'In that regard, the Court has stated that the [ECHR] has special significance'.⁸

Turning next to the EU's legislative incentives in the field of human rights, arguably it lacked a clear position on fundamental rights until the adoption of the EU Charter of Fundamental Rights (the 'Charter'), which was granted full legal

---

common to the Member States, as general principles of Community law.' The Treaty of Lisbon, amending the Treaty on European Union and the Treaty establishing the European Community, has slightly modified Art 6, adding, inter alia, reference to the Charter of Fundamental Rights of the European Union (the Charter).

² See, for example, Art 11(1) with respect to the Common Foreign and Security Policy.

³ Art 220(1) EC Treaty provides that 'The Court of Justice and the Court of First Instance, each within its jurisdiction, shall ensure that in the interpretation and application of this Treaty the law is observed.' It has been argued that 'here the word "law" must refer to something over and above the treaty itself; if correct, this means that Article 220 . . . not only entitles, but also obliges, the Court to take general principles into account': TC Hartley, *The Foundations of European Community Law*, 6th edn (2007), 132.

⁴ Art 230(2) lays down the grounds on which the ECJ may review the legality of Community acts, including an 'infringement of this Treaty or of any rule of law relating to its application'. It is normally considered that 'The phrase "any rule of law relating to its application" covers all those rules of Community law other than those in the Treaties themselves. This includes general principles of Community law': P Craig and G de Búrca, *EU Law*, 3rd edn (2003), 535. The general principles, of course, notably include fundamental rights. Thus when Art 35(6) EU Treaty entrusts the Court with 'jurisdiction to review the legality of framework decisions and decisions . . . on grounds of . . . infringement of this Treaty or of any rule of law relating to its application', it reinforces the supremacy of human rights over EU third-pillar action.

⁵ The importance of human rights was first recognized by the ECJ in *Stauder* (1969), where it underlined that fundamental human rights are 'enshrined in the general principles of Community law and protected by the Court': Case 29/69, *Erich Stauder v City of Ulm* (1969) ECR 419. A year later, *Stauder* was reinforced by *Internationale Handelsgesellschaft*, where the ECJ noted that 'respect for fundamental human rights forms an integral part of the general principles of law protected by the Court of Justice': Case 11/70, *Internationale Handelsgesellschaft mbH v Einfuhr- und Vorratsstelle für Getreide und Futtermittel* (1970) ECR 1125. In *Nold* (1974), one of the most important cases on human rights to date, the ECJ made it clear that when the protection of fundamental rights is at stake, inspiration may be drawn not only from the constitutional traditions common to the Member States, but also from international treaties for the protection of human rights binding on EU Member States: Case 4/73, *J Nold, Kohlen- und Baustoffgroßhandlung v Commission of the European Communities* (1974) ECR 491.

⁶ Hartley (2007) (n 3 above), 140.

⁷ *Nold* (n 5 above), para 13.

⁸ Opinion 2/94, *Accession by the Communities to the ECHR* [1996] ECR I-1759, para 33.

effect by the Lisbon Treaty and which entails a number of rights that apply to all individuals, not only EU citizens and residents, such as dignity rights (Articles 1–5)[9] and rights to various freedoms.[10] A general anti-discrimination clause has also been included,[11] although the effect of the Charter in practice may largely depend upon the ECJ and its interpretation of the scope of this clause,[12] particularly considering that it does not list discrimination on grounds of nationality or national origin among the prohibited grounds of discrimination.

In the context of PMSC activities, one situation where the Charter's provisions could play a complementary role is in a case where the damage suffered by an individual of the host state of a PMSC arises from discriminatory treatment in his or her employment by the PMSC. However, considering the narrow scope of the Charter's anti-discrimination clause, its relevance for a potential discrimination victim is limited. The same criticism applies to the EU's anti-discrimination legislation, all of which is carefully tailored to exclude difference of treatment based on nationality.[13]

What is more, besides demonstrating that their discrimination is not merely based on their nationality, potential victims of discrimination—or, in fact, of any other human rights violation—at the hands of PMSCs would also have to overcome the complex question of extraterritorial application of the EU's human rights legislation. If a territorial link can be established between the infringement of the human right in question and the EU (ie the scope of application of Community law), EU law may provide a remedy. If, however, no such direct territorial link can be established, the claimant will need to resort to the so-called 'effects doctrine', which has so far been mostly applied in the field of EU competition law, the prevailing view being that both the illegal act's direct effect *and* its implementation in the EU must be proven.[14] In sum, the extraterritorial application of the EU

---

[9] Human dignity (Art 1), Right to life (Art 2), Right to the integrity of the person (Art 3), Prohibition of torture and inhuman or degrading treatment or punishment (Art 4), Prohibition of slavery and forced labour (Art 5).

[10] Right to liberty and security (Art 6), Respect for private and family life (Art 7), Protection of personal data (Art 8), Freedom of thought, conscience and religion (Art 10), Freedom of expression and information (Art 11), Freedom of assembly and association (Art 12(1)), Freedom of arts and sciences (Art 13), Right to education (Art 14), Freedom to choose an occupation and right to engage in work (Art 15(1)–(2)), Right to property (Art 17).

[11] Art 21(1) mirrors Art 14 ECHR, providing that: 'Any discrimination based on any ground such as sex, race, colour, ethnic or social origin, genetic features, language, religion or belief, political or any other opinion, membership of a national minority, property, birth, disability, age or sexual orientation shall be prohibited.'

[12] Note that Art 51(2) of the Charter explicitly states that the Charter 'does not extend the field of application of Union law beyond the powers of the Union or establish any new power or task for the Union, or modify powers and tasks defined in the other Parts of the Constitution'.

[13] See, most pertinently, Art 3(2) of the Racial Equality Directive; Council Directive 2000/43/EC of 29 June 2000 implementing the principle of equal treatment between persons irrespective of racial or ethnic origin, OJ L 180, 19/07/2000 P 0022–0026; and Art 3(2) of the Employment Directive; Council Directive 2000/78/EC of 27 November 2000 establishing a general framework for equal treatment in employment and occupation, OJ L 303, 02/12/2000 P 0016–0022. Neither covers difference of treatment based on nationality.

[14] P Torremans, 'Extraterritoriality in Human Rights' in NA Neuwahl and A Rosas (eds), *The European Union and Human Rights* (1995), 281, 293.

human rights regime in the absence of a territorial link is unlikely to be successful for the victim of the type of human rights violations that are likely to occur in the context of PMSC action.

III. The Role of the ECJ and ECtHR in the Development of Human Rights

The ECJ has played a decisive role in the development of human rights. In its development of the law, the ECJ relies on the common constitutional principles and international treaties in force for the Member States, especially the ECHR and its application by the ECtHR. This is how important human rights such as human dignity, religious freedom, due process, procedural guarantees, and other rights have become part of Community law.[15] Ever since the ECJ first referred to the ECHR in *Rutili*[16] in 1975, its reliance on the ECHR and the case law of ECtHR has become much more frequent and comprehensive, although some argue that it has not yet 'proved itself to be a precursor in relation to the establishment of a high level of protection', but has rather merely 'followed the raising of the level of protection [of human rights] which has taken place "externally"'.[17]

Turning next to the relevance of ECJ jurisprudence to the operations of PMSCs, it must first be observed that, generally, national measures that fall outside the scope of Community law are not subject to review for compliance with general principles of EC law.[18] However, the tide may have changed slightly since the recent *Viking* case, where the ECJ recognized that protection of fundamental rights fell under the scope of Community law even in situations where the primary dispute at stake has arisen in an area of law that falls outside the scope of the Community's competence.[19] By analogy, it appears prima facie that the state

---

[15] K Stern, 'From the European Convention on Human Rights to the European Charter of Fundamental Rights: The Prospects for the Protection of Human Rights in Europe' in H-M Blanke and S Mangiameli (eds), *Governing Europe under a Constitution* (2006), 174.

[16] Case 36/75, *Rutili v Minister for the Interior* (1975) ECR 1219.

[17] H-J Blanke, 'Protection of Fundamental Rights Afforded by the European Court of Justice in Luxembourg' in Blanke and Mangiameli (eds) (n 15 above), 15, 277.

[18] As noted by the ECJ in the *ERT* case, '[the Court] has no power to examine the compatibility with the European Convention on Human Rights of national rules which do not fall within the scope of Community law': judgment in Case C-260/89, *Elliniki Radiophonia Tiléorassi* [1991] ECR I-2925, para 42. See also judgment in Case C-299/95, *Kremzow* [1997] ECR I-2629, para 19.

[19] In this case, the ECJ had to determine the delicate balance between a company's economic rights of free movement and the trade unions' social rights. The Court observed that 'even if, in the areas which fall outside the scope of the Community's competence, the Member States are still free, in principle, to lay down the conditions governing the existence and exercise of the rights in question, the fact remains that, when exercising that competence... Member States must nevertheless comply with Community law'; 'the right to take collective action... must... be recognised as a fundamental right which forms an integral part of the general principles of Community law the observance of which the Court ensures ...' (para 40). In this particular case, the ECJ concluded that the protection of economic rights prevailed over the fundamental social rights, because the restriction on the free movement right did not meet the high threshold of the proportionality test applicable in these types of circumstances: Case C-438/05, *International Transport Workers' Federation, Finnish Seamen's Union v Viking Line ABP, OÜ Viking Laine Eesti* [2007] ECR I-000.

of nationality of a PMSC whose acts may constitute a breach of fundamental principles of human rights—as enshrined in the Member State common traditions and human rights treaties applicable to them—could be bound to remedy such violations, even if the operation and the major activities of the PMSC in question were to fall outside the scope of the Community's competence. This assumption is further enforced by the ECJ's recognition that it is sufficient for a national measure to be within the 'scope' of Community law for Community general principles to apply—a more lenient and less clearly defined requirement than requiring a measure either to be an implementing measure or one which restricts the fundamental freedoms but comes within the ambit of an express derogation provided for in the treaty. In this context, three further observations must be made.

First, the ECJ has often exercised a high degree of creativity in recognizing situations as falling within the 'scope' of Community law and thus triggering rights review of national measures; there is a tendency towards the broad application of fundamental rights.[20] Secondly, the ECJ's interpretation of fundamental rights protected by the Community has also been extensive.[21] Finally, in what has become known as a process of judicial de-pillarization, the Court has understood its jurisdiction under the third pillar broadly, holding that individuals may invoke a framework decision adopted under Article 34(2) EU Treaty to create consistent interpretation of national law and that 'the obligation on the national court to refer to the content of a framework decision when interpreting the relevant rules of its national law is limited by general principles of law'.[22] Consequently, a Member State can be bound by the EU version of fundamental rights also when acting within the scope of rules on police and judicial cooperation in criminal matters. This is particularly relevant in the context of PMSCs because under international law they 'might be considered ... as agents of the state, and in this way, the normal rules for state responsibility would apply where the firm's activity is controlled by the state'.[23]

However, in most contexts where PMSCs have not been commissioned by a Member State but their activities have human rights implications, attribution to any of the Member States will be almost impossible because the exercise of governmental authority, normally understood, does not entail extraterritorial maintenance of peace and security.

---

[20] For example, in the *Carpenter* case, the UK was disallowed from expelling Mrs Carpenter, a national of the Philippines, because her separation from her husband 'would be detrimental to their family life and, therefore, to the conditions under which Mr Carpenter exercises a fundamental freedom'. The situation thus having come within the scope of Community law, the Court instructed the Member State in question that expulsion would be a disproportionate intervention in Mr Carpenter's privacy: see judgment in Case C-60/00, *Carpenter* [2002] ECR I-6279, para 39.

[21] For instance, in the above-mentioned *Carpenter* case the Court's view of what was required for an adequate protection of family life went beyond what in all likelihood would have been demanded by the ECtHR. Similarly, in the *Mangold* case, one of the most daring of the Court's forays into human rights law of all time, the Grand Chamber found that 'The principle of non-discrimination on grounds of age must ... be regarded as a general principle of Community law': judgment in Case C-144/04, *Mangold* [2005] ECR I-9981, para 74–5.

[22] Judgment in Case C-105/03, *Pupino* [2005] ECR I-5285, para 44.

[23] Andrew Clapham, *Human Rights Obligations of Non-State Actors* (2006), 320, references omitted.

Indeed, generally states have no obligation under their national law to require the PMSCs registered in their national territory to take account of human rights obligations in situations that fall outside their jurisdiction. Considering that the state hosting the PMSC will usually lack both the incentive and resources for effective enforcement of human rights, PMSCs, just like other multinational corporate enterprises, may appear to be operating in a legal vacuum.[24] As one author has put it, 'international law does not directly reach the corporate actor'.[25]

The ECtHR has made remarkable achievements in bridging this gap. However, the ECtHR's role in determining the scope of PMSC's obligations and the ensuing (state) responsibility is constrained by two aspects: first, the scope of the contracting state's duties to ensure respect for human rights, punish, and prevent such violations in situations where the breach of international law occurs at the hand of a private entity; and, secondly, the ECtHR's jurisdictional limits.

As to the first issue, although sometimes the ECtHR has taken a bold approach when determining the scope of the *positive* obligations of the contracting parties under the Convention,[26] overall the Court has remained careful when pronouncing itself on the state obligation to *prevent* the occurrence of human rights violations. Hence it appears unlikely, at least prima facie, that a state's responsibility could be invoked on grounds that it has failed to prevent human rights violations committed by a PMSC against a private party, unless, of course, the ECtHR's high threshold for finding a breach is satisfied.

As to the second issue, the exercise of the Court's jurisdiction, both personal and (extra)territorial, is very complex. The question whether Article 1 ECHR[27] places a territorial limitation on contracting states' duty to secure the rights and freedoms set forth in the ECHR was thoroughly considered by the ECtHR in *Bankovic*,[28]

---

[24] On the obligations of the home state and the hiring state in connection with services provided by PMSCs, see Ch 5 by Francioni and Ch 6 by Hoppe in this volume.

[25] O de Schutter, 'The Accountability of Multinationals for Human Rights Violations in European law' in P Alston, *Non-State Actors and Human Rights* (2005), 228.

[26] For example, in *Osman v UK*, a landmark case on state responsibility for alleged breaches of Art 2 ECHR (right to life), the Court was faced with the question of whether the failure of authorities to appreciate the threat posed to one private party by another private party and the consequent lack of intervention can amount to a violation of the state's positive obligation to protect the right to life. The Court responded by stating that state responsibility would only arise if 'the authorities knew or ought to have known at the time of the existence of a real and immediate risk to the life of an identified individual or individuals from the criminal acts of a third party and that they failed to take measures within the scope of their powers which, judged reasonably, might have been expected to avoid that risk' (emphasis added, para 116): *Osman v UK*, Appl no 23452/94 (28 October 1998). The fairly high threshold set by the ECtHR has also been satisfied in *Kontrová v Slovakia*, Appl no 7510/04 (31 May 2007); *Yasa v Turkey* (2 September 1998); *Mahmut Kaya v Turkey* (19 February 1998); *Akkoc v Turkey* (10 October 2000); *Killic v Turkey* (28 March 2000). For a more elaborate discussion of these issues, see Ineta Ziemele, 'Issues of Responsibility of Private Persons or Entities for Human Rights Violations: The Case-law of International Human Rights Courts and Monitoring Bodies', EUI Working Papers, Academy of European Law, WP 2009/08, <http://cadmus.eui.eu/dspace/bitstream/1814/11409/1/AEL_2009_08.pdf>, accessed 25 March 2010).

[27] Art 1 ECHR provides: 'The High Contracting Parties shall secure to everyone within their jurisdiction the rights and freedoms defined in Secion I of this Convention.'

[28] *Bankovic and ors v Belgium and 16 other states*, Appl no 52207/99 (2001) 41 ILM 517. The case arose out of the human rights violations allegedly committed by the NATO forces as a result of the

where the Court found no jurisdictional link between the persons who were victims of the act complained of and the respondent states, concluding that Article 1 must be understood as reflecting an 'essentially territorial understanding of jurisdiction',[29] since otherwise the phrase 'within their jurisdiction' used in Article 1 would be rendered superfluous.[30] While *Bankovic* has given rise to an extensive debate—and sometimes criticism[31]—in the legal doctrine, it is important to underline that the jurisdictional standard applied by the Court is twofold: territorial and personal.

To sum up, a respondent state may be held responsible for human rights violations carried out by a PMSC, as long as the respective connection as per *Bankovic* can be established, and the PMSC is found to have had effective control of the person or the territory where the illegal acts have been perpetrated.[32]

IV. ECJ and ECtHR: Diverging Views

An instructive example of different approaches taken by the ECJ and ECtHR to the protection of human rights is reflected in the cases concerning the control of acts of the United Nations Security Council. The cases before the ECJ arose in the context of Security Council resolutions requiring all states to freeze the assets of the persons identified as being associated with the Al-Qaeda network or the Taliban. A list of such persons was drawn up, yet they were not afforded any meaningful rights of

---

bombing of Belgrade. The applicants argued that the Court has jurisdiction to adjudicate the violation of their human rights since the illegal acts of the Respondent states have produced effect in the Federal Republic of Yugoslavia.

[29] Ibid, para 59–61.

[30] For the Court's earlier case law on the issue of jurisdictional limits, see *Cyprus v Turkey*, Appl nos 6780/74, 6950/75, 2 Eur Comm'n HR Dec & Rep72 (1975) and *Drozd and Janousek v France and Spain*, Appl no 12747/87, 240, Series A (1992), where the Court, in determining its "jurisdiction", made the following important observation: 'the term "jurisdiction" in Art 1 is not limited to the national territory of the High contracting parties; their responsibility can be involved because of acts of their authorities that occurred outside of their territories' (para 91).

[31] For criticism of the *Bankovic* judgment see, among others, E Roxstrom et al, 'The NATO Bombing Case (*Bankovic et al v Belgium et al*) and the limits of Western Human Rights Protection' (2005) 23 Boston University International Law Journal 55; O de Schutter, 'The Accountability of Multinationals for Human Rights Violations in European Law' in P Alston, *Non-State Actors and Human Rights* (2005), 228.

[32] For example, in the *Issa* case the ECtHR relied on its previous case law to recall that: 'a State may also be held accountable for violation of the Convention rights and freedoms of persons who are in the territory of another State but who are found to be under the former State's authority and control through its agents operating—whether lawfully or unlawfully—in the latter State... Accountability in such situations stems from the fact that Article 1 of the Convention cannot be interpreted so as to allow a State party to perpetrate violations of the Convention on the territory of another State, which it could not perpetrate on its own territory': *Issa and ors v Turkey*, Appl no 31821/96, ECHR 2004 (16 November 2004), para 67–8, 71. This has also been confirmed by the recent admissibility decision in *Al-Saadoon and Mufdhi v UK* (Decision on Admissibility of Appl no 61498/08), which arose out of the occupation of Iraq in 2003. In that case the Court found that 'given the total and exclusive *de facto*... and control exercised by the United Kingdom authorities over the premises in question, the individuals detained there... were within the United Kingdom's jurisdiction' (at para 88). See also *Al-Saadoon and Mufdhi v UK*, judgment on the merits of 2 March 2010.

defence. In order to implement that resolution, the Council of the EU first adopted a common position,[33] followed by the adoption of an EC regulation,[34] directly applicable in all Member States.

Mr Yasin Al-Qadi and an organization called Barakaat International Foundation were included in the respective list and consequently challenged the regulation before the Court of First Instance (CFI)[35] on grounds of lack of competence and infringement of the right to property protected by Article 1 of Protocol 1 to the ECHR; the right to a fair hearing; and the right to judicial process under Article 6 ECHR and ECJ case law. After the CFI dismissed the applicants' action, an appeal on points of law was brought before the ECJ. In what is commonly known as the *Kadi* judgment,[36] the ECJ ruled that:

> the obligations imposed by an international agreement cannot have the effect of prejudicing the constitutional principles of the EC Treaty, which include the principle that all Community acts must respect fundamental rights, that respect constituting a condition of their lawfulness which it is for the Court to review in the framework of the complete system of legal remedies established by the treaty.[37]

Having thus established the full applicability of the constitutional (namely general) principles of the EC Treaty, the Court checked the contested regulation against the EU version of fundamental rights and found a violation of the right to defence and effective judicial protection, as well as property.[38] Arguably, 'The bottom line of the judgment...is that the UN Charter and UN SC Resolutions, just like any other international law, exist on a separate plane and cannot call into question or affect the nature, meaning or primacy of fundamental principles of EC law'.[39]

By contrast, when confronted with a similar problem, the ECtHR adopted a different approach. In its *Behrami/Saramati* admissibility decision[40] the Grand Chamber had to rule on whether the ECtHR may adjudicate the alleged human rights violations by KFOR (a security presence established by a Security Council

---

[33] See Common Position 2001/154/CFSP concerning additional restrictive measures against the Taliban and amending Common Position 96/746/CFSP (OJ 2001 L 57, p 1).

[34] See Regulation (EC) no 467/2001 prohibiting the export of certain goods and services to Afghanistan, strengthening the flight ban and extending the freeze of funds and other financial resources in respect of the Taliban of Afghanistan, and repealing Regulation no 337/2000 (OJ 2001 L 67, p 1).

[35] See judgments in Case T-315/01, *Kadi* [2005] ECR II-3649; and Case T-306/01, *Yusuf and Al Barakaat International Foundation* [2005] ECR II-3533.

[36] See Joined Cases C-402/05 P and C-415/05 P, *Kadi and Al Barakaat International Foundation* (3 September 2008), nyr.

[37] Para 285.

[38] See paras 333–53, 354–71. Note as well that the ruling was given notwithstanding the fact that the Charter of the United Nations provides for the obligatory nature of Security Council's resolutions (Art 25) and their prevalence over other international agreements (Art 103), be they earlier or subsequent.

[39] G de Búrca, *The European Court of Justice and the International Legal Order after* Kadi, Jean Monnet Working Paper 01/09, 35, <http://www.jeanmonnetprogram.org/papers/09/090101.pdf>, accessed 30 March 2010.

[40] See *Behrami and Behrami v France*, Appl no 71412/01 (2 May 2007); and *Saramati v France, Germany and Norway*, Appl no 78166/01 (2 May 2007).

resolution and staffed by UN Member States) and UNMIK (an interim administration under UN auspices established by the same resolution) in Kosovo, following the forced withdrawal of Federal Republic of Yugoslavia forces and the conflict between Serbian and Albanian forces in 1999.

The ECtHR decided not to recycle its earlier *Bosphorus* case law, which concerned the relationship between the ECHR and EU measures.[41] Instead, the rationale in the *Behrami/Saramati* case was based on a strictly territorial argument.[42] The ECtHR also found the applications to be inadmissible because the reproached conduct was attributable not to the respondent states but rather to the United Nations, declaring that to decide otherwise 'would be [to] interfere with ... effective conduct of [the UN's] operations'.[43]

One may attempt to explain the divergent approaches between the ECtHR and the ECJ by saying that the former, being an international court proper, could not behave in the expansive manner of a supreme court, and that the latter simply used an opportunity to take a new step towards constitutionalizing the EU. Although itself a creation of international law, it now levitates as a constitutional entity, much like traditional states do, by dismissing any need for a superior international legal order by virtue of which it might be said to exist. However, the ECtHR has also sought to assert the constitutional quality of the ECHR structure,[44] yet it chose not to reconsider its view of the hierarchical position of international law in the name of human rights. It therefore appears that in substantial, if not procedural, terms the EU's general principles are on occasion capable of offering more protection to individuals than the ECHR. It must also be observed that the international standard is the minimum standard, while a domestic standard, either EU or national, may always go beyond the minimum standard. Since a Member State will always have to comply with lower and higher standards alike—national, regional, international—the most extensive standard in protecting a particular right will clearly be of advantage to the beneficiaries.

On the other hand, in a number of instances it could be argued that the EU falls below the standard of protection that would be required by the ECHR. This is

---

[41] In that case the ECtHR had ruled that it would not review a national measure implementing an EU measure where the latter left no discretion to the Member States' authorities, as long as there is no evidence of some dysfunction in the control mechanisms or a manifest deficiency in the protection of human rights; see *Bosphorus Airways v Ireland*, Appl no 45036/98 (7 July 2005), para 155.

[42] The ECtHR ruled:

In its judgment in [the *Bosphorus*] case, the Court noted that the impugned act ... had been carried out by the respondent State authorities, on its territory and following a decision by one of its Ministers ... The Court did not therefore consider that any question arose as to its competence, notably ratione personae, vis-à-vis the respondent State despite the fact that the source of the impugned seizure was an EC Council Regulation which, in turn, applied a UNSC Resolution. In the present cases, the impugned acts and omissions of KFOR and UNMIK cannot be attributed to the respondent States and, moreover, did not take place on the territory of those States or by virtue of a decision of their authorities (*Behrami/Saramati*, para 151).

[43] Para 149.

[44] See eg *Ireland v UK*, Appl no 5310/71 (18 January 1987), para 239 ff.

particularly the case with respect to fair trial rights.[45] Competition law is also a notoriously problematic area when it comes to ensuring full compliance by the Commission with the ECHR.[46] Similarly, in the area of development cooperation, human rights safeguards have been modelled in an explicitly political fashion.[47]

V. Direct and Indirect *Drittwirkung*

Having considered the content and the ensuing human rights obligations of the EU and its Member States, the application of human rights in relations between individuals must now be assessed. Horizontal applicability of human rights provisions—often referred to by the German noun *Drittwirkung*—is a perpetually vexing and contested issue of constitutional law. The first principal objection is that if human rights provisions were applicable in relations between individuals, this 'would put an end to private autonomy'.[48] A second important objection is that, given the legal-principle status of human rights and the highly abstract nature of rules, they are inappropriate for regulating the daily myriad of relationships between private parties, who cannot be expected to undertake a balancing of competing principles and to cope with the open texture of fundamental rights provisions. Nevertheless, whilst there may be good reasons for rejecting the idea of direct enforcement of human rights by one private party against another, known as direct *Drittwirkung*, opinions differ widely as to the permissibility of indirect or '*mittelbare*' *Drittwirkung*, ie the notion that human rights could or should guide the interpretation of private law rules and/or deny enforceability to private law obligations where they conflict with the state's obligation to ensure protection against abusive effects of private autonomy.

---

[45] For example, as far as fair trial rights are concerned, in *Emesa Sugar* case the ECJ rejected a litigant's request to submit observations in response to the Opinion of the Advocate General, principally because the latter has the same status as the judges and is 'not entrusted with the defence of any particular interest in the exercise of [his] duties' (see order of the Court in Case C-17/98, *Emesa Sugar (Free Zone)* [2000] ECR I-665, paras 11–12.) However, in a subsequent case on the status of the *commissaire du Gouvernement* of the French *Conseil d'État*, the ECtHR implied that conformity with Art 6(1) ECHR required that the parties may respond, if only in writing, to the *commissaire*'s opinion even after the closure of oral proceedings (see *Kress v France*, Appl no 39594/98 (7 June 2001), para 76). No such right is afforded to litigants before the Court. However, the ECtHR recently has drawn the distinction between the Advocate General of the ECJ and the commissaire when it decided not to follow the *Kress* case law in *Cooperatieve Producentenorganisatie Van de Nederlandse Kokkelvisserij UA v The Netherlands* (21 January 2009).

[46] For example, the prohibition of double jeopardy has been interpreted by the Court as requiring not that the same competition law infringement may not be pursued by the Commission and by a Member State, but simply that in setting a fine an earlier fine must be taken into account. See judgment in Joined Cases T-236/01, T-239/01, T-244–6/01, T-251–2/01, *Tokai Carbon and ors* [2004] ECR II-1181, paras 131–2.

[47] See L Bartels, *Human Rights Conditionality in the EU's International Agreements* (2007), 123 ff.

[48] DP Currie, *The Constitution of the Federal Republic of Germany* (1994), 186, quoted in M Tushnet, 'The issue of state action/horizontal effect in comparative constitutional law' [2003] 1 I Con 84.

While direct *Drittwirkung* is not required by the ECHR, the obligations imposed upon the Member States with respect to indirect *Drittwirkung* seem to be very extensive.[49] Under EC law, because 'No Treaty provision confers on the Community institutions any general power to enact rules on human rights',[50] there can be no question of direct *Drittwirkung*. The indirect *Drittwirkung*, by contrast, forms part and parcel of established case law.[51]

The EU human rights rules would generally affect PMSCs just as any other service providers. In fact, it is often argued that 'indirect horizontal effect may differ from direct horizontal effect in form; however, there is no difference in substance'.[52] Put more provocatively, however horizontal effect is formulated, in the final analysis it will always be direct.[53] That may be true from a radically substantive point of view. Yet, in reality, the extent to which human rights can be invoked against a private party depends also on rules of competence, standing, and interpretation. Consequently, as regards the applicability of human rights in private relations, the distinction between direct and indirect *Drittwirkung* does hold some value. The appropriate conclusion thus seems to be that human rights as general principles of EU law can be applicable to private relations, albeit indirectly.

VI. Judicial Remedies

Human rights violations carried out by PMSCs may give ground to both state responsibility as well as individual responsibility. Similarly, one may contemplate the invocation of responsibility of the PMSC's home state, contracting state, or host state before the ECtHR, discussed elsewhere in this book, on the grounds of violation of that state's positive obligation to observe human rights and prevent their infringement.

As far as the invocation of state responsibility before the ECJ is concerned, matters are more complex, not least because the ECJ is not a human rights court. In addition, matters are further complicated by the unclear locus standi of private parties before the ECJ when Community acts are challenged. Generally the ECJ's approach with respect to individual access to the Community courts has been

---

[49] For an elaborate discussion see I Ziemele, 'Issues of Responsibility of Private Persons or Entities for Human Rights Violations: The Case-law of International Human Rights Courts and Monitoring Bodies', EUI Working Papers, Academy of European Law WP 2009/08, <http://www.cadmus.eui.eu/dspace/bitstream/1814/11409/1/AEL_2009_08.pdf>, accessed on 15 August 2010, esp the commentary on the *Pla and Puncernau* case.

[50] Opinion 2/94 [1996] ECR I-1759, para 27.

[51] See, in particular, the *Schmidberger* case, where the ECJ found that the protection of fundamental rights, amongst them freedom of expression, 'is a legitimate interest which, in principle, justifies a restriction of the obligations imposed by Community law, even under a fundamental freedom guaranteed by the Treaty such as the free movement of goods': ECJ judgment in case C-112/00, *Schmidberger* [2003] ECR I-5659, para 74.

[52] *Viking* case (n 19 above), per AG Poiares Maduro, para 40.

[53] R Alexy, *A Theory of Constitutional Rights* (2002), 363.

restrictive. In fact, a number of scholars have observed that the present system is not always sufficient for protecting an individual's fundamental rights and have argued either in favour of an expansion of the ECJ's competence or its accession to the ECHR.[54]

Furthermore, in the context of PMSC (illegal) conduct, and in the (current) absence of any specific EU legislation in the field, action against a Member State on the grounds of the conduct of a PMSC—brought either by the Commission or indirectly by a private individual—is unlikely. That is so particularly because of the Commission's wide discretion whether or not to pursue a Community law infringement.[55] Also, the availability of remedies in national courts is subject to Member States' procedural autonomy, and, according to well-entrenched case law of the Court, Community law only requires that sanctions for its breach be equivalent to those penalizing violations of national law;[56] that they be effective, ie dissuasive;[57] and that they be proportionate.[58] It is difficult to see how these rather abstract requirements might be used by a private party successfully to argue that a Member State has failed to comply with the EU human rights regime by inadequately reining in PMSCs.

VII. Conclusion

There can be no doubt that fundamental rights are enforceable at the EU level. At the same time, any possible EU legislation imposing an obligation on the Member States with respect to the licensing of PMSCs as well as criminalization of their illegal conduct outside the EU will need to strike a balance between human rights and economic rights. In other words, although the ECJ has acknowledged that fundamental rights may constitute justifiable grounds for imposing restrictions on the free-movement provisions, any such restriction on, for example, the free movement of services, is likely to be interpreted very narrowly.

However, in the light of several recent cases, the possibility of enacting legislation requiring Member States to regulate the conduct of PMSCs can by no means be excluded. In the recent *Ship-Source Pollution*[59] case, which followed the ECJ's ruling in the *Environmental Crimes*[60] case, the Court ruled that the EU may enact first-pillar legislation thereby requiring Member States to adopt measures

---

[54] See, inter alia, A-M Roddik Christensen, *Judicial Accommodation of Human Rights in the European Union* (2007), 80. For a forceful and as yet unsuccessful criticism of the current practice see Case C-50/00 P, *UPA v Council* [2002] ECR I-6677, per AG Jacobs, para 33 ff.
[55] See eg Case 7/71, *Commission v France* [1971] ECRI-1003, para 5 ff.
[56] See eg Case 45/76, *Comet v Produktschap voor Siergewassen* [1976] ECR 2043, para 13.
[57] See eg Case 14/83, *Von Colson and Kamann v Land Nordrhein-Westfalen* [1984] ECR 1891, para 23.
[58] See eg Case C-167/01, *Kamer van Koophandel en Fabrieken voor Amsterdam v Inspire Art* [2003] ECR I-10155, para 62.
[59] Case C-440/05, *Commission v Council* (23 October 2007).
[60] Case C-176/03, *Commission v Council* [2005] ECR I-7879.

criminalizing certain conduct where such legislation is necessary for combating crimes of a considerable gravity—in these cases, in the field of environmental law. It is also hoped that the entry into force of the Lisbon Treaty on 1 December 2009 will have facilitated the way for eventual EU legislation imposing an obligation on the Member States with respect to the licensing of PMSCs, as well as the criminalization of their illegal conduct outside the EU.

5
The Role of the Home State in Ensuring Compliance with Human Rights by Private Military Contractors

Francesco Francioni

I. Introduction

Throughout the first decade of the new millennium, international law and international relations scholarship has engaged in a wide-ranging debate over the legal implications of the growing use of private military and security companies (PMSCs) in the provision of services hitherto considered to be an integral part of governmental functions.[1] Such services include support to regular armed forces in theatres of war, guarding of diplomats, intelligence-gathering, and management of detention and interrogation centres, to mention just the most important. Research and academic writing on this subject has been accompanied by policy initiatives aimed at providing an international framework of principles and standards to promote governance and oversight of these new actors on the international scene.[2]

An important part of this debate, and of the regulatory movement stemming from it, concerns the role of human rights law (and of international humanitarian law (IHL)) in the regulation of PMSCs. This is not so much because PMSCs must be considered inherently inimical to human rights, but rather because their growing role and importance raises legitimate questions as to the transparency of their

---

[1] D Avant, *The Market for Force: The Consequences of Privatizing Security* (2005); S Chesterman and Lehnardt, C, *From Mercenaries to Market: The Rise and Regulation of Private Military Companies* (2007); G Kummel, *Private Military and Security Companies: Chances, Problems, Pitfalls and Prospects* (2007); C Hoppe, *Passing the Buck: State Responsibility for the Conduct of Private Military Companies*, Thesis, European University Institute (2009). See also the contributions to the EJIL-Priv-War Symposium on Private Military Contractors and International Law in 19(5) (2008) EJIL.

[2] The most important of such initiatives is the so-called 'Swiss initiative' a state-driven project that has culminated with the adoption in September 2008 of a set of non-binding standards by 48 states, including the permanent members of the Security Council, and applicable to PMSCs operating in situations of armed conflict. Another initiative is the preparation of a Draft Convention on the Regulation, Oversight and Monitoring of Private Military and Security Companies by the UN Working Group on the Use of Mercenaries of the Human Rights Council (July 2009). For an overview and comment on such initiatives and other regulatory options, see J Cockayne et al, *Beyond Market Forces* (2009).

mandate and operations, the adequacy of existing national legislation for the prevention of abusive uses of force, and, more generally, the adaptability of existing international human rights standards to the conduct of PMSCs as business entities.

To avoid any misunderstanding as to a possible ideological bias against PMSCs, it is important to clarify that, from the viewpoint of the author, human rights (and IHL) play a double role in this area of international relations. On the one hand, they provide legal constraints on the activities of private contractors. Such constraints are especially important since, by definition, PMSCs are meant to bear and use arms and provide services which in most cases contemplate the use of force, such as support in combat, guarding of sensitive installations, and custody of prisoners. It is important, therefore, that the risk of abuse and the inevitable endangerment of life and personal integrity[3] be met by a clear understanding of the limits that human rights law places on the conduct of PMSCs.

On the other hand, human rights perform a protective function for the PMSCs themselves. With a few exceptions, these are people who work in situations of conflict or of institutional instability, and thus they are particularly in need of the protection of human rights to safeguard their lives and freedom when their profession puts them in situations of danger.

Having clarified this twofold role of human rights, this chapter will focus only on the first aspect of this role,[4] ie the limits and obligations that human rights law imposes on the relevant international actors involved in the commercial provision of private military and security services. More specifically, I will examine the place of the home state of the PMSC as the addressee of human rights obligations relating to the prevention and, if necessary, the redress, of injuries resulting from the activities of its PMSCs.[5] This focus on the home state is justified, in my view, by a number of considerations. First, doctrinal contributions have been directed so far mainly at the responsibilities of the 'hiring state', ie the state who buys the services.[6] Although the role of the hiring state remains important, since it may promote responsible behaviour and compliance with international standards by means of the procurement contract, the home state acquires a distinct relevance especially with respect to the commercial export of private military and security services. This is so because of the paramount importance attributed by international law to the exclusive territorial control exercised over the company by the state where the company has been legally created or where the centre of gravity of its management and operations is located. In some cases the territorial link results in the coincidence of the home state and the hiring state. This will have cumulative effects and possible

---

[3] The right to life and to personal integrity are not the only human rights that may be put at risk by the activities of private contractors. They are, though, the most important and most frequently affected by the abuse of force. For a survey of the relevant human rights potentially endangered by PMSCs, see Ch 3 by Lenzerini and Francioni and Ch 4 by Kalnina and Zeltins in this volume.
[4] The second aspect is treated by den Dekker and Myjer in Ch 9 of this volume.
[5] Obviously the use of the shorthand possessive adjective 'its' implies a reference to the relevant links connecting the company with the state where it has been incorporated or otherwise constituted, or registered, or where it has its headquarters, its managing centre, or the main business activity. For further discussion of these criteria, see section II of this chapter.
[6] See, in particular, Hoppe (n 1 above).

synergies of obligations and responsibilities under international law. Often, however, the home state and the hiring state are different. A PMSC registered in the United Kingdom may be hired by a governmental agency of Italy to provide security services in Afghanistan or in the Middle East. In this situation a distinct set of obligations arise under international law for the home state and the hiring state. These obligations exist in a relation of mutual complementarity and in turn they complement the independent human rights obligations of the state where the services are performed, and also of the individual under international humanitarian and criminal law.

A second consideration concerns the weak role of the 'host state'. In the case of the commercial export of military and security services in a foreign country or area where situations of armed conflict or of institutional instability prevail, one cannot realistically rely on the effective control of PMSCs by the host state, whose inability or incapacity to provide security and governance is the *raison d'être* of the resort to private contractors.

Third, the focus on the home states as a guarantor of human rights provides the most useful dimension in which to reconstruct and evaluate specific human rights obligations related to the supervision and control of PMSCs. One need only think of the obligation concerning the adoption of appropriate regulation on the licensing of PMSCs, on procedures for the issuance of export permits, of authorization for the bearing of arms, and on remedial processes in case of harm. These are public functions that go to forming the content of the international law obligation to prevent and remedy human rights violations within the jurisdictional sphere of the state. Compliance with this obligation is a matter of governmental function and may not be left entirely to the private, contractual arrangements of the hiring state with the private contractor. These arrangements are important in view of a progressive development of models and standards supportive of human rights. However, they cannot be the exclusive source of human rights obligations and guarantees: in the present state of the law, they lack transparency, are vulnerable to conflicts of interests between the company and the hiring state, and do not seem to offer a guarantee of effective enforcement in domestic law.[7]

A final consideration that can be noted at policy level concerns the present trend in the security market toward an ever-increasing concentration of small security firms into large military and security companies endowed with substantial assets, equipment, and personnel and with a stable connection of the parent company with the home state.[8] For this 'second generation' of large security companies it is

---

[7] A very recent example of these problems is the inconclusive result of the investigation and prosecution of the Blackwater contractors involved in the killing of 17 civilians and the wounding of many more innocent bystanders in the shooting that took place on 16 September 2007 in Nisour Square while they were escorting American officials in Bagdad. The federal court in Washington has simply dismissed the indictment of the guards on the grounds that the prosecution had repeatedly violated the rights of the accused. The decision has been reported by the *International Herald Tribune* (2 January 2010), 1, 3.

[8] See Ch 1 by Cusumano in this volume, where the author refers to the acquisition by Group4 of Wakenut in 2002, Securicor in 2004, and Armor Group in 2008.

more difficult to escape regulation and circumvent sanctions by quick dissolution or transfer to convenient offshore seats under different names. It is reasonable to assume that one consequence of this evolution will be an increasing relevance of the link of PMSCs with their home state, where stable and long-term demand for services is generated and where market incentives exist for the adoption of regulation and accountability standards.[9]

II. Definition and Context

Before we analyse the substantive legal basis of the home state's obligation to supervise and control the operations of PMSCs under international human rights law, two preliminary points need clarification. The first concerns the meaning of the expression 'home state'. In strictly legal terms the home state is the state of the company's nationality. In turn, this means the state in which the company was constituted by way of incorporation or registration as a legal person. This is the most widely accepted criterion of attribution of nationality to a corporation and this criterion remains decisive for the purpose of international law, as recognized by the ICJ in the 1970 judgment in the *Barcelona Traction* case.[10] However, the home state may be also that in which the company has its main management centre (*siege sociale*) or where the main object of its business is located. Sometimes these connecting criteria are used cumulatively or alternatively in domestic legislation. Sometimes they are used exclusively, with the result that the same company may be linked to more than one state and be treated as a national by more than one state. Pursuant to this hypothesis, as with individuals with plural citizenship, the international law solution is that the home state is that with which the company has a 'genuine link' or the prevalent substantial connection resulting from the possible aggregation of the criterion of incorporation with other criteria and with the criterion of the economic control of the corporation, ie the nationality of the shareholders who control the company.[11]

The second preliminary point to clarify concerns the general international law context in which the issue arises of the international responsibility and accountability for the conduct of PMSCs. This context has been characterized in the past ten years by a far-reaching attempt to shift the responsibility for violations of human rights from the state to corporate actors operating across national boundaries. This shift has been supported by international law literature[12] and also by the

---

[9] This obviously does not apply to 'single shot' companies competing for a single lucrative contract and often consisting of little more than a website and a roster of recruitable personnel. On this phenomenon, see J Cockayne, 'Make or Buy? Principal–Agent Theory and the Regulation of Private Military Companies' in Chesterman and Lehnardt (n 1 above).

[10] *Barcelona Traction, Light and Power Co Ltd* (*Belgium v Spain*), ICJ Reports, 1970.

[11] For the enunciation of the genuine link theory, see *Nottebohm* (*Liechtenstein v Guatemala*), ICJ Reports, 1955, 4 ff. For the endorsement of the principle of the dominant and effective nationality in international jurisprudence, *Ephanian v Bank Tejarat*, Iran–United States Claims Tribunal, 1983, 157, 166.

[12] A Clapham, *Human Rights Obligations on Non-State Actors: The Collected Courses of the Academy of European Law* (2006); S Ratner, 'Corporations and Human Rights: A Theory of Legal Responsibility',

practice of United Nations bodies. The UN Secretary General Kofi Annan in 1999 launched the famous 'Global Compact' intended to mobilize private resources and stimulate voluntary initiatives designed to bring about adherence to good standards of corporate conduct, including respect for human rights and labour rights. In 2003, the now defunct Sub-Commission for the Protection and Promotion of Human Rights adopted the draft 'Norms on the Responsibilities of Transnational Corporations and Other Business Enterprises'. The norms were not formally approved by the Human Rights Commission, but a new Special Representative of the Secretary General was appointed, namely Harvard professor John Ruggie, to continue the work within the new institutional framework of the Human Rights Council.[13] This wide-ranging effort is premised on the idea that the law of international human rights may also create obligations for private corporations. It does not necessarily postulate a radical shift of paradigm from states to private actors with respect to human rights obligations. However, the insistence on the role of corporate social responsibility, market tools, voluntary initiatives, and the (cap)ability of business corporations to deliver effective standards of human rights compliance certainly has the effect—intentionally or otherwise—of deflecting attention from the role of states in ensuring compliance with human rights.

Today, this project of reconceptualizing human rights obligations has become problematic. First, because, at a technical level, the direct application of international human rights norms to private actors presents more difficulties than originally thought, both from the viewpoint of the transplantability of primary obligations from the interstate system to non-state actors and from the viewpoint of the adaptability of secondary rules on the international responsibility for breach and of enforcement procedures.[14] Secondly, the transformation of human rights from obligations of the state into obligations extended directly to private actors is not sufficiently supported by judicial practice.[15] Thirdly, at a political level, the faith in the ability of the market to generate spontaneous forms of regulation to ensure respect for public goods, such as human rights, social justice, and environ-

---

(2001) 111 Yale Law Journal 443 ff; *Human Rights Standards and the Responsibility of Transnational Corporations*, ed MK Addo (1999).

[13] See his latest report in UN Doc A/HRC/11/13/, 22 April 2009.

[14] These difficulties have been recognized by the new special representative J Ruggie. In his first interim report he stated that the human rights norms elaborated by the Sub-Commission in 2003 'cannot also directly bind business because, with the possible exception of certain war crimes and crimes against humanity, there are no generally accepted international legal principles that do so. And if the Norms were to bind business directly, then they could not merely be restating international legal principles; they would need, somehow, to discover or invent new ones': Interim Report, April 2006. In subsequent reports, especially the last one of 22 April 2009, the Special Representative has adopted a more flexible approach admitting that certain international human rights norms are capable to create direct obligations for business entities. For this report, see n 12 above.

[15] The United States is the only state that systematically permits the hearing and the enforcement of human rights claims related to private actors' conduct under the Alien Tort Statute. For discussion on the jurisdictional aspects of this practice, see C Ryngaert, *Litigating Abuses Committed by Private Military Companies*, EUI Symposium on PMSCs, EJIL (n 1 above). A recent decision of the Court of Appeals, 2nd Circ., has denied the applicability of international law to business companies, therefore removing them from the reach of the ATS. *Kyobel v. Royal Dutch Shell*, Sept. 17, 2010 (on file with the author).

mental quality has been undermined by the gigantic market failures of recent years: global warming, increased poverty, and now the planetary financial crisis of devastating economic and social consequence for the ordinary life of people all over the world.

All this suggests the need to remain focused on the role of the state as guarantor of human rights and human security. Accordingly, in the following sections of this chapter, I will address two closely related questions: first, whether and to what extent the home state has the responsibility under international law to regulate and supervise its PMSCs in order to prevent or minimize human rights violations, including violations resulting in injuries abroad; then, I will address the question of the home state's obligation to ensure appropriate remedial process in the event of injuries caused by the PMSC in performing its services. This second question entails a verification of the effective access to justice for victims to have their civil claims heard, and of good-faith investigation, prosecution, and assistance in the prosecution of crimes arising from or connected to the performance of services by the PMSC.

III. The Boundaries of the Home State Responsibility

The nature and scope of the home state's responsibility in respect of the prevention and minimization of the risk of human rights injuries arising from, or incidental to, the provision and export of PMSCs can be analysed from two complementary perspectives: the perspective of general international law on state responsibility for wrongful acts, and that of the substantive scope of the obligations incumbent upon the state to respect, to ensure respect, and promote human rights.

In the first scenario, the conditions for the attribution to the home state of acts of the PMSC must be established on the basis of the pertinent rules of international law as reflected in the Articles adopted in 2001 by the International Law Commission (ILC). As we shall see in the following sections, these Articles are quite restrictive with regard to the possibility and criteria of imputation of private acts to the state.

In the second scenario, the question, in the opinion of this writer, is not so much the attribution or not of private acts to the state, but rather the proper delimitation of the scope of the home state's substantive obligation to respect, protect, assist, and ensure respect for human rights. The nature and sources of this obligation have been illustrated in the current literature.[16] It is important to point out here that the general obligation to protect human rights precedes the actual causation of a human right injury and, therefore, the analysis of its content and reach with regard to PMSCs is independent of the actual causation of a human rights infringement and, consequently, of the issue of attribution to the state of private acts. This obligation entails a commitment by the state to prevent human rights violations in its territory, and in areas and over entities subject to its jurisdiction and control, by the adoption of legislative, judicial, or administrative measures applicable to public

---

[16] See Lenzerini and Francioni; and Kalnina and Zeltins (n 3 above).

organs as well as to private parties. Such a general obligation to protect may be breached even before a concrete human rights violation materializes. One need only think of the case of the prohibition of *non-refoulement*,[17] which involves a duty to protect against potential danger, and of the failure to enact legislation implementing the international prohibition of torture,[18] which has been recognized in international practice as an independent ground of international responsibility.[19] In all these cases the responsibility may arise not so much as a consequence of the attribution to the state of a private act of torture or *refoulement* but due to failure by the state to comply with its positive obligation to protect against potential exposure to such danger.

In the following sections, I shall examine these two different perspectives of state responsibility for acts of PMSCs.

IV. The Imputability of PMSCs' Acts to the Home State

Under the 2001 ILC Articles there are several grounds of attribution to the state of acts of PMSCs.

Article 4 provides:

The conduct of any state organ shall be considered an act of the state under international law. Therefore, private military contractors may be considered organs of the home state to the extent that that state has made them part of its armed forces. To understand what 'part of the armed forces' actually means for the purpose of the status of 'state organ' one can look at the Third Geneva Convention, which defines the categories of persons entitled to the status of prisoners of war. Under Article 4 these categories include, besides the regular members of the armed forces of a Party...

2. Members of other militias and members of other volunteer corps, including those organised resistance movements...

4. Persons who accompany the armed forces without actually being members thereof, such as civilian members of military aircraft crews, war correspondents, supply contractors, members of labour units or of services responsible for the welfare of the armed forces, provided that they have received authorisation from the armed forces which they accompany.

So, to the extent that private military contractors are embedded in the armed forces of the home state, their acts are to be considered acts of the state and the home state may thus be considered directly responsible for them when they constitute violations of human rights under international law.

---

[17] On non-refoulement as a general principle of international law see F Lenzerini, *Asilo e Diritti Umani. L'evoluzione del Diritto D'asilo nel Diritto Internazionale* (2009), 378 ff.
[18] Convention against Torture, Arts 2, 4.
[19] '...the mere fact of keeping in force or passing legislation contrary to the International prohibition of torture generates International responsibility': *Furundzija* case, Trial Chamber ICTY, 10 December 1998, para 148 ff. See also *Velasquez-Rodriguez v Honduras*, IACtHR, Series C, no 4 (29 July 1988), para 175.

This hypothesis is, however, quite rare. Practice shows that PMSCs are seldom integrated into the armed forces. They rather operate on the basis of ad hoc contractual arrangements often with ministries and agencies different from the defence department of the government. Their chain of command is linked to the corporate structure of the PMSC rather than to the hierarchical structure of the armed forces.[20] So, realistically, the most useful basis for attributing misconduct by PMSCs to the home state must be found in the Articles concerning conduct of persons not organs of the state. The relevant provisions of the ILC Draft are Articles 5 and 8.

V. Conduct of PMSCs 'exercising elements of governmental authority': Article 5 ILC Draft

Article 5 of the ILC Draft provides:

the conduct of a person or entity which is not an organ of the State... but which is empowered by the law of that state to exercise elements of the governmental authority shall be considered an act of the State under international law, provided the person or entity is acting in that capacity in the particular instance.

In spite of the rather hermetic language contained in the reference to the 'exercise of elements of governmental authority', this Article is especially relevant to PMSCs because it clarifies that the legal status of a company, as a private entity rather than a public one, cannot be a criterion for excluding a priori the attribution of its acts to the state. The important factor is the empowerment of the company with a certain measure and form of governmental authority.

Careful analysis of this provision reveals that the path to attribution of PMSCs' misconduct to the home state under its criteria remains quite narrow. First, the 'empowerment' hurdle is high. Article 5 refers to empowerment 'by the law of that state', which prima facie would exclude a similar delegation of powers by way of contractual arrangements or by executive measures. To the best of this writer's knowledge, there are no cases where the constitution, registration, or licensing of a PMSC has been effected by law. Normally, the home state performs these functions either by administrative or quasi-judicial measures. Similarly, there are no known cases in which PMSCs have been hired by way of an Act of Parliament having the formal quality of a law of general application. Normally, the hiring occurs by contractual arrangements or administrative acts of public procurement. So, it would be absurd to interpret Article 5 in the restrictive sense of 'law' as specific statutory enactment designed to delegate governmental powers to the private actor. The correct interpretation of the term 'law' must be broader, which will encompass any governmental measure, including executive and judicial acts and even contractual arrangements entered into under the authority of

---

[20] On the chain of command, see M Frulli, 'Exploring the Application of Command Responsibility to Private Military Contractors' *Journal of Security and Conflict Law*, 15(3), 2010, <http:jcsl.oxfordjounals.org/content/early/2010/09/21/jcsl.krq016.abstract>.

the law by governmental agencies. This interpretation is supported by the French text of the Article, which speaks of governmental functions delegated '*par le droit*', not '*par la loi*', as well as by the ILC comment to Article 5[21] and a sturdy body of legal doctrine.[22]

Once we have overcome the above textual strictures, a second set of interpretative difficulties in respect of Article 5 arises in connection with the determination of the meaning of 'governmental authority'. PMSCs provide services on a commercial basis and are not inherently engaged in the exercise of governmental authority. The question, therefore, is what the governmental powers are that may be delegated to them and that can trigger the responsibility of the home state under Article 5. The comment to Article 5 states that:

> What is regarded 'governmental' depends on the particular society, its history and traditions. Of particular importance will be not just the content of the powers, but the way they are conferred on an entity, the purpose for which they are to be exercised and the extent to which the entity is accountable to government for their exercise.[23]

If we apply these criteria to PMSCs we can identify several categories of services which entail the exercise of governmental authority. They are, inter alia: (1) participation in hostilities through delegation of combat responsibilities; (2) arrest and detention of prisoners of war or of persons subject to criminal prosecution in peace time; (3) interrogation functions; (4) intelligence-gathering for governmental purposes; (5) maintenance of law and order in critical areas of armed conflict or weak governance. When a home state has chosen to delegate the performance of these functions, and of other governmental functions, to private military contractors, it is reasonable to presume that the latter are empowered with 'elements of governmental authority' and thus in principle are capable of triggering the responsibility of the state under Article 5. We must observe, however, that the text of Article 5 places a significant restriction on the possibility of imputing the responsibility to the home state on grounds of delegation of governmental powers: it is not enough that such delegation be effected by operation of law; it is necessary that the PMSC is acting in that capacity as an assignee of public functions in the particular situation in which the human rights violation is alleged to have occurred.[24] Thus, the killing or injuring of an innocent person by a PMSC employee in an off-duty fight at a pub, as recently occurred in Iraq, would not entail state liability, unless it was shown that there was a serious breach of due diligence in hiring and overseeing the perpetrator. The question, in any event, remains open whether in such a case the home state would be under an obligation to guarantee access to its courts and remedies to the victims. I shall return to this point in section VIII below.

---

[21] See para 2 of the Comment to Art 5, ILC Report 2001, UN doc A/56/10, 92.
[22] M Spinedi, 'La Responsabilità dello Stato per Comportamneti di Private Contractors' in M Spinedi et al (eds), *La Codificazione della Responsabilità Internazionale degli Stati alla prova dei Fatti* (2006), 77; University Centre for International Humanitarian Law, *Expert Meeting on Private Military Contractors: Status and State Responsibility for their Actions*, Geneva, 29–30 August 2005, Report, p 20, <http://www.ucihl.org/communication/privatemiltary-contractors-report.pdf>, accessed on 15 August 2010.
[23] Para 6 of the Comment (n 7 above).
[24] The last sentence of Art 5 reads: 'provided the person or entity is acting in that capacity in the particular instance'.

Outside of the core of inherently governmental functions described above, many of the services provided by PMSCs are purely commercial and in principle they do not entail any exercise of public authority. These services include provision of security for property or personnel, guarding including body guards, logistic support, escorting of convoys, and other similar security services that do not necessarily entail use of weapons and coercive activities. However, even in relation to such activities it would be wrong to exclude a priori the possibility of attribution to home states of the international responsibility for human rights violations by PMSCs. Even conduct that is essentially commercial may trigger the responsibility of the home state if that state had an obligation under international law to discharge certain positive duties in relation to the performance of activities outsourced to the PMSC. One can think of the provision of security for internationally protected persons or assets, such as diplomatic personnel and missions. In such cases the responsibility to protect cannot be circumvented if the state chooses to delegate the protective functions to private contractors rather than perform them directly.[25]

VI. PMSCs' Acts Performed on the Instructions or under the Direction or Control of the Home State

Article 8 of the ILC's Draft contemplates the possibility that the conduct of a person or group of persons be considered an act of state if that person or group of persons acted 'on the instruction of, or under the direction or control of that State in carrying out the conduct'. This criterion of attribution has been the source of intense doctrinal debate since the well-known ruling by the ICJ in the *Nicaragua* case. In that case the ICJ adopted a restrictive interpretation of the concept of control, which the Court construed as 'effective control' for the purpose of attribution of private acts to the state. This restrictive test was put into question by the International Criminal Tribunal for the Former Yugoslavia (ICTY) in the equally well-known decision in the *Tadić* case, which adopted the more liberal test of 'overall control'. Under the *Nicaragua* test, a PMSC would engage the home state liability for a violation of human rights only if it was proved that, in conducting the specific activity which infringed a human right, the company or its employees were acting under the effective control of the home state. Under the *Tadić* test—also known as the Cassese test—it is sufficient that the home state maintains a general or 'overall' control of a political–military nature over the private military contractors, without being necessary that it has directed the specific commission of the wrongful act by the private actor. To give an example, the *Tadić* test would permit the attribution to the home state of human rights violations arising from the use of interrogation techniques amounting to torture, simply on the basis of official directives permitting or mandating the use of such techniques, without the need to prove that in the particular instance the state instructed and controlled the conduct of the contractor in the actual administration

---

[25] In the same sense, see Spinedi (n 22 above), 78–9.

of the interrogation. The text of Article 8 uses language that departs from both the *Nicaragua* and the *Tadić* test. However, it is clear that the use of the alternative criteria of 'instructions', 'directions', or 'control' have the potential of slackening somewhat the very strict condition of effective control laid down in *Nicaragua*.

Further refinement of the *Nicaragua* and *Tadić* tests can be found in the more recent jurisprudence of the ICJ and of human rights courts. In the *Bosnian Genocide* case, the ICJ, having to decide whether the commission of atrocities by a group of persons in the Yugoslav war could be imputed to Serbia, avoided the language of its own judgment in the *Nicaragua* case and resorted to a factual analysis based on the concept of 'complete dependence'. As stated by the Court:

persons and groups of persons or entities may, for purposes of international responsibility, be equated with state organs even if that status does not follow from internal law, provided that in fact the person, groups or entities act in 'complete dependence' on the state of which they are ultimately merely the instrument. In such a case, it is appropriate to look beyond the legal status alone, in order to grasp the reality of the relationship between the person taking action and the state to which he is so closely attached as to appear nothing more than its agent.[26]

This approach, which may be called 'constructive agency', has the advantage of focusing on the objective situation of dependence of the private actor on the state rather than on the formal criterion of the instructions/direction or effective control, which may be difficult to prove especially in relation to acts that constitute violations of international human rights and even international crimes. The development of this doctrine by the ICJ arose in an interstate dispute where Bosnia was invoking the responsibility of Serbia for its involvement in the genocidal massacres of Srebenica. However, there is nothing in that judgment to prevent the application of this doctrine outside of interstate disputes. On the contrary, this doctrine was developed earlier in the specific context of human rights adjudication by the European Court of Human Rights. In the 2004 case of *Ilascu and ors v Moldova and Russia*, the Court was confronted with a complaint by a number of individuals who had been the victims of prolonged arbitrary detention in the self-proclaimed separatist Moldovan Republic of Transdniestria (MRT), a part of Moldovan territory bordering with Russia. The Court, after noting that the MRT had been set up with the decisive support of Russia and remained under its preponderant military, economic, and administrative influence, concluded that this dependence created a 'continuous and uninterrupted link of responsibility on the part of the Russian Federation' for the breach of human rights caused by the arbitrary detention of the applicants in the hands of the Transdniestrian separatist regime.[27]

These precedents support the view that when the home state uses a PMSC as an instrument of its own political and military policies, and the company has no will of its own or is in a position totally subordinating its commercial interest to the policy goals of the home state, then this state should not be allowed to invoke the private

---

[26] ICJ (26 February 2007), para 392.
[27] Judgment of 8 July 2004, para 393 ff.

character of the company to shield itself from the responsibility arising from wrongful acts that the company has committed in the implementation of the home state's policies.

But what about situations where it is neither possible to prove that the PMSC acted on the instruction, or under the direction or control, of the home state nor that it was in a position of complete dependence on the home state?

We shall address this hypothesis in the next section.

VII. The Responsibility to Protect and the Export of Military and Security Services

To go beyond the strictures of the formal rules of attribution laid down in the ILC's Articles, and elaborated in the judicial practice mentioned above, it is helpful to examine now the nature and scope of the substantive international human rights obligations of home states with respect to PMSCs organized in their territory. This is useful also in respect of military and security services that are exported from the home state, because most activities of PMSCs, especially those based in Europe and in the United States, are performed abroad. In this case, the home state's obligation to respect and ensure respect for human rights has been systematically eluded on the basis of the argument that the home state cannot be responsible for what happens outside of its territory and beyond its national jurisdiction. The position taken in this chapter is that this argument is intellectually unconvincing and even logically flawed. When we address the question of the export of military and security services that are capable of exposing a foreign population to the risk of human rights injuries, it is not a question of extending extraterritorially the reach of the home state's control over the PMSC's operation. On the contrary, it is simply a question of fully implementing *within the national territory* the principle of effective protection of human rights in relation to home-based PMSCs, in conjunction with the classical principle of effective territorial control recognized in international practice since the early cases of *Trail Smelter* (1941) and *Corfu Channel* (1948). The home state has full control and jurisdiction over the PMSCs organized under its law and established in its territory. This territorial competence and effective control makes it possible for the home state to discharge its due-diligence duty in order to prevent, minimize, and redress human rights violations arising from the commercial export of military and security services.

As already pointed out, the main gap in ensuring PMSCs' accountability for human rights compliance is the systemic failure of the host state to ensure adequate control over PMSC activities in the national territory. This failure is most often due to lack of institutional and enforcement capacity, which is reduced to a minimum in situations of armed conflict or of military occupation, as has been the case with Iraq and Afghanistan. But it may also depend upon the wilful support, or sympathetic acquiescence, of local authorities for the misconduct of the foreign military and security contractors. This is frequently the case in non-democratic states where

PMSCs provide security services to protect foreign economic interests, as is often the case with oil and gas corporations and other enterprises operating in the extractive industry—sometimes in hostile environments where the local population opposes such industries or their modus operandi on environmental, political, or social grounds. In these situations, relying on the territorial state for the prevention and remediation of human rights violations perpetrated by PMSCs may be unrealistic, since it is the territorial state that has authorized the foreign investment by appropriate concession agreement for the exploration and exploitation of its natural resources. The home state, on the contrary, is in a good position to prevent human rights violations arising from the commercial export of security services because it is able to regulate the PMSC 'at the source' by virtue of the effective territorial control it exercise over the centre of management of the company.

This approach, which the present author has developed earlier in the context of environmental harm[28] and of multinational enterprises,[29] is in the field of human rights and of PMSCs a fortiori rationally and morally desirable. In this field, all states are committed under the UN Charter and under general principles of international law to respect and contribute to respect for human rights 'for all without distinction as to race, sex, language or religion'. All states are also bound to 'take joint and separate action in cooperation with the Organisation for the achievement of the purposes set forth in Article 55 of the Charter'. This universalist approach, confirmed in the 1948 Universal Declaration, entails an obligation for every state not to knowingly allow the use of its territory and the conduct of persons subject to its jurisdiction to cause serious violations of human rights. This is a typical due-diligence obligation, not an obligation to ensure a given result. However, even within the limits of the flexible principle of due diligence, one can identify a number of standards of good behaviour that can objectively help to prevent and minimize the exposure to the risk of serious human rights violations by PMSCs even when they operate abroad.[30]

The first and most basic obligation of the home state in this respect is to prohibit the use of its territory by PMSCs to recruit, train, and send personnel abroad to be used in combat operations directed against the 'sovereignty, territorial integrity, and political independence of another State'. These words are lifted from the 1974 GA Resolution on the definition of aggression.[31] The same resolution includes in the

---

[28] F Francioni, 'Export of Environmental Harm by Multinational Enterprises: Can the State of Origin be held Responsible' in F Francioni and T Scovazzi (eds), *International Responsibility for Environmental Harm* (1991).

[29] F Francioni, *Imprese Multinazionali, Protezione Diplomatica e Responsabilità Internazionale* (1979), Ch 4; F Francioni, 'Four Ways of Enforcing the International Responsibility for Human Rights Violations by Multinational Corporations' in M-A Moreau and F Francioni (eds), *La Dimension Pluridisciplinaire de la Responsabilité Sociale de l'Entreprise* (2007), 154 ff.

[30] For a recent decision of the European Court of Human Rights confirming that the obligations arising from the European Convention cover also activities performed by state organs in foreign territory, see *Al-Sadoon v UK*, Appl no 61498/08 (2 March 2010).

[31] Article Definition of Aggression Resolution (1974) GA Res 3314 (XXIX) 1970. For purposes of individual criminal responsibility, a definition of aggression has been now provided also by the Review Conference of the Rome Statute of the International Criminal Court. Amendments to the Rome Statute were adopted after two weeks of intense debate and years of preparatory work, on 11 June 2010

legal definition of aggression the sending by or on behalf of the state of 'armed bands, groups, irregulars, or mercenaries, which carry out acts of armed force against another state of such gravity as to amount the acts listed above or its substantial involvement therein'.[32] The language of this definition does not explicitly refer to human rights. However, it is not difficult to interpret the expression 'political independence' as inclusive of the right to self-determination, which is the first human right recognized at Article 1 common to the two UN Covenants. At the same time, the terms 'groups', 'irregulars', or 'mercenaries' cover the commercial export of military services through private contractors, when the home state uses them as a conduit ('on behalf of the state') for indirect armed intervention in another state.[33] Therefore, home countries of PMSCs, in addition to hiring states, are bound under international law to implement this prohibition through appropriate regulation and judicial enforcement at the source. Of course, states have a wide margin of discretion in choosing the regulatory approach they deem fit. This is made clear by the variety of regulatory models that have emerged so far in domestic law.[34] In the event that the state decides to adopt a total ban on PMSCs, the problem will be only one of effective implementation of the ban. When, instead a state decides to permit or encourage the establishment of PMSCs in its territory, then the due-diligence obligation entails a certain number of positive duties that go beyond the basic prohibition of indirect armed attack against another state.

First, the home state is required as a minimum to subject the creation and operation of PMSCs in its territory to a system of permits or licences. This is essential in order to verify the ability of the management and employees to operate responsibly and avoid conduct that may result in human rights infringements. In this field, it is hard to maintain the application of a principle of *laissez-faire* according to which the PMSC should be considered as any commercial enterprise and be allowed to operate under the liberal principle according to which anything that is not expressly prohibited is permitted. This principle makes little sense in an industry that involves the systematic use of weapons and the implementation of coercive activities for which it is generally accepted that a special or general licence is required under domestic law. The requirement of a general licence for PMSCs, and of specific licences for the personnel, has the further social function of enabling home states to mandate the inclusion of human rights and international humanitarian law conditionalities in the licensing instrument, whilst ensuring transparency as to the actual operations in which the company is engaged.

---

in Kampala, Uganda. Notwithstanding the agreed definition, the Court will not be able to exercise its jurisdiction over the crime until after 1 January 2017 when states parties will decide to activate the jurisdiction.

[32] Ibid, Art 3(g).
[33] For a discussion of these issues, see Ch 20 by Fernandez, Beaucillon, and Raspail in this volume.
[34] For a collection of national reports on legislation applicable to PMSC, see <http://www.privwar.eu/?page_id=49>, as well as the comparative analysis by O Quirico, *National Regulatory Models for PMSCs and Implications for Future International Regulation*, EUI Working Papers, Max Weber Programme, MWP 2009/25.

Once a system of ex ante licences is in place, the home state must discharge its due-diligence duty by subjecting the export of hazardous military and security services and goods to authorization and monitoring procedures. This authorization mechanism is not revolutionary: it is already in force in Europe and in the United States as well as in many other countries in respect of export of arms and of sensitive 'dual use' technology, as well as in respect of dangerous chemicals and hazardous waste.[35]

In the event that PMSCs are engaged in the provision of sensitive security services to transnational business corporations—as is the case for oil and gas companies and other mineral extraction companies which operate in unstable environments in Africa, Latin America, and South Asia—the home state should acquire relevant information about the nature of such services and verify that their performance is compatible with the respect for human rights. It is well known, and currently it is the object of many civil actions before national courts, that security services of transnational corporations have been involved in serious human rights violations in the host countries, including forced relocation of people, arbitrary detention, and even extrajudicial killings.

To prevent and minimize these crimes, the home state can check on past practices of the relevant PMSC in comparable situations so as to detect precedents of abuses that should require suspension of a licence or the withholding of further export authorizations.

Since the home state reaps economic and financial advantages from the presence and operation in its territory of PMSCs—in terms of employment and tax revenues—it is reasonable to expect that, as part of its due-diligence obligation, it should allocate resources to establish a mechanism of systematic and reactive monitoring of PMSCs' activities. The systematic monitoring can be facilitated by the requirement of social-impact reports in the annual financial reports of the company as well as by the use of the home state diplomatic missions and military attachés—when available—in the host state of PMSCs' operations. Reactive monitoring, on the other hand, is important when situations of serious misconduct by PMSCs are disclosed and remedial action is required. In states where a large sector of private military contractors has developed, as in the United States and the United Kingdom, systematic and reactive monitoring can be greatly facilitated by the work of the competent international organizations, independent experts, trade unions, and non-governmental organizations, which often are in a better position than states to provide factual elements for investigation and possible prosecution of human rights abuses.

The typology of positive obligations outlined above is not intended to exhaust the whole range of the home state's responsibilities in preventing violations of human rights connected to the export of military and security services by PMSCs

---

[35] See K Meessen (ed), *International Law of Export Control* (1992); Rotterdam Convention on the Prior Informed Consent Procedure for Certain Hazardous Chemicals and Pesticides in International Trade, 10 September 1998, UNEP/FAO/PIC/CONF 2; Basel Convention on the Control of Transboundary Movement of Hazardous Wastes and their Disposal, 22 March 1989, repr 28 ILM 657 (1989).

based in its territory. It provides only an exemplification of objective and reasonable standards of due diligence that home states are bound to adopt in order to comply with human rights obligations and avoid international responsibility for failure to protect human rights in the face of foreseeable and potential danger.

VIII. The Duty to Ensure Access to Court and Judicial Protection

The responsibility to protect illustrated in the previous section is not limited to the due-diligence obligation to prevent foreseeable abuses by PMSCs: it also entails the duty to remedy and sanction such abuses if they actually occur. This is clearly the case when the PMSC operates abroad in violation of the operating licence or export permits. Depending on the seriousness of the violation, sanctions may consist of (1) the investigation and possible prosecution of personnel, (2) the requirement to remove individual members suspected of crimes, and (3) the suspension or revocation of the operating licence or of specific export authorizations. These requirements have been considered part of existing international law in recent efforts at regulating PMSCs, in particular in the code of conduct and good practices elaborated on the basis of the Swiss Initiative in 2008.[36] In addition, it is incumbent upon the home state to ensure access to courts and appropriate civil remedies, including reparation for damage, to victims of human rights abuses committed abroad by PMSCs. This is an integral component of the responsibility to protect since, more often than not, the host state in whose territory the PMSC operates is not in a position to offer adequate judicial protection either because of the lack of institutional capacity and stability, lack of PMSC's resources to satisfy reparation claims, or, as was the case in Iraq until 2008, because of blanket immunity granted to the PMSC under the law of the home state.[37]

IX. Procedural Obligations: Interstate Cooperation

Of course, the set of positive duties we have tried to identify as part of the general due-diligence obligation incumbent upon the home state of a PMSC can be reinforced and made more effective through appropriate international cooperation between the home state and other relevant actors. Such cooperation is particularly important with the host state. In order to ensure that its population, especially the civilian population, is not exposed to serious human rights violations by PMSCs, as we have seen in recent years, it is essential first of all that the home state and the

---

[36] See the Montreux Document, adopted in September 2008 and the comprehensive commentary on this intitiave and other regulatory options contained in the volume *Beyond Market Forces* (n 2 above).

[37] This is why the Iraqi government has reacted with rage to and bitter resentment to the recent decision of the United States federal court in Washington which has dismissed the charges against the private contractors accused of reckless killing of civilians in the 2007 shooting at Nisour Square in Baghdad. See n 7 above.

host state communicate and that that the export of security services by the former occurs in a context of transparency and information so that appropriate measures for the prevention of harm may be taken on both sides. Cooperation is also necessary, whenever the activities of PMSCs involve breaches of the law of the territorial state or international crimes, for the prosecution and criminal investigation including gathering of evidence and verification of the facts in situ. In many recent cases involving reckless killings of innocent civilians in Iraq, torture, sex crimes, and even prostitution rings run by a PMSC in Bosnia, the perception has been that the persons responsible for the offences and the companies hiring them did not live up to a level of accountability required by the seriousness of the offences. This perception was reinforced by the combined effect of immunity from local jurisdiction and jurisdictional hurdles for home-country prosecution, and sometimes by the very result of judicial proceedings often ending in acquittals—as in the very recent case of the private contractors responsible for the killing of 17 civilians in Baghdad in 2007[38]—or very tenuous sanctions. Cooperation between the home state and the territorial state can help prevent potential incidents and abuses by ex ante exchange of information and monitoring of PMSCs' activities. It can also help deal with actual abuses of personnel by cooperation between investigatory agencies, limitation of immunities, and eventual prosecution after the event.

X. Conclusion

This contribution has examined the question of the home state's responsibility for human rights violations connected to the conduct of private contractors from two distinct perspectives. The first is the perspective of the general rules of attribution under international law, and the conclusion reached in this context is that the home state responsibility will arise when the PMSC is actually integrated in the national armed forces, thus effectively acting as an organ of the state, and when the home state has delegated by law some measure of governmental authority to PMSCs operating in its territory and exporting military and security services to other countries. Practice shows that this delegation occurs when the home state authorizes combat functions, arrest powers, management of detention facilities, interrogation services, and law enforcement functions. By empowering PMSCs with this type of governmental function, the home states cannot escape the international responsibility for the way in which such functions are carried out. A second hypothesis of responsibility has been identified in relation to the situation where the PMSC acts on the instruction of, or under the direction or control of, the home state. In this context I have pointed out that in the recent practice of the ICJ and of human rights courts the restrictive test of 'effective

---

[38] See n 7 above.

control' is evolving into the broader criterion of 'complete dependence' of the non-state actor upon the state.

All these doctrines of attribution can be useful for imputing violations of human rights and international humanitarian law to the home state. However, as practice shows, PMSCs are not working only for governments and under the more-or-less vivid colour of law and public authority. They also provide services to business corporations and private actors in dangerous areas where security is needed. In these cases, the ILC Draft and the traditional rules of attribution of international responsibility for wrongful acts are less helpful. A complementary approach, as has been argued in this chapter, can be found in the law of international human rights and in the general obligation that this branch of international law places upon states to exercise their sovereignty in such a way as reasonably to prevent activities conducted in their territory from causing human rights violations to other people. The effective control exercised by the home state over the creation, licensing, and export authorizations of PMSCs, constitutes the most rational basis for the recognition of a due-diligence obligation to regulate PMSCs so as to prevent and minimize the risk of human rights violations by the PMSC, including when the company performs its services abroad. At the same time, the home state has the responsibility of ensuring perpetrators are appropriately sanctioned, and victims are appropriately recompensed for violations of human rights which occur in spite of preventive measures. This approach seems all the more propitious in the present international context in which PMSCs are emerging as a viable alternative to official armed and police forces in the performance of many activities hitherto considered governmental. In conjunction with the parallel obligations of the territorial state and of the hiring state—whenever this is a third state—this approach can enhance responsible standards of conduct and accountability of PMSCs at a time when their conduct has given rise to lamentable abuses and has led to the unfortunate perception that they can operate beyond the reach of the law.

6

Positive Human Rights Obligations of the Hiring State in Connection with the Provision of 'Coercive Services' by a Private Military or Security Company

Carsten Hoppe

I. Introduction

In the present contribution, I address the positive human rights obligations of the hiring state with respect to violations of human rights arising from the conduct of private military or security companies (PMSCs/contractors).[1] In particular the obligation to prevent such violations, and the obligations to legislate, investigate, prosecute, and punish are discussed. My analysis is limited to scenarios where PMSCs provide services in a theatre of conflict. Moreover, it addresses the provision of coercive services, defined as those services that explicitly entail or can be expected to entail in their execution an element of compelling individuals or groups by force or authority. Examples include combat, guarding and protection of persons or property, detention, and interrogation. A counter-example would be the provision of food services or construction, even if provided in a context of conflict.

Contractors provide such services not only on behalf of states, but also for international organizations, private companies, and non-governmental organizations. The present contribution, however, considers the specific scenario where a state enters into the contract with the PMSC, and analyses the responsibility arising out of this relationship.

The hiring state or contracting state as discussed in the present contribution is thus defined as the state that enters into an agreement with a PMSC to provide services, in contrast to the home state of the PMSC, and the territorial or host state, where the service is provided.[2]

---

[1] This chapter summarizes research conducted for my PhD dissertation entitled 'Passing the buck: State Responsibility for the Conduct of Private Military Companies'.
[2] Sometimes these labels will overlap. Note that in a situation of non-international armed conflict, for example, the hiring state could also be the territorial state.

In the following, section II introduces the duty to prevent violations arising from the conduct of PMSCs, and section III discusses the duties to legislate, investigate, and prosecute and punish. For each set of obligations, the International Covenant on Civil and Political Rights (ICCPR), the American Convention on Human Rights (ACHR), and the European Convention on Human Rights (ECHR) are considered separately.[3]

II. The Duty to Prevent

In the following I will set out to answer the question of when and how a state hiring a PMSC to provide coercive services in the context of a conflict has to take measures to prevent violations of human rights by these contractors. Different approaches to the question of when and how states have a positive obligation to prevent violations of human rights by private actors have been developed by the judicial and quasi-judicial bodies interpreting human rights instruments.

A. The International Covenant on Civil and Political Rights

The Covenant provides that every human being has the inherent right to life of which he or she shall not be arbitrarily deprived;[4] and that '[n]o one shall be subjected to torture or to cruel, inhuman or degrading treatment or punishment'.[5] These provisions are non-derogable, even in times of armed conflict.[6] The right to life and the prohibition of torture as interpreted by the Human Rights Committee (the Committee) imply positive obligations extending to the conduct of private actors.[7]

Hence, where there is a credible 'threat to the life of persons under their jurisdiction', of which the state should be aware, it has to intervene.[8] The state owes this duty to all persons within its territory and to all persons subject to its jurisdiction.[9]

---

[3] For a discussion of the African system of human rights protection see Ch 7 by Bakker in this volume, in section II.D.

[4] International Covenant on Civil and Political Rights, GA Res 2200A (XXI) A/6316, 21 UN GAOR Supp (no 16), 52; UN Doc A/6316 (1966), 999 UNTS 171, Art 6.1.

[5] Ibid, Art 7.

[6] Ibid, Art 4.2.

[7] UNCHR, General Comment no 06: The Right to Life (Art 6) 27 July 1982; UNCHR, General Comment no 07: Torture or Cruel, Inhuman or Degrading Treatment or Punishment (Art 7) 30 May 1982 UN Doc CCPR/C/Rev1, para 2; UNCHR, General Comment 20, Art 7 (Forty-fourth session, 1992) (1994) UN Doc HRI/GEN/1/Rev1, 30, paras 2; UNCHR, General Comment no 31: Nature of the General Legal Obligation Imposed on States Parties to the Covenant 26 May 2004 UN Doc CCPR/C/21/Rev1/Add 13; See also eg UNCHR, *Karina Arutyunyan v Uzbekistan*, Communication no 917/2000 2004 UN Doc CCPR/C/80/D/917/2000.

[8] UNCHR, *William Eduardo Delgado Páez v Colombia*, Communication no 195/1985 1990 UN Doc CCPR/C/39/D/195/1985; For further references see K Wiesbrock, *Internationaler Schutz der Menschenrechte vor Verletzungen durch Private* (1999), 137.

[9] UNCHR, General Comment no 31 (n 7 above), para 7.

States thus have to take reasonable and appropriate measures to protect individuals from harm at the hands of PMSC personnel. These include that the hiring state must take all feasible precautions to avoid contractors providing coercive services violating the right to life of individuals they encounter, and ensuring proper supervision and planning of their missions. The off-duty conduct of contractors must also be supervised if the state becomes aware that transgressions are likely to happen.

Let me now move on to the prohibition of torture or cruel, inhuman, or degrading treatment or punishment (Article 7). Here too, the Committee confirmed a 'duty to prevent' which applies to the conduct of PMSCs hired by the respective state,[10] given that the state has a duty to take measures beyond merely legislative ones 'to afford everyone protection... against the acts prohibited by article 7, whether inflicted by people acting in their official capacity, outside their official capacity or in a private capacity'.[11] These protections are especially strict in the context of interrogations.[12] Whilst the duty to prevent violations of Article 7 is one of conduct, states have to ensure that independent inspection of contractor operations is not only incorporated into the contract, but in fact implemented.

Where violations have already occurred, the duty to prevent a recurrence of a similar violation is heightened.[13] States may thus have a duty to scrutinize conduct of contractors, improve the regulation of contractors, change the planning of operations, or to terminate a contract where systematic violations have occurred.

B. The Inter-American System

The American Convention on Human Rights obligates its states parties to respect and ensure the rights contained in it,[14] and to take legislative and other measures necessary to that effect.[15] Article 4.1 contains the basic provision on the right to life, while Articles 5.1 and 5.2 protect the integrity of the person and prohibit torture or cruel, inhuman, or degrading treatment or punishment.[16] The Inter-American Court of Human Rights (IACtHR) has developed a rich jurisprudence on the issue of enforced disappearances, including the *Velásquez Rodríguez* case.[17]

---

[10] See UNCHR, General Comment no 07 (n 7 above), para 2.
[11] UNCHR, General Comment 20 (n 7 above), at para 2. See also, UNCHR, General Comment no 31 (n 7 above), para 8.
[12] See General Comment no 20 (n 7 above), para 11.
[13] See eg UNCHR, General Comment no 20 (n 7 above), para 17; see also eg *Arutyunyan v Uzbekistan* (n 7 above).
[14] American Convention on Human Rights, OAS Treaty Series no 36, 1144 UNTS 123, Art 1.1.
[15] Ibid, Art 2.
[16] Ibid, Arts 4 and 5.
[17] *Velásquez Rodríguez*, Inter-American Court of Human Rights, Series C, no 4 (29 July 1988).

Under the ACHR positive obligations to prevent violations of human rights are violated where a state fails to exercise due diligence to prevent the violation[18] by taking all reasonable measures.[19] The duty to prevent is broadly conceived.[20]

The IACtHR has also addressed the special situation of individuals in custody, which is very relevant to contractors providing interrogation services. The Court found that states have an elevated duty to protect the life and health of persons on their custody. Moreover, the burden of proof will be on the state to show that it is not responsible, once the petitioner has discharged the burden of evidence.[21]

The IACtHR has also specifically addressed the responsibility of states in relation to private conduct in conflict situations, chiefly in the context of the massacre cases brought against Colombia.[22]

Whilst in these cases known criminal organizations were at issue, and not per se legal entities, it remains interesting that, under the IACtHR's approach, constructive knowledge of the high risks posed by persons providing coercive services may be sufficient to trigger the obligation physically to prevent violations. Specifically, states can incur responsibility where they fail to prevent a violation of an individual's right to life[23] if the state Is aware of a situation of real and imminent risk for a specific individual or group of individuals and there is a reasonable possibility of preventing or avoiding that danger.[24]

The duty to prevent is still framed as one of due diligence, but may be heightened where the state has allowed the formation of or supported the paramilitary groups, and thus 'created' the danger.[25]

Moreover, the Court recognizes a duty to 'prioritize the protection' of especially vulnerable persons such as human rights defenders.[26] Recurring violations heighten this duty.[27] The Court in some cases even inferred a failure to observe due diligence from facts of the violation itself without the need for further inquiry into questions of fault, akin to a res ipsa loquitur approach.[28]

Where states should be aware of the high general risks that, for example, guard and protection contractors pose to the civilian population, they have to take measures to prevent violations of the right to life resulting from such activities. The duty to adopt these measures will be heightened where grave violations recur.

---

[18] However, the language of *Godínez Cruz*, distinguishing prevention and response leaves this possibility open. *Godínez Cruz*, Inter-American Court of Human Rights, Series C, no 5 (20 January 1989), para 182.

[19] For the duty to investigate see, *Velásquez Rodríguez* (n 17 above), paras 176–7.

[20] Ibid, para 175; see also, *Godínez Cruz* (n 18 above), para 185 (employing identical language).

[21] *Juan Humberto Sánchez*, Inter-American Court of Human Rights, Series C, no 99 (7 June 2003), para 111.

[22] See, among many others, *Valle Jaramillo*, Inter-American Court of Human Rights, Series C, no 192 (27 November 2008).

[23] Ibid, paras 76–8.

[24] Ibid, para 78.

[25] Ibid, passim.

[26] Ibid.

[27] Ibid, para 76.

[28] *Case of the Pueblo Bello Massacre v Colombia*, Inter-American Court of Human Rights, Series C, no 140 (31 January 2006), para 136.

Extending the analysis of the European Court of Human Rights (ECtHR) to contractors who, by their nature are only exercising their functions in the area due to the hiring state having 'created' them by contract, again the hiring state's duty to prevent will be heightened. Lastly, some activities of contractors may be so outrageous, such as, for example, some of the abuses at Abu-Ghraib, that the IACtHR would find a violation of the duty to prevent without the need for any further evidence of fault.

C. The European System

Article 1 ECHR contains a duty obligating states parties to 'secure' the rights contained in the Convention to individuals within their jurisdiction. The Convention rights most likely to be endangered by PMSCs providing coercive services are the right to life (Article 2), which remains applicable in an armed conflict if the state concerned does not derogate from it under Article 15, and the prohibition of torture (Article 3), which cannot be derogated from under any circumstances. Under Articles 2 and 3 ECHR, several specific positive duties have been derived by judicial and quasi-judicial bodies, including the duty to put in place an effective legal framework;[29] the duty to prevent breaches (even where the direct involvement of the state cannot be demonstrated); and the duty to investigate and, where applicable, prosecute.[30] There follows an examination of the duty to prevent, while the duties investigate and prosecute are discussed in Part III of this chapter.

In interpreting Articles 2 and 3 ECHR, the ECtHR has derived several specific positive duties, including a duty to prevent. Accordingly, in *W v UK*,[31] the Commission acknowledged that Article 2 not only mandates repressive measures but, rather, it also calls for preventive measures by the authorities, which can be conceptualized as entailing the proactive element of planning, and the reactive element of intervention in the face of imminent danger to an individual. In *McCann*, addressing an antiterrorist operation of British special forces against IRA suspects in Gibraltar, the ECtHR held for the first time that the planning of operations that threaten the right to life can fall short of the requirements of the Convention.[32]

Since then the Court has in *Andronicou and Constantinou* also confirmed its willingness to examine the planning and organization of operations of security forces.[33] Therefore states must observe due diligence in planning and organizing their activities. This duty applies no matter whether PMSC personnel form part of

---

[29] See eg *X and Y v Netherlands* (1985), Series A, no 91.
[30] Eg *Assenov and ors v Bulgaria*, Appl no 90/1997/874/1086, ECHR 1998-VIII, para 102.
[31] *W v UK*, Appl no 9348/81 (1987), Series A, no 121, 190 (dealing with a case of domestic abuse not halted by the authorities).
[32] *McCann and ors v the UK*, Appl no 18984/91 (1995), Series A, no 324, para 213; the majority of ten judges was faced with a dissent of nine judges who disagreed as to the facts and cautioned against the use of hindsight in the assessment of the state's decisions. *McCann*, Joint Dissenting Opinion, para 8.
[33] *Andronicou and Constantinou v Cyprus*, Appl no 25052/94, ECHR 1997-VI 52.

the security forces of a given state, by, for example, providing guarding and protection, or even combat services under a contract. However, given that in both cases the conduct of state organs was at issue, *McCann* and *Andronicou and Constantinou* do not offer reasoning that could directly apply to the conduct of most PMSC personnel. The *Ergi* case may offer some support for the position that the positive obligation to plan and organize is independent of the question of attribution. There, the Court clarified that the duty to plan operations includes factoring in the conduct of third parties without any relationship to the state such as the targets of security operations.[34] States a fortiori have a duty under the Convention to plan any security operation that poses a threat to the right to life, where they hire the third party.[35]

A specific duty to prevent violations of the right to life by specific operational measures was the central issue in the *Osman* case.[36] The Court was presented with a teacher infatuated with one of his pupils, who later attacked the boy and his father. The Court held that, beyond a duty to put in place an effective criminal law to deter the commission of offences and law enforcement to back it up, a state may have a duty to take operational measures to protect individuals whose lives are at risk.[37] The duty is limited to cases where there is a real and tangible risk emanating from a specific person for the life of another specific person, and the authorities knew or should have known of a real and immediate danger to the victim(s).[38]

With respect to how narrowly identifiable the danger and victims need to be, the Court held in *Mahmut Kaya* that the threatened individual(s) must be identified, but did not apply the same requirement with regard to the 'third party' posing that threat,[39] yet ultimately only referred to the fact that no investigations into the conduct of counterterrorist groups were taken.[40] In its subsequent jurisprudence the Court upheld this approach, and only in dictum hinted at situations in which society at large could be in danger.[41]

In many cases in which the uncontrolled or off-duty conduct of contractors poses a danger to the right to life of individuals or groups, the Court's test of close indentifiability is unlikely to be met. There is still no positive obligation of the state elaborated by the Court for the benefit of the population at large. However, if the

---

[34] *Ergi v Turkey* ECHR 1998-IV; see also C Droege, *Positive Verpflichtungen der Staaten in der Europaeischen Menschenrechtskonvention* (2003), 47–8; A. Mowbray, *The Development of Positive Obligations under the European Convention on Human Rights by the European Court of Human Rights* (2004).
[35] *McCann* (n 32 above) and accompanying text.
[36] *Osman v UK*, Appl no 23452/94, ECHR 1998-VIII.
[37] Ibid, para 115.
[38] Ibid, para 116.
[39] *Mahmut Kaya v Turkey*, Appl no 22535/93, ECHR 2000-III, para 86; see also *Akkoç v Turkey*, Appl nos 22947/93 and 22948/93, ECHR 2000-X (presenting parallel finding with regard to the duty to prevent); see also, *Kiliç v Turkey*, Appl no 22492/93, ECHR 2000-III.
[40] *Mahmut Kaya v Turkey* (n 39 above), para 100.
[41] In *Mastromatteo* a dangerous criminal had committed murder while on leave during his prison term. In dictum, the Court elaborated that nothing had indicated to the authorities a 'need to take additional measures to ensure that, once released the two did not present a danger to *society*': *Mastromatteo v Italy*, Appl no 37703/97, ECHR 2002-VIII, para 76 (emphasis added).

Court would be willing to expand the identification requirement for potential victims to a location, for example, the passers-by on a crowded marketplace, the positive obligation to prevent through intervention could be very relevant to contractor operations. The duty already covers situations in which organs of the hiring state observe or are otherwise alerted to imminent or ongoing violations of the right to life by contractors, no matter whether they are under the state's control at the time or not, or even if they are off duty.[42]

Article 3 ECHR is also very relevant to PMSC's activities, for example, with regard to interrogation services. With respect to violations of Article 2, in the specific situation of detained individuals, the ECtHR has stressed their vulnerable position as grounds for more extensive duties of the state to protect their right to life. Here, states are not only responsible for the actions of their own organs, but also have to ensure that these persons are not subject to potentially lethal attacks at the hands of third persons.[43] Specifically, Article 1 taken together with Article 3 imposes a positive duty on the state to protect individuals against abuse by third parties, particularly those who are especially vulnerable,[44] with the factors to be assessed including the area of cell room allocated to an individual detainee, hygiene, isolation, and strip searches, among others. Certain practices of interrogation preparation by contractors reported from Abu-Ghraib would clearly fall foul of these provisions.[45]

In its jurisprudence with respect to detainees as vulnerable individuals whose dignity has to be preserved, the ECtHR has thus demonstrated its willingness to assess the circumstances under which detainees are kept independent of the question whether the treatment occurs at the hands of the state or third parties. Therefore, the state cannot retreat to the position that any given abuse occurred without its involvement, but has positive duties to check that detainees are being granted their Article 3 rights. I examine these latter obligations below including their relevance to PMSCs providing coercive services in situations of armed conflict.

III. The Duties to Legislate, Investigate, Prosecute, and Punish

In addition to the positive obligation to prevent discussed above, the judicial and quasi-judicial bodies interpreting the ICCPR, the American Declaration on Human Rights, the ACHR, and the ECHR have all derived positive obligations of the state flowing from the right to an effective remedy and the provisions protecting the right to life and freedom from torture or cruel and inhuman

---

[42] Of course, this finding still has to be carefully limited to the situations where the Convention is applicable.
[43] *Gezici v Turkey*, Appl no 34594/97, paras 49–54.
[44] *A v UK*, Appl no 100/1997/884/1096, ECHR 1998-VI, paras 22; see also, *Kalashnikov v Russia*, Appl no 47095/99, ECHR 2002-VI; *Valašinas v Lithuania*, Appl no 44558/98, ECHR 2001-VIII, paras 102–6.
[45] See *Kalashnikov* (n 44 above); *Valašinas* (n 44 above), para 102.

treatment. These duties include a duty to legislate in conformity with the respective instruments, as well as the duties to investigate, prosecute, and punish offenders. I examine these latter obligations below, including their relevance to PMSCs providing coercive services in situations of armed conflict.

A. The International Covenant on Civil and Political Rights

Article 2.1 ICCPR sets out the obligation of state parties to 'respect and ensure to all individuals within its territory and subject to its jurisdiction' the rights enshrined in the Covenant.[46] Whilst only the wording of the right to life under Article 6 explicitly calls for protection 'by law', Article 2(3) adds the specific obligation of states to ensure that an effective remedy is available in cases of violations. The Human Rights Committee has consistently expressed the view that every violation of the Covenant triggers this obligation of the state party under whose power or jurisdiction the victim was at the time to provide for an effective remedy.[47] In its General Comment 31, the Committee stated that states have to take 'legislative, judicial, administrative, educative and other appropriate measures' to fulfil their obligations under the Covenant.[48] As interpreted by the Committee, the duties extend to the conduct of private persons.[49]

This chapter discusses two aspects of the duty to provide an effective remedy, namely the duty to legislate, on the one hand, and the duty to investigate, prosecute, and punish, on the other.

1. The Duty to Legislate

The Human Rights Committee has analysed the duty to legislate for the right to life with respect to the prohibition of torture or cruel, inhuman, or degrading treatment or punishment separately.

Regarding the duty to legislate, as interpreted by the Committee, the right to life requires that the state enact effective private and administrative law to protect it, and the necessary criminal law provisions.[50] This may be violated, for example, where the law allows security forces presumptions of self-defence where they kill on duty.[51] For 'particularly serious violations of human rights', including of the right to life, disciplinary or administrative measures will not qualify as effective remedies.[52]

---

[46] International Covenant on Civil and Political Rights (n 4 above), Art 2(1).
[47] UNCHR, *Basilio Laureano Atachahua v Peru*, Communication no 540/1993 1996, para 8.3.
[48] UNCHR, General Comment no 31 (n 7 above), para 7.
[49] Ibid.
[50] See eg Concluding Observations of the Human Rights Committee, Philippines, UN Doc CCPR/CO/79/PHL (2003), para 8.
[51] See eg UNCHR, *Pedro Pablo Camargo v Colombia*, Communication no 45/1979 1985, para 13.3.
[52] See eg UNCHR, *José Vicente and Amado Villafañe Chaparro, Luís Napoleón Torres Crespo, Angel María Torres Arroyo and Antonio Hugues Chaparro Torres v Colombia*, Communication no 612/1995, 14 June 1994, UN Doc CCPR/C/60/D/612/1995, para 8.2.

In its General Comment 31, the Committee elaborated on the duty to legislate. As interpreted, the duty necessitates the creation of an administrative structure to investigate allegations of violations, a duty which could be violated independently from, or in addition to, the duty to investigate.[53] It stressed that remedies need to take into account special vulnerabilities.[54] Moreover, referring to the conduct of state agents, the Committee expressed the view that 'impediments to the establishment of responsibility' such as immunities or the defence of having obeyed superior orders should be removed.[55]

Regarding the prohibition of torture or cruel, inhuman, or degrading treatment or punishment, the Committee has stressed that states also incur a duty to legislate in accordance with Article 7, to:

> protect both the dignity and the physical and mental integrity of the individual ... through legislative and other measures as may be necessary against the acts prohibited by article 7, whether inflicted by people acting in their official capacity, outside their official capacity or in a private capacity.[56]

The duty is viewed as interrelated with the duties to investigate, prosecute, and punish—a necessary, but on its own insufficient, element of the protection of Article 7 rights.[57] General Comment 31 also underlines the approach of the Committee that extends the duty to legislate in conformity with the Covenant to Article 7.[58]

The duty to legislate under the ICCPR constitutes an obligation of conduct. Some clear lines can, however, be drawn. Where states fail to provide mechanisms to ensure that PMSC personnel violating the right to life or acting in violation of Article 7, by, for example, torturing a detainee, are subject to criminal sanctions, they violate their obligations under the Covenant. States hiring PMSCs have to enact appropriate legislation that ensures contractors can be effectively prosecuted for such violations in the host state or in their own justice system to comply with the ICCPR. Where the judicial system of the host state cannot be expected to provide an effective forum, as will often be the case in a theatre of conflict, the hiring state will have to ensure the reach of its own justice system. In any event, affording contractors immunity from the host states' justice system (as was the case for contractors in Iraq during the coalition occupation), whilst at the same time failing to ensure that an alternative forum is available, violates the duty to legislate in conformance with the ICCPR.

Let me now turn to the duty to investigate, prosecute, and punish.

2. The Duty to Investigate, Prosecute, and Punish

The Human Rights Committee has held that states have to create administrative mechanisms to ensure prompt investigations of alleged violations, and that a failure

---

[53] UNCHR, General Comment 31 (n 7 above), para 15.   [54] Ibid.
[55] Ibid, para 18.   [56] UNCHR, General Comment no 20 (n 7 above), para 2.
[57] Ibid, paras 8, 14.   [58] UNCHR, General Comment 31 (n 7 above), para 8.

to investigate can in itself constitute a violation of the Covenant.[59] Similarly, states have a duty to prosecute where investigations substantiate allegations.[60] A failure to do so can constitute a separate violation of the Covenant,[61] as can amnesties or the existence of certain defences.[62] The approach thus expressed by the Committee permeates its reasoning in country reports[63] and individual complaints.[64]

Moreover, the Committee has emphasized the state's duty, in accordance with Article 2, para 3(a) of the Covenant, to provide an effective remedy, including a thorough and effective investigation producing adequate information.[65] Similarly, the Committee has highlighted the duty of states under Article 2.3 'to provide the victim and the author with an effective remedy' through investigation and prosecution of those responsible, irrespective of amnesty laws.[66] The Committee has repeatedly emphasized that the ICCPR does not contain an individual right to the prosecution of another individual by the state.[67] However, states have a duty to investigate thoroughly alleged violations of human rights, and to prosecute criminally, and where appropriate punish, the perpetrators of the violations.[68] The duty to prosecute and punish 'applies a fortiori in cases in which the perpetrators of such violations have been identified'.[69] As a minimum, states thus have to launch an investigation if they are informed or otherwise become aware of alleged violations of the right to life and, where they fail to take any such measures or delegate the investigation to the contractors themselves without result, the duty will be violated.

The prohibition of torture in Article 7 ICCPR does not contain an explicit duty to investigate, prosecute, and punish. However, it has been argued convincingly that the duty to ensure the rights contained in the Covenant extends these duties in principle to all of them. Moreover, Article 2.3 allows the interpretation that remedies have to be made available even where the state was not the author of the respective violation.[70] Moreover, in its General Comment 20 on the prohibition of torture, the Committee extends the duty to investigate, prosecute, and punish to persons 'acting in their private capacity'.[71] In *Cabal and Bertran v Australia* the Committee held that 'contracting out to the private commercial sector of core state activities which involve the use of force and the detention of persons

---

[59] Ibid, paras 8 and 15; see also, UNCHR, General Comment no 06 (n 7 above).
[60] UNCHR, General Comment 31 (n 7 above), para 18.
[61] Ibid.
[62] Ibid.
[63] See eg UNCHR, Concluding Observations of the Human Rights Committee, Congo (2000) UN Doc CCPR/C/79/Add 118, para 8.
[64] See eg UNCHR, *Mr S Jegatheeswara Sarma v Sri Lanka*, Communication no 950/2000 2003 UN Doc CCPR/C/78/D/950/2000, para 11.
[65] Ibid.
[66] UNCHR, *Basilio Laureano Atachahua v Peru* (n 47 above).
[67] UNCHR, *Arhuaco v Colombia*, Communication no 612/1995, 29 July 1997, CCPR/C/60/D/612/1995, para 8.8.
[68] Ibid.
[69] Ibid.
[70] M. Nowak, *UN Covenant on Civil and Political Right: CCPR Commentary*, 2nd edn (2005), 39–40, para 20.
[71] UNCHR, General Comment no 20 (n 7 above).

does not absolve a state party of its obligations under the Covenant, notably under Articles 7 and 10'.[72] The Committee also stressed that domestic law has to provide vehicles to file claims for abuse of Article 7 rights. Complaints are to be investigated promptly and impartially.[73] Amnesties are viewed to be 'generally incompatible' with this duty,[74] and this principle extends to the investigation of crimes of a former regime.[75] The duty to investigate, prosecute, and punish applies a fortiori where the perpetrators have already been identified.[76]

The Committee has already elaborated on the duty to investigate, prosecute, and punish in several country reports, for example, in its Concluding Observations on the situation in Sri Lanka, both in 2003 and 1995. The Committee specifically noted that allegations of 'torture, abduction and illegal confinement', as well as intimidation of witnesses, had to be investigated, and where applicable prosecuted and punished.[77] Similarly, it called on Congo to investigate, inter alia, violations of Article 7 by armed forces, as well as paramilitaries and militias, and to bring the perpetrators to justice.[78] In its Concluding Observations on Russia it found that the state should ensure that violations of Article 7, among others, are not committed with impunity '*de jure* or *de facto*'.[79] Similarly, in individual complaints under the Optional Protocol, the Committee has applied the same reasoning. Already in 1981, in *Lopez-Burgos*,[80] addressing the torture of a Uruguayan national detained by Uruguayan special forces on Argentinean soil with the help of Argentinean paramilitaries, it found that the state had a duty to investigate Article 7 violations,[81] even if they were committed by its agents outside the national territory.[82] In *Rodriguez v Uruguay*,[83] the petitioner and victim of the abuses chose to focus on the duty to investigate, prosecute, and punish, rather than the violations of Article 7 proper. He had suffered extreme acts of abuse including torture by (soiled) water, electric shocks, and hanging by his arms.[84] With respect to abuse in detention, the Committee has stressed that the duty to investigate arises

---

[72] UNCHR, *Mr Carlos Cabal and Mr Marco Pasini Bertran v Australia*, Communication no 1020/2001 2003, para 7.2.
[73] UNCHR, General Comment no 20 (n 7 above), para 14.
[74] Ibid, para 15; see also, UNCHR, *Rodríguez v Uruguay*, Communication no 322/1988 1994, para 12.4.
[75] UNCHR, *Rodríguez* (n 74 above), para 12.3.
[76] UNCHR, *José Vicente and Amado Villafañe Chaparro, Luís Napoleón Torres Crespo, Angel María Torres Arroyo and Antonio Hugues Chaparro Torres v Colombia*, Communication no 612/1995, 14 June 1994, para 8.8.
[77] See eg UNCHR, Human Rights Committee, Comments on Sri Lanka 1995 UN Doc CCPR/C/79/Add 56.
[78] UNCHR, Concluding Observations of the Human Rights Committee, Congo (n 63 above), paras 8, 12.
[79] UNCHR, Concluding Observations of the Human Rights Committee, Russian Federation, CCPR/CO/79/RUS (2003), para 13.
[80] UNCHR, *Sergio Euben Lopez Burgos v Uruguay*, Communication no R12/52 (6 June 1979) 1981.
[81] Ibid, para 11.3.
[82] *Sergio Euben Lopez Burgos v Uruguay* (n 80 above), paras 12.1–12.3.
[83] UNCHR, *Rodríguez* (n 74 above).
[84] Ibid, para 2.1.

at the point the state is made aware of the allegations, even if these allegations may not be formally reflected in later proceedings (in the specific case transcripts of domestic proceedings were lacking).[85]

From this extensive treatment, several basic conclusions can be drawn: regarding the right to life, states have to conduct thorough and effective investigations of alleged violations. These procedures have to be conducted quickly, and all persons responsible brought to justice. Amnesties or immunities violate the Covenant, and where the perpetrators of violations have been identified, it is imperative that investigation and, where appropriate, prosecution and punishment follow. States are therefore not free under the ICCPR to leave violations of the right to life to the disciplinary system of the contractor they hired, even if the contractor operates one.

The prohibition of torture in Article 7 ICCPR also extends to the actions of private individuals and specifically those of coercive service contractors. Complaints are to be investigated promptly and impartially, and again cannot be left to the PMSC itself. The duty to investigate, prosecute, and punish applies a fortiori where the perpetrators have already been identified, and amnesties or immunities cannot shield contractor personnel. The state has to observe due diligence in its efforts to investigate, prosecute, and punish violations by contractors to which it is alerted and to which the ICCPR applies. However, there is no need for a formal complaint to be brought.

To discharge their obligation of due diligence, the duty to investigate, prosecute, and punish thus constitutes a minimum obligation of conduct which states have to ensure. Beyond their duties to provide for a basic legislative and administrative structure and penal laws as already discussed, complaint mechanisms must also be in place by which violations can be brought to their attention. To that effect it will not suffice to have the duty of reporting resting with the contractor itself. Rather, independent structures for formal complaints with the hiring state have to be in place. Examples would include a clearly identified and publicized office in charge of complaints. Similarly, a hotline for reports of abuses could be relied on. In any event, the hiring state has to investigate any credible allegations that come to its attention, whether formal or not. Hence, where a state fails to investigate allegations outright, or fails to provide meaningful access to lodge complaints against contractors, it will have violated its international obligations. On the other hand, where such mechanisms exist, and a diligent investigation does not substantiate allegations, or does not lead to arrests, the state will have discharged its duty.

B. The Inter-American System

Also the Inter-American Commission on Human Rights and the IACtHR have derived duties to legislate, investigate, prosecute, and punish under the Inter-American system.

---

[85] See eg UNCHR, *Mr Abduali Ismatovich Kurbanov v Tajikistan*, Communication no 1096/2002 2003, para 7.4.

1. The Duty to Legislate

Article 2 ACHR, entitled 'Domestic Legal Effects', contains an explicit duty of states to legislate in accordance with the Convention.[86] Moreover, 'other' measures listed in Article 2 provide grounds for the further duty to investigate, prosecute, and punish, and Article 25 ACHR specifically enshrines a right of the individual to effective recourse to a court or tribunal for violations of fundamental rights.[87]

The duty enshrined in Article 2 ACHR obligating states to legislate in accordance with the Convention may act as a basis for the argument that states cannot simply tolerate contractors violating the right to life and the prohibition of torture because of the limited reach of existing laws. The duty constitutes an obligation of conduct. Where states fail to take any steps to ensure PMSC personnel violating the right to life, or acting in violation of the prohibition on torture, are not only subjected to disciplinary and administrative measures but also to criminal sanctions, they violate their obligations under the Covenant. This duty entails that states hiring PMSCs in situations where the ACHR is applicable have to enact appropriate legislation ensuring that contractors can be effectively prosecuted for such violations in the host state or in their own justice system. Where the judicial system of the host state cannot be expected to provide an effective forum—which, as noted above in relation to the ICCPR, is often the case in a theatre of conflict—the hiring state will have to ensure its own justice system can provide the forum. In any event, the enactment of legislation inconsistent with this obligation constitutes a direct violation of the ACHR.[88] Thus, affording contractors immunity from the host states' justice system whilst at the same time not ensuring an alternative forum is available would, as was the case under the ICCPR, also violate the duty to legislate under the ACHR.

2. The Duty to Investigate, Prosecute, and Punish

The Inter-American Commission on Human Rights (IAComHR) has in numerous country reports consistently found that the right to an effective remedy implies a duty of the state to investigate, prosecute, and punish violations.[89] The IACtHR for its part has developed a rich jurisprudence on the subject, holding consistently that the state has to investigate 'every situation involving a violation of the rights protected by the Convention'.[90] This duty extends to violations committed by

---

[86] American Convention on Human Rights, OAS Treaty Series no 36, 1144 UNTS 123, Art 2.
[87] Ibid, Art 25.
[88] See eg *Case of the Mapiripán Massacre v Colombia*, Inter-American Court of Human Rights, Series C, no 134 (15 September 2005), separate opinion of Judge Cançado Trindade, paras 6–7.
[89] See eg Report on the Situation of Human Rights in the Peruvian State of Cayara, Inter-American Court of Human Rights, OEA/SerL/V/II.83, Doc 32 rev (1993), Doc 32 rev (1993), para 48.3.
[90] See eg *Velásquez Rodríguez Case*, Inter-American Court of Human Rights, Series C, no 4 (29 July 1988), para 187.

individuals not attributable to the state,[91] and will be violated if they go uninvestigated or unpunished.[92] In fact, the Court even hints at possible responsibility based on complicity of the state where it failed to investigate.[93] Investigations are to be undertaken by the state, even without private initiative,[94] and the duty to investigate continues until the circumstances of the violation are clarified, possibly even when prosecution and punishment are no longer possible[95] (eg where the perpetrators are confirmed to have died).

In its subsequent jurisprudence, the IACtHR has routinely emphasized the duty of states parties to investigate, prosecute, and punish.[96] Failure to comply with the duty to investigate, prosecute, and punish results also in a violation of Article 1(1) of the Convention.[97]

Violations of the duty to investigate, prosecute, and punish leading to impunity[98] are viewed by the Court as fostering 'chronic recidivism of human rights violations, and total defenselessness of victims and their relatives'.[99] Hence, amnesties are incompatible with the duty to investigate, prosecute, and punish,[100] and existing laws to that effect may have to be repealed.[101] Similarly, undue delays or suspensions can also violate the duty.[102] Where the appropriate structures are lacking, states must in accordance with Article 1(1) and Article 4 (Right to life):

adopt any measures that may be necessary to create an adequate statutory framework to discourage any threat to the right to life; to establish an effective system of administration of justice able to investigate, punish and repair any deprivation of lives by state agents, or by individuals; and to protect the right of not being prevented from access to conditions that may guarantee a decent life, which entails the adoption of positive measures to prevent the breach of such right.[103]

---

[91] Ibid, para 172; *Bulacio*, Inter-American Court of Human Rights, Series C, no 100 (18 September 2003), para 111.

[92] *Velásquez Rodríguez Case* (n 90 above), para 176; see also, *Godínez Cruz Case*, Inter-American Court of Human Rights, Series C, no 5 (20 January 1989), para 187.

[93] *Velásquez Rodríguez Case* (n 90 above), para 177; see also, *Godínez Cruz* (n 92 above), para 188.

[94] See eg *Bulacio* (n 91 above), para 112; *Juan Humberto Sánchez*, Inter-American Court of Human Rights, Series C, no 99 (7 June 2003), para 132.

[95] *Velásquez Rodríguez Case* (n 90 above), para 181; *Godínez Cruz* (n 92 above), para 191.

[96] See eg *La Rochela Massacre*, Inter-American Court of Human Rights, Series C, no 163 (11 May 2007), operative para 9.

[97] *Cantoral Benavides*, Inter-American Court of Human Rights, Series C, no 69 (18 August 2000), para 104.

[98] For a definition of impunity by the Court see, *Bulacio* (n 91 above), para 120.

[99] *Paniagua Morales*, Inter-American Court of Human Rights, Series C, no 37 (8 March 1998), para 173.

[100] *Barrios Altos*, Inter-American Court of Human Rights, Series C, no 75 (14 May 2001), paras 41–4; *Bulacio* (n 91 above), paras 117–18; *Caesar v Trinidad and Tobago*, Inter-American Court of Human Rights, Series C, no 123 (11 March 2005), para 17; *Ituango Massacres*, Inter-American Court of Human Rights, Series C, no 148 (1 July 2006), para 402.

[101] *Servellón-García*, Inter-American Court of Human Rights, Series C, no 152 (21 September 2006), operative para 8.

[102] See eg *Juan Humberto Sánchez* (n 94 above), para 131.

[103] *Sawhoyamaxa Indigenous Community*, Inter-American Court of Human Rights, Series C, no 146 (29 March 2006), paras 152–3.

The investigation into alleged violations cannot simply be a mechanical execution of routine formalities, but rather the state 'must demonstrate that it has conducted an immediate, exhaustive, genuine and impartial investigation' and will prosecute and punish the offenders.[104] Moreover, where the state at one point had close control over the victims, the burden of proof shifts to the state as to the whereabouts of disappeared individuals, and proper investigations have to be taken.[105] In addition, the Court has specified guidelines for the investigation of extralegal executions.[106] Lastly, states parties to the Inter-American Convention against Torture have an additional specific duty to investigate and punish torture, as well as to enact the required legislation, under Articles 1, 6, and 8 of that instrument.[107]

How do the duties to legislate, investigate, prosecute, and punish contained in the ACHR impact upon the responsibility of states hiring contractors to provide coercive services in theatres of conflict and occupation? The IACtHR has recognized a broad duty of states to investigate all violations of rights granted in the ACHR. Where the ACHR applies, the hiring state will have to investigate alleged violations of contractors even where their conduct is not attributable to it, independent of the service they provide.[108] In addition, the state will have to initiate such investigations as soon as it becomes aware of them, even without private complaints.[109] Where the state did not exercise due diligence, and such violations go uninvestigated or unpunished, the state will be in breach of the ACHR.[110]

In a conflict to which the ACHR applies, immunities such as those granted to contractors of the United states in Iraq would violate the Convention,[111] and any state operating with coercive service contractors not otherwise subject to jurisdiction would need to create a statutory framework to discourage violations and to put in place an effective system of justice to investigate, prosecute, and punish them.[112] Especially relevant to interrogation and detention contractors, the burden of proof is reversed when investigating the whereabouts of individuals who disappeared after having been taken into custody.[113]

---

[104] *Cantoral Benavides* (n 97 above), para 104; *Bulacio* (n 91 above), para 112; *Juan Humberto Sánchez* (n 94 above), para 144.
[105] *Barrios Altos* (n 100 above), paras 135–6; *Bulacio* (n 91 above), paras 141–2; *Neira Alegría*, Inter-American Court of Human Rights, Series C, no 20 (19 January 1995), para 65.
[106] *Juan Humberto Sánchez* (n 94 above), paras 127–8.
[107] Inter-American Convention to Prevent and Punish Torture, OAS Treaty Series no 67, entered into force 28 February 1987, repr Basic Documents Pertaining to Human Rights in the Inter-American System, OEA/SerLV/II82 doc6 rev1, 83 (1992); see also, *Cantoral Benavides* (n 97 above), para 104.
[108] *Velásquez Rodríguez Case* (n 90 above), para 172; *Bulacio* (n 95 above), para 111.
[109] See eg *Bulacio* (n 91 above), para 112; *Juan Humberto Sánchez* (n 94 above), para 132.
[110] *Velásquez Rodríguez Case* (n 90 above), para 176; see also, *Godínez Cruz* (n 92 above), para 187.
[111] *Caesar v Trinidad and Tobago* (n 100 above), para 17; *Ituango Massacres* (n 100 above), para 402.
[112] *Sawhoyamaxa Indigenous Community* (n 103 above), paras 152–3.
[113] *Velásquez Rodríguez Case* (n 90 above), paras 135–6; *Godínez Cruz* (n 92 above), paras 141–2; *Neira Alegría* (n 105 above), para 65.

C. The European System

The ECHR as interpreted by the ECtHR also contains positive obligations to investigate, prosecute, and punish that can be relevant to states contracting with PMSCs for the provision of coercive services in the context of armed conflict. The ECtHR does not identify a separate duty to legislate flowing from the ECHR but the Court has addressed the issue in terms of the right to an effective remedy under Article 13 ECHR. The ECtHR has progressively developed the duties to investigate, prosecute, and punish in separate strands of jurisprudence with respect to the right to life and the prohibition of torture.

Starting with *McCann*,[114] the ECtHR has consistently held that the obligation to protect the right to life under Article 2 of the Convention, together with the duty under Article 1 to 'secure to everyone within [its] jurisdiction the rights and freedoms defined in [the] Convention', implies that there should be 'some form of effective official investigation when individuals have been killed as a result of the use of force'.[115] The duty to investigate violations of Article 2 is non-derogable even in armed conflict.[116]

Compensation without investigation does not satisfy the state's obligation to investigate, prosecute, and punish under the ECHR.[117] The state has to investigate allegations of violations of the right to life brought to its attention, even in the absence of a formal complaint.[118] The purpose of the investigation is to ensure the protection of the right to life through domestic legal norms, and 'in those cases involving state agents or bodies to ensure their accountability for deaths occurring under their responsibility'.[119] The state has to ensure that the investigation is conducted independently,[120] and is promptly executed and effective.[121] Of course this is an obligation of conduct, or means, rather than result—hence, the state has to take all reasonable steps available to investigate the alleged violation, including, where applicable, eyewitness testimony, forensic evidence, and autopsies.[122]

There also has to be an element of public scrutiny of the investigations.[123] Any deficiency in the investigation which undermines its ability to establish the cause of death or the person responsible will risk falling below this standard.[124] In the specific case of the disappearance in life-threatening circumstances (such as a civil

---

[114] *McCann and ors v UK* (n 32 above), para 161.
[115] *Kaya v Turkey* (158/1996/777/978), para 105; for reiterations of this formulation see eg *Angelova and Iliev v Bulgaria*, Appl no 55523/00, ECHR 2007, para 94.
[116] See eg *Akpınar and Altun v Turkey*, Appl no 56760/00, ECHR 2007.
[117] *Bazorkina v Russia*, Appl no 69481/01, para 117.
[118] See eg *Angelova and Iliev* (n 115 above), para 96.
[119] *Bazorkina* (n 117 above), para 117.
[120] See eg *McShane v UK*, Appl no 43290/98, para 95.
[121] See eg *Angelova and Iliev* (n 115 above), para 97.
[122] Ibid, para 95.
[123] See eg *McShane v UK* (n 120 above), para 98.
[124] *Bazorkina* (n 117 above), para 118.

war) of persons last seen in the custody of state agents, a duty to investigate arises.[125]

The ECtHR does not specifically identify duties to prosecute and punish flowing from Article 2 of the Convention. However, the ECtHR has interpreted Article 13 of the Convention (the right to an effective remedy), to the effect that required investigations must be able to assess whether the force used in such cases was or was not justified in the circumstances,[126] and to lead to the identification and punishment of those responsible.[127] Hence, combining Article 2 with Article 13, the ECtHR has developed a duty to prosecute alleged violations of Article 2 going beyond the duty to investigate flowing directly from Article 2.

The duty to investigate violations of the right to life under the ECHR extends to cases perpetrated by individuals not attributable to the state such as PMSC personnel.[128] The ECtHR routinely identifies a duty to investigate alleged violations of the prohibition of torture by relying on Article 13, the ECHR right to an effective remedy.[129]

According to the ECtHR, Article 13 thus implies a duty to investigate on the part of the state extending to both the right to life and the prohibition of torture. The implicit duty to investigate violations of Article 3 was recognized by the ECtHR in *Aksoy*, where the Court stated that where an individual has an arguable claim that he has been tortured by agents of the state, the notion of an 'effective remedy' implicit in Article 13 entails 'a thorough and effective investigation capable of leading to the identification and punishment of those responsible and including effective access for the complainant to the investigatory procedure'.[130]

Similar to the duty under Article 2, the state has to engage in a 'thorough and effective investigation capable of leading to the identification and punishment of those responsible'.[131] If the investigation into the violation of the right to life remains ineffective, this may at the same time give rise to a violation of the Article 13 duty to investigate alleged violations of Article 3 based on the same facts.[132] The Court has also applied this approach to circumstances not reaching the ECHR's threshold of torture, but qualifying as inhuman or degrading treatment.[133] While the Court has not explicitly stated whether the duty to investigate violations of Article 3 is non-derogable even in armed conflict, one would expect its observations regarding Article 2 to apply with equal force to violations of Article 3.

As we have seen, the ECtHR has interpreted the Convention to give rise to (1) a duty to investigate violations of the right to life flowing directly from Article 2; (2) a

---

[125] *Cyprus v Turkey*, Appl no 25781/94, ECHR 2001-IV, para 132.
[126] See eg *Kaya v Turkey* (n 115 above), para 87.
[127] Ibid, paras 106–8; *Ogur v Turkey*, Appl no 21954/93, ECHR 1999-III, para 88; *McKerr v UK*, Appl no 28883/95, ECHR 2001-III, para 121.
[128] *Osmanoğlu v Turkey*, Appl no 48804/99, para 87.
[129] See eg *Bazorkina* (n 117 above), paras 161–5.
[130] See eg *Aksoy v Turkey*, Appl no 21987/93, ECHR 1996-VI 26, para 98.
[131] See eg *Bazorkina* (n 117 above), para 161.
[132] Ibid, para 163.
[133] *Tekin v Turkey*, Appl no 52/1997/836/1042, ECHR 1998-IV; *Assenov and ors v Bulgaria*, Appl no 90/1997/874/1086, ECHR 1998-VIII; *Mikheyev v Russia*, Appl no 77617/01.

duty to investigate violations of the right to life *and* the prohibition of torture, flowing from Article 13 (the right to an effective remedy);[134] and (3) a duty to prosecute and punish that applies to both violations of the right to life and the prohibition of torture, implied by the duty to investigate flowing from the Article 13 right to an effective remedy, which mandates an investigation capable of ensuring the 'identification and punishment of those responsible'.[135] In sum, where the Convention applies, it is evident from the above analysis that states will have to investigate alleged violations of the right to life by contractors, no matter what coercive service they provide. As we have seen, even the acts of combat contractors would have to be investigated whenever individuals have been killed as a result of the use of force or treated in violation of Article 3. Moreover, the practice of the United States in Iraq, for example, to compensate victims without a publicized investigation[136] would not conform to the ECHR. Investigations conforming to the ECHR cannot be executed by the contractors themselves, or contractors within the same company, to ensure that independence is not compromised. It is doubtful whether an investigation by contractors could ever qualify as an official investigation under the ECHR. Whilst the obligation is one of conduct, even in a theatre of conflict the state has to take all reasonable steps available to investigate the alleged violation and, for example, try to obtain eyewitness testimony, forensic evidence, and conduct autopsies to ascertain the cause of death where applicable.

With regard to interrogation and detention, the hiring state has to investigate any disappearances of persons who were last seen in its custody. In all cases, the required investigations must be able to assess whether the force used was justified, and lead to the identification and punishment of those responsible. As a minimum, complete inaction by the state will of course constitute a violation of the obligation.

IV. Conclusion

As this chapter has demonstrated, hiring states have numerous positive obligations under human rights law that are highly relevant to PMSC operations in situations of conflict. Among these, the duty to prevent violations of the right to life and the prohibition of torture and cruel and inhuman treatment are pertinent. The interpretations of the International Covenant on Civil and Political Rights and the regional Conventions, by the respective judicial and quasi-judicial bodies provide for specific duties to oversee, control, and where necessary physically prevent conduct likely to threaten the right to life or to contravene the prohibition of torture and cruel and inhuman treatment. Where violations have already occurred

---

[134] For the clear statement that the Art 13 investigation duties apply both to violations of Arts 2 and 3 see *Mikheyev* (n 133 above).
[135] *Bazorkina* (n 117 above), para 161.
[136] Hearing on Private Security Contracting in Iraq and Afghanistan Before the House Committee on Oversight and Government Reform (Statement by Eric Prince, CEO of Blackwater International) 2007, <http://www.oversight.house.gov/documents/20071003153621.pdf>, accessed October 2009.

or have been alleged, the duty to investigate, prosecute, and punish as interpreted in by the Human Rights Committee, the IACtHR, and the ECtHR obligates states to provide for a structure facilitating the reporting of such allegations, quickly and effectively to follow up on them, and to ensure that they are properly processed through the system of justice. These provisions can, for the most part, be extended to the conduct of third persons and thus also to contractors providing coercive services, even where their conduct may not be attributable to the state.

7

Duties to Prevent, Investigate, and Redress Human Rights Violations by Private Military and Security Companies: The Role of the Host State

Christine Bakker

I. Introduction

By becoming parties to universal and regional human rights instruments, states have not only committed themselves to respect the rights enshrined in these Conventions; they have also accepted a number of duties or positive human rights obligations[1] which also come to play in their relations with private actors.

This chapter will focus on the question of which positive human rights obligations laid down in the main general human rights instruments[2] are relevant to those states on whose territory private military and security companies (PMSCs) operate. These states are referred to as 'host states'. First, the *obligations to prevent* human rights violations will be considered (section II) followed by an examination of the *obligations to investigate* violations, *to prosecute* their perpetrators, and *to redress* these violations by providing reparations to the victims (section III).

In practice, some limiting factors exist which complicate or even preclude compliance with these obligations. They include, in particular, the lack of institutional capacities and governmental structures; military occupation or other forms of 'effective control' exercised in the host state's territory by one or more third states in an armed conflict or post-conflict situation; and, finally, states may formally

---

[1] Positive obligations are understood as those obligations contained in human rights instruments which require states parties to take certain measures to ensure respect for these rights, as opposed to the negative obligations, requiring states parties to refrain from violating the human rights protected by these instruments themselves.

[2] The International Covenant on Civil and Political Rights; the European Convention on Human Rights; the American Convention on Human Rights, and the African Charter on Human and Peoples' Rights. The term 'general' refers to the scope of the instruments, covering a wide range of human rights, as opposed to 'specific' human rights instruments, addressing certain individual human rights, such as the UN Convention against Torture.

derogate from their human rights obligations by invoking a derogation clause included in the different human rights instruments.

It should be noted that the positive obligations to prevent and, to a certain extent, the obligations to investigate and punish human rights violations pertain to all states that are involved in the deployment of a PMSC. Besides the host state, these are the state which has concluded the contract with the PMSC (hiring state or contracting state)[3] and the state where the PMSC is registered (home state),[4] at least when they are parties to the human rights instruments from which the obligations derive.[5] Often the hiring state and the home state are the same, for example, when Blackwater—now Xe Services—or DynCorp are contracted by the United States or Control Risks by the United Kingdom, but this is not always the case. Therefore, the same obligations will generally apply to two or three states simultaneously.

In practice, the hiring state or the home state may be in a better position to comply with these obligations, for instance, when the hiring state exercises full control over PMSC activities and the host state is not involved in the supervision at all. On the other hand, if the effective control over a territory is first exercised by an occupying power, and this control is subsequently passed over to the host state, this entails consequences for the positive human rights obligations of the host state as well. It is especially in these transitional phases that there is a risk of a 'human rights void', where no state is actually taking the measures required to ensure the protection of these rights.

A. Lack of Institutional Capacities

The lack of institutional capacity often limits the de facto possibilities for the host state to comply with its positive human rights obligations. However, the degree to which these institutional capacities are dysfunctional varies from one state to another. Moreover, the institutional framework may evolve over time, for instance, with external support for reconstruction and institutional development, and/or due to improving economic and political conditions in a post-conflict situation. It is difficult to assess to what extent the host state is or is not capable of taking certain measures, and in which circumstances positive human rights duties (also) pertain to the contracting and home states. To date, the monitoring bodies of the main human rights Conventions have not developed any specific criteria in this regard.

However, the notion of the *inability* of a state to comply with certain obligations under international law is explicitly included in the Statute of the International Criminal Court (ICC Statute). In the context of its complementarity regime, the ICC Statute also foresees the situation in which a state is *unwilling* to genuinely investigate and prosecute international crimes. It is acknowledged that provisions of

---

[3] See Ch 6 by Hoppe in this volume.
[4] See Ch 5 by Francioni in this volume.
[5] See O de Schutter, *The Responsibility of States* in S Chesterman and A Fischer, *Private Security, Public Order* (2009), 27–45, 33 (obligations of the host state) and 34–44 (obligations of the home state). See also S Farrior, 'State Responsibility for Human Rights Abuses by Non-State Actors' (1998) 92 *Proceedings of the American Society of International Law* 299, cited by de Schutter, 33, n 29.

international criminal law cannot, by themselves, be applied to human rights law due to the differences between these two bodies of law in terms of their addressees and the nature of responsibility to which they give rise (individual criminal responsibility versus state responsibility). Nevertheless, this parallel could be helpful when considering in what circumstances a state will be considered to be incapable of complying with its obligations under human rights law. This is especially true as regards the positive obligations of states to investigate human rights violations and to prosecute the responsible persons.

The ICC Statute states, in Article 17(3), that in order to determine the *inability* of a state to comply with its obligation to investigate and prosecute in a particular case:

the Court shall consider whether, due to a total or substantial collapse or unavailability of its national judicial system, the State is unable to obtain the accused or the necessary evidence and testimony or otherwise unable to carry out its proceedings.

The terms 'total or substantial collapse or unavailability of its national judicial system' point to a rather high threshold. In other words, if the national judicial system is only partially 'collapsed' this would not be considered a sufficient justification for the state not to comply with its obligations under the statute.[6]

The criteria of a 'lack of central government' and 'a state of chaos due to the conflict or crisis' may be useful when analysing the inability of a state to comply with its international obligations including its positive human rights obligations.[7] These elements support the argument that the positive obligations of the host state of a PMSC deriving from human rights instruments to which it is a party, cannot be considered to be 'waived' in all situations where there is a lack of institutional capacities. However, there are situations in which these obligations are indeed suspended, at least temporarily.

B. Military Occupation or Effective Control by a Third State

Suspension of the human rights obligations of the host state may arise in the case of a military occupation by a foreign state in (part of) the state's territory; or in a situation not amounting to occupation, but where a third state nevertheless

---

[6] In this regard, the Office of the Prosecutor explained in a Policy Paper of 2003, that 'This provision was inserted to take account of situations where there was a lack of central government, or a state of chaos due to the conflict or crisis, or public disorder leading to collapse of national systems which prevents the State from discharging its duties to investigate and prosecute crimes within the jurisdiction of the Court': Paper on some policy issues before the Office of the Prosecutor, ICC-OTP 2003–4, September 2003, <http://www.icc-cpi.int>, accessed on 15 August 2010.

[7] Art 17(2) also enumerates some criteria for determining *unwillingness* of a state genuinely to investigate and prosecute: (a) the proceedings were or are being undertaken for the purpose of shielding the person concerned from criminal responsibility; (b) an unjustified delay in the proceedings; (c) the proceedings were not or are not being conducted independently or impartially. With regard to the two last-mentioned criteria, the Court will consider whether in the circumstances, such delays or the lack of independence or impartiality in the proceedings are inconsistent with the intent to bring the person concerned to justice.

exercises effective control over (part of) the territory. The positive human rights obligations then temporarily pertain to the state exercising such control. As outlined in previous chapters of this volume,[8] human rights courts and monitoring bodies, as well as the International Court of Justice (ICJ) and the International Criminal Tribunal for the former Yugoslavia (ICTY) have provided some clarification on the term effective control. It should be noted that the case law of the human rights bodies focuses on the extent to which the *foreign state* is bound to ensure the human rights obligations on the territory of the state where these operations are carried out (eg military operations by Turkey in Cyprus or Iraq; or by NATO member states in former Yugoslavia). However, it does provide some guidance on the consequences for the obligations of the host state as well. The main positions of the monitoring bodies will now be examined.

The European Court of Human Rights (ECtHR) emphasizes 'effective control' of a territorial area in a foreign state as the main criterion for extraterritorial application of the Convention,[9] whilst acts of state agents, exercising some authority or control may also constitute the basis for such an application.[10] These two criteria are still considered as exceptional situations.[11] The Court has underlined the essentially regional nature of the Convention and its primary application within the legal sphere of the contracting states.[12] At the same time, since 2004, the Court has also recognized the possibility of extraterritorial application in third states, in the same above-mentioned exceptional situations.[13] In March 2010 the Court confirmed in its judgment in *Al-Saadoon and Mufdhi v UK* that the establishment of jurisdiction over persons within the territory of a

---

[8] See Ch 4 by Kalnina and Zeltins, and Ch 5 by Francioni in this volume.
[9] *Loizidou v Turkey (prel obj)*, EComHR (1995), Series A, vol 310, para 62; *Cyprus v Turkey*, Appl no 25781/94 (2001), para 77; this position was confirmed in *Demades v Turkey*, Appl no 16219/90 (2003).
[10] ECtHR, *Cyprus v Turkey*, Appl nos 6780/74 and 6950/75, EComHR, 26 May 1975 (stating that 'the authorised agents of the state, including diplomatic or consular agents and armed forces, not only remain under its jurisdiction when abroad but bring any other person or property "within the jurisdiction" of that State, to the extent that they exercise authority over such persons or property. Insofar as, by their actions or omissions, they affect such persons or property, the responsibility of the State is engaged'); see also *X v Federal Republic of Germany*, Appl no 1611/62, EComHR (1965) (stating that conduct of diplomatic or consular representatives abroad affecting nationals of the sending state residing abroad may give rise to liability under the Convention); *W v Denmark*, Appl no 17392/90, EComHR (1992) (affirming that authorized agents of a state bring other persons or property under the jurisdiction of that state to the extent that they exercise authority over such persons or property); *Hess v the UK*, Appl no 6231/73, EComHR (1975) (confirming that a state is under certain circumstances responsible under the Conventions for the actions of its authorities outside its territory, even though this was rejected in this case).
[11] *Bankovič and ors v Belgium and ors*, Appl no 52207/99, ECHR (2001), para 71.
[12] Ibid, para 80.
[13] *Issa and ors v Turkey*, Appl no 31821/96, judgment (2004), paras 69–71; this position was reiterated in *Ben el Mahi and ors v Denmark*, Appl no 5853/06 (2006), 9; *Mansur PAD and ors v Turkey*, Appl no 60167/00 (2007), para 53; *Isaak and ors v Turkey*, Appl no 44587/98 (2006), para 19. The *Issa* judgment is also mentioned in *Stephens v Malta (no 1)*, Appl no 11956/07 (14 September 2009), para 49, as providing an example of the exceptional situations in which an extraterritorial application of the Convention is accepted.

third state, outside the regional sphere of the Convention, entails obligations to prevent violations of the European Convention Human Rights (ECHR).[14]

Whilst the Inter-American Commission on Human Rights (IAComHR) also bases its acceptance of extraterritorial application of the American Declaration and the American Convention on the criterion of effective control, this 'control' is not related to the territory, but rather to the acts of the state agents exercising authority or control in the foreign state.[15] Its interpretation of such control seems to be broader than that of the ECtHR, since the IAComHR also recognizes the shooting of civilian airplanes in international airspace as falling within that scope (as opposed to the more restrictive interpretation adopted by the ECtHR in *Bankovic*).[16]

The United Nations Human Rights Committee (HRC) has also linked the notion of 'effective control' to the persons or agents exercising such control rather than to the territory. It has adopted a more contextual approach, also considering the factual situation in relation to the *violation* which occurred.[17]

The case law of the ECtHR on extraterritoriality gives rise to some uncertainty as to its exact meaning.[18] In particular, the statement in *Bankovic* emphasizing that the Convention operates in an essentially regional context and notably within the legal space of its contracting parties, is at odds with its later decisions adopting the broader formulation of *Issa*, confirming the possible extraterritorial application in third states, even if they are not a party to the ECHR. These differences have led some national courts to selectively apply the European case law, thereby adding to the lack of clarity.[19]

---

[14] *Al-Saadoon and Mufdhi v UK* (3 March 2010), para 140:

> 'In the present case... the respondent State's armed forces, having entered Iraq, took active steps to bring the applicants within the United Kingdom's jurisdiction, by arresting them and holding them in British-run detention facilities (see *Al-Saadoon and Mufdhi v the United Kingdom* (dec.), Appl no 61498/08, §§ 84–9, 30 June 2009). In these circumstances, the Court considers that the respondent State was under a paramount obligation to ensure that the arrest and detention did not end in a manner which would breach the applicants' rights under Articles 2 and 3 of the Convention and Article 1 of Protocol no 13'.

[15] *American Declaration on the Rights and Duties of Man (1948); Victor Saldaño v Argentina*, IACtHR, Report no 38/99 (11 March 1999); *Coard and ors v US*, IAComHR, Report no 109/99, Case no 10.951 (29 September 1999).

[16] *Armando Alejandre Jr and ors v Cuba*, IACtHR, Report no 86/99, Case no 11.589 (29 September 1999), para 25; Bankovic (all above).

[17] *Saldias de Lopez v Uruguay*, HRC, Communication no 52/1979, CCPR/C/13D/52/1979; *Lopez Burgos v Uruguay*, HRC (1981), Communication no 52/1979, CCPR/C////13/D/1979, para 12.3; and *Celeberti de Casariego v Uruguay*, HRC (1981) Communication no 56/1979, para 10.3, stating that: 'Article 2(1) does not imply that the State Party cannot be held accountable for violations of rights under the Covenant which its agents commit upon the territory of another State, whether with the acquiescence of the Government of that State or in opposition to it.' In its Concluding Observations on Israel (2003), the HRC no longer refers to the notion of 'effective control', but states: 'In the current circumstances, the provisions of the Covenant apply to the benefit of the population of the Occupied Territories, for all conduct by [Israel's] authorities or agents in those territories that affect the enjoyment of rights enshrined in the Covenant and fall within the ambit of state responsibility of Israel under the principles of public international law': Concluding Observations on Israel (2003), UN Doc CCPR/CO/78/ISR, para 11.

[18] See also Ch 4 by Kalnina and Zeltins in this volume.

[19] *Issa* (n 13 above). The UK House of Lords in *Al-Skeini* has followed the Court's restrictive reasoning in *Bankovic*, while dismissing the *Issa* position. In this case, which concerned six Iraqi citizens

Based on the existing case law, the following example could be given of a possible application in practice. Whereas during the military occupation of Iraq by the United States and the Coalition Forces the positive human rights obligations of Iraq were suspended (and these obligations then pertained to the Coalition Forces), since the transfer of power to the newly elected government, in principle, these obligations pertain once again to the Iraqi authorities. Clearly, exceptions will occur as long as foreign forces provide substantial military support. To the extent that these forces—or PMSCs—as part of their operations again exercise 'effective control' over a certain area, or through their acts put Iraqi citizens under their authority or control, the foreign state will once again be bound to ensure the human rights of the individuals within that territory or under such control.

Indeed, the ECtHR has held that in a situation of effective control (military occupation of Turkey in Northern Cyprus):

> Turkey's 'jurisdiction' must be considered to extend to securing the entire range of substantive rights set out in the Convention and those additional Protocols which she has ratified, and that violations of those rights are imputable to Turkey.[20]

This means that in such a situation, the positive obligations of the host state in the occupied territory are considered to be suspended. On the other hand, it also implies that when the occupation comes to an end, these obligations would again have to be fulfilled by the host state. Moreover, in a situation of effective control exercised over, for example, a detention facility by the agents of a foreign state such as in *Al-Skeini*, the full range of positive obligations in respect of the individuals present in that facility pertain to the state exercising such control. This has also been confirmed by the ECtHR in the *Al-Saadoon* case.[21] Even though there are no specific cases concerning PMSCs, it is argued that the same conclusion could be drawn when the state exercises such effective control by delegating the task to guard a detention facility to a PMSC. As mentioned above, the case law and views of the IACtHR and the HRC recognize a broader scope of extraterritorial application, less strictly tied to the notion of effective control over *territory*. As a consequence, the threshold for recognizing the applicability of positive obligations of the hiring state or the home state of a PMSC is lower.[22]

---

who were killed by British troops in Iraq, the Law Lords found that only one of the incidents—which occurred in a British-run detention facility—fell within the scope of the Convention (and thus under the British Human Rights Act), since the UK had effective control over that detention facility. This selective application of certain elements of the Strasbourg case law, without a detailed consideration whether the other incidents in the case might fall under the second exception expressly mentioned by the Court itself, namely through the specific actions of its agents abroad, is regrettable. On the other hand, one could also welcome the fact that the House of Lords has expressly recognized the applicability of the UK's positive human rights obligations abroad—even in the territory of a non-state party to the ECHR—at least in those situations where it exercises effective control: *Al-Skeini and ors v Secretary of State for Defence*, UKHL, 2007.

[20] *Cyprus v Turkey* (n 6 above), para 77.
[21] n 14 above.
[22] Nevertheless, the recent decision of the ECtHR in *Al-Saadoon* (n 14 above), has confirmed its recognition of situations in which extraterritorial jurisdiction is also established over *persons* when they are arrested and detained by a foreign state in the territory of another state.

C. Derogation Clauses

Many international and regional human rights instruments include a provision enabling states parties to derogate from their obligations in exceptional situations.[23] However, such derogation or suspension is not permitted for certain fundamental rights.[24] On the other hand, the right not to be subjected to arbitrary or unlawful detention is not excluded from the derogation clause. This is one of the violations that could, in theory, be committed by a PMSC. Thus if the host state invokes the derogation clause and suspends all rights and obligations except those explicitly excluded, this state could not be held accountable for having failed to prevent such conduct. It becomes even more serious if the unlawful detention results in the 'enforced disappearance' of the detainees. In practice, these derogations have only been invoked in very few instances.[25]

Even though the host state of a PMSC may often be unable to comply with its human rights obligations due to the factors discussed above, this needs to be established on a case-by-case basis.

II. Positive Obligations to Prevent Human Rights Violations: Applying the Case Law on the General Obligation to Prevent to the Host State of PMSCs

The positive obligations to prevent human rights violations fall within the scope of the obligations to ensure respect for these rights. The general obligation included in each human rights instrument to respect and ensure the rights included therein to all persons within their jurisdiction, implies a series of other obligations which are more specifically geared towards the protection of each individual right, such as the right to life or the freedom from torture. In this section, the main elements of the

---

[23] International Covenant on Political and Civil Rights (ICCPR), General Assembly Res 2200A (XXI) of 16 December 1966, Art 4; ECHR Art 15; American Convention on Human Rights (ACHR), OAS Treaty Series no 36, 1144 UNTS 123, Art 27.

[24] The prohibition of torture is excluded from derogation in all instruments. The right to life cannot be derogated according to the ICCPR and the ACHR; the ECHR states that no derogation from this right can be made, 'except in respect of deaths resulting from lawful acts of war'. Also the freedom from slavery may not be derogated from according these three instruments. Moreover, the right to life (with the above specification in the ECHR), freedom from torture, and freedom from slavery may not be derogated even in a time of war or public emergency.

[25] The United Kingdom invoked the derogation clause of the ECHR on 18 December 2001 after the terrorist attacks of 9/11 in the United States, with a view to adopting provisions in the Anti-terrorism, Crime and Security Act 2001, granting the government an extended power to arrest and detain foreign nationals suspected of posing a risk to national security. The derogation specifically concerned Art 5(1) of the Convention, which prohibits arbitrary or unlawful detention. The derogation was challenged before the ECtHR in *A and ors v UK*, Appl no 3455/05, ECtHR (19 February 2009). The Court concluded that the derogating measures were disproportionate in that they discriminated unjustifiably between nationals and non-nationals (para 90).

A. UN Human Rights Committee

The general obligation to respect and ensure the rights enshrined in the ICCPR requires that states parties adopt legislative, judicial, administrative, educative, and other appropriate measures in order to fulfil their legal obligations.[26]

This implies that the host state must ensure that the acts amounting to violations of human rights—in particular the right to life, the prohibition on torture, the prohibition on slavery, and the prohibition on arbitrary or unlawful detention—are incorporated as crimes in its national criminal code. The host state should take administrative measures to exercise a minimum of control over the functions performed by PMSCs and over the selection of these corporations. To this end, it could consider establishing an authorization regime for PMSCs at the national level requiring these companies to obtain prior authorization to perform services within the host state's territory. In this regard, the host state could establish an authorization authority for PMSCs responsible for checking the background of each PMSC; their internal accountability procedures; the training provided to its personnel including on human rights, international humanitarian law (IHL), and the use of force; and their past involvement in human rights or IHL incidents. The granting of such an authorization could then be made conditional on the fulfilment of certain criteria in terms of training; accountability; chains of command; supervision by/reporting to military commanders of (most likely) the hiring state, depending on the role and functions performed by the latter state in the territory in a certain period of time.[27] If the host state lacks the institutional capacities and governmental structures to ensure an effective authorization system—which will often be the case—it could consider requiring the necessary safeguards and information from the hiring state, especially if this is also the home state of the corporation. This corresponds to the situation in Iraq and Afghanistan, where PMSCs are contracted by, in particular, the United States and the United Kingdom, each applying their own national requirements in this respect.

The HRC has also expressed itself on the question what the obligation to prevent entails in terms of more specific duties, as follows:

---

[26] Human Rights Committee, General Comment no 31, The Nature of the General Legal Obligation Imposed on States Parties to the Covenant, UN Doc CCPR/C/21/Rev1/Add13, 26 May 2004, para 7.

[27] Montreux Document on Pertinent International Legal Obligations and Good Practices for States related to Operations of Private Military and Security Companies during Armed Conflict (the Montreux Document), Montreux, 17 September 2008, repr 13(3) (2009) JC&SL, part of the Swiss Initiative, sets out a series of 'good practices' for the different states involved with PMSCs, including the territorial state. These practices also include such an authorization regime and provide a detailed description of the criteria that could be used for granting it. See Montreux Document, Good Practices, paras 24–52.

States have a due diligence obligation to prevent violations of the right to life, which may also include the duty to intervene where there is a credible threat to the life of persons under their jurisdiction.[28]

Since PMSCs usually do not operate under the command of the host state, this latter state will often not be able to foresee any threats to the life of persons by acts of such corporations. However, if the host state authorities are aware of such a threat, they are bound to intervene in order to prevent such a violation. The HRC also held that:

> The state party has to take 'legislative and other measures' to protect individuals against acts prohibited by Article 7 (prohibition on torture), even when they are inflicted by persons in their private capacity.[29]

This implies that the host state, when granting authorization to a PMSC—if an authorization regime exists in that state—or when it is informed that a PMSC contracted by another state will be given the task to exercise full authority, for example, over a detention centre, or to perform interrogation tasks, it should specifically require strict supervision over these tasks, in order to avoid the risk that torture or other inhumane or degrading treatment or punishment is inflicted upon detainees. Moreover, according to the HRC, the duty to prevent also entails the duty to prevent recurring violations through measures; which 'may require changes in the state party's laws or practices'.[30] The obligation to prevent recurring violations as recognized by the HRC is of particular relevance to PMSCs, considering the series of incidents in Iraq which repeatedly involved violations of the right to life and of the prohibition of torture. This means that the host state has to take measures to exercise increased control over PMSCs, and if necessary withdraw their authorization or license—if issued by the host state—or force the hiring state to terminate the contract with those companies involved in recurring violations. The Iraqi government has given a positive example in this regard by refusing, in January 2009, to renew the licence of the firm Blackwater to perform security services for the US in Baghdad.[31] This refusal was directly linked to the Nisour Square incident in September 2007, whereby 17 civilians were killed and several others injured by employees of that PMSC. Finally, the HRC established that:

> The positive obligations on states also entail protection of individuals against acts committed by private persons or entities that would impair the enjoyment of Covenant rights in so far as they are amenable to application between private persons or entities.[32]

---

[28] *Delgado Paez v Colombia*, UN Doc CCPR/C/39/D/195/1985 (1990).
[29] HRC, General Comment no 20: replaces General Comment 7 concerning prohibition of torture and cruel treatment or punishment (Art 7), (1992), UN Doc HRI/GEN/1/Rev1, 30, paras 2, 10, 13; see also HRC, General Comment no 31 (n 26 above), para 8.
[30] HRC General Comment no 31 (n 26 above), para 17.
[31] <http://edition.cnn.com/2009/WORLD/meast/01/29/iraq.blackwater/index.html>, accessed on 15 August 2010.
[32] HRC General Comment no 31 (n 26 above), para 8.

Therefore, the positive obligations as discussed above are, in principle, also valid with respect to PMSCs, and not only to acts of state agents.

B. The Inter-American Court of Human Rights (IACtHR)

The IACtHR has interpreted the duty to prevent violations of the ACHR both in general and in more specific terms. The main elements of the relevant case law are the following:

The duty to prevent includes 'all those means of a legal, political, administrative and cultural nature that promote the protection of human rights and ensure that any violations are considered and treated as illegal acts.'[33]

As indicated by the HRC, this general duty implies that the host state must incorporate the acts amounting to violations of human rights as crimes in its national criminal law and take administrative measures to ensure sufficient supervision of the authorization and licence of PMSCs operating in its territory.

The state must organize its governmental apparatus in such a way that it is capable of ensuring such protection.[34]

The establishment of an authorization authority for PMSCs, as mentioned above could be an example thereof.

Regarding due diligence and state responsibility for private acts, the test is the state's 'awareness of a situation of real and imminent risk for a specific individual or group of individuals, and of the existence of a reasonable possibility of preventing or avoiding that danger'.[35]

Such test of 'awareness' includes the situation where the state has actual knowledge of the real and imminent risk and the situation of 'constructive' knowledge, i.e. where the state ought to have known of the imminent risk.[36]

In theory, the host state should, as far as its military and police forces have sufficient capacity for doing so—which will most often not be the case in a conflict situation where PMSCs are employed to take over certain functions—endeavour to follow the threats to security in different parts of its territory and assess the risks and the possibilities of preventing or avoiding danger for individuals or groups who may be at risk through the operations of a PMSC. In practice, the host state will not always

---

[33] IACtHR, Series C, no 4 (29 July 1988), para 175; and *Godinex Cruz*, IACtHR, Series C, no 5 (20 January 1989), para 185. See also *Paniagua Morales and ors v Guatemala*, IACtHR, Series C, no 37 (8 March 1998); *Suarez Rosero v Ecuador*, IACtHR, Series C, no 35 (12 November 1997), para 65; *Villagran Morales and ors v Guatemala*, IACtHR, Series C, no 63 (19 November 1999), para 225; *Bamaca Velasquez v Honduras*, IACtHR, Series C, no 70 (25 November 2000), para 194; *Durand and Ugarte v Peru*, IACtHR, Series C, no 68 (16 August 2000); *Barrios Altos (Chumbipumba Aguirre v Peru)*, IACtHR, Series C, no 75 (14 March 2001).
[34] *Velazquez Rodriguez*, IACtHR, Series C, no 4 (29 July 1988), para 18.
[35] *Valle Jaramillo and ors v Colombia*, IACtHR, Series C, no 192 (27 November 2008), para 78.
[36] *Case of the Pueblo Bello Massacre v Colombia*, IACtHR, Series C, no 140 (31 January, 2006).

be in a position to comply with this obligation, precisely because if it *were* capable of doing so, there would probably not have been a need for PMSCs to intervene.

However, the situation may also occur that a host state is unwilling, rather than unable, to take any preventive measures. For example, the government in Colombia has not taken any steps to prevent human rights violations by PMSC employees who participate in the US-led Plan Colombia, which is aimed at reducing the production and traffic of narcotics. Human rights incidents have not been investigated and no prosecutions have followed, due to an immunity agreement with the United States. The possible unwillingness to take any preventive measures seems to be related to the ongoing internal armed conflict. The human rights abuses occurred in areas controlled by the non-governmental armed groups, which may negatively affect the government's priority to take measures protecting the population of those areas.[37]

C. European Court of Human Rights (ECtHR)

The case law of the ECtHR on the duty to prevent is quite extensive. An important dictum which may be of particular relevance for the host state of a PMSC is that 'Positive obligations of states include the duty to put in place an effective legal framework ...'.[38] In addition to the incorporation of the relevant crimes in the criminal code as mentioned above, a host state should also consider including corporate responsibility for acts amounting to serious human rights violations in its criminal legislation. It should avoid wherever possible, given the availability and capacities of its judicial system, the conclusion of immunity agreements with hiring states of PMSCs. However, where the judicial system is not functioning effectively, the host state must require guarantees from the hiring state that any crimes committed by the PMSC or its employees are duly investigated and prosecuted by the authorities of the contracting (or home) state. Moreover, the ECtHR has held that 'The duty to prevent breaches may include the duty to ensure an adequate planning of security operations threatening the right to life...'.[39] Since the ECtHR specifically applied this criterion to operations of security forces of the state itself, it is questionable whether this is also relevant for PMSCs which are employed by another state than the host state. This would only be the case if the host state is directly involved in the planning of the PMSC operations, which is unlikely in practice. Furthermore, the Court stated that:

---

[37] See I Cabrera and A Perret, *Colombia: Regulating PMSCs in a 'Territorial State'*, Priv-War Reports on National Legislation and Case-law, no 19/09, <http://priv-war.eu/wordpress/wp-content/uploads/2009/12/nr-19-09-col.pdf>, accessed on 15 August 2010.

[38] *X and Y v Netherlands*, Series A, no 91, para 23 (1985). See C Hoppe, 'Passing the Buck: State Responsibility for Private Military Companies' EJIL 19(5) (2008) 989–1014, 1001.

[39] *McCann v UK*, 21 EHRR 97 (1996), para 213. The Court found with ten votes to nine that the planning of an antiterrorist operation by British special forces against IRA suspects was a violation of the right to life. The planning and organization of another operation by Greek special forces was also considered to violate the right to life in *Andronicou and Constantino v Cyprus*, 1997-VI 52 (9 October 1997).

In limited circumstances a duty to take operational measures to protect individuals whose lives are at risk may arise.[40]

The duty is limited to cases where there is a real and tangible risk emanating from a specific person for the life of another specific person, and the authorities knew or should have known of a real and immediate danger to the victim(s).[41]

The life of individuals is especially at risk in combat operations, when any risks to the life of specific persons cannot usually be foreseen. Otherwise, the right to life is most often violated either by excessive violence in the performance of a duty which normally would not have entailed this risk or by arbitrary shootings (such as in the Nisoor Square incident in Iraq), which by their nature cannot be foreseen.

D. African Commission on Human and Peoples' Rights[42]

The AComHPR has also addressed the scope of the duty to prevent violations including by private actors. The following points should be noted in this regard:

An act by a private individual can generate responsibility of the state because of the lack of due diligence to prevent the violation or for not taking the necessary steps to provide the victims with reparation...[43]

The standard of due diligence describes the threshold of action and effort which a state must demonstrate to fulfil its responsibility to protect individuals from abuses of their rights. A failure to exercise due diligence to prevent or remedy violation, or failure to apprehend the individuals committing human rights violations gives rise to state responsibility even if committed by private individuals.[44]

The specific circumstances of the case and the rights violated, considering the means which are at the disposal of the State, although for non-derogable human rights the positive obligations of states would go further than in other areas.[45]

This criterion of means being 'at the disposal' of the state limits the scope of the due-diligence obligations to what is actually possible for a host state in the given circumstances (eg armed conflict, insufficient institutional structures, and capacities). The AComHPR has outlined three principles as to whether means are 'at the disposal' of the state:

1. There should be an 'analysis of the feasibility of effective state action' as well as the extent to which the state concerned could 'have foreseen the violence and taken measures to prevent it'.[46]

---

[40] *Osman v UK*, 1998-VIII 95, para 115.
[41] Ibid, para 116. See also *Mahmut Kaya v Turkey*, ECHR 2000-III, para 86.
[42] Hereafter, AComHPR.
[43] See *Zimbabwean Human Rights NGO Forum v Zimbabwe*, Communication no 245/2002, 2006, 2006 *AHRLR* 128, para 143.
[44] Ibid, para 147.
[45] See *Zimbabwean Human Rights NGO Forum v Zimbabwe* (n 43 above), para 155.
[46] Ibid, para 157.

The feasibility of such effective action and the possibility of foreseeing violence by PMSCs may be limited for the host state, but is not excluded.

2. Usually a single violation of human rights, such as individual cases of policy failure or sporadic incidents of non-punishment do not establish a lack of due diligence by a state;[47] a violation of due diligence occurs in the case of systematic failure of the state to provide protection of violations from private actors who deprive any person of his/her human rights.

Even such a systematic failure to provide protection from violations by PMSCs cannot always be attributed to the host state, especially when it lacks all the institutional capacities for doing so. However, to the extent that this institutional capacity is more developed or restored, the responsibility of the host state to exercise some form of control and take measures to prevent recurring violations by PMSCs (eg by withdrawing their authorization, or requiring the hiring state to terminate the contract with a PMSC which has been involved in several incidents) may increase.

3. The standard for establishing state responsibility in violations committed by private actors is more relative than for direct state action. Responsibility must be demonstrated by establishing that the state condones a pattern of abuse through pervasive non-action.[48]

If a host state condones a pattern of abuse, this will most often be due to a lack of institutional capacity. However, as mentioned above, a state may also be unwilling to take action to prevent or to sanction abuses, for example, if a PMSC would intervene in support of an armed opposition group or otherwise against then host state's interests. The threshold for establishing state responsibility for a failure to prevent violations by private actors is clearly higher than for violations by state agents.

III. Positive Obligations to Investigate, Prosecute, and Provide Reparations

The general obligation to ensure human rights included in the different human rights instruments also entails the obligation to provide an effective remedy for human rights violations. This obligation consists of two separate duties: on the one hand, the duty to investigate violations and to prosecute their perpetrators and, on the other hand, the duty to provide reparation to the victims of human rights violations or their family members.

A. Obligation to Investigate and Prosecute

The human rights-monitoring bodies have all developed consistent case law in which the duty to ensure the substantial rights, in combination with their obligation to guarantee the right to an effective remedy, includes the duty to investigate

---

[47] See *Zimbabwean Human Rights NGO Forum v Zimbabwe* (n 43 above), para 158 ff.
[48] Ibid, para 160.

serious human rights violations and to prosecute criminally those responsible.[49] These duties to investigate and prosecute form part of the positive obligations to ensure the rights protected by these instruments.[50] The monitoring bodies have developed some criteria for these investigations and prosecutions.[51] In particular, as stated in consistent case law of the Inter-American Commission and Court, investigations must be complete and impartial and they must be carried out effectively and independently.[52] The ECtHR affirmed for the first time in *Kaya v Turkey* that in the case of an arguable claim of unlawful killing by agents of the state, Article 13 (right to an effective remedy) entails, in addition to payment of compensation where appropriate, 'a thorough and effective investigation capable of leading to the identification and punishment of those responsible'.[53] The same formulation, implying a duty to prosecute has also been upheld for torture,[54] serious ill-treatment,[55] and the intentional destruction of a person's home and possessions by agents of the state.[56] In some cases concerning the violation of the right to life through Russian armed attacks on civilians in Chechnya, the ECtHR held that Article 13 is also violated when a criminal investigation into the attack lacked sufficient objectivity and thoroughness.[57]

---

[49] For a detailed analysis of this case law, see C Bakker, *The Obligation of States to Prosecute Employees of PMSCs for Serious Human Rights Violations*, EUI Working Paper, AEL Series, Priv-War Project (2009).

[50] Only the AComHPR has not recognized these duties. Whereas the Inter-American Commission and the Inter-American Court do not distinguish between 'serious' and 'other' human rights violations, this distinction is explicitly made by the ECtHR and the UN HRC. The criterion of 'seriousness' refers to the rights protected by the relevant instrument; only violations of the most fundamental human rights, including the right to life, the prohibition on torture, and the liberty of person carry the duty to investigate and to prosecute.

[51] On this point, see also Ch 6 by Hoppe in this volume.

[52] Eg IAComHR, Res 48/82, Case 6586 (Haiti), March 9, 1982, Conclusion, para 3; *Velasquez Rodriguez*, IACtHR, Series C, no 4 (29 July 1988), para 18; *Paniagua Morales and ors v Guatemala*, IACtHR, Series C, no 37 (8 March 1998); *Suarez Rosero v Ecuador*, IACtHR, Series C, no 35, para 65; *Villagran Morales and ors v Guatemala*, IACtHR, Series C, no 63 (19 November 1999), para 225; *Bamaca Velasquez v Honduras*, IACtHR, Series C, no 70 (25 November 2000), para 194; *Durand and Ugarte v Peru*, IACtHR, Series C, no 68 (16 August 2000); *Barrios Altos (Chumbipumba Aguirre v Peru)*, IACtHR, Series C, no 75 (14 March 2001); *Miguel Castro-Castro Prison v Peru*, IACtHR (25 November 2006), para 470(8); *Manuel Cepeda-Vargas v Colombia*, IACtHR, Series C, no 213 (26 May 2010), Preliminary Objections, Merits, and Reparations, para 8; '*Las Dos Erres' Massacre v Guatemala*, IACtHR (24 November 2009), Preliminary Objection, Merits, Reparations, and Costs, para 12; *Chitay Nech y otros v Guatemala*, IACtHR (25 May 2010), para 12.

[53] *Mahmut Kaya v Turkey*, Appl no 22535/93 (28 March 2000), para 107; and *Buldan v Turkey*, Appl no 28298/95 (20 April 2004), para 103. Some examples of older cases of the ECtHR are *Klass and ors v Germany* (6 September 1978), para 67; *Silver and ors v UK* (25 March 1983), para 113; *Leander v Sweden* (26 March 1987), para 77; and *Chahal v UK* (15 November 1996), para 154.

[54] *Mahmut Kaya v Turkey*, Appl no 22535/93 (28 March 2000), para 107 and *Buldan v Turkey*, Appl no 28298/95 (20 April 2004), para 134.

[55] *Tekin v Turkey*, Appl no 52/1997/836/1042 (9 June 1998), para 66; *Assenov and ors v Bulgaria*, 1998-VIII, 3264 (28 October 1998), para 102; *Mikheyev v Russia*, Appl no 77617/01 (26 January 2006), para 142.

[56] *Hasan Ilhan v Turkey*, Appl no 22494/93 (9 November 2004), para 121.

[57] *Isayeva v Russia*, Appl no 57950/00 (24 February 2004), para 229; *Isayeva, Yusupova and Bazayeva v Russia*, Appl nos 5747/00, 5748/00, and 57949/00 (24 February 2004), para 239; *Khashiyev and Akayeva v Russia* (24 February 2005, Final Text published 6 July 2005), para 185. See also *Kallis and Androulla Panayi v Turkey*, Appl no 45388/99 (29 October 2009); and *Satabeyeva v Russia*, Appl no 21486/06 (29 October 2009), para 119. For more details on the case law of the ECtHR see Hoppe (n 3 above).

Also the HRC has consistently taken the position that whenever a violation of one of the substantive provisions of the Covenant is established the state party has a positive obligation to provide an effective remedy to the victim. This obligation is considered as a consequence of the violation itself.[58] The HRC has gradually refined the criteria for what constitutes an effective remedy. The duty to prosecute those responsible for violations of the Covenant has also been recognized, for the first time, in 1982.[59] In its General Comment 31 the HRC specifically states that: 'A failure by a State to investigate allegations of violations could in and of itself give rise to a separate breach of the Covenant.'[60] Where these investigations reveal violations of certain Covenant rights, states parties must ensure that those responsible are brought to justice.[61] The Committee stresses that these obligations notably arise in respect of those violations recognized as criminal under either domestic or international law, such as torture, summary and arbitrary killings, and enforced disappearances.

Host states of PMSCs are, in theory, also bound to comply with these duties. This raises, again, the issue of their institutional capacities. Investigations of violations such as killings or torture require qualified legal experts, who can perform their duties immediately after the acts were committed. The same requirement of professional capacities applies to the prosecution of the persons who may be accused of the violations. Moreover, the immunity agreements concluded between host states and hiring states often render such investigations and prosecutions by the host state impossible from the outset, although this depends on the exact terms of the agreement.[62] The host state has the duty to assist the investigatory authorities of the hiring state to gather all possible evidence, such as providing logistical support and translation services when witnesses are interviewed.

B. Obligation to Redress Violations by Providing Reparations

The essence of the obligation to make reparations for an internationally wrongful act was defined by the Permanent Court of International Justice in the *Factory at Chorzów* case:

---

[58] UNHRC, Communication no 5/1977 (*Moriana Hernandez Valentini de Bazzano and ors v Uruguay*), views adopted on 15 August 1979, Selected Decisions of the Human Rights Committee under the Optional Protocol, vol 1, 40, para 10.

[59] UNCHR, views adopted on 21 October 1982 (*Dermit Barbato v Uruguay*), Selected Decisions of the UNHRC under the Optional Protocol, vol II, 112, 116, para 11, cited by C Tomuschat, 'The Duty to Prosecute International Crimes Committed by Individuals' in H-J Cremer and H Steinberger (eds), *Tradition und Weltoffenheit des Rechts* (2002), 315–49, 323. See also Views of 24 July 1984 (*Muteba v Zaire*), Optional Protocol, vol II, 160, para 13; Views of 4 April 1985, Optional Protocol, vol II, 176, para 16, both cited by Tomuschat, 323.

[60] HRC, General Comment no 31 (n 26 above), para 15.

[61] 'As with failure to investigate, failure to bring to justice perpetrators of such violations could in and of itself give rise to a separate breach of the Covenant': General Comment 31 (n 26 above), para 18.

[62] For a detailed analysis of the question of immunity for PMSC personnel in international law, see Ch 22 by Frulli in this volume.

The essential principle contained in the actual notion of an illegal act ... is that reparation must, so far as possible, wipe out all the consequences of the illegal act, and re-establish the situation which would, in all probability, have existed if that act had not been committed.[63]

This definition, often referred to as the principle of full reparation,[64] has subsequently been followed in several cases by the ICJ,[65] but also by regional human rights courts.[66] The IACtHR has developed specific criteria for the types of reparation which should be granted for serious violations. Although financial compensation is the most important form of reparation, the IACtHR has also required states to make a public apology or create a monument for the victims, especially in cases of massive human rights violations.[67] The HRC has also adopted a broad definition of the term reparations, which can involve restitution, rehabilitation, and measures of satisfaction, such as public apologies, public memorials, guarantees of non-repetition, and changes in relevant laws and practices, as well as bringing the perpetrators of human rights violations to justice.[68]

For the purpose of this analysis, financial compensation is the most relevant form of reparation to be considered. Since human rights violations involving PMSC personnel are more likely to consist of incidents related to small groups of individuals, rather than massive human rights violations with large numbers of victims, the other forms of reparations, such as public memorials and apologies, do not apply to these situations. In the context of this chapter, the main questions to consider are whether the positive obligation to provide reparation also covers conduct by private actors, such as PMSCs, and if so, whether this obligation also pertains to the host state of PMSCs, even when the PMSC is contracted by a third state. Regarding the first question, some assistance can be found in the jurisprudence of the ECtHR and the IACtHR. Indeed, in several cases where the injury suffered by a victim was inflicted by a private actor, but where the responsibility of the state was engaged for failing to take sufficient measures to prevent that injury, the state's obligation to provide reparation was confirmed.[69] Similarly, in *Pueblo*

---

[63] *Factory at Chorzów* (Merits), 1928, PCIJ, Series A, no 17, para 47.
[64] See C McCarthy, 'Reparation for Gross Violations of Human Rights Law and International Humanitarian Law at the International Court of Justice' in C Ferstman et al (eds), *Reparations for Victims of Genocide, War Crimes and Crimes against Humanity* (2009), 283, 285. For an analysis of several aspects of the question of reparations, see also M Du Plessis and S Peté (eds), *Repairing the Past? International Perspectives on Reparations for Gross Human Rights Abuses* (2007); and D Shelton, *Remedies in International Human Rights Law* (2005).
[65] See eg *Bosnia and Herzegovina v Serbia and Montenegro*, ICJ Reports (26 February 2007), Merits, para 460; *DRC v Uganda*, ICJ Reports 2005 (Merits), para 259, cited by McCarthy (n 64 above).
[66] See eg *Velasquez Rodriguez v Honduras*, IACtHR, Series C, no 7 (21 July 1989) (Reparation and Costs), para 26; *Papamichalopoulos and ors v Greece*, 21 EHRR 439 (31 October 1995), Just Satisfaction, para 34.
[67] See eg *Manuel Cepeda-Vargas v Colombia*, IACtHR, Series C, no 213 (26 May 2010), Preliminary Objections, Merits, and Reparations, paras 11–13; *'Las Dos Erres' Massacre v Guatemala* (n 52 above), paras 13–15; *Chitay Nech y otros v Guatemala* (n 52 above), paras 14–16.
[68] HRC, General Comment 31, para 16.
[69] *Kaya v Turkey*, Appl no 22535/93 (28 March 2000), para 138. In this same case the Court had not found it proved beyond reasonable doubt 'that agents of the State carried out, or were otherwise implicated in, the killing of the applicant's brother'. However, in the words of the Court, 'that does not preclude the complaint in relation to Article 2 from being an "arguable" one for the purposes of

Bello Massacre v Colombia, the IACtHR held that the state had violated its positive obligations to prevent serious violations of Articles 4 (Right to Life), 5 (Right to Humane Treatment), 7 (Right to Personal Liberty), and 19 (Rights of the Child).[70] The IACtHR subsequently awarded substantial amounts of financial compensation for pecuniary and non-pecuniary damages to the victims and their next of kin,[71] as well as other forms of reparation. These examples demonstrate that a state that fails to prevent serious human rights violations within its jurisdiction can be required to make reparations, even if the persons responsible for the violations were private actors.

This leads to the second question, whether this obligation also extends to the host state of a PMSC whose personnel becomes involved in such violations. The answer depends on the factual circumstances of each case. A priori, the host state, as the territorial state where a violation occurs, has the positive obligation to prevent such violations, to investigate, to prosecute, and thus also to provide reparations. These obligations are, in principle, only suspended in a situation of military occupation by a foreign state. Also in a situation of effective control exercised by a third state over (part of) the territory, or over a certain area, detention facility, or in certain other situations specified in the case law of the monitoring bodies, these positive obligations pertain to that third state.

In this regard, mention should be made of the *principle of concurrent causation* in customary international law. One commentator notes that: 'In circumstances where several states or a state and one or more private groups are responsible for conduct, which entails the international responsibility of the state, it is well established that any single responsible state is liable to provide full reparation for the damage caused by the wrongful act.'[72] This conclusion was also drawn in the ILC commentary on the Articles of State Responsibility, maintaining that where 'injury is caused by a combination of factors, only one of which is to be ascribed to the responsible state, international practice and the decisions of international tribunals do not support the reduction or attenuation of reparation for concurrent causes'.[73] When applying this principle to the positive obligations of states to provide reparations, this would support the position that even if the home state or the hiring state of a PMSC failed to comply with its obligation to prevent a violation and was therefore under an obligation to make reparation, the latter obligation could also pertain to the host state if it also failed to comply with the obligation to prevent.

Article 13'. Thus, the financial compensation was awarded, irrespective of the question whether the violation was committed by a state agent or a private actor, such as members of a contra-guerrilla group involving confessors or terrorists who 'were targeting individuals perceived to be acting against State interests with the acquiescence, and possible assistance, of members of the security forces' (para 91).

[70] *Pueblo Bello Massacre v Colombia*, IACtHR, Series C, no 140 (31 January 2006), Merits, Reparations, and Costs, para 140: 'The responsibility for the acts of the members of the paramilitary group in this case in particular can be attributed to the State, to the extent that the latter did not adopt diligently the necessary measures to protect the civilian population in function of the circumstances that have been described.'

[71] Ibid, paras 226–59.
[72] McCarthy (n 64 above), 296.
[73] Cited by McCarthy, ibid.

In the UN framework, a set of principles was adopted by the General Assembly in 2005, with a view to providing guidance for the implementation of the positive obligations to make reparations as included in the various human rights instruments.[74] Even though this document has no legally binding force, it does contain some guidance on the obligations of states and non-state actors to provide reparations. Notably, Article 15 of these basic principles states that private actors may also be liable for reparations.[75] This implies that if a PMSC or members of its personnel are found to be accountable for conduct amounting to a gross human rights violation, the PMSC or the employees may also be found liable for reparations to the victim of such violations. The PMSC or the employees concerned should provide reparation to the victims or compensate the state if the latter has already done so. The application of this principle would require the existence of effective mechanisms under domestic law for victims to claim reparations, as well as for the enforcement of reparation judgments.[76]

IV. Conclusion

The analysis in this chapter shows that the positive obligations of states to ensure human rights also pertain to the host states of PMSCs. Indeed, despite the tendency in the case law and views of the human rights courts and monitoring bodies that the jurisdiction of states—and thus their positive human rights obligations—may also apply extraterritorially, the general duty to ensure these rights is primarily conferred upon the state in whose territory violations may occur. Nevertheless, two main factual constraints have been examined, which may render it impossible for the host state to comply with these obligations: in the first place the lack of institutional capacities (including an appropriate legal framework, governmental structures, administrative bodies and judicial capacities), and in the second place a situation of military occupation or other form of effective control exercised by one or more foreign states, mostly in an international or internal armed conflict, which may result in a suspension of the human rights obligations of the host state.

In practice, PMSCs are most often deployed in situations of armed conflict or post-conflict situations, in which one or more third states[77] exercise either effective control or state agent authority over the individuals in the territory of the host state. Consequently, the positive human rights obligations will then generally be considered to pertain to these third states. Nevertheless, it is argued that these limiting

---

[74] Basic Principles and Guidelines on the Right to a Remedy and Reparations for Victims of Gross Violations of International Human Rights Law and Serious Violations of International Humanitarian Law, General Assembly Res 60/147 of 16 December 2005. See T van Boven, 'Victims' Rights to a Remedy and Reparation' in Ferstman et al (eds) (n 64 above), 19–40, 35.
[75] 'In cases where a person, a legal person, or other entity is found liable for reparations to a victim, such party should provide reparation to the victim or compensate the State if the State has already provided reparations to the victim.'
[76] See Basic Principles and Guidelines (n 74 above), Principle 17.
[77] Or possibly an international force under the command of NATO, the UN, or an ESDP operation.

factors vary from one state to the other, and may evolve over time. For example, when a military occupation comes to an end and governmental authority is transferred to a newly elected government, the host state will then regain its primary responsibility for complying with its positive human rights obligations. Moreover, when institutional capacities improve in a post-conflict situation, for example, with external support for institutional development, the limiting factor of lacking such capacities also diminishes. Therefore, host states should be aware of their positive obligations under human rights law and consider in each particular situation the extent to which they are bound and able to comply with these duties.

8

Adjudicating Human Rights Violations Committed by Private Contractors in Conflict Situations before the European Court of Human Rights

Giulia Pinzauti

I. Introduction

Adjudicating human rights violations committed in armed conflict is, broadly speaking, always a difficult task. War is no ordinary situation, and abuses committed in wartime are difficult to monitor and investigate. But the focus here is on the international mechanisms for the protection of human rights established by treaty. Human rights treaties, though still applicable in time of armed conflict,[1] are

---

[1] This contention is now warranted in the light of, inter alia, three pronouncements of the International Court of Justice (ICJ): the advisory opinions concerning the *Legality of the Threat or Use of Nuclear Weapons* and the *Legal Consequences of the Construction of a Wall in the Occupied Palestinian Territory*, and the judgment in the *Case Concerning Armed Activities on the Territory of the Congo (Democratic Republic of the Congo v Uganda)*. In the advisory opinion on *Nuclear Weapons*, the ICJ held that the protection offered by the International Covenant on Civil and Political Right (IICCPR) does not cease in time of war. ICJ, *Nuclear Weapons*, para 25. In the *Wall* opinion the Court extended this determination to human rights treaties in general, subsequently reaffirming this statement in the *Case Concerning Armed Activities on the Territory of the Congo*. ICJ, *Legal Consequences of the Construction of a Wall in the Occupied Palestinian Territory*, Advisory Opinion, 9 July 2004, ICJ Reports 2004, para 106; *Case Concerning Armed Activities on the Territory of the Congo (Democratic Republic of the Congo v Uganda)*, 19 December 2005, ICJ Reports 2005, para 216. The view that human rights law still applies in time of armed conflict has been upheld also by many UN bodies, by the UN International Commission of Inquiry on Darfur in its final Report, and by many distinguished legal scholars. For the practice of UN bodies with respect to the applicability of human rights in time of armed conflict see the detailed analysis by C Droege, 'The Interplay between International Humanitarian Law and International Human Rights Law in Situations of Armed Conflict' (2007) 40 *Israel Law Review* 310; International Commission of Inquiry on Darfur, 'Report of the International Commission of Inquiry on Darfur to the United Nations Secretary-General', 25 January 2005, paras 143–4. On the applicability of human rights in time of armed conflict see eg Y Dinstein, 'Human Rights in Armed Conflict' in T Meron (ed), *Human Rights in International Law: Legal and Policy Issues* (1984); L Doswald-Beck and S Vité, 'International Humanitarian Law and Human Rights Law' (1993) 33 IRRC 94; H-J Heintze, 'On the Relationship between Human Rights Law Protection and International Humanitarian Law', (2004) 86 IRRC 789; R Provost, *International Human Rights and Humanitarian Law* (2002).

not tailored to regulate armed strife, which is the realm of another body of international law, namely international humanitarian law (IHL). Thus, the hurdles for human rights bodies are even more numerous, due to the additional inherent limits of human rights adjudication at the international level. After all, the international bodies created to engender respect for human rights can only establish state responsibility, are subject to jurisdictional constraints, and have limited fact-finding capabilities. Case selection is high and the wait long, given the prerequisite that domestic remedies are exhausted. Gross violations, which might potentially give rise to hundreds of applications, are likely to overburden these organs, without being adequately dealt with. It can thus be argued that the supervisory bodies created to oversee respect for human rights are—at least broadly speaking—ill-suited to dealing with violations perpetrated in conflict situations.[2]

Notwithstanding the limits indicated above, in practice human rights supervisory bodies are currently amongst the few organs that deal with human rights violations perpetrated in time of armed conflict.[3] It can also be contended that, within the limits of the specific *petita* of the cases brought before them, the practice of those bodies is extremely significant. Not only have human rights bodies contributed to the repression of some egregious human rights violations that would have remained otherwise non-adjudicated, but they have also asked states to pay compensation to the victims.

What happens when the subject responsible for the violation of human rights in a situation of armed conflict is not a soldier or a policeman, but an employee of a private military and security company (PMSC)? In other words, how does the tendency towards the outsourcing of military and security functions to private actors affect the supervision and adjudication of human rights violations committed in conflict situations?

This chapter addresses the challenges posed to the supervision and adjudication of human rights violations committed in time of armed conflict by the increasing reliance on PMSCs. Though touching upon the jurisprudence of various international human rights bodies operating at the universal and regional level, this study focuses on the potential role of the European Court of Human Rights (ECtHR). After a brief introductory part on the ECtHR's role in overseeing respect for human rights in time of armed conflict (section II), it provides an overview of the relevant

---

[2] N Lubell, 'Challenges in Applying Human Rights Law to Armed Conflict' (2005) 87 IRRC 737.
[3] The practice of national courts is outside the scope of the present chapter, which is only intended to deal with supervision and adjudication of human rights violations at the *international* level. The specific protection systems existing in the field of IHL are few in number and have proven to be largely ineffective in practice. One of the distinguishing features of the human rights regime in comparison with IHL is the existence of individual complaints procedures at the international level for victims of alleged violations of human rights. By and large, human rights machinery is a lot more developed than the one in place under IHL. The unavailability of remedies under IHL, on the one hand, and the fairly developed system of guarantees existing under the human rights regime at the universal and regional level, on the other, may well have prompted victims to turn to human rights monitoring bodies. One can also mention non-governmental organizations (NGOs). The latter, however, can only *report* violations, but do not have adjudicatory powers of their own.

principles applicable in adjudicating instances of serious misconduct by PMSCs (section III). Then it addresses the main challenges the ECtHR will have to face if ever called upon to rule on the infringement of the ECHR by PMSCs acting in a situation of armed conflict (section IV).

The issue is novel. To the best of this author's knowledge, there is no instance so far where the responsibility of a state for acts of PMSCs has been affirmed or even invoked before the ECtHR. Setting the legal framework, however, is not a mere academic exercise. It is important, first, to reaffirm the idea that states have certain human rights obligations even when they delegate the exercise of sensitive functions to PMSCs, or host them on their territory. Secondly, if the current trend towards the outsourcing of military functions to PMSCs continues in the future, there is a possibility that the ECtHR might be called upon to adjudicate cases involving PMSC activities. Therefore, it is appropriate to be aware of the challenges the Court will eventually have to face well ahead of time.

II. The ECtHR's Role in Overseeing Respect for Human Rights in Situations of Armed Conflict

The ECtHR has dealt with cases arising out of an armed conflict in three situations: the military occupation of Northern Cyprus by Turkish troops, the emergency situation in South-East Turkey, and the armed conflict in Chechnya.[4] It declined to exercise jurisdiction over the complaint brought by the victims of the NATO bombing over the Belgrade TV station in 1999, as well as in post-conflict situations where the UN was involved as administering authority of the *locus commissi delicti*.[5] The Court will again be called upon to pronounce upon human rights violation in conflict situations by the interstate application brought by Georgia against Russia (as regards Russia's intervention in South Ossetia and Abkhazia), and in relation to torture and killings allegedly committed by British troops during the military occupation of Iraq.[6]

The Court's extensive practice speaks for itself as regards the significance of the Court's role in deciding on human rights violations perpetrated in both international and non-international armed conflicts. A unique feature of the ECtHR's case law, compared with that of other human rights adjudicatory bodies,[7] is that the

---

[4] For an overview of the ECtHR's case law see eg W Abresch, 'A Human Rights Law of Internal Armed Conflict: The European Court of Human Rights in Chechnya' (2005) 16 EJIL 741.
[5] *Bankovic and ors v Belgium and ors* (dec), Appl no 52207/99, Reports 2001–XII, 12 December 2001; *Behrami and Behrami v France and Saramati v France, Germany and Norway* (dec), Appl nos 71412/01, 78166/01, 2 May 2007, <http://www.echr.coe.int>, accessed on 18 June 2010.
[6] *Georgia v The Russian Federation*, Appl no 38263/08; *Al-Skeini and ors v UK*, Appl no 55721/07.
[7] Both the Inter-American Commission and Court of Human Rights (respectively, IAComHR and IACtHR) have made reference to IHL in their case law, although to a different extent. In its earlier case law the IAComHR held that it was competent to directly apply IHL. However, the IACtHR in its decision in the preliminary objections of the *Las Palmeras* case rejected that attitude, holding that human rights monitoring bodies are only competent on human rights issues. However, in its later case law, the IACtHR has consistently referred to the relevant rules and principles of IHL for interpretative

Court has made very little reference to the rules and principles of IHL. So far it has always applied legal standards that, although resembling those of humanitarian law, were derived solely from human rights norms (and particularly from Article 2 on the right to life), even when dealing with technical questions such as military objectives, precautionary measures in attack and collateral damage. This fact has not precluded the Court from effectively adjudicating the claim, by stretching the reach of the human rights provisions so as to cover exceptional situations of armed violence. However, in this author's view, the ECtHR would be empowered to (and actually should) make reference to IHL as an aid in interpretation. It should also apply the relevant IHL provisions, though only incidentally, whenever the more general human right norm at stake does not contain the necessary standards to adjudicate the matter brought before the court.[8] This application of IHL could be relevant also in adjudicating cases dealing with PMSCs' conduct.

III. Adjudicating Human Rights Violations Committed by Private Contractors: The Relevant Principles

I shall now briefly recall the general principles according to which a violation of human rights committed by private contractors can trigger the responsibility of the state, be it the home state, the hiring state, or the host state, depending on the circumstances of the case. In a nutshell, there are two ways in which human rights violations committed by private parties, such as the employees of PMSCs, engage the responsibility of the state: (i) when the violation can be attributed to the state; (ii) when the state fails to discharge its positive human rights obligations to prevent and redress the violation, even if the latter was perpetrated by private parties and was not attributable to the state.

A. Violative Conduct Attributable to the State

The grounds for attributing to the state acts of private parties under public international law are codified in the 2001 International Law Commission (ILC) Draft Articles on the Responsibility of States for Internationally Wrongful Acts.[9] As

---

purposes. See L Moir, 'Law and the Inter-American Human Rights System' (2003) 25 Human Rights Quarterly 182. The African Commission on Human and Peoples' Rights has also made reference to IHL in the inter-state case of *Democratic Republic of the Congo v Burundi, Rwanda, and Uganda*, Comm no 227/99, 2003, 2004 AHRLR, 19.

[8] G Pinzauti, 'The European Court of Human Rights' Incidental Application of International Criminal Law and Humanitarian Law: A Critical Discussion of *Kononov v Latvia*' (2008) 6 JICJ 1043, esp 1059 ff.

[9] For a commentary on those Articles and how they apply to the acts of private contractors see Ch 5 by Francioni in this volume, at sections IV–VI; M Spinedi, 'Private contractors: responsabilité internationale des entreprises ou attribution à l'Etat de la conduite des personnes privées?' (2005) 7 *International Law Forum du Droit International* 273.

has already been shown,[10] wrongdoings committed by PMSCs become acts of the state only under strict circumstances, namely if the contractors:

1. Act as state organs proper (Article 4 ILC Draft Articles), which is only the case if they are formally incorporated into the armed forces of the state.
2. Are empowered by the law of the state to exercise 'elements of governmental authority' (Article 5). The contours of this notion are blurred. An interesting view has been put forward, according to which PMSCs can be said to exercise elements of governmental authority when they have been contracted by the state to carry out: (i) combat functions; (ii) arrests and management of detention facilities; (iii) interrogations; (iv) intelligence gathering; (v) law-enforcement functions. In addition, a human rights violation can only be attributable to the state if it is perpetrated by the company's employees in the exercise of the above functions.[11] By and large, it is exactly in the exercise of those kinds of functions (rather than cleaning or cooking) that the commission of human rights violations is more likely to occur.
3. Act on the instructions, or under the direction or control of the state (Article 8). The ECtHR in its case law, consistent with the practice of other human rights supervisory bodies, has adopted a broader, less formalistic approach. The test applied by the Court is whether the acts of private individuals that breach the Convention were committed with the acquiescence or connivance of state authorities.[12]

B. Breach of the State's Positive Obligations

Independent of whether the conduct giving rise to human rights violations is attributable to the state, the home state, the hiring state, and the host state may incur responsibility for failure to discharge their positive human rights obligations because of lack of due diligence to prevent the violation or to respond to it. This holds true even when the violations perpetrated by private contractors qualify as purely private acts, and notwithstanding the fact that human rights treaties are only addressed to the contracting states and do not have direct horizontal effects.[13]

The human rights most relevant to PMSCs' activity are the right to life (Article 2 ECHR) and the right not to be subjected to torture and inhuman or degrading treatment or punishment (Article 3 ECHR). A survey of the various studies on the positive obligations of the states that are involved in the deployment of a PMSC[14] shows that the latter are all bound to respect, protect, and ensure respect for those

---

[10] See the contribution by Francioni (n 9 above), sections IV–VI.
[11] Francioni (n 9 above), section V.
[12] *Solomou and ors v Turkey*, Appl no 36832/97, 24 June 2008, para 46; *Isaak v Turkey*, Appl no 44587/98, 24 September 2008 (generally). Unless otherwise specified, the ECtHR's judgments quoted herein are available online on the Court's website at <http://www.echr.coe.int>, accessed on 15 August 2010.
[13] Contra see generally A Clapham, *Human Rights Obligations of Non-State Actors* (2006).
[14] See Francioni (n 9 above); Ch 6 by Hoppe and Ch 7 by Bakker in this volume.

rights. Though these obligations have been couched in slightly different terms by the various human rights monitoring bodies concerned, it can be argued that the following obligations (at a minimum) apply to the host state, the home state, and the contracting state.

First, the obligation to *prevent* human rights violations, which entails the obligation to enact adequate legislation to deter the commission of abuses and to implement an effective regulatory and monitoring system. When particularly important rights such as the right to life and physical integrity are at stake, the relevant states also have the obligation to take operational measures to protect individuals from violations, even when the latter are perpetrated by private parties. The responsibility of the state is triggered when the state authorities (i) knew or ought to have known of a real and immediate risk that a violation be committed and (ii) failed to take measures within their power to avoid that risk.[15]

Secondly, with regard to the obligation to *investigate, prosecute, and punish* those responsible for the violation, and to ensure the victims adequate compensation, it should be emphasized that the failure to comply with the above obligations constitutes a *violation* of the ECHR per se, even though the state at issue may not be directly responsible for the physical commission of the abuse.

IV. The Challenges

Let us now turn to the hurdles that the ECtHR admittedly would encounter in adjudicating human rights violations committed by private contractors.

A. Jurisdiction

Armed conflicts where PMSCs are deployed often occur in unstable countries outside Europe's borders. One of the reasons that may prompt a government to outsource certain tasks to private military contractors is exactly because they represent a readily available force that can be deployed outside the national territory on the basis of a contract (an act of a purely commercial nature), bypassing many of the bureaucratic steps that would normally be required if members of the state's armed forces were sent on a mission. This outsourcing of competences should not permit states to escape their human rights obligations. However, when trying to hold states accountable for the acts carried out by PMSCs on foreign territory, one is faced with the problem of jurisdiction.

---

[15] ECtHR, *Osman v UK*, Appl no 23452/94, Reports 1998-VIII, 28 October 1998. The approach adopted by the ECtHR in its case law is more restrictive than the parallel approach followed by the IACtHR. For a state to be held accountable of its failure to protect the right to life, it is necessary that the individual whose life is in danger be an identified person. In other words, there is no duty to protect the population at large. Conversely, it is not necessary that the same requirement be fulfilled with respect to the person posing the threat (it needs not be an identified individual). In the inter-American human rights system, the duty to prevent is more broadly conceived. See I Ziemele, 'Human Rights Violations by Private Persons and Entities: The Case-law of International Human Rights Courts and Monitoring Bodies', EUI AEL 2009/8, Priv-War Project, 15.

As is well known, the reach of human rights obligations is not unlimited. States parties to human rights treaties are bound to respect and ensure respect for those obligations to all individuals subject to their jurisdiction.[16] Jurisdiction is a prerequisite for the state's obligations (and, eventually, responsibility) under human rights conventions. It is a common feature of universal and regional human rights treaties that the sphere of jurisdiction is not limited to the state's national territory. Acts (or omissions) carried out by state agents outside the state's own territory, or that produce effects therein, may amount to the exercise of jurisdiction by the relevant state.

The alleged commission of human rights abuses by PMSCs outside the state's national territory raises interesting and complex legal problems. Before turning to those questions, I shall first point out that in certain circumstances jurisdiction is *not* an issue. For instance, the necessity of a jurisdictional link between the state and human rights violations committed extraterritorially does not arise with respect to the responsibility of the home state. On the one hand, the obligations of the home state, being the state where the company is based, are confined to regulating the export of military and security services in accordance with human rights standards; on the other hand, the home state also has the obligation to react to the commission of abuses by providing judicial remedies to the victims. In this regard the home state has, or at least should have, full control and jurisdiction over the PMSCs based in its territory. Thus, there is no need to prove that the state had control over the extraterritorial conduct of the PMSC. In plain language, the problem of extraterritoriality does not arise.[17] Similarly, that problem of extraterritorial jurisdiction does not crop up with regard to the obligations of the host state when that state is a party to the ECHR.

Where the problem of extraterritoriality does arise is with respect to the responsibility of the hiring state, whenever the services contracted out are performed outside its national territory. As we shall see, in the framework of the ECHR the question of jurisdiction becomes particularly thorny in those instances where the PMSCs are deployed in the territory of third states that are not parties to the ECHR. Many issues are still unsettled, and the ECtHR will have a chance of clarifying them in its future case law. Part of the impact of the ECtHR in ensuring accountability of hiring states for human rights violations committed by private contractors will depend on how the Court interprets the notion of jurisdiction.

1. Legal Standard for the Extraterritorial Application of the ECHR

In the ECtHR's jurisprudence, the test for determining whether acts performed by the contracting states outside their territory entail the extraterritorial applicability of the Convention has focused on whether the respondent state exercised 'authority and/or effective control' over the victims of the violation, or 'effective control' over the (foreign) territory where the violation allegedly took place. The court has also

---

[16] See Art 1 ECHR.
[17] Francioni (n 9 above), section VII.

repeatedly stressed the exceptional character of the exercise of extraterritorial jurisdiction by the contracting states.[18]

Moreover the Court in *Banković* seemed to place an additional limitation on the notion of jurisdiction for the purpose of Article 1 ECHR. In a famous obiter dictum it stated that the ECHR is a multilateral treaty operating 'in the legal space (*espace juridique*) of the Contracting States';[19] as such, the Convention does not apply to states that do not fall within this legal space, even with respect to the conduct of the contracting states. In this latter respect, the Court's jurisprudence is not entirely consistent. In subsequent case law, as we shall see, the ECtHR recognized the extraterritorial application of the ECHR in the territory of third states, though only in exceptional circumstances.

(a) **Authority and/or effective control test**
While the ECtHR placed emphasis on the element of *territorial control* as one of the main criteria for establishing the extraterritorial application of the ECHR,[20] other human rights monitoring bodies have recognized broader scope for the extraterritorial application of human rights obligations. Neither the American Declaration of the Rights and Duties of Man and the African Charter on Human and Peoples' Rights contain a jurisdictional provision. In the jurisprudence of the Human Rights Committee (HRC) and the IAComHR the relevant criterion for establishing the extraterritorial reach of the relevant treaties is 'authority and control',[21] or 'power or effective control'[22] over the *person* concerned, rather than the territory where the alleged violation is committed.[23]

In order to establish whether an individual is subject to the state's control, authority, or power (and hence, jurisdiction), international human rights bodies have looked at whether the state had the *direct ability to affect the individual's right* alleged to have been violated. In other words, an individual present in the territory of a foreign state may come within the jurisdiction of the respondent state through the acts of the latter state's agents, even when the respondent does not hold effective control over the territory. The criterion of the 'ability to affect' the enjoyment of a human right in order to establish a state's extraterritorial jurisdiction may seem

---

[18] *Banković* (n 5 above), para 71.
[19] Ibid, para 80.
[20] Ibid, para 71.
[21] IAComHR: *Salas and ors v The United States*, Case no 10.573, Report no 31/93, 14 October 1993; *Coard and ors v The United States*, Case no 10.951, Report no 109/99, 29 September 1999, para 37; *Armando Alejandro Jr and ors v Cuba* (also known as the '*Brothers to the Rescue*' case), Case no 11.589, Report no 86/99, 29 September 1999, para 23; *Victor Saldaño v Argentina*, Report no 38/99, 11 March 1999, para 19.
[22] HRC, General Comment no 31, Applicability of the ICCPR in time of war, CCPR/C/21/rev1/Add13, para 10.
[23] D Cassel, 'Extraterritorial Application of Inter-American Human Rights Instruments' in F Coomans and MT Kamminga (eds), *Extraterritorial Application of Human Rights Treaties* (2004) 175, 176–8; see also 'Written Comments by the Bar Human Rights Committee, the European Human Rights Advocacy Centre, Human Rights Watch, Interights, the International Federation for Human Rights' in *Al-Skeini* (n 6 above), para 12 ff.

overly broad. As a distinguished commentator pointed out, the applicability of that criterion could be restricted to those instances where it is possible to discern a *direct and immediate link* between the extraterritorial conduct of the state and the violation of the human rights of the individual or individuals concerned.[24] A typical example is the deprivation of the right to life. If the victim died or was seriously injured as a result of the direct actions of the agents of the state, even if in a territory that was not under the state's effective control, the individual can still be said to have been subject to the state's authority and control. Therefore, he was within the state's jurisdiction.

Significantly, the ECtHR applied this principle in a recent spate of decisions concerning events in Northern Cyprus. It held that Turkey was responsible for violating Article 2 ECHR (on the right to life) because of the shooting of several Greek-Cypriot individuals by Turkish agents in the UN buffer zone that divides the Greek-Cypriot side from the Turkish-Cypriot side of the island.[25] Notwithstanding the fact that Turkey exercised no control over the buffer zone (under UN control), the Court found that the victims in the relevant cases came under the authority and/or effective control (and therefore within the jurisdiction) of the respondent state as a result of the acts of the Turkish soldiers and/or officials and those of the 'Turkish Republic of Northern Cyprus'.[26] In addition, in a seminal decision as to admissibility in *Al-Saadoon and Mufdhi v UK* (on the arrest and detention of two Iraqi nationals by UK forces in Iraq), the Court found it established that the applicants fell within the jurisdiction of the respondent state from the moment of their arrest (in 2003, when the United Kingdom was an occupying power in Iraq) until 31 December 2008, when they were transferred to the Iraqi authorities. However, at the latter point in time the United Kingdom no longer exercised effective territorial control over Iraq (Iraqi sovereignty was restored with the end of the military occupation in June 2004). Nevertheless, the Court held that UK jurisdiction existed on the strength of the 'total and exclusive *de facto*, and subsequently also *de jure*, control exercised by the United Kingdom authorities over the premises in question' where the applicants were kept in detention.[27]

The determination of whether the state exercises control, authority, or power over the persons concerned has to be made on the facts of the case. There are, however, certain factual circumstances that admittedly should give rise to a *presumption of state jurisdiction*. These include arrest and detention effected by state organs on foreign territory and military occupation of a territory. In the practice of the ECHR organs, the HRC, and the IAComHR, those circumstances have always

---

[24] RA Lawson, 'Life after Bankovic: On the Extraterritorial Application of the European Convention on Human Rights' in Coomans and Kamminga (n 23 above), 83.

[25] In an attempt to quell a Greek-Cypriot demonstration that developed into a riot, Turkish forces opened fire on the crowd, killing or seriously injuring several unarmed individuals. See *Andreou v Turkey*, Appl no 45653/99, 27 October 2009; *Isaak v Turkey* (n 12 above); *Solomou v Turkey* (n 12 above).

[26] *Solomou v Turkey* (n 12 above), para 51.

[27] *Al-Saadoon and Mufdhi v UK* (dec), Appl no 61498/08, 30 June 2009, para 88.

been found to give rise to jurisdiction.[28] Both situations may be relevant to the operation of PMSCs.

It is further submitted that the extent to which a state must secure extraterritorially the rights set forth in the ECHR could depend on the extent of its control, authority, or power over the individual concerned, in the circumstances of the case.[29] From a practical point of view, the Court could apply the standard of review adopted as regards positive obligations to define, mutatis mutandis, the extent to which contracting parties are bound to secure the enjoyment of human rights when they act in an extraterritorial setting. The ECtHR has interpreted the scope of positive human rights obligations so as not to impose on states parties an impossible or disproportionate burden: they are only required to take the measures within their powers and that, judged reasonably, might have been expected to avoid the occurrence of a given violation of the Convention. Self-evidently, if we apply a similar standard to the extraterritorial conduct of a state party, the more effective the control the state exercises over the person or the territory, the broader the range of Convention's rights it is required to vouchsafe for the individuals concerned. It would be burdensome to require state agents who effect an arrest abroad to guarantee the right to private and family life or freedom of assembly to the individual who is being deprived of his liberty. However, those state agents acting abroad must undoubtedly treat the captured individual who is under their physical control according to Articles 2 and 3 ECHR. By the same token, when agents of the state are involved in a military operation on the territory of another state, even though effective control over the territory or physical control over the individuals concerned can be lacking, the intervening state can be said to exercise a sufficient degree of control over the lives of the inhabitants to be bound to respect their right to life. To use Cassel's words, 'where a State can kill a person outside its territory, it exercises sufficient control over that person to be held accountable for violating his right to life'.[30] The ECtHR clearly rejected this argument in *Banković*, where it had been put forward by the applicants. However, the Court's other case law seems to provide some support for that proposition, contrary to what was held in *Banković*. There are circumstances (such as the deprivation of liberty or the use of deadly force) in which the Court seems ready to accept that the responsibility of the state

---

[28] For the cases concerning arrest and detention see eg EComHR: *Illich Sanchez Ramirez v France* (dec), Appl no 28789/95, 24 June 1996; *Freda v Italy* (dec), Appl no 8916/80, 7 October 1980, DR 21, 250. ECtHR: *Al-Saadoon and Mufdhi* (n 27 above); *Öcalan v Turkey*, Appl no 46221/99, 12 March 2003. HRC: *Lopez Burgos v Uruguay*, Comm no R 12/52, 6 June 1979 (on the abduction of the applicant by Uruguayan agents in Argentina, that at the relevant time was not a party to the ICCPR); and *Lilian Celiberti de Casariego v Uruguay*, Comm no 56/1979, 29 July 1971 (on the abduction of the applicant by Uruguayan agents in Brazil, that at the relevant time was not a party to the ICCPR). IAComHR: *Coard v The United States* (n 21 above). For the case law dealing with military occupation see AComHPR, *DRC v Burundi, Rwanda and Uganda* (n 7 above); ECtHR: *Loizidou v Turkey*, Appl no 15318/89, Reports 1996-VI, 18 December 1996; *Cyprus v Turkey*, Appl no 25781/94, Reports of Judgments and Decisions 2001-IV, 10 May 2001; *Ilaşcu and ors v Moldova and Russia*, Appl no 48787/99, Reports 2004-VII, 8 July 2004. See also ICJ, *DRC v Uganda* (n 7 above); *Legal consequences of the Construction of a Wall in the Occupied Palestinian Territory* (n 7 above).

[29] Lawson (n 24 above), 105.

[30] Cassel (n 23 above), 177.

could be engaged with respect to securing the *specific* right or rights affected by the impugned acts, even without having to ensure the whole range of the Convention's rights.[31] This argument, amongst others, was run by the third-party interveners in the proceedings in *Al-Skeini*. As the case is currently pending before the Grand Chamber, the latter will have a chance to clarify the matter.[32]

(b) **The notion of** *espace juridique*
As regards the Court's holding in *Banković* that the ECHR is an essentially regional treaty that applies primarily within the European legal space, it is submitted that it would be high time for the Court to reconsider that statement. The reasons are as follows.

First, as a matter of judicial policy, the ECtHR should not allow any leeway to states parties to perpetrate with impunity on foreign territory violations they could not perpetrate on their own territory. The guarantor of human rights in the Council of Europe should avoid unconscionable double standards in overseeing respect for those rights.

Secondly, the jurisprudence of other human rights monitoring bodies does not support the existence of the *espace juridique* limitation. Suffice it to mention that the IAComHR in *Brothers to the Rescue* considered that the shooting down by the Cuban air force of two private planes flying in international air space brought the victims within Cuba's jurisdiction.[33] Similarly, the HRC has applied the ICCPR against state parties for acts committed by their agents on the territory of states that at the relevant time were not parties to the Covenant.[34]

Thirdly, the ECtHR has established the principle that in certain circumstances, the scope of the Convention may extend beyond the regional space of the contracting parties. The Convention has been considered applicable in territories outside the Council of Europe—for example, in Iraq,[35] Kenya,[36] Sudan,[37] Costa

---

[31] Eg in *Cyprus v Turkey* (n 28 above), para 77, the ECtHR held that where a state has effective overall control of an area outside its borders, it may be required to secure the entire range of the Convention's rights. This proposition seems to suggest that, lacking such overall control over the foreign territory, the state is *not* required to guarantee the entire range of the Convention's rights. However, the respondent may still be required to secure at least *some* of the rights set forth in the ECHR. As already mentioned, there are cases in which the respondent state has been found responsible of violating one or more Convention's rights in circumstances where (i) the impugned acts carried out by its agents abroad brought the individual concerned under the authority and/or effective control, and therefore within the jurisdiction, of the respondent state; (ii) the respondent state did not have effective control of the area where the violation occurred (and thus was not bound to ensure the entire range of the Convention rights).

[32] Written Comments by the Bar Human Rights Committee, the European Human Rights Advocacy Centre, Human Rights Watch, Interights, the International Federation for Human Rights' (n 23 above), para 15.

[33] *Brothers to the Rescue* case (n 21 above), para 23.

[34] *Lopez Burgos* (n 28 above); *Lilian Celiberti de Casariego* (n 28 above).

[35] *Al-Saadoon and Mufdhi* (n 27 above); *Issa and ors v Turkey*, Appl no 31821/96, 16 November 2004.

[36] *Öcalan* (n 28 above). However, consent by the territorial state is required.

[37] Eg EComHR *Illich Sanchez Ramirez* (n 28 above), concerning apprehension of the applicant by French authorities in Sudan.

Rica,[38] in a UN neutral buffer zone,[39] and in international waters.[40] Particularly significant is the recent decision in *Al-Saadoon and Mufdhi v UK*, where the Court found a violation of Articles 3, 13, and 34 ECHR for the applicants' transfer from two British-run detention facilities to Iraqi authorities (where they faced the risk of being subjected to the death penalty) by UK forces who had those individuals in their physical custody.[41] As a statement of principle (on the facts of the case the application was declared inadmissible) the Court's decision in *Pad v Turkey* is also noteworthy. The Court allowed the possibility of applying the Convention in Iran on the ground that:

> a State may be held accountable for violations of the Convention rights and freedoms of persons who are in the territory of another State which does not necessarily fall within the legal space of the Contracting States, but who are found to be under the former State's authority and control through its agents operating—whether lawfully or unlawfully—in the latter State.[42]

Admittedly, the above statement stands in sharp contrast with *Banković*. Also in *Behrami and Saramati* the Court did not resort to the notion of *espace juridique* to exclude the applicability of the Convention.[43] It could easily have done so because at the relevant time Serbia was not a party to the ECHR. However, it resorted to other grounds (and particularly to the fact that the respondents did not come within the Convention's scope *ratione personae*) to declare the applications inadmissible.

It would be tempting to say that the ECtHR's recent practice shows a departure from *Banković*. However, it is undeniable that the factual circumstances giving rise to the *Banković* case and the decisions mentioned above are different. *Banković* concerned an air strike in the territory of a sovereign country. It is not the same thing to state that the ECHR applies in a neutral zone, or in international waters, where no one is sovereign. Moreover, where the Court accepted the applicability of the ECHR on the territory of third states, it was either (i) a decision in principle (because the Court rejected the application on other grounds, or otherwise did not establish the responsibility of the respondent state);[44] (ii) a law-enforcement operation where the individual was in the physical control of agents of the

---

[38] *Freda* (n 28 above), concerning apprehension by Italian police in Costa Rica.
[39] See cases referred to in n 25 above.
[40] *Xhavara and ors v Italy and Albania* (dec), Appl no 39473/98, 11 January 2001, concerning the sinking in international waters of a ship carrying irregular Albanian immigrants by an Italian naval ship. The application was declared inadmissible for failure to exhaust domestic remedies. See also *Women on Waves and ors v Portugal*, Appl no 31276/05, 3 February 2009, concerning the ban on a ship chartered by the Women on Waves Foundation from approaching Portuguese territorial waters and entering Portugal.
[41] *Al-Saadoon and Mufdhi v UK*, Appl no 61498/08, 2 March 2010.
[42] *Pad and ors v Turkey* (dec), Appl no 60167/00, 28 June 2007, para 53.
[43] *Behrami and Saramati* (n 5 above). For a commentary on the case see M Sossai, 'Accesso alla Corte Europea dei Diritti Dell'uomo per Violazioni Compiute dalle Forze Armate Degli Stati Contraenti All'estero' in F Francioni et al (eds), *Accesso alla Giustizia Dell'individuo nel Diritto Internazionale e dell'Unione Europea* (2008) 197, 215.
[44] *Issa* (n 35 above); *Pad* (n 42 above).

state;[45] or (iii) a minor military operation, or the use of force by state agents, as opposed to a fully fledged armed conflict.[46] Against this background, *Al-Saadoon* is so far an isolated, though extremely significant, exception. In this latter case the Court did find a violation of the ECHR for acts committed by British forces in Iraq during the military occupation of the country and later on, when those forces were involved in the administration of detention facilities in the territory of a sovereign Iraqi state. However, this case may still be distinguished from *Banković* in that British forces were present on the ground, and held the applicants in their physical custody. Therefore, they clearly exercised authority and control over the individuals concerned.

The decisive test for the extraterritorial applicability of the ECHR will probably be the forthcoming decision in *Al-Skeini v UK*. Here, the Court is faced not only with alleged violations committed against individuals under the authority or control of agents of the respondent state (eg during detention), but also with the shooting of Iraqi nationals in the course of patrol operations by UK troops. In this case the question whether the UK exercised 'authority and control' over those individuals is more controversial. It will be interesting to see whether the Grand Chamber is ready to adopt a broad notion of authority and control that also encompasses the shooting of persons who were not in the immediate physical control of agents of the state.

2. Extraterritorial Jurisdiction and Acts of Private Parties

The cases discussed so far on the extraterritorial applicability of human rights treaties have one feature in common: the extraterritorial act giving rise to the infringement of human rights (and triggering the jurisdiction of the state) is carried out by *agents of the respondent state*. It is by virtue of the authority or control exercised by those state agents over the individuals concerned that the latter fall within the jurisdiction of the state. This renders the ECtHR competent to adjudicate the alleged violation.

How does the fact that the violation of human rights stems from an act carried out by PMSC personnel affect the extraterritorial applicability of the ECHR? As we have already seen, private military contractors can act as de jure or de facto agents of the state under public international law. However, this occurs only under the strict criteria defined in Articles 4, 5, and 8 ILC Draft Articles on state responsibility.[47] Does that mean that in all other instances (ie when the contractors do not qualify as agents of the state) the extraterritorial commission of human rights violations by PMSC personnel is outside the jurisdiction of the state, and thus of the ECtHR? The example of the Italian government hiring a PMSC based in the United Kingdom for the purpose of providing security to its agents in Afghanistan might help clarify this point. The function of guarding people and property in principle

---

[45] *Illich Sanchez Ramirez*, *Öcalan*, and *Freda* (n 28 above).
[46] *Issa* (n 35 above).
[47] See section III.A above.

does not entail the exercise of public authority, as the same PMSC could just as well be contracted by a private company for the provision of the same services. Let us also assume that one day the PMSC's employees on a government contract, during the performance of the contract, shoot on a crowd killing or injuring several civilians. Does the ECHR apply to those facts? That question also raises the problem of access to the Court. In other words, could the victims of that shooting bring a claim before the ECtHR alleging the responsibility of Italy?[48]

Whether the Court would be *willing* to entertain the claim is a different question. Let us now deal with the theoretical question of whether it would have jurisdiction to do so. In this author's view, the answer should be in the affirmative, for two reasons.

First, adopting a broad interpretation of the notion of 'state agents' that also encompasses PMSC personnel carrying out tasks entrusted by the state (even though not entailing the exercise of governmental authority *stricto sensu*),[49] the victims of the shooting would fall within Italy's extraterritorial jurisdiction. Indeed, the use of deadly force can be said to have placed the civilian victims under the power or authority of the contractors. If the latter can be considered 'state agents', then Italy's extraterritorial jurisdiction would be triggered (of course, this holds true only in the assumption that the Court rethinks its *Banković* decision). It is submitted that human rights monitoring bodies could adopt a broader standard for the attribution of acts of private contractors to the state (see below).

Secondly, let us not forget that the jurisdiction of the contracting states under Article 1 ECHR, as interpreted by the Strasbourg organs, extends to the application of *positive* human rights obligations. These obligations extend to the conduct of private parties. Adopting a functional notion of jurisdiction,[50] it can be argued that the reach of the state's positive obligations also extends extraterritorially, ie to the conduct of private parties abroad, when certain conditions are met. The rules on treaty interpretation as set out in the Vienna Convention on the law of treaties require interpreting Article 1 ECHR in light of the object and purpose of the treaty. The ECHR is an instrument for the protection of human rights. The Convention's special character as a human rights treaty, together with the need to interpret and apply it so as to render the human rights guarantees practical and effective, imply that the meaning attributed to the notion of jurisdiction cannot be restrictive. Extraterritorial jurisdiction for the purpose of applying the state's negative obligations requires authority and/or effective control over the victims of the violation, or effective control over territory. In addition, the violation has to be perpetrated by, or with the acquiescence of, agents of the state. Conversely, it seems reasonable to impute to a state its positive obligations with respect to extraterritorial violations

---

[48] On the basis of what has been already said, those applicants could bring a claim against the PMSC's home state (the United Kingdom), if that state allegedly infringed its positive human rights obligations to take all the measures in its power to prevent or react to the violation.
[49] See section IV.B below.
[50] P De Sena, *La Nozione di Giurisdizione Statale nei Trattati sui Diritti Dell'uomo* (2002), 125 ff.

Adjudicating Human Rights Violations Committed by Private Contractors 163

whenever it has the power and ability to prevent or redress the commission of the violation, independent of whether (i) it has effective control over the territory, and (ii) the violation was carried out by state agents or private parties.[51]

To sum up, in cases where PMSCs contracted by a state[52] commit human rights violations abroad, the question whether the extraterritorial act places the victims within the jurisdiction of the hiring state depends on: (i) how we interpret the rules of attribution, and particularly if we can consider the contractors as 'state agents'; and (ii) the scope of the state's *positive* human rights obligations to ensure respect for the human rights set forth in the Convention. We will address both issues in the next section.

B. Issues of Responsibility: Attribution to the State and Positive Human Rights Obligations

Shifting from the issue of jurisdiction to the actual attribution of responsibility to the state for acts of private contractors, the two major challenges seem to be (i) the attribution of the contractors' conduct to the state; (ii) the precise definition of the state's positive obligations, and the difficulty in applying them in practice.

1. Broadening the Rules on Attribution

As we have already mentioned, the criteria for attributing the conduct of private persons to the state as set out in the ILC Draft Articles are very restrictive. Only exceptionally are PMSC personnel formally incorporated into the armed forces of the state. The functional criterion based on the exercise of 'elements of governmental authority' covers a broad variety of services amongst those provided by PMSCs, and particularly the provision of coercive services. However, it admittedly leaves out the provision of other important services, such as security services (ie the guarding of property or personnel, escorting of convoys, and so on). Especially if the contractors carry weapons, even though only for defensive purposes, they are in a position to commit abuses. These wrongdoings, however, would not be attributable to the state. In addition, the requirement of control or direction under Article 8 is difficult to prove.

Human rights monitoring bodies in their jurisprudence have applied more lenient criteria for attributing to the state human rights violations carried out by private parties. The IACtHR, in particular, developed a very far-reaching concept of attribution, whereby the mere tolerance of infringements committed by private

---

[51] This reading of the reach of the state's positive obligations is consistent with the law as articulated by the ECtHR in *Ilaşcu*. One of the principles that can be drawn from the judgment is that jurisdiction for the purpose of establishing the reach of the state's positive obligations is not inextricably linked to effective territorial control. See *Ilaşcu* (n 28 above), paras 330–3. However, in that case it would seem that the reach of positive obligations is limited to the state's own territory, and does not extend to the territory of other states. See Nigro, 'Giurisdizione e Obblighi Positivi degli Stati Parti della Convenzione Europea dei Diritti Dell'uomo: Il Caso *Ilascu*', (2005) 88 Rivista di diritto internazionale 413, 434–5.
[52] On the scenarios where PMCs are contracted by other non-state actors see below, section IV.C below.

parties is enough to trigger the responsibility of the state.[53] Similarly, the test applied by the ECtHR is whether the acts of private individuals that breach the Convention were committed with the acquiescence or connivance of authorities of the state.[54] In addition, in cases where a state exercises overall control over the territory of another state, the Court imputed to the former not only the acts carried out by its agents, but also the acts of the local administration. The rationale of attributing to the occupying state the acts of the local administration is that it was in place thanks to that state's military or other (political and economic) support.[55]

In line with this approach, it is submitted that human rights supervisory bodies, including the ECtHR, could adopt a broad notion of 'state agents' for the purpose of attributing the contractors' conduct to the hiring state. Admittedly, this could be done in two ways (subject, of course, to the specificities of each case).

First, the ECtHR could adopt an expansive interpretation of the 'public' character of the nature and functions that PMSCs contracted by a state perform while acting on behalf of that state in a context of armed conflict. In the ECtHR's jurisprudence, the criteria taken into account to distinguish between governmental and non-governmental organizations are as follows: (i) the entity's legal status under national legislation, and the rights attached thereto; (ii) the nature of the activities it carries out; (iii) the context in which such activities are performed; and (iv) the entity's degree of independence from the political authorities.[56] Let us apply those criteria by analogy to inquire whether PMSC personnel can be considered public or private agents.

Under national legislation PMSCs unquestionably qualify as private entities, even though they may provide their services to public powers. However, the criteria mentioned above leave considerable leeway to the Court for taking into account the specific circumstances of armed conflict (a theatre that is traditionally associated with the activity of state organs, depending of course on the specific function discharged by the PMSC). Moreover, the Court would be also allowed to take into consideration the *rights* that the company enjoys under national (and, one may add, also international) law. Significantly, practice shows that PMSCs' employees are often granted immunity from jurisdiction on the strength of special legislative measures or by means of special agreements between the hiring state and the host state.[57] Immunity traditionally accrues to state organs. Indeed the rationale for

---

[53] *Case of the 'White Van' (Paniagua-Morales and ors v Guatemala)*, Series C, no 37, 8 March 1998, para 91.
[54] n 12 above.
[55] See eg *Cyprus v Turkey* (n 28 above), para 77; *Ilaşcu* (n 28 above), para 392, where the Court imputed to the Russian Federation the violations committed by the Moldovan Republic of Transdniestria, which survived by virtue of the military, economic, financial, and political support given to it by the Russian Federation.
[56] See *Case of Islamic Republic of Iran Shipping Lines v Turkey*, Appl no 40998/98, 13 December 2007, para 79. For a discussion of the ECtHR's case law on the attribution to the state of acts of private organizations exercising governmental functions see Ziemele (n 15 above), 21–2.
[57] See Ch 22 by Frulli in this volume. The author points out that in a large number of cases immunity does not stem from the application of immunity rules, but rather from the combination of loopholes in the law or from the unwillingness to proceed.

granting immunity to PMSCs employees is that they perform certain functions on behalf of the state that hired them. This is yet another indicator of the fact that private contractors, though formally not (or not always) agents of the state, often act as such, or simply replace state agents in carrying out their activity.

Therefore, from the totality of the elements just mentioned, the ECtHR may well decide to consider the contractors as agents of the state for the purpose of applying the ECHR.

Secondly, the Court may hold that the contract can be equated to the test of 'political and financial support' used to impute to states the acts of local administrations in a territory subject to their overall control.[58] The hiring state would be responsible for the acts of private contractors who contravene an international obligation of the state, no matter what the activity performed is, and irrespective of whether it entails the exercise of public authority proper. In this scenario, the responsibility of the hiring state would be established even if the company acted in full independence from the state. However, it seems reasonable to circumscribe the responsibility of the hiring state to acts of private contractors that (i) run contrary to an international obligation *of the state*; and (ii) are carried out *in the performance of the contract* only.

This second approach would imply stretching considerably the test of 'political and financial support', which so far has been applied to very different factual circumstances. It is needless to say that the institutional apparatus of a PMSC is radically different from a local public administration. Moreover, the hiring state would not necessarily have overall control over the territory in which the violations are committed. Nevertheless, using the contract as a source of political and financial support for the acts of PMSCs could be a useful tool to bring the actions of PMSCs within the scope of the ECHR.

The idea whereby a state that enters into a contract with a PMSC should be held accountable for *every act* carried out by the company that contravenes its international obligations has merit, and finds some support in scholarly writings.[59] The obvious rationale is that the state should not be allowed to escape international responsibility for wrongful acts by choosing to delegate the exercise of certain functions (that would normally be carried out by its agents) to private entities. It is a well-established rule of customary international law that a state is internationally responsible for the acts of its local governmental authorities (such as municipalities and regions). The state's responsibility arises irrespective of whether the conduct of the local administration: (i) entailed the exercise of elements of public authority; (ii) was contrary to the will of the state; or (iii) exceeded the limits of the administration's competences under national law. This reasoning could be applied, mutatis mutandis, to the case where the state delegated the exercise of certain functions to private entities, as opposed to a local public administration.[60]

---

[58] Ziemele (n 15 above), 25.
[59] Spinedi (n 9 above).
[60] Ibid, 279.

Admittedly, if the state faced a real risk of incurring international responsibility for the violations of human rights committed by PMSCs acting on its behalf it would have a strong incentive to regulate the activity of PMSCs ex ante, to supervise it thoroughly, and to investigate and punish any allegation of wrongdoings.

2. Scope of Positive Human Rights Obligations

It will be recalled that the difficulties in attributing the conduct of private contractors to the state do not arise in establishing whether the state violated its *positive* human rights obligations. Even when the (extraterritorial) violation committed by PMSC personnel cannot be attributed to the hiring state, the latter may still be held accountable for the failure to comply with its positive obligations, if the necessary conditions are met. Therefore, in this respect, attribution is not a challenge for adjudicating human rights violations.

The challenge, admittedly, is defining the exact scope of the state's positive obligations. The ECtHR derived those obligations by way of interpretation from Articles 1–3 and 13 ECHR. The adoption of a specific normative framework clarifying the relevant positive obligations of the home state, the host state, and the hiring state with respect to the activities carried out by PMSCs would certainly improve legal certainty, and would also enable the ECtHR to enforce positive human rights obligations more effectively.

Also the practical significance of positive obligations might be limited with regard to certain activities carried out by PMSCs. For instance, under the ECHR the standard of proof necessary for holding the state accountable for a failure to protect the right to life is particularly high, in that the ECtHR requires that the victim be an *identified individual*.[61] In practice, this standard is almost impossible to meet with regard to contractors involved in combat activities, or whenever lethal force is used uncontrollably against individuals or groups of individuals—unless, of course, the Court adopts a more flexible standard in the future. On the other hand, the obligation to protect the right to life and physical integrity has more realistic chances of being relevant for contractors involved in interrogations or the management of detention facilities. Here the detained or arrested individuals whose rights are at stake are clearly identified individuals, and also in a vulnerable position.

As regards the standard of constructive knowledge (the state 'knew', or 'ought to have known' of a real and imminent risk) necessary for holding the state accountable for its failure to take the reasonable measures, it would be much easier for the Court to apply this standard against the respondent if an effective authorization and monitoring system of PMSCs activities were in place. In that case, the state could not argue that the alleged abuses were beyond its control, and that it did not and could not know what was going on, say, miles away.

---

[61] See Hoppe (n 14 above), section II.C.

C. PMSCs Hired by Other Non-State Actors

Governments are so far the largest group amongst the consumers of the services provided by PMSCs, but they are not the only ones.[62] PMSCs can also be hired by private companies, NGOs and international organizations. In this latter scenario, the reach of human rights norms—that only apply to the state, as we have already said—inevitably has some limits.

Let us take the example of a Russian gas company hiring a French PMSC to provide security to its employees in Iraq. What is the reach of the human rights norms enshrined in the ECHR if the PMSC personnel commit abuses? Undoubtedly those personnel cannot be considered as agents of the Russian state, lacking any de jure or de facto link between the PMSC and that state. Therefore, the violation would not fall within Russia's jurisdiction for the purpose of attributing to it the direct responsibility for the violation. Similarly, in the case at hand, the reach of Russia's positive human rights obligations arguably does not extend so far as to require the state to prevent or react to the violation. Of course, Russia would be entitled to prosecute the alleged wrongdoers, should it be willing to do so, especially in case of inaction by the host state and the PMSC's home state. However, the state of nationality of the hiring company has only a residual duty. At the end of the day, the contractual relationship takes place between purely private subjects. Therefore, one cannot mandate the state of nationality of the hiring company to exercise tight control on the performance of the contract, as such interference would run contrary to the hiring company's market freedom. When human rights violations are committed by PMSCs hired by private companies the obligation to prevent and redress is incumbent upon the territorial state and the PMSC's home state (in our example, Iraq and France respectively), thereby leaving no gap in the protection.

I turn now to the scenario where a PMSC is hired by an international organization, such as the UN, the EU, or NATO. This hypothetical situation raises interesting issues of attribution and responsibility.[63] Organizations are not contracting parties of the ECHR (with the exception of the EU, that is expected to sign the Convention as the Lisbon Treaty has entered into force).[64] Thus, the ECtHR can only adjudicate wrongful acts that are attributable to the *member states* of the organization, whereas it has no jurisdiction ratione personae over the organization as such (again, this does not apply to the EU, if it accedes to the ECHR). In this hypothetical scenario, the Court would have to apply the test of 'authority,

---

[62] See the Report of the Political Affairs Committee, Parliamentary Assembly, Council of Europe, 'Private Military and Security Firms and the Erosion of the State Monopoly on the Use of Force', Doc no 11787, 22 December 2008, para 30.
[63] Here I will only deal with the prospect of adjudicating before the ECtHR the violations committed by the PMSCs. For a discussion of corporate and social responsibility see Ch 19 by White in this volume.
[64] The legal basis for the EU's accession to the ECHR is provided for in Art 6(2) TEU Lisbon, which entered into force on 1 December 2009, and by Art 17(1) of Protocol 14 to the ECHR.

command, and control' (according to the criteria defined in the ILC Draft Articles on the Responsibility of International Organisations) to determine whether responsibility for the violation lies with the organization or with the contributing states. There appear to be, however, several hurdles to the ECtHR's exercise of jurisdiction in case of alleged human rights violations committed by PMSCs hired by an international organization.

First, instead of allocating responsibility between the organization and the member states, the Court could easily dismiss the claim by arguing that responsibility only lies with the international organization, over which it has no jurisdiction. This is, mutatis mutandis, what happened in the *Behrami and Saramati* case.

Even in the assumption that the ECtHR accepted that the responsibility for the wrongdoing could somehow be attributed to one or more contracting states, a second problem that the Court would have to overcome is the application of the so-called '*Monetary Gold* principle'. According to the ICJ ruling in the *Case of the Monetary Gold Removed from Rome in 1943*, an international court cannot rule on the lawfulness of the conduct of a state when the judgment would imply an evaluation of the lawfulness of the conduct of another state that is not party to the case.[65] Whereas all EU member states are also members of the Council of Europe, the situation would be different if the UN or NATO were concerned. In this latter case, one could argue that the Court would not be empowered to decide the merits of the case, as it would be determining the rights and obligations of non-contracting parties to the Convention.[66]

Thirdly, in any event the Court may be prevented from exercising jurisdiction by the international organization's immunity.

D. Immunity

As already mentioned, both PMSCs and their employees are often granted immunity from jurisdiction (respectively, civil and criminal) of the host state and the contracting state. Contrary to what one may think, these immunities do not preclude human rights monitoring bodies from adjudicating the violations committed by the said PMSCs. Indeed, the immunities apply to the company and/or to its employees, whereas human rights bodies pronounce upon the responsibility of the state that hires or hosts them.

Under certain circumstances the granting of immunity to private contractors may entail a *separate violation* of human rights provisions. This is all the more acutely the case with blanket immunities. States parties have, indeed, the obligation to prosecute and punish the alleged wrongdoers. Affording contractors immunity

---

[65] *Case of the Monetary Gold Removed from Rome in 1943, 15 June 1954 (Italy v France, United Kingdom and United States of America)*, ICJ Reports 1954, 19. The principle was later applied eg in the *Case Concerning East Timor (Portugal v Australia)*, 30 June 1995, ICJ Reports 1995, 90, paras 23–35.

[66] This issue was raised, eg, in *Banković* and *Behrami and Saramati*. The ECtHR, however, avoided taking a stance on the matter as it dismissed the applications on other grounds. See *Banković* (n 5 above), para 83; *Behrami and Saramati* (n 5 above), para 153.

from the host state's justice system while providing no alternative avenue violates the state's positive obligation to legislate in keeping with human rights standards, and would thus constitute a separate violation of the ECHR.

Where immunity may bar the ECtHR from deciding upon alleged violations committed by PMSCs during armed conflict is in the hypothetical scenario where a PMSC is hired by an international organization. For instance, the ECtHR has already held that it lacks jurisdiction to scrutinize acts and omissions of contracting parties that are covered by resolutions of the UN Security Council.[67]

V. Concluding Remarks

The adjudication by the ECtHR of human rights violations committed by PMSC personnel in situations of armed conflict, for the time being, is only a theoretical possibility. It is not, however, a 'mission impossible', notwithstanding the many hurdles.

The ECtHR, like other human rights supervisory bodies, is playing a significant role in reviewing instances of gross misconduct in armed conflict. It is submitted that it could continue to do so also with respect to the conduct of private contractors, by holding states accountable for the violation of either their negative and/or positive obligations.

The fact that certain services are outsourced to PMSCs, while rendering adjudication more difficult in that it weakens the ties between the violation and the state, is no impediment. The Court could develop its own rules of attribution, broadening the strict criteria enshrined in the ILC Draft Articles on the responsibility of states for internationally wrongful acts, so as to render the hiring state directly responsible for any violation of its international obligations committed by PMSCs acting on its behalf.

In addition, states also have positive obligations in the field of human rights. In the great majority of cases, the obligation to discharge the positive obligation to prevent the violation and to respond to it is independent of the question of attribution. Therefore, the acts performed by private contractors are well within the purview of the international norms on human rights.

To a great extent, the ECtHR's role will depend on how it interprets the notion of jurisdiction. It would be desirable for it to bring its jurisprudence in line with that of other human rights monitoring bodies, which have interpreted jurisdiction as control, authority, or power over the *person* concerned, as opposed to the territory where the violation occurs. In providing for the extraterritorial application of the ECHR, arguably a flexible approach should be adopted. States could be asked to secure the rights of an individual outside their own territory to an extent commensurate with the degree of their control, authority or power over the

---

[67] *Behrami and Saramati* (n 5 above), para 149.

individual concerned. This possibility was, however, categorically ruled out by the ECtHR in *Banković*.

Major problems arise when PMSCs are contracted by subjects other than states. To the extent that human rights law only imposes obligations upon states, human rights courts are not the appropriate forum in which to hold non-state actors accountable.

9

The Right to Life and Self-defence of Private Military and Security Contractors in Armed Conflict

Guido den Dekker and Eric PJ Myjer

I. Introduction: The Problem of Armed Private Contractors

There is a growing international debate about the legal limitations on outsourcing tasks to private military and security companies (PMSCs) by states.[1] It would be going too far to consider the PMSC industry as such to be problematic from an international law perspective. Indeed, for the largest part, the private security sector counts as a regular economic sector. Within the European Union (EU) it is subject to the same rules as any other supply of services within the internal market.[2] Also, generally speaking in most states the sector is well regulated under domestic law. However, from an international law perspective problems arise when armed private contractors are hired to provide high-risk services in areas of (brewing) armed conflict.[3] The use of firearms by such contractors has the potential of challenging compliance with international humanitarian law (IHL) and human rights law. This is first of all relevant from the point of view of protecting the local civilian population in the areas of operation from the possible use of force by PMS contractors. Well-known instances of killings of unarmed civilians by private contractors demonstrate that this is a real threat, not to mention detainee abuse

---

[1] We will use the term PMS 'contractors' throughout this chapter because of the focus on personal self-defence. For the purpose of this chapter, PMS contractors are individuals working for private military and security companies (PMSCs) as defined in the Introduction to this volume.

[2] See G den Dekker, *The Regulatory Context of Private Military and Security Services at the European Union Level*, Priv-War National Report, Series 04/09 (2009), 8–11, <http://www.priv-war.eu>, accessed 15 August 2010.

[3] Opinions may differ as to what constitutes 'low-risk' or 'high-risk' services, tasks, or responsibilities. However, there are many concepts and suggestions about which of those are considered to be at the high or the low end of the violence spectrum. For example, Singer's categorization of private military firms according to the nature of their activities (military provider firms, military consulting firms, military support firms: see PW Singer, *Corporate Warriors: The Rise of the Privatized Military Industry* (2003)) is useful, even though categorizing the PMS industry is only ideal-typical.

and other reported cases of the use of force.[4] Even so, the perspective of protecting the PMS contractors themselves merits attention as well: it is a fact that large numbers of private contractors have been killed in operational areas.[5]

Apart from the potential applicability of the domestic laws of the territorial state, the contract is practically the only effective legal link between the PMS contractors operating on the ground and the hiring entities—mainly states.[6] If the prevention or regulation of the use of force by private contractors is meant to be accomplished via their contracts, a preliminary question is whether the rules of the contract are decisive in this respect or whether international law independent of the contract determines to what extent a private contractor in an armed conflict has the right to use force. Even though the regulation of the possession and use of weapons is first and foremost a matter of national law, the right for individuals under special circumstances to use a weapon, in particular for purposes of personal self-defence, has found recognition in international law as well. The origin of the right to exercise protective force in armed conflicts where threats of attack are threats of deadly force can be traced back to the most fundamental human right of all: the right to life.[7]

This chapter sets out to examine to what extent the right to life and its protection as recognized in international law has an impact upon the carrying and use of arms by PMS contractors in armed conflict. In the following sections, first the right to life and its protection by way of personal self-defence will be examined with reference to IHL and international criminal law (sections II and III). Then, the question will be addressed whether allowing private contractors arms in armed conflict can be a form of 'due diligence' on the part of the (hiring or territorial) state, and to what extent a pre-existing right to carry and use arms can be limited through the contract governing the relationship between the state and the private contractors (section IV). Next, the problem of armed PMS contractors in armed conflict is connected with the broader debate of the legality

---

[4] Eg the PMSC Executive Outcomes was criticized for using cluster bombs and other military methods that were questionable under IHL in Africa. In Iraq, security contractors employed as interrogators by CACI International and Titan were involved in the Abu Ghraib prison abuses. Also, Blackwater USA contractors have come under scrutiny for the apparently unjustified killing of seventeen Iraqi civilians while providing mobile convoy protection.

[5] Eg the Report *Employing Private Military Companies: A Question of Responsibility* of the Dutch Advisory Council on International Affairs to the Dutch Government, no 59, December 2007, 14, mentions that, 1,000 contractors have been killed in Iraq over the years (<http://www.aiv-advies.nl>, accessed on 15 August). Other sources estimated over 200 deaths and hundreds injured among subcontractors in Iraq as at January 2005: see A McDonald, 'Some Legal Issues concerning US Military Contractors in Iraq' in MN Schmitt and J Pejic (eds), *International Law and Armed Conflict: Exploring the Faultlines* (2007), 361. Well known is also the brutal execution of four PMS contractors of Blackwater in Iraq in 2004: see L Cameron, *International Humanitarian Law and the Regulation of Private Military Companies*, conference paper Basel Institute on Governance, 8–9 February 2007, 1, <http://www.baselgovernance.org>, accessed on 15 August 2010.

[6] But note that procedural obstacles can frustrate transnational litigation based on breach of contract or tort: see C Ryngaert, 'Litigating Abuses Committed by Private Military Companies', (2008) 19 EJIL 1035.

[7] W Kaufman, 'Is there a "right" to self-defense?' [2004] *Criminal Justice Ethics* 22, rightly asserts that the use of deadly force is only a small part of the broader right of self-defence which permits the use of defensive force only in proportion to the harm being threatened. Thus, if threatened with minor force, only minor force in self-defence may be used.

of outsourcing in light of the state monopoly on the use of force in international law (section V). Finally, a concluding section summarizes the most important findings (section VI).

II. Right to Life, International Law, and Armed Conflict

A. The Right to Life under International Human Rights Law

The right to life is often claimed to be the most important of all human rights because life is the precondition for the exercise of any other right.[8] In international law, it has found recognition in global and regional treaties and it is also part of customary international law. Although shared by virtually all national jurisdictions, the right to life is not absolute. This is already apparent from the International Convention on Civil and Political Rights (ICCPR) (Article 6), the American Convention on Human Rights (ACHR) (Article 4), and the African Charter on Human and Peoples' Rights (ACHPR) (Article 4), all of which prohibit the 'arbitrary' deprivation of the right to life. The European Convention on Human Rights (ECHR) stipulates in Article 2(2) that a deprivation of life is not contrary to the right as protected by it if it is the result of a use of force which is no more than absolutely necessary in defence of any person from unlawful violence, in order to effect a lawful arrest, or to prevent the escape of a person lawfully detained, or in action lawfully taken for the purpose of quelling a riot or insurrection. Although the other human rights instruments do not spell out the same exceptions as the ECHR, exceptions such as these can be read into the notion of 'arbitrary' deprivation of the right to life which is more flexible and wider than the strict enumerations of Article 2 ECHR.[9] In addition, the ECHR, the ICCPR, and the American and African human rights treaties explicitly take account of the possibility of lawful death sentences.[10] The EU for its part has included the right to life in strict terms, explicitly excluding the death penalty, in the EU Charter of Fundamental Rights.[11] As the EU will accede to the ECHR, an even more direct responsibility of the EU is created to abide by the provisions of the ECHR in the exercise of its functions.[12] Within (the jurisdiction of) EU member states the right to life is therefore protected through multiple international instruments.

---

[8] The Human Rights Committee (in CCPR General Comment no 6: The right to life (Art 6), 30 April 1982), called it 'the supreme right'; the ECtHR (in *K-HW v Germany*, Appl 37201/97, 22 March 2001) referred to it as 'the supreme value in the hierarchy of human rights'.

[9] N Petersen, 'Life, Right To, International Protection', 3, in *Max Planck Encyclopedia of Public International Law*, <http://www.mpepil.com>, accessed on 15 August 2010.

[10] See further EPJ Myjer, 'Uniform Justice and the Death Penalty' in J Doria, H-P Gasser, and M Cherif Bassiouni (eds), *The Legal Regime of the International Criminal Court: Essays in Honor of Professor Igor Blishenko* (2009), 927–42.

[11] See Charter of Fundamental Rights of the European Union, 18 December 2000, OJ 2000 C, 364/1, Art 2.

[12] The EU has already expressed that it is bound by the provisions of the ECHR through Art 6 of the Treaty on European Union (TEU) which provides that respect for human rights is one of the foundations of the EU. See further Ch 15 by Falco in this volume.

It is subject to debate to what extent and where (locus) the protection of human rights must be guaranteed by states. However, for the purposes of this chapter it suffices to observe that the right to life in principle applies to anyone anywhere in the world, and also in armed conflict. For in international armed conflict (IAC) as well as in non-international armed conflict (NIAC) and in situations of occupation, it is by now undisputed that international human rights law applies as lex generalis, thereby overlapping with, and filling gaps left by, IHL as lex specialis.[13] The human rights treaties stipulate that the articles guaranteeing the right to life cannot be derogated from in times of armed conflict or other severe public emergency.[14] Therefore also in those situations the 'arbitrary' deprivation of life is prohibited. The wording 'arbitrary' deprivation ensures that killings which result from lawful acts of war—'lawful' meaning in accordance with IHL—are allowed for.[15] This includes possible killings as a consequence of the legitimate exercise of the right of self-defence. To the drafters of Article 6 ICCPR the term 'arbitrary' was understood to mean both 'illegal' and 'unjust'.[16] This is in line with what the International Court of Justice (ICJ) observed, albeit in a different context, when it considered that arbitrariness goes beyond the notion of unlawfulness. It is something opposed to the rule of law; a willful disregard of due process of law, an act which shocks, or at least surprises, a sense of juridical propriety.[17]

As such, even the act of 'unlawful' killing may not be 'unjust' in the circumstances of a concrete case and therefore not 'arbitrary'. As will be argued in sections II.B and III below, in the same vein IHL recognizes, under conditions of proportional military necessity, 'excusable' rather than 'lawful' killings, which still qualify as lawful acts of war. Likewise, in international criminal law duress may provide an excuse to otherwise unlawful killings. In armed conflict, the test of what is an arbitrary deprivation of life falls to be determined primarily by the applicable lex specialis, namely the law applicable in armed conflict.[18] The reason is that human rights treaties contain no rules that either define or distinguish civilians from

---

[13] See *Legality of the Threat or Use of Nuclear Weapons,* Advisory Opinion of 8 July 1996, ICJ Rep 1996, 226, para 25; *Legal Consequences of the Construction of a Wall in the Occupied Palestinian Territory,* Advisory Opinion of 9 July 2004, para 106, <http://www.icj-cij.org>, accessed on 17 August 2010; *Case Concerning Armed Activities on the Territory of the Congo (DRC v Uganda)* (19 December 2005), para 216, <http://www.icj-cij.org>, accessed on 17 August 2010. See also Art 72 Additional Protocol (AP) I.

[14] See ICCPR Art 4(2); ACHR Art 27(2); ECHR Art 15(2). The ACHPR does not allow for derogation in state of emergency.

[15] See V Gowlland-Debbas, 'The Right to Life and Genocide: The Court and International Public Policy' in L Boisson de Chazournes and P Sands (eds), *International Law, the International Court of Justice and Nuclear Weapons* (1999), 320.

[16] See 'The Drafting History of Art 6 of the International Covenant on Civil and Political Rights: Note by the Editor' in B Ramcharan (ed), *The Right to Life in International Law* (1985), 43.

[17] See *Case Concerning Elettronica Sicula SpA (ELSI) (US v Italy),* 84 ILR 311 (20 July 1989), paras 124, 128.

[18] See *Legality of the Threat or Use of Nuclear Weapons* (n 13 above), para 25: 'Whether a particular loss of life, through the use of a certain weapon in warfare, is to be considered an arbitrary deprivation of life contrary to Art 6 of the [ICCPR], can only be decided by reference to the law applicable in armed conflict and not be deduced from the terms of the [ICCPR] itself.' This does not rule out that human rights law applies in armed conflict as lex generalis.

combatants and other military targets, or specify when a civilian can be lawfully attacked or when civilian casualties are a lawful consequence of military operations.[19] The next question is therefore how IHL regulates the right to life.

B. The Right to Life under International Humanitarian Law

IHL was designed specifically to regulate the conduct of hostilities in armed conflicts. It can be argued that for all practical purposes as soon as organized armed groups are engaged in fighting of some intensity an armed conflict has arisen and IHL becomes applicable in the situation.[20] This applies both to IAC and NIAC.[21] For IHL to be applicable it is not necessary that actual combat activities are taking place in a particular location but it should also not be too far away from it, for example, in the larger territory of which that location forms part.[22] The conflict situations in which PMS contractors typically operate will often qualify as armed conflicts under IHL. The protection of civilians and the civilian population, which, inter alia, finds expression in the fundamental principle of distinction between persons who participate directly in the hostilities and those who do not (civilians and persons *hors de combat*), is equally applicable to IAC and NIAC. All four Geneva Conventions list 'willful killing' of protected persons as a grave breach. The rules of minimum protection, which include a prohibition of violence to the life of persons taking no active part in the hostilities, apply both in IAC and NIAC.[23] Still, the distinction between IAC and NIAC is relevant because the differences in defining status under IHL may have a bearing on the protection of the right to life.

It is well known that in IAC a distinction as to status is made between combatants, civilians, and mercenaries.[24] The United States in the context of its 'war on terror' has at some point argued that certain persons should be qualified as 'unlawful enemy combatants' but this is not a status recognized in IHL.[25] The distinction based on status is linked to each person's right to participate directly in

---

[19] Cf *Tablada* decision, IACHR Report no 55/97, Case no 11.137, Argentina, OEA/Ser/L/V/II97, Doc 38, 30 October 1997, 44.
[20] See ME O'Connell, 'Defining Armed Conflict' (2008) 13(3) JC&SL 398. See also D Raab, '"Armed Attack" After the *Oil Platforms* Case' (2004) 17 LJIL 719–35.
[21] As to NIAC, AP II Art 1(2) indicates that internal disturbances and tensions do not qualify as armed conflicts. The ICTY has adopted the view that an armed conflict exists whenever there is resort to armed force by states or protracted armed violence between governmental authorities and organized armed groups or between such groups within a state (*Tadić* case, IT-94-1, Dec Interloc Appeal of 2 October 1995, para 70; *Boskoski* case, IT-04-82 (10 July 2008), paras 174–5).
[22] Cf ICTY *Celebici* case, IT-96-21-T (16 November 1998), para 185.
[23] See AP I Art 75(2)(a); AP II Art 4(2)(a). See also GC Common Art 3, and AP I Art 1(2); AP II, preamble (Martens clause).
[24] See in particular Arts 43, 47, and 50 AP I. See also Art 13 GC I, II; Art 4 GC III; Art 13 AP II. IAC under AP I includes wars of national liberation.
[25] M Sassòli and L Olston, 'The Relationship between International Humanitarian and Human Rights Law where it Matters: Admissible Killing and Internment of Fighters in Non-international Armed Conflicts' (2008) 90(871) IRRC 601; see also J Pejic,'"Unlawful/Enemy Combatants": Interpretations and Consequences' in Schmitt and Pejic (eds) (n 5 above), 335–55.

the hostilities or not.[26] Civilians shall not be attacked or killed; they enjoy immunity from attack. Civilians who are participating directly in the hostilities, however, lose this prerogative for as long as their direct participation lasts (Article 51(3) AP I). Such direct participation, even though it is not prohibited as such, does not give civilians a lawful right to attack or kill, but they can be lawfully attacked and killed by enemy combatants—or, they can be injured or killed by other civilians responding to the (imminent) attack through a legitimate exercise of self-defence. In brief, only combatants have a right under IHL to attack other persons and take their lives as part of their combat activities provided these other persons are themselves combatants or are otherwise participating directly in the hostilities. In IHL there are several, largely overlapping, definitions of combatant.[27] Today it is used as a term of status and is therefore not dependent on the nature of the activities displayed by the persons concerned.[28] Although not impossible if they fulfil combat functions on behalf of a party to an IAC,[29] the predominant view in the literature is that PMS contractors do not qualify as combatants under IHL.[30] This is also in line with the *rationale* of outsourcing tasks to private (legal) persons: the intention is that they do not belong to a state organ such as the armed forces. This means that in IAC, PMS contractors enjoy immunity from attack as civilians[31] (cf Article 50 AP I) unless and as long as they participate directly in the hostilities. They do not have the right to attack and kill adversaries under IHL. As mentioned, this does not rule out the use of force in self-defence.

In NIAC, IHL (Geneva Conventions (GCs) common Article 3 and AP II) does not award combatant status to any person. Civilians and persons *hors de combat*

---

[26] Cf Art 43(2) AP I: 'members of the armed forces of a Party to the conflict... are combatants, that is to say, they have the right to participate directly in hostilities'.

[27] See Hague Regulations on Land Warfare (1907) Art 1 which uses the broader term 'belligerents', GC III Art 4(A) in which the status of combatant is implicitly used to determine prisoner of war status, and Art 43(2) AP I.

[28] See CHB Garraway, 'Combatants: Substance or Semantics?' in Schmitt and Pejic (eds) (n 5 above), 320, 325.

[29] Eg it has been reported that PMS contractors (of Xe Company, formerly known as Blackwater) have been hired by the United States to assemble and load missiles and laser-guided bombs on remotely piloted aircraft to kill Al Qaeda leaders, at hidden bases in Afghanistan and Pakistan: see J Risen and M Mazzetti, 'CIA Said to Use Outsiders to Put Bombs on Drones', *New York Times* (20 August 2009).

[30] See eg E-C Gillard, 'Business Goes to War: Private Military/Security Companies and International Humanitarian Law', (2006) 88 IRRC 536; L Doswald-Beck, 'Private Military Companies under International Humanitarian Law' in S Chesterman and C Lenhardt (eds), *From Mercenaries to Market: The Rise and Regulation of Private Military Companies* (2007), 18; M Schmitt, 'Humanitarian Law and Direct Participation in Hostilities by Private Contractors or Civilian Employees' (2005) 5 Chicago JIL 531; D Ridlon, 'Contractors or Illegal Combatants? The Status of Armed Contractors in Iraq', (2008) 62 Air Force LR 219–29; and see for a plea why certain PMS contractors exercising coercive functions can be persons forming part of the armed forces, C Hoppe, 'Passing the Buck: State Responsibility for Private Military Companies', (2008) 19(5) EJIL 989–1014. For a discussion of views pro and contra combatant status of private contractors see Ch 10 by Sossai in this volume.

[31] See eg L Cameron, 'Private Military Companies: Their Status under International Humanitarian Law and its Impact on their Regulation', (2007) 88 IRRC 573–98; L Green, *The Contemporary Law of Armed Conflict*, 3rd edn (2008), 115; N Melzer, *Interpretative Guidance on the Notion of Direct Participation in Hostilities under International Humanitarian Law*, ICRC (2009), 38; McDonald (n 5 above), 377, 379.

shall be treated humanely. Acts of violence to life and person, including murder of all kinds, against these persons are and shall remain prohibited at any time and in any place whatsoever. These fundamental obligations, it can be argued, rest upon both government forces and non-state armed groups—AP II, Article 1(1) speaks of 'dissident armed forces or other organized armed groups'—since they are binding on 'each party to the conflict'.[32] As in IAC, civilians enjoy protection and shall not be the object of attack unless and for such time as they take a direct part in hostilities (Article 13(3) AP II). The question who can lawfully participate in the hostilities in NIAC is in principle determined by the domestic laws of the state involved.[33] Generally this will be confined to the members of the armed forces and, in some domestic systems, the law-enforcement units of (the legitimate government of) the state—usually the same state that has hired the PMS companies or has consented to their hiring. Non-state armed groups in a NIAC do not enjoy protection against attack by the regular armed forces (and, if applicable, the law-enforcement units) of the legitimate government of the territorial state. Opinions differ as to whether under IHL the 'core' of these non-state armed groups are considered to participate directly in the hostilities per se on the basis of their involvement ('membership') and can therefore be attacked at any time, or whether this still is only allowed when and as long as each of them participates directly in the hostilities and thus presents a danger to the opposing state forces.[34]

The relevant central question in both IAC and NIAC therefore is when private contractors participate directly in the hostilities.[35] One important factor is that in IHL there is no differentiation between offensive and defensive attack (cf Article 49 (1) AP I); participating in either combat action can amount to a direct participation in the hostilities.[36] Although no single definition of 'direct participation in the hostilities' has been established, it is generally accepted that direct participation implies a direct causal relationship between the activity engaged in and the harm done to the enemy at the time and place where the activity occurs. It consists of acts which by their nature and purpose are intended to cause actual harm to the personnel and equipment of the (armed forces of the) adverse party.[37] Hostilities have been broadly described[38] but even in a narrow sense would cover more than

---

[32] Cf L Zegveld, *Armed Opposition Groups in International Law: The quest for accountability* (2000), 17–18; Green (n 31 above), 347.

[33] See R de Nevers, 'Private Security Companies and the Laws of War', *Security Dialogue* 40(2) (2009) 172.

[34] Cf *Expert Meeting on the Right to Life in Armed Conflicts and Situations of Occupation*, University Centre for International Humanitarian Law, Geneva, 1–2 September 2005, 35–40, <http://www.adh-geneve.ch>, accessed on 17 August 2010. Cf also the discussion in Ch 12 by Vierucci in this volume.

[35] See on the topic of direct participation also Sossai (n 30 above).

[36] The term 'attack' means 'combat action' here. It covers defensive acts (particularly 'counter-attacks') as well as offensive acts: see Y Sandoz, C Swinarski, and B Zimmerman (eds), *Commentary on the Additional Protocols of 8 June 1977 to the Geneva Conventions of 12 August 1949* (1987), para 1880 (re Art 49(1)).

[37] See Sandoz, Swinarski, and Zimmerman (eds) (n 36 above), para 1679 (re Art 43), para 1942 (re Art 51).

[38] *Third Expert Meeting on the Notion of Direct Participation in Hostilities*, Summary Report, October 2005, 18, 22–3, <http://www.icrc.org>, accessed on 17 August 2010.

attacks and military operations and include the preparatory operations to and the return from the actual fighting as well as immediate threats of actual harm to the opposing forces.[39] The foregoing implies that PMS contractors who carry out functions such as guarding—ie deterring and protecting against attack—strategic buildings or military camps or convoys, or acting as private police forces in occupied territory, or those who are directly involved in the support of military operations even though not in active combat as such, for example, through the provision of fuel or ammunition, or strategic planning and training, run a risk of carrying out tasks which by their nature qualify as direct participation in the hostilities. In IAC, they could be legitimately attacked by combatants of the opposing forces regardless of their civilian status. In NIAC, the same would apply even though opposing non-state armed groups do not have a right under IHL to attack or kill them.

There may be circumstances in which the use of force against civilians in armed conflict can be justified even when they do not participate directly in the hostilities. In these situations targeting civilians, although not 'lawful', can be deemed 'excusable'. It could be argued that a person by virtue of his attachment to a military objective can become himself a military objective and thus a legitimate target under IHL even independent of the question whether the person is participating directly in the hostilities.[40] Applied as such, it can be argued that the private contractor driving a fuel truck to a base camp would not be participating directly in the hostilities as the act of transporting fuel is neither part of the actual fighting nor poses a direct threat of actual harm to the enemy, but he would still be a legitimate target himself because the truck he is driving qualifies as a military objective. An alternative view is that the driver cannot be attacked as such and remains under the protection of the law attaching to his civilian status, but that the truck can be attacked and destroyed because the truck is a military objective. Complying with this, however, requires very careful targeting and extreme accuracy of weapons which may not be compatible with the realities of even modern-day armed conflict.[41] Therefore, this type of situation is probably better analysed according to the concept of proportional collateral damage. Attacks that are expected to cause collateral damage are not prohibited as such, but they must not amount to an indiscriminate attack on civilians and the collateral damage expected from any

---

[39] See Sandoz, Swinarski, and Zimmerman (eds) (n 36 above), para 1943 (re Art 51).

[40] The text of Art 52 AP I does not rule out that others than objects—ie persons—can also be military objectives for the purpose of this clause. Moreover, in 1956 the ICRC proposed Draft Rules for the limitation of dangers incurred by the civilian population in time of war including a list of military objectives which mentioned first of all 'armed forces, including auxiliary or complementary organizations, and persons who, though not belonging to the above-mentioned formations, nevertheless take part in the fighting': see *List of Categories of Military Objectives according to Art 7(2) of the ICRC Draft Rules*, reprinted in Sandoz, Swinarski, and Zimmerman (eds) (n 36 above), 632.

[41] Cf MN Schmitt, 'Precision Attack and International Humanitarian Law' ICCR 87(859) (2005) 445, who asserts that as weaponry is becoming more precise, compliance with IHL is becoming increasingly demanding for an attacker.

attack must be proportional to the military advantage anticipated.[42] It follows that even if PMS contractors do not participate directly in the hostilities, the possibility cannot be ruled out that due to their presence in or near a military objective they can become objects of an attack which is 'excusable' under IHL.

III. Personal Self-defence and its Application in Armed Conflict

Violations of 'the laws and customs of war' is the generic term in IHL materializing the basis for individual criminal responsibility of violations of the laws applicable in armed conflict. In connection with international criminal law the area of reference is first of all the specific catalogue of internationally recognized war crimes: see in particular Article 8 Statute of the International Criminal Court (ICC).[43] Wilful killing and violence to life and person including murder are specified therein as a war crime in IAC and in NIAC, respectively. Still, not each and every killing or act of violence constitutes a (war) crime even if it is a wilful act. Personal self-defence to protect one's life against an immediate or imminent potentially deadly attack constitutes the prime exception. The right of individuals to defend themselves against attack is codified in most national legislations.[44] The individual right of self-defence is also recognized in international law. If not a human right in itself, the right to use force in self-defence against a potentially deadly attack is a necessary corollary to the right to life.[45] The use of defensive force has been described as a legitimate expression of individual autonomy and sovereignty.[46] In international criminal law, further to the fundamental principle of legality which characterizes this body of law, the right of personal self-defence has been expressly codified: see Article 31(1)(c) ICC Statute. This codification, which reflects provisions found in most national criminal codes, has even been referred to as a rule of customary international law.[47] In the application and interpretation of this right, as in general in the determination of the law under the Statute, the ICC has to take account of

---

[42] See H Fischer, *Collateral Damage*, Crimes of War project, <http://www.crimesofwar.org/thebook/book.html>, accessed on 17 August 2010. See also Art 51(5)(b)) AP I and see Art 8(2)(b)(iv) ICC Statute.

[43] See *Rome Statute of the International Criminal Court*, 17 July 1998, 2187 UNTS 3 (ICC Statute).

[44] See P Haggenmacher, 'Self-defense as a General Principle of Law and its Relevance to War' in P Eyffinger et al (eds), *Self-Defence as a Fundamental Principle* (2009), 14.

[45] See A Ashworth, 'Self-Defence and the Right to Life' (1975) 34(2) Cambridge LJ 283: 'If a legal system is to uphold the right to life, there must be a liberty to use force for the purpose of self-defence.' See on the discussion whether self-defence constitutes in itself a fundamental human right, contra, *Prevention of Human Rights Violations committed with Small Arms and Light Weapons*, Final Report submitted by Special Rapporteur B Frey to the Human Rights Council Subcommittee on the promotion and protection of human rights, A/HRC/Sub1/58/27, 27 July 2006, and, pro, DB Kopel, P Gallant, and J Eisen, 'The Human Right of Self-defense' (2008) 22(1) BYU Journal of Public Law 43–178.

[46] H Tonkin, 'Defensive use of Force under the Rome Statue' (2005) 6 Melb JIL 88; S Rosenne, 'Self-defense and the Non-use of Force: Some Random Thoughts' in Eyffinger et al (eds) (n 44 above), 61.

[47] See ICTY *Kordić and Cerkez*, IT-95-14/2-T (26 February 2001), para 451.

the established principles of IHL and international human rights law: see Article 21 ICC Statute. This implies that the right to self-defence has a limited scope since it is not particularly conceivable that self-defence could be successfully invoked before the ICC to justify crimes against humanity, the crime of aggression or, outside individual and isolated cases, grave breaches of IHL or war crimes.[48] It furthermore presupposes that the (imminent) attack against which the defence takes place is itself unlawful, irrespective of the culpability of the attacker.[49]

There is no right to exercise self-defence against lawful self-defence. This raises the difficult question how the difference between 'offensive' and 'defensive' violence can be identified, especially if it is supposed to be a response to an 'imminent' attack. There is no general answer to this question: all will depend on the concrete circumstances of the case, and regardless of whether the act attributed to the state in which the individual took part was itself lawful or not.[50] In any event, the use of force in self-defence must not itself amount to a direct participation in the hostilities. If this were otherwise, civilians could abuse the right to self-defence as a pretext for attacking, wounding, or killing adversaries as a direct participant in the hostilities, on the same footing as combatants.[51] This, too, implies that in general the scope of the right of self-defence must be interpreted restrictively.

In IAC, if the civilian is participating directly in the hostilities, he has no right of self-defence against enemy combatants, who can lawfully attack him, but only against (imminent) attack from other civilians whether they are participating directly in the hostilities or not. In NIAC the right of self-defence is in principle linked to the legality of force pursuant to the domestic law of the territorial state. IHL is in principle not concerned with domestic law enforcement. Besides criminal law, national administrative law is important in this respect as it normally indicates which persons have the right to carry arms and use force (against civilians) for purposes of law enforcement and the maintenance of public order. Similarly, it will also determine which persons in an emergency situation amounting to NIAC have the right to use force, ie may participate directly. Such direct participation does not generate a lawful right to attack the armed private contractors if they operate on the side of the legitimate government.[52] Human rights law plays a role in this as well.

---

[48] E David, 'Self-defence and State of Necessity in the Statute of the ICC' in Doria et al (eds) (n 10 above), 772, even considers self-defence to be totally unsuitable in respect of war crimes or gross violations of IHL.

[49] An insane or mistaken attacker is legally excused but his attack is not justified, therefore one may use defensive force against him: see Kaufman (n 7 above), 20.

[50] ICTY *Kordić and Cerkez*, n 47 above, para 452, and see Rosenne (n 46 above), 64, adding that 'Personal self-defense is always an individual and independent right'; see also Sandoz, Swinarski, and Zimmerman (eds) (n 36 above), para 1882 (re Art 49(1)): 'in the sense of [AP I] an attack is unrelated to the concept of aggression or the first use of armed force'. As such, it is self-explanatory that if the person concerned was involved in a self-defence operation conducted by one or more states in accordance with Art 51 UN Charter (a 'defensive operation conducted by forces' as it is referred to in the ICC Statute) this shall not in itself constitute a ground for excluding his individual criminal responsibility on the ground of self-defence (Art 31(1)(c) ICC Statute).

[51] Cf H Olasolo, *Unlawful Attacks in Combat Situations* (2008), 236–7.

[52] A structural exploitation of this typical situation—'legitimate' targets that in fact cannot be 'lawfully' attacked—may at some point in time perhaps bring new life to the now outdated idea that

It can be argued that the obligation to protect the right to life 'by law' (cf eg Article 6(1) ICCPR) requires that states enact domestic laws for emergency situations, including domestic armed conflict. To the extent that IHL addresses this matter, it would seem to allow self-defence by a civilian not participating directly in the hostilities in the NIAC if an unlawful threat or act of violence is directed against his/her life and person (cf Common Article 3 and Article 13(3) AP II). Outside armed conflict or occupation, the legality of the acts in view of the protection against arbitrary deprivation of life has to be assessed according to human rights law and general criminal law.[53] For example, if the 'attacker' is a law-enforcement officer or a member of the armed forces of the legitimate government of the territorial state who according to national law has the right to use force against civilians for purposes of law enforcement or maintaining public order, effectuating a lawful arrest or the lawful quelling of a riot can justify the use of deadly force against civilians.

The right to use force in personal self-defence is subject to a number of conditions. First of all, the application of force must serve a lawful aim or purpose. The policies of most states employing armed PMS contractors in armed-conflict areas seem to take this into account as it is indicated that the use of force by these contractors must be considered to constitute acts of self-defence which do not amount to direct participation in the hostilities, because the purpose of the use of force is not aimed at harming the enemy but at self-protection. However, to meet that end, the force used must be limited to the protection of the persons themselves or another person who is under (imminent threat of) attack, or of property which is essential for their survival (cf Article 31(1)(c) ICC Statute). Where contractors can use force in defence of their own life, this includes defence of the lives of other persons who are under (imminent) attack. In essence, defence of another person concerns protection of the same interests as defence of oneself. The defence of property generally has lesser strength than the defence of one's body, but the additional criterion—that the property must be essential for the survival of the persons in an armed conflict[54]—clearly limits the purpose of lawful self-defence in this respect. The final option mentioned in Article 31(1)(c) ICC Statute, namely the use of force in defence of property which is essential for accomplishing a military mission, would seem to be beyond the reach of private contractors. After all, it is hardly conceivable that a PMS contractor can defend property essential for

---

the laws of war must be interpreted such that direct participation of civilians is in fact prohibited and by itself constitutes a (war) crime. See for two examples of case law reflecting this idea, both relating to IAC and dating from the 1940s, Schmitt (n 30 above), 520–2.

[53] Cf R McLaughlin, 'The legal regime applicable to use of lethal force when operating under a United Nations Security Council Chapter VII Mandate authorizing "all necessary means"', (2008) 12 (3) JC&SL 394–7, referring to this as 'the law enforcement paradigm'.

[54] The use of force in defence of property essential for survival as a ground for excluding criminal responsibility is limited to the case of war crimes. One may think of the—remote—example of protecting water tanks of an outpost in the desert. The recognition of the defence of property in the ICC Statute is itself controversial: see eg WA Schabas, *An Introduction to the International Criminal Court*, 2nd edn (2004), 112.

the accomplishment of a military mission—ie a military objective—without thereby being required to participate directly in the hostilities.

In addition to the lawful aim or purpose, ie the repelling of an (imminent) unlawful attack, self-defence must fulfil the customary law requirements of necessity and proportionality. Necessity means that the defence must be against immediate, or at least imminent, danger caused by the attack. One may also identify immediacy of both the attack and the danger caused by it as a separate requirement, although it is often viewed as an element of necessity.[55] The condition of proportionality requires that the damage inflicted by the defensive force must be proportional to the (danger of the) attack.[56] Arguably, necessity and proportionality of self-defence should be strictly construed against persons unlawfully in possession of a weapon.[57] Only members of the armed forces and law-enforcement agents are supposed to reasonably resist the (danger of) attack in their capacity.[58] Others ought to avoid such situations if reasonably possible. Therefore generally speaking the (armed) PMS contractor who comes under attack must first try to remove himself from the danger provided he can safely do so, or call in the assistance of the armed forces, instead of trying to resist the (imminent) attack by using force. Only if the danger is life-threatening and there are no alternative solutions can killing in self-defence be lawful. A person who through his own negligence or fault creates a situation in which his life is endangered—leaving aside extreme cases of provocation[59]—still has a right of self-defence (since it is a justification not an excuse), albeit that a duty to retreat will be assumed earlier in circumstances of self-defence caused by own fault.

Human rights law, which as mentioned earlier applies as lex generalis in armed conflict, also incorporates the principles of proportionality and necessity as dominant factors in determining whether a killing was 'arbitrary' and thus contrary to the right to life as protected in human rights treaties.[60] The same criteria apply to the defensive use of force and firearms by law-enforcement officials, as indicated by the UN.[61] Under the ECHR, the enumerative list of exceptions to the right to life

---

[55] See B Sangero, *Self-defense in Criminal Law* (2006), 151.
[56] See Art 31(1)(c) ICC Statute.
[57] Cf Ashworth (n 45 above), 297–9.
[58] On violence applied by public authorities see B Mathieu, *The Right to Life in European Constitutional and International Case-Law* (2006), 57–70.
[59] Sangero (n 55 above), 316–17, gives the example of a person provoking and harming another after planning in advance both his provocation and also the reaction of the assigned 'aggressor' with the purpose of injuring the latter, in which case a lawful right of self-defence would not be recognized in most domestic legal systems.
[60] For example, the Human Rights Committee found a violation of Art 6 ICCPR because a killing by the Colombian police was unnecessary and disproportionate, and considered the policy of targeted killings of suspected terrorists by Israel to be arbitrary since other measures to arrest the suspected person had not been exhausted. The Inter-American Court has also used the requirements of necessity and proportionality as controlling standards.
[61] See 'Basic Principles on the Use of Force and Firearms by Law Enforcement Officials', adopted by the Eighth UN Congress on the Prevention of Crime and the Treatment of Offenders, 1990, principle 9, subsequently adopted in GA Res 45/166, 18 December 1999, para 4.

share a strict necessity and proportionality requirement ('absolutely necessary').[62] The European Court of Human Rights (ECtHR) has stated more than once that it will be no excuse for the state concerned to plead that its action was taken in the face of 'violent armed clashes' or that the scale of the 'incidence of killings' justified its action.[63] In UN peacekeeping missions, the right to self-defence of armed peacekeepers is somewhat wider than self-defence in other fields of international law, and includes resistance of attempts by forceful means to prevent the mission from discharging its duties under the mandate of the Security Council.[64] The Rules of Engagement (ROE) of the mission contain the customary elements of necessity and proportionality when force in self-defence is employed. In sum, self-defence and its legal limitations are firmly embedded in various branches of international law.

The question may be raised whether the threat of imminent death or serious bodily harm against the PMS contractor or another person can be justified or excused on grounds other than self-defence, namely military necessity or duress. Military necessity attaches to acts of the state, and thus in principle it can only exonerate the state concerned with the individual authors of the acts acting as its agents. Military necessity is not available as a codified individual defence in international criminal law, although situations can be thought of in which it could be raised.[65] Even then, in order to be admitted as an individual defence in criminal law, necessity would have to fulfil strict criteria, very similar to instances of duress.[66] Duress as a defence in international criminal law is based on the concept that in a given situation a person can be excused for disregarding his obligation to abide by the law because of a lack of freedom of will or choice in the face of an immediate threat.[67] It is clear from Article 31(1)(d) ICC Statute that force used in duress can only be excusable if strict criteria have been fulfilled, including that the situation leading to duress must not have been voluntarily brought about by the person invoking it.[68] Duress in international criminal law appears as a defence in

---

[62] This criterion, which applies to intended and unintentional deaths alike, is stricter and more compelling than the criterion 'necessary in a democratic society' used elsewhere in the ECHR; cf *McCann and ors v UK*, ECHR (1995), Series A, no 324, paras 147–50.

[63] See P Rowe, *Control over Armed Forces Exercised by the European Court of Human Rights*, DCAF Working Paper, Series no 56, August 2002, 4, <http://www.dcaf.ch/_docs/WP56.pdf>, accessed on 17 August 2010.

[64] See MC Zwanenburg, *Accountability under International Humanitarian Law for United Nations and North Atlantic Treaty Organization Peace Support Operations* (2004), 17–18.

[65] See E van Sliedregt, *The Criminal Responsibility of Individuals for Violations of International Humanitarian Law* (2003), 298; see also Schabas (n 54 above), 111.

[66] In one of the very rare examples, namely the ICTY *Orić* case, IT-03-68 (8 June 2005), involving command responsibility for not preventing pillage by some Bosnian Muslims of Srebrenica, taking livestock from Serb farms in the surrounding area, the Trial Chamber examined the existence of an imminent threat of serious and non-reparable damage to life: only way to avoid the damage, act non-disproportionate to the threat, situation not attributable to the agent who invokes necessity as conditions required for admitting the defence of necessity. See David (n 48 above), 774.

[67] K Ambos, 'General principles of criminal law in the Rome Statute', (1999) 10(1) Criminal Law Forum 27, however, notes that the wording in Art 31(1)(d) ICC Statute mixes up elements of duress and necessity.

[68] Cf ICTY *Erdemovic* case, IT-96-22 (17 October 1997), separate and dissenting opinion of Judge Cassese, para 16, with further references. Cf also 2001 ILC Articles on Responsibility of States for Internationally Wrongful Acts, Art 24, which excludes duress as a circumstance precluding

cases where suspects commit war crimes under coercion of their group or their military superiors threatening death or serious bodily harm if they do not comply. It is therefore unlikely that duress would be an available defence to the PMS contractor who has killed an adversary in order to save his life if self-defence is not available to him for that purpose, particularly because the danger of attack is likely the result of the voluntary decision of the PMS contractor to put himself in that position. Moreover, since there is no formal command structure in private companies, PMS contractors do not have to follow orders as in a military hierarchy. They can refuse hazardous assignments, possibly at the risk of forced resignation or losing the contract, but these consequences do not qualify as threats which could justify acts on the basis of duress.

IV. Private Contractors and the Right to Carry Arms

A. Allowing Arms to PMS Contractors as 'Due Diligence'

In most European states, private persons do not have the right to carry (or use) weapons, unless for limited, specific purposes such as hunting or sports for which a special licence or permission by the competent authorities is required. The same applies to private persons who want to take (their) weapons across the European borders. In contrast, in the United States a historically developed bias against too much government control has induced a strong protection of the personal right to keep and bear arms as the hallmark of personal freedom: the Second Amendment to the Constitution as it is nowadays interpreted protects an individual right to possess a firearm and to use that arm for traditionally lawful purposes, such as self-defence within the home.[69] Still, in general, the basic idea of this aspect of statehood is that the state through its armed forces and law-enforcement units guarantees security to its citizens and ensures their protection against the threat or use of force by others. However, precisely this type of state function is often partly or totally absent in the war-torn societies in which armed PMS contractors typically operate.

Even though the right to life attaches to individuals, the protection of this right through IHL and human rights law is in the form of negative and positive obligations addressed to states.[70] Whereas the negative obligation comes down to an obligation of the armed forces and law-enforcement units of the state not to attack the PMS contractors operating on their side, the 'link' with the PMS contractors (other than contractual)—be it territorial, jurisdictional, or by way of

---

wrongfulness for states if the situation of duress is due to the conduct of the state invoking it: UN Doc A/56/10 (2001).

[69] US Supreme Court *District of Columbia v Heller*, 128 SCt 2783 (2008); US Supreme Court *McDonald v City of Chicago*, no 08–1521, 28 June 2010.

[70] See Art 49 GC I, Art 50 GC II, Art 129 GC III, Art 146 GC IV, Art 85 AP I; and see eg Art 1 ECHR, Art 2 ICCPR. See on issues of state responsibility in this context, Hoppe (n 30 above). See also C Lenhardt, *Private Military Companies and State Responsibility*, IILJ Working Papers 2007/2, <http://www.iilj.org>, accessed on 17 August 2010.

control—may also bring into play positive obligations of the territorial and the hiring (or the home) states to prevent situations within their territory, jurisdiction, and/or control that are likely to threaten human life.[71] It may be difficult to argue that a state can ipso facto (meaning here: irrespective of contractual obligations, if any) have these type of positive human rights obligations towards PMS contractors in an armed conflict. After all, the contractors are not state agents and, when acting abroad, are not normally under the jurisdiction or control of their home state or the hiring state (if other than the territorial state), whereas the territorial state is rarely in the position to offer direct protection against attack from enemy combatants, local armed groups, and/or criminals. However, there is a tendency in the case law of international human rights courts and monitoring bodies to recognize that there exists a general due-diligence obligation to prevent human rights violations and to respond to any such violations as required by the law.[72] In the same vein, the International Court of Justice (ICJ) has identified a due-diligence obligation resting upon an occupying power under Article 43 Hague Regulations, to prevent the violation of human rights and IHL and to protect the inhabitants against acts of violence and not to tolerate such violence by any third party, including private actors such as rebel groups acting on their own account, in the occupied area.[73] The ICJ has also identified the conditions under which the obligation resting on the states parties to the Genocide Convention to employ all means reasonably available to them which might contribute to preventing genocide can be deemed fulfilled. This, according to the Court, depends on an assessment in concreto of the capacity to influence the actions of persons likely to commit, or in the process of committing, genocide effectively. This capacity in turn depends, among other things, on the geographical distance of the state concerned from the scene of the events and on the strength of the political, or other, links between the authorities of that state and the main actors in the events. The duty to prevent arises at the instant that the state concerned learns of, or should normally have learned of, the existence of a serious risk that genocide will be committed. Breaching this obligation does not require proof that the state concerned had the power to prevent the genocide; it is sufficient that it had the means to do so and that it manifestly refrained from using them.[74]

---

[71] On specific human rights obligations of hiring, home and other states, see Ch 5 by Francioni, Ch 6 by Hoppe, and Ch 7 by Bakker in this volume.

[72] Eg the Human Rights Committee recognizes a due-diligence obligation of states to prevent violations, including a duty to protect or physically intervene on behalf of individuals: see CCPR General Comment no 6 (n 8 above), paras 4–6. Cf also General Comment no 31, Human Rights Committee, UN Doc CCPR/C/21/Rev1/Add13 (2004). The Inter-American Court of Human Rights has been vigilant in its interpretation of a general due-diligence obligation with respect to the rights of the American Convention (eg the case of *Velásquez-Rodríguez v Honduras*). This tendency is also visible in the case law of the ECtHR (eg *McCann and ors v UK*, *Andronicou and Constantinou v Cyprus*, *Ergi v Turkey*, *Budayeva and ors v Russia*, *Osman v UK*). See also Gowlland-Debbas (n 15 above), 323; and see further I Ziemele, *Human Rights Violations by Private Persons and Entities: The Case-law of International Human Rights Courts and Monitoring Bodies*, AEL PrivWar working papers 2009/08, 15–16, <http://cadmus.eui.eu/handle/1814/11409>, accessed on 17 August 2010.

[73] See *Case Concerning Armed Activities in the Territory of the Congo* (n 13 above), paras 178–9.

[74] See *Case Concerning Application of the Convention on the Prevention and Punishment of the Crime of Genocide* (*Bosnia-Herzegovina v Serbia-Montenegro*), ICJ Rep 2007, paras 430–1, 438.

One may draw a parallel with the conditions under which the (individual) responsibility of superiors can arise for a failure to try to prevent grave breaches of IHL by their subordinates (Article 86(2) AP I).

The above discussion, although not relating as such to private contractors in armed conflict, indicates that human rights law and IHL share a similar concept of due-diligence obligations for states to act diligently upon serious risks of infringement of the rights of protected persons within their jurisdiction or under their control if caused by (threatening) unlawful acts of third parties whose conduct is not attributable to the state.[75] It can be summarized that the scope of this due-diligence obligation depends on the existence of a serious (ie a real and immediate) threat to the protected rights of the individual or group of individuals concerned; knowledge on the part of the state, in that the relevant state organ(s) knew or ought to have known of the threat; and the capacity of the state to take action to prevent or counter that threat. It would seem that the knowledge of the relevant state organ at the time, provided it was based on an honest belief to be valid, should be decisive even if it later turns out to be mistaken.[76] If this concept is applied to PMS contractors in an armed conflict, one may say that the territorial state—and also the hiring or even the home state if it is within their powers—has a due-diligence obligation to protect, by any precautionary measure available, the life of the private contractors against the risk of unlawful attack from third parties if this risk is, or should be, known to exist. Such a due-diligence obligation can, for example, be fulfilled by the state by ordering constant protection for PMS contractors by the armed forces or keeping military rescue teams on stand-by to interfere and evacuate the contractors if the situation in the area becomes life-threatening. This, however, may prove impossible to arrange and would largely diminish any added value of outsourcing because it does not help to release members of the armed forces to focus on combat. Another solution would be to prohibit private contractors from carrying out tasks which may give rise to threats to their lives. However, starting from the reality that in practice the presence of private contractors in armed conflict areas has been accepted in principle, it would seem that allowing—or providing—firearms for personal self-defence to the contractors under the circumstances constitutes a reasonable way to fulfil the due-diligence obligation regarding the protection of the right to life of PMS contractors in armed conflict. The idea that non-combatants may be equipped with (small) arms for self-defence is not completely alien to IHL see, for example, Article 13(2)(a) AP I (medical personnel). It has furthermore been submitted that under certain circumstances civilians that have been armed by their state to enable them to legitimately protect themselves in situations where the state itself cannot offer sufficient security or maintain order

---

[75] The element that the threat is caused by a third party who, in other words, is neither an agent of nor otherwise acting on behalf of the contractors' hiring (or home) state or the territorial state is an essential element in this respect: the obligation of states (organs) to take precautionary measures in the conduct of hostilities and to prevent that protected persons are affected by their attacks is more stringent and codified in IHL: see eg Art 57 and 58 AP I.

[76] Cf *McCann and ors v UK* (n 62 above), para 200.

might not be directly participating in the hostilities if their motivation for using force is only to put an end to the unlawful attacks directed against them.[77]

Allowing the contractors to carry arms does not mean that their use of force is a priori accepted as, or presumed to constitute, lawful self-defence. In fact, not only the use of defensive force but also the arming of private contractors must remain the exception not the rule. The availability of arms in private hands in unstable societies may easily lead to misuse and human rights violations.[78] Even apart from the potential dangers to local civilians in the areas of operation, allowing arms to PMS contractors may not help to protect their lives as a deterrent against unlawful attack but instead may invite an exchange of fire and could create confusion as to the possible combatant status of contractors who carry their arms openly.[79] Furthermore, not all threats of force are life-threatening and immediate or at least imminent, yet contractors may feel compelled to open fire, for example, due to miscalculation or out of fear. This hazard would be non-existent if they were unarmed. To separate the carrying of arms from their use in this respect is no more than theoretical. If the presumed or desired deterrent effect of the weapon fails, its use is inevitable. A logical proviso therefore is that the carrying of arms by PMS contractors should be permitted only if compatible with the domestic law of the territorial state or granted by its special permission.[80] In the absence of such domestic laws, the contract should at least make clear that the individuals who are allowed or provided with arms must be properly trained in the use of firearms and made fully aware of the conditions necessary for lawful use of force in the protection of their lives. Similarly, there should be procedures in place to report any use of force by contractors with deadly result and to conduct investigations into the events even when an unlawful killing by a contractor is merely alleged. Another proviso, which is also a logical counterpart of a due-diligence obligation in this respect, is that the arms should be carried only during the fulfilment of the contractual duties for purposes of self-protection. Once provided by the state, the weapons should be accounted for and handed over again to the proper authorities after the end of each mission and upon the contractors' leave.

All this raises the question of what happens if the territorial state or the hiring state refuses to allow arms to the PMS contractors and the PMS contractors then come under unlawful attack in the exercise of their contractual duties and receive no, or clearly insufficient, protection, with deaths resulting. It can be argued that the (hiring or territorial) state may have violated its due-diligence obligation to do

---

[77] See MN Schmitt, '"Direct Participation in Hostilities" and 21st Century Armed Conflict' in H Fischer et al (eds), *Crisis Management and Humanitarian Protection: Festschrift für Dieter Fleck* (2004), 520.
[78] See eg *Prevention of Human Rights Violations Committed with Small Arms and Light Weapons* (n 45 above); Z Yihdego, *The Arms Trade and International Law* (2007).
[79] Reportedly, in Iraq insurgents treated private contractors indistinguishably from the (Western) combatants: see D Barstow, 'Security Companies: Shadow Soldiers in Iraq', *The New York Times* (19 April 2004).
[80] There is no reason in principle why a PMS contractor operating abroad should be prohibited by the hiring state or his state of nationality or residence from carrying arms if the territorial state consents to it.

everything reasonably within its power to protect the contractors' right to life.[81] In extreme circumstances, it may even be argued that a contractor's non-compliance with the laws of the territorial state prohibiting the carrying of arms (or similarly, his non-compliance with rules of the territorial or the hiring state making the carrying of arms dependent on prior approval of eg the relevant commander in the area of operations) would be excusable given the lack of alternatives to protect his life effectively. It is thus clear that not only allowing, but also withholding, weapons to PMS contractors in armed conflict can under certain circumstances give rise to issues of due diligence, prudence, and precaution, and possibly responsibility, on the part of states.

B. Contractual Clauses and the Carrying of Arms

As the previous discussion indicates, the contract as a regulating tool has its limits as regards the controlling of the lawful use of force by private contractors in armed conflict. A contract which contains the clause that PMS contractors may only use their arms as ultimate resort in self-defence and only proportional to the danger, reiterates a rule of international law which applies independent of it. There is no difference in substance to contracts that are silent as to the issue of the use of firearms, although the fact that the individual contractor has been duly informed through the contract about his rights and duties under international law may play a role in the evaluation of the behaviour (eg for purposes of establishing responsibility) of the contractor, his company, and the (hiring or territorial) state. It can be presumed that if it is known or can be foreseen at the time by the state concerned that there will be 'inherent' serious risks to the lives of the contractors due to (the nature and the location of) the contractual tasks involved and no other means for protection (eg escorts by the armed forces of the state) can be provided, the right to carry and use arms for self-defence will logically be included in the contract, or at least will not be excluded by it.

This does not mean or imply that a contract could give the contractors a right to use force which goes beyond the limits set by international law. In particular, a right to use force which amounts to direct participation in the hostilities cannot be granted to PMS contractors (otherwise, a category of 'unlawful combatants' would be created). Similarly, a contract which purports to exclude the right to carry and use arms cannot set aside the right to protect one's life, including through force used in lawful self-defence. The contractual clause prohibiting the carrying and use of arms by PMS contractors (or a similar clause which eg makes the carrying of arms by the contractor dependent on special permission) is therefore set aside or 'overruled' if, in the exercise of the contractual tasks or duties, situations occur in which

---

[81] Arguably, the territorial state likely is well aware of the concrete circumstances on the ground in the designated areas of operation of the contractors, or at least it should be able to make accurate assessments as to the security situation on the ground. The hiring state presumably has the most frequent contacts with the contractors or their management and on that basis arguably has the capacity to exert influence on their behaviour.

the contractors' life is at stake and apart from defensive force no reasonable options for protection are available.[82] In that respect it may additionally be noted that even if an individual could 'renounce' his right to life and its protection by entering into a contract, such a contract generally would be considered void in domestic legal systems as being immoral or contrary to public order. It should be kept in mind that PMS contractors do not forfeit their right to life by engaging in dangerous duties in armed conflict even if the actions resulting from those duties at some point amount to a direct participation in the hostilities (then they 'only' forfeit their legal protection against attack). The same holds true where the contractor has consciously and by his own fault exposed himself to the danger to his life or has endangered the lives of others without his contractual obligations requiring this of him. But in those circumstances a 'need to retreat' instead of using defensive force will be presumed to exist and there will be no due-diligence obligation towards that contractor since these risks were not known or foreseeable for the state concerned.

It can be concluded that if the contract assigns the PMS contractors low-risk tasks, activities, or responsibilities, in places which for all practical purposes rule out as much as possible any serious hazard of deadly attack against them, a contractual clause prohibiting the carrying and use of arms cannot be set aside. The same applies if effective alternative means of protection are available to the contractors in the event of emergencies. In addition, those conditions in practice rule out the possibility that the territorial state or the hiring state (whichever seeks to prohibit the use of arms through the contract) knew or ought to have known at the time of the existence of a real risk to the life of the contractors concerned and failed to take precautionary measures which reasonably fell within its capacities. Still, the assessment as to whether or not PMS contractors should be allowed arms for the protection of their lives is also dependent on the concrete circumstances on the ground in the (planned) area of operation. Even extensive precautions or excessive diligence cannot always prevent miscalculations in such an assessment. As noted earlier, rapidly changing conditions on the ground can make it difficult to calculate whether the contractors will be exposed to life-threatening situations. This raises the more fundamental question whether, by default, states should allow PMS contractors to carry (and therefore use) arms for self-defence in order to be prepared for the eventuality of attack in the performance of their duties or, instead, should deny contractors arms in order to prevent the inherent risks such as violations of IHL and human rights law in the (planned) areas of operation as far as possible. With this question, the broader debate is entered whether outsourcing by states of certain functions to private parties is, or should be, permitted under international law.

---

[82] Outside the exercise of contractual tasks or duties, this assessment is of course different. Eg four US-hired private contractors were accused of violating the gun policy of their contract with the US military because they were not authorized to carry weapons when they were involved in a deadly shooting in Afghanistan in May 2009: although authorized to handle weapons in the exercise of their contractual duties (firearms training of the Afghan army) they were not allowed to have weapons with them at other times. See Jerry Markon, 'Two Defense Contractors Indicted in Shooting of Afghans', *Washington Post* (8 January 2010).

V. The Broader Context: The State Monopoly on the Use of Force

Although a fact of life today, it cannot be denied that the outsourcing by states of functions to armed private contractors operating in armed conflict comes close to challenging the state monopoly on the use of force. The state monopoly on the use of force can be inferred from the fundamentals of the collective security system, in which the threat or use of force is prohibited between states. Self-defence is the exception to this prohibition and can be exercised by states, for example, in the context of international arrangements for mutual assistance.[83] Security Council mandates for enforcement actions are addressed to states as well.[84] International organizations such as the UN, NATO, and the EU do not have standing armed forces available to them on a permanent basis. Even though the right to use force in international relations has been largely transferred to the UN, the military means to exercise that right are still held exclusively by states.

There can be little doubt that the outsourcing of combat functions ('warfare') by states to private parties goes against the foundations of the international legal system relating to collective security and the defence of national sovereignty, even though examples of contrary practice can be found.[85] Likewise, in IHL combat functions are meant to be allocated only to state organs (namely the armed forces). Civilians are expected not to participate directly in the hostilities and lose their right to immunity from attack when, and as long as, they do. The same is reflected in the ancient bias against mercenaries and in their lack of protection under IHL.[86] Another indicator for the existence of legal limits to the outsourcing of state functions to private parties can be found in the rule that the conduct of private persons or entities exercising elements of governmental authority shall be considered an act of the state under international law provided the person or entity is acting in that capacity in the particular instance.[87] It can even be argued that elements which are 'inherently governmental' cannot be outsourced at all and must be carried out by government employees only.[88] The question of exactly which

---

[83] Cf Arts 2(4) and 51 UN Charter; Art 5 NATO Charter. See further M Schmidl, *The Changing Nature of Self-defense in International Law* (2009), 34–6.

[84] Such a mandate can be addressed to an undefined number of states, eg S/Res/678 (1990), which authorized the Member States cooperating with the government of Kuwait to use all necessary means (ie including force) to implement previous resolutions, or even to a specific state; S/Res/221 (1966), which authorized the United Kingdom to stop vessels reasonably believed to be carrying oil to Rhodesia, by the use of force if necessary.

[85] See, in particular, the involvement of the South African company Executive Outcomes in the civil wars in Angola and Sierra Leone in 1995–7, and the Bahamas-based company Sandline International in Sierra Leone in 1997–8. Cf P Singer, 'Corporate Warriors: The Rise of the Privatized Military Industry and its Ramifications for International Security' *International Security* 26(3) (2001–2) 188, 206–7, 213–14.

[86] See eg PW Mourning, 'Leashing the Dogs of War: Outlawing the Recruitment and use of Mercenaries' (1981–2) 22 Va J Int'l L 589; S Brayton, 'Outsourcing War: Mercenaries and the Privatization of Peacekeeping' *J Int'l Affairs* 55(2) (2002) 303.

[87] See 2001 ILC Articles (n 68 above), Art 5.

[88] See S Chesterman, '"We Can't Spy...If We Can't Buy!": The Privatization of Intelligence and the Limits of Outsourcing "Inherently Governmental Functions"' (2008) 19 EJIL 1055.

services or functions fit the qualification 'inherently governmental' is subject to debate, but there is a wide consensus that combat functions ('warfare') are certainly part of them.[89] The 2008 Montreux Document[90] stipulates that, in determining which services can be contracted out to private parties and which cannot, states must take into account whether the particular service could cause PMS personnel to become involved in direct participation in the hostilities. This 'top-down' approach based on the use of force by states is consonant with the 'bottom-up' approach based on the right to life and its protection through self-defence as analysed in this chapter. After all, one way for states to fulfil the due-diligence obligation to protect the right to life is by determining whether outsourcing in a concrete instance will require private contractors to carry out tasks which involve serious risks of unlawful deadly attacks against them. If serious risks can be discerned and protection cannot be offered through alternative means, outsourcing to private parties should be avoided. The leading principle may be that states should allow PMS contractors to perform only those tasks and in those areas where their right to life is not endangered or can be effectively protected by the hiring or the territorial state if unexpected events occur. This does not rule out that contractors can be armed to enable lawful self-defence in emergency situations, but it is preferable that, as a matter of prudence and precaution, solutions are made available which minimize chances that force has to be used by the contractors.

A general prohibition on outsourcing tasks to PMS contractors 'with guns' would probably be the best guarantee against a whole range of risks pertaining to the abuse of arms, direct participation in the hostilities by non-combatants, and 'arbitrary' killings, and would also fit in well with the established principle of the state monopoly on the use of force. However, such a prohibition could not take away the contractors' right to protect their lives through self-defence against unlawful attack when necessary. The best alternative approach from the perspective of protecting the contractors would not be to try to reach agreement as to each and every typical 'governmental' task which should not be outsourced. Rather, agreement should be reached on the effects which should be avoided. As such, it is submitted that states should be prohibited from outsourcing functions or services to private contractors if it is known or can be foreseen that in the performance of the contract in the (planned) area of operation, either direct participation in the hostilities by the (armed) contractors is or will be necessary or inevitable or that the (armed) contractors cannot reasonably avert life-threatening dangers other than through a use of force which will exceed the limits of lawful self-defence. Below this threshold, outsourcing to (armed) private contractors would be permissible in

---

[89] See eg *Report on Private Military and Security Firms and Erosion of the State Monopoly on the Use of Force*, Council of Europe Venice Commission, CDL-AD (2009) 038, study no 531/2009, 29 June 2009, para 25, 29, <http://www.venice.coe.int>, accessed on 17 August 2010; J Elsea, 'Private Security Contractors in Iraq and Afghanistan: Legal Issues', *CRS Report* (7 January 2010), 16, <http://www.fas.org/sgp/crs>, accessed on 17 August 2010.

[90] See The Montreux Document on Pertinent International Legal Obligations and Good Practices for States Related to Operations of Private Military and Security Companies during Armed Conflict (Montreux Document), Montreux, 17 September 2008, repr 13(3) (2009) JC&SL 451–75.

principle, but there still exists a due-diligence obligation requiring states to assess to what extent there is, or likely will arise, a serious risk of harm to the lives of the private contractors when performing their contractual duties in the (planned) area of operation, and to take all protective measures available to them and corresponding to the risks involved. In assessing those risks, the circumstances 'on the ground' should be decisive and not the question of whether, or how, the contract arranges the carrying and use of arms by the contractors.[91]

In the absence of international legally binding documents on these precise matters—and as yet there are no such documents—the divergent interests of states create serious obstacles to negotiating, concluding, and implementing (uniform) rules on the outsourcing of tasks to (armed) PMS contractors in armed conflict. It must be acknowledged, however, that the PMS sector largely operates domestically, outside armed conflicts, and for the most part offers services which do not raise any serious concerns as to compliance with IHL and human rights law by or against the contractors. The pressing issue is therefore to single out the high-risk businesses in high-risk areas of operation. This requires careful coordination at the international level, in order to prevent businesses from simply changing their seat to states with a more lenient regulatory climate. In that respect, international organizations can fulfil an important harmonizing role.[92] The EU in particular is in a position to take steps, considering that many PMS companies are located in EU Member States and the EU is becoming increasingly active in areas of (armed) conflict, and that the regulatory capacity of the EU, comprising instruments which are directly binding in the Member States, goes beyond that of practically any other international organization.

VI. Concluding Remarks

In this chapter the extent to which the right to life and its protection through personal self-defence can impact on the carrying and use of arms by PMS contractors in armed conflict has been examined. It has been established that PMS contractors, who in principle qualify as civilians under IHL, can be legitimate

---

[91] From the perspective of active protection of the civilian population or prisoners of war *against* PMS contractors even stricter limitations on the outsourcing of tasks may be desirable, but this is outside the scope of the present chapter. See on human rights violations committed by private contractors Ch 8 by Pinzauti in this volume.

[92] See on the (potential) role of international organizations, especially the EU, in regulating PMS contractors eg A Bailes and C Holmqvist, *The Increasing Role of Private Military and Security Companies*, European Union DG External Policies study, October 2007; C Holmqvist, *Private Security Companies: The Case for regulation*, SIPRI policy paper 9 January 2005; E Krahmann, 'Regulating Military and Security Services in the European Union' in M Caparini and A Brayden (eds), *Private Actors and Security Governance* (2006), 189–212; J Hagmann and M Kartas, 'International Organizations and the Governance of Private Security' in M Caparini and A Brayden (eds), ibid, 285–304; H Born, M Caparini, and E Cole, *Regulating Private Security in Europe: Status and Prospects*, DCAF Policy Paper 20 (2007), 7–8. Clearly, self-regulation by the PMS industry itself (the 'supply side') can be relevant as well: see eg S Percy, *Regulating the Private Security Industry*, Adelphi Papers 384 (2006); and Ch 18 by Hoppe and Quirico in this volume.

targets in IAC and in NIAC if they participate directly in the hostilities or if their targeting can be deemed 'excusable' out of military necessity, for example, because they are functionally attached to military objects. It is submitted that the contract which governs the relationship with the PMS contractors cannot take away their right to carry and use arms for purposes of lawful self-defence, unless the performance of the contract in the area of operation poses no risk to the contractors' life or effective alternative means of protection are available in emergency situations.

States (hiring or territorial) have a general due-diligence obligation requiring them to assess to what extent there is a serious risk of harm to the lives of the private contractors when performing the contract in the (planned) area of operation, and to take all protective measures available to them and corresponding to the risks involved. In the event that other means of protection are not available, it is submitted that this due-diligence obligation may be fulfilled by allowing arms for personal self-defence to PMS contractors who operate in hostile environments where it is known or foreseeable that in the performance of their contract their lives will be at serious risk. It should be acknowledged that due to the often rapidly changing circumstances in zones of armed conflict, assessments as to the concrete dangers on the ground are very difficult to make. Moreover, armed contractors in highly unstable zones may in practice feel compelled to use force beyond the limits of lawful self-defence, thus committing (war) crimes.

It can therefore be concluded that as a matter of prudence and precaution, states should refrain from outsourcing tasks which, insofar as is known or foreseeable, necessitate PMS contractors carrying arms because of the risks involved in the regular performance of their contract in the area of operation, thus minimizing chances that defensive force must be used by the contractors. It is furthermore suggested that outsourcing should be prohibited if direct participation in the hostilities by the contractors is a necessary or inevitable consequence of the performance of their contract or if life-threatening dangers can only reasonably be averted by the contractors through a use of force which will exceed the limits of lawful self-defence (lawful aim, necessity, proportionality). Such prohibitions would also fit the principle of the state monopoly on the use of force.

PART III

INTERNATIONAL HUMANITARIAN LAW

10

Status of Private Military and Security Company Personnel in the Law of International Armed Conflict

Mirko Sossai

I. Introduction

The employment of private military and security companies (PMSCs) in recent war scenarios constitutes a challenge to the paradigm of the law of armed conflicts as a state-centric system based on the state monopoly of the use of force.[1] Nonetheless, various commentators have already shown that private contractors do not operate in a legal vacuum: the existing law of armed conflict provides a binding legal framework and contains the criteria for individuating the status of their staff. On the basis of the fundamental principle of distinction between combatants and civilians, the primary status of persons affected by an international armed conflict[2] is indeed crucial as it determines the rights and the privileges afforded by the law and the legal consequences deriving from the conduct of those persons.[3]

There seems to be little doubt that PMSC employees can fall into several categories, depending on both the function they perform and their relationship with a party to the conflict. Therefore, the focus of this chapter will be on both the qualification of the connection with the hiring state and the controversial notion of direct participation in hostilities.

II. The Relationship with the Hiring State

There is general agreement that a number of activities that were previously performed by regular military forces are now being outsourced to private contractors. Though most of them carry out functions that are unrelated to the conduct of hostilities, concern has been expressed about their possible involvement in combat

---

[1] J Cockayne, 'The Global Reorganization of Legitimate Violence: Military Entrepreneurs and the Private Face of International Humanitarian Law' (2006) 88 IRRC 459.
[2] On the issue of the role of PMSCs in Non-international armed conflicts, see Ch 12 by Vierucci in this volume.
[3] K Ipsen, 'Combatants and Non-combatants' in D Fleck (ed), *The Handbook of Humanitarian Law in Armed Conflicts* (2008), 79.

operations. The first problematic aspect is whether they should be considered as legitimate combatants under international humanitarian law (IHL), as traditionally only members of the armed forces (regular or irregular combatants belonging to a party to the conflict) enjoy the 'combatant privilege' in war.

A. Private Contractors as Legitimate Combatants

Though one cannot exclude that PMSC employees may fall within the category of mercenaries,[4] much debate has been devoted to the issue of the definition of membership of the armed forces, specifically whether it could include the private contractors' personnel in certain cases. It seems that the underlying crucial question relates to the legitimacy of outsourcing activities which are inherently governmental and military in nature. In this respect, one might wonder whether IHL sets specific limits to the state practice of hiring PMSCs.

The first step is to investigate whether the law of international armed conflict assigns certain tasks to the regular armed forces of the state, so that they cannot be carried out by private firms. This is the case of the appointment of the commander responsible for a prisoner of war camp: Article 39 of the Third Geneva Convention provides that every camp 'shall be put under the immediate authority of a responsible commissioned officer belonging to the regular armed forces of the Detaining Power'. In the same way, Article 99 of the Fourth Geneva Convention states that: 'Every place of internment shall be put under the authority of a responsible officer, chosen from the regular military forces or the regular civil administration of the Detaining Power.'

In addition, the corollary of the fundamental principle of distinction—according to which only combatants can lawfully directly participate in hostilities—is to define a criterion to determine what functions private companies may perform and what degree of control the state should exercise. It goes without saying that the discussion on the combatant status is limited to the situation of private contractors hired by states. In this regard, IHL identifies various categories of persons who can be combatants. The discussion among certain experts[5] has focused essentially on the category of de facto combatant status, identified by Article 4A(2), ie 'members of other militias and members of other volunteer corps belonging to a Party to the conflict', and on the key rule contained in Article 43 of the 1977 Additional Protocol I, which provides the definition of the members of armed forces. The reason why the relevant provisions of both instruments need to be taken into account is that Protocol I has not been ratified by 27 states, even though the recent ICRC study considers the rule on membership of the armed forces as evidence of customary law.[6]

---

[4] See Ch 16 by Mancini, Ntoubandi and Marauhn in this volume.
[5] The University Centre for International Humanitarian Law, 'Expert Meeting on Private Military Contractors: Status and State Responsibility for their Actions', August 2005; ICRC, 'Summary Report of Third Expert Meeting on the Notion of Direct Participation in Hostilities', Geneva, 23–5 October 2005 (hereinafter ICRC, '2005 Summary Report').
[6] See J-M Henckaerts and L Doswald-Beck (eds), *Customary International Humanitarian Law* (2005), I, 14 (Rule 4).

The category identified by Article 4A(2) comprises the members of irregular forces. Independent militias which are not formally incorporated into the state armed forces[7] are combatants if they belong to a party to the conflict and fulfil the four well-known conditions set out in the 1907 Hague Regulations:[8] that of being commanded by a person responsible for his/her subordinates; that of having a fixed distinctive sign recognizable at a distance; that of carrying arms openly; and that of conducting their operations in accordance with the laws and customs of war.

As for the requirement of 'belonging to a Party to the conflict', it refers at least to a de facto link between the militia or the volunteer group and the state: the International Tribunal for the Former Yugoslavia described the relationship in terms of control by the state and dependence by the group.[9] Therefore, the mere fact of fighting in support of a party is not sufficient for a PMSC to meet the criterion, though the amount of control that the state should exercise is not easy to assess. In any event, considering that the category was conceived with resistance movements in mind, the majority of commentators share the view that a private company, considered as a distinct group, could rarely match the four standards.[10] The last condition, requiring the general respect of the laws and customs of war, has been recognized as less problematic: a general and systematic disregard for IHL on the part of PMSCs has not been observed. The first condition could be met only by those structured companies which are hierarchically organized and provide some form of supervision analogous to command.[11] The other two criteria are intended to eliminate any risk of confusion with the civilian population: in particular, having a fixed distinct emblem does not require the wearing of a uniform. This seems to be satisfied by PMSC staff that do openly carry arms and wear military clothes: it is reported that in Iraq they have sometimes been confused by the civilian population with members of the regular armed forces. There is no unified policy among the contractors. Generally, the US Department of Defense (DoD) does not allow contractors' staff to wear military or military lookalike uniforms. However, certain contractor personnel may be authorized 'to wear standard uniform items for operational reasons'.[12]

The broader and more flexible criteria individuated by Article 43 of Protocol I might offer a viable solution to include the PMSC staff within the category of 'members of the armed forces' in certain circumstances. This provision establishes a common denominator applicable to all, supplementing the specific rules of Article 4

---

[7] For a discussion on the relevance of Art 4A(1) of the Third Geneva Convention, see E-C Gillard, 'Business Goes to War: Private Military/Security Companies and International Humanitarian Law', (2006) 88 IRRC 525, 533.

[8] See Art 1 of the Regulations Concerning the Laws and Customs of War on Land, The Hague, 18 October 1907.

[9] *Prosecutor v Dusko Tadić*, IT-94-1-A, 15 July 1999, paras 93–4.

[10] Cf E-C Gillard (n 7 above), 535; L Doswald-Beck, 'Private Military Companies under International Humanitarian Law' in S Chesterman and C Lehnardt (eds), *From Mercenaries to Market: The Rise and Regulation of Private Military Companies* (2007), 118.

[11] Cf MN Schmitt, 'Humanitarian Law and Direct Participation in Hostilities by Private Contractors or Civilian Employees' (2005) 5 Chicago JIL 511, 529.

[12] US DoD Instruction 3020.41, 3 October 2005, para 6.2.7.7.

of the Third Geneva Convention,[13] with a view to taking into account 'the new forces which have appeared on the modern battlefield in the course of the last few decades'. The definition under Article 43 is based on the following elements: that of acting on behalf of a party to the conflict; that of being organized; and that of being under a command responsible to that party for the conduct of its subordinates.

The most controversial aspect is therefore how to qualify the connection between the party to the conflict and the private contractor: the opinions expressed by the various experts could be grouped around two main positions with regard to the content of the crucial notion of 'command responsible to a Party'.

According to the first approach, what is required is formal incorporation by the state, in order to put the private contractors within the military chain of command and control. Therefore, membership of an armed force remains primarily regulated by domestic legislation. It has been argued that contractors' employees do not become members of the armed forces of a state simply by performing certain activities, if the state does not considers them as such.[14] This seems to be confirmed by Article 43(3), on the incorporation of paramilitary or armed law enforcement agencies, which provides an obligation of notification to the other parties of the conflict. In one author's view, the provision introduces a constitutive requirement, so that unincorporated agencies are civilian in nature for the purposes of humanitarian law.[15]

On the contrary, it has been argued that if private contractors have been entitled by a state to participate directly in hostilities on its behalf, they should be included within the members of the armed forces. Therefore, the second position adopts a functional approach: the requirements of international law that provide the fulfilment of certain conditions de facto are decisive.[16] In other words, the category identified by Article 43 covers all groups which have a certain qualified factual link to the regular armed forces.[17]

Against the background of these considerations, the first observation relates to the comprehensiveness of the definition provided by Article 43 which overcomes the distinction between regular and irregular armed forces: it follows that formal incorporation is not an unavoidable requirement. Nevertheless the functional approach needs further analysis and clarification, on the basis of the recent practice.

B. The 'Command Responsible' Requirement

The question of the 'combatant privilege' concerns an organized unit of employees of a private firm hired by the state for the provision of services which may amount

---

[13] J de Preux, 'Article 43' in Y Sandoz et al (eds), *Commentary on the Additional Protocols of 8 June 1977 to the Geneva Conventions of 12 August 1949* (1986), 506.
[14] ICRC, '2005 Summary Report', 77.
[15] Schmitt (n 11 above), 525.
[16] ICRC, '2005 Summary Report', 75.
[17] Doswald-Beck (n 10 above), 121, quoting M Bothe, KJ Partsch, and WA Solf, *New Rules for Victims of Armed Conflict: Commentary on the Two 1977 Protocols additional to the Geneva Conventions of 1949* (1982), 234.

to 'taking a direct part in hostilities'. Therefore, assuming that a state intends to confer such a mandate, it should make the effort to satisfy the criteria established by IHL, in order to confer combatant status on the PMSCs employees. As argued in the previous section, formal incorporation is not decisive according to the definition included in Article 43 of Protocol I. Under the functional approach, the problem of what the 'command responsible' condition entails lies at the heart of the analysis. This requirement, in conjunction with the existence of 'an internal disciplinary system', pursues, inter alia, the aim of enforcing 'compliance with the rules of international law applicable in armed conflict'.

On the one hand, it seems that the mere conclusion of the contract between the state and the private firm would not be sufficient to meet the condition, even though the document would contain clauses on the respect for the laws of war and the contractor would be required to submit reports to a governmental officer.[18] On the other hand, the formulation of Article 43 does not call for the existence of a military chain of command: the notion is flexible and it leaves open the possibility of a different kind of command, for instance, consisting of private individuals.

In other words, the 'command responsible' condition requires a certain degree of oversight by the party to the conflict. An accepted standard should meet the requirement provided by Article 43 of an internal disciplinary system, 'which covers the field of military disciplinary law as well as that of military penal law'.[19] What the hiring state must do is to establish appropriate supervision and control which includes the exercise of criminal jurisdiction over the contractor personnel. Against this background, the reading of the 'functional approach' for the determination of membership in armed forces by the ICRC's *Interpretive Guidance on the Notion of Direct Participation in Hostilities*[20] seems unconvincing. The document recognizes the situation of 'contractors and employees who, to all intents and purposes, have been incorporated into the armed forces of a party to the conflict, whether through a formal procedure under national law or *de facto* by being given a continuous combat function',[21] and concludes that 'Under IHL, such personnel would become members of an organized armed force, group, or unit under a command responsible to a party to the conflict and, for the purposes of the principle of distinction, would no longer qualify as civilians'.[22] However, the 'command responsible' criterion requires more than the mere 'express or tacit authorisation of the State party to the conflict'.[23]

There is no doubt that the first step would be to rigorously define the tasks in the contract and include specific provisions on the respect of the law of international

---

[18] *Contra* C Hoppe, 'Passing the Buck: State Responsibility for Private Military Companies', (2008) 19 EJIL 989, 1009.
[19] de Preux (n 13 above), 513.
[20] N Melzer (ed), *Interpretive Guidance on the Notion of Direct Participation in Hostilities under International Humanitarian Law* (2009) (hereinafter ICRC, *Interpretive Guidance*). See below, next section.
[21] Cf ibid, 34: The notion individuates 'a continuous function involving a direct participation in hostilities'.
[22] Ibid, 39.   [23] Ibid.

armed conflict, the violation of which should trigger consequences like contract suspension or termination, possible fines, and exclusion from future contracts. The contract should provide for appropriate training programmes in international human rights and humanitarian law.[24] Even though the United States considers contractors as civilians accompanying the armed forces, recent practice deserves particular attention, as it represents the unavoidable test case:[25] whilst in the early stages of the Iraqi operations the DoD lacked regulation on the presence and use of contractors, now a substantial number of documents have been published.[26] It is important to investigate how they cover the new functions of private firms and whether they set a certain trend with regard to the relationship with the armed forces. In this respect, a 2006 DoD directive requires 'contractors to institute and implement effective programs to prevent violations of the law of war by their employees and subcontractors, including law of war training and dissemination'.[27] However, implementation has been regarded as insufficient.[28]

In addition, under Protocol I, being 'responsible to a Party of the conflict' entails that the organized group has to answer to the party for its own actions. In the context of the use of private contractors in armed conflicts, it means not only that the contractor has to report to the hiring state but that the latter has to establish a supervision mechanism. Specific indications are unlikely to be found in the commentary to the Protocol; however, one might infer that the command of the regular armed forces should ensure a certain degree of control and coordination of the activities performed by private contractors.

The problem of the lack of control of PMSCs was dramatically demonstrated in the aftermath of the incident in the Nisoor Square on 16 September 2007, when Blackwater personnel, running an armed convoy through Baghdad, killed 17 civilians.[29] It was even reported that in some cases contractors were actually supervising governmental personnel, instead of the other way around.[30] On October 2007 the panel of experts appointed by the US Secretary of State published a report on

---

[24] The parties to a conflict are required to 'give orders and instructions to ensure observance' (cf Art 80(2) of Protocol I) of IHL.
[25] Various examples in this chapter will be taken from the Iraqi scenario since 2003. As a matter of law, the *occupatio bellica* following the end of major hostilities still constitutes a situation of international armed conflict. See, inter alia, A Roberts, 'The End of Occupation: Iraq 2004' (2005) 54 ICLQ 27; A Carcano, 'End of the occupation in 2004?' (2006) 11 JC&SL 58.
[26] D Isenberg, 'A Government in Search of Cover' in S Chesterman and C Lehnardt (eds) (n 9 above), 89.
[27] US DoD Directive 2311.01 E, 9 May 2006. This document and all the subsequent DoD issuances are available at <http://www.dtic.mil/whs/directives>, accessed on 17 August 2010.
[28] L Dickinson, 'Testimony before the United States Senate Committee on Homeland Security and Governmental Affairs', 27 February 2008, 8, <http://hsgac.senate.gov/public>, accessed on 17 August 2010.
[29] Memorandum to Members of the Committee on Oversight and Government Reform, 'Additional Information about Blackwater USA', 1 October 2007, 6.
[30] Cf the findings of the US internal investigation on the prison abuses at Abu Ghraib in Iraq, as regards the relationship between government officers and CACI employees: 'Several people indicated in their statements that contractor personnel were "supervising" government personnel'. See 'Investigation of the Abu Ghraib Detention Facility and 205th Military Intelligence Brigade', AR–15–6, 23 August 2004, 51–2.

personal protective services in Iraq, which recommended a series of measures to improve coordination, oversight, and accountability.[31] A Memorandum of Agreement between the Departments of State and Defense was then signed on 5 December 2007; the document represents a significant step towards the enhancement of procedures, since it states that US government private contractors running a convoy in Iraq 'will coordinate their movements' with either Coalition military or US Embassy operations centres in Baghdad. Improvements in how the US DoD manages PMSCs[32] have been reported by both the Special Inspector General for Iraq Reconstruction and the Commission on Wartime Contracting.[33]

The last aspect is the issue of criminal jurisdiction over contractor personnel. US practice shows that the trend moves towards the exercise of military jurisdiction over the employees of private firms. On 17 October 2006, the Uniform Code of Military Justice (UCMJ) was amended to extend jurisdiction over persons 'serving with or accompanying an armed force in the field' also during 'contingency operations';[34] courts-martial are authorized to try them for offences prohibited by the UCMJ.

To conclude, when a state hires an organized private unit for coercive services, the existence of the factual link required for 'membership in the armed forces' within the meaning of Article 43(1) is not unlikely, once the following three conditions are present: the contract defines precisely the tasks to be performed by the company, the state authorities assure adequate oversight and coordination of the activities, and the PMSCs employees are subject to criminal jurisdiction. The scenario appears to be more problematic when private companies are not contracted by the state directly, but subcontracted. In Iraq, for example, more than 20,000 individuals perform protective security functions for private firms under US government contracts.[35] The question of whether they act on behalf of a party to the conflict should be answered in the affirmative if the security services constitute an integral element of the prime contract performance.[36]

---

[31] P Kennedy et al, 'Report of the Secretary of State's Panel on Personal Protective Services in Iraq', 23 October 2007.

[32] See, recently, US DoD Instruction 3020.50, 22 June 2009. This document 'establishes policy, assigns responsibilities, and provides procedures for the regulation of the selection, accountability, training, equipping, and conduct of personnel performing private security functions under a covered contract during contingency operations'.

[33] US Special Inspector General for Iraq Reconstruction, 'Field Commanders see Improvements in Controlling and Coordinating Private Security Contractor Missions in Iraq', SIGIR 09-022, 28 July 2009; US Congress, House Committee on Oversight and Government Reform, Subcommittee on National Security and Foreign Affairs, 'Commission on Wartime Contracting: Interim Findings and Path Forward', 111th Cong, 1st sess, 10 June 2009.

[34] Under US law, 'Contingency operations' are those 'designated by the Secretary of Defense as an operation in which members of the armed forces are or may become involved in military actions, operations, or hostilities against an enemy of the United States or against an opposing military force'.

[35] See 'Private Security Contractors in Iraq: Background, Legal Status, and Other Issues', RL32419, July 2007, 6.

[36] Schmitt (n 11 above), 528.

III. Private Contractors Taking a Direct Part in Hostilities

When PMSCs employees have not been de jure or de facto incorporated into the armed forces of a party to a conflict and do not provide services amounting to direct participation in hostilities, they are clearly civilians under IHL. However, the precise definition of 'direct participation in hostilities' and its consequences has been a source of controversy in recent years. This crucial notion is used both in Article 43(2) and in Article 51(3) of Protocol I: to define the combatant privilege in the former; to express the loss of the civilians' right to protection from attack in the latter. The loss of immunity for a civilian participating in hostilities is also repeated in Additional Protocol II on the law of non-international armed conflicts.

The ICRC has sought to clarify the main issues at stake by organizing a series of expert meetings between 2003 and 2008: the outcome is the publication of the *Interpretive Guidance on the Notion of Direct Participation in Hostilities under IHL* in 2009.

A. The Constitutive Elements of the Notion

Since the two key components are that of 'hostilities' and that of 'direct participation', the approach taken by the ICRC *Interpretive Guidance* focuses on three constitutive elements of the two notions: whilst the 'threshold of harm' principle essentially addresses the first component, the other two requirements of 'direct causation' and 'belligerent nexus' qualify when a specific act amounts to 'direct participation'.[37]

To understand the first requirement, one should start from the description of 'hostile acts' as 'acts which by their nature and purpose are intended to cause actual harm to the personnel and equipment of the armed forces'.[38] As for the typology of harm, the Commentary to Protocol I seems to imply that only military objectives must be affected. However, this interpretation is too restrictive in present war scenarios, where the parties pursue their goals by also illegally attacking civilian objects.[39] The formulation included in the *Interpretive Guidance* takes into account this latter element as it provides that 'a specific act must be likely ... to inflict death, injury, or destruction on persons or objects protected against direct attack'.[40] That the definitions cover all hostile acts, both in offence and in defence,[41] is undisputed.

---

[37] ICRC, *Interpretive Guidance*, 46. It should be noted that such an approach was criticized by some members of the ICRC expert group, as it imposes inappropriate constraints on the scope of direct participation in hostilities.

[38] Sandoz et al (eds) (n 13 above), 618, para 1942. See *Prosecutor v Kordic and Cerkez*, IT-95-14/2-A, 17 December 2004, para 51; Inter-American Commission on Human Rights, *Third Report on Human Rights in Colombia*, Doc OEA/SerL/V/II102 Doc 9 rev 1, 26 February 1999, para 53.

[39] See *The Public Committee against Torture in Israel and ors v The Government of Israel and ors*, HCJ 769/02, 13 December 2006, para 33.

[40] ICRC, *Interpretive Guidance*, 47.

[41] See Art 49 Protocol I.

However, the qualification of protective security services might be delicate in certain circumstances, when it is not easy to distinguish defence against enemy attacks and against violence unrelated to the hostilities.

The qualification of the term 'harm' is still dubious: it should not be interpreted too broadly, to individuate every interference with the enemy's strategic goals. The *Interpretive Guidance* qualifies the notion of harm as comprising acts 'adversely affecting the military operations or military capacity of a party to the conflict'.[42] It definitely includes the establishment and exercise of control over military personnel (including detention), objects, and territory, as well as 'electronic interference with military computer networks'.

The second element appears to be less problematic. Its function is to explain that 'an act qualifying as "direct participation in hostilities" must have a "nexus" to a situation of armed conflict'.[43] At first sight, this criterion is similar to the requirement for the qualification of an act as a war crime.[44] But the 'belligerent nexus', as conceived by the *Interpretive Guidance*, is narrower since it requires not only that the act should be designed to harm a party to an armed conflict, but it must also be 'in support of a party to the conflict'.[45] During the expert meetings, the point was made that this latter requirement would prevent armed violence by independent groups, including certain non-state private contractors, during an international armed conflict from qualifying as direct participation in hostilities, unless their members operated in support of one of the parties.[46]

The third element—the existence of a causal correlation between the activity and the harm for the adversary—is the key principle.[47] The qualification of the term 'directness' lies at the core of the debate on the notion of 'direct participation'. Two main theoretical positions have been propounded: a narrow interpretation which prioritizes the protection of innocent civilians;[48] and a wider approach, in favour of finding participation in grey areas, aimed at encouraging civilians 'to remain as distant from the conflict as possible'.[49]

In this respect, the ICRC Commentary on Protocol I appears to favour a restrictive interpretation, as it affirms in the context of Article 43: 'Direct participation in hostilities implies a *direct causal* relationship between the activity engaged

---

[42] ICRC, *Interpretive Guidance*, 47.
[43] ICRC, '2005 Summary Report', 24.
[44] Cf G Mettraux, *International Crimes and the* Ad Hoc *Tribunals* (2005), 39, for a discussion on the substance and meaning of the nexus requirement for war crimes in the jurisprudence of the ad hoc International Criminal Tribunals.
[45] ICRC, *Interpretive Guidance*, 58.
[46] Cf ICRC, 'Summary Report of Fourth Expert Meeting on the Notion of Direct Participation in Hostilities', Geneva, 27/28 November 2006, 51.
[47] D Akande, 'Clearing the Fog of War? The ICRC's Interpretive Guidance on Direct Participation in Hostilities' (2010) 59 ICLQ 180, 187.
[48] Cassese, 'Expert Opinion on Whether Israel's Targeted Killings of Palestinian Terrorists is Consonant with International Humanitarian Law', para 12 ff, para 18, <http://www.stoptorture.org.il>, accessed on 17 August 2010.
[49] MN Schmitt, 'Direct Participation in Hostilities and 21st Century Armed Conflict' in H Fischer (ed), *Crisis Management and Humanitarian Protection, Festschrift für Dieter Fleck* (2004), 505.

in and the harm done to the enemy at the time and the place where the activity takes place.'[50] This suggests that a certain conduct should be regarded as an immediate sine qua non of the event adversely affecting the enemy. Of course, this does not exclude the existence of other concurrent causes. But, as recognized by one author, 'what counts is the immediate impact on the enemy'.[51] The *Interpretive Guidance* too interprets the element of direct causation as meaning that 'the harm in question must be brought about in one causal step'.[52]

In considering the spectrum of possibilities, direct participation is uncontested when a person uses weapons and other means to commit acts of violence in the course of military operations. On the other hand, a mere contribution to the general war effort does not fall within that category: working in a munitions factory, transport of food or humanitarian supplies, and building infrastructures are all certainly unproblematic examples.[53] However, a consistent number of activities already performed by PMSCs belong to the so-called grey area. One of the most problematic scenarios is when an individual contractor does not materially inflict the harm to the adversary. In complex military operations, what needs to be assessed is the kind of contribution that an individual makes to the production of the harm. The link between a certain activity and the subsequent harm for the enemy has been convincingly described as 'integration into combat operations':[54] a person directly participates in hostilities once his activity constitutes an indispensable contribution, within a military operation, to the direct infliction of violence.[55] This means that the notion of direct participation of hostilities comprises also activities which cause harm 'only in conjunction with other acts'.[56]

The above considerations help to evaluate the relevance of geographic proximity in the notion of direct participation and essentially lead to a reconsideration of the validity of the principle according to which the closer an activity occurs to the physical location of fighting, the more likely it will be considered combat.[57] It is questionable whether a civilian's proximity to the theatre of operations is in itself a decisive and qualifying element, absent any immediate link with the caused harm. The following sections will test and apply the three constitutive elements of the notion to the most important categories of activities performed by contractor personnel.

---

[50] de Preux (n 13 above), 516, para 1679.
[51] M Sassoli, 'Targeting: The Scope and Utility of the Concept of "Military Objectives" for the Protection of Civilians in Contemporary Armed Conflicts' in D Wippman and M Evangelista (eds), *New Wars, New Laws? Applying the Laws of War in the 21st Century Conflicts* (2005), 201.
[52] ICRC, *Interpretive Guidance*, 53.
[53] de Preux (n 13 above), 516.
[54] ME Guillory, 'Civilianizing the Force: Is the United States Crossing the Rubicon?' (2001) 51 Air Force LR 111, 134.
[55] ICRC, *Interpretative Guidance*, 54.
[56] N Melzer, *Targeted Killing in International Law* (2008), 342.
[57] Cf R Heaton, 'Civilians at War: Reexamining the Status of Civilians Accompanying the Armed Forces' (2005) 57 Air Force LR 155, 178.

B. Protective Security Services

The first category comprises the security services performed by private contractors in a situation of an international armed conflict. These include tasks such as guarding of military bases, checkpoints, work sites, and embassies; personal security of high-ranking officials; travel security for individuals; escorts for vehicle convoys moving equipment and supplies; event security; evacuation planning; and security advice and planning. As of September 2009, the total number of PMSC personnel performing security tasks for the US DoD was 12,684 in Iraq and 11,423 in Afghanistan.[58] To give one example, the three contracts concluded with the British firm Aegis provide a variety of services, including security escort teams, personal security, static guards, and antiterrorist force protection.[59]

In this context, it is noteworthy that the Instruction released by the DoD on 3 October 2005, which applies 'to all contractors and subcontractors at all levels, and their employees, authorized to accompany US Armed Forces', devoted a specific paragraph to the use of contractor personnel for security services—it specifies that: 'Contracts shall be used cautiously in contingency operations where major combat operations are ongoing or imminent. In these situations, contract security services will not be authorized to guard US or coalition military supply routes, military facilities, military personnel, or military property except as specifically authorized by the geographic Combatant Commander.'[60]

Public awareness for such security tasks is connected to the series of tragic incidents involving PMSCs in recent years. A report by Human Rights First reviews the events which occurred between 2004 and 2005 on the basis of official documents: these sources offer detailed accounts of roadside explosions, small arms attacks, and kidnappings.[61] On 4 April 2004, Blackwater personnel engaged 'in tactical military actions in concert with US troops' to defend the regional Coalition Provisional Authority headquarters in Najaf—a memorandum of the US House Committee on Government Oversight described the battle as follows: 'Blackwater became aware from staff for the US Ambassador to Iraq that there was an attack on Najaf and joined the fire fight. Several Blackwater personnel took positions on a rooftop alongside US Army and Spanish forces.'[62]

Security services usually entail the use of weapons. The events described above demonstrate that their legal characterization is problematic when the contractors are required to protect high-level individuals and certain sites: could their actions be qualified as the exercise of self-defence or do they amount to a direct participation

---

[58] M Schwartz, *Department of Defense Contractors in Iraq and Afghanistan: Background and Analysis*, US Congressional Research Service R40764, 14 December 2009.
[59] US Special Inspector General for Iraq Reconstruction, 'Oversight of Aegis's Performance on Security Services Contracts in Iraq with the Department of Defense', SIGIR-09-010, 14 January 2009, 9.
[60] US DoD Instruction 3020.41, 3 October 2005, para 6.4.
[61] Human Rights First, *Private Security Contractors at War: Ending the Culture of Impunity* (2008), 59.
[62] 'Additional Information about Blackwater USA' (n 29 above), 8.

in hostilities? To answer these questions, two variables have been considered: whether the persons or objects to be protected constitute a military objective and whether the attacker is a common criminal or belongs to a party of the conflict.[63] Since the law of armed conflicts does not distinguish between offensive and defensive operations, defending military objectives from the enemy amounts to taking a direct part in hostilities. The fact that contractor personnel were mandated to carry that task is not determinative.[64] The opposite case would be the provision of security for civilians against common crimes: such a situation amounts to a police operation.

As for the definition of military objectives; buildings; positions where combatants, their material, and armaments are located; and military means of transportation and communication fall within the category identified by the Article 52(2) of Protocol I. Other situations are more problematic. As for the characterization of dual-use facilities, this provision is based on two cumulative criteria: first, the object has to contribute effectively to military action; secondly, its destruction, capture, or neutralization has to offer a definite military advantage. The case of economic installations is of particular interest: after the Iraqi invasion, many attacks by insurgents against oil pipelines were reported. Erinys was one of the early contractors in Iraq and won an $80 million contract in the summer of 2003 to provide security for Iraqi oil refineries and pipelines.[65] It could be difficult to verify whether the attack against these installations was simply an attempt to loot by criminals or a military operation for diminishing the enemy's access to oil.[66] Here the element of the nexus with an armed conflict seems to be decisive: an evaluation of both the context in which a person bears arms and the nature of the exchange of fire led to the correct qualification of the conduct. The same approach should be applied when considering the case of private contractors protecting certain civilian objects.

It necessarily follows that humanitarian organizations do not lose the protection accorded by the law of international armed conflict, particularly by Articles 70–1 of Protocol I,[67] when they resort to private armed security.[68] Indeed, major international humanitarian actors, including UN agencies and non-governmental organizations, have increasingly relied on private security services in conflict

---

[63] Cf Schmitt (n 11 above), 538–9; Doswald-Beck (n 10 above), 129.

[64] In this context, see also *Prosecutor v Thomas Lubanga Dylo*, ICC-01/04-01/06, Decision on the confirmation of charges, 29 January 2007, para 263. The Chamber analysed the notion of 'active participation in hostilities' under Art 77(2) of Protocol I, which refers to the involvement of children in armed conflicts. Interestingly, it affirmed that the notion covered the use of children 'to guard military objectives, such as the military quarters of the various units of the parties to the conflict, or to safeguard the physical safety of military commanders'.

[65] See 'U.S. Soldier's Family brings Legal Action against British Private Security Firm', *The Guardian* (30 October 2007).

[66] Cf L Cameron, 'Private Military Companies: Their Status under International Humanitarian Law and its Impact on their Regulation' (2006) 88 IRRC 573, 591.

[67] See R Barber, 'Facilitating Humanitarian Assistance in International Humanitarian and Human Rights Law' (2009) 91 IRRC 371.

[68] B Perrin, 'Humanitarian Assistance and the Private Security Debate: An International Humanitarian Law Perspective', 11 December 2008, 17, <http://ssrn.com/abstract=1315006>, accessed on 17 August 2010.

situations, though this practice still represents the exception than the rule.[69] Concern was expressed that the use of commercial entities could compromise the reputation and the neutrality of aid agencies, as the private contractor could be associated and identified with a party to the conflict; this would result in increased risk of harm for the humanitarian operation.[70]

A different question is whether private companies could perform civil defence functions.[71] This does not seem precluded by the relevant norms of Protocol I, provided that private entities are authorized by the competent authorities, which retain control over their activities.[72] Interestingly, civilian civil defence personnel are permitted to carry light personal weapons for the purpose of maintaining order or for self-defence, though they may be disarmed by the occupying power for reasons of security.[73] Of course, the abuse of the civil defence emblem—for instance, to carry out covert raids—constitutes an act of perfidy, defined by Article 37 of Protocol I as an act 'inviting the confidence of an adversary to lead him to believe that he is entitled to, or is obliged to accord, protection under the rules of international law applicable in armed conflict, with intent to betray that confidence'. As the Commentary makes clear, the distinguishing feature of perfidy is 'the intention to mislead'.[74]

In conclusion, it is important to determine, on a more general level, whether the employees of private companies, as civilians, are allowed to carry weapons for self-defence purposes. In assessing the UK government's Green Paper, *Private Military Companies: Options for regulation*,[75] the House of Commons Foreign Affairs Committee recommended 'that private military companies be expressly prohibited from direct participation in armed combat operations, and that firearms should only be carried—and if necessary, used—by company employees for purposes of training or self-defence'.[76] Furthermore, the already mentioned Instruction released by the US DoD on 3 October 2005 affirms that contractor personnel may be authorized 'to be armed for individual self-defence'.[77]

---

[69] See A Stoddard, A Harmer, and V DiDomenico, *The Use of Private Security Providers and Services in Humanitarian Operations* (2008).

[70] See J Cockayne, *Commercial Security in Humanitarian and Post-Conflict Settings: An Exploratory Study*, IPI Policy Paper, 14 March 2006, 14. The ICRC, as a general rule, has excluded the armed protection for humanitarian assistance operations. See 'Principles and Action in International Humanitarian Assistance and Protection', resolution adopted at the 26th International Conference of the Red Cross and Red Crescent, (1996) 78 IRRC 69, para G.2.(c).

[71] See Arts 61–7 of Protocol I.

[72] Cf HP Gasser, 'Protection of the Civilian Populations' in Fleck (ed) (n 3 above), 237, 263.

[73] See Art 65(3) of Protocol I.

[74] de Preux (n 13 above), 438, para 1506.

[75] Foreign and Commonwealth Office, *Private Military Companies: Options for Regulations* (February 2002).

[76] House of Commons Foreign Affairs Committee, *Private Military Companies* (August 2002), 30, para 108.

[77] Instruction 3020.41, 3 October 2005, para 6.3.4. According to the US Army Field Manual: 'Contractor employees...cannot take an active role in hostilities but retain the inherent right to self-defense. Because of their civilian background, they may possess neither the training nor experience to actively participate in force protection measures, and the rules governing warfare preclude them from doing so except in self-defense.' FM 3–100.21, 'Contractors on the battlefield', 3 January 2003, para 6–3. For further analysis, see Ch 9 by den Dekker and Myjer in this volume.

IHL explicitly permits certain individuals to bear and use arms in individual self-defence. The International Criminal Tribunal for the former Yugoslavia confirmed the status of certain individuals as civilians who, strictly speaking, did not carry out military operations although they did bear arms.[78] There is also little doubt that the resort by civilians to armed force in personal self-defence should be distinguished from direct participation in hostilities, as it does not satisfy at least one of its constitutive elements; the ICRC *Interpretive Guidance* has rightly observed that: 'The causation of harm in individual self-defence or defence of others against violence prohibited under IHL lacks belligerent nexus.'[79]

C. Intelligence Activities

In one author's view, since September 2001 PMSCs have been as important to the US military's intelligence function as they have to its training, logistics, or equipment maintenance roles.[80] The tasks performed by private contractors have been divided into three main categories: the collection of information from interrogations or electronic means, the analytical function, and alleged participation in covert operations.[81]

The majority of commentators agree that information-gathering activities may constitute direct participation in hostilities. However, a distinction can be drawn between a person who gathers military intelligence in enemy-controlled territory (acknowledged to be directly participating in hostilities) and a civilian who retrieves data from satellites or listening posts, working in terminals located in his home country.[82] In this regard, one cannot exclude that private contractors may fall within the definition of spies according to Article 29(1) of the 1907 Hague Regulations: in fact, the category includes persons, irrespective of their primary status, who, acting clandestinely or under false pretences, gather information in the territory controlled by the adversary. The relevance of the notion of spy will be made clear in the section devoted to its legal consequences.

Although intelligence-gathering does not necessarily entail material damage to the enemy, certain operations could still fall within the notion of direct participation in hostilities: for instance, transmitting intelligence data to the attacking forces and providing analysis about the adversary for the purpose of the identification and localization of targets. The *Interpretive Guidance* includes also both wire-tapping the enemy's high command[83] and Computer Network Exploitation (CNE), which has been defined as 'the ability to gain access to information hosted on information

---

[78] *Prosecutor v Tadić*, IT-94-1-T, 7 May 1997, paras 640–3; *Prosecutor v Blaskic*, IT-95-14-T, 3 March 2000, paras 402–10. The Tribunal referred to the final report of the Commission of Experts established pursuant to SC Res 780 (1992), UN Doc S/1994/674, para 78.
[79] ICRC, *Interpretive Guidance*, 61.
[80] D Donald, 'Private Security Companies and Intelligence Provision' in A Alexandra, DP Baker, and M Caparini (eds), *Private Military and Security Companies: Ethics, Policies and Civil-Military Relations* (2008), 131.
[81] See 'Outsourcing US Intelligence', *International Herald Tribune* (27 August 2007).
[82] See Y Dinstein, *The Conduct of Hostilities under the Law of International Armed Conflict* (2004), 27.
[83] ICRC, '2005 Summary Report', 29.

systems and the ability to make use of the system itself'.[84] In line with the previous analysis, one should demonstrate a direct causal link between the intelligence information and the harm affecting the adversary.

Furthermore, the outsourcing of detainees' interrogation to private contractors and their involvement in the torture scandal at the Abu-Ghraib prison raises the issue of their legal qualification:[85] there seems to be little doubt that tactical and strategic interrogations aimed at obtaining relevant information at the operative level should be regarded as direct participation in hostilities.[86] Therefore, only legitimate combatants have the right to carry out such functions: it is noteworthy that the US *National Defense Authorization Act for Fiscal Year 2009* provided that 'interrogation ... is an inherently governmental function and cannot appropriately be transferred [by the Department of Defence] to private sector contractors'.[87]

D. The Maintenance of Combat Drones

A further type of function which is considered as direct participation is the maintenance and operation of a weapons system.[88] During the Iraqi invasion, contractors maintained and loaded weapons on many of the most sophisticated US weapons systems, such as the B-2 stealth bomber and the Apache helicopters.[89] In 2009 various press sources reported that PMSCs employees helped to load Hellfire missiles and laser-guided smart bombs on unmanned aerial vehicles or drones, remotely piloted by CIA to target Al-Qaeda members suspected of hiding in the Afghanistan–Pakistan border regions.[90]

As a good example of a contemporary complex military operation, an attack carried out by drones requires the simultaneous coordination of a number of persons, whose acts constitute an integral part of the mission. Therefore, the geographical proximity to the battle zone is relevant for the legal characterization of this kind of activity only insofar as it constitutes evidence of its indispensable contribution to a military operation. Conversely, performing routine maintenance which does not have an immediate causal link with an operation affecting the adversary, does not qualify as direct participation in hostilities.[91]

---

[84] J-F Quéguiner, *Direct Participation in Hostilities under International Humanitarian Law: Background Paper* (2003), <http://www.icrc.org>, accessed on 17 August 2010.
[85] See 'Article 15–6 Investigation of the 800th Military Police Brigade' (Taguba Report, 2004), <http://www.npr.org/iraq/2004/prison_abuse_report.pdf>, accessed on 17 August 2010.
[86] Cf Schmitt (n 11 above), 544.
[87] *Duncan Hunter National Defense Authorization Act for Fiscal Year 2009*, Public Law 110–417, 14 October 2008, sec 1057. See also 'Statement to Employees by Director of the Central Intelligence Agency Leon E. Panetta on the CIA's Interrogation Policy and Contracts', 9 April 2009, <http://www.tinyurl.com/dcdfaq>, accessed on 17 August 2010.
[88] Heaton (n 57 above), 202.
[89] PW Singer, *Can't Win With'Em, Can't Go To War Without'Em: Private Military Contractors and Counterinsurgency*, Brookings, Foreign Policy Paper no 4 (September 2007), 2.
[90] See, inter alia, 'CIA Said to Use Outsiders to Put Bombs on Drones', *New York Times* (21 August 2009). On the legal debate on the US policy of attacks by drones, see M O'Connell, 'Unlawful Killing with Combat Drones' in S Bronitt (ed), *Shooting to Kill: The Law Governing Lethal Force in Context* (2010); UN Doc A/HRC/14/24/Add6, Report of the Special Rapporteur on Extrajudicial, Summary or Arbitrary Executions, Philip Alston, Addendum: Study on Targeted Killings, 28 May 2010, 7.
[91] Guillory (n 54 above), 128.

E. Other Examples of Direct Participation

Another field of activity in which PMSCs could be involved is rescue operations of military personnel. They are regarded as examples of direct participation in hostilities: it is therefore legitimate to attack the rescuers to impede or prevent the rescue activity, but protection should be assured to medical personnel, units, or transports collecting the sick or wounded.[92] In this regard, it has been pointed out during the ICRC second expert meeting that care must be taken when concluding that rescue operations constitute direct participation in hostilities, because Article 18 of the First Geneva Convention encourages the civilian population to care for wounded military personnel.[93]

Finally, according to the US Air Force Commander's Handbook, the rescue of civilian or military hostages in situations of armed conflict might also amount to direct participation in hostilities.[94] However, it has been stressed that it rather constitutes a law-enforcement measure.[95]

The example of driving an ammunition truck was a source of much controversy during the expert meetings organized by the ICRC. Although the experts agreed that the truck itself was a legitimate military objective, there was no agreement on the lawfulness of directly attacking the driver.[96] By applying the three elements of the notion identified in the previous section, one can conclude that this kind of activity does not amount to a direct participation in hostilities, unless the driver delivers the ammunition to an active firing position at the front line. In any case, since the truck is a military target, the driver runs the risk of death or injury resulting from attacks on that target.[97]

As for advice and military training aimed at improving the capabilities of the regular armed forces, there is little doubt that they have a strategic importance but they do not necessarily produce an immediate direct impact on military operations.[98] The conclusion might be different if the training were essential for 'specific requirements of a particular combat operation'.[99]

---

[92] UK Ministry of Defence, *The Manual of the Law of Armed Conflict* (2004), 327.
[93] Cf ICRC, 'Report of the Second Expert Meeting: Direct Participation in Hostilities under IHL', The Hague, 25/26 October 2004, 13.
[94] US Air Force, *Commander's Handbook* (1980), paras 2–8: 'The rescue of military airmen downed on land is a combatant activity that is not protected under international law. Civilians engaged in the rescue and return of enemy aircrew members are therefore subject to attack.'
[95] Schmitt (n 11 above), 540.
[96] ICRC, 'Report of the First Expert Meeting: Direct Participation in Hostilities under IHL', The Hague, 2 June 2003, 4.
[97] Cf APV Rogers, *Law on the Battlefield* (2004), 12.
[98] Boldt, 'Outsourcing War: Private Military Companies and International Humanitarian Law' (2004) 47 German Y Intl L 502, 522. The private firm MPRI worked in the Balkans during the mid-1990s training the Croatian army. In 1995 Croatian forces performed unexpectedly well in the offensive against Serb forces in the Krajina region. MPRI denied playing any role in the attack, and maintained that its involvement was limited to classroom instruction. See Foreign and Commonwealth Office, *Private Military Companies: Options for Regulation* (n 75 above), 13.
[99] Cf Rule 29 (xii) of the *HPCR Manual on International Law Applicable to Air and Missile Warfare* (2009), <http://www.ihlresearch.org>, accessed on 17 August 2010.

IV. Legal Consequences Deriving from the Primary Status under the Law of International Armed Conflict

A. Contractor Personnel as Military Objectives

Having verified that employees of PMSCs may have combatant status, the first consequence in this specific circumstance is that attacks can be directed against them, unless they are *hors de combat*. On the contrary, if they are considered civilians, they are protected against attack 'unless and for such time as they take part in hostilities'. The main question to be addressed in this context is the temporal scope of loss of protection: the time requirement, rendered by the expression 'for such time', determines that the civilian who has ceased taking a direct part in hostilities regains his or her protection.

The dilemma has been expressed by the Israeli Supreme Court judgment in the *Targeted killings* case.[100] President Barak identified, on the one hand, 'a civilian who took a direct part in hostilities once, or sporadically, but detached himself from them (entirely, or for a long period) is not to be harmed'; on the other hand, there exists the 'revolving door' phenomenon, namely civilians who have joined an armed group and then claim the benefit of immunity from attack as soon as they have dropped their arms. President Barak recognized the existence of a grey zone between these two extremes, where international law has not yet crystallized: therefore, he pointed out the importance of case-by-case verification. The merit of this solution lies in the rejection of a radical application of the 'membership approach' in international armed conflicts, which might allow attacks against members of an armed group as such, whatever function they were fulfilling.

As for the contractors' activities, there is no doubt that a single employee performing an isolated act of direct participation in hostilities immediately regains the protection once the specific act in question is terminated. The most challenging scenario is represented by organized and structured PMSCs, which have entered into a contract with a state to perform activities amounting to direct participation in hostilities. Their employees are not legitimate combatants, unless they satisfy the functional criteria for membership in state armed forces.[101] As demonstrated above, in the present author's view, these criteria are more stringent than those outlined by the ICRC Interpretive Guidance: indeed, while participating in hostilities 'on behalf of' one party and against another, private contractors do not necessarily 'belong' to that party.[102]

---

[100] *The Public Committee against Torture in Israel and ors* (n 39 above), para 40.
[101] This does not exclude that PMSCs could become 'Organized armed groups operating within the broader context of an international armed conflict without belonging to a party to that conflict could still be regarded as parties to a separate non-international armed conflict provided that the violence reaches the required threshold': ICRC, *Interpretive Guidance*, 24.
[102] See also *Commentary on the HPCR Manual on International Law Applicable to Air and Missile Warfare* (2010), 119, <http://www.ihlresearch.org>, accessed on 17 August 2010.

In the case of employees of PMSCs as members of armed groups who do not belong to the state but who directly participate in hostilities during an international armed conflict, a viable solution remains the one reflected in the ICRC Interpretive Guidance: they 'cease to be civilians, and lose protection against direct attack, for as long as they assume their continuous combat function'.[103] This approach seems to strike the right balance: if a contractor's employee fulfils a function which implies taking a direct part in hostilities on a regular or continuous basis, then that individual 'would lose protection against direct attack for as long as that function was being fulfilled'.[104]

Suffice it here to recall that attacks directed against military objectives must be carried out in conformity with the relevant provisions of IHL, including the prohibition of means and methods of warfare 'of a nature to cause superfluous injury or unnecessary suffering', which constitutes an intransgressible principle of international customary law.[105] As regards the 'restraints on the use of force in direct attack', the ICRC *Interpretive Guidance* has introduced a specific standard, according to which 'the kind and degree of force which is permissible against persons not entitled to protection against direct attack must not exceed what is actually necessary to accomplish a legitimate military purpose in the prevailing circumstances'.[106] Such a requirement is based on the modern concept of military necessity under IHL[107] and it also resembles the approach taken by the Israeli Supreme Court, known as the '*least-injurious alternative*':[108] if a civilian 'taking a direct part in hostilities can be arrested, interrogated and tried, those are means that should be employed'.[109] Interestingly, the reasoning of the Court relies on the case law of the European Court of Human Rights.[110] Thus, in determining the precise amount of force to be used in a certain situation, the interaction between IHL—as ex specialis[111]—and human rights law is particularly fruitful. The priority of special law does not extinguish the relevant general law (ie human rights), which remains applicable and gives 'direction for the interpretation and application of the relevant special law and...become[s] fully applicable in situations not provided for by the latter'.[112]

---

[103] ICRC, *Interpretive Guidance*, 70.
[104] ICRC, '2005 Summary Report', 82.
[105] *Legality of the Threat or Use of Nuclear Weapons*, ICJ Reports (1996) 226, 257, para 78.
[106] ICRC, *Interpretive Guidance*, 77.
[107] Cf UK Ministry of Defence (n 92 above), 21–2: 'Military Necessity Permits a State (party) Engaged in an Armed Conflict to use Only that Degree and Kind of Force, not Otherwise Prohibited by the LOAC, that is required in order to achieve the legitimate purpose of the conflict, namely the complete or partial submission of the enemy at the earliest possible moment with the minimum expenditure of life and resources.'
[108] Cf A Cohen and Y Shany, 'A development of modest proportions', (2007) 5 J of Intl Criminal Justice 310, 313.
[109] *The Public Committee against Torture in Israel and ors* (n 39 above), para 40.
[110] *McCann v UK*, 21 EHRR (1995) 97.
[111] *Legality of the Threat or Use of Nuclear Weapons* (n 105 above), 240, para 25.
[112] 'Conclusions of the Work of the Study Group on the Fragmentation of International Law: Difficulties Arising from the Diversification and Expansion of International Law' (2006) in UN Doc A/61/10, para 251 ff.

Finally, the test case of the ammunition truck driver has demonstrated that the civilian employees of private companies, though not taking a direct part in hostilities, assume the risk of being injured because of their vicinity to military objectives. Therefore, subject to the principle of proportionality *stricto sensu*,[113] attacks directed against such targets are lawful if the civilian losses are not excessive in relation to the concrete and direct military advantage.

B. Criminal Liability

Once civilians taking a direct part in hostilities are captured, they may be prosecuted for the mere fact of fighting, in conformity with the applicable domestic criminal law.[114] In any case, they may not be punished without a trial. The law of international armed conflict also prescribes this in the specific case of espionage.[115] Moreover, under Article 5 of the Fourth Geneva Convention, civilian contractors directly participating in hostilities should not be 'deprived of the rights of fair and regular trial'.

Finally, civilian contractors who commit serious violations of IHL may be prosecuted for war crimes.[116] Since judicial proceedings against PMSC employees have been very rare, several commentators have already emphasized the difficulties and the limitations in the exercise of criminal jurisdiction.[117]

C. Legal Regime Applicable upon Capture

Once the members of private companies fall within the category of legitimate combatants, they should consequently be accorded the prisoner-of-war status if captured.[118] In addition, they are entitled to the same treatment if they satisfy the conditions to be qualified as civilians accompanying the armed forces under Article 4 of the Third Geneva Convention. Even if they fall within one of the previous categories, persons engaged in espionage are not entitled of prisoner-of-war status.[119]

---

[113] The principle of proportionality in attack is a rule of customary IHL: though it does not explicitly appear in treaty law, its content is enshrined in Arts 51(5)(b) and 57(2) of Protocol I. Cf Henckaerts and Doswald-Beck (eds) (n 6 above), I, 46; see Y Dinstein, 'Collateral Damage and the Principle of Proportionality' in Wippman and Evangelista (eds) (n 51 above), 211.

[114] See, inter alia, C Rousseau, *Le Droit des Conflits Armés* (1983), 68.

[115] Cf. Art 30 of the 1907 Hague Regulations.

[116] See C Lehnardt, 'Individual Liability of Private Military Personnel under International Criminal Law' (2008) 19 EJIL 1015.

[117] See Ch 21 by Quirico in this volume.

[118] There is no space here to deal with the implications deriving from the recognition of the customary character of the first part of Art 43(1) of Protocol I; since controversy relates to the subsequent Art 44—stating that 'Any combatant, as defined in Art 43, shall be prisoner of war'—one could infer that these individuals are combatants for the purpose of the conduct of hostilities but are not entitled to combatant privilege and prisoner-of-war status. Cf ICRC, *Interpretive Guidance*, 22; ICRC, 'Summary Report of Fourth Expert Meeting' (n 46 above), 15 ff.

[119] Art 29(1) of the Hague Regulations; Art 46(1) of Protocol I. The most controversial issue is whether civilians accompanying armed forces retain that status if they take a direct part in hostilities: see Ch 11 by Bartolini in this volume.

Contractors' employees who do not benefit from the protection of the Third Geneva Convention may be protected by the Fourth Geneva Convention, if they fall within the category of persons covered by Article 4 of that treaty. According to one author, the fact that a person has directly participated in hostilities is not a criterion for excluding the application of the Fourth Geneva Convention: he rightly observed that Article 5 uses the term 'protected persons' with regard to persons detained as spies or saboteurs as well as persons definitely suspected of or engaged in activities hostile to the security of the state or of the occupying power.[120]

Finally, it is worth recalling that, in relation to an international armed conflict, persons who are in the power of a party to the conflict and who do not benefit from more favourable treatment shall be treated humanely in all circumstances and are nevertheless entitled to certain fundamental guarantees under Article 75 of Protocol I.[121] In this context, one should stress the interaction between these guarantees and the fundamental human rights protected at both universal and regional level, in particular with regard to the deprivation of liberty, the conditions of detentions, and the procedural safeguards.

V. Concluding Remarks

The notion of 'direct participation in hostilities' is essential to whether contractors' personnel can be targeted. But it also offers a valuable tool for the debate on the equally fundamental question concerning the legitimacy of outsourcing activities which are inherently governmental. Since only legitimate combatants can directly participate in hostilities in the course of an international armed conflict, the notion defines a criterion to determine what functions private companies may perform and what degree of control the state should exercise. In fact, under Article 43 of Protocol I, employees of PMSCs could fall within the category of legitimate combatants, once the state establishes a certain qualified factual link between them and its regular armed forces.

The recent ICRC *Interpretive Guidance* offers a valuable analytical tool for the identification of conduct amounting to direct participation in hostilities: such acts should meet the three cumulative requirements of threshold of harm, direct causation, and belligerent nexus. The analysis conducted above on the tasks entrusted to employees of PMSCs permits a conclusion that the concept of direct participation in hostilities encompasses activities like protecting military objectives from adversary attacks, providing tactical intelligence data (including through interrogation techniques), maintaining or operating weapon systems in the course of complex military operations, and training troops for the execution of a specific military operation.

---

[120] See K Dörmann, 'The Legal Situation of "Unlawful/Unprivileged Combatants"' (2003) 85 IRRC 45, 50.

[121] Cf also Art 45(3) of Protocol I. On the fundamental guarantees under customary IHL, see Henckaerts and Doswald-Beck (eds) (n 6 above), I, 299.

Finally, the controversial example of driving an ammunition truck should not generally be qualified as direct participation in hostilities: civilian drivers enjoy immunity from targeting but the truck remains a legitimate military objective. It follows that individuals working for a PMSC in the surroundings of a military objective could be at risk of injury incidental to the attack of that target, as so-called 'collateral damage' under the principle of proportionality as set out in Article 51(5)(b) of Protocol I.

11

Private Military and Security Contractors as 'Persons who Accompany the Armed Forces'

Giulio Bartolini

I. Introduction: The Development of the Notion of 'Persons who Accompany the Armed Forces'

A possible legal issue related to the involvement of private military and security companies (PMSCs) in armed conflicts is the attribution of the classification of 'persons who accompany the armed force' to personnel belonging to these firms by the states who contract them. This hypothesis can involve a significant number of contractors as evidenced by recent national legal documents analysing the status of these individuals, such as the US Department of Defense (DoD) Instruction 3020.41,[1] which recognizes that certain civilian personnel supporting the US armed forces may be identified as 'persons who accompany the armed forces'. It is therefore necessary to analyse the legal consequences connected with this classification in relation to both the conduct of hostilities (section III below) and the position of these personnel once captured (section IV below). In this regard we shall first take into account the original framework provided by international humanitarian law for the attribution of this classification (section II below) and the challenges posed by recent armed conflicts, in which an increasing involvement of contractors operating in the heart of military operations has been recorded, in order to explore possible limits to attributing this status.

The category of 'persons who accompany the armed forces without actually being members' was introduced in early codifications of international humanitarian law in order to provide legal status for civilian personnel providing auxiliary services to armed forces. For centuries these individuals have participated in a series of significant functions, mainly connected with the logistical organization of the armies, such as preparing and selling food, welfare services, assistance to belligerent

---

[1] US Deparment of Defence, Instruction no 3020.41, *Contractor Personnel Authorized to Accompany the U.S. Armed Forces*, 3 October 2005.

convoys, for instance through beasts of burden.[2] Taking into account this framework, early codifications of international humanitarian law, such as the 1863 Lieber Code and the 1874 Bruxelles Project,[3] made reference to this notion. These rules had a significant influence on subsequent codifications, where we can find similar provisions, such as Article 13 of the regulations annexed to the 1899 Hague Convention II and to the 1907 Hague Convention IV.[4] Even more recent provisions, such as Article 4.A.4 GC III, make reference to these individuals, providing prisoner of war (POW) status to:

> Persons who accompany the armed forces without actually being members thereof, such as civilian members of military aircraft crews, war correspondents, supply contractors, members of labour units or of services responsible for the welfare of the armed forces, provided that they have received authorization from the armed forces which they accompany, who shall provide them for that purpose with an identity card similar to the annexed model.

These rules had the common aim of defining the legal status of these personnel once captured, taking into account divergent opinion in early writings on this issue.[5] Due to their performance of activities in the proximity of military units involved in belligerent campaigns, these individuals faced the risk of being captured. However, not being enrolled in state armed forces they could not claim the status of POW awarded to combatants on the basis of the relevant provisions. Similarly, taking into account the rudimentary character of the guarantees granted to civilians at the end of the nineteenth century these could not be relied on to safeguard their position. In fact, the Hague Conventions granted limited protection to the civilian population of the opposing state only in the case of occupation, whereas persons accompanying an army were usually captured in other situations during military operations in foreign territories. It was therefore considered necessary to extend POW status to such personnel at that time.

---

[2] See J Roth, *The Logistic of the Roman Army at War, 264 BC–AD 235* (1999), 91–115; PM Creveld, *Supplying War: Logistics from Wallentstein to Patton* (1986); JA Lynn (ed), *Feeding Mars: Logistic in Western Warfare from the Middle Ages to the Present* (1994).

[3] See Art 50 of the Instructions for the Government of Armies of the United States in the Field (Lieber Code), 24 April 1863: 'Moreover, citizens who accompany an army for whatever purpose, such as sutlers, editors, or reporters of journals, or contractors, if captured, may be made prisoners of war, and be detained as such.' A similar rule was included in Art 34 of the Project of an International Declaration concerning the laws and customs of war, adopted in Bruxelles in 1874. However, this document was not legally binding.

[4] See Art 13 of regulations annexed to the II 1899 Hague Convention on Laws and Customs of War on Land: 'Individuals who follow an army without directly belonging to it, such as newspaper correspondents and reporters, sutlers and contractors, who fall into the enemy's hands and whom the latter thinks fit to detain, are entitled to be treated as prisoners of war, provided they are in possession of a certificate from the military authorities of the army which they were accompanying.' On the drafting of this provision see J Brown Scott, *The Proceedings of the Hague Peace Conferences: The Conference of 1899* (1920), 57. An identical provision was included in the regulations annexed to the 1907 Hague Convention IV.

[5] For instance, according to GF Martens, *Précis du Droit des Gens Moderne de l'Europe* (1864), II, 243, it was not possible to retain auxiliary personnel as prisoner of war as they should be set at liberty. On the contrary, P Pradier-Fodèré, *Traité de Droit International Public Européen et Américain* (1897), VII, 161–6, admitted this possibility.

The development of the category of 'persons who accompany the armed forces' is connected to some basic characteristics. First, it may only be granted by the armed forces, whose authorities are responsible for attributing this status, through a specific authorization. Hence, contractors providing support to other branches of the state administration, such as civilian authorities, during an armed conflict, cannot claim this status.[6] Moreover, even if this element was not highlighted in these codifications, which mainly focused on the status of such individuals once captured, it could be maintained that these personnel should be classified as civilians as regards the conduct of hostilities, thus prohibiting direct attacks against them. This character, already highlighted by early legal scholars,[7] was confirmed in Article 50.1 Additional Protocol (AP) I, which excludes individuals referred to in Article 4.A.4 Geneva Convention (GC) III from the definition of combatants. Furthermore, referring to modern classifications, activities traditionally performed by contractors classified as 'persons who accompany the armed force' are not considered as direct participation in hostilities.[8] Finally, this notion may only be applied in international armed conflicts.

However, current belligerent scenarios determine a framework that differs in part from this typical representation of the phenomenon. First of all, an increasing recourse to civilians has been recorded due to the general trend towards a reduction in military personnel for political, military, and financial reasons. Moreover, the activities performed by civilians have changed to some extent. Apart from traditional duties, we can observe a constant trend towards the employment of contractors to maintain weapons and military systems, using them to transport troops and weapons, etc. This trend is also largely due to technological developments in modern armed forces, which have necessitated support services provided by specialized civilian technicians.

Furthermore, the majority of situations in which contractors are deployed with armed forces nowadays are alien to international armed conflicts. In many contexts these personnel are employed during non-international armed conflicts,[9] when foreign armed forces are supporting the legitimate government, such as the current situation in Afghanistan. Even if the technical notion of 'persons who accompany the armed forces' is not relevant in these conflicts,[10] it is still necessary to analyse the legal status of contractors. Similarly, these individuals play a vital role in post-

---

[6] See the Montreux Document on Pertinent International Obligations and Good Practices for States Related to Operations of Private Military and Security Companies during Armed Conflict (Montreux Document) (2008), 36: 'To qualify, civilians must have a real link with, i.e. provide a service to, the armed forces, not merely the State. This means that, for instance, contractors employed by civilian State authorities or by private companies do not fall into this category'; GD Solis, *The Law of Armed Conflict: International Humanitarian Law in War* (2010), 199.

[7] See eg A Mérignhac, *Les Lois et Coutumes de la Guerre sure Terre d'après le Droit International Moderne et la Codification de la Conférence de La Haye de 1899* (1903), 85.

[8] See n 26 below.

[9] For the involvement of PMSC in non-international armed conflicts see Ch 12 by Vierucci in this volume.

[10] See the Montreux Document (n 6 above), 36: 'The status of civilians accompanying the armed forces does not apply in non-international armed conflicts.'

conflict situations. In these cases, specific rules cannot be found in the IHL system and we must refer to other provisions, mainly those included in Status of Force Agreements (SOFAs), a topic that will be analysed by other authors.[11]

Nevertheless, apart from these latter scenarios, there are a number of hypotheses in which states may classify contractors as 'persons who accompany the armed forces' and in this chapter we shall examine legal issues related to these hypotheses, mainly focusing on aspects related to the conduct of hostilities and the status of these personnel once captured.

II. The Classification of Personnel Supporting the Armed Forces in Relation to the Conduct of Hostilities

The preliminary issue in relation to the conduct of hostilities is that of the legal status of contractors supporting armed forces, and especially their classification as civilians or combatants. Indeed where they have been granted the status of 'person accompanying the armed forces', it does not have any impact on this issue.

Generally speaking, 'persons who accompany the armed forces' should be excluded from the definition of combatants, as defined in Article 4.A.1–2 GC III and Article 43 AP I.[12] Similarly it could be argued that recourse to 'functional' criteria, as provided by the 2009 International Committee the Red Cross (ICRC) *Interpretative Guidance* on the notion of direct participation in hostilities,[13] could be sufficient to reach this conclusion. Moreover, even based on functional criteria there would be very few cases in which it could be affirmed that these contractors have, de facto, been given a 'continuous combat function'[14] by state armed forces.

Therefore, as a basic hypothesis, we can affirm that these individuals should be considered civilians. This solution was already envisaged in Article 50.1 AP I, according to which 'persons who accompany the armed forces' cannot be considered as combatants. This finding has also been adopted in the ICRC *Interpretative Guidance* and in the Montreux Document.[15]

---

[11] See Ch 22 by Frulli in this volume.
[12] See L Cameron, 'Private Military Companies: Their Status under International Humanitarian Law and its Impact on their Regulations' (2006) 863 IRRC 573, 582–7; Ch 10 by Sossai in this volume; G Bartolini, 'The Participation of Civilians in Hostilities' in M Momtaz and J Matheson (eds), *Rules and Institutions of International Humanitarian Law Put to the Test of Recent Armed Conflicts*, Hague Academy of International Law (in press), para II.A. For the possible qualification of this personnel as mercenaries see Ch 16 by Mancini, Ntoubandi, and Marauhn in this volume.
[13] See *Interpretative Guidance on the Notion of Direct Participation in Hostilities under International Humanitarian Law*, adopted by the Assembly of the International Committee of the Red Cross on 26 February 2009, (2008) 872 IRRC 991–1047.
[14] See ibid, 1001, 1006–9, 1010–11. For relevant materials related with expert meetings see <http://www.icrc.org/web/eng/siteeng0.nsf/html/direct-participation-article-020709>, accessed on 15 June 2010.
[15] See ICRC, *Interpretative Guidance* (n 13 above),1010, and the Montreux Document (n 6 above), 36.

III. Activities Performed by 'Persons who Accompany the Armed Forces' under International Humanitarian Law

Classification as civilians does not resolve the legal difficulties in evaluating the activities of such persons during an armed conflict. Independently of the armed conflict at issue, ie international or non-international, these personnel face the risk of being directly targeted once they take a 'direct part in hostilities'.[16] However, the usefulness of the notion of direct participation is open to question, as the two APs do not provide clear guidelines.[17]

Recently the ICRC in its *Interpretative Guidance* on this notion has proposed several cumulative criteria which need to be satisfied in order to establish whether or not the contribution provided by a civilian can qualify as direct participation (threshold of harm, direct causation, belligerent nexus).[18] For our purposes the key point of this issue is the criterion of 'direct causation', which has been defined as the need to ascertain that in activities performed by civilians there is 'a direct causal link between a specific act and the harm likely to result either from that act, or from a coordinated military operation of which that act constitutes an integral part'.[19] As persons accompanying the armed force usually participate in auxiliary activities conducted before the harm occurs, we should focus on the kind of contribution provided by the contractor in complex operations.

In fact these personnel are rarely involved in situations in which they materially and directly cause harm to the opposing party, for instance, cases in which they are personally responsible for direct fighting using military weapons or capturing enemy combatants or weapons.[20] It seems implausible to imagine such duties as being officially entrusted to these persons accompanying the armed forces, as combat operations are inherently governmental functions and cannot involve private sector performance.[21]

Nevertheless, in addition to their official duties, such personnel may make use of kinetic force during deployment in hostile areas. The classic situation would be a

---

[16] See Art 51.3 AP I and Art 13.3 AP II.
[17] See J Henckaerts and L Doswald-Beck, *Customary International Humanitarian Law* (2005), 21–2: 'A precise definition of the term "direct participation in hostilities" does not exist.'
[18] For further references see Ch 10 by Sossai in this volume; D Akande, 'Clearing the Fog of War? The ICRC's Interpretative Guidance on Direct Participation in Hostilities' (2010) 59 ICLQ 180–92; MN Schmitt, 'The Interpretative Guidance on the Notion of Direct Participation in Hostilities: A Critical Analysis' *Harvard National Security Journal* 1 (2010) 5–44.
[19] See ICRC, *Interpretative Guidance* (n 13 above), 1016.
[20] See Y Sandoz, C Swinarski, and B Zimmermann (eds), *Commentary on the Additional Protocols of 8 June 1977 to the Geneva Conventions of 12 August 1949* (1987), 516, para 1679 (hereinafter Commentary APs); Israeli Supreme Court (High Court of Justice), Case 769/02, *The Public Committee against Torture in Israeland ors v The Government of Israel and ors*, 13 December 2006, para 34 (hereinafter '*Targeted Killings* case'); UK Ministry of Defence, *The Manual of the Law of Armed Conflict* (2004), 54.
[21] See US Department of Defence Instruction 1100.22, *Guidance for Determining Workforce Mix*, 7 September 2006, 15–17. See similarly UK House of Commons Foreign Affairs Committee, *Private Military Companies*, August 2002, 30, para 108.

civilian who is charged with providing welfare services to troops, taking up arms in order to repel an ongoing attack on the military structures where he is performing his duties. Even if this activity is of an episodic nature, the support provided can be considered as direct participation, thus exposing the contractor to lawful direct attack.

Similarly, states expressly prohibit persons who accompany the armed forces from carrying out certain activities which are commonly considered as direct participation in hostilities. For instance, the US DoD Instruction no 3020.41 maintains that personnel authorized to accompany the US armed forces should not be employed to protect military objectives, such as 'US or coalition military supply routes, military facilities, military personnel, or military property'.[22] At the same time it is evident that a contractor employed to counter possible lootings and criminal acts would not be a direct participant in hostilities as the belligerent nexus is lacking.[23]

At the other end of the spectrum we can place activities that are commonly defined as 'indirect' participation. Such activities are related in an indeterminate manner to the overall war effort,[24] without it being possible to ascertain a definite causal link with specific harm subsequently caused to the opposing party during a coordinated military operation, as recognized by the ICRC *Interpretative Guidance*.[25]

The majority of functions carried out by persons who accompany the armed forces are generally considered as 'indirect' participation as they only provide general support. For instance, activities described in Article 4.A.4 GC III have been unanimously accepted by legal doctrine as not implying a loss of protection against direct attacks for persons involved,[26] which has also been confirmed by

---

[22] See US Department of Defence, *Instruction no 3020.41* (n 1 above), para 6.3.5.2. For a qualification of these activities as direct participation see J-F Quéguiner, *Direct Participation in Hostilities under International Humanitarian Law*, Humanitarian Policy and Conflict Research Working Paper, no 12, December 2003, 5; LL Turner and LG Norton, 'Civilians at the Top of the Spear' (2001) 51(1) Air Force Law Review 28; MN Schmitt, 'Humanitarian Law and Direct Participation in Hostilities by Private Contractors or Civilian Employees' (2005) 5 Chicago JIL 511, 538; L Doswald-Beck, 'Private military companies under international humanitarian law' in S Chesterman and C Lehnardt (eds), *From Mercenaries to Market: The Rise and Regulation of Private Military Companies* (2007) 115, 129; N Melzer, *Targeted Killing in International Law* (2008), 344.

[23] See APV Rogers, *Law on the Battlefield*, 2nd edn (2004), 11–12; Schmitt (n 22 above), 538–9; ICRC, *Interpretative Guidance* (n 13 above), 1028. The ICRC's *Interpretative Guidance* expands this possibility, identifying the guarding of captured military personnel as direct participation only when it is a means of preventing their liberation by the enemy, while other situations such as the suppression of riots or prevention of escapes, would not be qualified in such a manner due to the lack of a belligerent nexus (ibid, 1017, n 99, and 1028–9).

[24] See: Rogers (n 23 above), 9; F Kalshoven and L Zegveld, *Constraints on the Waging of War*, 3rd edn (2001), 99.

[25] According to the ICRC's document, connecting the notion of direct participation to an involvement in 'hostilities' implies considering activities that at a collective level are 'part of the general war effort or may be characterized as war-sustaining activities' as 'indirect' contributions of the civilian to hostilities: ICRC, *Interpretative Guidance* (n 13 above), 1020.

[26] See HP Gasser, 'Protection of the Civilian Population' in D Fleck (ed), *The Handbook of Humanitarian Law in Armed Conflicts*, 2nd edn (2008), 239; Doswald-Beck (n 22 above), 129: 'If the support role of a PMC is of the nature described in Article 4.A (4) of the Third Geneva

judicial decisions.[27] Of course, the list of activities contained in this provision has a purely descriptive function, and is not exhaustive; similarly, the terms employed in the article can be interpreted very broadly. For instance, notions such as 'welfare of the armed forces' can include services provided by persons working in canteens[28] or in structures providing billeting,[29] clothing,[30] medicine;[31] similarly, 'supply contractors' can involve reconstruction activities,[32] translation services, etc.

However, the most controversial issue regards certain activities that in current operations involve a large number of contractors, as here their participation may also be considered part of the contractual obligations of the industry that supplies military systems.[33] We refer to certain kinds of logistical support to armed forces, such as transporting troops or weapons, repairing weapons systems, loading weapons, or the management of complex technological systems such as those employed in reconnaissance activities. An evaluation of these activities in isolation would result in the impossibility of satisfying the required threshold of harm criterion, as the contractors are not causing it directly. However, the presence of this criterion may be determined when the harm arises 'from a coordinated military operation of which that act constitutes an integral part'.

Legal scholars have divergent views, some of them seeing these duties as an indirect participation in hostilities.[34] This position has recently been adopted by the US DOD Instruction no 3020.41, which characterizes 'transporting munitions...performing maintenance functions for military equipment' as 'indirect participation in military operations',[35] even if these activities can be carried out 'in a theatre of operations'.[36] Similarly, the 2004 UK Military Manual confirms that 'civilians working in military vehicle maintenance depots or...driving military transport vehicles are not' taking a direct part in hostilities.[37]

On the contrary, other authors and practice maintain that these activities may sometimes be considered as direct participation in hostilities, citing two slightly different reasons for this.

Convention...it would be difficult to see such activities as being "direct participation in hostilities" as this group is perceived as being civilian and benefiting from civilian immunity'; Schmitt (n 22 above), 531–2; APV Rogers, 'Unequal Combat and the Law of War' (2004) 7 YIHL 3, 21.

[27] See Israeli Supreme Court, *Targeted Killings* case (n 20 above), para 35, in which the Israeli Supreme Court has qualified 'logistical, general support' as examples of 'indirect participation' in hostilities.
[28] See US DoD Instruction no 3020.41 (n 1 above), para. 6.1.1.
[29] Ibid.
[30] See Israeli Supreme Court, *Targeted Killings* case (n 20 above), para. 34.
[31] See ibid, para 35; Rogers (n 24 above), 11.
[32] Schmitt (n 22 above), 545–6.
[33] N Boldt, 'Outsourcing War: Private Military Companies and International Humanitarian Law' (2004) 47 German YIL 502, 507.
[34] See Rogers (n 23 above), 10–11; M Sossai, 'Status of Private Military Companies' Personnel in the Laws of War: The Question of Direct Participation in Hostilities' (2008) 18 IYIL 89, 109.
[35] See US DoD Instruction no 3020.41 (n 1 above), para. 6.1.1.
[36] Ibid, para 2.2.
[37] UK Ministry of Defence (n 20 above), 54, para 5.3.3.

According to some scholars[38] when the contribution has been carried out in a tactical operation,[39] this activity qualifies as direct participation. In this case the integration of the civilian in a tactical combat operation provides an indispensable contribution to the direct infliction of violence and has an 'immediate impact' on the opposing party.[40] Classic examples would be contractors involved in managing remote-control identification systems in view of tactical operations, transporting weapons to an active fire position, and loading weapons in an airplane ready to operate.

The employment of persons who accompany the armed forces to upgrade, provide support to, and repair military weapons systems and using them to drive military vehicles transporting military equipment and personnel is to some extent a different issue. In these cases, while there could be cases of direct participation on the basis of the above-mentioned reasoning[41] (ie involvement in a specific tactical operation), the emphasis is also on geographical factors, such as the proximity of the civilian's activities to the operational combat area. According to several authors[42] and practice,[43] when these activities are carried out in the theatre of operations this implies direct participation, while some authors tend to define the relevant area for this qualification more narrowly by referring to activities performed 'within a combat zone' or involving movements to 'an operational combat area'.[44]

The guidelines provided by the ICRC provide additional elements for evaluation. The document specifies that 'individual conduct that merely builds up or maintains the capacity of a party to harm its adversary...is excluded from the

---

[38] See Schmitt (n 22 above), 534; Melzer (n 22 above), 341–6. For this latter author the involvement of the civilian in integrated military operations can be qualified as direct participation if he has a role in a 'concrete hostile act', 'tactical' activities, a 'concrete attack', etc.

[39] For a definition of the 'tactical level of war' see US DoD, Dictionary of Military and Associated Terms, Joint Publication 1-02 (as amended through 17/10/2007): 'The level of war at which battles and engagements are planned and executed to achieve military objectives assigned to tactical units or task forces.' For this reference see Schmitt (n 22 above), 542–3.

[40] See M Sassòli, 'Targeting: The Scope and Utility of the Concept of "Military Objectives" for the Protection of Civilians in Contemporary Armed Conflicts' in D Wippman and M Evangelista (eds), *New Wars, New Laws? Applying the laws of war in 21st century conflicts* (2005), 181, 201, according to which 'What counts is the immediate impact on the enemy'; Quéguiner (n 22 above), 3. See similarly ME Guillory, 'Civilianizing the Force: Is the United States Crossing the Rubicon? Role of Civilians under the Laws of Armed Conflict' (2001) 51 Air Force Law Review 111, 134; JR Heaton, 'Civilians at War: Reexamining the Status of Civilians Accompanying the Armed Forces' (2005) 57 Air Force Law Review 155, 177–80.

[41] Reference could be made to a contractor transporting munitions to an active fire position; in this case the predominant element would appear to be the involvement of the contractor in a tactical military operation more than geographical elements. See Israeli Supreme Court, *Targeted Killings* case (n 20 above), para 35.

[42] See WH Parks, 'Air War and the Law of War' (1990) 32(1) Air Force Law Review 132; Turner and Norton (n 22 above), 26–32; Guillory (n 40 above), 128; Boldt (n 33 above), 522; Heaton (n 40 above), 177; Schmitt (n 22 above), 544–5; Y Dinstein, *The Conduct of Hostilities under the Law of International Armed Conflict*, 2nd edn (2010), 150–1.

[43] According to the Israeli Supreme Court, *Targeted Killings* case (n 20 above), para 35, 'a person who operates weapons which unlawful combatants use, or supervises their operation, or provides service to them, be the distance from the battlefield as it may' is a clear example of direct participation in hostilities.

[44] Melzer (n 22 above), 344–5.

concept of direct participation in hostilities',[45] unless support such as transport, maintaining of weapons, etc implies the individual's integration in a 'specific military operation'.[46] However, recourse to this notion does not provide conclusive terms of reference. In fact the notion of 'military operation' is not defined in the APs. Only the Commentary includes some indications. For instance, in relation to Article 51 it identifies 'military operations' as 'all the movements and activities carried out by armed forces related to hostilities',[47] a solution similarly held in Article 48, which also provides a broader definition.[48] In other circumstances military operations have been identified as 'movements, manoeuvres and other action taken by the armed forces with a view to fighting'.[49]

Therefore, in order to prevent certain activities performed by contractors from being defined as direct participation, due to the broad definition of the notion of 'military operations' provided by the Commentary, the *Interpretative Guidance* adds a reference to the involvement of the individual in a 'specific' military operation. Although univocal indications are lacking, it seems that this term has primarily been interpreted in the document as qualifying the above-mentioned critical activities as direct participation once they are linked with 'tactical' operations,[50] such as military activities aiming to achieve a specific objective in relation to a concrete hostile act.

Nonetheless, the usefulness of this approach is difficult to sustain in certain cases. Reference could be made to a contractor charged with driving military vehicles transporting belligerent materials to support an armed force operating in foreign territories. In some cases it would be hard to ascertain the final destination of the vehicle when, for instance, it leaves a military installation. However, this determination is fundamental in establishing the individual's direct or indirect participation in hostilities, as his support in a specific tactical operation would certainly result in his loss of protection. The same could be said for personnel involved in repairing and maintaining military vehicles and weapons. When such activities are performed in enemy territories close to the contact zone, we could probably conclude, based on the *Interpretative Guidance*, that only personnel accompanying a military convoy and repairing military vehicles or weapons systems damaged during the ongoing military action can be considered as direct participants in hostilities. On the other hand, personnel performing identical activities in a military base a few kilometres away from the operation in question, on the repair of weapons systems damaged during the same action, would probably be excluded

---

[45] ICRC, *Interpretative Guidance* (n 13 above), 1021–3, 1008.
[46] Ibid, 1021–2.
[47] See *Commentary APs* (n 20 above), 615, para 1936.
[48] Ibid, 600, para 1875. This text also refers to dictionary definitions defying this notion as 'battles and manoeuvres of all kinds, taken as a whole, as carried out by armed forces in a defined area, with a view to gaining a specific objective'.
[49] See ICRC statement of 25 November 1981, 'Interpretation by the ICRC of Art. 53 of the Fourth Geneva Convention of 12 August 1949, with particular reference to the expression "military operations"', quoted in Melzer (n 22 above), 273.
[50] For references to involvement in tactical operations as cases of direct participation in hostilities see *Interpretative Guidance* (n 13 above), 1008, 1018, 1022, 1023, 1043.

from this classification. Similarly, we can refer to civilian personnel on board the military fleet engaged in maintaining the technical efficiency of ships involved in military activities. Once the ship reaches its geographical area of operation, it would be difficult to identify cases in which such personnel are alien from ongoing military operations.

The practical difficulties in identifying these different scenarios are evident. When these activities are carried out in close proximity to the area of performance of armed hostilities, several uncertainties could arise in referring to a criterion which qualifies these activities according to the temporal moment in which we can locate the contractors' activities, ie during or outside a specific military operation. Therefore, in such cases, recourse to the 'geographical' requirement could provide some further elements of reference for an evaluation of the situation at issue.

A. Activities Performed by Contractors and the Application of the Principle of Proportionality

Finally it must be stressed that the above-mentioned elements play an important role in the evaluation of the lawfulness of military actions. In fact loss of protection of persons who accompany the armed forces from direct attack can only be admitted when their conduct is qualified as 'direct' participation. Moreover, this conclusion also implies that injury to such individuals cannot be considered as 'collateral damage' in accordance with the application of the principle of proportionality, as recognized in legal practice.[51] Even if the wording of the relevant provisions does not specify this additional outcome, and notwithstanding the fact that civilians taking a direct part in hostilities maintain their legal status as civilians, it would be wrong to include injury to these individuals in the evaluation based on the principle of proportionality.

However, in certain circumstances any evaluation of the status of persons accompanying the armed forces seems to be of limited practical relevance in the actual conduct of hostilities. Even where some of the ambiguous activities carried out by contractors fall within the definition of indirect participation, the personnel involved face a significant risk of being held to have been lawfully injured during the performance of their duties due to their proximity to military objectives. In fact, these military actions can be justified on the basis of the principle of proportionality. For instance, it seems hard to consider the presence of contractors charged with repairing military vehicles and weapons systems in a military base as an insurmountable legal hurdle for potential enemy actions against these structures, given the application of the principle of proportionality. Obviously, a similar

---

[51] See Inter-American Commission on Human Rights, *Third Report on Human Rights Situation in Colombia*, OEA/SerL/V/II102, Doc 9 rev 1, 26 February 1999, para 54: 'Further, by virtue of their hostile acts, such civilians lose the benefits pertaining to peaceable civilians of precautions in attack and against the effects of indiscriminate or disproportionate attacks.' This position has been upheld by the Israeli Supreme Court, *Targeted Killings* case (n 20 above), para 46.

conclusion can be reached in relation to civilians driving military vehicles used for belligerent purposes.

IV. The Status of Captured 'Persons who Accompany the Armed Forces'

Once a contractor supporting armed forces is in the hands of the opposing party it is necessary to determine his position. The guarantees he benefits from under international humanitarian law will differ according to the kind of conflict he has been involved in and the activities performed.

A. The Attribution of POW Status in International Armed Conflicts

As outlined above, the development of the notion of 'persons who accompany the armed forces' in the nineteenth century was based on the need to provide a clear legal status for this kind of support personnel upon their capture by an enemy state during an international armed conflict. Therefore, even if these individuals are commonly considered civilians as regards the conduct of hostilities and do not have a legal entitlement to take a direct part in hostilities, they can claim POW status once in the hands of the enemy.

In order to admit this claim, Article 4.A.4 GC III requires that armed forces provide such individuals with special identity documents stating their identification as persons belonging to this particular category, as confirmed in national documents[52] regulating the issue of standard cards by military authorities on the basis of the specimen reproduced in GC III.[53] However, the absence of such a document cannot completely exclude the possibility of being granted POW status.[54] In fact, on this aspect Article 4.A.4 GC III clearly departs from previous codifications, such as Article 13 of the Hague Regulations or Article 81 of the 1929 GC, which required the 'possession' of an authorization from the military authorities, evidenced by these special ID cards. However, this requirement, which was also envisaged in earlier drafts of Article 4.A.4 GC III, was eventually modified in order to take into account events that occurred during the Second World War, when some individuals were deprived of this status owing to the loss of their cards.[55] However, since a person accompanying an armed force may lose the

---

[52] For national regulations dealing with this issue see US DoD, Instruction 1000.1, *Identity Cards Required by the Geneva Conventions*, 30 January 1974, which also 'cover...civilian personnel authorized to accompany the military forces in areas of combat' (ibid, 1–2); UK Command of the Defence Council, *Contractor Support to Operations*, 4th edn (2008), 4–4, para 414: 'When necessary a Geneva Convention ID Card will be issued by the PJHQ to contractors before deployment, dependant upon the nature of the Operation and in conjunction with legal advice'; and the specimen reproduced in UK Ministry of Defence (n 20 above), 464.

[53] See Geneva Convention III, Annex IV, A (Identity Card).

[54] See K Ipsen, 'Combatants and Non-combatants' in Fleck (ed) (n 26 above), 107; Turner and Norton (n 22 above), 66–70.

[55] J Pictet (ed), *The Geneva Conventions of 12 August 1949: Commentary* (1960), III, 64–5.

identity document due to contingent situations, the Commentary is clear in asserting that possession of this ID card is not an absolute condition, as the determining factor is the capacity in which the person was serving.[56] Therefore, the functions performed and circumstances in which the individual was captured alongside members of the armed force, are key elements in ascertaining his status.

B. Problems Raised by Recent Armed Conflicts

1. The Link between the Contractor and the Armed Forces or other Entities

Events that have occurred in recent armed conflicts have given rise to doubts concerning the categories of contractors that are entitled to claim POW status. This problem involves both the link between the individual and the armed forces or other entities and the kinds of activities the contractor can perform in order to subsequently claim this protection.

As regards the first issue, Article 4.A.4 GC III requires that these personnel are accompanying 'armed forces' and have received an 'authorization from the armed forces', as evidenced by the above-mentioned Geneva Convention ID card. These expressions imply that contractors working for other branches of a state, such as the civilian administration, cannot claim POW status. Obviously the same position would exist with regard to contracts with international or non-governmental organizations, private entities, and so on, ie a large part of the situations involving contractors.

However, the principal point regards the possibility of obtaining this status when the individual does not have a direct contractual relationship with the armed forces but with another entity, such as a PMSC or defence firm, which has a contract with the armed forces for the provision of a service and subcontracts it to individuals. The Montreux Document, for instance, seems to deny this possibility, claiming that 'contractors employed . . . by private companies do not fall into this category'.[57] This statement demands clarification. In particular, Article 4.A.4 GC III does not appear to imply the need to ascertain a formal and direct contractual link between the individual and the armed forces. On the contrary, it seems sufficient to establish that the services provided are not performed for another branch of the administration but for the benefit of the armed forces, whose authorities are responsible for the attribution of this status through the granting of authorization to accompany military units and the issue of the Geneva Convention ID card. As emphasized in pertinent national documents regulating these matters, the necessary element for a contractor to qualify as a person accompanying an armed force is the existence of a 'formal grant to the Contractor of the MoD's written permission to deploy personnel in support of military operations. This is an essential element of complying with the Geneva Convention 3 Article 3 (A) [*sic*]—civilians supporting

---

[56] Ibid, 65: 'The application of this provision is therefore dependent on authorization to accompany the armed forces, and the identity card merely serves as proof.'
[57] The Montreux Document (n 6 above), 36.

a military force',[58] as it provides that 'Contractors are brought under the protection of the Geneva Convention'.[59] As 'Contractor' is intended as 'The commercial entity or organisation that undertakes to supply resources, perform services or both for the authority', which is responsible for notifying the actual names of personnel accompanying the armed forces,[60] it does not appear relevant to establish a direct contractual relationship between the armed forces and the individual for the recognition of this status.

2. Kinds of Activities Performed by 'Persons who Accompany the Armed Forces' and POW Status

In relation to the second problem, ie the kinds of activities a contractor can perform in order to be granted POW status, many scholars hold that when persons accompanying the army are taking a direct part in hostilities, these individuals cannot claim this more favourable treatment notwithstanding the fact that they have been provided with the necessary identity document and have been classified as such by the pertinent state.[61]

This restrictive view is primarily based on the limited nature of the activities included in Article 4.A.4 GC III, which provides clear examples of indirect support to hostilities.[62] Notwithstanding the non-exhaustive character of the list contained in the Article, the possibility of expanding its application to persons required to take a direct part in hostilities is considered contrary to the ratio of the rule. The Hague Regulations established the specific category of persons who accompany armed forces in order to provide a clear status for these civilians once captured. When the detaining power preferred to keep these individuals imprisoned it was considered more favourable to provide them with the status of POW, especially due to the rudimentary nature of guarantees provided to civilians at that time. However, this particular class of civilian was also considered worthy of protection on the

---

[58] UK Command of the Defence Council, *Contractor Support to Operations*, JSP 567, 4th edn (2008), 2–2, para 0202. In the United Kingdom the responsibility to provide contractors with this authorization 'is vested in the Secretary of State for Defence and can be delegated to an appropriate Officer of the Crown'. Concerning the procedure see UK Ministry of Defence, *Defence Standard 05–129, Contractors on Deployed Operations* (2008), 5–6, para 6.1.7. In the United States, 'contingency contractor personnel', ie 'defense contractors and employees of defense contractors and associated subcontractors', are allowed by DoD authorities to accompany US military forces and are provided with the appropriate Geneva Convention ID card (see US Department of Defence Instruction 3020.41 (n 1 above), 24–5). 'Defense contractors' are classified as 'any individual, firms, corporations, partnership... that enters into a contract directly with the Department of Defense'.

[59] UK Command of the Defence Council (n 58 above), 4–1, para 401.

[60] Ibid, 4–1, para 403.

[61] See concordant opinions expressed at the University Centre for International Humanitarian Law (UCIHL), *Expert Meeting on Private Military Contractors: Status and State Responsibility for Their Actions* (2005), 15–17; ICRC, *Third Expert Meeting on the Notion of Direct Participation in Hostilities* (2005) (n 14 above), 123–4.

[62] See EC Gillard, 'Business Goes to War: Private Military/Security Companies and International Humanitarian Law' (2006) 862 IRRC 525, 536–9.

assumption that they were performing activities characterized as indirect participation in hostilities.

Moreover, a general overview of GC III does not support a very broad interpretation of the duties that can be performed by 'persons who accompany the armed forces', as it appears difficult to maintain that while Article 4.A GC III states that combatants (ie members of armed forces, militias, levée en masse) can only obtain POW status under strict conditions of legitimacy, other individuals, such as civilians accompanying the force, can be directly involved in hostilities and nevertheless benefit from POW status without complying with these minimum requirements, solely on the basis of the classification awarded by the armed forces they are accompanying. This position is also shared in the UK Military Manual which explicitly states that: 'Civilians who are authorized to accompany the armed forces in the field... remain non-combatants, though entitled to prisoner of war status, so long as they take no direct part in hostilities.'[63] Despite the fact that there is currently no case law on this issue, there are strong arguments at a theoretical level to support this view, which is generally maintained in both cases of constant performance of activities classified as direct participation by contractors and of sporadic acts.[64]

On the contrary, other authors, including recent authoritative national documents such as US DoD Instruction 1100.22 maintain that persons who accompany the armed force 'do not lose entitlement to POW status upon capture' even if they have taken a direct part in hostilities,[65] unfortunately without providing any additional argument to sustain this conclusion. This position has been asserted by legal scholars on the basis of certain formal arguments. In fact, under Article 51.3 AP I, civilians lose the 'protection afforded by this Section... as they take a direct part in hostilities'. However, this refers to Section I of Part IV, concerning general protection against the effects of hostilities. The specific issue of POW status is analysed in Section II of Part IV of AP I, but this position has been unanimously rejected by experts.[66] Other authors claim that there is 'no evidence that civilians authorized to accompany the armed forces who took a direct part in hostilities and were captured were denied prisoner of war status'[67] on the basis of historical analysis. However, the reconstruction provided does not seem particularly

---

[63] See UK Ministry of Defence (n 20 above), 40.
[64] See eg ICRC, *Fourth Expert Meeting on the Notion of Direct Participation in Hostilities, Summary Report* (2006) (n 14 above), 35–6. This conclusion, therefore, seems different from the position held in the preparatory document for the session, ie ICRC, *Background Document Working Sessions VIII and IX: Individual Contractors and Civilian Employees* (2005) (n 14 above), 12, according to which: 'The fact that they have directly taken part in hostilities should not affect their POW status under international humanitarian law as DPH is not per se an offence under that law, but they could potentially be tried for that offence by a state.' However, in the same document this assertion was considered subject to revision during the meeting.
[65] US Department of Defence, Instruction 1100.22 (n 21 above), 50, para E3.2.5.5.1.
[66] See eg UCIHL (n 61 above), 16–17.
[67] See Parks, 'Evolution of Policy and Law Concerning the Role of Civilians and Civilian Contractors Accompanying the Armed Forces: Expert Paper' (2005) (n 14 above), 9.

pertinent to this conclusion, as it mainly focuses on describing cases of the direct involvement of civilians in hostilities and fails to refer specifically to the legal treatment of these individuals once captured.[68]

As a remote hypothesis, in the case of contractors charged by the state to perform activities that imply a direct participation and consequently a 'continuous combat function', it is debatable whether or not they could benefit from POW status on the basis of pertinent provisions concerning combatants. In these cases, however, the notion of 'continuous combat function', employed by the ICRC document in order to classify an individual as a combatant in relation to the conduct of hostilities would be useless concerning his status once captured. Therefore it would be necessary to verify compliance with the requirements set out in Article 4.A GC III and in Articles 43–4 I AP on a case-by-case basis.

At a practical level it would appear somewhat difficult to deny POW status to personnel who are formally qualified as 'persons who accompany the armed forces'. It seems plausible to assume that the detaining power will rely primarily on the contractor's capacity to clarify his position, for instance by presenting the special Geneva Convention ID card. This document usually provides very limited information about the individual, mainly his corresponding military rank, which is necessary to award particular privileges during confinement in a POW camp, and only a single line is devoted to describing the functions performed on behalf of the armed forces.[69] While it has been correctly maintained in legal doctrine that 'their function should be stated in such a manner that they cannot be suspected of having taken a direct part in hostilities',[70] it would be not difficult to imagine that in relation to activities that may arouse legal doubts on the proper qualification of the contractor in question, the pertinent armed forces authorities would simply provide generic information about the type of support provided by the individual, thus allowing him to largely avoid legal problems once captured. In these cases, the detaining power will face difficulties in challenging the POW status of the person accompanying the armed forces, except for limited cases in which its authorities have a definite idea of the activities the contractor performed on the field before being captured, mainly through the evaluation of information provided in the capture report.[71]

---

[68] Among examples provided by the above mentioned author only in the case concerning contractors involved in the construction of the US naval base on Wake Island it seems that this personnel was granted POW status even if some of them supported the unsuccessful defence of the island during the Japanese assault.

[69] Eg the UK Ministry of Defence (n 20 above), 464 reproduces the specimen included in Annex IV of GC III, in which there is a single line aimed to specify that the contractor 'accompanies the Armed Forces as ...'. Similarly, the specimen of the ID card for civilians who accompany the armed forces included in the US DoD Instruction 1100.1 (n 52 above), 8, has a box devoted to clarify the 'service' provided by the contractor.

[70] See Ipsen (n 54 above), 107.

[71] See NATO Standardization Agreement (STANAG) 2044, *Procedures for Dealing with Prisoners of War*, 6th edn (without date).

C. Other Forms of Legal Status for Captured Contractors

If a contractor cannot benefit from POW status, even in situations in which the relevant state has not sought to attribute the special status of a 'person who accompanies the armed forces' to him, these individuals may benefit from other guarantees, in particular through the possibility of being considered 'protected persons', once the requirements set out in Article 4 GC IV are satisfied. This position is confirmed in the 2004 UK Military Manual. For this document, whilst POW status can only be accorded to civilians authorized to accompany the armed forces, 'other civilians, including officials...have the protection of Geneva Convention IV'.[72] Moreover, the protection granted by these rules is also relevant in cases in which the civilian has taken a direct part in hostilities as this hypothesis is not included among the criterion for exclusion from protection under Article 4 GC IV.[73] Attempts to deny this protection by referring to undefined notions such as unlawful or enemy combatants,[74] thus placing such individuals in a legal black hole, have been rejected by the majority of legal scholars.

In non-international armed conflicts, the qualification of this personnel as 'persons who accompany the armed forces' is not relevant, as POW status does not exist in these conflicts. Nevertheless, personnel supporting armed forces can also be employed in this kind of armed conflict and once they are *hors de combat*, they maintain basic guarantees provided under Article 3 of 1949 GC, in AP II, when applicable, as well as customary international humanitarian law.

The debate concerning the attribution of POW status to certain contractors does not have any influence on the additional potentially negative consequences connected to their possible direct participation in hostilities. If these contractors have been classified as civilians and taken a direct part in hostilities they can face negative consequences. Although direct participation cannot be considered as a war crime per se, implying the international criminal responsibility of the individual,[75] the civilian can face penal prosecution by the adversary state as he is not lawfully entitled to take part in hostilities.[76]

---

[72] UK Ministry of Defence (n 20 above), 148, para 8.15.
[73] See K Dörmann, 'The Legal Situation of Unlawful/Unprivileged Combatants' (2003) 849 IRRC 45–74; S Borelli, 'Casting Light on the Legal Black Hole: International Law and Detentions Abroad in the "War on Terror"', (2005) 857 IRRC 39, 50–2; M Sassòli, 'Query: Is there a Status of "Unlawful Combatant"?' in RB Jaques (ed), [2006] Issues in International Law and Military Operations 57–67.
[74] J Callen, 'Unlawful Combatants and the Geneva Conventions' (2004) 44 Virginia JIL 1025–72.
[75] See Inter-American Commission on Human Rights, *Report on Terrorism and Human Rights*, OEA/SerL/V/II116, 22 October 2002, para 69: 'Mere combatancy by such persons is not tantamount to a violation of the laws and customs of war, although their specific hostile acts may qualify as such'; Quéguiner (n 22 above), 10–11.
[76] See Dinstein (n 42 above), 36–7; Schmitt (n 22 above), 520; Heaton (n 40 above), 174; R Kolb, *Ius in bello. Le droit international des conflits armés*, 2nd edn (2008), 324.

V. Concluding Remarks

One of the key elements in recent armed conflicts is the predominant and multi-tasking role of contractors supporting the armed forces. However, their legal status can give rise to uncertainty mainly due to the transformation of their role in current war scenarios. Even the analysis provided by the ICRC Interpretative Guidance is far from settling this issue in a definitive way and, furthermore, it does not provide any indication concerning recent legal issues related to captured personnel.

Therefore states should pay more attention to this issue. Only a few of them have provided regulation of the legal problems related to the outsourcing of military and auxiliary functions to PMSC. Furthermore, in certain cases, the solutions adopted so far are unsatisfactory in that they are aimed principally at permitting the widest employment of these personnel in military operations. However, this can create legal problems for 'persons who accompany the armed forces'. Regarding the conduct of hostilities, on the one hand these situations may result in the classification of such individuals as civilians taking a direct part in hostilities or even combatants, whilst on the other hand, once captured, they may not benefit from POW status under the protection afforded to 'persons who accompany the armed forces', with the risk therefore of being prosecuted for their unlawful active involvement in hostilities.

12
Private Military and Security Companies in Non-international Armed Conflicts: *Ius ad Bellum* and *Ius in Bello* Issues

Luisa Vierucci

I. Introduction

This chapter attempts to fill the gap existing in legal literature[1] concerning *ius ad bellum* and *in bello* issues arising from the activities that private military and security companies (PMSCs) carry out in non-international armed conflicts (NIACs).[2] As far as *ius ad bellum* is concerned, all the main legal questions will be addressed, ranging from the legitimacy of intervening with the use of force in favour of the legitimate government to the issues arising in instances of intervention in support of an armed opposition group, including national liberation movements. As we shall see, the thorniest question concerns the limits of support provided to the legitimate government given the difficulties materializing in many internal conflicts of identifying the legitimate authority. Both on account of these hurdles and the prohibition on recruiting mercenaries, serious doubts arise as to the lawfulness under international law of recourse to PMSCs for activities in which the use of force is required.

---

[1] The focus of analysis has been the increased privatization of state functions in time of international armed conflict. See J-C Zarate, 'The Emergence of a New Dog of War: Private International Security Companies, International Law, and The New World Disorder' [1998] Stan J Int'l L 75–162; PW Singer, 'War, Profits, and the Vacuum of Law: Privatized Military Firms and International Law' [2004] Columbia J Transnat'l L 521–49; N Boldt, 'Outsourcing War: Private Military Companies and International Humanitarian Law' [2005] GYbIL 502–44; L Doswald-Beck, 'Private Military Companies under International Humanitarian Law' in S Chesterman and C Lehnardt (eds), *From Mercenaries to Market: The Rise and Regulation of Private Military companies* (2007) 115–38; E-C Gillard, 'Business Goes to War: Private Military/Security Companies and International Humanitarian Law' (2006) IRRC 525–72; C Hoppe, 'Passing the Buck: State Responsibility for Private Military Companies' [2008] EJIL 989–1014.

[2] In this chapter the notion of non-international armed conflict propounded by the International Criminal Tribunal for the former Yugoslavia will be adopted. Accordingly, any such conflict exists whenever there is 'protracted armed violence between governmental authorities and organized armed groups or between such groups within a State': International Criminal Tribunal for the former Yugoslavia, *Prosecutor v Tadić*, IT-94-1-AR72, Decision on the Defence Motion for Interlocutory Appeal on Jurisdiction, Appeals Chamber, 2 October 1995, para 70.

By contrast, the *ius in bello* analysis will be confined to the most unsettled aspects, namely: (i) the legal status of PMSCs and their members in a NIAC, and (ii) the international responsibility accruing to such companies if they qualify as armed groups. Only a brief analysis will be devoted to the scope of protection of PMSC members as well as the treatment they are entitled to when acting in a non-international conflict as the two issues do not raise special legal problems but stem from the solution given to legal status.

II. Resort to PMSC Services Implying the Use of Force in NIACs: A Legitimate Means to Re-establish Internal Peace or a Breach of International Law?

There are no specific rules in international law regulating the resort to armed force by PMSCs in time of armed conflict, including conflicts of a non-international character. Therefore the issue of the legitimacy of the use of PMSCs services which include combat activities has to be evaluated in the light of the principles and rules of international law relating to intervention in a NIAC. Those rules vary according to the type of entity in favour of which intervention takes place, namely: (1) intervention in support of the legitimate government; (2) intervention on the side of an armed opposition group; and (3) intervention in favour of a national liberation movement. In the present analysis this division will be followed.

A. The Freedom of the Legitimate Government to Request Foreign Armed Intervention

The principle whereby a state is free to resort to foreign intervention to help restoring internal order or defending the national unity and territorial integrity of the country can be considered as established in international law, as this is an attribute of sovereignty.[3] Its applicability is uncontroversial when the measures

---

[3] Cf Institut de Droit International, Commission on Present Problems of the Use of Force in International Law, Sub-group on Intervention by Invitation, *Draft Report on Intervention by Invitation*, 25 July 2007, 229 (hereafter: *IDI Draft Report* 2007). The Institut de Droit International had previously expressed a different position, consisting in the duty of third states to 'refrain from giving assistance to parties to a civil war which is being fought in the territory of another state', without distinguishing between assistance provided to the legitimate government and to other subjects (Art 2 (1) of the Resolution on the Principle of Non-Intervention in Civil Wars (1975)). This view was supported, at least to some extent, also by (a minority of) scholars, cf authors referred to in I Brownlie, *International Law and the Use of Force by States* (1963), 323. Brownlie himself, though not openly denying the existence of the freedom of the government to get foreign assistance, cautions that 'once intervention has commenced the requesting government ceases to be a completely free agent as its security rests on foreign aid'. Moreover, he stresses that it is undesirable that the legality of military operations should be related to controversial questions of internal law also because 'there is in international law no definition of "legitimate government"': ibid. We shall deal extensively with these questions in the following section.

which are the object of the request for intervention fall short of the use of force,[4] provided that some conditions are met. The question arises as to the lawfulness of resorting to foreign armed force on the part of the government given the prohibition of intervention in internal affairs and the ban on the threat and use of force in international relations. We shall focus on this very modality of intervention as that which properly falls under the scope of *ius ad bellum*.[5]

As it is well known, two PMSCs, Executive Outcomes and Sandline International, conducted military operations respectively in Angola in 1992–4 and Sierra Leone in 1995–8 in support of the government. Their direct participation in the conflict by means of military units providing combat services contributed to a major extent to the victory and restoration of the established government.[6] Although these instances remain isolated, the possibility of PMSCs' involvement in combat operations in internal conflicts cannot be excluded mainly for two reasons. In the first place, in many cases PMSC members deployed in a conflict area are armed in order to carry out their mandate, which does not necessarily include the use of force but may be limited to services such as providing security to certain personalities. However, if they happen to be the object of an attack in connection with the armed conflict and/or use offensive force, they become de facto involved in the hostilities. Secondly, some agreements expressly require the company to conduct combat activities.[7]

Clearly, the lawfulness of the intervention of foreign entities is subject to the existence of consent as a clause precluding wrongfulness.[8] Therefore it is crucial to analyse the conditions of validity of consent.

1. Consent as a Necessary Condition for the Lawfulness of Foreign Armed Intervention

The prohibition of using force does not operate in the presence of the government's consent to foreign intervention involving direct participation in hostilities.[9] In

---

[4] Typically those measures consists in providing training to security and/or military forces, guaranteeing security to specific persons (normally in position of responsibility within the government), or granting financial assistance.

[5] For the types of acts that constitute violation of the *ius ad bellum* see Ch 20 by Beaucillon, Fernandez, and Raspail in this volume.

[6] S Cleary, 'Angola: A Case Study of Private Military Involvement' in J Cilliers and P Mason (eds), *Peace, Profit and Power: The Privatisation of Security in War-torn African Societies*, Pretoria, Institute of Strategic Studies (1999), 164; I Douglas, 'Fighting for Diamonds: Private Military Companies in Sierra Leone', ibid, 195.

[7] See the Agreement for the Provision of Military Assistance between the Independent State of Papua New Guinea and Sandline International, 31 January 1997, according to which Sandline was contracted to 'Conduct offensive operations in Bougainville in conjunction with PNG [Papua New Guinea] defence forces to render the BRA [Bougainville Revolutionary Army] military ineffective and repossess the Panguna mine'.

[8] The discussion on whether the question of intervention by invitation should be dealt with as a matter of primary rules goes beyond the scope of this chapter. For interesting remarks on this question see T Christakis and K Bannelier, '*Volenti non fit Injuria*? Les Effets du Consentement à l'Intervention Militaire' AFDI (2005) 102–37.

[9] Art 20 of the Draft Articles on the Responsibility of States for Internationally Wrongful Acts adopted by the International Law Commission in 2001 lists consent among the clauses precluding wrongfulness.

order for consent to be valid, international law requires that certain conditions be fulfilled. First of all consent must be expressed by the competent authority, because it has to be attributed to the state in order to be valid under international law. This is the most delicate condition to be met in a situation of armed conflict where it can be difficult to identify the authority entitled to represent the state internationally. The situation is clear-cut if the rebels have not attained the status of insurgents (either by means of insurgent or belligerent recognition,[10] or else de facto through control exercised over a part of the state territory). In this case it is the de iure government that is entitled to express consent.

The situation is less clear-cut as to who the authority entitled to express consent will be in situations where unrest has attained the threshold whereby the armed opposition group is a subject of international law. In this scenario practice is not uniform and the legal literature has expressed divergent opinions. According to one view, effectiveness is the crucial criterion.[11] This means that the de facto government is the one competent to express consent on behalf of the state. Another position holds that recognition by third states or international organizations is the key factor, on the condition that this recognition endures over a certain period of time.[12] Such recognition entails a presumption of legitimacy in favour of the established government and it persists also if the government is faced with armed opposition in the country so long as the opposition has not acquired stable control over portions of the territory.[13] The issue of the identification of the legitimate authority representing a county is increasingly addressed by international organizations and in particular the UN Security Council. The Council increasingly identifies the government which the international community considers to be legitimate mainly due to the expansion of the UN role in the field of peace-building.[14] For example, in the case of the Ivory Coast the Security Council, acting under Chapter VII of the UN Charter, indicated the person who they deemed the legitimate holder of the office of president.[15] In addition, with Resolution 1546 (2004) the Security Council legitimized the Iraqi interim government whose effectiveness was highly debatable.[16] This type of intervention by the Security Council constitutes a form of recognition of the legitimate government. A third stance is represented by the assertion that it is the combination of effectiveness and recognition on the part of third states or international organizations that determines who the legitimate

---

[10] See nn 53 and 54 below as well as related text.
[11] A Tanca, *Foreign Armed Intervention in Internal Conflict* (1993), 35–6.
[12] Cf *IDI Draft Report* 2007, 248–9 and authors referred to in footnotes.
[13] If the opposition group has acquired portions of the territory then, depending on the circumstance, the principle of effectiveness calls for recognition of the legitimacy of the power exercised over that territory: L Doswald-Beck, 'The Legal Validity of Military Intervention by Invitation of the Government [1985] BYbIL 197 and V Grado, *Guerre Civili e Terzi Stati* (1998), 67.
[14] C Gray, *International Law and the Use of Force*, 3rd edn (2008), 113.
[15] Res 1721 (2006), para 5.
[16] Notable are those resolutions where the Council draws legal consequences from the identification of the legitimate government. On several occasions the UN body has affirmed the right of states to assist the legitimate government against opposition groups and has decreed an embargo only vis-à-vis armed opposition groups: Gray (n 14 above), 113.

authority to request foreign armed assistance is.[17] This seems to be the majority position and the one that best reflects recent practice. According to this view, governments such as those put in place by Hamas in the Gaza strip are not legitimate because, even if they satisfy the effectiveness criterion, they have not gained international recognition from the majority of the international community.

The approach followed by PMSCs as to the identification of the authority entitled to request foreign military assistance *durante bello interno* sheds no light on the matter. The agreement signed by Papua New Guinea and Sandline International on 31 January 2007 states that the company operates 'particularly in situations of internal conflict and only for and on behalf of recognized Governments'. During the second civil war in Angola (October 1992–November 1994), Executive Outcomes provided armed assistance to the recognized government of President Dos Santos when the government's effectiveness was in doubt given that the União Nacional para a Independência Total de Angola (UNITA) insurgents were controlling four-fifths of the Angolan territory.[18] The backing given by PMSCs to the government of Sierra Leone during the conflict of the mid-1990s is more complex, as power changed several times.[19]

This practice, which tends to indicate that according to PMSCs recognition alone is the key criterion for the validity of consent, is contradicted by evidence that the above companies operated in favour of armed opposition groups that would certainly not qualify as the recognized government of the country at the relevant time.[20] It is therefore not easy to defeat the impression that political or other criteria, rather than legal convictions, direct the choices of military firms in this field.

The difficulties inherent in the determination of the authority from which consent can validly emanate during a NIAC unsettle the content of the principle relating to the freedom of the legitimate government to request foreign armed assistance.[21]

At best, this principle is helpful to identify the two poles of a continuum. At one pole lie those situations where the government lacks the requirements (effectiveness and recognition) needed to express valid consent. In this case, third parties are under a duty to refrain from intervening militarily until the situation permits

---

[17] For a detailed analysis of this position see O Corten, *Le Droit Contre la Guerre* (2008), 432–46. This seems also to be the approach favoured in the *IDI Draft Report* 2007, 264.
[18] Cleary (n 6 above), 146.
[19] Initially, Executive Outcomes and Branch Energy signed an agreement with the government of Strasser which also included assistance in defeating the Revolutionary Unitary Front opposition group. Those agreements remained in place after the election of a new government led by Ahmad Tejan Kabbah. In the second phase, which started with the 25 May 1997 a *coup d'état* was led by Ernest Koroma which ousted President Kabbah, and it was Sandline International that helped with the restoration of the deposed president, who actually returned to power on 10 March 1998; cf Douglas (n 6 above), 179, 190–1.
[20] See allegations of PMSCs supporting UNITA between 1992 and 1995: Cleary (n 6 above), 149–50 and K O'Brien, 'Private Military Companies and African Security 1990–98' in Musah Abdel Fatau and J Kayode Fayemi (eds), *Mercenaries: An African Security Dilemma* (2000), 58–9.
[21] C Le Mon, 'Unilateral Intervention by Invitation in Civil Wars: The Effective Control Test Tested' *New York University Journal of International Law and Politics* [2003] 791.

identification of the authority which can validly express consent to intervention.[22] At the other extreme are those instances in which the opposition has received armed assistance from abroad. In this case both practice and *opinio iuris* indicate that third parties may supply direct military assistance to the legitimate government.[23] Apart from these two extremes, the dividing line between a lawful and an unlawful intervention based on valid consent remains blurred.

Other features of consent as a basis for intervention are the fact that consent should not be nominal (it has to be effective, expressed in clear terms, and not vitiated) and be given either before or at the time of intervention. Such features are usually uncontested in the case of intervention on the part of a PMSC as the contract tends to satisfy those requirements. Other conditions for the validity of consent pertain to the scope of intervention. The action of the invited entity must be limited to the purposes accompanying the invitation and shall respect the conditions posed by the government.[24]

Absent the above conditions, consent cannot be considered as valid and consequently the use of armed force on the part of the foreign entity does not qualify as an intervention by invitation but amounts to a forcible intervention and hence will be unlawful.

In short, valid consent is a *necessary* condition for the legality of intervention by invitation in a NIAC in those situations where it is possible to identify the legitimate authority to express it. Yet even when valid, consent is not a *sufficient* condition for the legality of the intervention, as we shall now see.

2. Legal Bases for Intervention Accompanying Consent

Consent is decreasingly invoked as the only justification for the intervention of a foreign state in support of the legitimate government in its struggle against an

---

[22] Corten expresses the same position (n 17 above), 446.
[23] Brownlie (n 3 above), 327 and Art 5 of the Resolution of the Institut de Droit International on *The Principle of Non-Intervention in Civil Wars* (1975) (n 3 above).
[24] Typically, the contract between a state and a PMSC sets the duration both of the intervention and the contract itself. Normally the duration of the contract is expressed in precise temporal terms but subject to the achievement of the purposes set out in the document, which cannot usually be foreseen with accuracy. In addition, the conduct of activities not foreseen at the moment when consent is expressed (which, in the case of a PMSC, is usually a contract) makes the intervention unlawful; cf Art 3(e) of UN General Assembly Res 3314(XXIX). Eg an inquiry has recently been ordered by the Philippine Senate aimed at verifying whether US troops also conducted open combat operations in the course of what were supposed to be merely joint United States–Philippines training exercises to fight rebels and terrorists in the south of the country. Most probably this inquiry will also look at the agreement of 4 March 2008 between the United States and DynCorp concerning provision of support services to United States troops in Mindanao till 2012: cf DynCorp website (<http://www.dyn-intl.com/news2008/news030408.aspx>, accessed on 17 August 2010), since the Philippine Constitution prohibits permanent military bases and the conduct of combat operations by foreign troops: 'Oversight Body to Probe US Troops' Involvement in Combat', *Businessworld*, vol XXII, no 49, Thursday, 2 October 2008, <http://www.bworldonline.com/BW100208/content.php?id=077>, accessed on 17 August 2010.

armed opposition group. Practice shows that consent, which is usually expressed in a contract, coexists with other legal bases for intervention.[25]

First, the maintenance of internal law and order usually constitutes the legal ground for intervention where PMSCs are involved.[26] For instance, Papua New Guinea engaged Sandline International 'to support its Armed Forces in the protection of its Sovereign territory and regain control over important national assets'.[27] Secondly, open support for the legitimate government during a NIAC is frequently grounded on self-defence. This occurs when there is evidence that the armed group fighting the government is receiving external aid. The legality of the intervention in favour of the government in this case is well established.[28] Thirdly, particularly since the early 1990s, intervention by invitation has more and more often been conducted either directly by the United Nations or under a Security Council authorization.[29] Interestingly, such a development also concerns situations in which consent of the government was present.[30] In these cases a UN Security Council resolution adopted by virtue of Chapter VII constituted the factor legitimizing intervention.

In short, these three elements attest to the increasing awareness of the international community that the conditions for valid consent to external armed force in a non-international armed conflict are prone to abuse because of the difficulties connected with the determination of the authority competent to express consent. They indicate that the principle whereby the legitimate government is free to invite foreign armed forces to curb internal armed opposition is becoming the object of increasing restraints.[31] The only case where such freedom remains unlimited relates to those situations where the Security Council authorizes intervention or opposition groups have received foreign armed assistance. It is submitted that it is also on

---

[25] Practice shows that since the establishment of the United Nations instances of intervention by virtue of a treaty stipulated ante facto have virtually disappeared; cf Grado (n 13 above) and Gray (n 14 above), 214. There is no evidence of agreements concluded between a state and a PMSC before a need for the latter's intervention arises.

[26] According to Corten (n 17 above), 461, 480–1, this legal basis shows the third-party intention to maintain a neutral attitude towards the conflict. In our opinion it is often difficult to distinguish between an operation aimed at maintaining law and order and direct intervention in the conflict.

[27] Sandline–PNG Agreement, preamble. As to assistance short of the use of force, mention can be made of an agreement signed between the Philippines and the United States which is based, inter alia, on fighting terrorists: see Panti, 'Changes in VFA on Hold, Adan Says', *Manila Times* (21 July 2008), <http://www.manilatimes.net/national/2008/july/18/yehey/top_stories/20080718top7.html>, accessed on 20 August 2010.

[28] See the detailed analysis by Corten (n 17 above), 467 ff and Brownlie (n 3 above), 327.

[29] Gray (n 14 above), 70 ff, 113 ff.

[30] Two requests for authorization to intervene forwarded to the Security Council are particularly relevant: the request for a multinational force intervening in Haiti to facilitate the return of the President Bertrand Aristide in 1994 and the request of Italy to conduct a humanitarian operation in Albania in 1997. In those instances the government (or deposed president) had openly expressed consent to intervention, but neither the Security Council nor Italy had deemed it sufficient to intervene militarily; extensively on those cases cf Corten (n 17 above), 439 ff.

[31] *IDI Draft Report* 2007, 31, concludes that 'International law does not prohibit any State to render military assistance to another State, subject, however to the latter's consent (request) and further legal conditions'.

account of the above developments that no formal attribution of combat responsibility to PMSCs can be recorded since the 1990s.

B. Limitations to the Freedom of the Legitimate Government to Request Foreign Armed Intervention

There are cases in which international law expressly forbids or limits resort to foreign armed intervention. We are referring to: (1) the use of force employed in contravention to the right to self-determination of peoples; (2) the prohibition on recruiting mercenaries; (3) recourse to assistance measures violating provisions set forth in a binding Security Council resolution; or (4) an agreement concluded between the government and an armed opposition group. Obviously, foreign armed assistance is also unlawful if it entails the breach of another international obligation incumbent upon the requesting and/or requested state.[32]

1. Respect for the Principle of Self-determination of Peoples

The freedom of the legitimate government to resort to foreign armed intervention is limited not only by the principles prohibiting the threat and use of force as well as interference in internal affairs but also by the principle of self-determination of peoples. Recourse to force (and any other form of foreign aid and assistance) aimed at enhancing repression by the government of a people fighting for its self-determination is prohibited.

It must first be stressed that this legal constraint is arguably pertinent to our analysis. Its relevance depends on the qualification of the nature of the armed conflict where a national liberation movement is fighting. With the adoption of Article 1(4) of Protocol I of 1977 additional to the four Geneva Conventions of 1949, the traditional view that such conflicts were internal in character has been abandoned in favour of applying the rules of humanitarian law pertaining to international armed conflicts, yet it cannot be said with certainty that Article 1(4) has crystallized into a customary norm.[33]

In any case, recourse to external aid and assistance to suppress a national liberation movement is prohibited regardless of the qualification of the conflict. This means that, for example, resort to the services of PMSCs in the territories occupied by Israel is in violation of the right of the Palestinian people to

---

[32] We refer in particular to the conventions limiting the use or transfer of certain weapons and to human rights rules.

[33] Cf N Ronzitti, *Le Guerre di Liberazione Nazionale e il Diritto Internazionale* (1974). A Cassese, *Self-Determination of Peoples: A legal reappraisal* (1995), 201–4. The ICJ advisory opinion on the *Legal Consequences of the Construction of a Wall in Occupied Palestinian Territory* of 9 July 2004 seems to be based on the assumption of the customary nature of the rule because it held that the construction of the wall in Palestinian occupied territories infringed the right of that people to self-determination and at the same time concluded in favour of the application of the *ius in bello* rules pertaining to international armed conflict.

self-determination, given that they consist of activities aimed at repressing the national liberation movement, regardless of the qualification of the conflict.[34]

It should be noted that, if one accepts the view propounded by some legal scholars whereby the principle of self-determination of peoples is a jus cogens rule,[35] consent cannot be invoked by the government as a circumstance precluding wrongfulness.[36]

The issue arises of the applicability of this prohibition to PMSCs when the conduct of the company is not attributable to a state. In this regard reference must be made to the various resolutions of the General Assembly that have condemned armed intervention in favour of a government repressing a people fighting for its self-determination not only through the envoy of national units or armed groups but also by way of mercenaries.[37]

2. Prohibition on Recruiting Mercenaries

International law does not ban aid or assistance in any form—be it training, equipment, or combat operations—by corporate companies per se. The only prohibition concerns resort to *individuals* who qualify as mercenaries.[38] The question then arises of the possible qualification of PMSCs members as mercenaries.[39] As is well known, it is difficult to classify PMSC members as mercenaries[40] both under the definition contained in Article 47 of Additional Protocol I of 1977 and the 1977 Organization of African Unity (OUA) Convention[41] or the 1989 UN Convention.[42]

---

[34] We shall underline that Israel is not a party to Protocol I. According to the NGO, Who Profits?, 'Private security firms guard settlements and construction sites in the occupied territories; some are also in charge of the day-to-day operation, security and maintenance of some of the checkpoints', <http://www.whoprofits.org/Involvements.php?id=grp_inv_population#grp_inv_secu>, accessed on 20 August 2010.

[35] While a few scholars recognize the jus cogens nature of the principle of self-determination (see A Cassese, *International Law*, 2nd edn (2005), 65–7), the International Court of Justice has defined self-determination as 'one of the essential principles of contemporary international law' which creates erga omnes obligations (*Case Concerning East Timor*, ICJ Reports, 1995, para 29) but stopped short of defining it as a peremptory rule of international law.

[36] In addition, according to Art 41(2) of the 2001 Draft Articles on the Responsibility of States for Internationally Wrongful Acts, a serious violation of a jus cogens rule entails the obligation, among others, not to render aid or assistance to the responsible state.

[37] Grado (n 13 above), 130.

[38] It is well known that the conditions to be fulfilled in order to be qualified as a mercenary are so stringent that make the category almost exclusively theoretical: see Art 47 Protocol I and the 1989 Convention.

[39] Debate in the Security Council on the Report of the Secretary General on the Protection of Civilians in Armed Conflict, S/PV5781, 20 November 2007, 8.

[40] However, this circumstance does not prevent states, even those not parties to any of the above conventions, treating the staff of these firms as mercenaries: cf statement by Russia, debate in the Security Council on the Report of the Secretary General on the Protection of Civilians in Armed Conflict, ibid.

[41] Convention on the Elimination of Mercenarism in Africa, Organization of African Union, 3 July 1977.

[42] International Convention against the Recruitment, Use, Financing and Training of Mercenaries, United Nations, 4 December 1989. On the applicability of this Convention and the Convention of the

However, recourse to mercenaries has the same *raison d'être* as recourse to PMSCs, namely lack of adequate combat resources or technical skills internally, as well as the employment of force in exchange for payment. The abhorrence towards mercenarism is also dictated by the necessity of maintaining order among the armed forces, an issue that is liable to arise also with respect to recruitment of PMSCs.

There are also differences between PMSCs and mercenaries. The main one relates to the fact that while mercenaries are almost exclusively used in situations that violate the self-determination of peoples and sovereignty of states,[43] this is generally not the case with PMSCs intervening in favour of a government. At the same time, it is difficult to envisage a PMSC taking control over a country up to the point of endangering its sovereignty.

Finally, two other factors that differentiate a PMSC member from a mercenary are the maintenance of a reputation as law-abiding organizations and their permanent existence as firms,[44] but these distinctions do not hold under closer scrutiny. Evidence that a government avoids choosing a certain PMSC specifically on account of a disreputable record of observance of the law is extremely scant. Competence and efficiency are the qualities that are predominantly desired by the entities engaging these firms. As to the character of permanency, many PMSCs reinvent themselves under new names with a certain degree of frequency.

On account of the similarity between the rationale behind the ban on mercenarism and the principal features of PMSCs, serious doubts arise as to the lawfulness under international law of recourse to PMSCs for activities in which the use of force is required.

3. *Respect for Security Council Resolutions*

Security Council resolutions adopted under Chapter VII of the Charter which require the withdrawal of foreigners from a certain country or decree an embargo on arms or other material, restrict the freedom of the government to involve a foreign actor in a NIAC. The obligation to respect and implement binding Security Council decisions rests primarily upon Member States that must ensure the observance of the Council's resolutions on behalf of the legal persons under their jurisdiction. For this reason the United Kingdom felt the urge to institute a parliamentary commission of enquiry when the violation of the arms embargo

---

Organization of African Union to PMSC personnel see Ch 16 by Mancini, Ntoubandi, and Marauhn in this volume.

[43] Commission on Human Rights, Report on the Question of the Use of Mercenaries as a Means of Violating Human Rights and Impeding the Exercise of the Right of Peoples to Self-determination, UN Doc E/CN4/1998/31, 27 January 1998, para 50.

[44] United Kingdom, Foreign and Commonwealth Office, *Private Military Companies: Options for Regulations* (2002), para 35.

imposed on Sierra Leone by Resolution 1132 (1997) committed by the British company Sandline was discovered.[45]

However, the obligation to respect and implement binding Security Council resolutions may be directly incumbent upon non-state actors. The practice of the Security Council in this sense is not long-standing but consistent.[46] For example, in Resolution 864(1993) the Council warned UNITA, an armed opposition group, that it would decree trade measures against the armed group and restrictions on the travel of personnel unless the group complied with the peace agreement and previous resolutions.[47] From this practice it follows that the Council believes that any entity which is the addressee of a binding resolution has the obligation of ensuring its respect by individuals or entities carrying out activities on its behalf. In other words, should an armed opposition group avail itself of the services of a PMSC and at the same time become the addressee of coercive measures taken by the Security Council, the reach of the resolution extends to the PMSC. In this case, infringement of a Council resolution by a PMSC constitutes an unlawful act under international law independently of the existence of a link between the firm and a state.

4. Respect for Special Agreements Concluded between Conflicting Parties

In the agreements concluded between conflicting factions in those conflicts where the PMSCs were involved for combat purposes, namely Angola[48] and Sierra Leone,[49] the parties committed themselves to ensuring that all foreign forces be withdrawn from the country. In these cases, the continuous presence of members of PMSCs of foreign nationality would have constituted a breach of the agreement.

C. Intervention in Favour of an Armed Opposition Group

It is a well-settled principle under international law that armed opposition groups cannot receive *any* form of aid or assistance from third states. According to the type of support provided, such activity would violate the principle of non intervention or amount to a violation of the prohibition of the threat and use of force.[50] Hence

---

[45] United Kingdom, House of Commons, Committee on Foreign Affairs, *Report of the Sierra Leone Arms Investigation (Second Report)*, 27 July 1998, para 93, <http://www.publications.parliament.uk/pa/cm199899/cmselect/cmfaff/116/11602.htm>, accessed on 20 August 2010.

[46] PH Kooijmans, 'The Security Council and Non-state Entities as Parties to a Conflict' in K Wellens (ed), *International Law: Theory and Practice—Essays in Honour of Eric Suy* (1998), 333–46.

[47] Security Council Res 864, 15 September 2003, para 26.

[48] Art 1.1 of Annex 1/A to the Memorandum of Understanding—Addendum to the Lusaka Protocol for the Cessation of Hostilities and the Resolution of the Outstanding Military Issues under the Lusaka Protocol concluded between the Angolan government and UNITA.

[49] Art 12 of the Lomè peace agreement signed on 30 November 1996 between the government of Sierra Leone and the Revolutionary United Front is particularly explicit in this respect and it also stands out as it expressly mentions Executive Outcomes as among the foreign troops that have to be repatriated.

[50] International Court of Justice, *Case Concerning Military and Paramilitary Activities in and against Nicaragua (Nicaragua v United States of America)*, ICJ Reports 1986 (27 June 1986), 126 (hereafter *Nicaragua* case).

there can be no doubt that prima facie the intervention of Sandline International in favour of the Revolutionary United Front in Sierra Leone, the combat operations conducted by Executive Outcomes in Angola on behalf of the UNITA opposition group, the actions allegedly conducted by DynCorp in favour of rebels in Colombia,[51] and MPRI involvement in arms trafficking from Uganda to the Sudanese People's Liberation Army,[52] all constitute a breach of international law.

The only exception admitted by traditional international law to the above rule relates to the existence of the recognition of belligerency[53] and, to some extent, the recognition of insurgency.[54] Following recognition of belligerency, third states are bound by neutrality rules. This means that they can offer any type of aid and assistance to the opposition group on the condition that they do it impartially; that is, they do not take a discriminatory attitude.[55] In the case of a recognition of insurgency, third states must abstain from intervening in favour of either party as they would otherwise influence the outcome of the conflict. Such recognition only allows third parties to make contact with the insurgents to safeguard their own interests, for example, for the sake of protecting their nationals on the territory under the control of the armed group.

D. Intervention in Favour of a National Liberation Movement

Another limitation posed by international law to the freedom of the legitimate government to resort to external aid and assistance in a case of internal conflict consists in the intervention of a third party in favour of a national liberation movement. A customary rule exists whereby a people that is forcefully deprived of its right to self-determination has the right to receive assistance by third states (so-called right of resistance). However, despite the contrary view being propounded by a number of non-Western states, a general rule of international law allowing the sending of troops to assist a national liberation movement cannot be said to have crystallized.[56] Therefore the legality of such assistance is limited to support short of

---

[51] PW Singer, *Corporate Warriors: The Rise of the Privatized Military Industry* (2003), 137.
[52] O'Brien (n 20 above), 62.
[53] For the view that the recognition of belligerency has fallen into desuetude see A Clapham, *Human Rights Obligations of Non-State Actors* (2006), 271 ff.
[54] According to a customary principle, when an armed opposition group acquires control over a portion of the territory with a certain degree of stability, they reach the status of insurgents: see R Jennings and A Watts (eds), *Oppenheim's International Law*, 9th edn (1992), 161–76. A recent example of a recognition of insurgency is the appeal made by the president of Venezuela on 17 January 2008 to the effect that the FARC armed opposition group be recognized as belligerents by the government of Colombia. Despite the endorsement of the Venezuela Parliament (K Janicke, 'Venezuelan Legislature Supports Belligerent Status for Colombian Rebels', 19 January 2008, <http://www.venezuelanalysis.com/print/3080>, accessed on 20 August 2010), there was no follow-up to the appeal either by the Colombian authorities or the international community.
[55] A distinct question is whether intervention by a PMSC as such in favour of an opposition group internationalizes the conflict. The answer must be in the negative unless the PMSC acts on behalf of a state.
[56] Ronzitti (n 33 above), 116–23; Cassese (n 33 above), 152–3, 199–2000; and Gray (n 14 above), 61.

III. The Legal Status of PMSCs in Non-International Armed Conflicts and their Scope of Protection

direct military intervention. For the reasons set out above[57] with respect to the similarities between the rationale underlying the prohibition of resorting to mercenaries and the main features of PMSCs, it is difficult to deny that this limitation also applies if the third party intervening in favour of a national liberation movement is a private military company.

Addressing the question of the legal status of PMSCs in NIACs is troublesome as in this type of conflict the very term 'status' was a source of controversy during the negotiations leading to Article 3 common to the Geneva Conventions of 1949 and additional Protocol II of 1977. It is a fact that even the expression 'party to a conflict' used in common Article 3 in 1949 appeared as subversive in 1977 and was therefore discarded in the final draft. In addition, the will of the contracting parties not to affect the legal status of the powers ratifying the above treaties was expressly voiced in common Article 3 (in fine) and was inserted also in Protocol II via the provision specifying that the Protocol did not modify the 'existing conditions of application' of Article 3 (Article 1, para 1). Although the issue of legal status in a NIAC is not as weighty as in an international conflict, as no prisoner of war status exists in a NIAC, the question of the existence of a link to a party to the conflict is necessary to establish the type of protection and treatment guaranteed by international law.

The vast majority of legal doctrine recognizes the applicability of common Article 3 and Protocol II to non-state actors,[58] thus admitting the relevance of the status also for the party confronting the legitimate government. Yet, in order to avoid contentious status issues, it has recently been proposed that the term 'fighter' be used for any person who takes direct part in hostilities in a NIAC.[59] Although we find merits in the use of the broad category of 'fighter', as a matter of clarity for the purpose of this chapter we will adhere to the categories that can be factually distinguished in a NIAC, namely: (1) persons belonging to the armed forces of the legitimate government; (2) persons belonging to an armed opposition group (regardless of whom they are opposing); (3) mercenaries; and (4) civilians. We shall examine the conditions for PMSC members to fall into each category, and whether a PMSC *as such* may be considered as a separate addressee of *ius in bello* obligations.

---

[57] See above, section II.B.2.
[58] See S Sivakumaran, 'Binding Armed Opposition Groups' [2006] ICLQ 369–94 and doctrine therein referred to.
[59] M Schmitt, C Garraway, and Y Dinstein, *The Manual on the Law of Non-International Armed Conflict: With commentary*, International Institute of Humanitarian Law (2006), para 1.1.2(a).

A. Persons Belonging to the Armed Forces of the Legitimate Government

International humanitarian law (IHL) uses the expression 'armed forces' with respect to both international armed conflicts[60] (Article 43 of Protocol I) and NIACs,[61] without defining it. The issue of definition has been discussed in legal literature where two main lines of interpretation have emerged.[62] According to some, the silence of IHL shall be construed as devolving the question entirely to domestic law. In our opinion this view is propounded also by the fact that Additional Protocol I of 1977 establishes an obligation to notify the other parties when a party to a conflict 'incorporates a paramilitary or armed law enforcement agency into its armed forces' (Article 43(3)).[63] Others hold that IHL adopts a de facto criterion whereby determination of membership in the armed forces of a state is based on the function a person carries out in an armed-conflict context.[64]

Restricting our analysis to the notion of armed forces that applies to NIACs,[65] the expression can only be found in Article 1(1) of Additional Protocol II of 1977 concerning the material field of application. The term is used both with reference to the armed forces of a High Contracting Party in the territory of which the armed conflict takes place and to 'dissident armed forces' with which the High Contracting Party is confronted.

According to the *travaux préparatoires* the expression 'armed forces' of a High Contracting Party 'means *all* the armed forces—including those which under some national systems might not be called regular forces'[66] but does not include 'other

---

[60] Cf Art 1 and 3 of Regulations Respecting the Laws and Customs of War on Land, Annex to 1907 Hague Convention IV. Art 43 of Protocol I of 1977 broadens the scope of the terms 'armed forces' so as to include those 'groups and units which are under a command responsible to [a] Party for the conduct of its subordinates', beyond 'all organized armed forces'. Yet it fails to define what are 'organized armed forces'.

[61] Cf Art 1(1) of Protocol II of 1977.

[62] For a summary of the main arguments see International Committee of the Red Cross (ICRC) and TMC Asser Institute, *Third Expert Meeting on the Notion of Direct Participation in Hostilities, Summary Report*, Geneva, 23–5 October 2005, 74–8.

[63] As explained in Y Sandoz, C Swinarski, and B Zimmermann (eds), *Commentary on the Additional Protocols of 8 June 1977 to the Geneva Conventions of 2 August 1949*, (1987) (hereafter: *ICRC Commentary on the Additional Protocols*), 517, paras 1682–3, Art 43(3) of Protocol I was added in order to clarify that police forces may become part of the armed forces in wartime according to the internal law of some countries. Had the Convention adopted a de facto standard, such clarification would have been redundant.

[64] In this sense see also *Expert Meeting on Private Military Contractors: Status and State Responsibility for their Actions*, University Centre for International Humanitarian Law, Geneva, 29–30 August 2005, 12.

[65] From the *ICRC Commentary on the Additional Protocols* (with reference to Art 43 of Protocol I, 509–11, esp para 1672), a distinction seems to emerge between the notion of armed forces of a state (ie 'regular armed forces') and the armed forces of other parties to a conflict (ie 'irregular armed forces') belonging to a national liberation movement, an organized resistance movement, and eventually also to an international organization.

[66] Emphasis in the original. This is the intention of the drafters of the Protocol as can be deduced by *Acts of the Diplomatic Conference on the Reaffirmation and Development of International Humanitarian Law applicable in Armed Conflicts*, Geneva (1974–7), X, 94 (CDDH/I/238/Rev1, 2). In relation to this point, the *ICRC Commentary on the Additional Protocols*, 1352, para 4462 adopts a position that is

governmental agencies the members of which may be armed' such as law-enforcement bodies and paramilitary agencies. The rationale seems to be that the latter organizations are normally not incorporated by internal law in the state's army.

The last remark indicates a difference between the notion of armed forces contained in the two additional protocols concerning notification to the counterpart of the incorporation of those units into the armed forces. Such a notification is compulsory only in international conflicts.[67] The purpose that the notification seeks to fulfil, ie facilitating distinction between combatants and civilians, would also justify its application in NIACs. Thus the question arises as to the reasons why this obligation of notification was not included in Protocol II. It is submitted that this absence has two motivations: on the one hand, armed opposition groups are expected to know the internal law of their country;[68] and, on the other, the parties to Protocol II were presumably reluctant to commit themselves to the obligation of notification to the opposition group because such a measure could be seen as legitimizing the group.

In brief, the above difference between the two protocols concerning a procedural matter does not warrant the conclusion that the notion of armed forces applicable in a NIAC is substantially different from that adopted in international conflicts.

Despite this, we are left with a dichotomy between regulation by domestic law and reliance on the functional criterion. It is suggested that IHL establishes a different regime according to the type of armed forces we are dealing with. Whereas membership in the regular armed forces of a High Contracting Party is governed by domestic law, membership in irregular forces (such as militias or volunteer groups) can also (and sometimes only) be established according to a functional criterion. Reference to the law of international armed conflicts helps with illustrating the matter.

The Third Geneva Convention of 1949 Relative to the Treatment of Prisoners of War clearly distinguishes between 'members of the armed forces of a Party to the conflict as well as members of militias or volunteer corps forming part of such armed forces' (Article 4(A)1) and 'members of other militias and members of other volunteer corps, including those of organized resistance movements, belonging to a Party to the conflict' (Article 4(A)2) and only obliges the latter group to respect the

---

arguably consonant with the *travaux* as it states that: 'The term "armed forces" of the High Contracting Party should be understood in the broadest sense. In fact, this term was chosen in preference to others suggested such as, for example, "regular armed forces", in order to cover all the armed forces, including those not included in the definition of the army in the national legislation of some countries (national guard, customs, police forces or any other similar force)).' As affirmed in the text, in our view the *travaux* can be interpreted in a different way, where they specify that 'according to the views stated by a number of delegations, the expression [armed forces] would not include other governmental agencies the members of which may be armed; examples of such agencies are the police, customs and other similar organizations'.

[67] Art 43(3) of Protocol I.
[68] This means that armed opposition groups are presumed to be aware of the fact that domestic law provides for incorporation of law enforcement bodies into the armed forces in time of armed conflict.

four conditions for lawful combatancy.[69] A terminological distinction is thus made between those members 'forming part' of the armed forces and those 'belonging to a Party to the conflict'. The difference is also in substance: the lawful combatancy criteria are implicit for members of regular armed forces whilst they are constitutive of status for irregulars.

One may object that the customary rule concerning the notion of lawful combatant does not correspond to that set out in Article 4(A)1 and Article 4(A)2 of the Third Geneva Convention because it has been superseded by the one included in Article 43 of Protocol I.[70] We are not convinced about the validity of this objection since most of the states that have not ratified the protocol have done so rightly to avoid equal treatment between regular and irregular armed forces. In other words, there is no coincidence—at least for the states not parties to Protocol I—between members of the armed forces and combatants: while all members of the armed forces are combatants, the opposite is not true.[71]

Domestic law definitely governs membership in the armed forces, whilst membership in irregular groups is regulated by IHL according to a de facto criterion based on the function a group carries out and the existence of the link with the government.[72] This means that under IHL the notion of combatant applicable in an international armed conflict is generally broader than the notion of armed forces adopted under domestic law.

The same is true also for NIACs. For example, in the Sudanese region of Darfur the Janjaweed militias were only exceptionally incorporated into the Sudanese armed forces, though belonging to a party to the conflict (the Sudanese government).[73] With respect to liability to attack and responsibility under international law, their treatment is the same as that accruing to members of the armed forces.

This issue is prominent with respect to PMSCs because it shows that lack of formal enlistment in the armed forces of a state in a NIAC[74] does not exclude the

---

[69] Also a literal reading of Art 1 (in fine) of the Regulations Respecting the Laws and Customs of War on Land, Annex to the 1907 Hague Convention IV, whereby: 'In countries where militia or volunteer corps constitute the army, or form part of it, they are included under the denomination "army"' induces to conclude that there may be militias or volunteer corps which, though qualifying as lawful combatants and having a link to a party to a conflict, cannot formally be classified as members of the armed forces.'

[70] J-M Henckaerts and L. Doswald-Beck, *Customary International Humanitarian Law* (2005), I, 16, resolutely affirm that the definition in Art 43 of Protocol I 'is now generally applied to all forms of armed groups who belong to a party to an armed conflict to determine whether they constitute armed forces...All those fulfilling the conditions in Article 43 of Additional Protocol I are armed forces'. Hence they implicitly conclude in favour of a coincidence between the notions of combatant and member of the armed forces as a matter of customary law (see rules 4 and 5).

[71] Eg members of armed resistance movements in occupied territory qualify as combatants but not as members of the armed forces.

[72] This distinction has been recently propounded also the by *ICRC Interpretative Guidance on DPH*, 31.

[73] *Report of the International Commission of Inquiry on Darfur to the UN Secretary General*, 25 January 2005, para 108.

[74] This is the exception and has occurred only in Sierra Leone, Zarate (n 1 above), 124, and was foreseen for the members of Sandline International in Papua New Guinea (according to Art 2.1(h) of the Agreement for the Provision of Military Assistance Between the Independent State of Papua New

qualification of private actors acting on behalf of the state as organs of that state under international law. This is so because IHL merely requires the satisfaction of a functional relationship between the non-state entity constituting an irregular armed force and the state. In short, only the *combination* of the domestic-law approach and the functional criterion allows encompassing the multiform phenomenon of PMSCs acting in NIACs as organs of a state—that is, members of the armed forces.

Finally, should a PMSC member fall under the category of armed forces or qualify as member of an irregular group having a link with the government, he/she does not enjoy immunity from attack.[75]

B. Persons Belonging to an Armed Opposition Group

A legal status is accorded by IHL to those armed groups that fulfil certain conditions that are today codified in Article 1 of Additional Protocol I of 1977 (organization, existence of a responsible command, control exercised over a part of the territory so as to enable the group to conduct sustained and concerted military operations and to implement the Protocol). When these features are present, the group attains the status of insurgents.[76] Some IHL treaty rules refer to non-state parties but fail to clarify the content of this notion.[77] In particular Article 3 common to the Geneva Conventions contains a reference to the obligations accruing to 'each Party to the conflict' in the case of non-international armed conflict occurring on the territory of one of the contracting parties,[78] but does not assist in identifying the precise content of the notion.

As a starting point we can assume that the notion of armed opposition group is narrower than the notion of non-state entity. This position has been adopted by the Institut de Droit International, which has specified that the expression 'non-state entity' 'includes' the entities that fulfil the conditions set forth in common Article 3 and additional Protocol II, hence admitting the existence of entities other than those provided for in IHL treaties.[79] However, lack of a normative definition of the

---

Guinea and Sandline International, 31 January 1997, all personnel of Sandline International were to be enrolled as 'Special Constables').

[75] This principle, which is now crystallized in a customary rule, can be considered applicable to NIAC also by virtue of Art 13(3) of Additional Protocol II. See also the *ICRC Commentary on the Additional Protocols*, with reference to Art 13 of Protocol II, 1453, according to which: 'Those who belong to armed forces or armed groups may be attacked at any time.'

[76] See Cassese (n 35 above), 124–31.

[77] See Art 1 of Hague Regulations of 1907, which refers to militia and volunteer corps, and also Art 8(2)(f) of the Rome Statute of the International Criminal Court.

[78] For a detailed analysis of this article in light of the *travaux préparatoires*, doctrinal positions, and the implications for a definition of the notion of armed opposition group, see L Zegveld, *Accountability of Armed Opposition Groups in International Law* (2002), 134–6.

[79] Institut de Droit International, *Resolution on the Application of International Humanitarian Law and Fundamental Human Rights, in Armed Conflicts in which Non-State Entities Are Parties*, Art I, para 2 (the authoritative text is French, where the word 'comprend' is used, while surprisingly in the English translation the term 'means' was preferred). One may think of national liberation movements, de facto entities not recognized as having the features to become parties to the Geneva Conventions such as Somaliland, and international organizations, as non-state entities other than armed opposition groups.

expression 'armed opposition group' and the great variety in which such entities manifest themselves raise the question of the features that a group must have in order to be subject to IHL rules. It can only be affirmed with a high degree of certainty that a certain level of organization is required for the group to qualify as an addressee of those IHL obligations relating to the parties to a conflict.[80]

Certain opposition groups have their own armed forces. Clearly those groups show a high degree of organization. In addition, their armed forces fall under the category of 'armed groups' as much as do 'dissident armed forces' as referred to in Article 1(1) of Additional Protocol II,[81] the only difference between the two being that the latter are composed of former members of the state's armed forces, whilst the former are not.[82]

Two hypotheses must be distinguished with respect to the possibility of PMSCs falling into the category of persons belonging to an armed group. In the first place, PMSC members contribute to the formation of an armed group; in the second place, a PMSC *as such* qualifies as an armed group. Practice shows that there have been examples of the first hypothesis. In those instances there was no doubt about the existence of a de facto link between the members of the PMSC and the party opposing the government. No evidence of the second hypothesis has been found; in any case a certain level of organization would have to be satisfied by the company to qualify as an armed group by virtue of IHL.[83]

If PMSC members or the PMSC as such fall into the category of armed groups, they are liable to lawful attack *durante bello interno*. It is however unclear whether they can be attacked at all times or only for the duration of their active participation in hostilities. This ambiguity stems from the unclear status of the members of an armed opposition group as combatants (in an a-technical sense) or civilians under customary law.[84] Nor are treaty rules helpful since there is only one article touching upon the issue and it merely stipulates that the protection of the treaty can be enjoyed by civilians 'unless and for such time as they take a direct part in hostilities' without further specification.[85]

---

[80] The avenue consisting in determining the elements proving the required level of organization of the group has been pursued by the International Criminal Tribunal for the Former Yugoslavia (ICTY). In a recent case, after having surveyed the factual elements that the ICTY judges had taken into account in previous cases to assess the level of organization attained by an armed group, the trial chamber divided those elements into five broad groups, namely: presence of a command structure; capacity of the group to carry out operations in an organized manner; level of logistics; level of discipline and ability to implement the basic provisions of Art 3 common to the Geneva Conventions; representative character of the group and ability to speak with one voice: *Prosecutor v Boskoski and Tarkulovski*, trial judgment, 10 July 2008, paras 199–203. These indicative factors are relevant to our analysis as they were devised to be used in situations of non-international armed conflicts.

[81] For the assimilation of the notion of 'dissident armed forces' with 'the essential idea of an "insurrectional movement"' see the Commentary of the International Law Commission to the Draft Articles on the Responsibility of States for Internationally Wrongful Acts (n 9 above), 115, para 9.

[82] *ICRC Commentary on the Additional Protocols*, 1351, para 4460.

[83] In this case those criteria apply *ratione personae* and not *ratione materiae*.

[84] APV Rogers, *Law on the Battlefield*, 2nd edn (2004), 32–3, and Henckaerts and Doswald-Beck (n 70 above), I, 19. Extensively on this point specifically concerning PMSCs in NIAC, see Doswald-Beck (n 1 above), 129–31.

[85] Art 13(3) of Protocol II.

On this point only the *ICRC Commentary on the Additional Protocols* is unequivocal as it clarifies that 'Those who belong to armed forces or armed groups may be attacked at any time.'[86] Some state practice, for instance a series of acts carried out by the US-led operation *Enduring Freedom* in Afghanistan, tend to indicate that members of armed opposition groups are assimilated to members of armed groups rather than civilians taking a direct part in hostilities, as they are made the object of attack even when they do not take a direct part in hostilities. The recent *ICRC Interpretative Guidance on the Notion of Direct Participation in Hostilities under IHL* convincingly argues in favour of the mutual exclusiveness of the notions of organized armed groups and civilians[87] on the basis of the 'wording and logic' of common Article 3 to the Geneva Conventions and Additional Protocol II, and it concludes that in NIACs 'organized armed groups constitute the armed forces of a non-State party to the conflict'.[88] Interestingly, according to this study, under IHL 'the decisive criterion for individual membership in an organized armed group is whether a person assumes a continuous function for the group involving his or her direct participation in hostilities', ie if the person assumes 'continuous combat function'.[89] The study explicitly applies this criterion to PMSCs.[90]

C. Mercenaries

Only in extremely rare instances may PMSC staff fall under the current definition of mercenary.[91] The question does not change in relation to NIACs, as the two relevant conventions on mercenaries[92] are generally considered applicable irrespective of the type of conflict the mercenary fights.[93] We only briefly mention that, should a PMSC member qualify as a mercenary, he/she would be a legitimate objective of attack. It is however unclear whether for protective purposes a mercenary is assumed to be a member of an armed group or a civilian taking a direct part in hostilities.

In addition, a member of a PMSC who qualifies as a mercenary would be liable to national criminal proceedings against him for having committed an illicit act,[94]

---

[86] *ICRC Commentary on the Additional Protocols*, 1453, para 4789.
[87] *ICRC Interpretative Guidance on DPH*, 27–9.
[88] Ibid, 36.
[89] Ibid, 33.
[90] Ibid, 39.
[91] See Zarate (n 1 above), esp 120–45; Boldt (n 1 above), 532–5; and Cameron, 'Private Military Companies: Their Status under International Law and its Impact on Their Regulation' (2006) IRRC 580–2.
[92] OUA Convention for the Elimination of Mercenarism in Africa (1977) and the International Convention against the Recruitment, Use, Financing and Training of Mercenaries (1989).
[93] The only difference is that the OUA Convention defines a mercenary by reference to his/her fighting in 'armed conflict' (see Art 1), while the International Convention's definition covers also participation in a 'concerted act of violence aimed at: (i) Overthrowing a Government or otherwise undermining the constitutional order of a State; or (ii) undermining the territorial integrity of a State' (Art 2(a)).
[94] Despite the obligation to introduce national legislation criminalizing not only the conduct but also recruit of mercenarism, very few states have done so to date.

D. Civilians

The category of civilians is residual with respect to combatants (in an a-technical sense), including mercenaries.[95] It is unclear whether armed groups are to be assimilated to civilians or to members of the armed forces, but a trend is developing in the sense that they should be equated to members of the armed forces (see section III.B above).

PMSC members are likely to fall into the category of civilians in two cases in particular: first, if they are not formally enlisted as forming the armed forces of the territorial state and have no link to the state; and secondly if they accompany the armed forces of a state.[96]

The determination of the treatment owed to those PMSC members qualifying as civilians depends upon them taking a direct part in hostilities.[97] Despite the recent endeavour of the ICRC,[98] the notion of direct participation in hostilities remains largely unsettled.[99] For the purposes of this chapter what ought to be emphasized is that the question of direct participation in hostilities for PMSC personnel is as delicate as for any other individual and should be addressed with extreme caution. Each situation has to be dealt with on a case-by-case basis. Most importantly, no difference exists between the application of this notion in international and non-international armed conflicts.

---

[95] The definition of civilian given in Art 50 of Protocol I, whereby all those who do not qualify as combatants are civilians, was deleted during the simplification process preceding the adoption of Protocol II. Yet the definition is certainly customary, see Henckaerts and Doswald-Beck (n 70 above), I, 17, where it is affirmed the existence of a customary rule according to which 'civilians are persons who are not members of the armed forces'. For the reasons explained in Section II.B.2, we believe that the customary rule defines as civilians all persons who are not 'combatants' (instead of 'members of the armed forces').

[96] The inclusion of civilians accompanying an armed group into the category of 'civilians' may be problematic in a NIAC as it is doubtful whether armed groups should be equated to the armed forces or to civilians taking active part in hostilities for the purpose of attack. The *ICRC Interpretative Guidance on DPH*, 34, assimilates them to civilians when they accompany both the state's armed forces and armed groups because they do not perform a 'continuous combat function'.

[97] See Art 13(3) of Protocol II, according to which 'Civilians shall enjoy the protection afforded by this Part, unless and for such time as they take a direct part in hostilities'.

[98] The *ICRC Interpretative Guidance on DPH* establishes a complex system to determine whether an individual participates directly in hostilities by requiring the cumulative existence of three elements: threshold of the harm likely to result from direct participation in hostilities; direct causation between the act and the harm likely to result either from that act, or from a coordinated military operation of which that act constitutes an integral part; and belligerent nexus (the act must be specifically designed to directly cause the required threshold of harm in support of a party to the conflict and to the detriment of another).

[99] The analysis of the notion of direct participation in hostilities has been thoroughly carried out in Ch 10 by Sossai in this volume.

IV. The Treatment of Members of PMSCs whose Liberty Has Been Restricted

Absent prisoner-of-war status in a NIAC, a member of a PMSC who falls into the power of the adverse party will be subject to the treatment provided for under domestic law. This treatment shall satisfy, as a minimum, the guarantees included in Article 3 common to the Geneva Conventions and, if Additional Protocol II is applicable, also the rules of Part II, III, and IV of the Protocol. In particular, persons taking direct part in hostilities (including those PMSCs members that so qualify) are liable to prosecution for criminal offences related to the armed conflict in the competent state. The only exceptions relate to the immunity which may be granted to foreigners by virtue of a treaty[100] and the commitment undertaken by the parties to Protocol II to take into consideration the granting of amnesty.

Needless to say, despite this embryonic umbrella protection afforded by IHL, PMSC members, as any other person who falls into the hands of the opposing group in a NIAC, remain under the protection of applicable international human rights law.

V. Responsibility of the Armed Opposition Group in Favour of Whom the PMSC is Providing Services[101]

A. Armed Opposition Groups as Addressees of IHL Obligations

The principle whereby armed opposition groups in general—not only those qualifying as insurgents—have obligations under IHL is well established. The theoretical bases of such a principle, which are counter-intuitive given the fact that such groups are not signatories to any IHL treaty and often repel rules of a customary nature because they are uninvolved in their formation, are manifold and pertain to the application to armed groups of the law of treaties,[102] the reach of

---

[100] The immunity from the jurisdiction of Iraq for PMSC members working on behalf of the United States is well known. The Coalition Provisional Authority Order no 17 restricted the functional immunities to the acts performed in the execution of the contract provided the acts were carried out 'pursuant to the terms and conditions of a contract or any sub-contract thereto' (Section 4, para 3). As consequence of the serious accidents in which PMSCs members were actively involved, a new Status of Forces Agreement was adopted in December 2008 excluding immunity for such personnel employed by the US Department of Defence. Also the 17 September 2003 agreement stipulated between the United States and Colombia (<http://www.state.gov/documents/organization/96767.pdf>, accessed on 20 August 2010) in order to exempt US troops operating in Colombia from surrender to the International Criminal Court includes immunity for contractors.

[101] Clearly the reflections that will be elaborated in this section apply also where the PMSC as such qualifies as an armed group.

[102] A Cassese, 'The Status of Rebels under the 1977 Geneva Protocol on Non-international Armed Conflicts' [1981] ICLQ 416–39.

customary rules,[103] the binding character of international rules via municipal law,[104] and the signing of special agreements with the government or other armed groups aimed at implementing IHL rules in a specific conflict.[105]

Also the principle that armed opposition groups may be held accountable under IHL can be said to be recognized in contemporary international law. Elements of international practice relating in particular to the United Nations are uniform and conspicuous.[106]

Yet the precise content of the legal consequences stemming from this principle remains largely to be determined, as we shall now see.[107]

B. Consequences Arising from the Violation of an IHL Obligation by an Armed Opposition Group

A preliminary issue concerns the nature of the obligation incumbent upon armed groups and the type of responsibility that ensues from its violation. If the obligation has a customary character, for example, the rules relating to the protection of civilians, its erga omnes nature entails that, upon violation, responsibility arises both towards the injured entity and all other members of the international community. If the breach concerns a treaty rule (not of a customary nature), the international responsibility of the armed group arises erga omnes partes.

This conclusion is supported by Article V of the Resolution on the Application of International Humanitarian Law and Fundamental Human Rights, in Armed Conflicts in which Non-State Entities are Parties, adopted in 1999 by the Institut de Droit International, according to which: 'Every State and every non-State entity participating in an armed conflict are legally bound vis-à-vis each other as well as all other members of the international community to respect international humanitarian law in all circumstances.'[108]

---

[103] M Sassoli, 'Transnational Armed Groups and International Humanitarian Law', Harvard University Occasional Papers Series (Winter 2006), 14.

[104] Sivakumaran (n 58 above), 369–94

[105] E Roucounas, 'Peace Agreements as Instruments for the Resolution of Intrastate Conflict' in UNESCO, *Conflict Resolution: New Approaches and Methods* (2000), 116–21. In addition, armed opposition groups may unilaterally bind themselves to IHL rules though a specific declaration to that effect.

[106] Zegveld (n 78 above), 133, n 1, for reference to the various positions taken by the International Law Commission with respect to the Draft Articles on the Responsibility of States for Unlawful Acts; UN report on Darfur (n 73 above), paras 254–6, 285–8; UN Doc A/HRC/7/39, Report of the United Nations High Commissioner for Human Rights on the Situation in Colombia, 29 February 2008, paras 44–8. For further practice concerning UN bodies see A Clapham, 'Extending International Criminal Law beyond the Individual to Corporations and Armed Opposition Groups' [2008] JICJ 916–18.

[107] Henckaert and Doswald-Beck (n 70 above), I, 536.

[108] Art V of the resolution, which is available at <http://www.idi-iil.org/idiE/resolutionsE/1999_ber_03_en.PDF>, accessed on 20 August 2010. This point must have been harshly debated within the Institut because the revised draft resolution found that the obligation to respect IHL pertained to states only and it was due to the international community.

1. State Responsibility

The state may be held responsible for violations of IHL committed by an armed opposition group if the group forms a new government or a new state. This principle has been included in Article 10 ILC Draft Articles on the Responsibility of States for Internationally Wrongful Acts of 2001, despite the scant practice upon which it is grounded.[109]

The state may also incur international responsibility for acts of an armed group if it has not taken all the measures that were necessary to guarantee the observance of the law, both at a preventive and a repressive level, on the part of the acting group. In this case the breach of an international obligation by the state consists of an omission; in other words, the state violates a due-diligence obligation.

An example of a due-diligence obligation stemming from IHL rules is contained in Article 1 of the four Geneva Conventions whereby the parties undertake 'to respect and ensure respect' for the conventions.[110] This obligation also covers NIACs as it is expressly engaged 'in all circumstances'. However, the 'flexibility'[111] inherent in the due-diligence concept allows room for consideration of the *degree* of control exercised over a certain territory. Indeed, it would be improper and ineffectual to require the state to adopt preventive measures with respect to acts of armed groups carried out in the part of the territory over which the government does not exercise effective control.[112] Therefore the factual situation reduces the scope of the obligation to respect and ensure respect for those measures that are still in the power of the state to take. This conclusion is warranted also by the fact that, in case of stable control of a territory by an armed opposition group, the latter acquires the status of insurgents and hence enjoys a degree of international personality which certainly entails respect for IHL rules. This *ratio* underlies the conclusion reached in the only judicial pronouncement connected to this issue, the *Congo v Uganda* case in the International Court of Justice (ICJ), according to which the occupying power bears responsibility for acts of private actors 'including rebel groups acting on their own account'.[113] Finally, any other conclusion would render

---

[109] P Dumberry, 'New State Responsibility for Internationally Wrongful Acts by an Insurrectional Movement' [2006] EJIL 605.

[110] Further investigation on the material scope of IHL positive obligations would be appropriate but exceeds the objective of this chapter.

[111] On the 'flexibility' of the concept of diligence, also with respect to the degree of control exercised by the state over parts of its territory see R Pisillo-Mazzeschi, 'The Due Diligence Rule and the Nature of the International Responsibility of State' [1992] GYbIL 44.

[112] The European Court of Human Rights, *Ilascu* case (n 54 above), para 347, has affirmed that the positive obligations of a state stemming from the 1950 European Convention on Human Rights and Fundamental Freedoms concerning parts of the territory over which the state exercises no control do not include those activities which would be 'ineffectual'. In that case the contention pertained to judicial investigations that, according to the applicants, Moldovan authorities were bound to conduct in the territory of the internationally unrecognized Moldavian Republic of Transdniestria, where Moldavia had no control.

[113] *Case Concerning Armed Activities in the Territory of the Congo (Democratic Republic of the Congo v Uganda)*, ICJ Reports, (19 December 2005), para 179.

Article 10 of the Articles on the Responsibility of States for Internationally Wrongful Acts—which affirms the international responsibility of an insurgent movement that has gained power—meaningless.

On the contrary, when a state is confronted with an opposition group not controlling a portion of the territory with a certain degree of stability, the interplay between IHL and human rights rules militates in favour of the application of the standards that were set out in a clear-cut manner by the European Court of Human Rights in the judgment *Ergi v Turkey*.[114] There the respondent state was found responsible for having taken 'insufficient precautions'[115] to protect the life of the civilian population not only from the fire of the security forces but also from the firepower of the members of the opposition group.[116] Again, this suggestion is in line with the Articles on the Responsibility of States for Internationally Wrongful Acts, which implicitly establish responsibility of the state also for atrocities committed by an unsuccessful armed group committed in its territory.

A distinct but connected question concerns the issue whether an armed opposition group can be held accountable for violation of a due diligence obligation stemming from IHL rules. Practice[117] shows that the obligation to protect civilians from hostilities is certainly also incumbent upon those groups.[118] What practice does not clarify is whether, and eventually to what extent, in the case of breach of a positive obligation, there is a *concurrent* responsibility between the territorial state and the armed group.

2. International Criminal Responsibility

The individual criminal responsibility of members of an armed group, including those holding a position of command, is so settled in international law that it deserves no further examination.

More complex is the question of the international criminal responsibility of the group as such. The concept of joint criminal enterprise elaborated by the ad hoc

---

[114] *Case of Ergi v Turkey*, ECHR (28 July 1998).
[115] Ibid, para 81.
[116] Ibid, para 80. In the same paragraph it is specified that the Court agrees with the Commission's reasoning whereby: 'Even if it might be assumed that the security forces would have responded with due care for the civilian population in returning fire against terrorists caught in the approaches to the village, it could not be assumed that terrorists would have responded with such restraint. There was no information to indicate that any steps or precautions had been taken to protect the villagers from being caught up in the conflict.' Note that the Court was not applying IHL rules but Art 2 of the European Convention on Human Rights and Fundamental Freedoms.
[117] Zegveld (n 78 above), 79–84. Cf also Security Council resolutions (eg Res 1674, 28 April 2006, where it is stated that '*parties* to armed conflict bear the primary responsibility to take all feasible steps to ensure the protection of affected civilians'); and some agreements between conflicting parties (eg Art 2(1) of the Protocol on the Improvement of the Humanitarian Situation in Darfur, 9 November 2004, according to which the parties commit themselves 'to take all steps required to prevent all attacks, threats, intimidation and any other form of violence against civilians by any Party or group, including the Janjaweed and other militias').
[118] G Abi-Saab, 'Non-international Armed Conflicts' in UNESCO, *International Dimensions of Humanitarian Law* (1988), 274.

criminal tribunals, as well as the notion of group responsibility enshrined in Article 25(3)(d) of the statute of the International Criminal Court might be the way to ensure criminal responsibility both of the group as such and of its members.[119] However, recourse to this modality of enforcing the accountability of a group is not unanimously viewed as the panacea. Concerns relating to the resurfacing of collective notions of guilt make this hypothesis less appealing than it might appear at first sight.[120]

3. Obligation to Give Full Reparation

A few elements of practice may be taken as an indication that the obligation incumbent upon armed groups to the effect that they make full reparation is increasingly accepted in international law.[121] For example, the General Assembly Resolution of 2006 on Basic Principles and Guidelines on the Right to Remedy and Reparation for Victims of Gross Violations of International Human Rights Law and Serious Violations of International Humanitarian Law implicitly recognizes this principle.[122]

By contrast, only very few agreements concluded between an armed opposition group and a government contain undertakings by the group with respect to the clauses relating to the procedural and substantial right of a victim to reparation. The Agreement on Accountability and Reconciliation between the Government of Uganda and the Lord's Resistance Army of 29 June 2007, as supplemented by the annex of 19 February 2008, is the best example of the wide-ranging engagement that an armed group may take with respect to reparation issues, but its relevance as an element of international practice is tainted by the fact that the document was concluded with a view to avoiding the surrender of the leaders of the Lord's Resistance Army to the International Criminal Court, following the issue of arrest warrants against them.[123] Another example is offered by the Darfur Comprehensive Peace Agreement, which is very comprehensive in relation to the issue of reparation. The relevant clauses are couched in terms that bind equally the government and the signing armed groups (Sudan People Liberation Movement/Army and the Justice and Equality Movement) and recognize the 'inalienable right' of 'war-affected victims' to reparation.[124] Furthermore, this right is enunciated with

---

[119] Clapham (n 106 above), esp 919–26.
[120] M Sassoli and LM Olson, 'The Decision of the ICTY Appeals Chamber in the *Tadić* Case: New Horizons for International Humanitarian and Criminal Law?' (2000) IRRC 747–56.
[121] As it has been pointed out by Zegveld (n 78 above), 152–5, the applicability to armed groups of the rules of attribution pertaining to states needs clarification. It should be pointed out that recourse to this form of responsibility may be quite fruitful as armed groups, unlike states, do not enjoy immunity from foreign jurisdiction.
[122] UN GA Res 60/147, 21 March 2006. Art IX(15): 'In cases where a person, a legal person, or other entity is found liable for reparation to a victim, such party should provide reparation to the victim or compensate the State if the State has already provided reparation to the victim.'
[123] A Dworkin, 'The Uganda-LRA War Crimes Agreement and the International Criminal Court (Updated)' (25 February 2008), <http://www.crimesofwar.org/onnews/news-uganda2.html>, accessed on 20 August 2010.
[124] Arts 199–213 of the Darfur Peace Agreement, Abuja, 5 May 2006.

respect to a very wide category of damages suffered, including 'physical or mental injury, emotional suffering or human and economic losses', provided that they were suffered in connection with the conflict. This right would be a corollary to the right to an effective remedy in the case of serious violations of human rights and would also apply to armed opposition groups.

Beyond this, only in exceptional instances have armed groups provided reparations on a unilateral basis.[125]

In the light of the above practice, the conclusion is warranted that the practice concerning the obligation incumbent upon armed opposition groups to grant reparation is at an emerging stage.[126]

VI. Conclusions

This chapter addresses both *ius ad bellum* and *ius in bello* issues arising from the activities that PMSCs carry out in non-international armed conflicts.

The *ius ad bellum* analysis hinges upon a distinction between the right of the legitimate government—and to some extent of national liberation movements—to have recourse to PMSCs services implying the use of force during a NIAC, and the prohibition on using PMSCs for combat purposes on the part of armed opposition groups.

The difficulties inherent in the determination of the authority from which consent can validly emanate during a NIAC makes the content of the principle relating to the freedom of the legitimate government to request foreign armed assistance more unsettled than it may prima facie appear. The principle may be helpful only to identify the two poles of a continuum, at the one end of which lie those situations where resort to foreign armed force by the government is prohibited, namely when the government lacks the requirements (ie effectiveness and recognition) necessary to express valid consent; whereas at the other extreme are those instances in which resort to foreign armed force is allowed, ie in cases when the opposition group has received armed assistance from abroad. In the former case, third parties are under a duty to refrain from intervening militarily until the situation permits identification of the authority which can validly express consent to intervention; in the latter situation, on the contrary, third parties may provide armed assistance to the legitimate government.

Apart from these two extremes, the dividing line between a lawful and an unlawful intervention based on valid consent emanating from the legitimate government remains blurred. In any case, the rationale behind the recruitment of mercenaries, which is shared by recourse to a PMSC in wartime, dramatically

---

[125] E-C Gillard, 'Reparation for Violations of International Humanitarian Law' (2003) IRRC 535, referring to the excuses offered by the Colombian ELN armed group in 2001 for having provoked the death of children and destruction of civilian buildings in the course of an act of war.
[126] Henckaerts and Doswald-Beck (n 70 above), I, 550.

questions the lawfulness under international law of recourse to PMSCs for activities in which the use of force is required.

As far as the *ius in bello* inquiry is concerned, the question of the status of a PMSC in a NIAC is addressed, as the scope of protection from attack and standards of treatment in case of deprivation of liberty flow from such a determination. The analysis has focused on the definition of armed forces applicable, according to IHL, in NIACs. This issue is prominent with respect to PMSCs because the lack of formal enlistment in the armed forces of a state does not exclude the qualification of PMSC personnel as organs of the state under international law, provided they are part of an irregular force which has a functional link with the state party to the conflict. Despite this broad notion of organ (armed forces) of the state, only very rarely do PMSCs fall into this category. At the same time, the unclear content of the notion of armed opposition group shows that in very few instances PMSC members qualify as members of such a group or as an armed opposition group per se. Indeed the vast majority of PMSC members qualify as civilians. Whether they are civilians *tout court* or civilians taking an active part in hostilities is a de facto analysis that depends on the actual activity they carry out rather than on the contractual engagement.

As to the responsibility aspect of PMSC actions, only the neglected question of the international liability of armed opposition groups has been examined with special emphasis being placed on the due-diligence obligations accruing both to the group and the state.

13

Children's Rights: The Potential Impact of Private Military and Security Companies

Christine Bakker and Susanna Greijer

I. Introduction

In this chapter the normative framework for the protection of children's rights at the international and European Union (EU) levels will be examined with the aim of considering how the rights of children[1] may be affected by private military and security companies (PMSCs) in a conflict or post-conflict situation. The chapter is divided in two parts. It first addresses the existing norms which are most relevant to the intervention of PMSCs at the international level, as laid down in instruments of international humanitarian law (IHL), human rights law, and international criminal law (section II).[2] Considering the possibility that the EU may play a more active role in ensuring compliance by PMSCs with human rights and IHL, this chapter then analyses the existing European legal framework for the protection of children, both within the EU and with regard to its external relations (section III).[3]

II. Protecting Children's Rights: Evolving Norms at the International Level

A. General Protection of Children's Rights

Specific norms for the protection of children in armed conflict exist in the context of IHL, in particular in the two Additional Protocols to the Geneva Conventions. In recent decades, several human rights instruments have also been adopted specifically addressing children's rights, including in armed conflict. After providing a brief overview of these instruments, specific analysis will be devoted to the instruments that prohibit the recruitment of children into armed forces or groups

---

[1] In this chapter, the term 'children' is used for persons below the age of 18 years, in accordance with the definition in Art 1 of the Convention on the Rights of the Child.
[2] By Christine Bakker.
[3] By Susanna Greijer.

and the act of using them to actively participate in the hostilities of an armed conflict. The analysis focuses on the relevance of these provisions for PMSCs, considering whether PMSC employees can be held accountable for violations of the rights included therein.

1. Human Rights Instruments

The 1989 Convention on the Rights of the Child (CRC) is the most comprehensive human rights instrument specifically geared towards the protection of children.[4] The CRC sets out the rights of children, who are defined as 'every human being below the age of 18 years unless under the law applicable to the child, majority is attained earlier' (Article 1). The CRC covers both civil and political rights, and social and economic rights, as well as provisions originating from IHL, adapting them to the specific situation and needs of children. One of its basic principles is that in all actions concerning children, the best interest of the child must be a primary consideration. Together with the general obligation to ensure the rights of the child,[5] this implies that in all circumstances where a child is involved, the measures normally required to ensure respect for human rights may not be sufficient, and specific measures must be taken to protect the rights enshrined in the CRC.

The children's rights laid down in the CRC which are most likely to be violated by PMSCs in an armed conflict or in its aftermath when the security situation is still fragile are the right to life;[6] the right not to be subjected to torture or other cruel, inhuman, or degrading treatment or punishment;[7] the right not to be deprived of their liberty unlawfully or arbitrarily;[8] the right to be protected from all forms of trafficking[9] as well as from all forms of sexual exploitation and sexual abuse;[10] and the right of persons who have not reached the age of 15 years not to be recruited by armed forces and not to take a direct part in hostilities.[11]

The general obligation contained in this Convention that states parties must respect and ensure the rights enshrined therein entails a number of positive obligations, in particular the obligations to prevent violations of these rights and to provide an effective remedy when a violation has occurred, including reparations for the victims.[12]

---

[4] The 1966 International Covenant on Civil and Political Rights contains a general provision recognizing that '(e)very child shall have, without any discrimination as to race, colour, sex, language, national or social origin, property or birth, the right to such measures of protection as are required by his status as a minor, on the part of his family, society and the State' (Art 24(1)).

[5] CRC Art 3: 'In all actions concerning children, whether undertaken by public or private social welfare institutions, courts of law, administrative authorities or legislative bodies, the best interests of the child shall be a primary consideration'. CRC Art 4: 'States Parties shall undertake all appropriate legislative, administrative, and other measures for the implementation of the rights recognised in the present Convention'.

[6] Ibid, Art 6.
[7] Ibid, Art 37(1).
[8] Ibid, Art 37(2).
[9] Ibid, Art 35.
[10] Ibid, Art 34.
[11] Ibid, Art 38(2). For more details on this particular right, see below.
[12] For a detailed analysis of these obligations, see Ch 5 by Francioni, Ch 6 by Hoppe, and Ch 7 by Bakker in this volume. See also section II of Ch 3 by Lenzerini and Francioni in this volume.

2. IHL Instruments

Special care must be taken that children do not become victims of armed operations and that schools or places where children gather are not targeted for such operations. Under IHL, specific provisions protecting children are included in the Fourth Geneva Convention,[13] in particular Article 14(1), regarding hospital and safety zones to protect from the effects of war, inter alia, children under 15; Article 17, requiring the removal of children from besieged or encircled areas; and Article 23(1), concerning the free passage of all consignments of essential foodstuffs, clothing, and tonics intended for, amongst others, children under 15.

Apart from these child-specific provisions, IHL contains a vast body of rules designed to protect civilians, which also apply to children. Therefore, grave breaches of the Geneva conventions, including rape, sexual violence, and torture also occur when children are victims of such war crimes. As is well known, states are required to respect and to ensure respect of the Geneva Conventions in all circumstances (common Article 1 of these conventions). Therefore, in principle all the states involved in the deployment of a PMSC in a situation of armed conflict (the contracting state, the home state, and the host state) are bound to ensure the protection of children as outlined in the above-mentioned provisions. Although the scope of some of these provisions goes beyond the tasks conferred upon PMSCs, these companies should be made aware of these specific IHL obligations, as well of the general provisions protecting civilians, in order to avoid any violations thereof in the course of their operations.

3. International Criminal Law Instruments

The statutes of the Special Court for Sierra Leone (SCSL), the International Criminal Tribunal for Rwanda (ICTR), and the International Criminal Court (ICC) also include several provisions concerning children. Given the geographical and temporal limitations of the SCSL and the ICTR, they have no relevance for current and future PMSC activities. However, the following provisions of the ICC Statute may apply to acts of PMSC employees, if the jurisdictional conditions are met: apart from the recruitment of children into armed forces or groups and using them actively to participate in hostilities, which will be discussed below, children can become victims of several other international crimes which are defined either as war crimes or as crimes against humanity. These include rape, sexual slavery, enforced prostitution, forced pregnancy, enforced sterilization, and any other form of sexual violence also constituting a grave breach of the Geneva Conventions (ICC Statute, Articles 8(2)(b)(xxii) and 8(2)(e)(vi)). These same crimes are also included as crimes against humanity (ICC Statute, Article 7(g)), adding 'any other form of sexual violence of comparable gravity'. Of these crimes, rape and sexual violence against

---

[13] Convention (IV) Relative to the Protection of Civilian Persons in time of War, Geneva, 12 August 1949, UNTS no 973, vol 75, 287.

girls have been committed by PMSC employees, and should therefore be included among the risks for children posed by the use of such companies.

4. Violations of these Rights by PMSC Employees

Several incidents have been reported in the press or by human rights organizations of children becoming victims of violence or abuse by PMSC employees. In most cases, these incidents have not been investigated and no prosecutions have been launched against those responsible. In Colombia, children have been victims of sexual abuse by PMSC agents. According to a press report,[14] in October 2004 employees of a US PMSC, together with US marines, committed acts of sexual violence against three minors and widely distributed videos of the abuse among the local population. The marines and private contractors worked as advisors to Colombian military personnel on the Tolemaida Air Base, near the town of Melgar. No investigations or prosecutions have been launched, since US military personnel and private contractors benefit from an immunity agreement between the United States and Colombia.[15]

Concerning Guatemala, there have been reports that: 'Non-state actors with links to organized crime, gangs, private security companies, and alleged "clandestine groups" committed hundreds of killings and other crimes.'[16] However, no details were provided on the specific involvement of PMSCs.

Children were also among the victims of the Nisour Square incident in Iraq, in which 17 civilians were killed and 20 others injured by employees of the PMSC Blackwater International in September 2007. At least one of the persons killed was a child (an 11-year-old boy) and several children were injured after a grenade was thrown into a nearby school.[17] Although five of these employees were indicted by the District of Columbia in December 2008, the charges were dismissed on 31 December 2009, based on a violation of the rights of the defendants.[18]

Due to the absence or incompleteness of investigations in these incidents, very scarce information is available, including about the names of the PMSCs and the nationality of the employees who were allegedly involved. Therefore, the question whether they benefited from any immunity agreement cannot be answered, except

---

[14] <http://www.elcorreo.eu.org/esp/article.php3?id_article=4747>, accessed on 20 August 2010.
[15] Bi-national Agreement, 17 September 2003.
[16] US State Department, Country Reports on Human Rights Practices 2006: Guatemala, 6 March 2007, <http://www.state.gov>, cited by <http://www.childsoldiersglobalreport.org>, 155, both accessed on 20 August 2010.
[17] *New York Times*, 10 November 2009, 'Blackwater Said to Pursue Bribes to Iraq after 17 Died', <http://www.nytimes.com/2009/11/11/world/middleeast/11blackwater.html?_r=1>, accessed on 20 August 2010. The indictment represented the first prosecution under the Military Extraterritorial Jurisdiction Act (MEJA) to be filed against non-Defence Department private contractors. This was not possible prior to the 2004 amendments to MEJA that specifically expanded the reach of MEJA to non-Defense Department contractors who provide services 'in support of the mission of the Department of Defense overseas'. According to the above press report, senior management of this company agreed to pay up to US$1 million to Iraqi officials to keep them from criticizing the company and from providing information to the authorities investigating these crimes.
[18] <http://www.nytimes.com/2010/01/01/us/01blackwater.html>, accessed on 20 August.

in the Colombian example, where this was indeed the case. Nevertheless, despite the lack of details, this overview shows that reports do exist about the violation of children's rights by PMSC personnel, which confirms the risk of such violations through the employment of PMSCs, as well as the need to prevent them.

B. Recruiting and Using Children in the Hostilities of an Armed Conflict

The recruitment of children by the parties to an armed conflict and the use of children in hostilities are explicitly prohibited in various international conventions, both of IHL and of human rights law. Even though it may seem unlikely that PMSCs recruit children to work for them, such situations have occurred in practice. Indeed, in Afghanistan, boys under 18 years of age have been seen working for private security companies. According to a senior government official, cited in a report of Integrated Regional Information Networks (IRIN) of December 2007,[19] this occurred particularly in the Kandahar and Helmand provinces.[20] Even though the information of such under-age recruitment by PMSCs is scarce, it is not at all inconceivable that in certain African, Asian, or Latin American states, such recruitment may occur, either directly by a PMSC or through subcontracting. In particular in developing countries, minors might be willing to join such a corporation for economic reasons. PMSC personnel should therefore be aware of this risk and receive adequate information to avoid such underage recruitment.

1. International Humanitarian Law

The first Additional Protocol to the Geneva Convention applicable to international armed conflicts stipulates that: 'The Parties to the conflict shall take all feasible measures in order that children who have not attained the age of 15 years do not take a direct part in hostilities and, in particular, they shall refrain from recruiting them into their armed forces' (Article 77(2)). The same provision further states that in recruiting amongst those persons who have attained the age of 15 but not the age of 18, the parties to the conflict 'shall endeavour to give priority to those who are oldest'. The provision in Additional Protocol II, which concerns armed conflicts of a non-international character, goes even further, in the sense that it broadens the prohibition: 'Children who have not attained the age of 15 years shall neither be recruited in the armed forces or groups nor allowed to take part in hostilities.'[21] The main elements of these provisions have also been included in the statutes of

---

[19] See <http://www.irinnews.org/PrintReport.aspx?ReportId=75904>, accessed on 20 August, report of 19 December 2007. IRIN, Humanitarian News and Analysis is a project of the UN Office for the Coordination of Humanitarian Affairs.

[20] Two private security companies working in those provinces at that time declined to comment and turned down requests by IRIN to visit their headquarters. The same report signals that according to the Afghanistan Independent Human Rights Commission, child-soldiers are also being recruited and in some cases sexually abused by the Afghan police and various militias supporting the police, as well as by the Taliban.

[21] Art 4 (Protocol II, on non-international armed conflicts).

the International Criminal Court (ICC) and the Special Court for Sierra Leone (SCSL), albeit with some refinements, as will be shown below.

2. International Criminal Law

The Rome Statute of the ICC and the Statute of the SCSL also set the minimum age for the recruitment of children into armed forces or groups or using them to actively participate in the hostilities of an armed conflict at 15.[22] The distinction between voluntary and compulsory recruitment is explicitly made in the Statutes of the ICC and the SCSL, which speak of 'conscripting or enlisting children under the age of 15 into armed forces (or groups)'[23] or 'using them to participate actively in hostilities'.[24] While the term 'conscription' refers to compulsory recruitment, 'enlistment' is used for situations where children voluntarily join armed forces or groups. Therefore, even if children were not obliged or forced to become actively involved in an armed conflict, but allegedly joined one of the parties voluntarily, this does not diminish the criminal responsibility of the adults who are responsible for their enlistment or use in hostilities. This is a clear recognition of the fact that children, even if they participate themselves in the commission of crimes as members of an armed force or group, they are first and foremost considered as *victims* of the crime of their recruitment or enlistment.

In May 2004, the SCSL held that the conscription, enlistment, and use in hostilities of children under the age of 15 constitute crimes under customary international law.[25] By establishing the 'criminalization' of underage recruitment and use of children in hostilities under customary law, the SCSL also confirmed the applicability of this norm to all states. The SCSL has convicted several persons for this crime[26] and one last case including the same charge is still under consideration.[27]

In the first cases before the ICC, underage recruitment constitutes the principal charge. In the case *Prosecutor v Thomas Lubanga Dyilo*, the trial of which started in January 2009, the charges include the enlisting and conscripting children under the age of 15 years into the FPLC, the military wing of the Union des Patriotes Congolais (UPC),[28] and using them to participate actively

---

[22] Rome Statute Art 8(2)(b)(xxvi) for international armed conflicts and Art 8(2)(e)(vii) for armed conflicts not of an international character; and the Statute of the Special Court for Sierra Leone, Art 7.

[23] The term 'and groups' is only included in Rome Statute, Art 8(e)(vii), concerning non-international armed conflicts.

[24] n 22 above. The same interpretation of the term 'recruitment' was given by the International Committee of the Red Cross on the relevant articles of the two Additional Protocols. See A Smith, 'Child Recruitment and the Special Court for Sierra Leone: Some Considerations' (2004) 2 *Journal of International Criminal Justice* 1154–62

[25] *Hinga Norman*, SCSL-2004-14-AR72(E), SCSL Appeals Chamber (31 May 2004), paras 52–3.

[26] See *Prosecutor v Sankoh, Bockarie, Kallon and Gbao* (*the RUF Accused*), SCSL-04-14-T (2 August 2007); SCSL-2004-16-PT (20 June 2007) and SCSL-04-15.

[27] *Prosecutor v Charles Taylor*, SCSL-03-01, trial taking place in The Hague.

[28] Comment between brackets added.

in hostilities.[29] The Pre-Trial Chamber clarified the terms 'conscription' and 'enlistment'[30] and provided a detailed and rather broad interpretation of the term 'active participation in hostilities', which is not limited to participation in combat.

In the *Armed Forces Revolutionary Council* case,[31] the SCSL determined that:

Any labor or support that gives effect to or helps maintain operations in a conflict constitutes active participation. Hence, carrying loads for the fighting faction, finding or acquiring... ammunition or equipment, acting as decoys, carrying messages, making trails or finding routes, manning checkpoints or acting as human shields are examples of active participation as much as fighting and combat.[32]

In the *Lubanga* decision on confirmation of charges, the ICC Pre-Trial Chamber takes the same approach and also mentions spying, scouting, and sabotage as examples of active participation.[33] This broad interpretation clearly lowers the threshold for holding the accused responsible for the crime of using children actively to participate in hostilities.[34] In the case *Prosecutor v Germain Katanga and Mathieu Ngudjolo Chui*[35] before the ICC, the charges also include the war crime of using children to participate actively in hostilities. Although the outcome of the trials before the ICC are still awaited, the priority given to the prosecution of crimes against children in these first cases before the ICC confirms the recognition of the serious nature of these crimes at the international level.

---

[29] ICC-01/04-01/06, 29 January 2007, conclusion, <http://www.icc-cpi.int> accessed on 20 August 2010.
[30] *Lubanga* (n 29 above), para 245. The cited instruments are the CRC; the Optional Protocol on the Involvement of Children in Armed Conflicts; ILO Convention no 182 on the Worst Forms of Child Labour; and the Conclusions of the Committee on the Rights of the Child.
[31] *Prosecutor v Brima (AFRC)*, SCSL-2004-16-T, judgment, SCSL Trial Chamber II, 20 June 2007, <http://www.sc-sl.org/AFRC.html>, accessed on 20 August 2010. A second conviction followed a few months later, also involving the enlistment of children in an armed force or group, in the *Civil Defence Forces* case. *Prosecutor v Fofana (CDF)*, SCSL-04-14-T, Judgment, SCSL Trial Chamber II, 2 August 2007, <http://www.sc-sl.org/CDF.html>, accessed on 20 August 2010.
[32] *AFRC* Judgment (n 27 above), para 737.
[33] The examples mentioned in the *AFRC* judgment also fall within the range of activities mentioned in the *Lubanga* decision (n 30 above), paras 261-3. However, the two Chambers seem to have a different opinion on the activity of delivering food to an armed force or group; according to the SCSL this does constitute an active participation in hostilities; whereas the Pre-Trial Chamber explicitly excludes this example from the scope of this specific crime (*Lubanga*, para 262).
[34] It should be noted, however, that under IHL persons who actively participate in hostilities are considered as combatants. Combatant status, in its turn, can weaken the protection of these children, compared with civilians. It is clear that the purpose of the ICC chamber and the SCSL was to increase the level of protection of the minors, so that obviously, the higher level of protection of civilians (and even a higher one because of their young age) must be provided, also by PMSCs when they may be confronted with children carrying out such tasks.
[35] Mr Katanga acted as the main commander of the FRPI, an armed group in the Ituri region and subsequently as a general in the armed forces of the DRC, whereas Mr Ngudjolo Chui was the highest-ranking commander of the *Front des nationalistes et intégrationnistes* (FNI).

3. Relevance of the IHL and ICL Provisions for PMSCs

The provisions of IHL are explicitly designed to apply both to states and to individuals, since their violation may give rise to both state responsibility and individual criminal responsibility. By its very nature, the ICC statute provides for the possibility of prosecuting individuals for the international crimes included therein. Therefore, individuals, including managers or other employees of PMSCs, can in principle be held accountable for the crime of recruiting children or using them actively to participate in armed conflict.

The question then arises whether a PMSC manager or employee who recruits a child to work for its company, or uses them to participate in the hostilities of an armed conflict, falls within the scope of the relevant provisions, which only speak of recruitment into 'armed forces or groups'. According to Article 43(1) of Protocol I, the term 'armed forces' refers to 'all organized armed forces, groups and units which are under a command responsible to that Party for the conduct of its subordinates'.[36] IHL provides several bases for considering PMSC employees as members of the armed forces, if certain criteria are met. However, the debate among scholars and other experts on the exact interpretation of these provisions is still ongoing.[37] In practice, states employing a PMSC usually do not contract them as part of their armed forces, but rather for specific security services and with their own internal command structure. Therefore, while PMSC employees may, under certain conditions, be regarded as members of the armed forces of a state, this is rather an exception than a general rule.

The term 'armed groups' is not defined in IHL instruments related to international armed conflicts. However, in the context of non-international conflicts, Protocol II refers to groups which, 'under responsible command, exercise such control over a part of its territory as to enable them to carry out sustained and concerted military operations'.[38] Even though a PMSC might in practice exercise such control in a certain territory, it generally would do so on behalf of the state (or possibly another entity) by which it is contracted. In particular, the scenario in which a PMSC acts as an armed group—for example, as an armed opposition group—has not occurred in practice.[39] Therefore, the conclusion seems warranted that PMSCs cannot generally be considered to fall within the scope of the term 'armed groups' under IHL; this would be an exceptional situation, in which several criteria must be fulfilled.[40]

This leads to the question whether the act of 'using a child to actively participate in hostilities' also constitutes a violation of IHL, even though the child is not recruited into armed forces or groups, but by a PMSC instead. The provisions in the two Additional Protocols do not speak of 'using' children to take part in the armed conflict; they require states 'to take all feasible measures in order that

---

[36] Additional Protocol I, Art 43(1).
[37] See Ch 10 by Sossai, section I A, and Ch 12 by Vierucci, section III B, in this volume.
[38] Additional Protocol II, Art 1.
[39] For a more detailed analysis of this question, see Vierucci (n 37 above), section III.B.
[40] Ibid.

children under 15 years do not take a direct part in hostilities' (AP I, Article 77(2)), and 'Children who have not attained the age of 15 years shall neither be recruited in the armed forces or groups *nor allowed to take part in hostilities*' (AP II, Article 4, emphasis added).

On the other hand, the ICC Statute explicitly speaks of 'using them to participate actively in hostilities'.[41] The element of recruitment (or conscription, enlistment) is separated from the element of using the children to participate in hostilities. Consequently, these are two distinguishable acts each of which may give rise to individual criminal responsibility.[42] Therefore, the ICC Statute provides a more explicit definition of the separate crime of 'using' children than the two additional protocols. When states parties to the ICC have incorporated the definitions of the Rome Statute into their national criminal code, the relevant provision could therefore be used to prosecute PMSC managers or other employees who allegedly used children under 15 years to actively participate in hostilities before their national court, provided that it has jurisdiction over that particular crime.[43] In theory, the responsible PMSC employees could also be prosecuted before the ICC itself, if the necessary conditions under the complementarity regime are met.

4. Human Rights Law

Several international and regional human rights instruments adopted since 1990 establish a minimum age of 18 years for compulsory recruitment by armed forces and for the use of children to actively participate in hostilities. The minimum age of 18 for such recruitment is included in the 1999 Convention no 182 of the International Labour Organization (ILO) on the Worst Forms of Child Labour. At the regional level, the 1990 African Charter on the Rights and Welfare of the Child is the first to prohibit the recruitment or direct participation in hostilities *or internal strife* of anyone under the age of 18. These human rights instruments thus go beyond the minimum age determined by the existing instruments of international humanitarian law, as well as the Statutes of the ICC and the SCSL.

The CRC Optional Protocol on the Involvement of Children in Armed Conflict (OPAC), which entered into force in 2002, distinguishes between armed forces and

---

[41] Art 8(2)(b)(xxvi), applicable to international armed conflicts and Art 8(2)(e)(vii), applicable to non-international armed conflicts.

[42] This is also confirmed by the ICC Elements of Crimes: Art 8(2)(b)(xxvi): '1. The perpetrator conscripted or enlisted one or more persons into the national armed forces *or used one or more persons to participate actively in hostilities*. 2. Such person or persons were under the age of 15 years' (emphasis added); Art 8(2)(e)(vii): '1. The perpetrator conscripted or enlisted one or more persons into an armed force or group *or used one or more persons to participate actively in hostilities*. 2. Such person or persons were under the age of 15 years'; and Art 8(2)(b)(xxvi): '1. The perpetrator conscripted or enlisted one or more persons into the national armed forces *or used one or more persons to participate actively in hostilities*. 2. Such person or persons were under the age of 15 years' (emphasis added).

[43] A national court can only try such a case if it can exercise either territorial jurisdiction when the crime was committed on its own territory; or active personality when the suspect has the nationality of the forum state, passive nationality, when the victim has the nationality of the forum state, or in exceptional cases, universal jurisdiction.

armed groups as follows: armed forces may not use children below 18 years of age to take a direct part in hostilities; *compulsory* recruitment is banned below 18 years; and for *voluntary* recruitment states shall raise the minimum age from 15 years (as set out in the CRC, Article 38(3)) with certain specific conditions.[44] For non-state armed groups, states shall take all feasible measures to prevent the recruitment or use in hostilities of persons under 18 years.[45] The Committee on the Rights of the Child has consistently emphasized that a state party to this Protocol should explicitly criminalize the recruitment of children and their use in armed conflicts as prohibited by the OPAC. It has also held that states parties should establish territorial jurisdiction and extraterritorial jurisdiction based on active and passive nationality for these offences.[46]

5. Relevance of these Human Rights Provisions for PMSCs

This overview shows that the human rights provisions related to the recruitment and use of children in armed conflict are more stringent than those under IHL. The notion that non-state actors are also bound to comply with these instruments is increasingly accepted, both in judicial practice and in legal literature.[47] The extent to which such horizontal effect applies depends on the approach adopted in each national jurisdiction. In any event, each human rights instrument imposes on its states parties certain positive obligations to prevent violations of the rights enshrined therein within their jurisdiction, and to investigate and try those responsible for such violations. PMSC employees who engage in such violations must therefore, in principle, be held accountable for their acts through national investigations and prosecutions.

Even though the OPAC is the most far-reaching human rights instrument for the question considered here, its applicability to PMSCs seems to be more limited than the provisions of the ICC Statute. Indeed, the OPAC appears to link the recruitment and use of children directly to armed forces[48] or 'armed groups distinct from the armed forces of a state'.[49] As argued above, the qualification of PMSC employees as members of armed forces, or of the PMSC as an armed group, although not excluded, is rather an exception than a general rule.[50] However, as stated in its preamble,[51] the purpose of the OPAC is to *increase* the protection of

---

[44] Optional Protocol on the Involvement of Children in Armed Conflict, Arts 1–3. To date, this Protocol has been ratified by 123 states.
[45] Ibid, Art 4.
[46] See eg CRC/C/OPAC/BGR/CO/1, 5 October 2007, (Bulgaria), para 7(a)–(b); CRC/C/OPAC/CRI/1, 15 January 2007 (Costa Rica), para 7(c).
[47] For more details on this point and the notion of *Drittwirking* of human rights, see Ch 3 by Kalnina and Zeltins in this volume.
[48] OPAC, Arts 1–2.
[49] OPAC, Art 4(1).
[50] See nn 40–1 above and accompanying text.
[51] OPAC, Preamble, paras 5–6: noting the adoption of the Rome Statute of the International Criminal Court, in particular, the inclusion therein as a war crime of conscripting or enlisting children under the age of 15 years or using them to participate actively in hostilities in both international and non-international armed conflict; considering therefore that to strengthen further the implementation

children from involvement in armed conflict, compared to the provisions in the ICC and the CRC. Therefore, it could be argued that the higher standards of protection of the OPAC should be considered to apply to all actors who may potentially recruit minors for their participation in hostilities, including PMSCs. If this reasoning is followed, then the minimum age for PMSCs to recruit employees would be 18 under all circumstances, since there can be no question of *compulsory* recruitment by a private actor.

6. UN Resolutions and Other Initiatives on Child-Recruitment in Armed Conflict

A series of resolutions have been adopted in the United Nations Framework, including by the UN Security Council (SC) and the UN General Assembly calling for the prevention, termination and criminalization of unlawful recruitment of children in armed conflict.[52] The issue of children and armed conflict was added to the permanent agenda of the SC in 1998. Since then, the SC has adopted a series of Presidential Statements and resolutions condemning the recruitment and use of children in armed conflict, culminating in the provision of possible targeted measures against states that do not take action to end such violations. Moreover, in February 2007, a set of standards was endorsed which go beyond the existing legally binding instruments, the so-called 'Paris Commitments'.[53] Although the standard-setting value of these documents is limited, they do indicate that a consensus may be evolving according to which states are increasingly willing to also raise the minimum age for *voluntary* recruitment to 18 years.[54]

C. Confrontation of PMSCs with Children Participating in Hostilities

Apart from the recruitment of minors by PMSCs themselves, another way in which private contractors may risk violating children's rights is when they are confronted with children who are actually participating in hostilities as part of the armed forces or an armed group. Children are being used to participate in a large number of armed conflicts around the world, including in Afghanistan, Iraq, Colombia, and

---

of rights recognized in the Convention on the Rights of the Child there is a need to increase the protection of children from involvement in armed conflict.

[52] UNGA Res A/48/157, March 1994; UNGA Document A/S-27/2, October 2002: *A World Fit for Children*; SC Res 1261 (1999); SC Res 1314 (11 August 2000); SC Res 1332 (2000); SC Res 1341 (2001); SC Res 1355 (2001); SC Res 1460 (2003); SC Res 1539 (2004); SC Res 1612 (2005); SC Res 1882 (2009), and yearly reports of the Secretary General on Children and Armed Conflict.

[53] *Paris Commitments to Protect Children from Unlawful Recruitment or Use by Armed Forces or Armed Groups*, and *Paris Principles on Children Associated with Armed Forces or Armed Groups*. These documents were endorsed at a conference convened by the French government and UNICEF, with participants partly at ministerial level from 58 countries, as well as representatives of intergovernmental organizations and of 30 NGOs. By September 2009, the number of states having endorsed the Paris Commitments and Principles was 84.

[54] *Paris Commitments*, para 4.

several countries in Africa such as the Demoratic Republic of Congo (DRC), Uganda, and the Central African Republic.[55] Since PMSCs are also increasingly deployed in conflict situations around the world, it is far from inconceivable that employees of these companies may be confronted with children taking part in hostilities and carrying arms.[56] Such a confrontation may require a response that is different from a comparable situation in which the persons involved are adults. Since IHL does not provide any specific guidelines on how to deal with such a situation, it is the responsibility of each state whose armed forces—or contracted PMSCs—are involved in an armed conflict to take appropriate preventive measures. At the same time, the armed forces or private contractors who are faced with such a situation in practice need to find an appropriate answer in each concrete case. Some possible measures were mentioned by a high-ranking military expert who has specialized in human rights training, at a conference on child-soldiers held in Turin in November 2009, where he addressed the more general scenario of soldiers of a national army who may encounter child-soldiers in the course of a conflict.[57] In the planning and preparation phase, intelligence should be gathered to ascertain whether child-soldiers are involved in a conflict, who the commanders are, and what the numbers are. The personnel to be deployed should be educated about the modalities of the use of force against children, and about their legal accountability. In the conduct phase, encounters with child-soldiers should be avoided if possible; but in case of a confrontation, certain safeguards should be taken. Some additional suggestions for ensuring respect of children's rights by PMSCs will be made in the Concluding Remarks.

III. The European Union and the Protection of the Rights of the Child

During the last few years the EU has paid special attention to children's rights and protection, and has adopted several instruments that address different types of child abuses. Some of these instruments are part of the EU's internal policy, and relevant only for the Member States, whereas others play an important role in the EU's external relations. The latter aim at influencing the conduct of other countries and constitute an integral part of the EU's important role in the promotion of human rights.

This second part of the chapter provides an overview of the existing European legal framework for the protection of children, both within the EU and with regard

---

[55] According to the International Coalition 'Stop the Use of Child Soldiers', in 2007 an estimated number of 250,000 children were directly involved in hostilities, in 17 armed conflicts.
[56] Although the term 'child-soldiers' is often used to refer to children recruited into armed forces or groups, the authors of this chapter prefer to use the more general terms of children, or children participating in hostilities, since children who do not participate as 'soldiers' but perform other tasks are also entitled to the protection provided under the relevant legal provisions.
[57] Oral intervention by General Flaviano Godio, Vice Director, Post Conflict Operations Study Center, made at the International Conference *Childhood Spoiled by War: Child Soldiers*, Turin, 16 November 2009, organized by the Istituto per gli Studi di Politica Internazionale (ISPI), the International Institute of Humanitarian Law, San Remo (IIHL) and the Italian Red Cross. Since General Godio did use the term child-soldiers in his intervention, this term is exceptionally used in the context of the points he made.

to its external relations. The risk that these instruments may prove insufficient to adequately guarantee children's rights, especially in view of an increased use of PMSCs, is then addressed.

A. Children's Rights in the EU

Although all EU members have ratified the UN Convention of the Rights of the Child (CRC) and are bound to respect the rights it establishes, the EU as such does not have general competence in matters of fundamental rights, including children's rights, under the treaties. Nevertheless, the EU seeks to facilitate Member State compliance with the CRC through various actions, such as funding and policy measures.[58] Importantly, in accordance with Article 6:2 of the Treaty on the European Union (TEU), the EU must respect fundamental rights in all its actions.[59]

1. The EU and Generic Children's Rights

Whilst the European Convention of Human Rights (ECHR), which is binding for all the Member States of the Council of Europe (and to which all EU members are party), has no specific article on children's rights, the EU has created instruments of its own that address the rights of the child.[60]

Moreover, children's rights were identified as a top priority in the EU strategic objectives for 2005–9, in which the important goal of the EU to ensure the respect for human rights, and especially the rights of the child, was emphasized.[61] The EU Commission has also adopted the document, 'Towards an EU Strategy on the Rights of the Child', which clearly highlights the significant role that the EU could play in promoting children's rights in international forums and third country relations. In fact, the document sets forth that the respect for children's rights must be ensured and mainstreamed in all internal and external EU policies, as well as when drafting both EC legislative and non-legislative actions that may affect

---

[58] <http://ec.europa.eu/external_relations/human_rights/child/index.htm>, accessed 19 June 2010.
[59] Council of the European Union, Consolidated Version of the Treaty on European Union, OJ 2010/C 83/13, Art 6. See also Commission of the European Communities, Towards an EU Strategy on the Rights of the Child, COM(2006) 367 final, Brussels, para 1:3, Legal basis for an EU strategy; and J Klabbers, *An Introduction to International Institutional Law* (2002), 264.
[60] Eg Art 24 European Charter of Fundamental Rights, OJ 2007/C 303/01, explicitly recognizes children's rights:

1. Children shall have the right to such protection and care as is necessary for their well-being. They may express their views freely. Such views shall be taken into consideration on matters which concern them in accordance with their age and maturity.
2. In all actions relating to children, whether taken by public authorities or private institutions, the child's best interests must be a primary consideration.
3. Every child shall have the right to maintain on a regular basis a personal relationship and direct contact with both his or her parents, unless that is contrary to his or her interests.

[61] 'Europe should be the point of reference worldwide for the practical application of fundamental rights. A particular priority must be effective protection of the rights of children, both against economic exploitation and all forms of abuse, with the Union acting as a beacon to the rest of the world': Commission of the European Communities, *Strategic Objectives 2005–2009*, COM(2005) 12 final, Brussels, at para 2.3, Common responsibilities for common values.

these rights.⁶² This was followed, in 2008, by a Communication on behalf of the Commission to the Council and others⁶³ on the 'special place of children in EU external action', addressing the need for placing children at the centre of EU external relations.

2. The EU and the Protection of Children in Armed Conflict

The above-mentioned instruments demonstrated the European commitment to guarantee compliance with children's rights in general, but were lacking in any specific measures related to children's rights. However, the adoption of the EU 'Guidelines on Children and Armed Conflict' (hereinafter the Guidelines) in 2003, which were updated in 2008,⁶⁴ represents an example of European involvement in more specific issues regarding the child. This fundamental step towards a greater protection of children's rights in the EU's external policy sets out the following main objective:

> to influence third countries and non state actors to implement international human rights norms and standards and humanitarian law, as well as regional human rights law instruments and to take effective measures to protect children from the effects of armed conflict, to end the use of children in armies and armed groups, and to end impunity.⁶⁵

To date, the EU has been active in a series of projects that relate to children and armed conflict. Some of these, such as the programmes for the protection or rehabilitation of children involved in armed conflict in Colombia, Nepal, and Sri Lanka, have been funded by the European Initiative for Democracy and Human Rights (EIDHR). Other activities, including (emergency) child protection, have been funded in countries such as Lebanon, Liberia, and Burma/Myanmar by the EU Humanitarian Aid Office (ECHO).⁶⁶

Among the tools for action envisaged in the Guidelines, and that the EU could use in its relations with third countries, various forms of diplomatic action are listed, but, more importantly, the imposition of targeted measures is considered an option.⁶⁷ Whereas the other tools are limited to dialogue and cooperative measures, paragraph 19 of the Guidelines explicitly introduces the possibility of resorting to stronger means if necessary. This is a clear sign of the importance that children's rights have gained in the EU and its Member States. Thus far, the initiatives undertaken by EU agencies have not included such measures, but this in no way excludes future situations requiring such action.

---

⁶² Towards an EU Strategy on the Rights of the Child (n 59 above), para III.1.3.
⁶³ Communication from the Commission to the Council, the European Parliament, the European Economic and Social Committee and the Committee of the Regions, Brussels (2008).
⁶⁴ Council of the European Union, 'Update of the EU Guidelines on Children and Armed Conflict', Brussels, 5 June 2008.
⁶⁵ Council of the European Union, 'EU Guidelines on Children and Armed Conflict', 8 December 2003, para 6.
⁶⁶ Summary of CAAC-related EU projects. See also <http://ec.europa.eu/echo/index_en.htm>, accessed on 19 June 2010.
⁶⁷ EU Guidelines (n 65 above), para 19.

3. Children's Rights and Military Operations

The Guidelines are also relevant to EU military operations, and could therefore possibly also be relevant to military activities carried out by PMSCs. The text notably states that the review of implementation of the Guidelines has to be effected in close cooperation with Heads of mission and EU military commanders.[68] In 2006, an implementation strategy for the 'Guidelines on Children and Armed Conflict' was adopted by the Council of the European Union (hereinafter: the Council), in which EU Special Representatives (EUSRs) and Heads of European Security and Defence Policy (ESDP) missions are encouraged to use the Guidelines in their work. The Council also adopted the 'Checklist for the Integration of the Protection of Children Affected by Armed Conflict into ESDP Operations', intended for use in mission planning and support, as well as in the field.[69] The goal is to ensure that child rights and protection concerns are consistently addressed throughout the entire process of ESDP operations, including both planning and implementation phases. In order to do so, the Checklist suggests that each component taking part in a mission consider how to deal with child protection issues. A major element in the Checklist is that the rules of engagement for the ESDP forces shall address key child-protection concerns, including the involvement of children with fighting forces.[70]

As regards the personnel, any violation of children's rights should be investigated by law-enforcement authorities and specialists. When intervening in armed conflicts, ESDP personnel must call upon the parties to the conflict to protect children, especially from abduction and recruitment, and seek agreements with such parties to end these practices. Along with the above-mentioned activities to guarantee respect for the rights of the child, the EU, and all its Member States, ought to advocate accountability for crimes against children, and support justice and truth-seeking mechanisms.

With regard to training on children's rights, the updated version of the Guidelines also explicitly mentions that the question of the protection of children should be adequately addressed in the planning process of an operation, as well as in any of the different approaches whether the mission is of a preventive nature, carried out during an ongoing armed conflict or in a post-conflict context.[71] The EU does not specify any particular mechanisms for training on children's rights within each Member State, leaving this to the discretion of each Member State.

---

[68] Ibid, para 20(c).
[69] <http://ec.europa.eu/external_relations/human_rights/child/index_en.htm>, accessed on 19 June 2010.
[70] 'Note by the Council of the European Union Regarding Checklist for the Integration of the Protection of Children Affected by Armed Conflict in ESDP Operations', Brussels, 26 May 2006.
[71] Update of the 'EU Guidelines on Children and Armed Conflict' (n 64 above).

B. Implementing EU Rules for the Rights of the Child in Relation to PMSC Activity

1. Children's Rights and PMSCs

The EU currently has no specific regulations on PMSC activity, whereas the normative and policy framework for the protection of the rights of the child has been growing steadily over the last few years. The European Council has emphasized the situation of children in armed conflict or post-conflict contexts.[72] However, doubts can be raised as to whether the existing instruments are sufficient to guarantee that these rights are not, or will not be, violated by the presence or use of PMSCs. There are known to be active military companies in at least four EU countries:[73] the United Kingdom, Denmark, the Netherlands, and France. These companies operate both at home and abroad, in countries such as Iraq, Afghanistan, Bosnia, Kosovo, Colombia, Nigeria, Sudan, and the Democratic Republic of Congo. Other PMSCs from the United Kingdom, the United States, and South Africa have also been involved, militarily and otherwise, in Sierra Leone, Uganda, etc.

The work tasks differ depending on where the company and its agents are deployed. Likewise, the risks are far from the same and can change quite drastically depending on whether the context is European or that of a country where, for instance, the frequent use of child soldiers represents or has represented a serious problem. So far, there have been no recorded casualties, nor any litigation or controversies, regarding violations of children's rights in relation to PMSC activity.[74] Nevertheless, with the increase in missions and operations carried out by PMSCs, and with these companies being (partly) European, the risk that the rights of the child, binding upon all EU Member States, might be disregarded or violated cannot be ignored. Moreover, the confidentiality that still surrounds PMSC contracts raises issues regarding responsibility for eventual violations of human and children's rights and, arguably, even more so given that the activity of these companies is steadily expanding.

EU Member States clearly have obligations with regard to children's rights, but the main problem with regards to PMSCs is that, for the time being, it seems impossible to know whether these obligations are actually being respected or even taken into consideration by PMSCs. No proper monitoring body exists to report on violations, and no control is presently being exercised over contracts that have been concluded between the companies and their 'employers' (ie states or international organizations). These actors thus appear as though they are situated, at least partially, in a grey area of the law, and defining their obligations under international,

---

[72] Note by the Council of the European Union on the promotion and protection of the rights of the child in the EU's external action, 27 May 2008, esp paras 24–9, <http://register.consilium.europa.eu/pdf/en/08/st09/st09739.en08.pdf>, accessed 19 June 2010.

[73] See draft PMCs and PSCs database, edited by Chiara Altafin, <http://www.priv-war.eu>, accessed on 20 August 2010.

[74] At least not that include European PMSC agents. See section II.A.4 and II.B for examples of recorded violations.

European and national laws is problematic. The rights and protection of the child, however, form part of the framework of all these legal regimes and must therefore be respected at all times.

2. *The Importance of EU Action*

It must be highlighted that, although particular attention has been accorded to children in armed conflict, and although situations of armed conflict represent a frequent context for Western PMSCs operating abroad, the existing European instruments for the protection of the rights of the child have not been developed with specific considerations for PMSC activities.

Moreover, most of the existing instruments presented above concern situations where it is presupposed that the EU or its Member States will not be the actor committing a violation, but the one promoting the 'remedy' or engaging in negotiations with third states in order to ensure their compliance with human rights and children's rights. These types of development cooperation measures may prove rather limited when it comes to the protection of children's rights during PMSC operations, where the PMSC agents could actually become the 'violators' of these rights.

The EU has, with regard to its external relations, declared itself to be a promoter of human rights (and of children's rights in particular) and has, through its actions in this sphere, proven that it takes this role seriously. Therefore, it is certainly justified for the EU to be concerned with the risks that the use of PMSCs represent for human rights and children's rights, and eager to control those risks in order to limit violations to any extent possible.

IV. Concluding Remarks

As this chapter demonstrates, a comprehensive body of international human rights instruments and specific IHL provisions exist, aimed at the protection of children in armed conflict. These international legal instruments impose specific obligations on states in terms of prevention and sanctioning of children's rights. Therefore, in the authors' view, there is no immediate need for the adoption of additional international legal standards specifically focusing on PMSCs and the rights of the child at the international level. There is, rather, a need for an improved compliance by states with the existing international obligations in this field, as suggested in the first part of the report.

The main measures to be taken are, *first*, the inclusion of a firm requirement in contracts with PMSCs, as well as in the licence awarded to these companies by their home state, to provide adequate training to their personnel on the specific measures to be taken to protect children and their rights as laid down in IHL and human rights instruments, in the broader context of the training on human rights and IHL. *Secondly*, the contracting state and the host state should require the PMSC to take due account of the specific protection of children from the beginning of the planning and organization phase of the operations. If a PMSC is contracted to intervene in a country where children are actively participating in an armed conflict, its employees should be specifically informed about the risks involved and the protective measures to take. *Thirdly*, adequate supervision should be ensured throughout the command structure between the home state, the contracting state, and within the PMSC itself, with particular attention to minimizing the risks for children during their operations on the ground. *Finally*, measures should be taken by the states involved in the deployment of PMSCs to ensure accountability of PMSC employees for acts amounting to violations of children's rights or international crimes against children before their national courts. PMSC personnel should also be made aware that they could be held individually accountable for violations against children, and that the young age of possible victims may constitute an aggravating factor in the sentencing for certain acts.[75]

Specific regulation at the EU level may contribute to improving such compliance with the existing international norms. As the second part of this chapter has shown, there is a framework of European instruments for the protection of the rights of the child, both with regard to the EU as such and to its external relations. However, these instruments may prove insufficient to guarantee the non-violation of children's rights on behalf of European PMSCs, especially when these companies are deployed in conflict or post-conflict contexts.

The EU has manifested its determination to play an active role in the protection of children affected by armed conflict, both in written form, through the instruments illustrated in this chapter, as well as in practice, through field activities under as taken in many affected countries. This determination is now challenged by a new form of actor, the PMSCs, and to fulfil its self-appointed mission as a guardian of human rights, the EU will have to consider ways to regulate PMSC activity in the future.

---

[75] See D Tolbert, 'Children and International Criminal Law: The Practice of the International Criminal Tribunal for the Former Yugoslavia (ICTY)' in K Arts and V Popovski (eds), *International Criminal Accountability and the Rights of Children* (2006), 147, 153. The citations are from ICTY, *Prosecutor v Kunarac and ors,* IT-96-23T and IT-96-23/1-T, trial judgment, para 874, and from the appeal judgment, para 355.

14

Women and Private Military and Security Companies

Ana Filipa Vrdoljak

I. Introduction

Recent press coverage of the role of private military and security companies (PMSCs) in conflict and post-conflict operations has invariably involved women. Women have been PMSC employees and brought actions against their employers for sexual assault;[1] or have been civilian victims of private contractors operating forced prostitution rings.[2] Armed conflict, belligerent occupation, and civil strife are by definition necessarily violent for all participants, be they civilians, combatants, or PMSC employees. However, for women it heralds an exacerbation in existing violence, discrimination, and inequalities. The increasing engagement of PMSCs in conflict, post-conflict, and transition situations in the provision of security and other services has brought their activities and operations starkly to the fore—particularly as they relate to women specifically and gender-related issues more generally.[3]

Lack of clarity about the application of international law norms and inadequacies of existing regulatory regimes covering PMSCs have reinforced concerns about transparency and accountability in respect of gender-related violence, harassment, and discrimination. Whilst international humanitarian law and human rights law has dedicated or 'special' provisions for women, feminist legal scholars have done much to expose the gendered nature of these branches of international law.[4] In recent decades, the United Nations' campaign of mainstreaming of women's issues

---

[1] US Department of Defence (DoD), Office of Inspector General, 'Efforts to Prevent Sexual Assault/Harassment Involving DOD Contractors during Contingency Operations', Report No D-2010-052 (10 April 2010), 1.
[2] See E Krahmann, 'Transitional States in Search of Support: Private Military Companies and Security Sector Reform' in S Chesterman and C Lehnardt (eds), *From Mercenaries to Market: The Rise and Regulation of Private Military Companies* (2007), 105 ff; and C de la Vega and A Beck, 'The Role of Military Demand in Trafficking and Sexual Exploitation' (24 February 2006), cited in 'Protection of Human Rights and Fundamental Freedoms when Countering Terrorism', Note by the Secretary General, 3 August 2009, UN Doc A/64/211, 21.
[3] See S Schulz and C Yeung, *Private Military and Security Companies and Gender* (2008), 13–16.
[4] See JG Gardam and MJ Jarvis, *Women, Armed Conflict and International Law* (2001).

has impacted significantly on relevant human rights law,[5] and the International Committee of the Red Cross (ICRC) has actively sought to investigate and address women's concerns.[6] However, as explained below, there has been limited flow-on of these concerns into the sphere of PMSCs.

This chapter focuses on the main issues and legal concerns raised by the impact of the privatization of war on women, both as PMSC employees and civilians. Section II highlights how armed conflict, civil unrest, occupation, and transition generally have a detrimental effect upon the lives of women with particular reference to safety, displacement, health, and economic disadvantage. Section III provides a summary of existing international humanitarian law and human rights provisions in this field. Section IV examines recent developments within the United Nations (and its members states), the work of the ICRC, and international criminal law jurisprudence shaping these existing protections. Section V considers the key recommendations of recent international and international initiatives covering PMSCs and women.[7]

II. Women, Armed Conflict, and Post-Conflict Situations

The premise of 'special' provisions for women in international humanitarian law and human rights law is that armed conflict, post-conflict, and transition impact differently on women. This premise is difficult to substantiate because of the limitations in available data.[8] Nonetheless, recent academic research and fact-finding by intergovernmental and non-governmental bodies have borne this assumption out in a number of key areas. When interpreting such information it is always crucial to bear in mind that women are not a monolithic group; rather, their diverse experiences are coloured by a multitude of social, economic, and cultural factors.[9] However, a base commonality of experience in key areas like violence, displacement, health, and economic disadvantage provides grounds for reform of international law and the practices of international organizations, states, and PMSCs.

---

[5] SC Res1325, 31 October 2000, UN DocS/Res/1325 (2000), and Fourth World Conference on Women, Action for Equality, Development and Peace, Beijing Declaration and Platform for Action, UN Doc A/Conf177/20 (1995) (Beijing Platform for Action), para 136.

[6] See C Lindsey, *Women Facing War: ICRC Study of the Impact of Armed Conflict on Women* (2001); and Statement of Renée Guisan, ICRC delegate to the Fourth World Conference on Women, Beijing, 4 September 1995, <http://www.un.org/esa/gopher-data/conf/fwcw/conf/una/950912110707.txt>, accessed on 10 April 2009.

[7] Montreux Document on Pertinent International Legal Obligations and Good Practices for States Related to Private Military and Security Companies in Armed Conflict, 17 September 2008, UN Doc S/2008/636; Schulz and Yeung (n 3 above); and DoD Office of Inspector General (n 1 above).

[8] Report submitted by the Special Rapporteur on Violence against Women Perpetrated and/or Condoned by the State during Armed Conflict, 23 January 2001, UN Doc E/CN4/2001/73, para 133 calling on states to develop and improve national data collection disaggregated by gender. See also WHO, *Ethical and Safety Recommendations for Researching, Documenting and Monitoring Sexual Violence in Emergencies* (2007).

[9] UN Doc E/CN4/2001/73, para 48; and SC Res 1261 (1999) of 25 August 1999, para 10.

A. Violence against Women (VAW)

Women, both as PMSC employees and civilians interacting with PMSCs, experience elevated levels of physical and mental violence during armed conflict, post-conflict and transition which encompass death, summary or arbitrary executions, torture, cruel, inhuman, and degrading treatment, rape, forced prostitution, forced terminations and sterilizations and other forms of sexual assault, abduction, persecution, harassment to themselves and to their family members.

Whilst all available statistics record that armed conflict and occupation generally have a disproportionate impact on civilian populations in respect of mortality, women (and children) make up the majority of civilian deaths in affected territories. For example, a peer-reviewed John Hopkins School of Public Health-led survey of civilian deaths after the 2003 invasion of Iraq comparing deaths prior to the conflict found a substantial spike in violent deaths, especially among women and children.[10] These findings were confirmed in a follow-up study covering the three years after the invasion which showed a significant increase in the number of civilian deaths.[11] The civilian death toll since 2006 has remained elevated.[12] The proliferation of small arms (including firearms, landmines, car bombs, and suicide bombers) in militarized zones has amplified this trend, with both the John Hopkins and Iraq Body Count surveys showing that increasingly violent civilian deaths are attributable to such munitions. There are corollary statistics for injuries not occasioning death. In addition, the likelihood of extrajudicial killings rises exponentially for women during armed conflict.[13] In conflicts in Mexico and Guatemala, evidence has emerged of women being deliberately targeted because of their gender (femicide).[14] These trends can be extrapolated for private contractors, for instance, a survey in Israel indicated a link between incidents of domestic violence and homicide and firearms licensed to private security guards.[15]

---

[10] See G Burnham et al, 'Mortality after the 2003 Invasion of Iraq: A Cross-sectional Cluster Sample Survey' *The Lancet* 368 (2006) 1421.

[11] See G Burnham et al, 'The Human Cost of the War in Iraq: A Mortality Study 2002–2006', <http://www.jhsph.edu/refugee/publications_tools/iraq/Human_Cost_of_WarFORMATTED.pdf>, accessed on 10 April 2009. Cf Iraq Family Health Survey Study Group, 'Violence-related Mortality in Iraq' *The New England Journal of Medicine* 358 (2008) 484.

[12] See Iraq Body Count, Documents Civilian Deaths from Violence, <http://www.iraqbodycount.org/database/>, accessed on 10 April 2009. Also in respect of Afghanistan see OO Bilukha et al, 'Death and Injury from Landmines and Unexploded Ordinances in Afghanistan' *Journal of American Medical Association* 290(5) (2003) 650.

[13] Report of the Special Rapporteur on Extrajudicial, Summary or Arbitrary Executions, Philip Alston, Preliminary Note on the Mission to Afghanistan, 29 May 2008, UN Doc A/HRC/8/3/Add6, paras 19–23; and Report submitted by the Special Rapporteur on Violence against Women, Its Causes and Consequences, M Radhika Coomaraswamy, 26 January 1998, UN Doc E/CN41998/54 (1998 UN VAW Report), Part 1A, paras 9–10.

[14] 'In-depth Study on all Forms of Violence against Women', Report of the Secretary General, 6 July 2006, UN Doc A/61/122/Add1, para 127.

[15] R Mazali, 'The Gun on the Kitchen Table: The Sexist Subtext on Private Policing in Israel' in V Farr, H Myrttinen, and A Schnabel (eds), *Sexed Pistols: The Gender Perspectives on Small Arms and Light Weapons* (2009), 246.

Whilst rape and sexual violence are not solely experienced by women,[16] data highlights that female civilians, combatants, and by extension PMSC employees, are at a substantially increased risk of suffering such violence during armed conflict, occupation, and transition.[17] The growing awareness of the use of sexual violence especially against women during the Bosnian conflict and in Rwanda in the 1990s, the military sexual slavery of Korean 'comfort' women by the Japanese during the Second World War, and the ongoing work of the UN Special Rapporteur on Violence Against Women since 1994 has led to greater consciousness of its deployment as a method of violence, brutality, and warfare against the enemy and its civilian population.[18] The UN Special Rapporteur, Radhika Coomaraswamy, in her 1998 report, observed: 'sexual violence against women... is seen and often experienced as means of humiliating the opposition... It is battle among men fought over the bodies of women.'[19]

Sexual violence encompasses various acts including forced prostitution, sex trafficking, forced sterilizations, forced abortions, forced impregnation, and pregnancies and so forth.[20] Data has highlighted that PMSC employees are as likely to perpetrate such crimes as are regular armed forces.[21] It is unsurprising given that, as noted above, PMSC recruits are often drawn from regular armed forces. For example, DynCorp Aerospace Technology UK Ltd employees were implicated in sex slavery in Bosnia by Human Rights Watch before a US congressional hearing

---

[16] Eg sexually targeted interrogation techniques allegedly used by contractors and military personnel at Abu Ghraib Prison, Iraq: see Tabuga, Article 15–6 of the Investigation of the 800th Military Police Brigade, Department of Defense, US Government (2004).

[17] See 'In-depth Study' (n 14 above), Table 1, 45; UN Doc E/CN4/2001/73, paras 67–113; UN, '15 Years of the UN Special Rapporteur on Violence against Women, Its Causes and Consequences (1994–2009): A Critical Review' (2009) (15 years UNSRVAW Report), 3, <http://www2.ohchr.org/english/issues/women/rapporteur/docs/15YearReviewofVAWMandate.pdf>, accessed on 10 March 2009. Researchers of peacetime data on rape and sexual violence highlight that it is difficult to obtain accurate information, suspecting underreporting because of ongoing trauma, social stigma and fear of 'punishment' (eg honour killings, stoning). Under-reporting is further exacerbated during armed conflict and occupation because of displacement and lack of access to health services: UN Department of Economic and Social Affairs, Statistics Division, The World's Women 2005: Progress in Statistics, UN Doc ST/ESA/STAT/SerK/17 (2006), 78. See also Reproductive Health Response in Conflict Consortium, *Gender Based Violence Tools Manual for Assessment and Program Design, Monitoring and Evaluation in Conflict-affected Settings* (2004).

[18] Preliminary report submitted by the Special Rapporteur on Violence Against Women, Its Causes and Consequences, M Radhika Coomaraswamy, 22 November 1994, UN Doc E/CN41995/42 (1994 UN VAW Report), paras 274–83; and Report of the UN High Commissioner for Human Rights, 'Systematic Rape, Sexual Slavery and Slavery-like Practices during Armed Conflicts', 11 July 2006, UN Doc A/HRC/Sub1/58/23.

[19] 1998 UN VAW Report (n 13 above), para 12. See also Report submitted by the Independent Expert on the Situation of Human Rights in the Democratic Republic of the Congo, UN Doc E/CN4/2006/113, 23.

[20] See 'In-depth Study' (n 14 above); and *Prosecutor v Issa Hassan Sesay, Morris Kallon and Augustine Gbao* (the RUF accused), trial judgment, Special Court for Sierra Leone, Case No SCSL-04-15-T, 25 February 2009.

[21] Integration of the Human Rights of Women and the Gender Perspective: Written Statement by Human Rights Advocates, 28 February 2006, UN Doc E/CN4/2006/NGO/85, paras 15–18; and Gumedze, 'Sexual Exploitation and Sexual Abuse: The Need for Special Measures within Private Security/Military Industry', *ISS Today* (16 January 2007), <http://www.iss.co.za/pgcontent.php?UID=14854>, accessed on 7 July 2010.

in 2002.²² A subsequent US Department of Defence (DoD) Inspector General report found the situation was fuelled by the lack of any requirement for private contractors to report or punish employees engaged in such conduct.²³

Victims of such violence are not confined to civilian populations. Civil suits filed in the United States against PMSCs by women highlight that contractor employees can also be victims of sexual violence and harassment.²⁴ The US DoD instigated an internal investigation into the reporting and prosecution of sexual assaults following an escalating disquiet pertaining to allegations concerning US military personnel in Iraq and Kuwait which led to the adoption of 'Direction and Instruction for prevention, reporting and response'.²⁵ A 2010 DoD audit precipitated by a Congressional request following the handling of a complaint of sexual assault against a Kellogg, Brown, and Root Services Inc (KBR) employee by other KBR employees at Camp Hope, Baghdad, found that the ratio of DoD contractors to military service personnel was equal in Iraq and Afghanistan.²⁶ However, civilian contractors are not subject to the DoD Directive or Instruction.

The evolving responses to rape and sexual violence against women in contemporary international law and the UN system are examined in section III below.

B. Health

Women as PMSC employees and civilians are at an elevated risk of contracting sexually transmitted diseases through sexual violence including rape (and deliberate infection),²⁷ and transfusion of infected blood products during pregnancy or childbirth.²⁸ For countries in the midst of armed conflict or transition, disruption to societal structures and governmental services necessarily has a knock-on effect on provision of health services.²⁹ Their treatment is compromised by systemic discrimination, lack of information, lack of access to affordable treatment, etc.³⁰ In

---

[22] US Department of Defense, Office of Inspector General, Assessment of DOD Efforts to Combat Human Trafficking, Phase II—Bosnia-Herzegovina and Kosovo, Case no H03188433128, 8 December 2003, 15, <http://www.dodig.mil/fo/foia/HT-Phase_II.pdf>, accessed on 7 July 2010. See also Krahmann (n 2 above), 105 ff; and de la Vega and Beck (n 2 above).
[23] Ibid.
[24] DoD Office of Inspector General (n 1 above).
[25] DoD Directive 6495.01, Sexual Assault Prevention and Response (SAPR) Program, 6 October 2005, revised 7 November 2008; and DOD Instruction 6495.02, Sexual Assault Prevention and Response Program Procedures, 23 June 2006, revised 13 November 2008. See also US Department of Defense, Armed Forces 2002 Sexual Harassment Survey, DMDC Report no 2003-026 (November 2003), <http://www.defense.gov/news/Feb2004/d20040227shs1.pdf>, accessed on 7 July 2010.
[26] DoD Office of Inspector General (n 1 above), 9.
[27] NGO Working Group on Women, Peace and Security, 'Fact Sheet on Women and Armed Conflict', 23 October 2002, <http://www.iwtc.org/212.html>, accessed on 10 April 2009.
[28] Lindsey (n 6 above), 112.
[29] See Lindsey (n 6 above), 119–20; 'The Impact of Armed Conflicts upon Children', Report submitted pursuant to the resolution adopted by the General Assembly A/RES/48/157 to the Fifty First Session of the United Nations General Assembly, UN Doc A/51/306, 26 August 1966, 150; and UNHCR, 'Sexual Violence Against Refugees: Guidelines on Prevention and Response' (1995), Section 3.9.
[30] 15 years UNSRVAW Report (n 17 above), 22–3; UN Inter-Agency Standing Committee, 'Guidelines for HIV/AIDS Intervention in Emergency Situations' (nd), 9–11, 32–3, <http://data.unaids.org/Publications/External-Documents/IASC_Guidelines-Emergency-Settings_en.pdf>, accessed on 10 April 2009; and 1998 UN VAW Report (n 13 above), Part II.

turn, there is greater likelihood of women dying from the disease once they have contracted it.[31] However, much focus in recent years has been placed on addressing the devastating impact of the lack of access to treatment in the area of reproductive health, including protection against and treatment for sexual violence, and sexually transmitted diseases.[32]

Recent US military audits reveal the inadequacy of responses by PMSCs to psychological harm suffered by employees subjected to sexual assault and sexual harassment.[33] Further, post-traumatic stress disorder (PTSD), manifest in private contractors returning from Iraq,[34] can also impact adversely upon the physical and psychological well-being of their families, particularly when it manifests itself as domestic violence.[35]

C. Displacement

A DoD report has noted testimony of former employees of PMSCs implicating other employees in human trafficking.[36] The likelihood of death, injury, sexual violence, disease and infection, and discrimination, especially economic disadvantage, is aggravated by human trafficking and other forms of displacement occasioned by armed conflict, belligerent occupation, and civil unrest.[37] The likelihood of death and physical and mental harm increases with the breakdown of familial, social, and economic structures; and lack of access to food, health care, and other resources.[38] The need to address the plight of women and girls within refugee camps and settlements was recognized in Security Council Resolution 1325 (2000) (para 12).[39] Sex or gender is not a ground for the granting of asylum under the

---

[31] UNAIDS, 'Report on the Global AIDS Epidemic 2008' (2008), 47.
[32] CA Palmer et al, 'The Emerging Policy Agenda for Reproductive Health Services in Conflict Settings' *Social Science and Medicine* 49 (1999) 1691; UNFPR, *Manual for Reproductive Health Kit in Crisis Situations*, 2nd edn (2003); and WHO, *Reproductive Health during Conflict and Displacement: A Guide for Programme Managers* (2000), 10–15. See Policies and Practices that Impact on Women's Reproductive Rights and Contribute to, Cause or Constitute Violence against Women, UN Doc E/CN4/1999/68/Add4; Intersections of Violence against Women and HIV/AIDS, UN Doc E/CN4/2005/72; and GA Res S-26/2, Declaration on Commitment on HIV/AIDS of 27 June 2001.
[33] DoD Office of Inspector General (n 1 above), 14.
[34] Study conducted by DynCorp indicated that 24% of its employees showed PTSD symptoms: see J Risen, 'Contractors back From Iraq Suffer Trauma from Battle', *The New York Times* (5 July 2007).
[35] Schulz and Yeung (n 3 above), 8; and DD Tucker, 'Domestic Violence, PTSD and Brain Injury: Military and Civilian Challenges' (2009), <http://www.ncdsv.org/images/MFLJ_Domestic%20Violence%20and%20PTSD_Tucker_Pt%201_4-2009.pdf>, accessed on 7 July 2010.
[36] DoD Office of Inspector General (n 22 above).
[37] 'Political Economy and Violence against Women', Report of the Special Rapporteur on Violence against Women, Its Causes and Consequences, Y Ertürk, UN Doc A/HRC/11/6/Add6 (2009), paras 59, 63–4. See UNHCR, *Statistical Yearbook 2007: Trends in Displacement, Protection and Solutions* (December 2008), 7–8; Lindsey (n 3 above), 65 ff; and WHO, *Clinical Management of Rape Survivors: Developing Protocols for Use with Refugees and Internally Displaced Persons* (2005).
[38] 1998 UN VAW Report, Part III D (1) (n 13 above); and UNHCR, 'Handbook for the Protection of Women and Girls' (January 2008), 9–11.
[39] In respect of internal displacement see Guiding Principles on Internal Displacement, 11 February 1998, UN Doc E/CN4/1998/53/Add2, Principles 7(3)(d), 18(3), 19(2), 20(3).

Convention Relating to the Status of Refugees (Refugee Convention).[40] However, the UNHCR has adopted guidelines on gender-related persecution under of Article 1A(2) of the Refugee Convention urging states to give adequate weight to gender elements when assessing asylum applications.[41]

Further, women are less frequently interned or detained than men; consequently, when they are, facilities are less likely to accommodate their needs.[42] Furthermore, when detention occurs there is a greater propensity for women to be subjected to gender-specific torture.[43] As security services are increasingly being contracted out to civilian companies rather than being undertaken by military forces or the police, there have been growing calls for PMSC employees to undergo mandatory gender-awareness training and for private contractors to increase their intake of female recruits and provide a work environment conducive to their retention.[44]

D. Economic Disadvantage

Existing data highlights that female combatants experience significant economic disadvantage compared with their male counterparts and this is reflected in inequality in earnings; and underrepresentation in leadership roles (and exclusion from certain positions).[45] As PMSC employees are predominantly recruited from the military and police service, these trends are replicated in these companies, with women segregated and confined to unskilled and repetitive work.[46]

Armed conflict and post-conflict situations exacerbate the existing economic disadvantage and discrimination usually experienced by local women.[47] In many areas of the world, women are primarily responsible for the development and maintenance of natural resources, especially land, to sustain themselves and their families. Rape of women has been used as a means of disrupting and halting

---

[40] 18 July 1951, in force 22 April 1954, 189 UNTS 150.
[41] UNHCR, Guidelines on International Protection: Gender-related Persecution within the Context of Article 1A(2) of the 1951 Convention and/or 1967 Protocol Relating to the Status of Refugees, UN Doc HCR/GIP/02/01, 7 May 2002, paras 5, 6, 9. See also UNHCR, 'Sexual and Gender-based Violence against Refugees, Returnees, and Internally Displaced Persons: Guidelines for prevention and response', May 2003, 14, 20.
[42] See Gardam and Jarvis (n 4 above), 33–5; and Lindsey (n 6 above), 164–5.
[43] Report of the Special Rapporteur on Torture and Other Cruel, Inhuman or Degrading Treatment or Punishment, M Nowak, 15 January 2008, UN Doc A/HRC/7/3, paras 41–3.
[44] DoD Office of Inspector General (n 1 above); and Schulz and Yeung (n 3 above), 3, 14.
[45] US General Accounting Office, 'Gender Issues, Trends in Occupational Distribution of Military Women', September 1999, GAO/NSIAS-99-212; UK Ministry of Defence, 'Women in the Armed Forces: A Report by the Women in the Armed Forces Steering Group' (May 2002), <http://www.mod.uk/NR/rdonlyres/A9925990-82C2-420F-AB04-7003768CEC02/0/womenaf_fullreport.pdf>, accessed on 10 April 2009; and *Mrs Sirdar v Army Board and SofS for Defence*, ECJ Judgment C-273/97, 26 October 1999; and NATO, 'Recruitment and Retention of Military Personnel' (RTO-RT-human RightsM-107) (2007).
[46] BH Erickson, P Albanese, and S Drakulic, 'Gender on a Jagged edge: The Security Industry, Its Clients and the Reproduction and Revision of Gender' *Work and Occupations* 27(3) (2000) 295; and Schulz and Yeung (n 3 above), 16.
[47] 1998 UN VAW Report (n 13 above), Part I D.

agricultural activity and food supplies.[48] Non-agricultural livelihood, however, is affected by systematic discrimination which is experienced by women more acutely during such social upheaval and its related effects, like permanent or ongoing injury and trauma.[49] With the underrepresentation of female PMSC recruits, this situation is further amplified in operations involving traditional societies where local women may be forbidden from interacting with male contractors.[50]

III. Women and International Humanitarian Law

Whilst women are covered by general protections afforded under international humanitarian law, human rights law, international criminal law, and 'special' international humanitarian law protections, the limitations of these provisions for the protection of female PMSC employees and female victims of PMSCs is widely acknowledged.[51] This section provides a brief overview of these 'special' provisions.[52] It should be noted that Security Council Resolution 1325 (2000) requires that 'all parties to an armed conflict... respect fully international law applicable to the rights and protection of women and girls, especially civilians, in particular the obligations applicable to them' under the 1949 Geneva Conventions and their 1977 Additional Protocols, the 1951 Refugee Convention and its 1967 Protocol, the Convention on the Elimination of All Forms of Discrimination Against Women of 1979 and its 1999 Optional Protocol, the Convention on the Rights of the Child and its two Optional Protocols, and the Rome Statute of the International Criminal Court.

Early codification of international humanitarian law provided implicit and explicit protection for women. Article 46 of the Convention (IV) respecting the Laws and Customs of War on Land, and the 1907 Hague Regulations provide that during belligerent occupation: 'Family honour and rights, the lives of persons... must be respected.'[53] The Commission on the Responsibility of the Authors of the War and on Enforcement of Penalties established by the 1919 Versailles Peace

---

[48] UN Doc A/HRC/11/6/Add6(2009), para 62.
[49] Economic and Social Policy and its Impact on Violence against Women, R Coomaraswamy, UN Doc E/CN4/2000/68/Add5; and 'Summary: Informal debate of General Assembly, Promotion of Gender Equality and Empowerment of Women 6–8 March 2007', <http://www.un.org/ga/president/61/letters/Them.deb.gender-report.pdf>, accessed on 10 April 2009.
[50] Schulz and Yeung (n 3 above), 4.
[51] Ibid, 10–11; and DoD Office of Inspector General (n 1 above).
[52] For more detailed and critical treatment, see Gardam and Jarvis (n 4 above) generally; H Durham, 'International Humanitarian Law and the Protection of Women' in H Durham and T Gurd (eds), *Listening to the Silences: Women and War* (2005), 95; and J Gardam, 'Women and Armed Conflict: The Response of International Humanitarian Law', ibid, 109.
[53] 18 October 1907, in force 26 January 1910, 208 *Parry's CTS* (1907) 77; 2(supp) (1908) AJIL 90, being a replication of Art 46 of the Convention (II) with Respect to the Laws and Customs of War on Land and its annex: Regulations concerning the Laws and Customs of War on Land, and Annex: Regulations, 29 July 1899, in force 4 September 1900, 187 *Parry's CTS* (1898–99) 429, 1(supp) (1907) AJIL 129.

Conference listed rape and the abduction of women and girls for enforced prostitution as war crimes.[54]

Under the non-discrimination provisions of the four 1946 Geneva Conventions and two 1977 Additional Protocols (Geneva Law), differentiated treatment on the grounds of sex is permissible as long as the effect is favourable to the affected targeted group.[55] These Articles are made subject to the tacit acknowledgement of the specific concerns of women addressed by the 'special' provisions concerning sexual violence, pregnant women and mothers of young children, female internees, and female prisoners of war. Common Article 3(1)(c) of the Geneva Conventions concerning 'outrages against personal dignity' and Article 14 of Geneva III Convention, and Article 12 of Geneva I and II Conventions replicate the obligation contained in Article 46 of the Hague Regulations—that is, 'women shall be treated with the regard due to their sex'. These provisions do not impose obligations as such but supplement those relating to sexual violence and protection of pregnant women and mothers with young children.[56]

The Geneva Conventions have specific provisions pertaining to sexual violence against women. Article 27(2) of Geneva IV provides that: 'women shall be especially protected against any attack of their honour, in particular against rape, enforced prostitution, or any form of indecent assault'.[57] This provision does not extend to acts of the state of which women are nationals. Article 75(2)(b) of Additional Protocol I prohibits 'at any time and in any place whatsoever, whether committed by civilian or by military agents... outrages upon personal dignity, in particular humiliating and degrading treatment, enforced prostitution and any form of indecent assault' against women and men.[58] Rape is specifically mentioned in Article 76 covering women and children, which extends the protection afforded under Article 27 of Geneva IV to all women on the territory of parties to the conflict.[59] In respect of non-international conflicts, Article 4(2)(e) of Additional

---

[54] 14 (1920) AJIL 95.
[55] See Art 12 of the Geneva Convention for the Amelioration of the Condition of the Wounded and Sick in Armed Forces in the Field (Geneva I), 12 August 1949, in force 21 October 1951, 75 UNTS 31; Art 2 of the Geneva Convention for the Amelioration of the Condition of Wounded, Sick and Shipwrecked Members of Armed Forces at Sea (Geneva II), 12 August 1949, in force 21 October 1951, 75 UNTS 85; Art 16 of the Geneva Convention Relative to the Treatment of Prisoners of War (Geneva III), 12 August 1949, in force 21 October 1951, 75 UNTS 135; Art 27 of the Geneva Convention Relative to the Protection of Civilian Persons in Time of War (Geneva IV), 12 August 1949, in force 21 October 1951, 75 UNTS 287; Art 74 of the Protocol Additional to the Geneva Conventions of 12 August 1949, and Relating to the Protection of Victims of International Armed Conflicts (Additional Protocol I), 8 June 1977, in force 7 December 1978, 1125 UNTS 3; and Art 4 of the Protocol Additional to the Geneva Conventions of 12 August 1949, and Relating to the Protection of Victims of Non-International Armed Conflicts (Additional Protocol II), 8 June 1977, in force 7 December 1978, 1125 UNTS 609.
[56] J Pictet et al, *Geneva Convention Relative to the Protection of Civilian Persons in Time of War* (1958), 385.
[57] Ibid, 205. See J Pictet et al, *Geneva Convention Relative to the Treatment of Prisoners of War* (1960), 147–8. For critique of the use of 'honour' to protect women within international humanitarian law see C Lindsey, 'The Impact of Armed Conflict on Women' in Durham and Gurd (n 52 above), 21.
[58] Y Sandoz et al (eds), *Commentary on the Additional Protocols of 8 June 1977 to the Geneva Conventions of 12 August 1949* (1987), para 3133 ff.
[59] Ibid, para 3151.

Protocol II requires that 'outrages upon personal dignity, in particular humiliating and degrading treatment, rape, enforced prostitution and any form or indecent assault... against [all persons who do not take a direct part or who have ceased to take part in hostilities] are and shall remain prohibited at any time and in any place whatsoever'.

Neither the grave-breaches provisions within the 1949 Geneva Conventions, nor Additional Protocol I, specifically mention rape or sexual violence. Nonetheless, Article 147 of Geneva IV Convention covering 'torture or inhuman treatment, including biological experiments, wilfully causing great suffering or serious injury to body or health' and Article 85(3)(b) concerning injury to civilians have the potential to be read broadly to cover such acts. In addition, the Rome Statute defines war crimes to include 'rape, sexual slavery, enforced prostitution, force pregnancy... enforced sterilisation, or any other form of sexual violence also constituting a grave breach of the Geneva Convention'.[60] Taking this beyond the context of armed conflict and belligerent occupation, it is listed as a crime against humanity in the Rome Statute,[61] with similar provisions included in the statutes of recent international and hybrid criminal tribunals.[62] In addition, the Rome Statute includes gender as one of the discriminatory grounds for persecution.[63] The jurisprudence of the international criminal tribunals in respect of sexual violence is discussed in section IV below.

The Geneva Conventions also provide special protection for women during pregnancy, as mothers and in their role as care givers for children (and the sick and elderly). Whilst this emphasis on the 'traditional' role of women by international humanitarian law has been criticized by feminist scholars,[64] the reality is that

---

[60] Arts 8(2)(b)(xxii) (international conflict) and 8(c)(vi) (non-international conflict) of the Rome Statute of the International Criminal Court, 17 July 1998, in force 1 July 2002, UN Doc A/CONF183/9; 37 ILM 1002 (1998); 2187 UNTS 90 (Rome Statute). See also Art 4(g) of the Statute of the International Criminal Tribunal for Rwanda, SC Res 955 of 8 November 1994 as adopted and amended to SC Res 1717 of 13 October 2006 (ICTR Statute); Art 3(e), Art 2(g) of the Statute of the Special Court for Sierra Leone, in Agreement between the United Nations and the Government of Sierra Leone on the Establishment of a Special Court for Sierra Leone, SC Res 1315 of 14 August 2000, 2178 UNTS 138 (Statute of the Special Court for Sierra Leone) with Art 15(4) requiring the office of the prosecutor give due consideration to the appointment of staff including prosecutors and investigators experienced in gender-related crimes. See also Art 7(2)(f) of the Rome Statute concerning 'force pregnancy' is defined as the specific intent of 'affecting the ethnic composition of any population or carrying out other grave violations of international law'; and Art 7(2)(c) covering 'enslavement' which is defined to include 'exercise of such power in the course of trafficking in persons, in particular women and children'. The UN VAW Special Rapporteur has criticized the specific intent require for forced pregnancy: UN Doc E/CN4/2001/73, para 18.
[61] Art 7(1)(g) of the Rome Statute.
[62] Art 5(g) (Crimes Against Humanity), Updated Statute of the International Criminal Tribunal for the former Yugoslavia, GA Res 827 of 25 May 1993, amended by GA Res 1166 (1998), 1329 (2000), 1411 (2002), 1431 (2002) 1481 (2003), 1597 (2005) and 1660 (2006) (ICTY Statute); Art 3 (h) ICTR Statute; Art 2(g) of the Statute of the Special Court for Sierra Leone; Art 5 (rape) of the Law on the Establishment of Extraordinary Chambers in the Court of Cambodia for the Prosecution of Crimes committed during the period of Democratic Kampuchea, with the inclusion of amendments as promulgated on 27 October 2004 (NS/RKM/1004/006).
[63] Art 7(3) of the Rome Statute.
[64] Gardam and Jarvis (n 4 above).

it remains a role which women fulfil especially during armed conflict and belligerent occupation and it is important that special provisions address it covering medical treatment,[65] food,[66] safety,[67] and penal law and the death penalty.[68]

Given that security operations relating to both civilians and prisoners of war are increasingly being contracted to PMSCs, commentators have emphasized the need for these companies to ensure adequate numbers of female employees and the provision of gender-awareness training for all staff.[69] International humanitarian law provides that female civilian internees are also afforded special protection even when they are not pregnant or mothers with dependant children. Article 75(5) of Additional Protocol I requires that female internees be provided with quarters separate from those of men and under immediate female supervision, and where families are detained or interned 'they shall whenever possible, be held in the same place and accommodation as a family unit'. Equivalent provision relating to non-international armed conflict is found in Article 5 of Additional Protocol II. Where women are interned with men who are not members of their family as an 'exceptional and temporary measure' they must be provided with 'separate sleeping quarters and sanitary conveniences' (Article 85 of Geneva IV). In addition, female internees shall only be searched by a woman (Article 25 of Geneva IV). When disciplinary punishment is meted out to female internees, their sex should be a factor taken into account (Article 119 of Geneva IV). The protections afforded female prisoners of war is more limited than those extended to female civilian internees.[70]

IV. Prohibition of Sexual Violence

The 'special' provisions in respect of women in international humanitarian law today can only be understood within the context of the significant developments which have occurred within international law and international institutions since they were initially drafted. This section focuses on efforts to address violence against women as an example, to illustrate how international criminal law, the advocacy of NGOs like ICRC, and the UN's mainstreaming of women's issues have shaped the law and best practice in military and security operations generally.

---

[65] Arts 38(5), 50, 91, and 127 of Geneva IV; Declaration on the Protection of Women and Children in Emergency Situations of 1974, GA Res 3318(XXIX), 14 December 1974, para 6. See also Declaration on the Elimination of Violence against Women, GA Res 48/104, 20 December 1993.
[66] Arts 23 and 89 of Geneva IV; and Art 70 of Additional Protocol I.
[67] Arts 14, 17, and 132 of Geneva IV.
[68] Art 76(2)–(3) of Additional Protocol I; and Art 6(4) of Additional Protocol II. The ICRC commentary suggesting that despite the qualified phrasing, it constitutes a prohibition on the execution the death penalty until the child is no longer dependent: ibid, para 3167. See also Art 6(5) of the International Covenant on Civil and Political Rights, 16 December 1966, in force 23 March 1976, GA Res 2200A (XXI), 21 UN GAOR Supp (no 16), 52, UN Doc A/6316 (1966), 999 UNTS 171.
[69] See Schulz and Yeung (n 3 above), 3.
[70] Arts 14, 25, 29, 97, and 108 of Geneva III.

A. Jurisprudence of International Criminal Tribunals

The work of the International Criminal Tribunal for the former Yugoslavia (ICTY) and the International Criminal Tribunal for Rwanda (ICTR) have done much not only for the enforcement of international humanitarian law and international criminal law but also the evolution of the interpretation of existing law, particularly the recognition of rape as a grave breach. Both governing statutes list rape as a crime against humanity and the ICTR enumerates it and other forms of sexual violence as a violation of Common Article 3 of the 1949 Geneva Conventions.[71] The Security Council when adopting the ICTY statute expressed 'once again its grave alarm at continuing reports of widespread and flagrant violations of international humanitarian law... including reports of... organised and systematic detention and rape of women'.[72] The jurisprudence of these tribunals has not only extrapolated from the notion of rape[73] and other sexual violence (including enslavement and sexual slavery)[74] as being not only war crimes, and crimes against humanity per se, but has included them within the definition of persecution (on the grounds of gender even though not explicitly contained in their respective governing statutes),[75] torture,[76] and genocide.[77]

---

[71] Art 5(g) ICTY Statute; Arts 3(h) and 4(g) ITCR Statute. The Tokyo International Military Tribunal referred to sexual crimes in its indictment; both the Nuremberg and and Tokyo Tribunals held evidence in respect of them, but neither mentioned rape in their judgments. Rape had also been listed as a crimes against humanity in Art II(1)(c) of the Control Council Law no 10, 20 December 1945, *Official Gazette of the Control Council of Germany,* no 3, 22 covering the trial of war criminals by the Allied military governments, but no charges relating to rape were brought under this law.

[72] SC Res 827, 25 May 1994, UN Doc A/RES/827. For summary of the UN investigations of reports of sexual violence during the early years of the Yugoslav and Rwandan conflicts, see Gardam and Jarvis (n 1 above), 148–60.

[73] *Prosecutor v Jean-Paul Akayesu,* ICTR-96-4-T, trial judgment, 2 September 1998, para 688; *Prosecutor v Zejnil Delalić and ors,* IT-96-21-T, trial judgment, 16 November 1998 (Čelibići), para 495; *Prosecutor v Anto Furundžija,* IT-95-17/1-T, trial judgment, 10 December 1998, para 271; *Prosecutor v Dragoljub Kunarac and ors,* IT-96-23-T and IT-96-23/1-T, trial judgment, 22 February 2001, paras 460 and 495; and *Prosecutor v Miroslav Kvočka and ors,* IT-98-30-T, trial judgment, 2 November 2001.

[74] *Kunarac and ors,* trial judgment (n 73 above), paras 540, 542. See 'Systematic Rape, Sexual Slavery and Slavery-like Practice during Armed Conflict', Report of the UN High Commissioner for Human Rights, 11 July 2006, UN Doc A/HRC/Sub1/58/23.

[75] *Prosecutor v Sylvester Gacumbtsi,* ICTR-2001-64-T, trial judgment, 17 June 2004, paras 321–33, and *Prosecutor v Sylvester Gacumbtsi,* ICTR-2001-64-T, appeals judgment, 7 July 2006, paras 102–3, 147–57; *Prosecutor v Alfred Musema,* ICTR-96-13, trial judgment, 27 January 2000, paras 962–6; *Prosecutor v Laurent Semanza,* ICTR-97-20-I, trial judgment, 15 May 2003, paras 477–9; *Prosecutor v Duško Tadić,* IT-94-1-T, trial judgment, 7 May 1997, para 715; *Prosecutor v Vlatko Kupreskić,* IT-95-16-T, trial judgment, 14 January 2000, para 627; *Kvočka,* trial judgment (n 73 above), paras 196–7, 233–4; *Prosecutor v Radislav Krstić,* IT-98-33-T, trial judgment, 2 August 2001, paras 617–18; *Furundžija,* trial judgment (n 73 above), para 172; and *Prosecutor v Zejnil Delalić and ors,* IT-96-21-A, appeals judgment, 20 February 2001 (Čelibići appeals judgment).

[76] *Akayesu,* trial judgment (n 73 above), para 594; *Semanza,* trial judgment (n 75 above), paras 482–5; and *Prosecutor v Anto Furundžija,* IT-95-17/1-A, appeals judgment, 21 July 2000, para 111. Cf *Kunarac,* trial judgment (n 73 above), paras 473, 482, 497; and *Kvočka* trial judgment (n 73 above), para 139 making a distinction between the definition of torture under international humanitarian law and human rights law, with the later found to be too restrictive. See also UN Doc A/HR/7/3.

[77] *Gacumbtsi,* trial judgment (n 75 above), paras 259–92; *Akayesu,* trial judgment (n 73 above); and *Musema,* trial judgment (n 75 above), para 933.

This jurisprudence has aided and reinforced the ongoing transformation occurring within international law in understanding and redefining violence against women. Feminist legal scholars and the UN Special Rapporteur on Violence against Women (who has presented reports on this topic since 1994) have cautioned against international humanitarian law reinforcing patriarchal notions of female sexuality and failing to address the violence visited by rape and other forms of sexual violence.[78] It was noted that by protecting the victim's 'honour' international humanitarian law was reaffirming stereotypical notions of women concerning purity, chastity, and virginity, linking the crime to the morality of the victim and reinforcing the shame associated with such acts. Instead, they promoted a reinterpretation which emphasized the role of rape and other forms of sexual violence as a weapon of violence during the armed conflict against combatants and civilians used by state militaries, militia, peacekeeping forces, and other non-state actors.[79] This transition from rape as a crime against honour (Geneva IV) to recognition of rape in limited form (Additional Protocols), through to its recognition within the definition of persecution and torture in the jurisprudence of contemporary international criminal tribunals, has facilitated this transformation, which is reflected in the Rome Statute.

This transformation has not only affected the understanding of sexual violence against women in international law, especially international humanitarian law, but it has had an impact upon the appointment of judicial officers,[80] prosecution, and enforcement procedures and practices of international courts through the recruitment and training of investigatory and prosecutorial staff in gender issues and gender-related crimes;[81] the tailoring of remedies to the needs of women and girls;[82] the involvement and needs of women in repatriation and rehabilitation; and post-conflict reconciliation and reconstruction efforts.[83]

---

[78] Report of UN Special Rapporteur on Violence Against Women, Y Ertürk, Mission to the Democratic Republic of the Congo, 28 February 2008, UN Doc A/HRC/7/6/Add4; and 1998 UN VAW Report, Part I (n 13 above).

[79] See SC Res 1820 (2008) of 19 July 2 008, sixth preambular recital.

[80] Art 36(8)(a)(iii) and (b) of the Rome Statute.

[81] Art 42(9)of the Rome Statute; for ICTY and ICTR see UN Division for the Advancement of Women, 'Sexual Violence and Armed Conflict: United Nations Response', <http://www.un.org/womenwatch/daw/public/w2apr98.htm>, accessed on 8 April 2009; and Art 15(4) of the Statute of the Special Court for Sierra Leone requires the office of the prosecutor to give due consideration to the appointment of staff including prosecutors and investigators experienced in gender-related crimes.

[82] Eg in the context of the 1990 Gulf War, see UN Compensation Commission Decision no 3, 'Personal Injury and Mental Pain and Anguish' in R Lillich (ed), *The United Nations Compensation Commission*, (1995), 404; and UN, 'Reports and Recommendations made by the Panel of Commissioners concerning Part One of the Second Instalment of Claims for Serious Personal Injury or Death (Category 'B' Claims)', S/AC26/1994/4, 15 December 1994, 10, para 17. See Gardam and Jarvis (n 4 above), 87–92.

[83] SC Res 1325, para 8. See 'Women and Peace and Security', Report of the Secretary General, 25 September 2008, UN Doc S/2008/622.

B. International Committee of the Red Cross and Red Crescent

The protection of women has always been part of the remit of the ICRC. This has now been extended to cover gender and PMSCs with the finalization of the Montreux Document. However, until the late twentieth century, women were often subsumed within the general category of civilian populations, or the sub-category of 'women and children'. However, the organization has from time to time addressed the specific concerns of women; for example, during the Second World War it raised awareness of the needs of female prisoners of war, and this was then reflected in Geneva III Convention.[84] It was instrumental in garnering recognition that rape during the Yugoslav conflicts constituted 'wilfully causing great suffering or serious injury to body and health' being a grave breach under the 1949 Geneva Conventions,[85] and the gradual acknowledgement of sexual violence against women.[86] The ICRC stressed the need to enforce international humanitarian law provisions, the reaffirmation that rape conducted in armed conflict was a war crime, and the need to specially train investigators and prosecutors.

In 1995, the ICRC contributed to the Fourth World Conference on Women, with the Beijing Platform for Action Critical Area E: Women and Armed Conflict recognizing that systematic rape was being used 'as a tactic of war and terrorism'.[87] Its 2001 Women Facing War report targeted specific areas of concerns for female civilians, including safety (covering personal safety, sexual violence, freedom from arbitrary displacement, and freedom of movement), and legal issues (personal documentation, access to effective remedy). This report formed the basis of subsequent documents detailing legal developments concerning international humanitarian law obligations and enforcement, and best practice in these areas including violence against women.[88] Going forward, the ICRC projected the need to reinforce the role of women in peacekeeping and stability operations, and target amendments to military manuals and military training.[89] For example, the US Uniform Code of Military Justice (UCMJ) defines sexual assault committed by DOD civilians and contractors accompanying armed forces in contingency operations as a criminal offence punishable by court martial.[90] The effectiveness of the application of these provisions and their extension to non-US companies has been

---

[84] ICRC, *Women and War* (1995).
[85] ICRC, Update on Aide, memoire of 3 December 1992. See also Final Declaration of the International Conference for the Protection of War Victims, para 13, in 296 ICCR (1993) 337.
[86] Res 2B, Final Declaration of the International Conference for the Protection of War Crimes, in 310 ICCR (1996) 63.
[87] Para 135, Beijing Platform for Action 1995.
[88] Lindsey-Curtet et al, 'Addressing the Needs of Women Affected by Armed Conflict: An ICRC Guidance Document' (March 2004), Part 1.2.
[89] ICRC, International Humanitarian Law and Gender, Report Summary, International Expert Meeting, 'Gender Perspectives of International Humanitarian Law', 4–5 October 2007, Stockholm (2007).
[90] DoD Office of Inspector General (n 1 above), 2. The contracts are also covered by the US Military Extraterritorial Jurisdiction Act (MEJA), 35.

challenged.[91] These advances in respect of military and security operations generally form the background to the specific recommendations for PMSCs contained in the Montreux Document, discussed below, adopted through the efforts of the ICRC.

C. Mainstreaming Women's Issues within the United Nations

The slow response to women's issues, particularly violence against women by the ICRC was likewise reflected within the United Nations. However, when it did gradually respond the developments have largely been felt in the field of human rights, international criminal law and UN organizational reform. The Declaration on the Protection of Women and Children in Emergency and Armed Conflict adopted by the General Assembly in 1974 did not explicitly refer to sexual violence during armed conflict, nor did the Convention on the Elimination of All Forms of Discrimination against Women (CEDAW) adopted five years later. However, CEDAW does require states parties to take appropriate measures to eliminate discrimination against women by any person, organization, or enterprise.[92]

As with the ICRC, the UN response coincided with the outrage engendered by the sexual violence evidenced during the Yugoslav and Rwandan conflicts. The notion of violence against women as a violation of human rights was finally reflected in the general recommendation on 'Violence against Women' adopted by the Committee monitoring CEDAW in 1992. The UN Declaration on the Elimination of Violence against Women adopted the following year which requires states to 'exercise due diligence to prevent, investigate and, in accordance with national legislation, punish acts of violence against women' whether perpetrated by the state or private persons.[93] This declaration recognizes that women are especially vulnerable to violence during armed conflict. Also in 1993, the Vienna Declaration and Programme of Action stated that the violation of the human rights of women during armed conflict 'including murder, systematic rape, sexual slavery, and forced pregnancy, require a particularly effective response'.[94]

As mentioned above, the Platform of Action adopted by the Fourth World Conference on Women in Beijing in 1995 also address this issue. The Beijing Declaration also reiterated the obligation on states to exercise due diligence in preventing, investigating, and prosecuting sexual violence against women by non-state actors.[95] From this initiative arose Resolution 1325, adopted by the Security Council on 31 October 2000, which continues to guide the work of the UN and its member states in this area. Article 11 of Resolution 1325 'emphasizes the

---

[91] Schulz and Yeung (n 3 above), 12; and C McGreal, 'Rape Case to Force US Defence Firms into the Open', *The Guardian* (15 October 2009).
[92] GA Res 34/180 of 18 December 1979, in force 3 September 1981, 34 UN GAOR Supp (no 46), 193, UN Doc A/34/46, 1249 UNTS 13, esp Art 2.
[93] GA Res 48/104, 20 December 1993, Art 4(c).
[94] Art 38 of the Vienna Declaration and Programme of Action, adopted by World Conference on Human Rights on 25 June 1993, UN Doc A/CONF157/23.
[95] UN Doc E/CN4/1995/42, para 72.

responsibility of all States to put an end to impunity and to prosecute those responsible for genocide, crimes against humanity, and war crimes including those relating to sexual and other violence against women and girls, and in this regard *stresses* the need to exclude these crimes, where feasible from amnesty agreements'.

These developments need to be understood within the broader United Nations' movement for mainstreaming issues related to women following the Beijing Conference, including peacekeeping and building operations.[96] Most UN organs, its agencies, and increasingly member states are reporting their progress in the implementation of Resolution 1325. Furthermore, the Security-General delivered the In-depth Study on all forms of Violence against Women in 2006 which enumerated several areas in need of reform including:

- 'surveillance of sexual violence in conflict and post conflict situations, with due attention to ethical and safety considerations, is needed urgently in order to establish more effective prevention and remedial services';[97]
- comprehensive services for victims of sexual violence;[98]
- the need to bridge the gap between international and national laws especially in respect of 'protect[ing] women in conflict, post-conflict and refugee and internally displaced persons settings' to enable victims of violence to seek redress and relax asylum requirements for such persons.[99]

V. Recent Recommendations Covering PMSCs

In her 2001 report on violence against women perpetrated or condoned by states during armed conflict, UN Special Rapporteur Radhika Coomaraswamy made special mention of the 'particular difficulties in enforcing international standards with regard to non-State actors' and called on additional pressure to be placed on them to comply with international humanitarian law.[100] Recent international initiatives (like the Montreux Document on Pertinent International Legal Obligations for States Related to PMSCS in Armed Conflict, and OSCE-UN Instraw Toolkit on Gender and PMSCs) and national reviews and recommendations (eg the US DoD Inspector General audits) in response to growing awareness of the lack of regulation covering PMSCs, particularly in their dealings with women,

---

[96] See the Windhoek Declaration and the Namibia Plan of Action on Mainstreaming Gender Perspective in Multidimensional Peace Support Operations, Windhoek, Namibia, 31 May 2000, UN Doc A/55/138, Annex I; C Bunch, 'Women and Gender' in TG Weiss and S Daws, *The Oxford Handbook on the United Nations* (2007) 496, 501; UN-STRAW, *Securing Equality: Engendering Peace: A Guide to Policy and Planning on Women, Peace and Security*, UN SCR 1325 (2006); and NGO Working Group on Women, Peace and Security, *From the Local to the Global: Making Peace Work for Women* (2006), Ch 2.
[97] In-depth Study (n 14 above), para 227.
[98] Ibid, para 334.
[99] Ibid, para 382.
[100] UN Doc E/CN4/2001/73, para 47.

have emphasized four areas requiring urgent action: vetting personnel, education and ongoing training of personnel, reporting, and investigation and accountability.

First, the Montreux Document recommends that past conduct of the PMSCs or their personnel, including reliable attested record of sexual offences, become criteria for awarding of contracts.[101] Such a requirement is imperative because regulation of PMSCs remains primarily confined to self-regulation and contractual obligations.[102] The UN-Instraw Report simply requires that PMSCs improve 'vetting standards... to ensure [that] those who have committed human rights violations or gender-based violent crimes be excluded'.[103]

Secondly, most recent initiatives have placed primary emphasis on the need to strengthen recruitment, deployment, and ongoing gender-awareness training. Gender has been defined by the ICRC as 'culturally expected behaviour of men and women based on roles, attitudes and values ascribed to them on the basis of their "sex"'.[104] The Montreux Document requires contracting, host, and territorial states, when selecting and authorising PMSCs, to take into account that their personnel are:

sufficiently trained, both prior to deployment and on an ongoing basis, to respect relevant national, international humanitarian and human rights law; and to establish goals to facilitate uniformity and standardisation of training requirements. Training could include general and task- and context-specific topics, preparing personnel for performance under the specific contract and in the specific environment, such as... gender.[105]

The UN-Instraw Review makes a similar recommendation. The 2010 DoD Inspector General audit in the United States found that, of the ten DoD contractors reviewed, eight 'did not have policies or training requirements for sexual assault prevention and response'.[106] In its recommendation, the DoD has recommended that contractual requirements be designed to ensure that civil contractors 'are aware of the DOD definition of sexual assault and require contractors to report sexual assault to Military law enforcement'.[107] To this end, the framework established under Resolution 1325 should be extended to encompass PMSCs; and the EU, Council of Europe, and countries like Denmark, the United Kingdom, and Sweden, which are viewed as examples of good practice, should tailor their existing programmes and serve as examples for other states.[108]

Thirdly, PMSCs should report gender-based violence to the appropriate civilian and military authorities. The UN-Instraw Review recommended that states and

---

[101] The Montreux Document on Pertinent International Legal Obligations and Good Practices for States Related to Private Military and Security Companies in Armed Conflict, 17 September 2008, UN Doc S/2008/636, 14, 20, 25. See also UN Doc E/CN4/2001/73, 13, 19, 24.
[102] Schulz and Yeung (n 3 above), 9.
[103] Ibid, 17.
[104] Lindsey-Curtet et al (n 88 above), 7.
[105] Montreux Document (n 107 above), paras 128, 130.
[106] DoD Office of Inspector General (n 1 above), i.
[107] Ibid.
[108] Cf J Valenius, 'Gender Mainstreaming in EDSP Missions', *Chaillot Paper* no 101 (May 2007).

PMSCs develop national and international standards for the monitoring and reporting of sexual and physical violence perpetrated by PMSCs particularly in post-conflict situations.[109] The DoD Inspector General audit found that only one of the ten respondents had an external reporting procedure to military law enforcement, with three respondents explicitly indicating they did not have such a procedure.[110] The Sexual Assault Advisory Council established by the DoD is presently considering how reporting requirements currently in place for military personnel can be extended to encompass DoD civilians and contractors.[111]

Fourthly, recent initiatives in this field have emphasized the need for accountability of PMSCs. Special Rapporteur Coomaraswamy ended her 2001 report by recommending states ensure that perpetrators of war crimes and human rights abuses are prosecuted and victims are eligible for compensation.[112] The Montreux Document reaffirms that this obligation to prosecute covers contracting, home, and territorial states.[113] As noted previously, there has been a push to extend the application of codes of military justice in respect of sexual assault to cover civilian contractors. For example, the US Uniform Code of Military Justice already covers acts perpetrated by DoD civilians and contractors accompanying US forces in contingency operations.

VI. Conclusion

It is clear that if current trends persist, security and related operations previously undertaken by armed forces and police will predominantly be provided by private contractors. For civilian populations, particularly women, who are dependent on effective security in post-conflict and transition situations for their physical and psychological well-being, the effective regulation and accountability of PMSCs are imperative. For this reason, recent reviews of the activities of PMSCs and existing regulatory regimes have emphasized the need for gender-awareness education, and recruiting and retention of female employees.[114]

Feminist scholars and women's NGOs have done much to raise awareness concerning women's issues cross the board and have pushed for law reform within the United Nations and its member states in the last half century. Nowhere has this work been felt more clearly than in challenging and changing understandings of the impact of sexual violence (particularly during armed conflict and civil unrest) on women. This work focuses on breaking down the divide between private/unregulated and public/regulated. Consequently, the gains made in recent years should

---

[109] Schulz and Yeung (n 3 above), 17.
[110] DoD Office of Inspector General (n 1 above), 8, Table 1.
[111] DoD Office of Inspector General (n 1 above), 14.
[112] UN Doc E/CN4/2001/73, para 135.
[113] UN Doc S/2008/636, paras 6, 12, 17, 21.
[114] Schulz and Yeung (n 3 at p.4.

not be eroded by stealth through the privatization of war and through its contracting out to PMSCs. It is incumbent on states that PMSCs and their personnel come within the ambit of the relevant legal standards for their own protection, for the protection of civilians with whom they interact, and to reinforce the effectiveness of their operations.

15

Private Military and Security Companies and the EU's Crisis Management: Perspectives under Human Rights and International Humanitarian Law

Valentina Falco

I. Introduction

Concerns about compliance by private military and security companies (PMSCs) with human rights law (HRL) and international humanitarian law (IHL) are among the main driving forces behind the growing calls for regulation of private contractors' activity in the field of crisis management.

The European Union (EU), in its recently developed capacity as a security actor, is not immune to these calls. Indeed, as is well known, the definitive integration of the so-called 'Petersberg Tasks'[1] into the Union's constituent instrument[2] provided an unequivocal legal basis for the EU's direct involvement in a wide range of civilian and military operations,[3] thereby laying the ground for the resort to private

---

[1] The 'Petersberg Tasks' were first set out in the 'Petersberg Declaration' adopted at the Ministerial Council of the Western European Union (WEU) in June 1992. They included 'humanitarian and rescue tasks, peacekeeping tasks and tasks of combat forces in crisis management, including peacemaking': see Petersberg Declaration of the Western European Union Council of Ministers, para II.4, 19 June 1992, <http://www.weu.int/documents/920619peten.pdf>, accessed on 20 August 2010.

[2] Some authors point to the adoption of the Treaty of Amsterdam in 1997 as 'the moment when the EU became a military actor', since it is under that Treaty the 'Petersberg Tasks' were actually integrated into the Union's constituent instrument: see A Treacher, 'From Civilian Power to Military Actor: The EU's resistable transformation' (2004) 9 European Foreign Affairs Review 59. However, it is only with the removal of any reference to the WEU in Art 17 of the Treaty of Nice that the EU itself assumed direct responsibility for the conduct of the Tasks, rather than leaving that to another organization: see RA Wessel, 'The EU as a Black Widow: Devouring the WEU to Give Birth to a European Security and Defence Policy' in V Kronenberger (ed), *The European Union and the International Legal Order: Discord or Harmony?* (2001), 405, 423.

[3] Art 43 of the Treaty of Lisbon has further extended the 'Petersberg Tasks' so as to include joint disarmament operations, military advice and assistance tasks, conflict prevention and post-conflict stabilization, see Treaty of Lisbon amending the Treaty on European Union and the Treaty establishing the European Community, signed in Lisbon on 13 December 2007, entered into force on 1 December 1 2009, OJ 2007 C 306/1. In the present chapter, the numbering of Treaty on European

contractors within the framework of the Union's Common Security and Defence Policy (CSDP).[4]

However, with regard to the employment of PMSCs by the EU, the recent debate on possible legislative and regulatory solutions has (with a few notable exceptions)[5] mainly focused on aspects related to trade in military equipment, export and brokering of arms, and defence procurement.[6] A comprehensive approach—taking into account and preliminarily assessing the sources of HRL and IHL obligations under EU law, as well as the specific legal and operational framework in which private contractors provide their services—is key to developing satisfactory regulatory options at EU level.

This chapter thus aims to verify whether and to what extent HRL and IHL rules and principles have been incorporated into the EU's legal order, with a particular focus on the CSDP. In view of that aim, the chapter surveys existing and potential sources of obligations under HRL and IHL for the EU personnel engaged in civilian missions and military operations within the context of the CSDP. Finally, by way of conclusion, it endeavours to assess which of these sources may be binding on PMSCs contracted in the framework of the CSDP, and to identify viable approaches in order to ensure more effective compliance by such companies with HRL and IHL.

II. The Role of Human Rights in the EU Legal Order: An Overview[7]

As is well known, as an international organization the EU is bound by international law—including international HRL—either by way of general international law or by way of treaty law.

Union articles as amended by the Treaty of Lisbon refers to the consolidated version of the TEU published by the Council of the EU, see Consolidated Version of the Treaty on European Union, OJ 2010 C 83/13 (hereinafter TEU Lisbon).

[4] Although the present chapter retains the denomination 'Common Security and Defence Policy' as used in the Treaty of Lisbon, sporadic references will also be made to the former denomination ('European Security and Defence Policy') and its abbreviation (ESDP) when dealing with the pre-Lisbon legal and operational framework.

[5] See, esp, GR den Dekker, *The Regulatory Context of Private Military and Security Services at the European Union Level*, Priv-War Project National Report Series no 4/09 (2009), 2–3, 18–24, <http://priv-war.eu/wordpress/wp-content/uploads/2009/05/nr-04-09-eu.pdf>, accessed on 7 September 2010; A Bailes and C Holmqvist, *The Increasing Role of Private Military and Security Company*, European Parliament Study (2007), 22 ff; C Holmqvist, *Private Security Companies: The Case for Regulation*, Stockholm International Peace Research Institute Policy Paper no 9 (2005), 57; ND White and S MacLeod, 'EU Operations and Private Militray Contractors: Issues of Corporate and Institutional Responsibility' (2008) 19 EJIL 965, 984–988.

[6] See, inter alia, J Hagmann and M Kartas, 'International Organisations and the Governance of Private Security' in A Bryden and M Caparini (eds), *Private Actors and Security Governance* (2006), 285, 292–3; E Krahmann, 'Regulating Military and Security Services in the European Union', ibid, 189–212.

[7] For a more comprehensive analysis of the issues touched upon in this section, see Ch 3 by Francioni and Lenzerini, and Ch 4 by Kalnina and Zeltins in this volume. See also references to HRL in section IV of the present chapter.

A. HRL Obligations under General International Law

It is commonly accepted that international organizations are subject to the rules of general international law.[8] With specific reference to the EU's legal framework, the European Court of Justice (ECJ) has reaffirmed on several occasions the applicability of customary international law to the European Community (EC),[9] recognizing its binding force as a source of EU law. In the *Racke* case, for instance, the Court found that 'The European Community must respect international law in the exercise of its powers. It is therefore required to comply with the rules of customary international law...'.[10]

The ECJ judgment in the *Intertanko* case has further confirmed the Court's well-established jurisprudence on the matter, by stating that 'the powers of the Community must be exercised in observance of international law, including provisions of international agreements in so far as they *codify customary rules of general international law*'.[11] As the customary[12] (and even jus cogens)[13] status of a number of core human rights is uncontroversial, the relevant HRL treaty provisions would appear to fall within the scope of the Court's dictum.

Although mainly referring to the EC, on the whole the ECJ's case law on the matter 'appears to be based on the idea that customary international law...is directly applicable in the *EU* legal order'[14] (and thus also binding on the EU when acting under the framework of the ESDP/CSDP). The ECJ's judgment in the *Pupino* case seems to corroborate this stance. In this judgment, the Court argued that 'in accordance with Article 6(2) EU, the *Union* must respect fundamental rights...as general principles of law',[15] thus appearing to suggest that, although

---

[8] See eg *Interpretation of the Agreement of 25 March 1951 between the WHO and Egypt*, Advisory Opinion, ICJ Reports (1980), 73, 89–90, para 37 ('International organizations are subjects of international law and, as such, are bound by any obligations incumbent upon them under general rules of international law ...').

[9] See, inter alia, Joined Cases 21–4/72, *International Fruit Company v Produktschap voor Groenten en Fruit* [1972] ECR 1219; Case C-286/90, *Anklagemyndigheden v Peter Michael Poulsen and Diva Navigation Corp* [1992] ECR I-6019; Case T-115/94, *Opel Austria v Council* [1997] ECR II-39; Case C–162/96, *Racke v Hauptzollant Mainz* [1998] ECR I–3655 (hereinafter *Racke* case).

[10] *Racke* case, para 45.

[11] Case C-308/06, *The Queen v Secr'y of State for Transp* [2008] ECR, para 51 (hereinafter *Intertanko* case) (emphasis added).

[12] Based on the jurisprudence of the International Court of Justice, Ahmed and de Jésus Butler mention, among such 'core rights', the right to self-determination; the prohibition of genocide; freedom from racial discrimination including apartheid and the prohibition of slavery; freedom from arbitrary detention and the right to physical integrity; and protection against denial of justice: T Ahmed and I de Jésus Butler, 'The European Union and Human Rights: An International Law Perspective' (2006) 17 EJIL 771, 779.

[13] Eg the right to life; the prohibition on torture; the right to equality before the law and non-discrimination; the prohibition of slavery: ibid, 779–80.

[14] See A Rosas, 'The European Court of Justice and Public International Law' in J Wouters, A Nollkaemper, and E de Wet (eds), *The Europeanisation of International Law* (2008), 71, 80. Rosas' observation is particularly pertinent now that the Treaty of Lisbon has removed the separation between the EU and the EC by subsuming the latter entity within the former.

[15] Case C-105/03, *Criminal Proceedings against Maria Pupino* [2005] ECR I-5285, para 58 (emphasis added). See also Case 4/73, *Nold v Commission* [1974] ECR 491 (hereinafter *Nold* case);

former Article 6(2) only referred to 'fundamental rights as general principles of *Community* law', such rights are equally binding on the *Union*.[16] Therefore, although the judgment concerned a Third Pillar case, some commentators have inferred from it the EU's obligation to also respect these rights in its non-EC activities, including the Common Foreign and Security Policy (CFSP) and the ESDP/CSDP.[17] This interpretation appears to be confirmed by subsequent practice in the Treaty of Lisbon, Article 6(3) which currently provides that 'fundamental rights, as guaranteed by the European Convention for the Protection of Human Rights and Fundamental Freedoms and as they result from the constitutional traditions common to the Member States, shall constitute general principles of the *Union*'s law'.[18]

B. HRL Treaty Obligations

Besides general international law, the EU is, in principle, also bound by international HRL treaties to which it is a party. On 30 March 2007 the EC signed its first human rights treaty (the United Nations Convention on the Rights of Persons with Disabilities).[19] As far as the EU is concerned, it should be recalled that while Article 37 TEU Lisbon (formerly Article 24 TEU) endows the Union with the necessary competence to conclude international agreements, accession to international treaties (including HRL-related ones) by the EU also depends on the rules and mechanisms provided for in the treaties themselves.[20] The European Convention on Human Rights (ECHR) is a prime example in this respect: Article 6(2) of the Treaty of Lisbon envisages the EU's accession to the ECHR[21]—at the same time,

---

Opinion 2/94, 1996 ECR I-01759, para 33; Case C-94/00, *Roquette Frères SA v Directeur general de la concurrence, de la consommation et de la repression des fraudes, and Commission of the European Communities* [2002] ECR I-09011, para 23; *Kadi* case, para 304 (reaffirming that the protection of fundamental rights forms 'part of the very foundations of the Community legal order'). For a valuable, up-to-date overview of the ECJ jurisprudence in the field of human rights, see J Callewaert, '"Unionisation" and "Conventionisation" of Fundamental Rights in Europe: The Interplay between Union and Convention Law and its Impact on the Domestic Legal Systems of the Member States' in J Wouters, A Nollkaemper, and E de Wet (eds), *The Europeanisation of International Law* (2008), 109, 110–16; E Defeis, 'Human rights and the European Court of Justice: An Appraisal' (2008) 31 Fordham Int'l LJ 1104, 1104–17.

[16] In this sense, see F Naert, 'Accountability for Violations of HRL by EU Forces' in S Blockmans (ed), *The European Union and Crisis Management: Policy and Legal Aspects* (2008), 375, 388 (emphasis added). See also Callewaert (n 15 above), 111 (arguing that 'the general principles of Community law ... form the legal basis upon which, according to Article 6(2) TEU, compliance with fundamental rights is to be ensured under Union law').

[17] See Naert (n 16 above), 388 (emphasis added).

[18] Emphasis added.

[19] United Nations Convention on the Rights of Persons with Disabilities, UN Doc A/61/611, adopted on 13 December 2006, entered into force on 3 May 2008, 46 (2007) ILM 443.

[20] N Tsagourias, 'EU Peacekeeping Operations: Legal and Theoretical Issues' in M Trybus and ND White (eds), *European Security Law* (2007) 102, 117–18.

[21] European Convention for the Protection of Human Rights and Fundamental Freedoms, 4 November 1950, 213 UNTS 220 (hereinafter ECHR).

Article 17(1) of Protocol 14 to the ECHR[22] provides that: 'The European Union may accede to this Convention.' This may possibly lead to direct responsibility of the EU under the ECHR system for violations of the Convention by PMSC personnel when employed by the EU.[23]

III. Ensuring Compliance with HRL in the CSDP

Despite the clear HRL obligations binding on the EU, traditionally, the main focus of the Union's human rights policy has been on the promotion of human rights in third countries,[24] rather than on the EU's own compliance with international human rights standards. Even the seven EU human rights-related Guidelines[25] adopted by the Council since 1998 are generally concerned with respect for human rights in non-EU Member States, placing on EU bodies and agents mere reporting obligations, at most.[26]

In any event, in recent years the EU seems to have become increasingly aware of the importance of ensuring compliance with human rights standards in its own conduct. This awareness has resulted in major efforts to integrate human rights into the legal framework for the EU's crisis-management operations conducted within the institutional and operational context of the ESDP/CSDP.[27]

---

[22] Protocol no 14 to the European Convention on Human Rights and Fundamental Freedoms, amending the Control System of the Convention, Art 17 (May 13, 2004), 194 ETS 247 (providing that the EU may accede to the Convention) (entered into force on 1 June 2010).

[23] Cf Hagmann and Kartas (n 6 above), 293.

[24] See, inter alia, Council Conclusions on Human Rights and Democratisation in Third Countries, Brussels, 12 December 2005, <http://www.consilium.europa.eu/uedocs/cmsUpload/st14960.en05.pdf>, accessed on 20 August 2010; EU Guidelines on Human Rights Dialogues with Third Countries (2009 update), <http://www.consilium.europa.eu/uedocs/cmsUpload/16526.en08.pdf>, accessed on 20 August 2010; Guidelines to EU Policy Towards Third Countries on Torture and Other Cruel, Inhuman or Degrading Treatment or Punishment (hereinafter EU Guidelines on Torture), <http://www.consilium.europa.eu/uedocs/cmsUpload/8590.en08.pdf>, <http://www.consilium.europa.eu/uedocs/cmsUpload/8590.en08.pdf>, accessed on 20 August 2010.

[25] EU Guidelines on Death Penalty (2008 update), <http://www.consilium.europa.eu/uedocs/cmsUpload/10015.en08.pdf>, accessed on 20 August 2010; EU Guidelines on Torture; EU Guidelines on Human Rights Dialogues with Third Countries; EU Guidelines on Children and Armed Conflict (2008 update), Council Doc no 10019/08, 5 June 2008; European Union Guidelines on Human Rights Defenders, <http://www.consilium.europa.eu/uedocs/cmsUpload/16332-re01.en08.pdf>, accessed on 20 August 2010; EU Guidelines for the Promotion and Protection of the Rights of the Child, <http://www.consilium.europa.eu/uedocs/cmsUpload/16031.07.pdf>, accessed on 20 August 2010; EU Guidelines on Violence against Women and Girls and Combating all Forms of Discrimination against Them, Council Doc no 16173/08, 24 November 2008, <http://www.consilium.europa.eu/uedocs/cmsUpload/16173cor.en08.pdf>, accessed on 20 August 2010.

[26] See eg European Union Guidelines on Human Rights Defenders, paras 8–10; EU Guidelines on Torture, 4 ('In their periodic reports, the EU Heads of Mission will include an analysis of the occurrence of torture and ill-treatment and the measures taken to combat it. The Heads of Mission will also provide periodic evaluation of the effect and impact of the EU actions'); EU Guidelines for the Promotion and Protection of the Rights of the Child, 23 ('In countries covered by country-strategies on violence against children, EU Heads of mission should include this subject in their regular human rights reporting and should also report ad hoc on relevant developments, as appropriate').

[27] See M Koskenniemi, 'Foreword' in T Pajuste, *Mainstreaming Human Rights in the Context of the European Security and Defence Policy*, The Erik Castrén Institute Research Reports, no 23/2008

In June 2001, in its conclusions on the EU's role in promoting human rights and democratization in third countries, the Council reaffirmed the EU's commitment to '"mainstreaming" human rights and democratisation in EU policies and actions',[28] further adding that 'the process of "mainstreaming" human rights... objectives into *all* aspects of EU external and internal policies should be intensified'.[29] As Pajuste notes,[30] it is in the 2002 Annual Human Rights Report that 'mainstreaming' was defined for the first time in the EU system as 'the process of integrating human rights (respect for universal and indivisible human rights, fundamental freedoms and the rule of law) into all aspects of policy decision-making and implementation'.[31]

The Council also stressed the need to 'enhance consistency and coherence of the human rights dimension in CFSP political dialogues and other actions, including in the field of conflict prevention and crisis management'.[32] Since then, the Council has increasingly and consistently reaffirmed in its conclusions 'the importance of the systematic consideration of human rights, gender and children affected by armed conflict in the planning and conduct of ESDP missions and operations, including their mandates and staffing, and in the subsequent lessons learned process'.[33]

Nowadays, human rights standards, including those related to children in armed conflict and to gender issues,[34] are taken into account and systematically included in the planning, conduct, and evaluation of all ESDP/CSDP operations and missions.[35] With specific regard to training, the recent Draft Comprehensive Annual Report on ESDP and ESDP-related Training (CART) 2010 is a breakthrough in clarifying that 'Training needs of *contracted personnel* recruited into CSDP Missions should be also addressed in an appropriate manner', including with respect human rights and gender aspects.[36] The report further points out that such

(2008), i (noting that 'The Union has embarked upon a declared policy of integrating human rights in its various activities, including its security and defence operations').

[28] Council Conclusions on the European Union's Role in Promoting Human Rights and Democratisation in Third Countries, 25 June 2001, para 3. The same commitment was reiterated in the Annual Report on Human Rights 2001, 10, <http://www.consilium.europa.eu/uedocs/cmsUpload/HR2001EN.pdf>, accessed on 20 August 2010.

[29] Ibid, para 12 (emphasis added).

[30] See Pajuste (n 27 above), 34.

[31] Council of the European Union, Annual Report on Human Rights 2002, 19, <http://www.consilium.europa.eu/uedocs/cmsUpload/HR2002EN.pdf>, accessed on 20 August 2010.

[32] Ibid, para 6 (emphasis added).

[33] Council Conclusions on ESDP, Doc no 10087/09, Brussels, 18 May 2009, paras 28–9; Council Presidency Report on ESDP, Doc no 10748/09, Brussels, 15 June 2009, para 88.

[34] The present chapter will only briefly touch upon ESDP/CSDP instruments on gender issues and children in armed conflict. These topics are specifically dealt with in Ch 13 by Bakker and Greijer and Ch 14 by Vrdoljak in this volume.

[35] EU Annual Report on Human Rights 2008, endorsed by the Council of the European Union on 27 November 2008, Doc no 14146/2/08, 5, 11, <http://www.consilium.europa.eu/uedocs/cmsUpload/st14146-re02.en08.pdf>, accessed on 20 August 2010. Cf H Hazelzet, 'Human Rights Aspects of EU Crisis Management Operations: From Nuisance to Necessity' *Int'l Peacekeeping* 13 (2006) 564, 570 ('References to human rights are by now included in most of the key documents').

[36] Draft Comprehensive Annual Report on ESDP and ESDP-related Training (CART) 2010 (hereinafter Draft CART 2010), Doc no 9472/10, para 18. The Draft CART 2010 was agreed by

areas 'may also apply to the military training domain as appropriate':[37] therefore, the recommendation would also appear to have important implications for private military contractors that may be employed by the EU.

Reportedly, clear human rights obligations for the EU-led troops are laid down in the concepts of operations (CONOPS), operation plans (OPLANs) and rules of engagement (ROEs).[38] A major obstacle to a comprehensive analysis of these instructions lies in the fact that they are not in the public domain. However, declassified excerpts of certain mission-specific planning documents[39] seem to confirm, prima facie, that the EU's operational planning and rules of engagement take into account internationally recognized standards of human rights law,[40] thus complying with the Council's requirement in this respect.[41]

Specific obligations for the EU troops to abide by HRL may legitimately be expected to be found in the instruments adopted by the Council of the EU in order to lay down the legal status of Union-led military operations. However, no reference to possible human rights obligations of the EU-led troops and contracted personnel has thus far been included in the instruments providing the legal basis for the ESDP/CSDP operations and missions.[42]

The same applies to the Status of Forces Agreements (SOFAs) and Status of Mission Agreements (SOMAs) concluded by the EU. This gap is rather unfortunate, as these instruments determine the terms and conditions of the presence of the EU forces in the host/transit states, defining their status, activities, privileges, and immunities.[43] A possible, partial exception may be found in a standard clause included in several agreements between the EU and host states, which stipulates that EU personnel 'shall respect the laws and regulations of the Host State and shall

---

the Political and Security Committee (PSC) at its meeting on 4 June 2010, see 'I/A' Item Note from the PSC to the Permanent Representatives' Committee/Council, Doc no 10713/10, 4 June 2010.

[37] Draft CART 2010, ibid, para 18.

[38] See F Naert, 'An EU Perspective' in International Institute of Humanitarian Law (ed), *International Peace Operations and International Humanitarian Law* (2008), 61, 62.

[39] See Doc no 11359/07 Restreint UE of 29 June 2007 on Mainstreaming Human Rights and Gender into European Security and Defence Policy: Compilation of Relevant Documents, 11359/07 EXT 1, 9 October 2007.

[40] See Naert (n 38 above), 62 ('In practice...[the EU's] operational planning and rules of engagement take into account internationally recognised standards of human rights law').

[41] Council of the European Union, Mainstreaming of Human Rights into ESDP, Doc 11936/4/06 REV 4, 3 ('human rights elements should be incorporated into the full range of planning documents for ESDP missions, including the Concept of Operations (CONOPS), the Operation Plan (OPLAN) and rules of engagement. These documents should incorporate elements related to both respect for human rights *by ESDP missions* and the way in which the mission should promote respect for human rights in the mission area') (emphasis added).

[42] A partial exception to this can be found in Art 12(2) of the joint action approving EU Navfor Somalia, providing that no one 'may be transferred to a third State unless the conditions for the transfer have been agreed with that third State in a manner consistent with relevant international law, notably international law on human rights': see Council Joint Action 2008/851/CFSP of 10 November 2008, OJ 2008 L 301/33.

[43] See, inter alia, A Sari, 'Status of Forces and Status of Mission Agreements under the ESDP: The EU's Evolving Practice' (2008) 19 EJIL 67 (providing an exhaustive analysis of the EU's Status of Forces Agreements).

refrain from any action or activity incompatible with the objectives of the operation'.[44] Similarly, the EU SOFA (concluded by the EU Member States in order to clarify the status of military and civilian personnel seconded to the EU) refers to 'the duty to abstain from any activity inconsistent with the spirit of this Agreement'.[45] While activities constituting a violation of HRL would arguably fall within the scope of the said clauses, such references still appear far too abstract to guide the EU forces on questions of practical application.

Furthermore, it should be noted that EU SOFAs and SOMAs do not apply to 'commercial contractors or personnel employed locally'.[46] Therefore, HRL obligations possibly laid down therein would not, in principle, be binding upon the employees of PMSCs.

Finally, with regard to the in-mission implementation of HRL standards, mention should be made of the inclusion of human rights focal points, gender advisors and experts on children affected by armed conflict[47] in most of the recent ESDP/CSDP operations and missions.

For instance, in the EUFOR Tchad/RCA operation focal points for human rights issues were appointed for each national contingent. Drawing on the information provided by the national focal points, monthly human rights reports were drafted by the EUFOR Tchad/RCA Legal Advisor at the Operations Headquarters. Furthermore, the Gender Adviser appointed to the Operations Headquarters conducted, inter alia, gender training and proposed a comprehensive structure for monitoring and reporting.[48] Undoubtedly, 'the integration of human rights,

---

[44] Eg Agreement between the European Union and the Republic of Chad on the status of the European Union-led forces in the Republic of Chad, 6 March 2008, OJ 2008 L 83/40 (hereinafter EU–Chad SOFA); Agreement between the European Union and the Central African Republic on the status of the European Union-led forces in the Central African Republic, 16 April 2008, OJ 2008 L 136/46, Art 2(1) (hereinafter EU–CAR SOFA).

[45] Agreement between the Member States of the European Union concerning the status of military and civilian staff seconded to the institutions of the European Union, of the headquarters and forces which may be made available to the European Union in the context of the preparation and execution of the tasks referred to in Art 17(2) of the Treaty on European Union, including exercises, and of the military and civilian staff of the Member States put at the disposal of the European Union to act in this context, 17 November 2003 (hereinafter EU SOFA), OJ 2003 C 321/6, Art 3.

[46] Agreement between the European Union and Georgia on the status of the European Union Monitoring Mission in Georgia, OJ 2008 L310/31, Art 1(3)(c) (hereinafter EUMM Georgia SOMA). It is worth noting that the EU's practice with regard to the definition of the subjective scope of application of SOMAs and SOFAs has evolved over the years. Eg the Concordia SOFA of 2003 provided that it would not apply to 'personnel *locally hired, including* contractors' (Art 1(3)(h)) (emphasis added), thus potentially leaving some room for its application to *international* contractors. The formulation of the clause has been amended in more recent SOMAs and SOFAs, which have expressly excluded from their scope of application 'commercial contractors or personnel employed locally' (EUMM Georgia SOMA, Art 1(3)(c)), or, even more specifically, 'personnel employed locally *and* personnel employed by international commercial contractors' (EU–Chad and EU–CAR SOFAs, Art 1(3)(f); Agreement between the European Union and the Somali Republic on the status of the European Union-led naval force in the Somali Republic in the framework of the EU military operation Atalanta, 15 January 2009, OJ 2009 L10/29, Art 1(3)(g)) (emphasis added).

[47] EU Annual Report on Human Rights 2008, 11.

[48] Ibid.

gender and the protection of children in armed conflicts in the conduct of the operation... has been an important aspect of its work'.[49]

EULEX Kosovo has a Human Rights and Gender Unit, which not only ensures compliance of EULEX Kosovo policies and decisions with human rights and gender standards but also constitutes an entry point for all third parties' complaints related to alleged breaches of the code of conduct.[50] EUSEC RD Congo and EUPOL RD Congo share a gender advisor, as well as a Human Rights/Children and Armed Conflicts expert, and the Gender Adviser in EUPOL Afghanistan provides advice to the Afghan authorities on gender policy in the Afghan National Police.[51]

However, none of the advisory and reporting procedures mentioned above seems to involve PMSC personnel at any level.

IV. The Relevance of IHL to the CSDP

As recalled above,[52] the integration of the 'Petersberg Tasks' in the EU's constituent instrument has provided, since 2001, an explicit and unequivocal legal basis for the direct engagement of EU-led troops in military operations. According to the prevailing view, the fifth type of mission mentioned in Article 43(1) TEU Lisbon (formerly Article 17(2) of the Treaty of Nice), 'tasks of combat forces in crisis management, including peacemaking', should be interpreted as 'wide enough to cover large-scale military operations, including genuine warfare against a regular army'.[53]

Furthermore, whilst it is generally accepted that the CSDP will by no means lay down the foundations of an EU army responsible for the defence of the Member States,[54] it is undeniable that the EU is gradually adding military capabilities to its considerable economic power.[55] As the presence of armed military personnel

---

[49] Council of the EU, ESDP Presidency Report on ESDP, Doc 10748/09, Brussels, 15 June 2009, para 89.
[50] Ibid.
[51] Ibid.
[52] See Introduction to this volume.
[53] SG von Kielmansegg, 'The Meaning of Petersberg: Some considerations on the Legal Scope of ESDP Operations' (2007) 44 CML Rev 629, 648. See also R Gosalbo Bono, 'Some Reflections on the CFSP Legal Order' (2006) 43 CML Rev 337, 349, n 28 (arguing that 'it follows from the terms "including peacekeeping" in Art 17(2) TEU, that all types of military and civilian crisis management actions fall within the scope of the TEU'); and Naert (n 38 above), 61.
[54] P Koutrakos, *EU International Relations Law* (2006) 459; G-J van Hegelsom, 'The Relevance of IHL in the Conduct of the Petersberg Tasks' in 'The Impact of International Humanitarian Law on Current Security Trends: Proceedings of the Bruges Colloquium', 26–7 October 2001, (2002) 25 Collegium 109, 113. Art 42(1) TEU Lisbon explicitly points out that: 'The performance of these tasks shall be undertaken using capabilities provided by the Member States.'
[55] M Trybus, 'With or Without the EU Constitutional Treaty: Towards a Common Security and Defence Policy?' (2006) 31 Eur L Rev (2006) 145, 146; W. Wallace, 'Is there a European Approach to War?' in C Reed and D Ryall (eds), *The Price of Peace: Just War in the Twenty-first Century* (2007) 37, 50.

represents the preliminary and most basic condition for the applicability of IHL,[56] the relevance of this body of law to the conduct of the CSDP should not be underestimated.

The most prominent achievement of the ESDP/CSDP's 'strikingly dynamic development'[57] has been the deployment since 2003 of more than 10,000 military personnel, contributed by Member States but also partly by non-Member States, engaged in seven EU-led military operations:[58] Concordia[59] (the EU's first-ever military operation), in the former Yugoslav Republic of Macedonia (FYROM); Artemis[60] and EUFOR RD Congo,[61] in the Democratic Republic of Congo; EUFOR Althea,[62] in Bosnia-Herzegovina (still ongoing); EUFOR Tchad/RCA,[63] deployed in Eastern Chad and North Eastern Central African Republic until March 2009; and the recently launched EU NAVFOR and EUTM Somalia operations.[64]

---

[56] G-J van Hegelsom, 'International Humanitarian Law and Operations Conducted by the European Union' in G Beruto (ed), *International Humanitarian Law, Human Rights and Peace Operations* (2009) 107, 111.

[57] B Koopmans, *Developing the European Foreign Security and Defence Policy Without the Constitution?*, Studia Diplomatica 59 (2006) 129.

[58] Due to space constraints, an overall assessment of the factual background of each of the ESDP military operations cannot be provided here. For an up-to-date overview of the military missions conducted by the EU see the relevant documents and factsheets in the ESDP section of the Council of the EU website: <http://www.consilium.europa.eu/ESDP>, accessed on 20 August 2010. See also F Naert, 'ESDP in Practice: Increasingly Varied and Ambitious EU Security and Defence Operations' in M Trybus and ND White (eds) [2007] European Security Law 61; D Nickel and G Quille, 'In the Shadow of the Constitution: Common Foreign and Security Policy: European Security and Defence Policy Adapting to a Changing External Environment', (February 2007) Jean Monnet Working Paper, 13–19; N Tsagourias, 'EU Peacekeeping Operations: Legal and theoretical issues' in M Trybus and ND White (eds), *European Security Law* (2007), 102, 107–10.

[59] Council Joint Action no 2003/92/CFSP of 27 January 2003 on the European Union Military operation in the former Yugoslav Republic of Macedonia, OJ 2003 L 34/26.

[60] Council Joint Action no 2003/423/CFSP of 5 June 2003 on the European Union military operation in the Democratic Republic of Congo, OJ 2003 L 143/50.

[61] Council Joint Action 2006/319/CFSP of 27 April 2006 on the European Union military operation in support of the United Nations Mission in the Democratic Republic of Congo (MONUC) during the election process, OJ 2006 L 116/98.

[62] Council Joint Action 2004/570/CFSP of 12 July 2004 on the European Union military operation in Bosnia Herzegovina, 2004 OJ L25/10; Council Decision 2004/803/CFSP of 25 November 2004 on the launching of the European Union military operation in Bosnia and Herzegovina, OJ 2004 L 353/21.

[63] Council Decision 2008/101/CFSP of 28 January 2008 on the launching of the European Union military operation in the Republic of Chad and in the Central African Republic (Operation EUFOR Tchad/RCA), OJ 2008 L34/39.

[64] Council Joint Action 2008/851/CFSP of 10 November 2008 on a European Union military operation to contribute to the deterrence, prevention and repression of acts of piracy and armed robbery off the Somali coast, [2008] OJ L301/33; Council Decision 2008/918/CFSP of 8 December 2008 on the launch of a European Union military operation to contribute to the deterrence, prevention and repression of acts of piracy and armed robbery off the Somali coast (Atalanta), [2008] OJ L330/19; Council Decision 2010/197/CFSP of 31 March 2010 on the launch of a European union military mission to contribute to the training of Somali security forces (EUTM Somalia), OJ 2010 L 87/33.

Private Military and Security Companies and the EU's Crisis Management 309

At least three of these operations (ie Concordia, Althea, and EUFOR RD Congo) were conducted in post-conflict contexts[65] and no involvement of the EU-led forces in situations triggering the application of IHL has been reported.[66] Therefore, with respect to such operations, HRL can certainly be identified as the relevant legal regime primarily governing the conduct of the EU troops on the ground.

However, the possibility of a deterioration of the situation in theatre—and of a subsequent escalation of confrontations involving EU military personnel—cannot be ruled out. This is notably the case for those operations (such as Artemis and EUFOR TCHAD/RCA) deployed in volatile, hostile environments and authorized to take all necessary measures (including the use of armed force beyond self-defence) to fulfil their mandate. In light of the above, it appears all the more necessary to verify whether and to what extent the EU—in its capacity as a military actor—has integrated IHL into its legal order.

As is well known, a major legal obstacle in the actual applicability of *jus in bello* to the EU as such (ie as a military actor distinct from its troop-contributing Member States) lies in the fact that international and regional organizations are not—and cannot be—parties to the relevant treaty instruments of IHL, as (according to the prevailing interpretation) those instruments are only open for signature and ratification by states.[67]

Nevertheless, in its judgment in the *Intertanko* case mentioned above, the ECJ stated that the EC should abide by provisions of international agreements to which it is not a party 'in so far as they *codify customary rules of general international law*'.[68] Since the customary nature of a large part of the rules of IHL is now widely acknowledged,[69] the relevant treaties can certainly be assumed to fall within the scope of the Court's ruling.

Furthermore, as recalled above, it is generally accepted that the EU is subject to the rules of general international law.[70] Some authors have maintained that within the varied range of operations subsumed under the general definition of 'Petersberg Tasks', customary IHL would serve as a valuable normative constant, ensuring the

---

[65] This has led Trybus to qualify such missions as 'second-hand operations at the 'low end' of security, M Trybus, 'On the future of the common Security and Defence Policy envisaged in the EU Constitutional Treaty' (2005) 61 *Merkourios* 46, 52.

[66] See Naert (n 58 above): '(Almost) all ESDP operations so far did not include active participation in hostilities.'

[67] More precisely, pursuant to the standard accession clause included in the four Geneva Conventions (Arts 60, 59, 139, and 155 respectively), accession to the Conventions shall be open to 'any Power'. However, the term 'Power' has traditionally been interpreted as encompassing states only. See JS Pictet (ed), *Commentaire à la I Convention de Geneve* (1952–9), 459.

[68] *Intertanko* case, para 51.

[69] For specific EU practice in this respect, see Statement by Ms Anna Sotaniemi, Legal Adviser, Permanent Mission of Finland to the United Nations, on behalf of the European Union, UN 61st Session, VI Committee, Agenda Item 75: Status of the Protocols Additional to the Geneva Conventions of 1949 and relating to the protection of victims of armed conflicts, 18 October 2006, New York ('the Geneva Conventions enjoy universal acceptance, and most of the provisions of the Conventions and their 1977 additional protocols are generally recognised as customary law').

[70] See section II.A above.

uniform application of *jus in bello* to all contributed troops, irrespective of their nationality and of the objective and scope of each operation.[71]

However, it could be argued that customary rules—unwritten by definition as they are—may prove of little value in providing hands-on operational guidance to the troops on the ground. For the purpose of clarifying the EU's obligations under *jus in bello*, it may thus be useful to also look at the EU's internal legal order, to see whether and to what extent it regulates the conduct of the EU as a military actor.

A. The EU's Constituent Instrument: An IHL-Oriented Analysis

At first glance, the preliminary outcome of an IHL-oriented analysis of the EU treaty foundations may prove rather disappointing, as the TEU does not make any reference whatsoever to *jus in bello*, nor does it explicitly place any constraints on the behaviour of the troops engaged in CSDP military operations. Reportedly, during the negotiations of the Amsterdam Treaty, the ICRC attempted unsuccessfully to persuade the EU Member States to include references to IHL in the sections of the Treaty dealing with foreign and security policy. In particular, in 1996 it proposed to the Council Presidency that the Treaty provision on the common defence policy should read as follows: 'All decisions relating to a common defence policy and actions of the Union which have defence implications shall be in conformity with international humanitarian law and help ensure its respect.'[72] Nevertheless, despite the efforts made by the ICRC, Member States have not filled this major gap, which has also remained unaddressed in the Treaty of Lisbon.

In principle, the absence of any reference to IHL in the TEU does not rule out the possibility that some of its provisions may be interpreted as paving the way for the recognition of IHL principles as part of the EU's legal order. It is submitted that the Union's duty to respect *jus in bello* may be inferred, in the first place, from an expansive reading of the well-established (internal) obligation to respect human rights mentioned above,[73] further developed over the years by the ECJ and now enshrined in the EU's constituent instrument. Within this framework, due consideration should be paid to the concept of general principles of Union law, as well as to the influence of the judgments of the European Court of Human Rights (ECtHR) on the EU legal order, as they may both serve as a bridge for the integration of IHL principles the EU legal order.

Former Article 6(1) TEU already laid some legal ground for the incorporation of IHL into the EU legal order.[74] In fact, it would have been difficult to maintain that principles 'so fundamental to the respect of the human person'[75] such as those informing IHL should not be subsumed under the formula stated in the said

---

[71] T Ferraro, 'Le Droit International Humanitaire dans La Politique étrangère et de Sécurité Commune de l'Union Européenne' (2002) 84 IRRC 435, 460–1.
[72] Quoted in L Doswald-Beck, 'Implementation of International Humanitarian Law in Future Wars' in M Schmitt (ed), *The Law of Armed Conflict: Into the Next Millennium* (1998) 39, 61–2.
[73] See section II.
[74] In this sense, see Naert (n 58 above), 97; Tsagourias (n 20 above), 117.
[75] *Nuclear Weapons* case, para 78.

provision, and thus guide the EU and its multinational troops. This guidance would thus have been by virtue of both international and EU law.

The suggested IHL-oriented interpretation of former Article 6(1) TEU would also indirectly concern former preambular paragraph 3 TEU,[76] as well as former Article 11(1) TEU (which, as recalled above, includes the development and consolidation of 'democracy and the rule of law, and respect for human rights and fundamental freedoms' among the objectives of the CFSP).[77]

Subsequent practice appears to confirm the dynamic interpretation of former Article 6(1) TEU suggested above. Significantly, the Treaty of Lisbon expressly upholds (for the first time in the history of the EU)[78] 'respect for the principles of the United Nations Charter and *international law*'[79]—a formula that seems to encompass all branches of this *corpus juris*, thus including IHL. By the same token, the constitutionalization of 'respect for human dignity' among the founding values and guiding principles of the Union's external action on the international scene[80] echoes the very *raison d'être* of IHL.[81] Reference to international law is also made in the new Article 3(5) TEU Lisbon, which provides for the EU's commitment to 'contribute . . . to the strict observance and the development of international law' in its relations with the wider world, and in Article 21(2) TEU Lisbon, reaffirming that 'the Union shall define and pursue common policies and actions . . . in order to consolidate support for democracy, the rule of law, human rights and the principles of international law'.

Finally, basic principles of IHL (ie impartiality, neutrality, and non-discrimination) have now been integrated in the new Article 214(2) of the Treaty on the Functioning of the European Union,[82] which will govern the EU's humanitarian aid policy. According to this provision, the Union's operations in the field of humanitarian aid will have to comply with the principles mentioned above as

---

[76] Confirming the EU Member States' 'attachment to the principles of liberty, democracy and respect for human rights and fundamental freedoms and of the rule of law'.
[77] Cf Naert (n 38 above), 62: 'Articles 6 and 11 of the EU Treaty clearly entail international law obligations for the EU and its institutions, including with regard to human rights and arguably also international humanitarian law.'
[78] Neither the TEU nor the TEC contained any provision on the relationship between the EU/EC and international law: see PJ Kuijper, 'Customary International Law, Decisions of International Organizations and Other Techniques for Ensuring Respect for International Legal Rules in European Community Law' in J Wouters, A Nollkaemper, and E de Wet (eds), *The Europeanisation of International Law* (2008), 87, 87–8.
[79] Art 21(1) TEU Lisbon (emphasis added).
[80] Ibid.
[81] See eg *Prosecutor v Zejnil Delalić, Zdravko Mucić, Hazim Delić And Esad Landžo* ('*Čelebići Case*'), IT-96-21, Appeals Chamber (20 February 2001), para 143. 'The fundamental humanitarian principles which underlie international humanitarian law], the object of which is the respect for the dignity of the human person, developed as a result of centuries of warfare and had already become customary law at the time of the adoption of the Geneva Conventions because they reflect the most universally recognised humanitarian principles.'
[82] In the present chapter, the numbering of Treaty on the Functioning of the European Union (hereinafter TFEU) articles refers to the consolidated version of the TFEU published by the Council of the EU, see Consolidated Version of the Treaty on the Functioning of the European Union, OJ 2010 C 83/47.

well as, more generally, with 'the principles of international law'. The groundbreaking impact of such provisions on the relationship between IHL and the EU legal order is indisputable.

A further argument in support of the IHL-oriented reading of the TEU's human rights provisions suggested above is drawn from a soft law instrument, namely the EU Guidelines on Promoting Compliance with International Humanitarian Law.[83] Despite their non-binding character, the Guidelines represent the most complete and comprehensive EU act in the domain of IHL so far, providing a useful overview of the EU's approach to *jus in bello*.

After reaffirming that 'The European Union is founded on the principles of liberty, democracy, respect for fundamental rights and fundamental freedoms' (ie using precisely the same wording as former Article 6(1) TEU), paragraph 3 of the Guidelines acknowledges for the first time that 'the goal of promoting compliance with IHL' is included among those principles, thus providing a progressive interpretation of the EU foundations explicitly encompassing IHL.

Such an interpretation seems to corroborate at a general level the approach already taken by the Council in two regulations (ie in legally binding instruments)[84] of 1999[85] (now repealed). In particular, Recital 8 of the regulation's preamble stated that:

human rights within the meaning of this Regulation should be considered to encompass respect for international humanitarian law, also taking into account *the 1949 Geneva Conventions and the 1977 Additional Protocol thereto*, the 1951 Geneva Convention relating to the Status of Refugees, the 1948 Convention on the Prevention and Punishment of the Crime of Genocide and other acts of international treaty or customary law.[86]

Although for the specific purposes of the Guidelines (aimed as they are at promoting compliance with IHL among non-Member States),[87] 'measures taken by the EU and its Member States to ensure compliance with IHL in their own conduct, including by their own forces' are not covered by their provisions,[88] arguably it would be, to say the least, paradoxical if such an expansive, far-reaching reading of

---

[83] EU Guidelines on Promoting Compliance with International Humanitarian Law, OJ 2005 C 327/4 (hereinafter EU Guidelines on IHL). See also the recent technical update of the Guidelines, OJ 2009 C 303/06. For an in-depth analysis of the Guidelines see section IV.C below.
[84] See Art 249, recital 2 TEU: 'A regulation shall have general application. It shall be binding in its entirety and directly applicable in all Member States.'
[85] See Council Regulation 975/1999/EC of 29 April 1999 laying down the requirements for the implementation of development co-operation operations which contribute to the general objective of developing and consolidating democracy and the rule of law and to that of respecting human rights and fundamental freedoms, OJ 1999 L 120/1; Council Regulation 976/1999/EC of 29 April 1999 laying down the requirements for the implementation of Community operations, other than those of development cooperation, which, within the framework of Community cooperation policy, contribute to the general objective of developing and consolidating democracy and the rule of law and to that of respecting human rights and fundamental freedoms in third countries, OJ 1999 L 120/8.
[86] Emphasis added.
[87] See section IV.C below.
[88] EU Guidelines on IHL, para 2.

the EU foundational document were contradicted by the behaviour of the EU's own troops in the field.

As far as Article 6(3) TEU Lisbon (formerly Article 6(2) TEU) is concerned, its potential significance for purposes of mainstreaming IHL into the EU legal order appears twofold. First, although Article 6(3) TEU Lisbon mentions the ECHR but no other international human rights treaties, ECJ case law consistently refers to 'international treaties for the protection of human rights on which the Member States have collaborated or of which they are signatories' as sources of inspiration and guidance.[89] It could be argued by analogy that, since all EU Member States are parties to the Geneva Conventions and their Additional Protocols, these treaties may well serve as particularly authoritative sources of inspiration in the formation of general principles of EU law. It follows from the above that, if the relevant treaty provisions of IHL were to achieve the status of 'general principles of the Union's law', they would impose legal obligations upon the EU institutions not only by way of general international law, but also as a matter of EU law.

B. The Legal Status of the CSDP Military Operations and IHL

As noted above with regard to HRL, Council acts forming the legal basis of EU military operations, as well as the relevant agreements with host states, are generally silent on the legal obligations of EU-led personnel under *jus in bello*.[90] The same is true of the agreements concluded with non-EU, troop-contributing nations that are not parties to the same humanitarian law treaties as the EU Member States, such as Turkey and Morocco.[91] A partial exception can be found in two provisions included in the *Concordia* SOFA[92] between the EU and the former Yugoslav Republic of Macedonia (FYROM), which may be interpreted as an implicit commitment to abide by principles of HRL and IHL. Article 2(1) of the agreement stipulates, inter alia, that the EU-led forces (EUF) 'shall refrain from any action or activity incompatible with the impartial and international nature of the operation'. Furthermore, Article 9 states that 'The EUF will... respect international conven-

---

[89] For recent examples, see *Kadi*, para 283; Case C-349/07, *Sopropé—Organizações de Calçado Lda v Fazenda Pública*, 18 December 2008.

[90] As Naert notes, 'It is remarkable that respect for international humanitarian law is never mentioned, except in the case of the AMIS Supporting Mission via the AU SOMA': Naert (n 58 above), 97.

[91] See eg Agreement between the European Union and the Republic of Turkey on the participation of the Republic of Turkey in the European Union-led Forces in the former Yugoslav Republic of Macedonia, 4 September 2003, OJ 2003 L 234/23; Agreement between the European Union and the Kingdom of Morocco on the participation of the Kingdom of Morocco in the European Union military crisis management operation in Bosnia and Herzegovina, OJ 2005 L 34/47. It should be recalled that in all the military operations undertaken by the EU, personnel have also been contributed by non-EU Member States. Among them, Turkey—which participated in the Concordia, Althea, and EUFOR RD Congo—and Morocco—which took part in the Althea operation—are not parties to the two Additional Protocols of 1977.

[92] Council Decision 2003/222/CFSP of 21 March 2003 concerning the conclusion of the Agreement between the European Union and the FYROM on the status of the European Union-led Forces (EUF) in the FYROM, O: J 2003 L 82/46 (hereinafter Concordia SOFA).

tions... regarding the protection of the environment'[93] and 'of cultural heritages and cultural values'.[94] Arguably, international provisions binding on the EU troops deployed in the FYROM should thus have included also the relevant IHL treaties, namely 1954 Hague Convention on the Protection of Cultural Property in the event of armed conflict and a number of rules laid down in the 1977 Protocols to the Geneva Conventions.[95]

However, as noted above,[96] it should be recalled that locally and internationally hired contractors are generally not regarded as EU personnel for purposes of the application of SOMAs and SOFAs: therefore, PMSC staff are, in principle, not bound by possible IHL obligations laid down therein.

C. EU Soft Law and IHL

The EU has been sometimes criticized for considering IHL 'as a subset of human rights law' rather than as a field in its own right, and for not giving *jus in bello* 'the prominent place which it deserves'.[97] The adoption in recent years of a number of soft-law instruments expressly concerned with IHL shows, however, that this *corpus juris* is not considered as irrelevant to the EU's external action; on the contrary, these instruments reflect growing recognition under the EU legal order of IHL as a discrete field of international law. Therefore—although not legally binding—they deserve careful consideration, since they may prove a useful interpretative tool to clarify the EU's approach to IHL issues.

Among these instruments, the above-mentioned EU Guidelines on Promoting Compliance with IHL[98] hold a pivotal position, to the extent that—as one commentator has noted—they 'represent the common legal understanding of EU Member States on this field of law'.[99] The Guidelines were elaborated by COJUR (the Council working group dealing with questions of general international law) upon an initiative by Sweden,[100] and were later adopted by the Council. The aim of the Guidelines is to set out operational tools for the EU and its institutions and bodies to promote compliance with IHL.[101] To this end, the first part of the Guidelines provides a restatement of the present state of the law (with respect to eg the sources of IHL, its scope of application, its relationship with HRL, and to the

---

[93] Concordia SOFA, Art 9(1).
[94] Ibid, Art 9 (2).
[95] Eg Art 53 of Protocol I and Art 16 of Protocol II (on the protection of cultural objects and places of worship); Art 55 of Protocol I (laying down the prohibition to use of methods or means of warfare that are intended or may be expected to cause widespread, long-term and severe damage to the natural environment).
[96] See section III above.
[97] See R Desgagné, 'European Union Practice in the Field of International Humanitarian Law: An Overview' in V Kronenberger (ed), *The European Union and the International Legal Order: Discord or Harmony?* (2001), 455, 455.
[98] n 83 above.
[99] F Hoffmeister, 'The Contribution of EU Practice to International Law' in M Cremona (ed), *Developments in EU External Relations Law* (2008), 37, 100.
[100] Ibid, 51.
[101] EU Guidelines on IHL, para 1.

principles of individual responsibility), while the second part sets forth operational guidelines (aimed at EU representatives in the world) on reporting on and assessing 'compliance with IHL by third states and, as appropriate, non-State actors operating in third States'.[102]

On the one hand, the Guidelines should be intended as a political reference paper[103] mainly concerned with the promotion of *jus in bello* among third countries,[104] and limiting themselves to placing reporting, monitoring,[105] and dissemination[106] obligations[107] on the relevant EU bodies and actors. Once again, it should be recalled that paragraph 2 of the Guidelines—while reaffirming the 'commitment of the EU and its Member States to IHL' and stressing that 'the same commitment extends to measures taken *by the EU* and its Member States to ensure compliance with IHL in their own conduct'[108]—excludes such measures from the scope of application of the Guidelines. However, despite this exclusion, the provision is not without significance, as it consistently acknowledges the EU as an autonomous military actor endowed with the capacity to undertake autonomous obligations under IHL. The increasing emphasis placed by the Guidelines on the EU's commitment to 'promote compliance' with IHL should not be underestimated either, as it may be interpreted as de facto upholding the general principle of IHL aiming 'to ensure respect' for the Geneva Conventions 'in all circumstances'.[109] The ICRC's hailing of the Guidelines as an 'important initiative' marking the 'renewed commitment of the European Union and its Member States toward the protection and assistance of victims of armed conflict worldwide'[110] would appear to confirm this interpretation.

Turning to regulatory efforts aimed at the EU troops in the field, two ESDP/CSDP instruments appear to be particularly significant with respect to IHL, ie the

---

[102] Ibid, para 2.
[103] Hoffmeister (n 99 above), 37.
[104] See EU Guidelines on IHL, para 2.
[105] Ibid, para 15.
[106] Ibid, para 16(h).
[107] Ibid (emphasis added). Arguably, the term sits uncomfortably with the soft law nature of the Guidelines.
[108] Emphases added.
[109] As is well-known, the principle has found explicit recognition by the ICJ in *Nicaragua v United States*:

> the Court considers that there's an obligation on the United States Government, in terms of Article 1 of the Geneva Conventions, to 'respect' the Conventions and even 'to ensure respect' for them 'in all circumstances', since such an obligation does not derive only from the Conventions themselves, but from the general principles of humanitarian law to which the Conventions merely give specific expression.

See *Nicaragua v United States*, para 220.

[110] See ICRC Opinion Paper, 'Support of the ICRC to the Implementation of the EU Guidelines on Promoting Compliance with International Humanitarian Law 1', 23 November 2006 (on file with author). The author is indebted to Stéphane Kolanowski and Geneviève Vercruysse-Toussaint, from the ICRC Delegation in Brussels, for their invaluable help.

EU Draft Guidelines on Protection of Civilians in EU-led Crisis Management Operations,[111] and the Generic Standards of Behaviour for the ESDP Operations.[112]

The Draft Guidelines were agreed in November 2003 by a working party of the Council of the EU,[113] and lay down, for the first time, a potential legal framework specifically aimed at ensuring the protection of civilians where EU operations are conducted. In this respect, they appear to uphold the European Council conclusions of July 2003, which had reaffirmed 'the endeavours made by the EU to ensure that special protection, rights and assistance needs of civilians are fully addressed in all EU-led crisis management, in full compliance with the applicable obligations of Member States under relevant international law and under relevant UN Security Council resolutions'.

In particular, Article 2 of the Draft Guidelines stipulates that 'the EU will, in co-ordination with the UN and other relevant international organisations, take all appropriate measures to facilitate, including through co-ordinated support and assistance, respect of international norms for the protection of civilians',[114] while Article 7 provides that: 'Bearing in mind their obligations under national and international law, States contributing personnel deployed in EU-led crisis management operations should in particular ensure monitoring and reporting of alleged violations of human rights, international humanitarian or international criminal law.'[115] Finally, Article 8 states that: 'Suitable training in the areas mentioned above should be provided to personnel deployed in EU-led crisis management operations... In the preparation of relevant training curricula, guidelines and materials, particular emphasis will be placed [inter alia] (a) on human rights, international humanitarian, refugee and international criminal law.' However, the normative value of the Draft Guidelines remains uncertain, because unlike other non-binding instruments, they have not even been adopted by the EU Council, but—as mentioned above—have simply been agreed upon by the CIVCOM, a Council working party endowed with mere advisory functions.

The Generic Standards of Behaviour were elaborated by the Council Secretariat[116] in May 2005, pursuant to a request by the Political and Security Committee 'to develop a generic document on standards of behaviour to be used when planning for future ESDP operations'.[117] Their complementary nature with respect to legal obligations of international law (including IHL) is explicitly indicated in

---

[111] See Draft Guidelines on Protection of Civilians in EU-Led Crisis Management Operations, Council Doc no 14805/03, 14 November 2003.
[112] Generic Standards of Behaviour for the ESDP Operations, Council Secretariat Doc no 8373/3/05 REV 3 Annex, 18 May 18 2005.
[113] Council Decision no 2000/354/CFSP of 22 May 2000, setting up a committee for civilian aspects of crisis management, OJ 2000 L 127/1.
[114] Emphasis added.
[115] Emphasis added.
[116] According to Art 240(2) TFEU: 'The Council shall be assisted by a General Secretariat, under the responsibility of a Secretary General appointed by the Council.'
[117] Generic Standards of Behaviour, 2.

their text.[118] The Standards are particularly useful in that they reaffirm, clarify, and develop at EU level fundamental principles of *jus in bello* concerning, inter alia, the dissemination of IHL among the ESDP personnel[119] and the obligation to prosecute alleged violations of IHL committed by such personnel.[120] For the purposes of this contribution, it is also important to recall that the Generic Standards should be adhered to by 'all personnel' (paragraph 3), and that, unlike the usual practice within the EU SOFAs, within the meaning of the Standards, the term 'personnel' also includes internationally contracted civilian personnel and locally contracted civilian personnel.

However, as with the Draft Guidelines on Protection of Civilians (which they aim to complement),[121] there is a considerable degree of uncertainty as to the legal value of the Standards. They appear (as their title suggests) to be intended as a mere disciplinary instrument,[122] and thus do not appear to be legally binding. Nevertheless, a subsequent interpretation provided by the EU Portuguese Presidency in 2007 suggests a different conclusion.[123]

Finally, as far as the planning documents for the EU military operations are concerned, the declassified OPLAN of the EUPOL Afghanistan police mission[124]—although not relating to an ESDP military operation—explicitly stipulates that the EU personnel 'will respect local authorities, the law of the land of the host country, their local culture, traditions, customs and practices unless they contradict with International Humanitarian Law (IHL) or Human Rights',[125] thus setting an indirect obligation to respect these legal regimes. In the

---

[118] Ibid, para 4: 'The standards of behaviour are complementary to the legal obligations of personnel. Personnel must apply the provisions of international law, including, when applicable, the law of armed conflict, and the laws of the contributing state.'

[119] Generic Standards of Behaviour, 4–5: 'Pre-deployment training of personnel, carried out nationally as well as by the EU, should include training and education on prescribed standards of behaviour. Particular attention should be given to international law, including international humanitarian law and human rights issues, gender issues and child rights issues.' Cf, inter alia, Fourth Geneva Convention, Art 144.

[120] Generic Standards of Behaviour, para 6: 'Personnel should report any alleged violations by personnel of human rights and international humanitarian or international criminal law. An investigation of each complaint and where relevant subsequent prosecution should be ensured by the competent authority.' Cf Arts 49, 50, 129, 146 common to the Geneva Conventions, as well as Art 85 of Additional Protocol I.

[121] Generic Standards of Behaviour for the ESDP Operations, 1.

[122] Ibid, 3: 'Not adhering to the required standards of behaviour is misconduct and may result in disciplinary measures.'

[123] See Statement by HE Ambassador João Salgueiro, Permanent Representative of Portugal to the United Nations, on behalf of the European Union, United Nations 62nd Session of the General Assembly—Security Council Open Debate on Women, Peace and Security, New York, 23 October 2007: 'In the EU context [the preventive dimension with regard to gender-based violence in conflict and post-conflict situations] includes the development of rules of conduct as the Generic Standards of Behaviour, *which are binding on ESDP staff* ...' (emphasis added), <http://www.europa-eu-un.org/articles/en/article_7443_en.htm>, accessed on 20 August 2010.

[124] Council Joint Action no 2007/369/CFSP of 30 May 2007 on establishment of the European Union Police Mission in Afghanistan (EUPOL AFGHANISTAN), OJ 2007 L 139/33.

[125] OPLAN for the EUPOL Afghanistan Police Mission, Council Doc no 10132/07, 185.

declassified OPLANs, emphasis is frequently placed on the need for both the induction and the in-mission training of ESDP personnel to include IHL.[126] The acknowledgement of such an obligation with regard to a *police* mission may strengthen a fortiori the claim that IHL should be respected in the context of the EU *military* operations, as the latter appear to be even more likely to trigger the applicability of *jus in bello*.

It should be emphasized, however, that none of the instruments mentioned above is legally binding; indeed, they are generally regarded as internal directives aimed at setting disciplinary and professional standards for EU-led military troops.[127] As such, although they incorporate (at least to a certain extent) principles of *jus in bello*, they cannot lay the ground for EU obligations *stricto sensu* under IHL,[128] especially since (unlike HRL) they are not supported by explicit references in EU primary law.

Finally, it should be noted that, unlike with human rights and gender advisors, there is no specific IHL expert attached to the EU-led operations. IHL expertise is provided by the legal advisors present at the Council's General Secretariat, in the Member States, in the Operation Headquarters and in the Force Headquarters.[129]

V. Conclusions

The expanding role and functions of PMSCs within the EU's crisis-management operations[130] make it crucial to clarify the legal framework in which their personnel must operate. This is all the more so with respect to their obligations under HRL and IHL, in order to prevent possible violations of these legal regimes by private contractors in the context of EU-led civilian and military missions. In principle, HRL and IHL may be binding on private companies acting within the framework of the CSDP not only as a matter of international law, but also as a matter of EU law, to the extent that the Union incorporates the relevant legal standards into its internal legal order.

This chapter has shown that HRL (and, to a lesser extent, IHL) principles have indeed been increasingly mainstreamed into the CSDP legal and operational framework. Over the past few years the EU has made significant self-regulatory

---

[126] See eg OPLAN for the ESDP SSR Police Mission in the Democratic Republic of Congo, Council Doc no 9770/07, para 61; CONOPS for the EUPOL Afghanistan Police Mission, Council Doc no 8199/07, para 145; OPLAN for the EUPOL Afghanistan Police Mission, ibid, 291.

[127] See eg C Gossiaux, 'Les Règles d'engagement Norme Juridique Nouvelle?' *Revue de Droit Militaire et de Droit de la Guerre* 40 (2001) 159, 172–3.

[128] Despite their non-binding character, however, the role of soft-law instruments in the EU legal order should not be underestimated. See eg F Beveridge and S Nott, 'A Hard Look at Soft Law' in P Craig and C Harlow (eds), *Lawmaking in the European Union* (1998), 285; F Snyder, 'Soft Law and Institutional Practice in the European Community' in S Martin (ed), *The Construction of Europe: Essays in Honour of Emile Noël* (1994), 197.

[129] See Naert (n 16 above), 350.

[130] The 'increasing cooperation' between the EU and PMSCs has been acknowledged eg by the European Defence Agency: see European Defence Agency, *Future Trends from the Capability Development Plan* (2008), 53.

efforts in this direction, and concerns about ensuring respect of HRL and *jus in bello* by the EU-led troops now permeate large parts of the CSDP legal architecture.

Nevertheless, such efforts have thus far resulted mainly in a number of soft law, non-binding instruments (eg guidelines and generic standards of behaviour), whose legal effects and normative scope are often rather ambiguous. Such uncertainty appears to reflect the general lack of clarity surrounding the CSDP legal framework, characterized as it is by a variety of actors and a range of 'ill-defined'[131] legal tools. Furthermore, as emphasized by a recent study, there is a well-founded risk that such documents 'remain just that, and that they have a somewhat limited impact on policy and operational decisions on the ground'.[132]

Beyond rare exceptions, no mention of HRL or IHL obligations concerning EU-led troops is made in Council acts approving or launching the operations, nor in the agreements with host, transit, or non-EU troop-contributing states. This also applies to civilian missions with respect to which the possibility of resorting to security contractors was already envisaged in the relevant joint actions.[133] References to HRL and IHL are known to be included in the operational planning documents and rules of engagement, but such instruments are not in the public domain.

As for the relevance of the aforementioned legal standards for PMSC personnel, it is debatable whether possible obligations placed by the EU on its civilian and military personnel under HRL and IHL would also bind private contractors, as they are expressly excluded from the scope of application of SOFAs,[134] SOMAs,[135] and ROEs. PMSC staff are not included in the command and control structure, their relationship with the Operations Commander (in military operations)[136] or the Head of Mission (in civilian operations) being contractual in nature. At present, the only ESDP/CSDP self-regulatory act explicitly providing for the application of HRL and IHL to internationally and locally contracted civilian personnel is the Generic Standards of Behaviour in ESDP Operations of 2005. As noted above, however, this instrument only has disciplinary value.

Some commentators have advocated the subordination of contracted security personnel to the military chain of command, arguing that: 'When serving with the armed forces, contractors would be subject to service regulations and discipline to ensure that they conformed to the norms of military behavior and the laws of war.' It has also been maintained that: 'Incorporating contractors into a state's armed forces would... permit oversight and accountability, as well as ensuring that troops from a provider firm obeyed military commands.'[137]

---

[131] P Eeckhout, *External Relations of the EU* (2004), 420.
[132] T Hadden (ed), *A Responsibility to Assist* (2009), 107.
[133] Eg Council Joint Action 2005/190/CFSP of 7 March 2005 on the European Union Integrated Rule of Law Mission for Iraq, EUJUST LEX, OJ 2005 L 62/37, Art 11(3).
[134] See sections III and IV.B above.
[135] Ibid.
[136] It should be recalled that, according to Council's sources, private security companies have thus far only been employed within the framework of civilian missions: see Reply by the Council to Written Question by Glynn Ford (PSE) to the Council, E-3061, 14 July 2008.
[137] JK Wither, 'European Security and Private Military Companies: The Prospects for Privatized "Battlegroups"' (2005) 4 *The Quarterly Journal* 107, 122. For further regulatory proposals at the CFSP/CSDP level, see Ch 1 by E Cusumano in this volume, 34–36.

A solution of this kind might possibly ensure greater uniformity of HRL and IHL standards applicable to CSDP missions and operations, creating a common legal, training, and reporting[138] regime for all the personnel engaged in such operations. However, given the EU's concerns for the 'integrity of the military chain of command' even as regards EU civilian actors,[139] the feasibility of such a proposal is dubious.

On the contrary, the contracts concluded between the Operation Commander/Head of Mission and PMSCs may prove to be a key tool for guaranteeing compliance by private contractors with HRL and IHL.[140] Standard clauses could be drafted, for example, clauses reiterating the obligations binding on PMSC staff under HRL and IHL, requiring that contractor personnel receive adequate training in HRL and IHL, and imposing a duty to periodically report to the Operations Commander and to the Human Rights Advisor.

---

[138] According to para 36(b) of the EU Military C2 Concept (Council of the EU, Doc 11096/03, 3 July 2003, partially declassified), 'The reporting by the OpCdr, drawing on information compiled *within the military chain of command*... may include suspected crimes against international humanitarian law and crimes against humanity' (emphasis added).

[139] Ibid, paras 50–1.

[140] Eg Art 8(3) Council Joint Action 2008/736/CFSP of 15 September 2008 on the European Union Monitoring Mission in Georgia, EUMM Georgia, OJ 2008 L 248/26: 'The conditions of employment and the rights and obligations of international and local civilian staff shall be laid down in the contracts between the Head of Mission and the members of staff.'

16

Old Concepts and New Challenges

Are Private Contractors the Mercenaries of the Twenty-first Century?

Marina Mancini, Faustin Z Ntoubandi, and Thilo Marauhn

I. Introduction

Irrespective of the so-called peace dividend[1] and a reduction of military expenditure and public security forces, since the end of the cold war states and international organizations have outsourced military and security functions to private military and security companies (PMSCs), with a significant impact on the strategic environment. Contractors are even hired to provide services in situations of armed conflict, with their employees now working alongside armed forces in conflict zones. Insofar as contractors are assigned tasks formerly performed by military personnel, the question arises whether they are mercenaries in a new form. Not surprisingly, the UN Working Group on the use of mercenaries, in its 2007 Report to the General Assembly, stated that PMSCs' contractors represent 'new modalities of mercenarism'.[2]

In the sections below, we will discuss whether and to what degree contractors may be labelled mercenaries under both treaty law and customary law. Based on this analysis, we will review whether the established concept of 'mercenaries' can be adopted to meet the challenges arising from what has been called the 'privatization of war'.[3]

---

[1] CW Kegley and MG Hermann, 'A Peace Dividend? Democracies' Military Interventions and their External Political Consequences' (1997) 32 *Cooperation and Conflict* 339, 339–40.
[2] UN Doc A/62/301, 24 August 2007, Report of the Working Group on the Use of Mercenaries as a Means of Violating Human Rights and Impeding the Exercise of the Right of Peoples to Self-Determination, 20.
[3] The notion of 'privatization' has even found its way into legal literature. See, among others, N Stinnett 'Regulating the privatization of war' (2005) 28 *Boston College International and Comparative Law Review* 211.

II. Treaty Law on Mercenaries

For analytical purposes, it is useful to distinguish between (1) the law applicable to armed conflict, insofar as it has a bearing on mercenaries and (2) treaties specifically addressing the question of mercenaries.

A. Mercenaries under the Law of Armed Conflict

The first instrument that is of relevance in this regard is the 1907 Hague Convention (V) Regarding the Rights and Duties of Neutral Powers and Persons in Case of War on Land.[4] This treaty does not explicitly include the term 'mercenary' in its text. However, it contains a number of provisions which may be interpreted as implicitly prohibiting states parties from allowing 'mercenary activities'[5] to be performed in their territory in order to assist a party to the conflict.[6] Articles 4 and 5 of Hague Convention V seek to prevent the territory of neutral powers from being used as a recruiting base for parties to the conflict. In addition, Articles 16 and 17 reserve the status of 'neutral' to individuals whose state of nationality is not participating in the war and who do not take up arms to fight alongside or against a belligerent. Whilst these provisions prohibit the formation of mercenary bands or the establishment of mercenary recruiting agencies in the territory of neutral powers for the purpose of fighting in armed conflicts abroad, they do not per se outlaw mercenary activities occurring in the territory of the belligerents.

The 1977 Protocol Additional to the Geneva Conventions of 12 August 1949, and Relating to the Protection of Victims of International Armed Conflicts[7] constitutes the first international humanitarian law treaty specifically to address the issue of mercenaries. This is done in Article 47, which was adopted by consensus at the Diplomatic Conference of 1977. For the first time in the history of modern international law, this provision defines the status of the mercenary, on the one hand, and seeks to determine who may qualify as a mercenary, on the other.

---

[4] Convention Regarding the Rights and Duties of Neutral Powers and Persons in Case of War on Land (1908) Supp 2 *American Journal of International Law* 117, which was adopted at the Second International Peace Conference in The Hague on 18 October 1907 and entered into force on 26 January 1910.

[5] For practical reasons, the term 'mercenary activities' is used in this chapter to refer to the mercenary and all his attributes and activities; unless otherwise specified, it will be used interchangeably with the term 'mercenarism'.

[6] For a discussion of The Hague Convention's impact on mercenaries, see S Percy, *Mercenaries: The History of a Norm in International Relations* (2007), 94 ff, 167 ff. See also J Hagman and M Kartas, 'International Organisations and the Governance of Private Security' in A Bryden and M Caparini (eds), *Private Actors and Security Governance*, (2006) 4 DCAF Yearbook 285, 287; TS Milliard, 'Overcoming Post-colonial Myopia: A Call to Recognize and Regulate Private Military Companies' (2003) 176 *Military Law Review* 1, 20–1.

[7] Protocol Additional to the Geneva Conventions of 12 August 1949, and Relating to the Protection of Victims of International Armed Conflicts, 1125 UNTS 3.

Article 47(1) provides that 'a mercenary shall not have the right to be a combatant or a prisoner of war'. Mercenaries may be distinguished by the fact that they are neither combatants as required by Article 4 of Geneva Convention III, nor civilians in the sense of Article 5 of Geneva Convention IV, as a result of having actively participated in the armed conflict. If they were to be held captive by the enemy party, they would be liable under Additional Protocol I to criminal prosecution for acts of violence in connection with the conflict—which would in fact be lawful if performed by a combatant—and for the sole fact of having taken a direct part in the hostilities.[8] Whilst mercenaries lack the specific protection of combatants, they are not, however, 'outlaws'.

Mercenaries who find themselves in the power of the enemy belligerent must always be treated humanely as required by the principle of humanity. Since they do not benefit from a more favourable treatment under Article 47(1), mercenaries are automatically entitled to the minimum rights and treatment pursuant to Article 75 of Additional Protocol I afforded to any other person.[9]

In addition, Article 47(2) defines a mercenary as:

any person who (a) is specially recruited locally or abroad in order to fight in an armed conflict; (b) does, in fact, take a direct part in the hostilities; (c) is motivated to take part in the hostilities essentially by the desire for private gain and, in fact, is promised, by or on behalf of a Party to the conflict, material compensation substantially in excess of that promised or paid to combatants of similar ranks and functions in the armed forces of that Party; (d) is neither a national of a Party to the conflict nor a resident of territory controlled by a Party to the conflict; (e) is not a member of the armed forces of a Party to the conflict; and (f) has not been sent by a State which is not a Party to the conflict on official duty as a member of its armed forces.

The foregoing definition thus enumerates six conditions that must be fulfilled cumulatively to qualify as a mercenary. However, among all these conditions, the pursuit of private gain stands as the most determining factor and constitutes the main source of contention, in the definition of mercenary.[10]

Yet, Article 47 of Additional Protocol I has been criticized in many respects.[11] As regards the cumulative fulfilment of all the requirements of paragraph (2), legal scholars assumed that it would be almost impossible for anyone to qualify as a mercenary; consequently, Article 47 would remain of little importance. It was also contended that the requirement of monetary gain would exclude those who take part in hostilities for mere 'adventure' and those who are ideologically supporting a particular party to the conflict.

---

[8] See J de Preux, 'Article 47' in Y Sandoz, C Swinarski, and B Zimmermann (eds), *Commentary on the Additional Protocols of 8 June 1977 to the Geneva Conventions of 12 August 1949* (1987), 571, 575, para 1796.
[9] Ibid, 576, para 1798.
[10] Ibid, 578, para 1807: 'for the protagonists of this article, this is the crux of the matter'.
[11] See, among others, A Cassese, 'Mercenaries: Lawful Combatants or War Criminals?' *Zeitschrift für ausländisches öffentliches Recht und Völkerrecht* 40 (1980) 1.

B. Treaties Specifically Addressing the Question of Mercenaries

During the 1970s and the 1980s, two treaties were concluded which specifically address the question of mercenaries. They are the 1977 Organization of African Unity (OAU)Convention for the Elimination of Mercenarism in Africa[12] and the 1989 International Convention against the Recruitment, Use, Financing and Training of Mercenaries.[13]

The 1977 OAU Convention for the Elimination of Mercenarism in Africa was adopted by the Council of Ministers of the OAU[14] countries at its 29th session held in Libreville, Gabon. It constitutes the most tangible reaction of African states to mercenary activities that were carried out in various parts of Africa in the 1960s and 1970s.[15] The main objective of this instrument is to define the crime of mercenarism and to set out appropriate measures for its elimination.

The definition attributed by the OAU Convention to the term 'mercenary'[16] is taken almost verbatim from Article 47(2) of Additional Protocol I of 1977. The only nuance being that, contrary to Additional Protocol I, the OAU Convention does not require that material compensation promised to the mercenary by a party to the conflict be substantially in excess of that promised or paid to combatants of similar ranks and functions in the armed forces of that party. Under this Convention, the crime of mercenarism is committed whenever an individual, group of persons, or the state uses armed violence to oppose a process of self-determination, stability, or the territorial integrity of another state, by engaging in the commission of any of the prohibited acts. The listed prohibited acts include sheltering, organizing, financing, assisting, equipping, training, promoting, supporting, and employing bands of mercenaries. Acts consisting of enlisting, enrolling, or attempting to enrol them are also prohibited. In addition, states must refrain from allowing any of the listed acts to be carried out in any territory under their control or jurisdiction, or from affording facilities for transit, transport, or other operations of bands of mercenaries. Pursuant to Article 1(3), any person—natural or juridical—whose conduct amounts to an act of mercenarism is punishable for an offence against peace and security in Africa.

---

[12] OAU Doc CM/817 (XXIX) Annex II Rev 1, which was adopted on 3 July 1977 and entered into force on 22 April 1985. See KO Kufuor, 'The OAU Convention for the Elimination of Mercenarism and Civil Conflicts' in A-F Musah and JK Fayemi (eds), *Mercenaries. An African Security Dilemma* (2000), 198–209.

[13] UN Doc A/RES/44/34, which was adopted on 4 December 1989 and entered into force 20 October 2001. For a discussion of its development, see A Layeb, 'The Need for an International Convention against Mercenaries and Mercenarism', (1989) 1 *African Journal of International and Comparative Law* 466.

[14] Replaced by the African Union in 2000.

[15] On the role of mercenaries during decolonization, see, inter alia, PW Singer, *Corporate Warriors: The Rise of the Privatized Military Industry* (2003), 37–8.

[16] On the definition, see II Drews, 'Private military companies: The New Mercenaries?—An International Law Analysis' in T Jäger and G Kümmel (eds), *Private Military and Security Companies* (2007), 331, 333.

Article 3 is a mere reiteration of the provision of Additional Protocol I Article 47 (1), which stipulates that mercenaries shall not be entitled to the status of combatants and of prisoners of war. Article 5 provides for state responsibility in respect of acts or omissions constituting a crime of mercenarism, whereas Article 6 requires contracting parties to take all necessary measures to eradicate mercenary activities in Africa. These include an obligation on parties to prevent any person present on their territory from engaging in any of the acts prohibited under Article 1; to prevent entry into or transit through their territory of mercenaries or their equipment; to prohibit any mercenary activities on their territory directed against any OAU Member State or African people engaged in their struggle for liberation; to inform other OAU Member States of any known mercenary activities; and to take all necessary legislative and other measures to ensure the immediate entry into force of the OAU Mercenary Convention. Article 7 goes on to provide for the imposition of the severest penalties, including capital punishment, for the crime of mercenarism. This provision may have to be reinterpreted in light of developing trends in international law, which tend to reject capital punishment as an appropriate penalty for serious international crimes.[17] However, a state imposing such a severe penalty on a mercenary would not be in strict violation of international law, if a decision to that effect has been made following an open and fair trial and if other fundamental guarantees accorded to non-combatants have been respected. Furthermore, Articles 8 and 9 introduce the principle of *aut dedere aut judicare*, which makes the crime of mercenarism an extraditable offence under the OAU Convention. It is noteworthy that a mercenary, according to Article 11 of this Convention, 'shall be entitled to all the guarantees normally granted to any ordinary person by the State on whose territory he is being tried'. This provision has to be read together with Article 3, in that it extends the application of fundamental guarantees to mercenaries who are standing trial and safeguards their inalienable human rights.

Despite the declared intention of the drafters of the OAU Convention to rid the African continent of the phenomenon of mercenarism, this instrument suffers from a number of deficiencies. In effect, it does not create or establish any supranational monitoring body or enforcement mechanisms. Instead, it relies on states for compliance through the adoption of domestic legislation. To date, only South Africa, which is not even party to this Convention, has adopted an anti-mercenary law, whereas other OAU states have failed to fulfil their obligations under the Convention. In addition, the Convention has been ratified by only a small number of states.[18] Moreover, the OAU Convention suffers from the deficiencies inherited from Article 47(2) of Additional Protocol I, which makes the classification and consequent prosecution of someone as a mercenary almost impossible. Finally, the OAU anti-mercenarism regime is ambiguous, in that it prohibits the use of

---

[17] See eg Art 24 of the 1993 Statute of the International Criminal Tribunal for former Yugoslavia; Art 23 of the 1994 Statute of the International Criminal Tribunal for Rwanda; Art 77 of the 1998 Statute of the International Criminal Court; and Art 19 of the 2002 Statute of the Special Court for Sierra Leone.

[18] See section III below.

mercenaries against OAU Member States, but does not prohibit its use by OAU Member States themselves. This criticism is strengthened by the fact that, since the adoption of the OAU Convention, a number of African States did not hesitate to recruit mercenaries to fight in internal conflicts.[19] Nevertheless, the OAU Convention goes beyond Article 47 of Additional Protocol I, in that it does not only define and specify the status of the mercenary, but it also criminalizes the mere fact of being a mercenary.

The International Convention against the Recruitment, Use, Financing and Training of Mercenaries was adopted in 1989 by the UN General Assembly. In line with its forerunners,[20] the UN Mercenary Convention attempts to define the status of the mercenary and to set out the modalities for the elimination of mercenarism. It adopts a two-pronged definition, with the first part similar to Article 47(2) of Additional Protocol I, except that it excludes the requirement that the non-national recruit 'does in fact take a direct part in the hostilities'.[21] The second part extends the context within which mercenary activities may take place to include 'any other situation' in which any non-national is recruited to participate in 'a concerted act of violence aimed at (i) overthrowing a Government or otherwise undermining the constitutional order of a state; or (ii) undermining the territorial integrity of a State'; and is 'motivated to take part therein essentially by the desire for significant private gain and is prompted by the promise or payment of material compensation'.[22] In this respect, the UN Convention applies irrespective of whether a mercenary is involved in an international or in a non-international armed conflict.

The omission from the UN instrument of the mention 'does in fact take a direct part in the hostilities' makes the foreign recruit a mercenary, irrespective of his actual participation in hostile or prohibited acts. It may, for example, suffice that the recruit is aware of the objectives of his recruitment in order to be defined as a mercenary, even if he has not yet acted in pursuance of the achievement of those objectives. The UN Convention goes even further since it implies that any alien who, in peacetime, takes part in any violent activity aimed at provoking a change of regime in a state through a *coup d'état* may be considered a mercenary.[23] In addition, the UN Convention makes the recruitment, use, financing, or training of mercenaries an offence under international law, whether perpetrated by mercenaries themselves or by any other person.[24] Moreover, direct participation by mercenaries in the hostilities or in any concerted act of violence constitutes an offence in terms of Article 3. By the same token, any attempt and/or complicity to commit any of the offences set forth in the Convention constitute an offence.[25] As with the OAU Convention, states parties to the UN instrument undertake not

---

[19] See section IV below.
[20] Namely Art 47 of Additional Protocol I and the OAU Convention.
[21] Art 1(1) of the UN Convention.
[22] Ibid, Art 1(2).
[23] See Milliard (n 6 above), 61–2.
[24] Art 2.
[25] Art 4.

only to make the offences set forth therein punishable by appropriate penalties, but also to cooperate in their prevention.[26] Furthermore, Article 15 makes the offences set forth in the Convention extraditable offences, whereas Articles 9(2), 10, and 12 require states parties to either try or extradite suspected offenders. Unlike the OAU Convention, the UN Convention contains a saving clause which stipulates that it shall apply without prejudice to the 'law of armed conflict and international humanitarian law, including the provisions relating to the status of combatant or of prisoner of war'.[27]

The UN Convention has also been subject to criticism.[28] Critics argue that the profit-motive requirement in the definition of mercenary should not be considered relevant because it might be difficult to prove that the person was motivated to take part in hostilities essentially by the desire for monetary gain. Another line of argument is that the elimination of the private gain motive would facilitate the prosecution of those mercenaries who fight in order to defend a certain ideology or just to quench their thirst for adventure. Perhaps the main drawback to the UN Convention is the lack of interest in its ratification. This is due, in large part, to its strict definition requirements, which deprive its text of any effective basis for prosecution. In this respect, the UK House of Commons Foreign Affairs Committee has deplored the fact that the 'definition of mercenary used in the UN Convention is impossible to employ in British courts' and 'parts of the Convention definition were "too vaguely" drafted for use in a court of law'.[29]

III. Customary Law

According to the ICRC study on customary international humanitarian law, the definition of mercenary contained in Additional Protocol I has nowadays achieved the status of customary law. Rule 108 of this study reads as follows: 'Mercenaries, as defined in Additional Protocol I, do not have the right to combatant or prisoner-of-war status. They may not be convicted or sentenced without previous trial.' The study clarifies further that: 'State practice establishes this rule as a norm of customary international law applicable in international armed conflicts.'[30]

This finding seems somewhat hasty. In the *North Sea Continental Shelf* cases, the International Court of Justice stressed that, for a conventional rule to become a customary rule:

an indispensable requirement would be that within the period in question, short though it might be, State practice, including that of States whose interests are specially affected, should have been both extensive and virtually uniform in the sense of the provision invoked;

---

[26] Arts 5–6.
[27] Art 16(b).
[28] See Milliard (n 6 above), 59–61, and elsewhere.
[29] House of Commons Foreign Affairs Committee, Ninth Report: Private Military Companies, Session 2001–2002, para 22, <http://www.publications.parliament.uk/pa/cm200102/cmselect/cmfaff/922/92202.htm>, accessed on 20 August 2010.
[30] J-M Henckaerts and L Doswald-Beck (eds), *Customary International Humanitarian Law*, I: *Rules* (2005), 391.

and should moreover have occurred in such a way as to show a general recognition that a rule of law or legal obligation is involved.[31]

As regards Article 47(2) of Additional Protocol I, this requirement is not met at the moment.

Although it has been in force for nearly 33 years, Additional Protocol I has not yet achieved the universal adherence which the four Geneva Conventions of 1949 have won. As of August 2010, 24 states were still required for this instrument to achieve a status similar to that of the Geneva Conventions.[32] Among them is the United States. In 1987, the Deputy Legal Adviser of the US Department of State Michael J Matheson affirmed: 'We do not favor the provisions of Article 47 on mercenaries, which among other things introduce political factors that do not belong in international humanitarian law, and do not consider the provisions of Article 47 to be part of current customary law.'[33]

As regards participation in the OAU Convention and the UN Convention, the situation is even less convincing. As of August 2010, only 30 Member States of the African Union had ratified the OAU Convention,[34] while only 32 states were parties to the UN Convention. Notably, none of the major world powers are among these.[35]

A close scrutiny of state practice reveals that the definition of mercenary contained in Additional Protocol I has not been as generally adopted by states as it ought to be. It is embodied, subject to some changes, in the legislation of a few states. Both the criminal codes of France and the Russian Federation are worthy of note in this respect.

Article 436–1 of the French Criminal Code, as modified by Law no 2003–340 of 14 April 2003 relating to the repression of mercenary activities, provides for the punishment by five years' imprisonment and by a fine of €75,000 of anyone who fulfils the conditions as set forth in Article 47(1) of Additional Protocol I, other than that of not being a resident of territory controlled by a party to the conflict.[36]

---

[31] *North Sea Continental Shelf*, Judgment, ICJ Reports (1969) 3, 43.

[32] As of August 2010, 194 states are parties to the Geneva Conventions of 1949, while only 170 are parties to Additional Protocol I. See the list of the states parties to the Geneva Conventions and to Additional Protocol I on the website of the ICRC, <http://www.icrc.org/ihl.nsf/CONVPRES?OpenView>, accessed on 20 August 2010.

[33] 'Sixth Annual American Red Cross-Washington College of Law Conference on International Humanitarian Law: A Workshop on Customary International Law and the 1977 Protocols Additional to the 1949 Geneva Conventions, Session One: The United States Position on the Relation of Customary International Law to the 1977 Protocols Additional to the 1949 Geneva Conventions, Remarks of Michael J Matheson' (1987) 2 *American University Journal of International Law and Policy* 419, 426.

[34] See the list of the states parties to the OAU Convention on the website of the African Union at <http://www.africa-union.org/root/au/Documents/Treaties/treaties.htm>, accessed on 20 August 2010.

[35] See the list of the states parties to the UN Convention on the website of the United Nations Treaty Collection at <http://treaties.un.org/Pages/ViewDetails.aspx?src=TREATY&mtdsg_no=XVIII-6&chapter=18&lang=en>, accessed on 20 August 2010.

[36] The English version of the French Criminal Code and of Law no 2003-340 is available on the website Legifrance, at <http://www.legifrance.gouv.fr>, accessed on 20 August 2010. For a comment on Law no 2003-340, see V Capdevielle and H Cherief, *The Regulation of Private Military and Security*

Article 359 of the Russian Criminal Code, which is headed 'Mercenarism', provides for the punishment of recruitment, training, financing, and use of mercenaries in an armed conflict as well as participation as a mercenary in an armed conflict. A note below the provision clarifies that 'a mercenary shall be deemed to mean a person who acts for the purpose of getting a material reward, and who is not a citizen of the state in whose armed conflict or hostilities he participates, who does not reside on a permanent basis on its territory, and also who is not a person fulfilling official duties'.[37]

Furthermore, a relatively small number of military manuals adopt the definition of mercenary provided by Additional Protocol I.[38] Among these, both the Canadian Manual of Law of Armed Conflict at the Operational and Tactical Levels of 2001[39] and the British Manual of the Law of Armed Conflict of 2004[40] deserve mention. They reproduce that definition in Article 319(1) and in Chapter 4 (10.1) respectively. The incorporation of the Additional Protocol I definition, however, cannot be overestimated, as the British case shows. The Green Paper on 'Private Military Companies: Options for Regulation', published by the Foreign and Commonwealth Office in 2002, stressed that 'a number of governments including the British Government regard this definition as unworkable for practical purposes'.[41]

Finally, there is almost no domestic case law regarding the definition of mercenary as it is enshrined in Article 47 of Additional Protocol I.[42]

IV. Do the Old Concepts Meet the New Challenges?

As explained above, the various elements of the definition of mercenary enumerated in treaty law and in customary law are cumulative. For a contractor to be considered a mercenary all of the conditions must be met. Does this definition of mercenary meet the challenges arising from the phenomenon of PMSCs? In the following section we will examine each element of the definition in the light of current problems related to PMSCs.

Services in France, 24–8, available on the website of the Project PRIV-WAR, at <http://priv-war.eu/?page_id=49>, accessed on 20 August 2010.

[37] The English version of the Russian Criminal Code is available on the website Legislationonline at <http://www.legislationline.org/documents/section/criminal-codes>, accessed on 20 August 2010. For a comment on Art 359 of the Russian Criminal Code, see S Novicka, *The Regulatory Context of Private Military and Security Services in the Russian Federation*, 19–21, available on the website of the Project PRIV-WAR, at <http://priv-war.eu/?page_id=49>, accessed on 20 August 2010.

[38] Henckaerts and Doswald-Beck (n 30 above), 393.

[39] Canada National Defence, Law of Armed Conflict at the Operational and Tactical Levels, B-GJ-005-104/FP-021, 2001-08-13, available on the website of the Canada National Defence, at <http://www.cfd-cdf.forces.gc.ca/sites/page-eng.asp?page=3481>, accessed on 20 August 2010.

[40] UK Ministry of Defence, *The Manual of the Law of Armed Conflict* (2004).

[41] Foreign and Commonwealth Office, HC 577, Private Military Companies: Options for Regulation 2001–2002, London, February 2002, 7, available on the website of the Foreign Office, at <www.fco.gov.uk/resources/en/pdf/pdf4/fco_pdf_privatemilitarycompanies>, accessed on 20 August 2010.

[42] See Capdevielle and Cherif (n 36 above), 31–2.

A. Recruitment

Article 47(2) of Additional Protocol I, Article 1(1) of the OAU Convention, and Article 1(1) of the UN Convention all require that mercenaries be 'specially recruited locally or abroad in order to fight in an armed conflict'. This definition is broadened under Article 1(2) of the UN Convention. As the nature of the employer is not specified, it may be argued that the employer may also be a company contracted by a state to provide military or security services in an armed-conflict zone. While most of the contracts between companies and recruits are not accessible to the public, those between companies and governments are sometimes available online.[43] It is possible to infer some of the content of the former from the latter.

During the 1990s, some governments hired PMSCs to conduct offensive operations against insurgents and to regain control of their territory. In 1993, the Angolan government contracted Executive Outcomes, a South African company now dissolved, to train the Angolan army and to direct operations against the rebel movement Uniao Naçional para a Indipendencia Total de Angola (UNITA). Executive Outcomes personnel engaged in combat alongside Angolan troops and were decisive in regaining government control of major cities and access to important natural resources.[44] In 1995, Executive Outcomes was hired by the Sierra Leone government to train its troops and to help them defeat the rebels of the Revolutionary United Front (RUF); operations were successful within a few months.[45] Finally, in early 1997, the government of Papua New Guinea entered into a contract with Sandline International, a London-based company now dissolved, to defeat the Bougainville Revolutionary Army (BRA), a secessionist movement operating in Bougainville, and regain control over the island. Under the contract, Sandline would 'provide personnel and related services and equipment to...conduct offensive operations in Bougainville in conjunction with PNG defence forces to render the BRA military ineffective and repossess the Panguna

---

[43] Eg the most valuable contracts concluded by the US government with PMSCs for work in Afghanistan and Iraq in the periods 2001–3 and 2004–6 are available on the website of the Center for Public Integrity, respectively, at <http://projects.publicintegrity.org/wow/resources.aspx?act=resources>, accessed on 20 August 2010 (Project Windfalls of War I) and at <http://projects.publicintegrity.org/WOWII/database.aspx?act=toponehundredcontracts>, accessed on 20 August 2010 (Project Windfalls of War II).

[44] For a full account of the involvement of Executive Outcomes in the Angolan civil war, see: J-C Zarate, 'The Emergence of a New Dog of War: Private International Security Companies, International Law, and the New World Disorder', (1994) 34 *Stanford Journal of International Law* 75, 94–5; KA O'Brien, 'Private military companies and African security 1990–1998' in Musah and Fayemi (n 12 above), 43, 51–2; Foreign and Commonwealth Office, HC 577, Private Military Companies: Options for Regulation 2001–2002 (n 41 above), 11; Singer (n 15 above), 107–10; Percy (n 6 above), 209–10.

[45] For a full account of the involvement of Executive Outcomes in the Sierra Leone civil war, see Zarate (n 44 above), 95–8; Foreign and Commonwealth Office, HC 577, Private Military Companies: Options for Regulation 2001–2002 (n 41 above), 12; Singer (n 15 above), 110–15; Percy (n 6 above), 210–12.

mine'.⁴⁶ It would also train the Papua New Guinea Special Forces in tactical skills specific to this purpose, gather intelligence on the BRA, and provide follow-up operational support. Shortly after the arrival of Sandline personnel, however, the overall commander of the Papua New Guinea defence forces publicly condemned the contract. The ensuing mass protests against the Sandline deployment forced the government to cancel the contract. As a result, Sandline staff left the country.⁴⁷ It is possible to read all three contracts in a way that the recruited personnel meet the recruitment requirement laid down in mercenary-related treaty law.

Similar conclusions may be drawn from recent operations. PMSCs have been primarily hired by the US and the UK governments and, to a lesser extent, by other governments to supply a wide variety of armed services in both Afghanistan and Iraq, after the interventions in 2001 and 2003 respectively. Major PMSCs in Afghanistan and Iraq include Blackwater, DynCorp International, MPRI, Triple Canopy, EOD Technology, Aegis, ArmorGroup, Control Risks, and Erinys.⁴⁸ Most of the services provided in both countries relate to security. They include the protection of fixed or static sites, such as government buildings (static security); the protection of individuals travelling through unsecured areas (security escorts); the protection of convoys travelling in the same areas (convoy security); and full-time protection of high-ranking individuals (personal security details).⁴⁹ Comprehensive figures on armed security contractors now working in Iraq and Afghanistan are not available. However, according to the US Department of Defense, as of September 2009, its armed security contractors in Iraq were 11,162, of which 5% were Americans, 18% were Iraqis, and 77% were third-country nationals;⁵⁰ whilst those in Afghanistan were 10,712, of which 1% were Americans, 90% were Afghans, and 9% were third-country nationals.⁵¹ The armed security contractors operating in Iraq and Afghanistan are often citizens of developing countries with a military or police background. In many cases, they are

---

⁴⁶ The text of the contract is available on the website of the Australian National University, at <http://coombs.anu.edu.au/SpecialProj/PNG/htmls/Sandline.html>, accessed on 20 August 2010.

⁴⁷ On the engagement of Sandline International by the Government of Papua New Guinea, see L Ebbeck, 'Mercenaries and the "Sandline Affair"' *Australian Defence Force Journal* 133 (1998) 5; T McCormack, 'The "Sandline Affair": Papua New Guinea Resorts to Mercenarism to End the Bougainville Conflict' (1998) 1 *Yearbook of International Humanitarian Law* 292; Zarate (n 44 above), 98–9; Singer (n 15 above), 191–6; Percy (n 6 above), 211–12.

⁴⁸ Blackwater, DynCorp International, MPRI, Triple Canopy, and EOD Technology are based in the United States while Aegis, ArmorGroup, Control Risks, and Erinys are based in the United Kingdom. Since 2008 ArmorGroup is part of G4S Risk Management. In 2009 Blackwater changed its name to Xe. Currently, according to the UN Working Group on the use of mercenaries, up to 80% of the PMSCs are registered in the United Kingdom and in the United States. See UN Doc A/64/311, 20 August 2009, Report on the Question of the Use of Mercenaries as a Means of Violating Human Rights and Impeding the Exercise of the Right of Peoples to Self-Determination, 5.

⁴⁹ M Schwartz, *The Department of Defense's Use of Private Security Contractors in Iraq and Afghanistan: Background, Analysis, and Options for Congress*, CRS Report for Congress, 19 January 2010, 2, <http://opencrs.com/document/R40835/2010-01-19/>, accessed on 20 August 2010.

⁵⁰ Ibid, 6.

⁵¹ Ibid, 9.

recruited by subsidiary companies, that have been tasked with the selection and training of personnel by the PMSC contracting with the government.[52]

As far as recruitment 'in order to fight in an armed conflict' is concerned, one should note that the contract between the company and the recruit specifies the theatre of operations where the recruit shall provide the security service and the period of time for which he shall work, generally a certain number of months. Usually, the hazardous nature of the job is emphasized. Thus, the contract signed by Hondurans recruited in 2005 by Triple Canopy, through a subsidiary, for the protection of fixed facilities in the so-called 'Green Zone' of Baghdad stipulated that the recruit would be 'exposed to great risk and immediate danger and to the many risks associated with a hostile environment, including but not limited to the threats inherent in a war situation'.[53] According to the UN Working Group on the use of mercenaries, 'former military personnel and ex-policemen are recruited as "security guards", but once in low-intensity armed conflicts or post-conflict situations, they become in fact private soldiers militarily armed'.[54] As a matter of fact, armed security contractors often receive ad hoc military training before being dispatched to Iraq or Afghanistan.[55]

Contractors are 'recruited to fight in an armed conflict', even if they do not conduct offensive operations, but are engaged to protect military objectives (eg ammunition trucks or military depots), which as such may be lawfully targeted by the enemy. It has been rightly argued that 'the phrase "to fight" under international humanitarian law is not synonymous with an offensive attack'.[56] The nature of the act of violence, offensive or defensive, is irrelevant. What matters is the subject against which it is committed. Only acts of violence against enemy forces constitute 'attacks' within the meaning of Article 49(1) of Additional Protocol I. According to this provision, '"attacks" means acts of violence against the adversary, whether in offence or in defence'. Consequently, armed security contractors cannot be considered as recruited to fight in an armed conflict if they are hired to protect military

---

[52] See the cases illustrated in the following reports: UN Doc A/HRC/4/42/Add1, 20 February 2007, Report of the Working Group on the Use of Mercenaries as a Means of Violating Human Rights and Impeding the Exercise of the Right of Peoples to Self-Determination, Addendum, Mission to Honduras, 7 ff; UN Doc A/HRC/7/7/Add2, 4 February 2008, Report of the Working Group on the Use of Mercenaries as a Means of Violating Human Rights and Impeding the Exercise of the Right of Peoples to Self-Determination, Addendum, Mission to Peru, 6 ff; UN Doc A/HRC/7/7/Add4, 4 February 2008, Report of the Working Group on the Use of Mercenaries as a Means of Violating Human Rights and Impeding the Exercise of the Right of Peoples to Self-Determination, Addendum, Mission to Chile, 8 ff.

[53] UN Doc A/HRC/4/42/Add1, 20 February 2007 (n 52 above), 10. For other examples, see the following reports: UN Doc A/HRC/7/7/Add2, 4 February 2008 (n 52 above), 11; UN Doc A/HRC/7/7/Add4, 4 February 2008 (n 52 above), 10.

[54] UN Doc A/HRC/7/7, 9 January 2008, Report of the Working Group on the Use of Mercenaries as a Means of Violating Human Rights and Impeding the Exercise of the Right of Peoples to Self-Determination, 24.

[55] See the cases mentioned in the following reports: UN Doc A/HRC/4/42/Add1, 20 February 2007 (n 52 above), 8, 11; UN Doc A/HRC/7/7/Add2, 4 February 2008 (n 52 above), 7, 10; UN Doc A/HRC/7/7/Add4, 4 February 2008 (n 52 above), 9 ff.

[56] L Cameron, 'Private Military Companies: Their Status Under International Humanitarian Law and its Impact on their Regulation' (2006) 88 IRRC 573, 581.

objectives against common criminals.⁵⁷ However, it is unthinkable that, in a situation of armed conflict, those protecting a military objective may be ordered to react only if the attack comes from common criminals. Besides, it may be very difficult to discern the nature of the attacker on the spot.⁵⁸

B. Direct Participation in the Hostilities

Both Article 47(2) of Additional Protocol I and Article 1(1) of the OAU Convention require that mercenaries 'in fact, take a direct part in the hostilities'. In contrast, the UN Convention does not require direct participation in hostilities or in a concerted act of violence for a person to qualify as a mercenary. Notwithstanding the importance attached to the notion of direct participation in hostilities in international humanitarian law, there is no conventional definition at hand.

In May 2009, the ICRC published interpretive guidance on this notion, consisting of ten recommendations and a commentary.⁵⁹ According to Recommendation IV, 'the notion of direct participation in hostilities refers to specific acts carried out by individuals as part of the conduct of hostilities between parties to an armed conflict'.⁶⁰ The commentary makes it clear that 'direct participation' must be interpreted in the same way in international and non-international armed conflicts.⁶¹

Recommendation V lists three criteria all of which must be fulfilled for a specific act to amount to direct participation in hostilities. First, the act must reasonably be expected 'to adversely affect the military operations or military capacity of a party to an armed conflict or, alternatively, to inflict death, injury, or destruction on persons or objects protected against direct attack'.⁶² Secondly, there must be a direct causal link between the act and the harm likely to result from it or from a coordinated military operation of which it is an integral part,⁶³ and, according to the commentary, 'direct causation should be understood as meaning that the harm in question must be brought about in one causal step'.⁶⁴ Thirdly, the so-called belligerent nexus is required, ie 'the act must be specifically designed to directly cause the required threshold of harm in support of a party to the conflict and to the detriment of another'.⁶⁵

---

⁵⁷ On this point, see Report of the Expert Meeting on Private Military Contractors: Status and State Responsibility for their Actions, University Centre for International Humanitarian Law, Geneva, 29–30 August 2005, 26–7, available on the website of the Geneva Academy of International Humanitarian Law and Human Rights, at <http://www.adh-geneva.ch/experts_meetings/year.php?year=2005>, accessed on 20 August 2010; Cameron (n 56 above), 589–91; L Doswald-Beck, 'Private Military Companies under International Humanitarian Law' in S Chesterman and C Lehnardt (eds), *From Mercenaries to Market: The Rise and Regulation of Private Military Companies* (2007) 115, 122.

⁵⁸ With regard to this, see Report of the Expert Meeting on Private Military Contractors: Status and State Responsibility for their Actions (n 57 above), 27; Cameron (n 56 above), 589–90.

⁵⁹ N Melzer, *Interpretive Guidance on the Notion of Direct Participation in Hostilities under International Humanitarian Law*, ICRC, May 2009, <http://www.icrc.it/web/eng/siteeng0.nsf/htmlall/p0990?opendocument>, accessed on 20 August 2010. See Ch 10 by Sossai, at section III, in this volume.

⁶⁰ Ibid, 16.
⁶¹ Ibid, 45.
⁶² Ibid, 16. See C Pilloud and J Pictet, 'Article 51' in Sandoz et al (n 8 above), 613, 619, para 1944.
⁶³ Melzer (n 59 above), 16.
⁶⁴ Ibid, 53.   ⁶⁵ Ibid, 17.

Recommendation VI makes it clear that the notion of direct participation in hostilities includes preparations for the execution of the act, as well as deployment to and return from the location of execution of the act.[66]

Many acts carried out by PMSC contractors are covered by the notion of direct participation in hostilities as specified in the ICRC's interpretive guidance. Clearly, taking part in offensive combat operations qualifies as direct participation in hostilities. It is noteworthy that the Policy Directives issued by the US Embassy in Baghdad in May 2008 prohibit contractors working for the Department of State and the Agency for International Development from engaging 'in offensive combat operations, alone or in conjunction with US, Coalition or host nation forces'.[67] Similarly, the Multi-National Force–Iraq Fragmentary Order 09–109 of March 2009, applicable to contractors working for the US Department of Defense, states that 'taking a direct or active part in hostilities other than self defense (eg engaging in combat actions with hostile forces) is strictly prohibited'.[68] However, there are some examples of contractors involved in offensive operations. Thus, in December 2009, the *New York Times* revealed that security contractors from Blackwater had taken part in clandestine CIA raids against individuals suspected of insurgency in Iraq and Afghanistan.[69]

Engaging in defensive combat also constitutes direct participation in hostilities. As has been rightly pointed out, 'international humanitarian law does not draw a distinction between offensive or defensive operations'.[70] Indeed, the ICRC's interpretive guidance regards 'the defence of military personnel and other military objectives against enemy attacks' as direct participation in hostilities.[71] Several instances of defensive combat involving security contractors in Iraq and Afghanistan have been reported. Thus, in Najaf, Iraq, on 4 April 2004 Blackwater's contractors tasked with the protection of the Coalition Provisional Authority headquarters repulsed an attack by hundreds of Shiite militia members, with combat lasting for more than three hours.[72]

PMSCs are often engaged in preparatory measures for the performance of hostile acts by armed forces. The ICRC's interpretive guidance considers such preparatory

---

[66] Ibid, 17. See Pilloud and Pictet, 'Article 51' (n 62 above), 618–19, para 1943.

[67] US Embassy Baghdad Iraq, Policy Directives for Armed Private Security Contractors in Iraq, May 2008, Directive II, para B.10, <http://baghdad.osac.gov/page.cfm?pageID=5314>, accessed on 20 August 2010.

[68] MNF-I Frago 09-109, Overarching Frago for Requirements, Communications, Procedures, Responsibilities for Control, Coordination, Management and Oversight of Armed Contractors/DOD Civilians and Private Security Companies (PSC), March 2009, Annex C, para 3.A.

[69] J Risen and M Mazzetti, 'Blackwater Guards Tied to Secret CIA Raids', *The New York Times* (11 December 2009), A1, <http://www.nytimes.com/2009/12/11/us/politics/11blackwater.html>, accessed on 20 August 2010.

[70] E-C Gillard, 'Business Goes to War: Private Military/Security Companies and International Humanitarian Law', (2006) 88 IRRC 525, 540. See also Cowling, 'Outsourcing and the Military: Implications for International Humanitarian Law' (2007) 32 *South African Yearbook of International Law* 312, 329.

[71] Melzer (n 59 above), 38 (commentary on Recommendation III). See also MN Schmitt, 'Humanitarian Law and Direct Participation in Hostilities by Private Contractors or Civilian Employees' (2004) 5 *Chicago Journal of International Law* 511, 538.

[72] D Priest, 'Private Guards Repel Attack on US Headquarters', *The Washington Post* (6 April 2004), A1.

measures as direct participation, stating: 'If carried out with a view to the execution of a specific hostile act, all of the following would almost certainly constitute preparatory measures amounting to direct participation in hostilities: equipment, instruction, and transport of personnel; gathering of intelligence; and preparation, transport, and positioning of weapons and equipment.'[73] As regards the instruction of military personnel, training provided by the US-based company MPRI to the Croatian army in 1994–5 is worth mentioning. Though the contract between the Croatian government and the US company officially only provided for education in democratic principles and civil–military relations, several military analysts have suggested that MPRI's contractors also trained the Croatian army in tactics, pointing to the stunning offensive, codenamed 'Operation Storm', that the latter launched against the Croatian Serb forces in the Krajina region in August 1995.[74]

Also, many contractors working for the US government have been tasked with gathering intelligence useful for US operations in Iraq. This highly sensitive task is generally performed by means of drones, the analysis of satellite data, or the interrogation of detainees.[75] Interestingly, as stated by the US Congressional Budget Office, contractor personnel also 'analyze intelligence data, which they may transmit in the form of targeting coordinates to unmanned aerial vehicles or other manned or unmanned platforms that fire weapons'.[76]

As regards the positioning of weapons, the role of Blackwater's contractors in the CIA covert programme for the assassination of Al Qaeda's leaders by means of remotely piloted drones is worth recalling. In August 2009, the *New York Times* revealed the existence of a contract between the CIA and Blackwater, under which the company's contractors were tasked with assembling and loading Hellfire missiles and 500 lb laser-guided bombs onto Predator aircraft, at the CIA hidden bases in Afghanistan and Pakistan.[77] The contract was cancelled by the CIA in December 2009.[78]

In response to some of these developments, the legally non-binding 2008 Montreux Document, elaborated on the ICRC and the Swiss government's initiative,

---

[73] Melzer (n 59 above), 66 (commentary on Recommendation VI).
[74] See M Thompson, M Calabresi, and A Stiglmayer, 'Bosnia: Generals for Hire', *Time* (15 January 1996), <http://www.time.com/time/magazine/article/0,9171,983949-1,00.html>, accessed on 20 August 2010; Foreign and Commonwealth Office, HC 577, Private Military Companies: Options for Regulation 2001–2002 (n 41 above), 13; Singer (n 15 above), 125–7.
[75] On this point, see N Boldt, 'Outsourcing War: Private Military Companies and International Humanitarian Law' (2004) 47 *German Yearbook of International Law* 502, 508–9; Schmitt (n 71 above), 543 f.
[76] The Congress of the United States, Congressional Budget Office, Contractors' Support of US Operations in Iraq, August 2008, 22, <http://www.cbo.gov/ftpdocs/96xx/doc9688/08-12-Iraq Contractors.pdf>, accessed on 20 August 2010.
[77] J Risen and M Mazzetti, 'CIA Said to Use Outsiders to Put Bombs on Drones', *The New York Times* (21 August 2009), A1, <http://www.nytimes.com/2009/08/21/us/21intel.html>, accessed on 20 August 2010.
[78] M Mazzetti, 'Blackwater Loses a Job for the CIA', *The New York Times* (12 December 2009), A8, <http://www.nytimes.com/2009/12/12/us/politics/12blackwater.html>, accessed on 20 August 2010.

with the participation of governmental experts from 17 other countries, encourages states, in determining which services may not be contracted out, carried out on their territory, or exported, to consider 'whether a particular service could cause PMSC personnel to become involved in direct participation in hostilities'.[79] Building upon existing treaty law on mercenaries, the Draft of a Possible Convention on Private Military and Security Companies, submitted by the UN Working Group on the use of mercenaries to the Human Rights Council in July 2010, establishes an outright ban on direct participation of contractors in hostilities. It requires parties 'to take such legislative, administrative and other measures as may be necessary to prohibit and make illegal the direct participation of PMSCs and their personnel in hostilities, terrorist acts and military actions' in violation of international law.[80]

C. Motivation

Article 47(2) of Additional Protocol I, Article 1(1) of the OAU Convention, and Article 1(1) of the UN Convention all require that a mercenary be 'motivated to take part in the hostilities essentially by the desire for private gain' and in fact be 'promised, by or on behalf of a Party to the conflict, material compensation'. Article 1(2) of the UN Convention adapts these requirements to concerted acts of violence outside an armed conflict. It only adds the adjective 'significant' to 'private gain' and envisages the possibility of a mercenary being prompted by actual payment, instead of a simple promise, of material compensation.

It is the desire for private gain which is the main element that distinguishes a mercenary from a volunteer. As de Preux points out, 'in contrast to a volunteer who is moved by a noble ideal, the mercenary is considered to offer his services to the highest bidder, since he is essentially motivated by material gain'.[81]

When considering personnel of PMSCs, the desire for private gain appears to be the primary motivation for accepting high-risk jobs and, except for local nationals, to be dispatched to countries very far from home. As a matter of fact, the UN Working Group on the use of mercenaries found that many of the contractors interviewed on its field missions were essentially motivated by private gain.[82] It has

---

[79] Montreux Document on Pertinent International Legal Obligations and Good Practices for States Related to Operations of Private Military and Security Companies during Armed Conflict (Montreux, 17 September 2008), Part II, paras 1, 24, 53, <http://www.icrc.org/Web/Eng/siteeng0.nsf/html/montreux-document-170908>, accessed on 20 August 2010. For a comment, see J Cockayne, 'Regulating Private Military and Security Companies: The Content, Negotiation, Weaknesses and Promise of the Montreux Document' (2008) 13 *Journal of Conflict and Security Law* 401.

[80] Art 8 of the Draft of a Possible Convention on Private Military and Security Companies (PMSCs), attached to UN Doc A/HRC/15/25, 2 July 2010, Report of the Working Group on the Use of Mercenaries as a Means of Violating Human Rights and Impeding the Exercise of the Right of Peoples to Self-Determination.

[81] de Preux (n 8 above), 579, para 1807.

[82] UN Doc A/HRC/7/7, 9 January 2008 (n 54 above), 15. See also the following reports: UN Doc A/HRC/4/42/Add1, 20 February 2007 (n 52 above), 16; UN Doc A/HRC/7/7/Add2, 4 February 2008 (n 52 above), 20; UN Doc A/HRC/7/7/Add3, 8 January 2008, Report of the Working Group on the Use of Mercenaries as a Means of Violating Human Rights and Impeding the Exercise of the

to be stressed that usually PMSC personnel are paid much more than equivalent members of the armed forces of their home country.[83] A memorandum of the Committee on Oversight and Government Reform of the US House of Representatives of 1 October 2007[84] revealed that a protective security specialist from Blackwater in Iraq cost the US government six to nine times more than an equivalent soldier.[85] Even though the US Congressional Budget Office observed that 'the billing rate is greater than an employee's pay because it includes the contractor's indirect costs, overhead, and profit',[86] it is beyond doubt that Blackwater's security contractors earned considerably more than equivalent military personnel. According to many sources, the salaries offered by PMSCs induce many soldiers in various countries to resign in order to work as contractors.[87] In addition, it is noteworthy that PMSCs apply different salary scales depending on the individual's nationality. As reported by the chairperson of the UN Working Group on the use of mercenaries, José Luis Gómez del Prado, PMSCs apply a hierarchical pyramid model to their contractors in Iraq and Afghanistan:

At the top of the hierarchical pyramid model are the United States employees who are the best paid and have the best facilities. Under the Americans are the 'expatriates' (mainly Australians, Canadians, British and South Africans). They receive good salaries but less than the Americans. Under the expatriates are the third-country nationals (Chileans, Fijians, Nepalese, Rumanians, Hondurans, Peruvians, Colombians, Nigerians, Polish etc.). Their salaries vary according to the needs and can fluctuate from USD 1000 to 3000 monthly. At the bottom of the pyramid are the Iraqis or Afghans who are the least paid.[88]

D. Nationality and Residence

Under Article 47(2) of Additional Protocol I, Article 1(1) of the OAU Convention, and Article 1(1) of the UN Convention, a mercenary must be 'neither a national of

---

Right of Peoples to Self-Determination, Addendum, Mission to Fiji, 12; UN Doc A/HRC/7/7/Add4, 4 February 2008 (n 52 above), 19.

[83] See Singer (n 15 above), 77; Boldt (n 75 above), 534; Report of the Expert Meeting on Private Military Contractors: Status and State Responsibility for their Actions (n 57 above), 25; Z Salzman, 'Private Military Contractors and the Taint of a Mercenary Reputation', (2008) 40 New York University Journal of International Law and Politics 853, 885; M Scheimer, 'Separating Private Military Companies from Illegal Mercenaries in International Law: Proposing an International Convention for Legitimate Military and Security Support that Reflects Customary International Law', (2009) 24 American University International Law Review 609, 627.

[84] Committee on Oversight and Government Reform, 'Additional information about Blackwater USA: Memorandum, October 1, 2007' in Blackwater USA, Hearing before the Committee on Oversight and Government Reform: House of Representatives, 110th Congress, 1st Session, October 2, 2007, Serial no 110–89, 176, <http://oversight.house.gov/index.php?option=om_content&task=view&id=3912&Itemid=2>, accessed on 20 August 2010.

[85] Ibid, 189.

[86] The Congress of the United States, Congressional Budget Office, Contractors' Support of US Operations in Iraq (n 76 above), 14.

[87] See Singer (n 15 above), 77; Schmitt (n 71 above), 515; Salzman (n 83 above), 885; UN Doc A/HRC/7/7/Add3, 8 January 2008 (n 82 above), 11.

[88] Gómez del Prado, 'Private Military and Security Companies and the UN Working Group on the Use of Mercenaries' (2008) 13 Journal of Conflict and Security Law 429, 437–8.

a Party to the conflict nor a resident of territory controlled by a Party to the conflict'. Article 1(2) of the UN Convention adapts this requirement to concerted acts of violence committed outside an armed conflict. It stipulates that a mercenary must be 'neither a national nor a resident of the State against which such an act is directed'.

This requirement has been strongly criticized as leading to unwarranted distinctions, when applied to the personnel of PMSCs.[89] The armed conflict between the US-led coalition and Iraq has been cited as an illustrative case. US, UK, and Australian contractors dispatched to Iraq during the conflict as well as Iraqi contractors did not meet the requirement. In fact, they were nationals of a party to the conflict and, following the establishment of the Coalition Provisional Authority, Iraqi contactors were also residents of territory controlled by a party to the conflict. By contrast, Honduran, Peruvian, Chilean, and the other third-country contractors working in Iraq during the conflict fulfilled the nationality and residence requirement. Therefore, the latter could be labelled as mercenaries, provided that they met the other conditions set forth in Article 47(2) of Additional Protocol I, Article 1(1) of the OAU Convention, and Article 1(1) of the UN Convention. On the contrary, the former could not be considered as mercenaries, even if the other conditions were met.[90] Moreover, it has been pointed out that contractors can be easily granted citizenship by a belligerent so that they fall outside the definition of mercenary.[91]

E. Membership of the Armed Forces

Article 47(2) of Additional Protocol I, Article 1(1) of the OAU Convention, and Article 1(1) of the UN Convention all state that a person can be considered a mercenary only if he is neither a member of the armed forces of a state party to the armed conflict nor a member of the armed forces of a third state, sent by that state on official duty. With regard to concerted acts of violence outside an armed conflict, Article 1(2) of the UN Convention analogously provides that a person can be labelled mercenary only if he is not a member of the armed forces of the state on whose territory the act of violence is committed and has not been sent by a state on official duty.

---

[89] See Gillard (n 70 above), 569–70.; Cowling (n 70 above), 338; Gaston, 'Mercenarism 2.0? The Rise of the Modern Private Security Industry and its Implications for International Humanitarian Law Enforcement' (2008) 49 *Harvard International Law Journal* 221, 233; Sossai, 'Status of Private Military Companies' Personnel in the Laws of War: The Question of Direct Participation in Hostilities' (2008) 18 *Italian Yearbook of International Law* 89, 91.

[90] See Report of the Expert Meeting on Private Military Contractors: Status and State Responsibility for their Actions (n 57 above), 25; Cameron (n 56 above), 582; Gillard (n 70 above), 569; Doswald-Beck (n 57 above), 123; Gaston (n 89 above), 233.

[91] See Foreign and Commonwealth Office, HC 577, Private Military Companies: Options for Regulation 2001–2002 (n 41 above), 7; Boldt (n 75 above), 534; Pw Singer, 'War, Profits, and the Vacuum of Law: Privatized Military Firms and International Law' (2004) 42 *Columbia Journal of Transnational Law* 521, 533; C Walker and D Whyte, 'Contracting Out War?: Private Military Companies, Law and Regulation in the United Kingdom' (2005) 54 *International and Comparative Low Quarterly* 651, 679.

Almost all the personnel of PMSCs fulfil both these requirements. Indeed, many contractors are former military personnel. PMSCs prefer hiring former members of the national militaries so as to minimize the costs of training and evaluation of personnel. As for the requirement of not being a member of the armed forces of a belligerent state or of the state on whose territory the act of violence is undertaken, states can easily prevent it being met by incorporating contractors into their armed forces. By this simple mechanism, they can prevent the personnel of PMSCs working for them being considered mercenaries, even if all the other conditions set forth in Additional Protocol I, the OAU Convention, and the UN Convention are fulfilled.[92] For example, the 1997 contract between the government of Papua New Guinea and Sandline International stipulated that Sandline's personnel dispatched to Papua New Guinea were to be enrolled as 'Special Constables', but were to hold 'military ranks commensurate with those they hold within the Sandline command structure'. As members of the Papua New Guinea armed forces, Sandline's contractors could not have been labelled mercenaries.[93]

V. Conclusion

The analysis carried out suggests that only a very limited number of private contractors fall within the definitions of mercenary laid down in treaty law. As illustrated above, these definitions, which do not form part of customary law, list numerous conditions that must be cumulatively met before a person can be labelled mercenary. Thus, should the personnel of PMSCs not fulfil any one of the aforementioned conditions (eg the nationality and residence requirement) they will not be deemed to be mercenaries.[94]

The UN Working Group on the use of mercenaries has in fact come to this very conclusion. As regards the so-called 'private security guards', it has affirmed that 'although their activities have characteristics in common with mercenarism, save in exceptional cases they do not fit the technical definition provided in the International Convention against the Recruitment, Use, Financing and Training of Mercenaries'.[95]

After a thorough study of the practice of PMSCs and various field missions to states of different geographical areas, the UN Working Group has concluded that many activities performed by PMSCs cannot be considered as mercenary activities

---

[92] Gillard (n 70 above), 561 f.
[93] On this point see Ebbeck (n 47 above), 17; Foreign and Commonwealth Office, HC 577, Private Military Companies: Options for Regulation 2001–2002 (n 41 above), 7.
[94] Scheimer (n 83 above), 622–3, 631.
[95] UN Doc A/HRC/7/7/Add5, 5 March 2008, Report of the Working Group on the Use of Mercenaries as a Means of Violating Human Rights and Impeding the Exercise of the Right of Peoples to Self-Determination, Addendum, Latin American and Caribbean Regional Consultation on the Effects of the Activities of Private Military and Security Companies on the Enjoyment of Human Rights: Regulation and Monitoring (17–18 December 2007), 7. See also Gómez del Prado (n 88 above), 440.

under the existing international treaties.[96] It has found that 'many private military and security companies are operating in a "grey zone", which is not defined at all, or at the very least not clearly defined, by international legal norms',[97] and that 'new international regulations, most likely in the form of a new international convention with an accompanying model law, are needed in order to bring private military and security companies fully out of the legal "grey zone"'.[98] The Draft of a Possible Convention on Private Military and Security Companies, submitted by the UN Working Group on the use of mercenaries to the Human Rights Council in July 2010, aims at satisfying this need.[99]

---

[96] UN Doc A/HRC/10/14, 21 January 2009, Report of the Working Group on the Use of Mercenaries as a Means of Violating Human Rights and Impeding the Exercise of the Right of Peoples to Self-Determination, 10 f.

[97] Ibid, 11. See also UN Doc A/HRC/4/42/Add1, 20 February 2007 (n 52 above), 6; UN Doc A/HRC/7/7/Add2, 4 February 2008 (n 52 above), 6; UN Doc A/HRC/7/7/Add3, 8 January 2008 (n 82 above), 6.

[98] Ibid, 12. See also UN Doc A/63/325, 25 August 2008, Report of the Working Group on the Use of Mercenaries as a Means of Violating Human Rights and Impeding the Exercise of the Right of Peoples to Self-Determination, 17–18.

[99] See n 80 above.

PART IV

ACCOUNTABILITY AND RESPONSIBILITY OF PRIVATE CONTRACTORS

17

The Role of International Regulatory Initiatives on Business and Human Rights for Holding Private Military and Security Contractors to Account

Sorcha MacLeod

I. Introduction

It is axiomatic that private military and security companies (PMSCs) operate and contract for commercial gain and as such they fall naturally within the scope of the rapidly evolving international initiatives which address, in general terms, the accountability and responsibility of *all* business actors for human rights violations. Much of the existing literature has tended to address PMSC industry-specific responses but this chapter takes a different approach and focuses on some of the key international business and human rights or corporate social responsibility (CSR) initiatives which are of broad application, and considers to what extent they can ensure the accountability and responsibility of PMSCs. In particular, the chapter examines the implications of the work of the UN Secretary General's Special Representative on business and human rights (SGSR), John Ruggie, especially in relation to the due-diligence requirement, as well as the impact of the UN Global Compact and the Organization for Economic Cooperation and Development's (OECD) Guidelines for Multinational Enterprises. The chapter concludes that while there are positive and negative aspects to a business and human rights approach to regulating PMSCs, the weaknesses of the existing international initiatives, in particular their voluntary nature and lack of individual redress, outweigh the strengths. It further concludes that the protection of human rights would be better achieved by an overarching international regulatory architecture which builds upon the existing business and human rights initiatives rather than piecemeal, industry, or sector-led regulatory development.

The examples employed are by no means intended to be exhaustive but rather highlight how principles elaborated via business and human rights and CSR initiatives at the international and regional level apply to PMSCs. Given that these initiatives apply to business actors generally, it is essential that any attempt to regulate PMSCs take account of them.

II. The Development of Business and Human Rights Regulatory Initiatives

The idea that business actors are more than mere economic players, and have an expansive societal role has a long history[1] but it is not until the latter part of the twentieth century that a variety of different international and regional organizations, each aiming to make business actors liable for their misbehaviour and human rights violations in particular, sought to create regulatory systems applicable to business under the corporate social responsibility (CSR) banner. These CSR principles emerged as a reaction to globalization and the ensuing 'widespread growth of commerce and the reach of business'.[2] This growth was accompanied by serious misconduct by many commercial actors which cut across industries and escaped regulatory capture because of the transnational nature of the unethical behaviour and the inability or unwillingness of host and home states to hold businesses to account.[3] Organizations such as the UN and OECD, adopted a variety of regulatory mechanisms largely in response to campaigns by civil society which demanded that business actors be held accountable for their actions, especially in relation to human rights violations, labour rights, and environmental degradation, and particularly in developing nations.

Companies which had been able to operate in a multitude of overseas territories subject to little scrutiny, free from much regulatory constraint and acting with impunity, found themselves and their activities to be the focus of inspection and analysis at a global level almost overnight.[4] Or to put it another way, they became 'vulnerable' to 'brand tarnishing, to investor resistance, to shareholder resistance'.[5]

---

[1] See the 1930s debate around the stakeholder theory of corporate governance: AA Berle, 'Corporate Powers as Powers in Trust' (1931) 44 Harv L Rev 1049; AA Berle, 'For Whom Corporate Managers are Trustees' (1932) 45 Harv L Rev 45 (1365); EM Dodd, 'For Whom are Corporate Managers Trustees?' (1932) 45 Harv L Rev 1145. For an overview see eg CA Harwell Wells, 'the Cycles of Corporate Social Responsibility: An Historical Perspective for the Twenty-first Century' (2002) 51 U Kan L Rev 77. See also the work of the UN Centre on Transnational Corporations in eg T Sagafi-nejad and JH Dunning, *The UN and Transnational Corporations: From Code of Conduct to Global Compact* (2008), 89–123; see also P Muchlinski, *Multinational Enterprises and the Law*, 2nd edn (2007), 15–21.
[2] Center for Human Rights and Global Justice/Human Rights Watch, 'On the Margins of Profit: Rights at Risk in the Global Economy', vol 20(3), no 3(G), February 2008 (hereinafter 'On the Margins of Profit'), 50.
[3] For examples of businesses violating human rights see Report of the Special Representative of the Secretary General on the Issue of Human Rights and Transnational Corporations and Other Business Enterprises, John Ruggie, Business and Human Rights: Mapping International Standards of Responsibility and Accountability for Corporate Acts, UN Doc A/HRC/4/35, 19 February 2007. See also generally 'On the Margins of Profit' (n 2 above).
[4] J Parkinson, 'The Socially Responsible Company' in MK Addo (ed), *Human Rights Standards and the Responsibility of Transnational Corporations* (1999), 49–62, 49.
[5] L Henkin, 'The Universal Declaration at 50 and the Challenge of Global Markets' (1999) 25 Brook J Int'l L 17, 24.

This was not as a result of positive 'corporate initiative'; rather it was 'the result of reputational disaster'.[6] NGOs and other 'norm entrepreneurs'[7] disseminated evidence of their wrongdoings, galvanizing public opinion and stimulating media interest.[8] The UN SGSR on business and human rights, John Ruggie describes the phenomenon:

> Each day, allegations of human rights abuses make their way to the public through various channels. Increasingly, companies are the subjects of these allegations. Whether through official reports or more informal means, various parties—NGOs, trade unions, States, media outlets, communities, shareholders and individuals—express concern over corporate-related human rights abuses.[9]

PMSCs, along with every other transnational business actor, are thus likely to find their activities under increasing civil society scrutiny.

It was against this backdrop that rapid development of a business and human rights paradigm took place throughout the 1990s and early years of the new millennium, albeit one upon which there was little agreement between states, international organizations, business, and civil society. While at least one entity, the UN Sub-Commission on the Promotion and Protection of Human Rights, sought to establish internationally binding rules in relation to the responsibility of business for human rights violations in the form of a multilateral covenant,[10] others such as the UN Global Compact (UNGC) and the EU relied upon the voluntary participation of business in adhering to wider CSR principles.[11] Still others, in particular the OECD, road tested new hybrid methods, combining binding international rules for states with domestic implementation via national contact points (NCP).[12] Such developments took place alongside the establishment of industry-

---

[6] G Chandler, Keynote Speech, JUSTICE/Sweet & Maxwell conference, 'Corporate Liability: Human Rights and the Modern Business', 12 June 2006, 2, <http://www.business-humanrights.org/Links/Repository/791944>, accessed on 18 June 2010.

[7] HH Koh, 'How is International Human Rights Law Enforced?' (1999) 74 Ind L J 1397, 1409; H Koh, 'Bringing International Law Home' (1998) 35 Hous L Rev 623, 646.

[8] See eg 'On the Margins of Profit' (n 2 above) which sets out specific instances of business violating human rights across a variety of sectors.

[9] Report of the Special Representative of the Secretary General on the Issue of Human Rights and Transnational Corporations and Other Business Enterprises, Addendum 2, Corporations and human rights: A survey of the scope and patterns of alleged corporate-related human rights abuse, A/HRC/8/5/ADD2, 23 May 2008, 8 (hereinafter 'Ruggie Survey 2008').

[10] Eg UN Norms on the Responsibilities of Transnational Corporations and Other Business Enterprises with Regard to Human Rights, UN Doc E/CN4/Sub2/2003/12/rev2 (2003).

[11] Eg UN Global Compact, <http://www.unglobalcompact.org/HowToParticipate/Business_Participation/How_To_Join_the_Global_Compact.html>, accessed on 14 June 2010; and the EU, Communication from the Commission to the European Parliament, The Council and the European Economic and Social Committee, Implementing the Partnership for Growth and Jobs: Making Europe A Pole of Excellence on Corporate Responsibility, COM(2006) 136 Final, 22 March 2006, 2.

[12] OECD, Guidelines on Multinational Enterprises, Revision 2000 (2008). For an analysis of the effective of the different approaches see S MacLeod, 'Stuck in the Middle With You?: Alternative Approaches to Realising Accountability for Human Rights Violations by Business' in D French, M Saul, and ND White (eds), *International Law and Dispute Settlement: New Problems and Techniques* (2010), 87–107.

specific initiatives[13] as well as the creation of codes of conduct by individual business actors. In general, the UN, OECD, and EU mechanisms focus on broad CSR standards, encompassing human rights, environmental, and labour issues, and the principles elaborated apply to business actors across the board, drawing no distinction between different industries or commercial sectors. Thus they are applicable to PMSCs.

This chaotic and disparate state of affairs was deemed unsatisfactory by UN Secretary General Kofi Annan and in 2005 he appointed Professor John Ruggie of Harvard University as the Secretary General's Special Representative on Business and Human Rights with a mandate to identify the issues around business and human rights and to come up with some solutions.[14] Ruggie was granted an initial two year mandate[15] by the Commission on Human Rights which was extended by one year in order to enable to complete the final report under that mandate and he was granted a further three year mandate in 2008.[16] In 2008 in Ruggie's final report under his 2005 mandate, he described the problem thus:

> The business and human rights debate currently lacks an authoritative focal point. Claims and counter-claims proliferate, initiatives abound, and yet no effort reaches significant scale. Amid this confusing mix, laggards—States as well as companies—continue to fly below the radar.[17]

This lack of coherence is reflected within the PMSC sector with the emergence of international initiatives in the form of the Voluntary Principles on Security and Human Rights[18] and the Montreux Document[19] as well as codes of conduct established by trade bodies, the British Association of Private Security Companies,[20] and its US counterpart, the International Peace Operations Association.[21]

Ruggie's 2008 report also unveiled the benchmark standard of 'Protect, Respect, and Remedy' which pinpoints the three principles that ought to apply in regulating corporate behaviour. This benchmark standard encompasses several important ideas. Significantly the Protect, Respect, and Remedy agenda recognizes that the primary duty to protect human rights rests with states *but* that businesses do have a

---

[13] Eg the Kimberley Process Certification Scheme for rough diamonds, <http://www.kimberleyprocess.com/>, accessed on 18 June 2010.
[14] Human Rights and Transnational Corporations and Other Business Enterprises, Human Rights Res 2005/69, 20 April 2005.
[15] Ibid.
[16] Mandate of the Special Representative of the Secretary General on the Issue of Human Rights and Transnational Corporations and Other Business Enterprises, Human Rights Council Res 8/7, 18 June 2008.
[17] 'Protect, Respect, and Remedy: A framework for business and human rights', Report of the Special Representative of the Secretary General on the Issue of Human Rights and Transnational Corporations and Other Business Enterprises, John Ruggie A/HRC/8/5 7 April 2008 (hereinafter 'Protect, Respect, and Remedy').
[18] <http://www.voluntaryprinciples.org/>, accessed on 20 June 2010.
[19] <http://www.icrc.org/web/eng/siteeng0.nsf/htmlall/montreux-document-170908/$FILE/ICRC_002_0996.pdf>, accessed on 20 June 2010.
[20] BAPSC <http://www.bapsc.org.uk/key_documents-charter.asp>, accessed on 20 June 2010.
[21] IPOA <http://www.ipoaworld.org/eng/codeofconduct/87-codecodeofconductv12enghtml.html>, accessed on 20 June 2010.

baseline responsibility to respect human rights and, perhaps most crucially, that there is a requirement to establish an adequate and appropriate remedy for any human rights abuses, which fulfils the dual functions of punishment and redress. According to Ruggie, these three principles together 'form a complementary whole in that each supports the others in achieving sustainable progress'.[22]

Aiming to provide a focal point for the business and human rights debate and implement the Protect, Respect, and Remedy agenda, the 2008 Special Representative mandate conferred by the Human Rights Council specifically authorizes Ruggie, among other things, 'to identify, exchange and promote best practices and lessons learned' in the field of business and human rights and to consult with 'international and regional organizations', among others, on relevant issues.[23] He is also required to report annually to the Human Rights Council and General Assembly.[24]

Obviously these duties are to be carried out while taking account of the underlying principles of Protect, Respect, and Remedy, namely that the primary duty of the *state* is to protect citizens from human rights abuses, that the active obligation incumbent upon *business* is to respect and protect human rights (essentially to 'do no harm'),[25] and that the necessity of ensuring access to adequate remedies for those who have suffered human rights violations at the hands of business is paramount. Importantly, businesses must exercise 'due diligence' when carrying out commercial activities to ensure that human rights requirements are met; furthermore, this due-diligence requirement extends to the supply chain.[26] Ruggie defines due diligence as:

> a process whereby companies not only ensure compliance with national laws but also manage the risk of human rights harm with a view to avoiding it. The scope of human rights-related due diligence is determined by the context in which a company is operating, its activities, and the relationships associated with those activities.[27]

This contextual approach is significant, because it thus appears that different circumstances may warrant different standards of behaviour from business actors and seems to establish variable degrees of due diligence. Potentially this will impose higher standards of behaviour for those businesses operating in conflict zones and is therefore likely to be of considerable importance for PMSCs.[28] In his 2010 Report, SGSR Ruggie elaborates on what due diligence means for business actors in practice and there is a clear focus on what Harold Koh calls 'norm-internalization'—that is,

---

[22] Protect, Respect, and Remedy (n 17 above), para 9.
[23] 4(e) and (g) Human Rights Council Res 8/7, Mandate of the Special Representative of the Secretary General on the Issue of Human Rights and Transnational Corporations and Other Business Enterprises, 18 June 2008.
[24] Ibid, 4(h).
[25] Protect, Respect, and Remedy (n 17 above), paras 24, 54–5.
[26] Ibid.
[27] Ibid, para 25.
[28] See discussion below.

the process whereby rules 'transform from being some kind of external sanction to becoming an internal imperative'.[29]

Ruggie identifies four 'essential' elements which will enable business actors to perform human rights due diligence. First, there should be 'a statement of policy articulating the company's commitment to respect human rights' accompanied, secondly, by 'periodic assessment of actual and potential human rights impacts of company activities and relationships'.[30] Thirdly, he insists that these 'commitments and assessments' be integrated 'into internal control and oversight systems'. And finally, the company must track and report on its performance.[31] It is Ruggie's view that:

> Company-level grievance mechanisms perform two functions: under the tracking and reporting component of due diligence, they provide the company with feedback that helps identify risks and avoid escalation of disputes; they can also provide remedy ...[32]

So there are two clear strands to Ruggie's proposals, first, *preventing* human rights abuses by business actors and, secondly, ensuring that the victims of such abuses have *effective access to redress*. Undoubtedly the provision of effective remedies for human rights violations by business is the area most in need of urgent attention and in the opinion of Ruggie is seriously 'underdeveloped', 'patchwork', and 'flawed' and can only be satisfactorily addressed by combining the three principles of Protect, Respect, and Remedy.[33] In order to address this inchoate state of affairs, Ruggie has outlined the minimum substantive and procedural elements required for an effective remedy, clearly drawing on established human rights discourse.[34] An effective remedy should be 'legitimate', 'accessible', 'predictable', 'equitable', 'rights-compatible', and 'transparent', which in essence means that it ought to be independent, non-discriminatory, fair, and with clearly defined procedures.[35] It is not at all clear whether the internal grievance procedures proposed in the 2010 Report will meet these requirements for an effective remedy. In particular, any business-based redress mechanism will struggle to attain legitimacy and raises issues of enforceability.

Ruggie's project, rightly or wrongly, is the key global business and human rights project of the moment and so it is appropriate to view the examples identified throughout this chapter through a Ruggie lens. As will be demonstrated, some, but not all, of the Ruggie criteria are met by existing international initiatives.

In order to move towards implementation of the Protect, Respect, and Remedy framework, SGSR Ruggie's Preliminary Work Plan and 2010 Report outline the

---

[29] n 7 above, 1400.
[30] Report of the Special Representative of the Secretary General on the Issue of Human Rights and Transnational Corporations and Other Business Enterprises, John Ruggie A/HRC/14/27, 9 April 2010, para 83.
[31] Ibid.
[32] Ibid.
[33] Protect, Respect, and Remedy (n 17 above), paras 26, 87.
[34] See eg D Shelton, *Remedies in International Human Rights Law*, 2nd edn (2006), 7–10.
[35] n 17 above, para 92.

so-called 'operational phase' of the Mandate and represent a response to those critics who were unhappy with what they perceived to be a merely principled approach to the problem, lacking in concrete action.[36] It is evident that a multi-stakeholder approach is crucial to this phase and SGSR Ruggie is very keen to see 'what works, what doesn't, and where the gaps are' by drawing upon the experiences of all international institutions involved with business and human rights.[37]

This high-profile experiential methodology is to be welcomed as in recent years there has been reluctance in some quarters, most notably on the part of the EU, to learn from the business and human rights/CSR practice of others.[38] SGSR Ruggie is seeking to amass this shared information to create what is described as 'a backdrop to the mandate's own processes of developing guiding principles'.[39] It is Ruggie's belief that in doing so it will 'strengthen the overall international architecture in the business and human rights domain'.[40] The question is whether existing initiatives have anything positive to contribute to this architecture.

In submitting his final report under the original mandate Ruggie recognizes throughout that the 'Protect, Respect, and Remedy' mantra is simply a framework for action and acknowledges that it is merely a baseline, or starting point, and clearly indicates the aspiration for practical tactics for moving the process forward. In his 2010, report he begins to outline some practical responses including the corporate internalization of the 'responsibility to respect'[41] and judicial and non-judicial mechanisms which will 'operationalize' the framework.[42] For example, he recommends strengthening the OECD mechanism, which is examined later in this chapter, as well as ensuring that legal barriers to responsibility are removed.[43]

Such progress is heavily dependent upon states, however, and while it is clear that some, like Norway, for example, are supportive of Ruggie's goals, the fact remains that many states remain resolutely opposed to the imposition of direct human rights obligations upon business and seek to limit their role to respecting human rights principles.

---

[36] Preliminary Work Plan Mandate of the Special Representative on the Issue of Human Rights and Transnational Corporations and other Business Enterprises, 1 September 2008–30 June 2011 (10 October 2008), <http://www.reports-and-materials.org/Ruggie-preliminary-work-plan-2008-2011.pdf>, accessed on 20 August 2010 (hereinafter 'Ruggie Work Plan'). For civil society criticisms of Ruggie see eg Earthrights International, 'Ominous outlook for the norms', 22 March 2006, <http://www.earthrights.org/legalfeature/ominous_outlook_for_the_un_norms.html>, accessed on 20 August 2010; Á deRegil, 'Business and Human Rights: Upholding the Market's Social Darwinism', Report by Jus Semper, October 2008, <http://www.jussemper.org/Resources/Corporate%20Activity/Resources/BHRRUpholding_Mkts_Darwinis.pdf>, accessed on 20 August 2010.
[37] Ruggie Work Plan (n 36 above), 3.
[38] See S MacLeod, 'Reconciling Regulatory Approaches to Corporate Social Responsibility: The European Union, OECD and United Nations Compared', (2007) 13 European Public Law 671–702; see also ND White and S MacLeod, 'EU Operations and Private Military Contractors: Issues of Corporate and Institutional Responsibility' (2008) 19 EJIL 965–88.
[39] Ruggie Work Plan (n 36 above), 3.
[40] Ibid, 4.
[41] Ruggie Report 2010 (n 30 above), para 123.
[42] Ibid, paras 96–113.
[43] Ibid, paras 98–100 and 103–13 respectively.

350   *Accountability and Responsibility of Private Contractors*

Thus it is clear that while there have been significant developments in attempting to regulate the behaviour of business actors in relation to human rights, concerns remain about the initiatives and principles established. This is reflected in the mandate and work of SGSR Ruggie. In particular, disagreements remain regarding the voluntary status of the initiatives, their lack of coherence, and the nature and content of the obligations relevant to business actors. Nevertheless, despite the theoretical differences and disordered development of the global business and human rights agenda, some of the initiatives developed offer helpful and workable methods for ensuring business accountability. The development of the due-diligence principle is especially important. The next section of the chapter examines both the positive and negative aspects of some of the existing initiatives and considers their impact on PMSC regulation.

III. The Possibilities and Limitations of a Business and Human Rights Approach to PMSC Regulation

This section of the chapter outlines some of the strengths and weaknesses of a business and human rights/CSR approach to PMSC regulation, especially in its attempts to address business entities directly at the international level rather than the traditional international law approach where obligations are placed upon states to control or regulate those non-state actors (including companies) within their jurisdictions. It is this conservative view of international human rights law which allows business actors to escape international legal regulation.[44] Importantly, as will be seen below, this conservative approach has become reflected in the work of SGSR Ruggie.

Several anomalies in this conservative approach can be identified, however, upon an examination of how corporations have been treated by states historically (in the case of the Dutch and British East India Companies in the seventeenth century) and in more recent times (where, eg, companies have been allowed to bring claims against states for unlawful expropriations). It can be demonstrated that states have clearly considered corporations to be subjects of international law or at least capable of engaging international responsibility in a derivative manner.[45] In many ways, therefore, the application of hard international obligations to business actors remains the exception rather than the rule.

Today it is generally accepted that private business actors, including PMSCs, are capable of violating, and do violate, human rights.[46] In the PMSC context, the killing of civilians by Blackwater USA in Bahgdad's Nisour Square in 2007 is

---

[44] But see Ch 5 by Francioni in this volume on a proposed expansive notion of human rights 'jurisdiction'.
[45] ND White and S MacLeod, 'EU Operations and Private Military Contractors: Issues of Corporate and Institutional Responsibility' (2008) 19 EJIL 965, 969.
[46] See eg Ruggie Survey 2008 (n 9 above); and generally 'On the Margins of Profit' (n 2 above).

notorious and highlighted the lack of accountability and responsibility of such businesses and has underlined the urgent need for regulation.[47] Human rights protection mechanisms and rules, however, have failed to keep up with such developments and accordingly, are 'unrelated fragments of responses'[48] and, as emphasized above, are disparate in nature, relying almost without exception upon the voluntary engagement of business.

Most states adhere to a traditional perception of the subjects of international law, which leads to a situation whereby international human rights law is interpreted as only imposing direct obligations upon states and not business actors. Despite calls from civil society for human rights obligations to be imposed directly on business actors, pressure by states has ensured that the status quo is maintained.

Like the Montreux Document,[49] initiatives such as the UN's Global Compact and the OECD's Guidelines on Multinational Enterprises, focus on reminding *states* of their obligations under international human rights law rather than imposing direct legal responsibility upon business actors. This approach is widely rejected by civil society but holds much currency among states[50] and, disappointingly, has influenced SGSR Ruggie.

In 2008 when he launched his Protect, Respect, and Remedy framework, Ruggie was open to the idea that international human rights law applied directly to business actors. The benchmark framework requires states to protect human rights, business actors to respect them, and for states to provide a remedy but SGSR Ruggie has recently confirmed his adherence to a narrower state-centric view of international law. In his 2010 report to the Human Rights Council, Ruggie states that 'respecting rights is not an obligation that current international human rights law generally imposes directly on companies'.[51] SGSR Ruggie does, however, take the view that the state duty to protect against human rights abuses extends to protection 'against other social actors, including business, who impede or negate

---

[47] For an outline of the Nisour Square incident see S Chesterman and A Fisher, 'Private Security, Public Order' in S Chesterman and A Fisher (eds), *Private Security, Public Order: The Outsourcing of Public Services and its Limits* (2009), at 222–6, at 222. On the failed criminal prosecution in the United States see Ch 21 by Quirico in this volume.

[48] Presentation of Report to United Nations Human Rights Council Professor John G Ruggie Special Representative of the Secretary General for Business and Human Rights, Geneva, 3 June 2008, 2, <http://www.business-humanrights.org/Documents/Ruggie-Human-Rights-Council-3-Jun-2008.pdf>, accessed on 14 June 2010; see also 'On the Margins of Profit' (n 2 above), 50.

[49] ICRC/Swiss Federal Department of Foreign Affairs, The Montreux Document on Pertinent International Legal Obligations and Good Practices for States Related to Operations of Private Military and Security Companies during Armed Conflict, August 2009, <http://www.icrc.org/web/eng/siteeng0.nsf/htmlall/montreux-document-170908/$FILE/ICRC_002_0996.pdf>, accessed on 14 June 2010.

[50] See eg Letter to Professor John Ruggie from the UK's Legal Adviser Daniel Bethlehem QC, dated 9 July 2009, <http://www.reports-and-materials.org/UK-Foreign-Office-letter-to-Ruggie-9-Jul-2009.pdf>, accessed on 14 June 2010.

[51] Ruggie Report 2010 (n 30 above), para 55. See also Letter to Daniel Bethlehem, UK Legal Adviser 14 July 2009, <http://www.reports-and-materials.org/Ruggie-letter-to-UK-Foreign-Office-14-Jul-2009.pdf>, accessed 14 June 2010.

those rights'.[52] Thus Ruggie's present position is that only states are required to protect human rights while business actors are expected to respect human rights standards and to utilize due diligence in their commercial activities to ensure that the standards are observed.

Even if this conservative approach to the application of international human rights standards is maintained—that is, that there are no direct and hard legal obligations incumbent upon business—nevertheless business actors are finding that their behaviour is being scrutinized to a greater extent and that they are being asked increasingly to account for their actions, albeit via non-judicial, more informal mechanisms. Notwithstanding their limitations, existing business and human rights initiatives, while not ensuring full accountability, responsibility, and ultimately remedies for human rights violations in a binding regulatory form, *do* provide an assortment of limited alternative responses to bad business behaviour. As Amartya Sen asserts, the protection of human rights 'need not...be confined only to making new laws'.[53]

By looking to the UN's Global Compact[54] and the implementation of the OECD's Guidelines on Multinational Enterprises[55] with its attendant National Contact Points, a number of common positives and negatives can be identified which will be of guidance for regulating PMSCs.[56] This section of the chapter pinpoints some theoretical concerns before identifying various weaknesses and strengths of some of these initiatives.

A. Theoretical Considerations

Despite the views of many states and SGSR Ruggie, business and human rights initiatives reflect a shifting paradigm, one where it is becoming increasingly difficult to contend that international human rights law does not apply directly to private actions.[57] Andrew Clapham describes two trends in particular which underpin this new paradigm and which are driving the redefinition of 'the parameters of the public and private spheres' and means that non-state private actors ought to bear direct human rights obligations.[58] First, he categorizes business actors (among others) as one of the emerging 'new fragmented centres of power' and concludes that their rise means that:

---

[52] Report of the Special Representative of the Secretary General on the Issue of Human Rights and Transnational Corporations and Other Business Enterprises, John Ruggie, A/HRC/11/13, April 2009, para 13.

[53] A Sen, 'Human Rights and the Limits of Law,' (2006) 27 Cardozo L Rev 2913, 2919.

[54] For general information on the Global Compact see 'UN Global Compact: Corporate Citizenship in the Global Economy', <http://www.unglobalcompact.org/docs/news_events/8.1/GC_brochure_FINAL.pdf>, accessed on 13 January 2010.

[55] OECD, Guidelines (n 12 above), <http://www.oecd.org/dataoecd/56/36/1922428.pdf>, accessed on 13 January 2010.

[56] For more on the Global Compact and the OECD Guidelines see MacLeod (n 12 above).

[57] A Clapham, *Human Rights in the Private Sphere* (1993), 343 (hereinafter 'Clapham').

[58] Ibid, 137.

the individual now perceives authority, repression, and alienation in a variety of new bodies, whereas once it was only the State which was perceived... to exhibit these characteristics.[59]

In such circumstances, it makes sense to protect the individual from the abuse of power no matter the source of the abuse, including PMSCs and other business actors.

The second relevant trend is that narrow, traditional conceptions of the 'private sphere' have become outdated and must be 're-evaluated'.[60] So the 'classical distinction... which identifies the public with the nation-State and the private with the free market' must be re-examined because: 'The public/private distinction can quickly become a weapon utilized in order to deny or claim jurisdiction.'[61] It is precisely this problem that the business and human rights initiatives were implemented to circumvent.

While there are few specific references to PMSCs by the various initiatives, absent express exclusion, it is therefore appropriate to conclude that PMSCs as commercial entities are included within the scope of these established business and human rights initiatives. Indeed the approach has been less about the types of business involved and more about the business environment in which they are operating. There is, nevertheless, divergence of opinion as regards the development of principles governing business in conflict zones and crucially whether PMSCs ought to be treated as a separate concern.

The OECD, UN Global Compact, and SGSR Ruggie have all highlighted the particular importance of regulating business behaviour *in general* within conflict or weak governance zones—that is, where the state is unable or unwilling to discharge its obligations. The OECD has a Risk Awareness Tool[62] while the Global Compact has instigated policy dialogues and published guidance on doing business in conflict zones.[63] These initiatives are applicable to business actors in a broad sense and aim to help establish a culture of 'conflict sensitive business practices'.[64] Likewise, SGSR Ruggie does not refer to PMSCs as a distinct category of business requiring specific regulation but he has, however, indicated his concerns about business operations within conflict zones noting in his 2010 Report that:

The worst corporate-related human rights abuses occur amid armed conflict over the control of territory, resources or a government itself—where the human rights regime cannot be expected to function as intended and illicit enterprises flourish. However, even reputable firms may become implicated in abuses, typically committed by others; for example, security forces protecting company installations and personnel.[65]

---

[59] Ibid.
[60] Ibid.
[61] Ibid.
[62] OECD, 'Risk Awareness Tool for Multinational Enterprises in Weak Governance Zones', <http://www.oecd.org/dataoecd/26/21/36885821.pdf>, accessed on 18 June 2010.
[63] See generally UN Global Compact, K Ballentine and V Haufler, 'Enabling Economies of Peace: Public Policy for Conflict-sensitive Business', February 2009, <http://www.unglobalcompact.org/docs/issues_doc/Peace_and_Business/Enabling_Economies_2009.pdf>, accessed on 18 June 2010.
[64] Ibid, 4.
[65] Ruggie Report 2010 (n 30 above), para 44.

Non-governmental organizations (NGOs) are split on the issue as regards the development of principles governing business in conflict zones and crucially whether there ought to be a PMSC sector-specific approach to regulation. Some, such as ActionAid, argue that 'business is business' and that SGSR Ruggie should be creating principles applicable to all business enterprises irrespective of the existence of a conflict in the host state.[66] Others, such as Amnesty International, make direct reference to PMSCs on the basis that 'there are specific accountability issues' because of the contractual relationships between PMSCs and states.[67] Amnesty is particularly concerned with what it regards as state failure to protect human rights standards and the apparent immunity granted to PMSCs, particularly in Iraq and Afghanistan. The NGO is keen to ensure that 'States cannot contract out of human rights responsibilities' as a consequence of commercial dealings. PMSCs are singled out for attention and Amnesty has encouraged SGSR Ruggie 'to look at the role played by private military and security contractors in conflict and beyond'.[68] Ruggie's response has been to convene 'a group of States in informal, scenario-based, off-the-record brainstorming sessions to generate innovative and practical approaches for preventing and mitigating corporate abuses in these difficult contexts'.[69]

SGSR Ruggie treats business actors operating in conflict zones as a special case, which has implications both for PMSC regulation and for the business and human rights agenda generally, given that his work is extremely influential in determining the direction of that agenda. Such an approach weakens the protection of human rights. It is inherent in the very nature of human rights that there ought to be universal rules applicable to *all* businesses irrespective of the host state and the business environment.

Though the business and human rights/CSR movement is an important development at the international level, and one that may develop eventually into a recognition of international legal persons with duties and rights at the international level, it is contended that an effective model of regulation requires at its core binding international standards applicable to states, supervised at the international level but implemented and enforced against PMSCs at the national level. Though there should also be mechanisms of accountability and remediality at the international level against PMSCs (and states) to complement those at the national level and to provide a safety net for individuals denied justice at the national level. Clearly supervised international treaty standards, binding on states, and implemented and enforced at the national level, are therefore the basis for an effective hybrid model.

---

[66] Letter from ActionAid to SGSR Ruggie, 30 June 2008.
[67] Amnesty International Submission to the Special Representative of the Secretary General on the Issue of Human Rights and Transnational Corporations and Other Business Enterprises, IOR 40/018/18/2008, 1 July 2008, 4.
[68] Ibid.
[69] Ruggie Report 2010 (n 30 above), para 45.

B. The Strengths of a Business and Human Rights-based Approach to PMSC Regulation

It is possible to identify six key strengths emanating in particular from the Global Compact and the OECD Guidelines which may be effective in holding business actors to account.

First, both the Global Compact and OECD systems adopt a top-down–bottom-up approach, whereby each initiative relies upon the top-down application of general international human rights standards as well as bottom-up implementation of those standards at the national level. The Global Compact does this through its Local Networks which promote the GC as a policy initiative and disseminate information about human rights. The OECD requires adherent states to implement the Guidelines via national contact points using a specific instance procedure (SIP).

Under the OECD Guidelines any 'interested party' may lodge a complaint, via the SIP, alleging extraterritorial wrongdoing by a business operating from an OECD adherent state. The UK SIP is one of the better examples of a SIP, with several cases resulting in complaints against transnational business actors being upheld. Importantly, in the UK context several NGOs have lodged successful complaints.[70] Once a complaint is lodged, voluntary mediation may be undertaken, otherwise determinations are made regarding the behaviour of the enterprise with reference to the Guidelines and recommendations are made. The determination and recommendations are made public via a UK government website.[71] It is important to note that PMSCs are not excluded from the remit of the SIP. There have been no complaints brought against PMSCs so far, but two important UK determinations, while not involving PMSCs, upheld complaints of human rights violations against businesses operating in conflict zones.[72] It is not hard to envisage, therefore, that PMSCs could find themselves the subject of complaint and thus be held accountable via this existing mechanism without the need for an industry-specific mechanism.

The second strength of both the GC and the OECD initiatives, is that they are multi-stakeholder in nature. That is, they actively involve relevant actors in the CSR process, namely states, business actors, NGOs, trade unions, industry bodies, and other members of civil society such as academics. It has become generally accepted that a multi-stakeholder CSR mechanism which engages all relevant

---

[70] Eg Global Witness, Survival International, and RAID.
[71] <http://www.bis.gov.uk/policies/business-sectors/low-carbon-business-opportunities/sustainable-development/corporate-responsibility/uk-ncp-oecd-guidelines/cases>, accessed on 18 June 2010.
[72] Final Statement by the UK National Contact Point for the OECD Guidelines for Multinational Enterprises: Afrimex (UK) Ltd, 28 August 2008, URN 08/1209 (Afrimex Final Statement); Final Statement by the UK National Contact Point (NCP) for the OECD Guidelines for Multinational Enterprises: Das Air, 21 July 2008, both available at <http://www.bis.gov.uk/policies/business-sectors/low-carbon-business-opportunities/sustainable-development/corporate-responsibility/uk-ncp-oecd-guidelines/cases>, accessed on 18 June 2010.

parties is to be preferred.[73] Witness the substantial criticism that the EU attracted when it abandoned its multi-stakeholder approach to CSR and chose to engage only with representatives of business.[74]

Thirdly, both projects demonstrate elements of transparency. According to SGSR Ruggie, an effective CSR mechanism 'must provide sufficient transparency of process and outcome to meet the public interest concerns at stake and should presume transparency wherever possible; non-State mechanisms in particular should be transparent about the receipt of complaints and the key elements of their outcomes'. The Global Compact and the UK NCP both offer examples of how a measure of transparency can be achieved. So, for example, the Global Compact asks that member companies voluntarily produce an annual report indicating their compliance with its human rights, environmental, and anti-corruption principles,[75] while, as indicated above, the UK NCP publishes its determinations and recommendations regarding corporate violations of human rights on the Department for Business, Innovation and Skills (BIS) website.[76]

A fourth strength of the GC and OECD projects is that business accountability is a key factor. Accountability mechanisms are a crucial element of any business and human rights initiative for holding business enterprises responsible for violations of human rights standards in order to hold them to their obligations. So, for example, the GC utilizes 'naming and shaming' techniques to highlight members who fail to report as required.[77] Companies can be permanently delisted from the Global Compact for failure to adhere to its principles and this information is published on the GC website.[78] The OECD Guidelines entail a more formal accountability mechanism because they impose obligations upon adherent states to establish an NCP to implement and promote the Guidelines and also to create a SIP.[79] As indicated above, the SIP may investigate complaints against businesses incorporated in the adhering state in relation to human rights violations and offers

---

[73] See eg Human Rights Council Resolution 8/7, Mandate of the Special Representative of the Secretary-General on the issue of human rights and transnational corporations and other business enterprises, 18 June 2008, para 4(e), (f), and (g). The SGSR is required to engage with a variety of stakeholders: <http://ap.ohchr.org/documents/E/HRC/resolutions/A_HRC_RES_8_7.pdf>, accessed on 14 January 2010.

[74] For an overview of the NGO position, see the European Coalition for Corporate Justice Advocacy Briefing, 'Corporate Social Responsibility at EU level: Proposals and Recommendations to the European Commission and the European Parliament', November 2006, <http://www.europarl.europa.eu/meetdocs/2004_2009/documents/dv/eccadvocacybriefing112006_/eccadvocacybriefing112006_en.pdf>, accessed on 14 January 2010.

[75] Global Compact 'Communicating Progress' 7 August 2009, <http://www.unglobalcompact.org/COP/index.html>, accessed on 14 January 2010.

[76] n 71 above.

[77] <http://www.unglobalcompact.org/NewsAndEvents/news_archives/2009_10_07.html>, accessed on 13 January 2010.

[78] The list of companies delisted includes several household names, eg Avon Brazil, Addecco Australia, and Radisson SAS Hotels Bulgaria, <http://www.unglobalcompact.org/docs/news_events/9.1_news_archives/2009_10_07/Delisted_List_10_07_2009.pdf>, accessed on 18 June 2010.

[79] Decision of the OECD Council on the Guidelines on Multinational Enterprises, June 2000 (hereinafter 'Council Decision 2000') in the OECD Guidelines on Multinational Enterprises, Review 2000 (Paris: OECD, 2000), 31–2.

some accountability. NGOs have highlighted that 'the importance of an NCP publicly finding companies to have been in breach of the Guidelines should not be underestimated.'[80] Public acknowledgement of a complaint is powerful in itself and if the complaint is upheld by the state-backed NCP, it is vested with a great deal of authority.

The increasing use of domestic mechanisms by business and human rights initiatives has enabled the enhanced promotion and dissemination of information regarding human rights standards and so yields a fifth strength. A large part of the Global Compact's work involves disseminating information about human rights standards. This is done by the GC itself and increasingly by the domestic Local Networks.[81] As mentioned above, the OECD NCPs are required to promote the standards established in the Guidelines.[82] Furthermore, statements by NCPs serve to clarify the scope of the Guidelines as well as helping to establish expected standards of business behaviour in relation to human rights. For example, in 2005 the Norwegian NCP issued clear guidance to a Norwegian-based company, Aker Kværner, regarding its wholly owned US subsidiary KPSI.[83] It found that both parent and subsidiary had provided maintenance services at the US prison at Guantanamo Bay and that these services 'at least in part can be considered to have affected the inmates.'[84] In its conclusion, the NCP:

> emphasized the importance of continuous assessments by Norwegian companies of their activities in relation to human rights in general, adding that the provision of goods or services in situations like Guantanamo Bay require 'particular vigilance.'[85]

The NCP also criticized Aker Kværner for failing to undertake 'a thorough and documented assessment of the ethical issues in connection with its tender for the renewal of the contract in 2005' and recommended that the company establish and apply a clear CSR policy across its operations. NCPs can therefore proffer strong and clear guidance to specific businesses while clarifying more generally the CSR standards which business actors are expected to implement.

A final strength of CSR is that, although the existing international system of CSR initiatives is chaotic and disparate resulting from too many different isolated projects, in recent years there has been improved cooperation and cross-fertilization of ideas, principles, and standards.[86] This integration has gathered momentum as a

---

[80] OECD Watch/J Oldenziel, J Wilde-Ramsing, and P Feeney, '10 Years On: Assessing the Contribution of the OECD Guidelines for Multinational Enterprises to Responsible Business Conduct', OECD Watch, June 2010, 22.
[81] UN Global Compact, 'Annual Review 2008' (UN Global Compact Office, New York, March 2009), 18–22, <http://www.unglobalcompact.org/docs/news_events/9.1_news_archives/2009_04_08/GC_2008AR_FINAL.pdf>, accessed on 14 January 2010.
[82] Council Decision 2000 (n 79 above).
[83] OECD NCP (Norway), Forum for Environment and Development v Aker Kværner ASA, Cuba 2005, <http://baseswiki.org/en/OECD_NCP_(Norway),_Forum_for_Environment_and_Development_vs._Aker_Kv%C3%A6rner_ASA,_Cuba_2005>, accessed on 28 June 2010.
[84] Ibid.
[85] Ibid.
[86] Protect, Respect, and Remedy (n 17 above), para 105.

direct result of SGSR Ruggie's involvement. Consequently, there is an increasingly coherent approach to bad business practices and this means that growing numbers of businesses are falling within the CSR/business and human rights framework as the regulatory net widens. So, for example, at the international level, the OECD is updating its Guidelines with regard to SGSR Ruggie's work on the due-diligence principle as part of its 2011 Review.[87] Furthermore, the due-diligence approach has been implemented in relation to the supply chain by the UK NCP in making its determination and recommendations with regard to Afrimex (UK) Ltd in 2008.[88]

Afrimex is a British company which has been engaged in the mining of coltan and cassiterite in the Democratic Republic of Congo over a number of years. As such, its activities fall squarely within the scope of the OECD Guidelines and the remit of the UK NCP. After a mediated outcome between the company and the complainant NGO failed, the UK NCP concluded that, while operating in a conflict zone, Afrimex failed to exercise due diligence—that is, it had failed to take measures 'to become aware of, prevent and address adverse human rights impacts' in relation to its own direct activities and importantly also in relation to its supply chain.[89] The NCP specifically upheld the complaints regarding the use of child labour and forced labour in mines within a conflict zone which supplied minerals to companies linked to Afrimex, rather than to Afrimex itself. It was determined in a strongly worded Final Statement that Afrimex had failed to meet the requirements of a multitude of provisions of the OECD Guidelines, in particular Guidelines II and IV:

> Afrimex applied insufficient due diligence on the supply chain and this remains the case. The UK NCP expects UK business to respect human rights and to take steps to ensure it does not contribute to human rights abuses. Afrimex did not take steps to influence the supply chain and to explore options with its suppliers exploring methods to ascertain how minerals could be sourced from mines that do not use child or forced labour or with better health and safety. The assurances that Afrimex gained from their suppliers were too weak to fulfil the requirements of the Guidelines.[90]

In making its recommendations, the UK NCP advised Afrimex to adopt the due-diligence standard and in particular to require that its suppliers 'do no harm'. Furthermore, it was recommended that the company implement an effective CSR policy which adhered to international human rights standards and a monitoring mechanism to ensure compliance by suppliers.

Thus it can be seen that existing business and human rights initiatives are useful regulatory models for achieving a measure of business accountability and establishing and disseminating the clear standards of behaviour expected of business actors. Weaknesses become apparent, however, when it comes to enforcement and remedies and the Afrimex case is a stark example of the problems which can arise.

---

[87] Terms of Reference for an Update of the OECD Guidelines for Multinational Enterprises, 4 May 2010, 3, <http://www.oecd.org/dataoecd/61/41/45124171.pdf>, accessed on 18 June 2010.
[88] n 72 above.
[89] Ibid.
[90] Ibid.

C. The Weaknesses in a Business and Human Rights-based Approach to PMSC Regulation

While there are significant positives about the existing international CSR initiatives, there are also some important negatives.

First, as mentioned, no international CSR initiative offers an enforceable mechanism for protecting human rights. Nor are enforceable remedies available for those who have suffered human rights violations at the hands of business actors. Consider the GC and OECD examples. Both the Global Compact and the OECD Guidelines lack specificity in their references to human rights standards which has implications for any realistic attempt at enforcement. (This vagueness could equally be considered a strength as both initiatives encompass all human rights.) Victims of human rights abuses perpetrated by business actors need an *effective* remedy and clearly enunciated rights upon which to base a claim. Furthermore, the GC is firmly voluntary or a 'strategic policy initiative' providing CSR leadership and highlighting best practice and it relies upon business enterprises to become involved of their own accord.[91] The GC was never intended to ensure accountability for bad business behaviour and in any event rogue businesses will choose not to participate in a voluntary initiative.

Likewise, the OECD Guidelines are not legally binding upon enterprises which means, for example, that the while the UK NCP is empowered to make determinations regarding the behaviour of UK-registered companies in order to ensure that the United Kingdom complies with its own international obligations, any recommendations made cannot be enforced.[92] So, for example, Afrimex has ignored the UK NCP's recommendations, intimating that there was no need for it to implement them because it was no longer operating in the DRC.[93] The NGO Global Witness asked the 'UK government to carry out an independent verification of Afrimex's claim that it has ceased trading in minerals' on the basis that its investigations support the contention that Afrimex has not suspended its Guidelines-breaching activities in DRC.[94] Furthermore, the NGO encouraged the UK government to utilise the provisions of UN Security Council Resolutions 1856[95] and 1857[96] and report Afrimex to the UN Sanctions Committee. As this was not forthcoming, in

---

[91] Overview of the GC at <http://www.unglobalcompact.org/AboutTheGC/>, accessed on 20 August 2010. See also <http://www.unglobalcompact.org/HowToParticipate/Business_Participation/index.html>, accessed on 18 June 2010.
[92] OECD Guidelines (n 12 above), 17, para 1, 'Concepts and Principles'.
[93] Global Witness, '"Faced with a Gun, What can You Do?" War and the Militarisation of Mining in Eastern Congo', Report, July 2009. For the background to the Afrimex complaint see p 68 ff, <http://www.globalwitness.org/fwag/index.html>, accessed on 17 August 2010.
[94] ibid, 69
[95] UN Security Council Resolution 1856(2008) The Situation Concerning the Democratic Republic of Congo, S/RES/1856 (2008), 22 December 2008, <http://daccess-dds-ny.un.org/doc/UNDOC/GEN/N08/666/94/PDF/N0866694.pdf?OpenElement>, accessed on 17 August 2010.
[96] UN Security Council Resolution 1857(2008) The Situation Concerning the Democratic Republic of Congo, S/RES/1857 (2008), 22 December 2008, <http://daccess-dds-ny.un.org/doc/UNDOC/GEN/N08/666/43/PDF/N0866643.pdf?OpenElement>, accessed on 17 August 2010.

July 2010 the NGO sought judicial review of the UK government's failure to refer the case to the Sanctions Committee and is awaiting judgment.[97] While a finding against the UK government will be significant for businesses operating in the DRC it will have less of an impact on the application of the OECD Guidelines in general and the weaknesses remain.

To a certain extent, the existing business and human rights initiatives reflect a 'victim-oriented', as opposed to a state-based, approach and have much to contribute to any attempt to regulate PMSCs; nevertheless, while these have served to expose the failings of the business sector, especially in respect of human rights violations, lack of enforcement remains an issue. The Protect, Respect, and Remedy framework requires redress for those affected by human rights violations and neither the Global Compact nor the OECD NCPs provide this. This is a fundamental flaw and must be rectified if they are to meet Ruggie's criteria, particularly in the case of the OECD SIP which is closest to a redress mechanism.

Secondly, in light of the lack of enforcement mechanisms there is no effective deterrent to business misbehaviour. Reputational carrots will always help to ensure that high street names adhere to CSR standards but the problem lies with those rogue businesses which are unwilling to behave and are immune to reputational stimuli. Many in civil society would argue that it is the lack of enforcement mechanisms and a deterrent factor that renders CSR initiatives weak and ineffectual. Nevertheless, the use of alternative methods in the initiatives discussed in this chapter has undoubtedly made *some* business actors respect human rights and consider and uphold their social responsibilities. Even where a complaint against a company has been upheld, as in the Afrimex case, the lack of follow-up and monitoring procedures limits severely the impact of a negative determination.[98]

IV. Conclusion

If, as SGSR Ruggie has concluded, all businesses have the obligation to respect human rights and all violations must be remedied, current business and human rights/CSR initiatives are deficient, especially in relation to remedying human rights violations.

Because of the transnational nature of business in the twenty-first century, international regulation is imperative in order to hold *all* business actors accountable and responsible for their behaviour, this is particularly true of so-called rogue business actors who deliberately seek to avoid regulatory mechanisms through choice of jurisdiction. The PMSC industry is as susceptible to rogue elements as any other sector—witness Blackwater USA's withdrawal from the International

---

[97] Global Witness, 'Global Witness takes UK Government to Court for Failing to List UK Companies Trading Congo Conflict Minerals for UN Sanctions', Press Release, 26 July 2010, <http://www.globalwitness.org/media_library_detail.php/1032/en/global_witness_takes_uk_government_to_court_for_failing_to_list_uk_companies_trading_congo_conflict_minerals_for_un_sanctions_>, accessed 17 August 2010.

[98] <http://oecdwatch.org/cases/Case_114/?searchterm=afrimex>, accessed on 1 July 2010.

Peace Operations Association when an investigation into the Nisour Square killings became inevitable. It must also be recognized, however, that neither international regulation nor national regulation alone is sufficient to capture bad business behaviour.

Regulation of PMSCs should take the form of a top-down–bottom-up hybrid approach which mirrors some of the existing international business and human rights/CSR initiatives. A hybrid approach can harness the benefits of international standards together with national implementation. The approach should be multi-stakeholder in nature, ensuring both accountability and transparency. Most importantly it should be victim-centred and act as a deterrent to human rights violations by business, as well as providing an effective, transparent, and enforceable remedy for those who suffer as a result of such violations. Existing business and human rights projects meet some but crucially not all of these criteria. As it stands, PMSCs do fall within the scope of the international business and human rights initiatives discussed within this chapter but given their voluntary nature and lack of enforcement mechanisms, there is not enough to ensure proper accountability for human rights violations.

18

Codes of Conduct for Private Military and Security Companies

The State of Self-regulation in the Industry

Carsten Hoppe and Ottavio Quirico

I. Introduction

The object of this chapter is to present and assess the state of self-regulation initiatives, often identified under the heading of corporate social responsibility, in private military and security companies (PMSCs). The chapter focuses on Codes of Conduct (CoC), including best practices and ethics declarations initiated by firms. Where pertinent, other initiatives developed outside the industry but applicable to it, including, for example, the Voluntary Principles on Security and Human Rights (VPSHR), will be touched upon.

The analysis addresses the state of self-regulation or corporate social responsibility initiatives developed within the PMSC industry. Corporate social responsibility (CSR), for our purposes, can be defined as 'a concept whereby companies integrate social and environmental concerns in their business operations and in their interaction with their stakeholders on a voluntary basis'.[1] The focus of the chapter, however, is narrower than the complete PMSC industry, in that it specifically addresses only instruments that are designed to, at least in part, apply to the provision of coercive services in contexts of armed conflict. Hence, ethics statements or CoC developed by firms providing exclusively non-coercive tasks, such as food services, as well as those not containing any language specifically relevant to the provision of coercive services, have not been considered in detail.

The chapter first classifies CoC, and subsequently sets out to analyse them with regard to different mechanisms: licensing regimes, the contract, the activity of PMSCs, resort to force, and risk assessment. Furthermore, issues of liability and different regulatory techniques are explored. Lastly, the chapter considers the implementation and enforcement of CoC. Under this heading the few existing

---

[1] European Commission Green Paper, Promoting a European Framework for Corporate Social Responsibility, COM(2001) 366, 6, para 20, <http://eur-lex.europa.eu>, accessed 15 June 2010.

examples of formal enforcement provisions tied to CoC in the industry are considered. Moreover, the chapter assesses the viability of initiatives that rely solely on the market to achieve compliance.

II. Voluntary Regulation and Private Codes of Conduct

The label 'Codes of Conduct' encompasses a variety of initiatives that are differently designated as 'ethical codes', 'private regulation', 'private codes of conduct', or 'voluntary principles'. Such initiatives have different origins.

The expressions 'voluntary principles', 'self-regulation', and 'ethical codes' propose the idea that PMSCs willingly submit to regulation that is not (only) imposed by an external public subject. In particular, the reference to 'ethical codes' entails a CSR approach.[2] Frequently, PMSCs set up regulation in collaboration with other actors, especially non-governmental organizations (NGOs), states, and governmental organizations. Thus, the VPSHR are standards applicable to corporate social responsibility commonly elaborated by the United States, the United Kingdom, the Netherlands, Norway, NGOs, and private companies.[3] They concern business companies operating in the extractive and energy sectors, whereas a specific section lays down fundamental rules when such companies hire private contractors for ensuring security. These principles are a constant reference for PMSCs' CoC. The Sarajevo CoC for PSCs is a set of rules elaborated by PSCs and clients in collaboration with NGOs and governmental agencies (Sarajevo Process).[4] Mainly 'private' by nature, it represents the most developed voluntary regulation specifically targeting PSCs.

For improving the quality and effectiveness of self-regulation, the project of a common CoC for PMSCs has been put forward.[5] The process of participation in this universal CoC is envisaged as gradual, initially including adhesion only to core duties and exclusion of external monitoring bodies.[6] Such a Code should combine the interests of the companies, stakeholders, groups in civil society, and it should be internally accepted by the companies. Participation in the common CoC is envisaged as a prerequisite for licensing and awarding of public and private contracts.[7] A common CoC represents a remedy against the multiplication of voluntary rules,

---

[2] On the definition of CSR see M Moraru, 'A Critical Survey of Mechanisms for Institutionalizing CSR in Business Organisations' in MA Moreau and F Francioni (eds), *The Pluridisciplinary Dimension of Corporate Social Responsibility* (2007), 201, 203.
[3] See the VPSHR, <http://www.voluntaryprinciples.org>, accessed on 15 June 2010.
[4] Cf the Sarajevo CoC for PSCs, <http://www.seesac.org>, accessed on 15 June 2010.
[5] See N Rosemann, *Code of Conduct: Tool for Self-regulation for Private Military and Security Companies*, Centre for the Democratic Control of Armed Forces, Occasional Paper no 15 (2008), 19 ff. See also Swiss Federal Department of Foreign Affairs (FDFA), *Draft Code of Conduct for Private Military Companies and Private Security Companies* (2010), <http://www.dcaf.ch>, accessed on 15 June 2010.
[6] Cf Rosemann (n 5 above), 37, 39.
[7] Ibid, 39.

which create fragmented regulation, and is likely to foster predictability and equal competitive conditions.[8]

The expression 'private regulation' sticks to the nature of the subject establishing a determinate regulatory framework, ie private companies. Therefore, it defines CoC elaborated exclusively by single private companies (individual codes) or associations of private companies (group codes). At the basis of private CoC lays the idea that PMSCs have direct knowledge of what happens in the field and thus are able to provide appropriate regulation.

Private CoC have different scopes of application. First, this depends on the nature of the activity provided by the company. In fact, the label 'PMSC' covers a very wide range of practices. Some enterprises, which might fall within the scope of the label 'PSCs', for instance, AECOM, simply offer technical and management support services to a broad range of markets, not necessarily concerned with the security sector, from transport to energy and environment. Other companies, for example, Dyncorp, operate exclusively in the security sector. In this respect, the distinction between PMCs, PSCs and other business enterprises looks simplistic. Secondly, the approach may vary, since some CoC generally target the activity of PMSCs, whereas others concern specific matters, such as armed operations. Thirdly, CoC can have an individual or federative nature. Our analysis takes into account a relevant range of PMSCs and CoC, with special regard to coercive services that might entail violations of human rights and international humanitarian law (IHL).

At the level of individual CoC, we focus particularly on Dyncorp,[9] G4S,[10] Blue Sky/Guardian Security Consultant,[11] Control Risks Group,[12] Xe,[13] Sharp End International,[14] and Secopex.[15]

At the federative level, in the UK PMSCs operating overseas that satisfy strict disciplinary procedures can join the British Association of Private Security Companies (BAPSC),[16] whose constitution was recommended by the Green Paper on PMSCs.[17] The idea is that a trade association provides assurances of respectability, by promoting business opportunities for lawful companies while outlawing disreputable companies. In fact, according to the BAPSC Charter, the Association aims to: (1) promote, enhance, and regulate the interest and activities of UK-based firms and companies that provide armed security services outside the UK; (2) represent

---

[8] Ibid, 24.
[9] See <http://www.dyn-intl.com>, accessed on 15 June 2010.
[10] See <http://www.g4s.com>, accessed on 15 June 2010.
[11] Cf <http://www.BlueSkysc.org>, accessed on 15 June 2010. Blue Sky appears to have become defunct since the initial research for the present chapter was completed. However, Guardian Security Consultant seems to have copied at least in part the corporate social responsibility mechanisms of Blue Sky. Whether there are overlaps in the ownership structure of the two companies remains unclear at the time of publication.
[12] See <http://www.controlrisks.com>, accessed on 15 June 2010.
[13] Cf <http://www.xecompany.com>, accessed on 15 June 2010.
[14] See <http://www.sharpendinternational.com>, accessed on 15 June 2010.
[15] Cf <http://www.secopex.com>, accessed on 15 June 2010.
[16] See <http://www.bapsc.org.uk>, accessed on 15 June 2010.
[17] Cf the Green Paper on PMSCs: Options for Regulation (2002), <http://www.fco.gov.uk>, accessed on 15 June 2010.

the interest and activities of the member companies in the matter of proposed legislation. 'Armed security services' are broadly conceived of as involving recruitment, training, equipping, coordination, and employment of persons who bear lethal arms.[18] At the regional level, in the EU the representatives of the Confederation of European Security Services (CoESS) and the Trade Union Federation Uni-Europa issued a CoC for companies and employees operating in the private security sector. It is considered that in the near future 20,000 companies will operate in the security sector within the EU, employing some 1,100,000 personnel.[19] The aim is to harmonize the rules governing this area of services. CoESS and UNI-Europa wish to emphasize the need for companies and employees to incorporate the principles of the Code in their activities.[20] The Private Security Company Association of Iraq (PSCAI) gathers PMSCs operating in Iraq.[21] In this case, the federative criterion is the 'host' state territory, ie the place where the activity of the companies takes place. The association adopted a CoC within the framework of its Charter for PMSCs active in Iraq.[22] At the international level, the International Peace Operations Association (IPOA) aims to improve accountability by promoting high operational and ethical standards for PMSCs.[23] The IPOA CoC, first adopted in 2001 and lastly revised in 2005, seeks to ensure respect for ethical standards by member PMSCs operating in conflict and post-conflict situations.[24]

III. The Content of Codes of Conduct: Basic Substantive Rules

A. Compliance with the Licensing Regime

According to national legislations and voluntary CoC, private contractors are usually required to comply with precise standards for practicing military and security services. Basically, PMSCs and their employees must satisfy strict professional qualifications, not pose a threat to state security, and be clear of judicial condemnations. These requirements are checked through targeted licensing procedures in the 'home' state, ie the state where the company is registered.[25]

---

[18] BAPSC Charter, Preamble, <http://www.bapsc.org.uk/key_documents-charter.asp>, accessed on 20 August 2010.
[19] CoESS/Uni-Europa, CoC and Ethics for the Private Security Sector, I, <http://www.coess.org>, accessed on 15 June 2010.
[20] Ibid, III-15.
[21] See <http://www.pscai.org>, accessed on 15 June 2010.
[22] PSCAI Charter, Section 9, <http://www.pscai.org/Docs/PSCAI_Charter_Final.pdf>, accessed on 20 August 2010.
[23] <http://ipoaworld.org/eng>, accessed on 15 June 2010.
[24] IPOA CoC, Version 12, Preamble, <http://www.ipoaworld.org/eng/codeofconduct.html>, accessed on 20 August 2010.
[25] See O Quirico, *National Regulatory Models for Private Military and Security Companies and Implications for Future International Regulation*, EUI MWP Working Paper 2009/25, 2–4, <http://www.eui.eu>, <http://priv-war.eu>, accessed on 15 June 2010.

Along these lines, the Sarajevo CoC fosters a fair and transparent licensing system for PMSCs, regardless of the size of the companies concerned. In the absence of satisfactory regulation, firms are requested to federate and adopt self-regulation.[26] IPOA backs the idea that PMSCs must disclose information to legal authorities, and thus supports a transparent licensing regime.[27] The BAPSC requires its members to build and promote open and transparent relations with UK governmental departments and relevant international organizations (IOs).[28] The CoESS/Uni-Europa CoC provides that a company active in the sector, or wishing to enter the sector, satisfies the conditions imposed by national regulations, in order to obtain the permits and authorizations needed by the company, its management, and its staff. Professional associations of private security companies should ensure that all of their members comply with this obligation. According to CoESS and UNI-Europa licences should be granted on an independent basis, by following fair and transparent procedures applied in the same way to all companies, irrespective of their size.[29] Insofar as possible, the Code also envisages that any internal organizational procedures are made transparent.[30] In the same vein, Sharp End International supports accountability and transparency in the military, security, peacekeeping, and stability operations industry.[31]

Specific regulation is usually elaborated with regard to trafficking and brokering of goods related to PMSCs' activities, such as arms, dual-use goods and technologies—in particular nuclear materials—and strategic goods. The main purpose is to limit the supply of technology or strategic goods to countries proscribed, specifically for reasons of proliferation, security, or terrorism. Thus, Dyncorp fosters governmental licensing and authorization for export, especially by conferring with the US Trade Compliance Department before export operations.[32] The Code of Practice of Guardian Security Consultant requires compliance with export licensing and control imposed by the UK government and the EU, which affect products in its overseas markets.[33]

In view of the licensing of personnel, the Sarajevo CoC provides the successful completion of training, especially concerning the use of the (armed) force for employees authorized to carry (fire)arms.[34] Transparency is achieved by requiring firms to register employees, including records of background checks and security incidents.[35] The CoESS/Uni-Europa CoC states that it is particularly important to select new employees on the basis of objective criteria, allowing a fair evaluation of candidates' professional qualities and moral values. The Code demands the setting of effective procedures for compliance with rules on personnel background.[36] It is also important that newly recruited employees receive basic, specific, and ongoing training, so much that the Code envisages the granting of licences on the condition that

---

[26] Sarajevo CoC, 2.2.   [27] IPOA CoC, 2.   [28] BAPSC Charter, Preamble.
[29] CoESS/UNI-Europa CoC, III-3.   [30] Ibid, III-2.
[31] See <http://www.sharpendinternational.com/how.html>, accessed on 20 August 2010.
[32] Dyncorp CoC, Fairness and Honesty in Business, 4.
[33] See <http://www.guardiansec.org/GSC/ethical-code_GSC_eng.html>, accessed on 20 August 2010.
[34] Sarajevo CoC, 2.4.   [35] Ibid, 2.20(f)(j).   [36] CoESS/UNI-Europa CoC, III-4.

companies can demonstrate not only their own quality and reliability, but also that of their employees through training programmes.[37] Following these guidelines, Xe declares to look for people of the highest calibre and to recruit very qualified personnel. Applicants may be requested to prove physical fitness and psychological attitudes as well as to provide specific certifications, depending on the purpose of the employment. Background checks and personal and employer references are completed on all prospective employees.[38]

B. The Hiring Contract

PMSCs provide services to different subjects, namely states, IOs, NGOs, transnational corporations, and other private entities. According to public and voluntary regulation, agreements normally follow the principle of the freedom of contract, but they cannot be contrary to the foundations of the law and morality. Specific national rules set up regulation for the hiring contract, in particular with regard to governmental outsourcing.[39]

Within this frame, the Sarajevo CoC prohibits unfair relationships with competitors, fosters federation links,[40] and requests firms to reject contracts that violate national or international law.[41] The VPSHR foresee that contracts between PMSCs and the hiring companies include the rules embodied in the Voluntary Principles and Guidelines, where appropriate. Contracts should also provide for investigation of unlawful or abusive behaviour as well as necessary disciplinary action.[42] IPOA requires PMSCs to contract solely with legitimate and recognized states, IOs, NGOs, and private companies, by carefully considering their accountability, whereas engagement with clients thwarting international peace efforts is prohibited.[43] IPOA also demands that the hiring contract specifies mandate, restrictions, goals, benchmarks, criteria for withdrawal, and accountability.[44] CoESS and Uni-Europa elaborated a guide for the awarding of security contracts based on fair competition.[45] The BAPSC requests its members not to accept contracts which are likely to involve criminal activities or breaches of human rights and compels PMSCs to decline contracts when the services provided might adversely affect the military or political balance in the country of delivery.[46]

At the level of individual CoC, Sharp End International declares to supply services and training only to legitimate governmental bodies and lawful organizations.[47] Control Risks takes into account ethical, reputational, and legal issues before accepting new assignments and clients.[48] Guardian Security Consultant,

---

[37] Ibid, III-5.
[38] See <http://www.xecompany.com/ProfessResources.html>, accessed on 20 August 2010.
[39] See Quirico (n 25 above), 4–7.   [40] Sarajevo CoC, 2.17.   [41] Ibid, 2.1.
[42] See <http://www.voluntaryprinciples.org>, accessed on 20 August 2010.
[43] IPOA CoC, 4.   [44] Ibid, 8.1.
[45] See <http://www.css.ba/docs/the%20sarajevo%20client%20guidelines.pdf>, accessed on 20 August 2010. See also CoESS/Uni-Europa CoC, III-12.
[46] BAPSC Charter, 4–5, 7.
[47] See <http://www.sharpendinternational.com/how.html>, accessed on 20 August 2010.
[48] See <http://www.controlrisks.com/default.aspx?page=7>, accessed on 20 August 2010.

Secopex, and Xe promote a client-oriented attitude by fostering impartiality, confidentiality, and a holistic approach to customers' needs.[49]

C. The Activity of Private Military and Security Companies

The country where the activity of PMSCs takes place, ie the 'host state', is not necessary the same as the 'home state' and the 'hiring state'.[50]

By sticking to this basic categorization, the VPSHR compel firms to observe the policies of the contracting company in the matter of ethical conduct and human rights, the law of the host state, emerging best practices, and human rights. In particular, the VPSHR require that firms respect the Universal Declaration of Human Rights (UDHR) and the International Labour Organization (ILO) Declaration on Fundamental Principles and Rights at Work.[51] The Sarajevo CoC requires firms to refrain from acting in a manner that would be contrary to the letter and the spirit of international law or the national law of the host country.[52] Specifically, it calls for compliance with the UDHR and the European Convention on Human Rights (ECHR).[53] The Project for a common CoC demands basic respect for the right to life, bodily integrity, ban on torture, freedom of movement, and non-discrimination.[54]

Private federative CoC compel PMSCs and their personnel to abide by voluntary rules and national and international law, especially in the matter of international human rights and IHL. IPOA requires compliance with the UDHR, the Geneva Conventions and their Additional Protocols, the Chemical Weapons Convention, as well as the VPSHR. IPOA generally demands that PMSC personnel behave humanely with honesty, integrity, objectivity, and diligence[55] because respect for ethical imperatives is considered essential for effective security and peace.[56] The CoESS/Uni-Europa CoC requires firms and their personnel to respect and improve regulation of activities within the EU. In countries where national regulation is non-existent or underdeveloped, the Code assumes that companies, their employees, and representatives are responsible for promoting the development of appropriate regulation.[57] The members of PSCAI are requested to abide by the law of Iraq and to further the aims of the democratically elected Iraqi government. They must also insist upon behaviour consistent with international rules and promote acceptable practices based on the rights and dignity of the Iraqi people. According to the CoC adopted by PSCAI, the task of PMSCs consists primarily in deterrence, so that firms and their employees may not conduct law-enforcement functions and

---

[49] See <http://www.xecompany.com/ProfessResources.html>; <http://www.secopex.com/index.php/ethique>; <http://www.guardiansec.org/GSC/ethical-code_GSC_eng.html>, all accessed on 20 August 2010.
[50] See Ch 5 by Francioni in this volume, section I.
[51] See <http://www.voluntaryprinciples.org>, accessed on 20 August 2010.
[52] Sarajevo CoC, 2.1.   [53] Ibid, 2.7.
[54] See Rosemann (n 5 above), 30; *Draft Code* (n 5 above), 3 ff.
[55] IPOA CoC, 6.13.   [56] Ibid, 9.   [57] CoESS/Uni-Europa CoC, III-1.

must recognize the role of Iraqi officials in enforcing security.[58] The BAPSC imposes respect for the home state law, ie UK law, the host-state law and international law, in particular humanitarian law and human rights. It specifically requires that PMSCs grant a high level of professional skill and expertise when host countries have inadequate legal frameworks. According to the BAPSC Charter, PMSCs must balance their activity with the legitimate concerns of persons who might be affected by security services.[59]

Also individual CoC promote respect for existing national and international law. The Code of Practice of Guardian Security Consultant fosters compliance in particular with the Geneva Conventions, the UDHR, and the law of the host country. PMSC personnel are expected to conduct themselves with honesty, integrity, objectivity, and diligence.[60] G4S and Sharp End International promote respect for international law, human rights, and United Nations (UN) sanctions.[61] According to its declaration of ethics, Secopex abides by the UDHR; the Geneva Conventions; the Convention against the Recruitment, Use, Financing and Training of Mercenaries; the fundamental principles of the UN; as well as the decisions of the UN and the EU.[62]

Pursuant to national legislation, PMSCs and their employees might incur criminal responsibility for violation of both international and domestic law. Below this threshold, violations are often subject to administrative procedures and entail sanctions such as fines and cancellation of permits.[63] The activity of PMSCs is likely to overlap in particular with mercenarism. Thus, it has been suggested that voluntary CoC adopt their own notion of 'mercenarism', in order to foster clarity with regard to both individuals and the companies.[64] Nevertheless, given that profits are the core aim of PMSCs, it is hard to achieve self-limitation in the matter.

D. Resort to (Armed) Force

States tend to exclude PMSCs from direct participation in hostilities. Therefore, resort to (armed) force is officially allowed only in very specific cases. In general, carrying and using (fire)arms is authorized only for a narrow list of activities, subject to a licensing system and permitted only to people having due training in arms handling. Outside these limits, the use of (fire)arms is a criminal breach, exceptionally authorized in the case of self-defence.[65]

---

[58] PSCAI CoC, Art 48(a–e).
[59] BAPSC Charter, Preamble, 6.
[60] See <http://www.guardiansec.org/GSC/ethical-code_GSC_eng.html>, accessed on 20 August 2010.
[61] G4S, Corporate Responsibility Report—Policies, 4 ff; <http://www.sharpendinternational.com/how.html>, accessed on 20 August 2010.
[62] See <http://www.secopex.com/index.php/ethique>, accessed on 20 August 2010.
[63] See Quirico (n 25 above), 13 ff.
[64] Cf Rosemann (n 5 above), 28.
[65] See Quirico (n 25 above), 9–10.

Along these lines, since an absolute ban on the use of the armed force is not likely to be accepted by PMSCs, the Project for a common CoC envisages resort to (armed) force only by way of self-defence.[66] The VPSHR and the Sarajevo CoC require PMSCs to provide only pre-emptive and defensive services, thus banning the participation of PMSCs in activities that are the exclusive competence of state military or law enforcement authorities. As a consequence, (armed) force should be used when strictly necessary, in a way proportionate to threats and according to precise rules of engagement. The VPSHR and the Sarajevo CoC also request firms to maintain high levels of technical and professional proficiency with regard to the use of (fire)arms. Furthermore, they recommend compliance with best international practices, in particular the UN Principles on the Use of Force and Firearms by Law Enforcement Officials and the UN Code of Conduct for Law Enforcement Officials.[67] The Sarajevo CoC envisages also the development of Standard Operating Procedures (SOPs) for: (a) the usage, storage, accounting, maintenance, ownership, and registration of weapons; and (b) the safe loading and unloading of firearms.[68]

According to these guidelines, IPOA requests PMSCs potentially involved in armed hostilities to establish with clients appropriate rules of engagement,[69] aiming to minimize casualties and damage, though preserving the individual right to self-defence.[70] IPOA also requires PMSCs to control and account for weapons and ammunitions utilized by their employees.[71] Only 'appropriate' weapons, common to military, security, and law-enforcement operations are allowed,[72] whereas PMSCs should refrain from resorting to illegal arms, especially toxic, chemical, and long-term effect weapons, namely by taking account of the Chemical Weapons Convention.[73] PSCAI compels PMSCs to abide by the rules on the use of force defined by the laws of Iraq and the laws of armed conflicts, ensuring that security staff are trained in these regulations.[74] According to its pre-emptive aims, the BAPSC provides that PMSCs' services are designed primarily to deter potential aggression. Therefore, the use of weapons is allowed only in a defensive mode as a last resort against an armed attack or for evacuation.[75] Furthermore, the BAPSC compels PMSCs not to provide governments or private bodies with lethal equipment when human rights are likely to be infringed.[76]

E. Remarks on Regulatory Techniques

Private CoC basically exploit two different regulatory techniques. A first technique consists in recalling rules set up by other legal instruments. In fact, private CoC tend to follow common patterns, by embodying national and international law in force, human rights, and acknowledged moral rules.[77] In particular, private CoC

---

[66] Cf Rosemann (n 5 above), 30–1; *Draft Code* (n 5 above), 3–4.
[67] See <http://www.voluntaryprinciples.org>, accessed on 20 August 2010; Sarajevo CoC, 2.4, 2.6.
[68] Ibid, 2.6. [69] IPOA CoC, 9.2.1. [70] Ibid, 9.2.2.
[71] Ibid, 9.4.1. [72] Ibid, 9.4.2. [73] Ibid, 9.4.2.
[74] PSCAI CoC, Art 48(f). [75] BAPSC Charter, 1. [76] Ibid, 8.
[77] See eg IPOA CoC, Preamble.

constantly refer to the Geneva Conventions and well-established voluntary regulation, specifically the VPSHR. The clearest example is the declaration of ethics of Secopex, which exclusively includes references to international conventions.[78] In this respect, issues of utility and interpretation arise, both at the individual and corporate levels.

At the individual level, though it is possible to regard physical persons as the primary addressees of some international obligations, especially in light of several recent instruments on criminal responsibility,[79] the question arises as to what extent individuals are really bound by international norms. An exemplary case is that of the Geneva Conventions, the applicability of which to PMSCs' personnel is rather controversial. In fact, the Geneva Conventions set up different classifications of subjects within the law of armed conflicts, in particular the distinction between 'civilians' and 'combatants'.[80] Therefore, it is essential to ascertain the category of subjects to which PMSCs' personnel belong, because different consequences stem from different classifications. For instance, civilians are not legitimate targets of attacks and cannot directly participate in hostilities. By contrast, private CoC refer to the Geneva Conventions in a fairly general way, not in a technical manner, and thus they cannot help to establish to what extent these rules might apply. In this regard, the declaration of ethics of Secopex is exemplary, insofar as it states that the company *'d'une manière générale adhère à la Convention de Genève de 1949'*.[81] It is true, nevertheless, that the clarification of the scope of application of the international instruments is ultimately a task of states and international law, rather than a duty of PMSCs.

At the corporate level, international subjectivity is highly controversial. In fact, since international law is traditionally conceived of as a matter of interstate relationships, it is not clear whether or not corporations are directly bound by international conventions. The controversy is general and maintained also in the field of human rights. For instance, the fact that the UDHR addresses 'all nations,... every individual and every organ of society' is not unanimously considered a statement sufficient directly to bind private corporations.[82] In the case of a negative answer, the reference of private CoC to international instruments, especially in the matter of human rights and IHL, would hardly be relevant. In the case of a positive answer, the question arises once again as to what extent international instruments apply to PMSCs. This is particularly important by considering that international jurisdictions lack the means to enforce human rights violations perpetrated by private corporations. Within this frame, the value of the contribution that private CoC

---

[78] See <http://www.secopex.com/index.php/ethique>, accessed on 20 August 2010.
[79] See A Orakhelashvili, 'The Position of the Individual in International Law', (2001) 21 California Western International Law Journal 241, 269.
[80] See Arts 43, 48, 50 of Additional Protocol I to the Geneva Conventions.
[81] See <http://www.secopex.com/index.php/ethique>, accessed on 20 August 2010.
[82] For an exhaustive presentation of the debate in the matter see F Francioni, 'Four Ways of Enforcing the International Responsibility for Human Rights Violations by Multinational Corporations' in Moreau and Francioni (n 2 above), 163–9; P Acconci, 'Accountability of Multinational Enterprises for Human Rights: Is Anything going Differently?' ibid, 121 ff.

bring to the debate by simply referring to international instruments is doubtful. For instance, one might wonder what the legal effect is of the statement that Sharp End International 'abide by all UN sanctions, International Law and its interpretations'.[83]

A second technique adopted by voluntary CoC consists in directly governing conduct, which could help to add binding rules when the application of existing legal norms is uncertain. Nevertheless, the language employed is not really rigorous, so that voluntary CoC do not prove very helpful in creating a significant legal framework for PMSCs.[84] A good example is the individual Code of Guardian Security Consultant, which stipulates that GSC personnel assess 'all possible implications of the situations' that clients face, 'tell the customers what they need to know, not just what they want to hear', 'fully understand and respect the need for client confidentiality', and 'go to great lengths' to understand each client's particular security requirements.[85] The language employed is broad, so that the content of the rules is not clearly defined. The tendency to generalization is stressed by redundant adjectives and adverbs such as 'all possible', 'fully', 'great'. It is also difficult to ascertain the exact meaning of expressions such as 'what they need to know' rather than 'what they want to hear'. On the one hand, it is certainly difficult to elaborate a detailed regulatory framework. On the other hand, regulation is void if the content of obligations is elusive. Naturally, distinctions must be taken into account. For instance, the group CoC issued by CoESS and Uni-Europa in the matter of relations with clients is an example of a fairly well-drafted regulation.[86] In fact, it does not enter into details which would be probably excessive for a group code, but provides a sufficiently strict regulatory framework, in coordination with national regulations.

IV. Procedural Rules

A. Enforcement Provisions Built into Existing Initiatives

Industry-driven self-regulation initiatives such as the CoC we have already introduced presuppose that firms include obligations in CoC that they may otherwise not be formally required to uphold. Examples include human rights treaties. Other obligations, such as provisions of national law, while formally binding on them, may be difficult to enforce due to problems of the local legal system in the conflict-ridden areas in which PMSCs routinely operate. However, the inclusion of obligations in a CoC will in any event only be credible and effective in adding to the

---

[83] See <http://www.sharpendinternational.com/how.html>, accessed on 20 August 2010.
[84] For a comprehensive view of the problems related to the language of private CoC see C Hoppe, 'Corporate Social Responsibility at the Frontline? The Case of the Private Military Companies' in Moreau and Francioni (n 2 above), 82–4.
[85] See <http://www.guardiansec.org/GSC/ethical-code_GSC_eng.html>, accessed on 20 August 2010.
[86] See CoESS/Uni-Europa CoC, III-12.

accountability of a given firm, if it is tied to an additional enforcement mechanism.[87] Accordingly, a CoC cannot be effective if both the act of committing to a code *and* the compliance with it are entirely voluntary, and breaches remain without consequence. Enforcement in this regard may simply mean that the firm would face a credible risk of damaging its reputation if it violates the provisions of its code of conduct. Yet, by tying the CoC into contracts with clients, it could also be mandated that such a firm will face, for example, a contractual penalty on top of existing other legal and non-legal consequences, which will add an incentive to comply with the norm in question. Presently, there are very few examples of clear enforcement mechanisms in the industry. Taken at face value, most initiatives seem rather to rely on market mechanisms to ensure compliance. As we will discuss below, this reliance may often be misplaced. Thus, with a view to achieving more effective and credible CoC, the inclusion of enforcement mechanisms beyond mere market control is highly desirable.

Regarding the two existing group CoC, great differences become immediately apparent, with the BAPSC's Charter not containing any specific mechanism, and IPOA's CoC being tied to an elaborate, if not very strict, enforcement mechanism. The BAPSC has a process in place designed to screen new members and to promote provisional members to full membership status.[88] However, there are no additional means of implementation of the Charter of the BAPSC in the members' internal operations. Similarly, the initiative lacks any external mechanisms offering incentives for compliance of members, to reprimand members, or otherwise enforce violations of the BAPSC Charter. There is no formalized way of addressing complaints. Related to the absence of implementation processes, the BAPSC Charter lacks any formal monitoring procedures, and no efforts regarding transparency, oversight mechanisms, and third-party stakeholder input into the process are apparent.

Formally, IPOA follows a very different model with an intricate procedure ostentatiously dubbed 'Enforcement Mechanism'. As regards external enforcement, the IPOA Code of Conduct already threatens that members who fail to uphold a provision 'may be subject to dismissal from IPOA'.[89] Moreover, the Code incorporates the so-called 'IPOA Enforcement Mechanism', a system allowing complaints by third parties. The IPOA Enforcement Mechanism in principle allows anyone to lodge a written complaint against a member of IPOA for violations of the IPOA Code of Conduct.[90] In addition, the Enforcement Mechanism provides a process—not legally binding—in which the Standards Committee of the International Peace Operations Association (SCIPOA) addresses complaints against a

---

[87] The term 'enforcement mechanism' is used here in a broader sense than 'legally enforceable'. We use it to refer to means that compel observance of or compliance with a norm. In that sense, a CoC that does not formally refer to any other enforcement mechanism likely assumes that enforcement will be by way of market pressure and/or public opinion.

[88] See <http://bapsc.org.uk/membership-membership_criteria.asp>, accessed on 20 August 2010.

[89] IPOA Enforcement Mechanism, para. 11, <http://ipoaworld.org/eng/compliance02eng.html>, accessed on 20 August 2010.

[90] Ibid, para 2.1.

member company. The SCIPOA is composed of designees of the members. Complaints are received by a chief liaison officer designated by IPOA, and initially screened by a three-member 'Task Force' of the SCIPOA, no member of which may be affiliated with the company to which the complaint relates. The task force can then decide to throw out the complaint as 'specious or irrelevant to the Code's provisions'.[91] Otherwise the complaint will be forwarded to the full SCIPOA for review. Rejections by the Task Force can be appealed by complainants.[92] The full SCIPOA, composed of designees of all firms elected to the IPOA Board, can then decide to either impose corrective measures and sanctions, or reject the complaint.[93] Appeals by companies subject to complaints, but not by complainants, are possible.[94] Final decisions of the SCIPOA are to be publicized upon the conclusion of the hearings.[95]

Sanctions to be imposed by the SCIPOA may include probation, or exclusion from IPOA, or 'other disciplinary measures'.[96] Sanctions (presumably other than suspension or exclusion) are to be monitored by a Compliance Monitoring Committee.[97] The decision to exclude a member is subject to appeal, must be ratified by the Board of IPOA and IPOA Executive Committee, can be subsequently rescinded, and the member can be readmitted to IPOA after six months.[98] All participants in the Enforcement Mechanism (except the complainant) have to sign non-disclosure agreements.[99] While submissions by the complainant are deemed public unless a special request for confidentiality is made, all submissions by IPOA members are deemed confidential absent a special waiver by the member.[100]

A crucial weakness of the mechanism is that a member company that withdraws from IPOA before or even while a complaint is being addressed will not be subject to the process, and can thus avoid the 'noisy breakup' that represents the only true enforcement mechanism available to IPOA. This happened, when the first member company threatened with dismissal, Blackwater, withdrew its membership just after investigations into its business by IPOA were started, and accordingly all investigations into its conduct by the SCIPOA were halted. The only public statement by IPOA regarding the issue was a press statement acknowledging the withdrawal, and declaring that Blackwater was a member in good standing before it withdrew from IPOA.[101] Moreover, it has been pointed out that neither the CoC, nor the so-called Enforcement Mechanism obliges members to react to a complaint by submitting information regarding the alleged conduct. Lastly, neither the CoC nor the Enforcement Mechanism provide for internal or independent monitoring of compliance with the CoC and the norms referred to in it.

---

[91] Ibid, para 2.2.10. [92] Ibid, paras 3.3–3.13.
[93] Ibid, para 4.2.4. [94] Ibid, para 4.6. [95] Ibid, para 2.1. [96] Ibid, para 5.6.
[97] Ibid, para 6.1–6.10. [98] Ibid, paras 6.13–6.14, 6.16, 7.7.
[99] Ibid, Section 8. [100] Ibid.
[101] IPOA Statement Regarding the Membership Status of Blackwater USA, <http://www.ipoaworld.org/eng/press/131-20071012blackwatermembershipwithdrawal.html>, accessed on 20 August 2010.

Besides the two group CoC by the BAPSC and IPOA, the industry has brought about numerous CSR initiatives by individual firms. As we have seen, most of those statements contain broad language that is concerned with customer relations and employee welfare and remain largely irrelevant to the specific risks PMSC activities pose in terms of violations of human rights (other than, potentially, the rights of the employees), and violations of IHL. Similarly, those individual CoC do not contain specific enforcement mechanisms, with the exception of Blue Sky, which advertises that its activities are overseen by an Ethical Overview Committee. According to company publications, the Overview Committee consists of 'individuals of international standing and unimpeachable integrity who are neither shareholders nor employees of Blue Sky.' Specifically, the three individuals currently composing the committee are Martin Bell, former BBC international correspondent and Member of Parliament, Dr David Shattock, a retired police Chief Constable, and General Sir Rupert Smith, former NATO Deputy Supreme Allied Commander. The Ethical Overview Committee reviews all Blue Sky operations, and has the power to veto any activity undertaken by Blue Sky if it deems the activity runs counter to Blue Sky's ethical standards. Blue Sky also operates an appeals process open to 'anyone with a legitimate involvement in its operations (whether as sponsor, client, employee or in any other capacity)'. It is not clear whether this mechanism would allow for complaints by third-party victims of harmful conduct of Blue Sky personnel.

B. Challenges for Purely Market-based Enforcement

In what follows, we seek to discuss factors that will tend to limit the effectiveness of CoC as means to achieve greater compliance with, and greater accountability for violations of human rights and IHL in the PMSC industry. First, we will discuss incentive problems for initiatives that do not include enforcement mechanisms but rather seek to rely entirely on the market, such as reputation costs, in order to ensure compliance with the norms they seek to promote. Secondly, monitoring problems that will tend to undermine the effectiveness of CoC will be discussed.

PMSCs are corporate entities motivated, at least among other things, by profit. They operate in a market, and this market will to a large degree guide their decision-making. The market brings together supply and demand. However, it has been suggested that the PMSC industry does not face a competitive market.[102] This has important implications: only if clients actually value compliance with human rights or IHL obligations expressed in CoC, *and* if clients have sufficient market power to bargain for it will firms compete in terms of that value. On the one hand, as has been suggested for the PMSC industry, if clients face a sellers' market, so that there is simply little or no alternative for a given provider, there is no competition, and hence firms will escape with as few obligations as possible. This in turn would mean that firms would not subscribe to CoC, or at least not to those ensuring effective enforcement. On the other hand, even if there is some competition, it is not clear

---

[102] See eg J Cockayne, *Commercial Security in Humanitarian and Post-Conflict Settings: An Exploratory Study* (2006), 10.

that clients will bargain for efficient CoC with respect to human rights, IHL, or other norms. One does not have to go as far as to suggest that clients of PMSCs do specifically contract with firms with a bad reputation in that regard, but clients may simply be indifferent to these values. If that is the case, firms will have little incentive to compete in terms of compliance with these norms.

The fact that there are some firms that employ CoC incorporating human rights and IHL obligations cannot without more dispel these concerns, as PMSCs could simply be engaging in window-dressing. Much depends on whether the potential stigma stemming from a violation of human rights or IHL will in fact be passed on to the client. Assuming the stigma is not passed on, for example, because the majority of such incidents are usually not highly publicized, clients will have very little incentive to put pressure on PMSCs to comply. On the other hand, recent reports of PMSCs allegedly flouting IHL and human rights, such as the shooting at Nisoor Square in Iraq, suggest that public awareness of abuses by PMSCs is rising.

Even if the stigma is actually passed on, ie a client will be connected to the violation, there are still two possibilities: either the client cares about its reputation in that respect, or not. Here, we can envision several scenarios, depending on the nature of the client, be it a state, a corporation, or even an NGO. At least for states and corporations, plausible illustrations can go either way. An unpopular government of a failing state could care less than another state about its reputation with respect to human rights, and might be happy to run the risk of violations to hire the cheapest PMSC available. On the other hand, a solid democracy with a healthy civil society might well care a lot about its reputation, and be willing to pay a premium to be able to contract private military services that reliably conform to its values. At the least we would expect the latter to ensure plausible deniability in case violations still occur. Similarly, we would expect to encounter corporations on either end of the spectrum, depending on the importance of their brand name for their operations. As for NGOs we may, if somewhat naively, hope that they would mostly fall on the side of a real interest in accountability of PMSCs, not only because they likely will have a brand name that would be damaged. However, there are numerous anecdotal accounts of NGO personnel in the field hiring security without inquiring into their human rights records. A key difference between these players may, however, be that states, unlike corporations or NGOs, may be held responsible internationally if their conduct falls below a certain threshold and/or violates a norm of international law, which may add an incentive for them to bargain for effective human rights and IHL protection.[103]

What we loosely referred to as 'passing on stigma' immediately above, can be more properly framed as the issue of whether, in turn, the client of the PMSC cares for either a market (in the case of a corporate client) or a civil society (in the case of states and NGOs) that values compliance with human rights and IHL. However,

---

[103] For a discussion of PMSCs and state responsibility see C Hoppe, 'Passing the Buck: State Responsibility for Private Military Companies' (2008) 19 European Journal of International Law 989, 989–1014.

even taking this for granted,[104] a second assumption necessary for such pressure to be exerted is the availability of information about the market and its players. Anyone who has researched in the PMSC field can attest to the fact that this is far from the case. While some PMSCs are forthcoming with information, most industry representatives still stress that the nature of their business does not allow them to discuss information contained in their contracts. Moreover, obtaining information about the subject in issue here, ie violations of human rights or IHL in a conflict situation, is inherently very difficult, even though NGOs and the press, with the help of modern technology, help to fill this gap. Accordingly, even if a client would be inclined to assess performance of a contract on the basis of compliance with a code of conduct that includes a commitment to human rights and IHL, reliable information may be lacking. Even assuming competition, and clients who bargain for human rights and IHL compliance, the industry reportedly still contains a significant amount of firms that are not repeat players. If a firm is thus able to reorganize, and in the process loses its tainted reputation, it has no incentive to honour its human rights commitments.

In sum, we find that the market in which PMSCs operate shows many signs that tend to counteract PMSCs' incentives to submit to effective CoC with respect to human rights and IHL. However, we currently lack the data to test these findings empirically. What we can take away from this discussion, however, is that we have a strong indication that the market for PMSCs cannot, with respect to incentives, be easily compared to, for example, the apparel industry, where such players as Nike or Levi's have faced tremendous pressure to submit to CoC with respect to labour rights. The imperfections in the market suggest to us not that CSR initiatives and CoC could not play a beneficial role, but rather that, for the time being, firms will have to rely on enforcement mechanisms beyond the market alone if their CSR efforts are to be taken seriously.

C. One More Caveat: Monitoring

A second crucial aspect that sets the PMSC industry apart from others is the difficulty effectively to monitor the conduct of PMSC employees. First, monitoring in a conflict zone generally proves very difficult. This will of course vary depending on the service provided. It will be much easier to monitor activities that take place indoors or in a small, confined area, and in groups, such as the detention services provided by PMSC personnel. Monitoring becomes increasingly difficult as activities approach the front line and are conducted covertly and/or over a widespread area and by individuals, such as mobile protection services. The above points are especially valid if we envision external monitoring provided by accounting firms or NGOs, which would in turn have to be protected in the theatre of operations, creating substantial additional costs.

---

[104] On the limits of brand value and hence effective CSR pressure see RJ Liubicic, 'Corporate Codes of Conduct and Product Labelling Schemes' (1998) 30 Law and Pol'y Int'l Bus 111, 139.

Accordingly, the financial burden to ensure effective monitoring may simply become too high, especially for small operators. In a competitive market in which clients care about human rights and IHL, those operators should be priced out of the market. While we have already outlined our doubts as to the composition of the market at present, this may be a point where growing consolidation will likely help, in that bigger companies, being able to provide somewhat better monitoring, have an incentive to compete in that regard and thus push the benchmark up.

Lastly, we should address problems of monitoring related to PMSC personnel: first, the quick personnel fluctuation in the industry will complicate effective monitoring, as an employee may already be employed for a different company potentially in a different geographic region, which makes inquiries into allegations difficult. Moreover, PMSC personnel may seek out employers that subject them to less control, either out of fear of liability or simply to increase job security. This effect is especially significant in the PMSC industry where a key objective of the CoC goes beyond the traditional CSR concern for labour rights—for the benefit of the employees—and rather addresses violations of human rights and IHL primarily bestowed upon others. Similarly, where CoC incorporating human rights and IHL are already in place, there is a danger that PMSC personnel will not report abuses for fear of job losses or tainting the reputation of their firm.[105]

Having demonstrated that, both with respect to incentives for firms to submit to effective CoC and with respect to monitoring, we find strong indicators that suggest to us that effective CSR will be difficult to achieve in the PMSC industry, and, particularly, that reliance on the market alone seems to be misplaced.

V. Conclusion

Different categories of private CoC exist. Basically, these initiatives can be divided into federative and individual. Federative codes are created by associations of PMSCs at the international, regional, and national levels. Their aim is to foster business opportunities for lawful companies whilst excluding corporations that do not comply with commonly defined rules. Individual codes are autonomously elaborated by single companies and should match the federative regulation, if the firm subscribes to any. Altogether, private CoC tend to refer to voluntary, national, and international rules existing in the matter of licensing, contracts, services, and resort to force, but they also add complementary norms.

As for the licensing regime, transparency is supported from the standpoint of the corporations and their personnel. Thus, PMSCs are required to disclose information to governments concerning both their status and that of their employees in order to obtain the licences necessary for the exercise of their activity. The purpose is to ascertain the lawfulness of the companies and the skill of their personnel. Transparency is fostered especially with regard to trafficking of arms, strategic

---

[105] For a discussion of these effects in other industries see Liubicic (n 104 above), 139, with further references.

goods, dual-use technologies, and resort to (armed) force. Once they come into existence, PMSCs are supposed to negotiate only with carefully selected subjects practicing legal activities; contracts should be negotiated by bearing in mind clients' satisfaction, but must anyway be consistent with the principle of fair competition and cannot interfere with public policies.

The provision of services is regulated through constant reference to human rights instruments, in particular the Geneva Conventions, the UDHR, and the VPSHR. Attention is paid to the protection of life, physical integrity, equality, non-discrimination, freedom of movement, and association. PMSCs and their personnel are expected to abide by not only domestic law, but also international law, and to promote the development of appropriate regulation in countries where respect for fundamental rights is not sufficiently granted. Within this frame, resort to (armed) force is allowed under very strict conditions, basically for defensive purposes and in a manner proportionate to threats. The UN Principles on the Use of Force and Firearms by Law Enforcement Officials and the UN Code of Conduct for Law Enforcement Officials provide essential guidelines in the matter.

Technically speaking, the language of private CoC is often vague; therefore, problems of interpretation arise. In fact, on the one hand, references to existing public and voluntary regulation do not specify the extent to which such norms apply to PMSCs and their personnel. This is highly problematic with regard to international rules, namely IHL, the application of which to non-state subjects is controversial. On the other hand, it is sometimes difficult to define precisely the content of the rules embodied in private CoC. Whereas a certain level of abstraction is understandable with respect to federative codes, it is less tolerable for individual CoC.

With respect to enforcement provisions, great differences become immediately apparent regarding the two existing group CoC, with the BAPSC's Charter not containing any specific mechanism, and IPOA's Code of Conduct being tied to an elaborate, if not very strict, enforcement mechanism. The BAPSC has a process in place designed to screen new members and to promote provisional members to full membership status, yet lacks any additional means of implementation offering incentives for compliance of members, or to reprimand members or otherwise enforce violations. Formally, IPOA follows a very different model with an intricate procedure. As regards external enforcement, the IPOA CoC already threatens that members who fail to uphold a provision may be subject to dismissal from IPOA. Moreover, the Code incorporates the so-called 'Enforcement Mechanism', a system allowing complaints by third parties. This system in principle allows anyone to lodge a written complaint against a member of IPOA for violations of the IPOA CoC. Yet, one crucial weakness of the process is that a member company that withdraws from IPOA before or even while a complaint is being addressed will not be subject to the process, and can thus avoid the 'noisy breakup' that represents the only true sanction available to IPOA.

Besides the two group CoC by the BAPSC and IPOA, the industry has spawned numerous CSR initiatives by individual firms which remain largely irrelevant to the specific risks PMSC activities pose to human rights and IHL. Similarly, these individual CoC do not generally contain specific enforcement mechanisms.

Furthermore, we have seen that numerous challenges for purely market-based enforcement remain. In that regard, it has been suggested that the PMSC industry does not face a competitive market. Thus, if clients face a sellers' market, so that there is simply little or no alternative for a given provider, there is no competition and hence firms will get away with the minimum of obligations. The fact that there are some firms that employ CoC incorporating human rights and IHL obligations cannot without more dispel these concerns, as PMSCs could simply be engaging in window-dressing. Much depends on whether the potential stigma stemming from a violation of human rights or IHL will in fact be transmitted to the client, with recent reports of PMSCs allegedly interfering with IHL and human rights, such as the shooting at Nisoor Square in Iraq, suggesting that public awareness of PMSCs' abuses is rising. Even if the stigma is actually passed on, ie a client is connected to the violation, the desired effect will only be achieved if the client cares about its reputation, which is apparently not always the case. Similarly, concerns about lack of information and non-repeat players remain, as do the inherent difficulties of monitoring in a conflict environment. In sum, we find that the market in which PMSCs operate shows many signs that counteract PMSCs' incentives to submit to effective CoC with respect to human rights and IHL. The imperfections in the market suggest to us not that CSR initiatives and CoC cannot play a beneficial role, but rather that, for the time being, firms must rely on enforcement mechanisms beyond the market itself if their CSR efforts are to be taken seriously.

19

Institutional Responsibility for Private Military and Security Companies

Nigel D White

I. Introduction

This chapter analyses the issues of legal responsibility arising from the discernible trend among international organizations, including regional organizations, to use the services of private military and security companies (PMSCs). It has been argued in the literature that suitably controlled and regulated use of PMSCs by the UN, EU, and other organizations would bring significant benefits, not only cost-savings but a removal of institutional dependence on voluntary and possibly poorly equipped contributions from member states. While recognizing the benefits to organizations that the greater use of PMSCs might bring, the chapter is concerned with issues of accountability when human rights abuse has been committed by PMSCs. While the wrongful actions of regular troops are attributable to governments, the most relevant test for private contractors is whether the government was in effective control of the conduct in question. The chapter considers whether this effective-control test is the most appropriate one for private contractors working for organizations or for troops-contributing nations (TCNs) involved in institutionally mandated peace operations.

II. The 'Inevitable' Rise of PMSCs

There is a discernible trend among states and international organizations, including regional organizations to use the services of PMSCs.[1] This trend has been recognized by the British government, which has increasingly relied upon PMSCs in the post-Cold War period. In the foreword to the 2002 Green Paper on 'Private Military Companies: Options for Regulation', the then Foreign Secretary Jack Straw stated that the massive military establishments of the Cold War were a thing of the past, and that 'States and international organizations are turning to the private sector as a

---

[1] H Wulf, *Internationalizing and Privatizing War and Peace* (2005), 42.

cost effective way of procuring services which would otherwise have been the preserve of the military'. Although mainly used by governments, principally the United States and the United Kingdom, the Foreign Secretary goes on to state that a 'further source of demand for private military services would be international organizations' enabling them to 'respond more rapidly and more effectively in crises'.[2] Kevin O'Brien is even firmer on the growing role of PMSCs within UN peace operations when he writes that 'it is clear that the United Nations is moving towards a situation (particularly through DPKO [Department of Peace Keeping Operations]) where PMSCs will be used in ever-greater capacities from their current existence as protectors and defenders of humanitarian aid operations in zones of conflict'.[3] It has been argued that suitably controlled and regulated use of PMSCs by the EU and other organizations would bring significant benefits, not only cost-savings but a removal of each organization's dependence on voluntary and possibly poorly equipped contributions from member states.[4] While identifying the benefits to organizations that the greater use of PMSCs would bring, Jack Straw also recognized that the use of PMSCs raises 'important concerns about human rights, sovereignty and accountability'.[5]

PMSCs are attractive to governments for a number of reasons other than the official one given of cost-savings. Indeed the financial argument itself is not necessarily determinative. Within Europe there are a large number of individuals serving in the armed forces of states (with over 200,000 each in Britain, France, and Germany), but only a small fraction is rapidly deployable. Rather than employing PMSCs to play this role, it might legitimately be asked whether it would be more cost-effective to spend defence budgets more sensibly to ensure military effectiveness—after all, taxpayers across Europe are already paying to maintain inefficient armies. Putting money to one side, the issue is as much one of ideology—the desire to outsource all services to the market is strong in the United States and the United Kingdom, and it is no coincidence that these are the countries where the vast majority of PMSCs are based, though Russia and China are starting to develop their industries using a vast surplus of well-trained military professionals. Further, with the number of military interventions increasing there is not only financial pressure but also democratic pressure to restrict the losses sustained by regular armed forces in foreign conflicts. Such democratic pressure and indeed democratic control is not the same for employees of PMSCs. MPs can criticize the government for losses of service personnel, and indeed if reforms in the United Kingdom are carried out, Parliament will have a say on issues of deployment of British soldiers in the future,[6] but the same democratic concern does not seem to apply to PMSCs. Though they are not considered to be mercenaries due to the narrow definition of what

---

[2] *Hansard*, HC 577, 12 February 2002, 4.
[3] KA O'Brien, 'What Should and What Should Not be Regulated?' in S Chesterman and C Lenhardt (eds), *From Mercenaries to Market: The Rise and Regulation of Private Military Companies* (2007), 45.
[4] J Patterson, 'A Corporate Alternative to United Nations Ad Hoc Military Deployments' (2008) 13 Journal of Conflict and Security Law 215.
[5] *Hansard*, HC 577, 12 February 2002, 4.
[6] ND White, 'International Law, the United Kingdom and Decisions to Deploy Troops Overseas' (2010) 59 ICLQ 814.

constitutes a mercenary in international law,[7] employees of PMSCs are viewed by some with similar distaste since they are doing their jobs for financial reward.

Finally, PMSCs are potentially attractive to governments because, unlike the regular armed forces for which the government bear 'automatic' responsibility, this is not the case for PMSCs employed by the government. The actions of PMSCs have to be attributed to the government if responsibility for wrongful acts is to ensue, and attribution under the orthodox test of international law occurs when there is 'effective control' of the acts of the PMSCs by the state or its agents. Though governments may be liable for a failure to control the action of the PMSCs if they, for example, commit human rights abuse, this is not the same as attributing the human rights abuse directly to the government. The issue is made even more complex if PMSCs play a role in UN, EU, or NATO peace operations, which traditionally have been composed of troops from member states (TCNs) acting under the authority (sometimes command and control) of the organization.

It is with this issue of institutional responsibility and the test to be applied in international law that this chapter is concerned. It argues that due to structural changes in the international legal order, with the rise in significance of non-state actors, the traditional test of effective control is inadequate for attribution to organizations such as the UN, NATO, or the EU, and to insist upon such a test would be to allow international organizations to escape direct liability for injurious acts committed under their authority.

III. Non-state Actors in International Law

Given the traditional focus on the state as principal right holder and duty bearer in international law, the use of PMSCs by international organizations does indeed raise complex issues of responsibility and accountability. There are conceptual difficulties in attributing legal responsibility to both international organizations and the companies that provide military and security services. Although very different entities, international organizations and corporate entities are classified as non-state actors and as such both represent challenges to the domination of the international legal order by sovereign states. International organizations acting in a collective security sphere challenge the traditional domination of the application of military force by states. The provision of security, potentially combat, personnel by private companies also challenges the domination of the state in military matters. With organizations such as the UN, EU, and NATO providing authority for the deployment of operations, and PMSCs potentially providing at least some of the forces, the state, though still important, is no longer omnicompetent in the application of military measures.

Of course when injurious acts are committed by PMSCs, morally speaking responsibility lies with the actor—the individual and the company they work for;

---

[7] See Art 1(1) of the International Convention against the Recruitment, Use, Financing and Training of Mercenaries 1989.

but while there are certain voluntary codes of practice and a growing literature on corporate social responsibility, corporations (including PMSCs) do not have the requisite level of autonomy to be subjects of international law and thereby to be responsible for internationally wrongful acts.[8] Companies and individuals may of course be liable before the domestic courts of the host state, though until 2009 PMSCs in Iraq had immunity from local courts.[9]

In contrast to corporations, international organizations have reached the stage of possessing objective legal personality making them responsible in their own right for breaches of international law. When PMSCs are used by organizations the issue is one of attribution and the chapter draws on accepted institutional practice on peacekeeping to show that organizations can be responsible for the acts of PMSCs over which the organization exercises authority and control. The chapter then uncovers the remedies that might be available in international law to victims of PMSC abuse against the authorizing organization. Of course this does not discount remedies that might be available against the individual employee or contractor, or against the company, but given their limited status in international law there are issues of whether international laws are applicable to them except in limited circumstances (such as under the Rome Statute on the ICC in the case of individuals suspected of committing war crimes, crimes against humanity, or genocide).

IV. The Responsibility of Organizations

Alongside states, intergovernmental organizations with certain features are established as subjects of international law, with separate will and personality, and with rights and duties on the international stage. With this status achieved the responsibility of organizations for breaches of international law is undeniable at least in theory. Full recognition, though, has been a slow process. Though the separate personality of the UN was confirmed by the International Court in 1949,[10] it was not until 1980 that the Court made it clear that organizations were 'subjects of international law and, as such, are bound by any obligations incumbent upon them under general rules of international law, under their constitutions or under international agreements to which they are a party'.[11] Further, in 1999 the Court stated that immunity from local legal processes enjoyed by an organization does not

---

[8] ND White and S Macleod, 'EU Operations and Private Military Contractors: Issues of Corporate and Institutional Responsibility', (2008) 19 EJIL 965, 967–70, 977–84.
[9] Coalition Provisional Authority Order 17, 27 June 2004, gave immunity to US Dept of Defense Contractors (approx 100,000 in Iraq). The Iraq/US SOFA of 17 November 2008 states that 'Iraq shall have the primary right to exercise jurisdiction over United States contractors and United States contractor employees' (Art 12(2)). This came into force on 1 January 2009.
[10] *Reparations for Injuries Suffered in the Service of the United Nations*, Advisory Opinion [1949] ICJ Rep 174, 179.
[11] *Interpretation of the Agreement of 25 March 1951 between the WHO and Egypt*, Advisory Opinion [1980] ICJ Rep 73, 89–90.

absolve it from responsibility for its unlawful acts.[12] The process of codification started soon after, with the International Law Commission (ILC) making good progress towards a draft code of articles on institutional responsibility deliberately using the 2001 Articles on State Responsibility as a model, the ILC declaring that 'they should be regarded as a source of inspiration, whether or not analogous solutions are justified with regard to international organizations'.[13]

In considering in general the international legal responsibility of organizations, the Special Rapporteur on the matter, Giorgio Gaja, identified that responsibility attaches only to organizations with separate personality.[14] While the UN's personality has been clear since 1949, in contrast was a lack of clarity on the international legal personality of the EU since its creation in 1992 until the Treaty of Lisbon came into force in December 2009. There is limited discussion of NATO's international legal personality, though the little that there is indicates that it possesses such.[15]

A rhetorical organization, one discussing matters and adopting recommendations, will not normally violate international law. In contrast an organization that is operational, with missions in the field, and with those missions performing functions such as peacekeeping and peace-building will be bound by those general norms of international law that are customary as well as jus cogens—those peremptory rules of international law that could be said to underpin the international legal order—prohibiting gross violence on the international stage. The ILC's Special Rapporteur recognized the applicability of the latter stating that the failure of the UN to prevent genocide in Rwanda in 1994 constituted a breach of an international obligation. He stated further that 'difficulties relating to the decision-making process could not exonerate the United Nations'.[16] Furthermore, it is clear that 'omissions are wrongful when an international organization is required to take some positive action and fails to do so',[17] and that both states and organizations are under a duty to suppress and prevent the commission of genocide.

Though there is general recognition that institutions are bound by jus cogens,[18] there may still be doubt about whether organizations can be bound by customary law, which after all, in the traditional ethos of international law, is made by states

---

[12] *Difference Relating to Immunity from Legal Process of a Special Rapporteur of the Commission on Human Rights, Advisory Opinion* [1999] ICJ Rep 62, 88.
[13] ILC Report on the Work of its Fifty-Fourth Session, UN Doc A/57/10, 232 (ILC Report, 2002).
[14] G Gaja, 'First Report on Responsibility of International Organizations', UN Doc A/CN4/532, 26 March 2003, 8.
[15] CF Amerasinghe, *Principles of the Institutional Law of International Organizations*, 2nd edn (2005), 72; HG Schermers and NM Blokker, *International Institutional Law*, 4th edn (2003), 995.
[16] G Gaja, 'Third Report on Responsibility of International Organizations', UN Doc A/CN.4/553, 13 May 2005, 4.
[17] Ibid, 3.
[18] ILC Report on the Work of its Fifty-Fifth Session, UN Doc A/58/10 (2003), 47 (ILC Report, 2003).

for states. This 'flat-earth' view of international law is exemplified by the Permanent Court's statement in the *Lotus* case of 1927,[19] but even by that date such an approach was not fully accurate given the existence of international organizations, principally the League of Nations, whose creation challenged the contractual model of international law.[20] Though the ILC stated in 2005 that 'for an international organization most obligations are likely to arise from the rules of the organization' or the internal law deriving from the constituent treaty as developed by practice, it did concede that the same sort of obligations that apply to states can apply to organizations, namely 'a customary rule of international law, a treaty or a general principle within the international legal order'.[21] Mainstream institutional lawyers agree with Amerasinghe stating that 'there are situations in which organizations would be responsible under customary international law for the acts of their servants or agents, when they are acting in the performance of their functions, or of persons or groups acting under the control of organizations, such as armed force in the case of the UN'.[22] It is worth noting that in his discussion of whose acts can be imputed to an organization, Amerasinghe writes about 'organs, servants, agents or independent contractors'.[23] More precise analysis of the issue of attribution for the acts or omissions of independent contractors will be undertaken in the next section.

In sum, international organizations exercise functions in their own right on the international stage and possess powers identified by Gaja as 'legislative, executive or judicial', more generally 'governmental'[24] or 'sovereign',[25] which can only be explained as evidence of a new international actor whose personality is not just a theoretical construct. Mainstream international legal literature contains many references to the development of this power no matter how imperfect it might be.[26] In other words, it should no longer be seen as controversial. Furthermore, once it is accepted that organizations legitimately exercise a wide range of powers and functions it is 'likely that the organization concerned will have acquired obligations under international law in relation to those functions, and the question of the existence of breaches may arise more frequently'.[27] With constitutional development comes institutional responsibility.

---

[19] *The Case of the SS Lotus*, PCIJ, Series A, no 10 (1927), 18.
[20] A McNair, 'The Functions and Differing Character of Treaties', (1930) 11 British Yearbook of International Law 100, 112; H Lauterpacht, 'The Covenant as the Higher Law', (1936) 17 British Yearbook of International Law 54.
[21] ILC Report on the Work of its Fifty-Seventh Session, UN Doc A/60/10 (2005), 87–8 (ILC Report, 2005).
[22] Amerasinghe (n 15 above), 400.
[23] Ibid.
[24] Gaja 2003 (n 14 above), 12.
[25] D Sarooshi, *International Organizations and their Exercise of Sovereign Powers* (2005).
[26] I Brownlie, 'The United Nations as a Form of Government' in JES Fawcett and R Higgins (eds), *International Organization* (1974), 26–7.
[27] Gaja 2003 (n 14 above), 15.

V. Attribution to Organizations

One of the key issues that makes organizational responsibility more complex, and therefore will lead to some differences in the principles of institutional responsibility when compared to those of state responsibility, is that there is often a question of whether responsibility lies with organization or member states (or both). This issue becomes acute when considering institutionally mandated peace operations consisting of troops supplied by TCNs. In general terms, for such peace operations the UN has only accepted responsibility for forces acting under its authority, command, and control. This normally means that it accepts liability for unlawful acts done by peacekeepers acting within their functions, but not for the acts of troops which are part of coalitions of the willing operating under a Security Council mandate but under the command and control of contributing state(s).[28]

Putting aside issues of individual criminal responsibility, the problem of where responsibility lies for unlawful acts committed by peacekeepers normally involves a choice between organization and the TCN. However, there is no reason why those choices that apply to peacekeepers should not also apply to private individuals or contractors employed by international organizations. This would indicate that in principle the organization should be responsible for unlawful acts committed by contractors acting under its authority, command, and control. If the contractors are not employed directly by the organization, but are employed by TCNs contributing to an operation under UN authority then the issue becomes more complex, but essentially comes down to who has authority, command, and control over the contractors in relation to the acts in question. If neither state nor organization has such control then, unless a less stringent test of attribution is to be used, the issue must be considered solely from the perspective of corporate responsibility. However, with corporations not normally responsible under international law, it is essential that we consider the rules on attribution closely.

The test of authority, command, and control may appear a stringent one and, furthermore, one that might not be sufficient to impute the actions of PMSCs to organizations. In peacekeeping practice though the threshold for attribution does not appear as strict as the terminology implies. Authority, command, and control may exist formally but in practice the level of control is less. For a start it is notable that the UN accepts responsibility for peacekeepers under its 'command' and 'control' despite the fact that disciplinary competence and criminal jurisdiction over UN peacekeepers remains with the TCN.[29] This illustrates the reality that the level of command and control exercised by the UN over peacekeepers is not complete or fully effective. Add to this the practice by national contingent commanders of referring controversial UN commands to their governments for approval

---

[28] I Scobbie in R-J Dupuy (ed), *A Handbook on International Organizations* (1998), 891. See also G Gaja, Second Report on Responsibility of International Organizations, UN Doc A/CN.4/541, 2 April 2004, 16–17.

[29] Gaja 2004 (n 28 above), 19.

before they act upon them.[30] With neither ordinary peacekeepers subject to UN military discipline (an essential component of 'control' not just accountability), nor fully under UN 'command', then the reality is that though there is UN 'authority' over peacekeepers there is only partial 'command' and 'control'.

The level of organizational control was a key issue in the *Behrami* case of 2007,[31] when the European Court of Human Rights identified that the failure to clear up cluster bombs in Kosovo, in the period after Serb withdrawal in June 1999, was attributable to the UN and not France as a contributing nation to the NATO force (KFOR) whose troops were deployed to the area in question. Though the UN administration of Kosovo (UNMIK) did have responsibility for mine clearance at the time of the explosion, it is doubtful whether it and not France (or KFOR) was in control of the conduct in question or the area in which the bombs were located.[32] Though the Court's judgment is not without problems,[33] especially in not endorsing the notion that contributing states as well as the UN could be responsible,[34] there are some benefits to recognizing that when the UN authorizes a force and furthermore does purport, subject to what was said above, to exercise command and control over it then it should bear, or at least share responsibility, especially when the UN is purporting to govern the territory in which the force is placed.

The Court stated that the key question was 'whether the Security Council maintained ultimate authority and control so that operational command was only delegated'.[35] With UN-commanded peace operations regularly being given mandates that contain Chapter VII elements after the Brahimi Report of 2000, and national- or multinational-commanded forces increasingly forming part of hybrid operations under a Chapter VII mandate, it seems appropriate to revise the simple cold war division of peacekeeping (for which the UN accepts responsibility) and coalitions (for which it does not). While coalitions of the type authorized in Korea and the Gulf (1991), subject to limited Security Council control, remain outside any revised test of attribution, peacekeeping and peace operations (even with robust mandates) should be within such a test unless it is shown that the level of control is clearly inadequate.

The above argument would suggest that within peace operations acts of individuals (peacekeepers or contractors) can be attributed to the authorizing organization even if individuals' primary loyalties and duties lay with another actor (the TCN or corporation). Simply put, if an organization authorizes a peace operation and purports to exercise control over it, it should bear the responsibility for acts or

---

[30] T Thakur and D Banerjee, 'India: Democratic, Poor, Internationalist' in C Ku and H Jacobson (eds), *Democratic Accountability and the Use of Force in International Law* (2003), 176, 198.
[31] *Behrami and Saramati v France, Germany and Norway*, ECHR Grand Chamber Decision as to Admissibility of Application nos 71412/01 and 78166/01.
[32] But see ibid, paras 5–7, 126.
[33] Ibid, para 132.
[34] A Sari, 'Jurisdiction and International Responsibility in Peace Support Operations: The *Behrami* and *Saramati* Cases', (2008) 8 Human Rights Law Review 151, 159.
[35] *Behrami* case (n 31 above), para 133.

omissions of individuals, whether troops drawn from contributing states or employees of PMSCs, working within that operation if those acts or omissions violate norms of international law. The ILC, though, draws a difficult distinction between attribution of responsibility to the UN and attribution of individual conduct which they confine to acts that were under the effective control of the organization.[36] This seems to signify that the attribution of responsibility for the acts of peacekeepers is established in principle if they are under UN command and control, but for the actual attribution of conduct it is necessary to establish effective control by organization or TCN.[37]

The International Court of Justice adopted a strong test of attribution for acts of individuals to states in the *Nicaragua* case of 1986,[38] reaffirmed in the *Bosnia v Serbia* decision of 2007. In restating the 'effective control' test in the latter case the Court made it clear that while it was not necessary to show a relationship of 'complete dependence' with the state, it must be proved that the persons who performed the wrongful acts must have either acted in accordance with the state's instructions or under its effective control, and that these instructions were given, or effective control exercised, 'in respect of each operation in which the alleged violations occurred, not generally in respect of the overall actions taken by the person or group of persons having committed the violations'.[39]

It is the latter point that distinguishes the test of 'effective control' from that of 'overall control' adopted by the ICTY where, in the words of the International Court of Justice, the Appeals Chamber of the ICTY took the view that the actions of the Bosnian Serbs could be attributed to the Former Republic of Yugoslavia (FRY) on the basis of the overall control exercised by the FRY over the Bosnian Serbs without there being 'any need to prove that each operation during which acts were committed in breach of international law was carried out on the FRY's instructions, or under its effective control'.[40] The International Court dismissed the 'overall control' test in the following terms:

The 'overall control' test has the major drawback of broadening the scope of State responsibility well beyond the fundamental principle governing the law of international responsibility: a State is responsible only for its own conduct, that it to say the conduct of persons acting, on whatever basis, on its behalf.[41]

Of course this depends on how narrowly or widely we construe 'acting on behalf' of a state. Consider a state that does not simply sponsor terrorists but is in overall control of them, knowing that they have committed atrocious acts against civilians

---

[36] ILC Report on the Work of its Sixty-First Session 2009, UN Doc A/64/10, 56, 62 (ILC Report 2009).
[37] Ibid, 64–6.
[38] *Case Concerning Military and Paramilitary Activities in and Against Nicaragua (Nicaragua v United States), Judgment*, [1986] ICJ Rep 14, 62–4.
[39] *Case Concerning the Application of the Convention on the Prevention and Punishment of the Crime of Genocide (Bosnia and Herzegovina v Serbia and Montenegro), Judgment*, [2007] ICJ Rep paras 400–7.
[40] Ibid, para 402.
[41] Ibid, para 406.

and will do so again, but that state is not in effective control of the particular atrocious act in question. According to the now orthodox 'effective control' test state responsibility is not engaged at least directly for the acts in question though 'lesser' levels of responsibility may be engaged for 'supporting' or 'harbouring' the terrorists, or failing to exercise 'due diligence' in preventing the terrorists from operating from its territory.[42] While it is true that a state's responsibility will be directly engaged when PMSCs are empowered to exercise elements of 'governmental authority'[43] such as guarding prisoners, for most PMSC activities a 'control' test is the most appropriate. The question then becomes whether it should be the 'effective control' test formulated in the *Nicaragua* case and developed further in the ILC's Articles on State Responsibility of 2001,[44] or a test embodying some lesser degree of control.

There is no doubt that the 'effective control' test has become central in the international regime governing state responsibility. It is interesting to note that in the 2008 Montreux Document on PMSCs the 17 states involved adopted the *Nicaragua*/ILC test in relation to attribution for the wrongful acts of PMSCs.[45] With the ILC seemingly endorsing the 'effective control' test in its draft articles on institutional responsibility, at least for the conduct of organs of states (including troop contingents) placed at the disposal of international organizations,[46] the 'effective control' test arguably seems to have become accepted as the method of attribution to international organizations as well as states. In this view the judgment of

---

[42] *Corfu Channel Case* [1949] ICJ Rep 18.
[43] Art 5 Articles on Responsibility of States 2001.
[44] Ibid, Art 8.
[45] Montreux Document on Pertinent International Legal Obligations and Good Practices for States Related to Operations of Private Military and Security Companies during Armed Conflict, 17 September 2008, which in part states:

> Although entering into contractual relations does not in itself engage the responsibility of Contracting States, the latter are responsible for violations of international humanitarian law, human rights law, or other rules of international law committed by PMSCs or their personnel where such violations are attributable to the Contracting State, consistent with customary international law, in particular if they are:
>
> a) incorporated by the State into its regular armed forces in accordance with its domestic legislation;
> b) members of organised armed forces, groups or units under a command responsible to the State;
> c) empowered to exercise elements of governmental authority if they are acting in that capacity (i.e. are formally authorised by law or regulation to carry out functions normally conducted by organs of the State); or
> d) *in fact acting on the instructions of the State (i.e. the State has specifically instructed the private actor's conduct) or under its direction or control (i.e. actual exercise of effective control by the State over a private actor's conduct).* [emphasis added]

[46] 'The conduct of an organ of a State or an organ or agent of an international organization that is placed at the disposal of another international organization shall be considered under international law an act of the latter organization if the organization exercises effective control over that conduct': Art 6 of the Draft Articles on the Responsibility of International Organizations, ILC Report 2009 (n 36 above), 21.

the ECtHR in *Behrami* is an aberration, a piece of judicial policy-making designed primarily to prevent the application of the ECHR to peace operations.[47]

Nevertheless, the 'overall control' test in the *Tadić* case, or 'the ultimate authority or control test' in *Behrami*, arguably better reflects the realities of the growth of non-state actors in international law whether insurgents, terrorists,[48] or PMSCs who may not necessarily be the agents of the state, but may well be under sufficient influence and control by a state or organization. Not to impute responsibility for violations committed by such actors to the state or organization exercising authority and overall control of them would, in the words of the ICTY, enable those states and organizations to escape 'international responsibility by having private individuals carry out tasks that may or should not be performed by...officials'.[49]

Whatever the merits of the different approaches to state responsibility, it appears that, in peacekeeping practice at least, institutional responsibility is engaged when the institution is in overall control of conduct in question. The fact that peace operations consist of contingents drawn from TCNs signifies that it is unrealistic to expect the UN to have effective control of the operation in all its aspects since issues of national command get in the way of achieving that high standard. Thus, when considering the attribution of acts or omissions of PMSCs to organizations, the fact that the organization might not exercise complete control over them should not necessarily be a bar to imputing responsibility. In contrast to this argument the orthodoxy seems to be that the test should start from the individual violation in question to see whether it was the state or organization in effective control of the conduct that led to the violation.[50] But in the circumstances of a UN-mandated and commanded multifunctional military operations, deployed in semi-hostile circumstances and potentially increasingly consisting of a mixture of TCN troops and PMSCs, the chances of making such a precise determination of control seems unlikely and, besides which, is contrary to UN practice that accepts at a general level at least responsibility for violations committed by persons operating under its authority and control.

The ILC's approach to attribution in the case of organizations is unclear. Its approach is not to adopt a test of attribution for acts of individuals in the sense of Article 8 of the 2001 Articles on State Responsibility, which provided that the conduct of individuals shall be attributed to a state if the individuals are 'acting on the instructions of, or under the direction or control of, the State in carrying out the conduct'. Instead, we have to look at the ILC's general test of attribution to organizations (draft Article 5), as well as its test for state organs placed at the disposal of organizations (draft Article 6).

---

[47] KM Larsen, 'Attribution of Conduct in Peace Operations: The Ultimate Authority and Control Test' (2008) 19 EJIL 509, 531.
[48] A Cassese, 'The *Nicaragua* and *Tadić* Tests Revisited in the Light of the ICJ Judgment on Genocide in Bosnia', (2007) 18 European Journal of International Law 649, 665–7.
[49] *Prosecutor v Tadić*, IT-94-1-A, 15 July 1999, para 117.
[50] O de Schutter, 'The Responsibility of States' in S Chesterman and A Fisher (eds), *Private Security, Public Order: The Outsourcing of Public Services and its Limits* (2009), 23 28; C Lehnardt, 'Peacekeeping', ibid, 212–14.

The ILC's general test for attribution for institutions is found in draft Article 5, paragraph 1 of which states that 'the conduct of an organ or agent of an international organization in the performance of functions of that organ or agent shall be considered as an act of that organization under international law whatever position the organ or agent holds in respect of the organization', and in paragraph 2 states that 'rules of the organization shall apply to determine the functions of its organs and agents',[51] which leaves it unclear whether PMSCs employed by an organization to perform security services would be covered. Draft Article 2(c) does though define 'agent' to include 'officials and other persons or entities through whom the organization acts', which is potentially broad enough to include private contractors.[52]

Here, the ILC is offering a test of 'acting in performance of functions' for individuals working for organizations in draft Article 5 yet, as already stated, it adopts an 'effective control' test for state organs (including national contingents) put at the disposal of international organizations in draft Article 6. Neither clearly covers PMSCs, though the former seems nearer. However, while (arguably customary) practice on peacekeeping establishes that organizations accept responsibility for operations over which they have 'overall control', or in the phrase of the Court in *Behrami*, 'ultimate authority and control', this contradicts the orthodox test in state responsibility—that of 'effective control' of conduct—which, the dominant view argues, should apply to other international legal persons such as organizations.[53]

There are strong arguments to be made that overall control is a better test for attribution of conduct to states so that a government should not be able to escape responsibility by acting through non-state actors. However, the purpose of this chapter is to contend that the arguments are even stronger when considering institutional responsibility. Organizations do not have their own forces so there is no real situation in which they control their armed forces as a state does. Thus the starting point for states and organizations is radically different. Organizations have to rely on troops from TCNs and increasingly personnel from PMSCs. In these circumstances organizations are unlikely to have fully effective control over conduct performed under its authority and in its name, though there will normally be some significant level of control. Not to attribute responsibility in these circumstances would be to absolve organizations from the consequences of their decisions to authorize military operations where there is a strong likelihood of injurious acts occurring (though they may still be liable for lack of due diligence in failing to prevent or respond to the violations).[54] This is not to say that the others actors concerned—the TCNs or the corporations—should not also bear some responsibility,

---

[51] ILC Report 2009 (n 36 above), 21.
[52] Ibid, 20. But see the UN's General Conditions of Contract, Second Interim Revision, OLA Version, 9 February 2006, section 1, which states in part that a contractor 'shall have the legal status of an independent contractor vis-a-vis the United Nations. The contractor's personnel and sub-contractors shall not be considered in any respect as being the employees or agents of the United Nations.'
[53] Larsen (n 47 above), 526.
[54] C Lenhardt, 'Private Military Companies and State Responsibility' in Chesterman and Lenhardt (eds) (n 3 above), 152–3; ILC Report 2009 (n 36 above), 65.

but legal problems of suing corporations, and indeed factual problems of making the TCNs liable for the injurious acts of, say, French or Ukrainian troops in a UN or NATO operation, means that it is important that organizations take their share of responsibility.

In conclusion, where the UN, EU, or NATO has authorized a peace operation and purports to exercise overall though not always effective control over it, the acts or omissions of troops and PMSC employees should be attributable to the organization if they amount to breaches of human rights law or, if appropriate, international humanitarian law. This reflects the reality that organizations such as the UN do not exercise effective control over the conduct of peace operations undertaken under their authority. Of course this does not mean that a higher standard of control is not desirable or achievable. Indeed, organizations may be able to control PMSCs more effectively by means of detailed contracts containing mechanisms of accountability than they can the contingents of member states. Even for those operations not under the overall control of the organization there might still be responsibility on the part of the organization, not for the violations in question but for the lack of due diligence in preventing or responding to such violations.

VI. Remedies

If the wrongful acts or omissions of PMSCs are attributable to the international organization, as well as having an obligation to 'perform the obligation breached', to cease the breach, and guarantee non-repetition,[55] the draft articles on institutional responsibility provide that the 'responsible international organization is under an obligation to make full reparation for the injury caused by the internationally wrongful act'.[56] Gaja gives an example of the statement of the UN Secretary General on the applicability of international humanitarian law to UN forces 'when they are engaged as combatants in situations of armed conflict' which will entail the international responsibility' of the UN, and 'its liability in compensation for violations of international humanitarian law committed by members of United Nations forces'.[57] The UN has paid compensation in a number of peacekeeping operations, but the evidence cited is largely from earlier forces especially the Congo in the early 1960s where the UN force was engaged in fighting with insurgents and mercenaries. It is difficult to gauge whether the UN has been consistent,[58] but there is no reason to assume that it (or other organizations such as the EU) will not compensate for damage caused by wrongs committed by PMSCs acting under its authority and control.

---

[55] G Gaja, Fifth Report on Responsibility of International Organizations, UN Doc A/CN4/583, 2 May 2007, 7.
[56] Draft Art 34; ILC Report 2009 (n 36 above), 29.
[57] Gaja, 2007 (n 55 above), 15; citing UN Doc A/51/389, para 16.
[58] See analysis of practice in MC Zwanenburg, *Accountability under International Humanitarian Law for United Nations and North Atlantic Treaty Organization Operations* (2004), 240–51.

Forms of reparation can include restitution (to re-establish the position which existed before the wrongful act was committed), compensation (covering any financially assessable damage, including loss of profits), and satisfaction (which may take the form of an expression of regret or a formal apology).[59] Though remedies are in principle available, access to them is limited. The hit-or-miss forum shopping by victims (as in *Behrami*) is not satisfactory. There needs to be an increase in access to remedies whether judicial, legal, or non-legal. The *Kadi* case before the European Court of Justice shows that victims of international wrongful acts committed by international organizations may obtain redress,[60] but access to European Courts is of course not often available. If the complainants are from non-EU countries but in territory under the control of an EU operation then responsibility for human rights abuses committed by EU forces or contractors employed by them may arise according to a number of European Court of Human Rights cases, though the question of whether the Convention applies outside the European legal space is subject to an ongoing debate.[61] As regards non-legal mechanisms, the EU established an office of the ombudsperson in 1992, 'empowered to receive complaints from any citizen of the Union... concerning instances of maladministration in the activities of Community institutions or bodies'.[62]

In general terms institutions do not have consistent or systematic mechanisms for claims to be made against them and remedies granted to those who have suffered loss as a result of a wrongful act committed by the organization or by its agents or those employed by it: witness the reluctance of the Security Council to grant redress to individuals wrongly suspected of terrorist links and listed for the purposes of targeted sanctions. Though targeted sanctions were first imposed in 1999, it was not until 2009 that the Security Council established an office of the ombudsperson to receive and handle complaints of wrongful listing.[63] Regional courts apart, there is no international court that will countenance claims brought by victims of abuse, though it is possible that the activities of PMSCs may well be subject to the scrutiny and criticism of the various treaty bodies created by human rights instruments, possibly as a result of an individual complaint. The World Bank Inspection Panel created in 1993 is a useful model that could be adopted to deal with the responsibility of the UN or EU in its security operations. Matters of serious international concern should be subject to more general inquiries, such as those conducted by the UN into its failings in the Rwandan genocide of 1994 and Srebrenica in 1995, but these should be followed up by the establishment of claims commissions enabling individuals to have access to justice.

Finally the jurisdictional immunity of organizations before national courts should not be interpreted by the organization as giving it, its agents, and contractors

---

[59] Draft Arts 34–9, ILC Report 2009 (n 36 above), 30.
[60] Joined Cases C-402/05 P and C-415/05 P, *Yassin Abdullah Kadi, Al Barakaat International Foundation v Council of the European Union and Commission of the European Communities* (3 September 2008).
[61] *Bankovic and ors v Belgium and ors*, Appl no 52207/99 (12 December 2001).
[62] Art 195 EC Treaty.
[63] SC Res 1904, 17 December 2009.

absolute immunity from local courts, but only granting a restrictive or functional immunity for those acts committed in the course of performing the functions designated to them by the organization. Violations of customary human rights law or humanitarian law cannot be justified as being part of an organization's functions and so immunity should not be claimed. Even if immunity is still applicable and there is no waiver of immunity by the executive head, the organization is still obliged to provide alternative methods for settling the claim.[64] Immunity cannot be used to deny the right of access to remedies.

VII. Conclusion

It is extremely difficult within the current international legal order to make companies that supply security or military services directly accountable for violations of international humanitarian law or human rights law when deployed as part of UN, EU, or NATO authorized peace operations. Furthermore, the development of corporate social responsibility by means of soft international and European law does not guarantee any improvement, and this situation will persist until voluntary regulation is matched to a strong institutional framework providing accountability for abuses. Of course it would be desirable for PMSCs and corporations generally to be subjects of international law and consequently directly be subject to obligations. Indeed, the establishment of other non-state actors with legal personality, such as international organizations, shows that there is no conceptual impediment to recognizing corporations as subjects of international law; it simply reflects a lack of political will. Furthermore, a strengthening of corporate social responsibility and the development of effective remedies within this would improve victims' chances of access to justice. Despite these possibilities it has been argued in the chapter that the wrongful acts or omissions of PMSCs should be attributable to organizations under whose authority they operate and who are under the overall control of the organization. It has been argued that this is the level of control that organizations have exercised over peacekeepers in peace operations where it is accepted that responsibility is be attributed to the institution, and that this level should be recognized as applicable to PMSCs. This will help to ensure an acceptable level of accountability for the acts of PMSCs operating under the authority of an international organization, pending the development of corporate responsibility and more effective corporate accountability on the international plane.

---

[64] Art VIII, s 29 of the Convention on Privileges and Immunities of the United Nations, 1946. See generally R Buchan, H Jones and ND White, 'The Externalization of Peacekeeping: Policy, Responsibility and Accountability', (2010) 14 Journal of International Peacekeeping (forthcoming).

20

State Responsibility for Conduct of Private Military and Security Companies Violating *Ius ad Bellum*

Charlotte Beaucillon, Julian Fernandez, and Hélène Raspail

This chapter addresses the question of whether or not a state can be held responsible for breaches of *ius ad bellum* arising from the acts of private military and security companies (PMSCs), and is part of an attempt to assess the role of international law in the governance of the still rather unregulated phenomenon of PMSC activity on the international scene.[1]

Historically, the problems associated with the activities of either the mercenaries or PMSCs have never led states to adopt specific norms, national or international, relating to their international responsibility in case of an illicit use of armed force with the help of such private combatants. The UN Convention on Mercenarism even states that, 'The present Convention shall be applied without prejudice to . . . [t]he rules relating to the international responsibility of States',[2] setting aside any specific question that could arise from this practice.[3]

Though they historically proceed from a single phenomenon, it is nowadays uncontroversial that mercenaries and PMSCs should be distinguished from each other, as they differ.[4] (See the definition of PMSCs proposed in the Introduction to this volume.[5])

For the sake of clarity, the Montreux Document proposes a categorization of the different relationships between a state and a PMSC:

---

[1] This chapter aims at exploring state responsibility for the acts of PMSCs and will therefore not address the issue of individual criminal responsibility of the PMSCs and their personnel. For such an approach, see below, Part V of the present volume.
[2] UN International Convention against the Recruitment, Use, Financing and Training of Mercenaries, Art 16.
[3] For an approach of state responsibility in regional international law on mercenaries, as crystallized under the patronage of the Organization of African Unity, see Ch 16 by Mancini, Ntoubandi, and Marhaun in this volume.
[4] See Ch 1 by Consumano and Ch 2 by Ronzitti in this volume.
[5] See the Introduction by Francion and Ronzitti in this volume.

'Contracting States' are States that directly contract for the services of PMSCs, including, as appropriate, where such a PMSC subcontracts with another PMSC.... 'Territorial States' are States on whose territory PMSCs operate.... 'Home States' are States of the nationality of a PMSC, i.e. where a PMSC is registered or incorporated; if the State where the PMSC is incorporated is not the one where it has its principal place of management, then the State where the PMSC has its principal place of management is the 'Home State'.[6]

In the absence of any lex specialis ruling the responsibility of the state for the acts of PMSCs, the present study is necessarily rooted in general public international law. According to the International Law Commission (the ICL) Draft Articles on State Responsibility, for a state to be responsible for the acts of a PMSC, a breach of *ius ad bellum* has to be characterized, and it is to be attributed to the state.[7] Indeed, Draft Article 1 states that 'every international wrongful act of a State entails the international responsibility of that State', while Draft Article 2 explains: 'there is an internationally wrongful act of a State when conduct consisting of an action or an omission (a) is attributable to the State under international law; and (b) constitutes a breach of an international obligation of the State'.[8]

Ius ad bellum encompasses the international rules on the use of force by states. It is well known that the entry into force of the UN Charter in 1945 grounded the general prohibition of the use of force by states in their international relations.[9] However, it must be clear that not every use of force amounts to a violation of *ius ad bellum*: the general prohibition contained in Article 2(4) of the UN Charter is accompanied with UN Charter-based, as well as arguably customary, exceptions. Indeed, the use of force can be considered lawful—with unequal certainty, which will be discussed later—in putative self-defence operations, peacekeeping and peace-enforcing operations, as well as in operations where states claim to be protecting their own rights under public international law.

This chapter will first address the question of whether or not a state can be held responsible for the acts perpetrated by a PMSC. It will then be examined whether, defined *lato sensu*, *ius ad bellum* would imply that states must abide by certain positive obligations of due diligence and to regulate the use of force by the PMSCs at the domestic level.

---

[6] 'Montreux Document', Swiss Initiative, in Cooperation with the International Committee of the Red Cross, on Private Military and Security Companies, 17 September 2008 (Preface, a. 9). For a comment, see, inter alia, J Cockayne, 'Regulating Private Military and Security Companies: The Content, Negotiation, Weaknesses and Promise of the Montreux Document' *Journal of Conflict and Security Law* 13 (2008) 10.

[7] We will extensively refer to the *Draft Articles on State Responsibility* of the International Law Commission (hereafter, 'the Draft Articles'), endorsed by the UN General Assembly in its Res 56/83 of 28 January 2002. But we will generally prefer the text of the *Draft Articles with Commentaries*, as published in the *Yearbook of the International Law Commission*, 2001, vol II, Part Two, 30–143.

[8] Draft Articles (n 7 above), 32–6.

[9] Art 2(4) of the UN Charter.

I. State Responsibility Arising from the Acts of a PMSC

According to the ILC Draft Articles on State Responsibility, a state is responsible in international law when a violation of an international obligation can be attributed to it.[10] The question of whether a state can be held responsible for the acts of a PMSC implying the use of armed force is therefore twofold, and will be dealt with in terms of both the existence of a violation of *ius ad bellum* (A) and the attribution of this breach to the State (B).

A. *A Violation of* Ius ad Bellum *by a PMSC*

As has been stressed before, not every use of force amounts to a violation of *ius ad bellum*. We will first examine the conditions of the lawful use of force, and then we shall characterize what a violation of *ius ad bellum* consists of.

1. *Disregarding the Conditions of the Lawful use of Force*

The limits to the prohibition on the use of force in international relations have been discussed before, and significantly since the entry into force of the San Francisco Charter.[11] We therefore do not intend to revisit the issue exhaustively, but only to examine the conditions of exercise of the three categories of military operations that can be considered, with variable certainty, consistent with *ius ad bellum*: self-defence operations, peace operations, and humanitarian interventions.[12] Indeed, in practice states do tend to argue that they are using force consistently with *ius ad bellum*. However, regardless of the political attempts to justify the use of force ex post facto, when PMSCs are acting outside the strict legal conditions of the lawful use of force, an issue of violation of *ius ad bellum* arises.

---

[10] Cf Arts 1 and 2, Draft Articles (n 7 above), 32–6.
[11] The related literature is obviously too dense to be recalled here in its entirety, but we cite the following selection: the two courses given by Wehberg at the Hague Academy of International Law, before and after the entry into force of the UN Charter. See H Wehberg, 'Le Problème de la Mise de la Guerre hors la Loi' (1928-IV) 24 RCADI 151–305; and H Wehberg, 'L'interdiction du Recours à la Force. Le Principe et les Problèmes qui se Posent' (1951-I) 78 RCADI 7–121. For more recent approaches, see also M Virally, 'Commentaire de l'article 2§4 de la Charte' in J-P Cot and A Pellet (eds), *La Charte des Nations Unies, Commentaire Article par Article*, 2nd edn (1991), 115–28; N Schrijver, 'Commentaire de l'article 2§4 de la Charte' in J-P Cot, A Pellet, and M Forteau (eds), *La Charte des Nations Unies, Commentaire Article par Article*, 3rd edn (2005), 437–66; A Randelzhofer, 'Article 2.4' in B Simma (ed), *The Charter of the United Nations: A Commentary*, 2nd edn (2002), 112–36; O Corten, 'The Controversies over the Customary Prohibition of the Use of Force: A Methodological Debate' [2005] EJIL 803–22.
[12] For a study on the question of whether or not State consent can be the basis of an intervention by PMSCs to support the legitimate government of a State, see Ch 12 by Vierucci in this volume.

a) Disregarding the legal conditions of self-defence

The 'inherent right of self-defence' of the state is the necessary corollary of the prohibition of the use of force,[13] as confirmed the International Court of Justice (ICJ) in its *Legality of threat or use of nuclear weapons* advisory opinion.[14] This right, however crucial it may be, is not absolute. First, self-defence is a subsidiary right of states, since the primary responsibility for the maintenance of international peace and security rests on the UN Security Council acting on behalf of the UN member states.[15] Therefore, the exercise of self-defence is only possible until the UN Security Council seizes the question. Deriving from this subsidiarity, self-defence is to be exercised immediately, and the measures taken are to be 'proportional to the armed attack and necessary to respond to it'.[16] Insofar as this right is exercised collectively, it is necessary that the attacked state both considers itself as such, and explicitly calls for third states' intervention.[17]

b) Disregarding the legal conditions of 'Peace Operations'

Peace-enforcement and peace-keeping operations constitute the second group of cases in which the use of force is considered lawful. On the one hand, peace-enforcement operations are military operations authorized by the UN Security Council on the basis of Articles 39 and 42 of the UN Charter, deciding to use force in order to maintain or restore peace.[18] Such operations are composed of national troops, made available by the UN Member States.[19] As said before, these operations are grounded on a decision of the Security Council under Chapter VII of the UN Charter. From a *lege lata* perspective, a possible breach of *ius ad bellum* would occur if the operation had not previously been authorized by the UN Security Council.[20] On the other hand, subsequent practice of the UN shows that

---

[13] We consider self-defence to be the only exception *stricto sensu* to Art 2(4) of the UN Charter. This core concept of the law of international security is nevertheless difficult to reconcile with the international law of state responsibility. In its Draft Articles, the ICL eventually decided to consider self-defence a circumstance precluding wrongfulness: a secondary norm of international law, in the sense of HART's *Concept of Law* (cf Draft Art 21, 74–5). However, as Art 51 of the UN Charter states, self-defence is a *right* of the state, this is, a primary rule of international law. We therefore respectfully disagree with the choice of the ICL, though acknowledging the difficulties of the exercise, and would stress that self-defence is no mere excuse for the use of force: it is never a wrongful act of the state.

[14] ICJ, Advisory Opinion of 8 July 1996, *Legality of the threat or use of nuclear weapons*, Advisory Opinion, ICJ Rep 1996, §96, 263.

[15] Art 24(1) of the UN Charter.

[16] *Military and paramilitary activities in and against Nicaragua* (*Nicaragua v United States of America*), Merits, Rec 1986, §176, 94 and §237, 122, ICJ (27 June 1986).

[17] *Case Concerning Military and Paramilitary Activities in and against Nicaragua* (n 16 above), §195, 103–4, and §232, 120.

[18] Indeed, Art 24(1) of the Charter grants the UN Security Council the primary responsibility to maintain international peace and security, and Chapter VII resolutions benefit from the primacy of Art 103 of the UN Charter.

[19] The troops are made available on an ad hoc basis, unlike Art 43 of the UN Charter provides. Art 43 has never been implemented because of the reluctance of the UN members to conclude the planned 'special agreements' with the Security Council, which would have made troops available on a more permanent basis.

[20] Here again, we acknowledge the ongoing debate on the legality of ex post facto and implicit authorizations from the UN Security Council, without actually entering the discussion.

peacekeeping operations[21] can be agreed on a conventional basis, whereby the consent of the state hosting the mission on its territory is obtained, and the mission of the deployed troops is limited. As former UN Secretary General Boutros Boutros-Ghali recalled, when so-called Chapter VI *bis* operations are at stake, the 'three particularly important principles [to consider] are the consent of the parties, impartiality and the non-use of force except in self-defence'.[22] So, for example, a violation of *ius ad bellum* would occur, were the troops to use force outside self-defence,[23] thereby going beyond their conventional mandate.[24]

c) Operations where states claim to protect their own rights under public international law

This is the most controversial case: when a state unilaterally intervenes in another country, claiming to exercise its own right to protect its citizens and national interests abroad. Such operations are illustrated by concrete examples as the hostage-rescue raid conducted by Israel on 4 July 1976 on the Entebbe airport in Uganda, the French operation Shaba in Zaire in 1978, or the 1980 US operation in Iran aimed at rescuing its diplomatic staff. In these situations, it is arguable whether strict conditions must be complied with to ensure the legality of the intervention, since there is no consensus that this kind of operation is lawful at all. On the other hand, there is no reverse consensus clearly outlawing these operations, because of the very fact that states claim to be protecting their own rights under public international law. Furthermore, state practice shows that these operations survived the entry into force of the San Francisco Charter and its Article 2(4). In any event, from a pragmatic standpoint, general principles of international law should nevertheless apply here. At the very least the intervention should be necessary and proportionate. Therefore, from this perspective the acts of PMSC personnel should be evaluated according to a teleological criterion, ie in light of the aims of the intervention on an *ad hoc* basis.

2. *Legal Characterization of the Breach of* Ius ad Bellum *by a PMSC*

The breach of *ius ad bellum* by a PMSC—that is, the unlawful use of force by a PMSC—can receive different legal characterizations, ranging from coercive intervention in the internal affairs of a state, to armed attack. As we will see later, the legal characterization of the breach of *ius ad bellum* varies according to the relationship between the state and the PMSC. It is well known that the notions

---

[21] A/47/277–S/24111, 17 June 1992, *An Agenda for Peace Preventive Diplomacy, Peacemaking and Peace-keeping*, §20.
[22] A/50/60–S/1995/1, 3 January 1995, *Supplement to an Agenda for Peace: Position Paper of the Secretary General on the Occasion of the Fiftieth Anniversary of the United Nations*, §33.
[23] In this very case, note that self-defence does not refer to the right of the state, but to the right of the individual involved in fighting. This case goes beyond the scope of this chapter and we will not develop it further. Note that it is dealt with in terms of the right to life of PMSC contractors in Ch 9 by den Dekker and Myer in this volume.
[24] In this case, the breach of *ius ad bellum* amounts to an ultra vires act.

of armed attack and aggression are left undefined by the UN Charter,[25] and were defined in 1974 by the UN General Assembly (UNGA).

In the distinct context of individual criminal liability, the definition of aggression given by the 1974 UNGA resolution has been further elaborated, challenged and confirmed. First, it was discussed and finally rejected by the ILC when working on a Draft Code of Crimes against the Peace and Security of Mankind.[26] Then, in the context of the creation of the International Criminal Court (ICC), the 1974 UNGA definition served as a basis for the definition of the *crime* of aggression in the Court's Statute. However, although included in Article 5 of the Statute of the International Criminal Court as a prosecutable offence, no definition of the crime of aggression could be agreed upon. The Special Working Group on the Crime of Aggression, established by the Assembly of the Parties to the Rome Statute to cope with the lack of definition of aggression in Article 5 of the Statute, presented a draft amendment to the Statute of the Court in February 2009.[27] The discussions of the Assembly of the Parties to the Rome Statute during the Review Conference of the Rome Statute, which was held in Kampala from 31 May to 11 June 2010, led to the adoption by consensus of a resolution on 'The Crime of Aggression', which confirms the pertinence of the 1974 UNGA resolution. Article 8 *bis* of the Statute is indeed introduced, and states:

1. For the purpose of this Statute, 'crime of aggression' means the planning, preparation, initiation or execution, by a person in a position effectively to exercise control over or to direct the political or military action of a State, of an act of aggression which, by its character, gravity and scale, constitutes a manifest violation of the Charter of the United Nations.

2. For the purpose of paragraph 1, 'act of aggression' means the use of armed force by a State against the sovereignty, territorial integrity or political independence of another State, or in any other manner inconsistent with the Charter of the United Nations. Any of the following acts, regardless of a declaration of war, shall, in accordance with United Nations General Assembly resolution 3314 (XXIX) of 14 December 1974, qualify as an act of aggression ...[28]

---

[25] We acknowledge here the problem of the linguistic differences between the English and French versions of the Charter, which refer in the former to 'armed attack' (Art 51) and 'aggression' (Arts 39) and in the latter only to 'aggression' (Arts 39 and 51), and will therefore consider both terms to be identical for the purposes of this chapter.
[26] Doc A/51/10, Report of the International Law Commission on the Work of its 48th Session, 6 May–26 July 1996, UN GAOR, 51st Sess, Supp no 10, Art 16, 42–3.
[27] ICC Doc ICC-ASP/7/20/Add1, Assembly of States Parties, Report of the Special Working Group on the Crime of Aggression, 30.
[28] RC/Res 6, 'The Crime of Aggression', adopted at the 13th plenary meeting, on 11 June 2010, by consensus. Advance version 28 June 2010 available at <http://www2.icc-cpi.int/iccdocs/asp_docs/Resolutions/RC-Res.6-ENG.pdf>, accessed on 20 August 2010. It falls out of the scope of this chapter to examine more than the definition of the crime of aggression. We will therefore only stress that the Resolution on the Crime of Aggression also states that there are two triggers to the jurisdiction of the Court: a referral by the Security Council, or a referral by a state or the prosecutor. States parties may opt out of the crime of aggression by declaration, and the ICC will not have jurisdiction over nationals of non-states parties. The jurisdiction over the crime of aggression may be activated from 1 January 2017. Finally, the amendments will be reviewed seven years after the beginning of the Court's exercise of jurisdiction. For further insight on the negotiations leading to the adoption of Art 8 bis, see the report by the American non-Governmental Organizations Coalition for the International Criminal Court,

Although it is acknowledged here that the 1974 UNGA resolution definition of aggression is often considered unsatisfactory, and that the very aim of defining aggression has been challenged,[29] the 1974 UNGA proposal is still an incontrovertible element of the definition in our study.

According to resolution 3314 (XXIX), adopted by the UNGA in 1974: 'Aggression is the use of force by a State against the sovereignty, the territorial integrity or political independence of another State, or in any other manner inconsistent with the Charter of the United Nations, as set out in this Definition.'[30] The resolution then provides for a list of cases considered as acts of aggression, such as wrongful attack, bombardment, blockade, etc.[31] Article 3(g) of the 1974 resolution stipulates that an act of aggression can consist of: 'The sending by or on behalf of a State of armed bands, groups, irregulars or mercenaries, which carry acts of armed forces against another State of such gravity as to amount to the acts listed above, or its substantial involvement therein.'[32] Such a form of aggression is also referred to as indirect aggression, insofar as 'the home State uses [the PMSCs] as a conduit ("on behalf of the State") for indirect armed intervention against another State'.[33] Consequently, the resolution expressly recognizes that a PMSC can perform or contribute to an act of aggression by a state, when the conditions of legality of the missions we considered above are not met. This is indeed the position of the ICJ in the *Nicaragua* case, when dealing with the right of self-defence in customary international law, as reflected by Article 3(g) of the above mentioned 1974 resolution:

> The Court sees no reason to deny that, in customary law, the prohibition of armed attacks may apply to the sending by a State of armed bands to the territory of another State, if such an operation, because of its scale and effects, would have been classified as an armed attack rather than as a mere frontier incident had it been carried out by regular armed forces. But the Court does not believe that the concept of 'armed attack' includes not only acts by armed bands where such acts occur on a significant scale but also assistance to rebels in the form of the provision of weapons or logistical or other support. Such assistance may be regarded as a threat or use of force, or amount to intervention in the internal or external affairs of other States.[34]

The decision of the ICJ in the *Nicaragua* case has an impact on the legal characterization of acts that violate *ius ad bellum*, and that are attributable to a state, ranging

---

Report on the Review Conference of the Rome Statute of the International Criminal Court, Kampala, Uganda, 31 May–11 June 2010, <http://www.amicc.org/docs/RC.pdf>.

[29] For a recent critique of the crime of aggression and on its potential repercussions in terms of controversial uses of force, cf A Paulus, 'Second Thoughts on the Crime of Aggression' in (2009) 4 European Journal of International Law 1119–24.

[30] Res 3314(XXIX), *Definition of Aggression*, 14 December 1974, Annex, Art 1.

[31] Ibid, Annex, Art 3.

[32] Ibid, Annex, Art 3(g).

[33] As expressed by F Francioni, 'The Responsibility of the PMSCs Home State for Human Rights Violations arising from the Export of Private Military and Security Services', EUI Working Paper, AEL 2009/18, Academy of European Law, Priv-War Project, 11.

[34] *Case Concerning Military and Paramilitary Activities in and against Nicaragua* (n 16 above), §195, 103–4.

from armed attack to mere intervention into the internal affairs of a state. According to the *Nicaragua* decision, a strong relationship—more than mere support—has to exist between the state and the PMSC in order for an armed attack to be attributed to the state. For instance, the case of peacekeeping operations based upon the consent of the territorial state is expressly foreseen in Article 3(e) of the 1974 Resolution of the UN General Assembly: 'The use of the armed forces of one State, which are within the territory of another State, with the agreement of the receiving State, in contravention of the conditions provided for in the agreement or any extension of their presence in such territory beyond the termination of the agreement'[35] amounts to an act of aggression. This legal characterization of the aggression depends, as we will see in the next section, on attribution of the acts of PMSCs to the state and on their relationship—that is, whether the state is the contracting state, the territorial state, or the home state. A contrario, in cases where the state is only providing support to the acts of the PMSC personnel—where there is no close relationship between the state and the PMSC—only a threat or use of force, or a coercive intervention in the internal affairs of a State, could be attributed to the state, but not an act of aggression.

It must now be determined to what extent and in what conditions acts of PMSCs violating *ius ad bellum* can be considered acts of a state so as to trigger its international responsibility.

B. *Attribution to the State of Acts of the PMSCs Violating* Ius ad Bellum

Two alternative criteria may be used to attribute breaches of *ius ad bellum* to a state.[36] In the first situation, when the PMSC exercises elements of governmental authority, and according to the conditions set up by the ICL Draft Articles, the behaviour of the PMSC is exclusively attributable to the contracting state (1). In the second case, the breach may be attributable to the contracting state, to the territorial state, or to the home state, provided the state either instructs the PMSC to act, or exercises direction or control over it (2).

1. *Exercise of Elements of Governmental Authority*

The criterion of the exercise of governmental authority is referred to in Article 5 of the ILC Draft Articles on State responsibility.[37] The preparatory works of the ILC[38] as well as the final commentary on the Draft Articles are useful, as they extensively refer to the case of PMSCs: the entities referred to:

---

[35] UNGA Res 3314(XXIX) (n 30 above).
[36] On the attribution of violation of IHL violations to a state in case a PMSC qualifies as an armed group, see Vierucci (n 12 above), 19–20.
[37] Draft Articles (n 7 above), 38.
[38] A/CN4/246 and Add1–3, 'Third Report on State responsibility, by Mr Roberto Ago, Special Rapporteur, the Internationally Wrongful Act of the State, Source of International Responsibility' in *Yearbook of the International Law Commission*, 1971, vol II, 278–80.

may include public corporations, semi public entities, public agencies of various kinds and even, in special cases, private companies... For example, in some countries private security firms may be contracted to act as prison guards and in that capacity may exercise public powers such as powers of detention and discipline pursuant to a judicial sentence or to prison regulations. Private or State-owned airlines may have delegated to them certain powers in relation to immigration control or quarantine.[39]

For the acts of a PMSC to be attributed to the state, two conditions have to be met: first, the PMSC has to be empowered by the law of the state; secondly, it has to be empowered to exercise elements of governmental authority.

The empowerment of the PMSC by the law of the state is a strict requirement, based upon the strength of the authorization that a sovereign state addresses to private groups through its legislative or executive organs.[40] In that respect, it is a widely accepted principle of international law that a state may be held internationally liable for its internal laws and regulations.[41] Passing an Act of Parliament or adopting a regulation granting a PMSC the power to exercise part of the governmental authority is therefore the one and only condition necessary to link the future acts of the PMSC to the state. The 'authorizing' Act of the state consists in a limited delegation of the exercise of governmental or sovereign powers to a PMSC, which will enjoy a high degree of discretion when acting. Finally, one might wonder whether the internal authorizing Act of the state may be adopted either ex ante or ex post. In the latter case, the Act or regulation could be interpreted as expressing the consent of the state to endorse the acts that had already been perpetrated.[42]

Secondly, the mandate should authorize the exercise of 'governmental authority'. This concept is not defined by the ILC, and is expressly left to a case-by-case appreciation. However, in the situations we are dealing with here, which imply the use of force, and given the state-owned nature of defence activities, there is little doubt that the condition of governmental authority would be met. In this context, the fact that PMSC personnel wear arms could be one of the factors to consider. A contrario, in cases where a PMSC carries out a mixed activity (ie military and commercial), only the part amounting to the exercise of governmental authority would be attributable to the state under Draft Article 5. The question then follows of the attribution to the state of ultra vires acts of PMSC personnel whilst exercising elements of governmental authority. As recalled in the Commentary of Draft Article 7 ICL, the rule according to which the conduct of an entity empowered to exercise elements of governmental authority is to be attributed to the state, is a well-recognized customary norm of international law.[43] In other words, all acts of the PMSC are to be attributed to the empowering state, if, and only if, these ultra

---

[39] Draft Articles (n 7 above), 43.
[40] Previous work of the ICL shows that a looser link than an actual legislative act or regulation has been considered to attribute the acts of private persons to the state, provided that the missions had been given by public authorities: cf A/CN4/246 and Add1–3, 'Third Report on State Responsibility, by Mr Roberto Ago' (n 38 above), 79–80.
[41] *Certain German Interests in Polish Upper Silesia*, PCIJ, Merits, Series A, no 7 (25 May 1926), 19.
[42] *United States Diplomatic and Consular Staff in Tehran*, ICJ Rep 1980 (24 May 1980), 35, §74.
[43] n 7 above, 45–7.

vires acts can still be linked to the delegated governmental functions. In this case, the PMSC is treated as if it were an organ of the state.

In practice, as has already been shown in the context of the Priv-war project, the criterion of the existence of a national act empowering a PMSC is problematic. Indeed, H Cherif mentioned in his report a case of arbitration in Papua New Guinea, where the Tribunal refused to interpret the constitutional provision regulating the raising of special forces, which required the prior adoption of an Act of Parliament. In the main, the Tribunal argued that the interpretation of the constitution had to be left to national courts. However, despite the fact that in this case the PMSC had not been previously empowered by an Act of Parliament, the contract was considered valid in international law.[44]

Our conclusion on the attribution to a state of acts of a PMSC under Draft Article 5 is twofold. First, in terms of the relationship between the PMSC and the state, it appears that acts of a PMSC can only be attributed to the contracting state. As we have demonstrated, the requirements of Draft Article 5 are even stricter, since the state not only has to be contracting with a PMSC, but also has to do so by virtue of its own law. This of course does not exclude the purely practical possibility that the contracting state is also the home state. Similarly one could imagine, in the case of self-defence operations, that the contracting state might also be the territorial state. Secondly, in terms of the legal characterization of the acts of the PMSC, which violate *ius ad bellum*, it should be stressed that it is only where a PMSC exercises elements of governmental authority that an act of aggression can with certainty be attributed to the state. As we showed in the previous section when examining the definition of an act of aggression, the ICJ considers that mere support by a state to armed groups would not suffice to attribute responsibility for an armed attack to the supporting state. Rather, the actions of the PMSC would need to be on a large scale, and the relationship between the state and the PMSC the strongest possible.[45] This strong relationship would be characterized here by the empowering Act or regulation enacted by the state.[46]

2. Instructions, Direction, or Control

We now turn to the examination of Draft Article 8, which sets up the other criterion for attributing the conduct of a PMSC to a state: instruction, direction, or control—these three conditions being understood as a gradation, from a con-

---

[44] H Cherif, 'A Brief Analysis of the Case Law Relating to Private Military Companies and Mercenaries: Filling or Revealing the Lacunae through Jurisprudence', 14, Report produced in 2009 in the context of Working Package no 3 of the Priv-War project.
[45] See section I.A.2 above.
[46] It goes beyond the scope of this study, which is focused on the violations of *ius ad bellum*, to address the question of state responsibility for human rights violation and protection. Cf Francioni (n 33 above), 6–8, 13, and C Bakker, *Private Military and Security Companies: Positive Human Rights Obligations of the Host State*, EUI Working Paper, AEL 2009/20, Academy of European Law, Priv-War Project, 17.

crete action on the part of the state (giving instructions), to a legal fiction linking acts to a state (directing and controlling troops).

The most straightforward situation falling within the scope of Draft Article 8 is instruction, when the state *de facto* requires PMSC personnel to adopt certain behaviours in breach of *ius ad bellum*. An example of this is given in the Commentary of the Article itself, where private persons or groups are recruited by the state and act as 'auxiliaries' without being part of the regular forces of the state.

Two international courts have given different interpretations to the criterion of 'direction and control' by a state.[47] The ICJ first interpreted restrictively the criterion of 'effective control' in the *Nicaragua* case, when examining the activities of military forces in Nicaragua: 'such acts could well be committed by members of the contras without the control of the United States. For this conduct to give rise to legal responsibility of the United States, it would in principle have to be proved that that State had effective control of the military or paramilitary operations in the course of which the alleged violations were committed.'[48] More than ten years later, in the context of individual criminal responsibility, the International Tribunal for the former Yugoslavia (ICTY) expressly disagreed with the standard set up by the ICJ in the context of state responsibility, considering that 'The degree of control may...vary according to the factual circumstances of each case.'[49] Since then, however, the ICJ has twice confirmed its interpretation of the criterion of 'effective control' in order to establish state responsibility; in 2005 in the *Case Concerning Armed Activities on the Territory of the Congo*,[50] and in 2007 in the *Genocide* case. In the latter case the Court clarified its position: 'the particular characteristics of genocide do not justify the Court in departing from the criterion elaborated in the Judgment in the case concerning Military and Paramilitary Activities in and against Nicaragua...The rules for attributing alleged internationally wrongful conduct to a State do not vary with the nature of the wrongful act in question in the absence of a clearly expressed lex specialis.'[51]

Then one must ask whether or not ultra vires acts can be attributed to a state. When a state authorizes, directs, or controls the acts of PMSC personnel, but the addressees go beyond those orders or directions, the ultra vires acts can nevertheless be attributed to the state if they remain connected to the mission. Indeed, as the Commentary on Draft Article 8 stresses, an ultra vires act will still be attributable to the state, although 'particular instructions may have been ignored'.[52]

---

[47] The ICL chose to consider that instruction, direction and control are disjunctive conditions, although international Courts have treated 'direction and control' as a single condition.
[48] *Case Concerning Military and Paramilitary Activities in and against Nicaragua* (n 16 above), 64–5, §115. Emphasis added.
[49] *Prosecutor v Dusko Tadić*, IT-94-1-A (1999), ILM, vol 38, no 6 (11 November 1999), 1541, §117.
[50] *Armed activities on the territory of the Congo (Democratic Republic of the Congo v Uganda)*, ICJ Rep 2005 (19 December 2005), 56, §160.
[51] *Application of the convention on the prevention and punishment of the crime of genocide (Bosnia and Herzgovina v Serbia and Montenegro)*, Merits, ICJ Rep 2007 (26 February 2007), 143, §401. See also 142–9, §396–412.
[52] Draft Articles (n 7 above), 48–9.

In considering the relationship of the state to the PMSC, the criterion of instruction, direction or control can apply in order to attribute PMSC acts to the territorial state and the home state as well as to the contracting state.[53] On the other hand, however, the legal characterization of attributable acts is more restricted. Indeed, as has already been demonstrated when examining the definition of acts of aggression[54] and the exercise of elements of governmental authority,[55] in order to attribute to the state PMSC acts that would qualify as an armed attack, a strong relationship between the state and the PMSC is needed, mere control by the state not being sufficient. It is thus very unlikely that acts of a PMSC amounting to acts of aggression could be attributable to a state under the criterion of instruction, direction, and control. Accordingly, where a state simply supports the actions of a PMSC, it would be possible to attribute to that state a threat or use of force, or an intervention in the internal affairs of a state but not an act of aggression.

In conclusion, the establishment of state responsibility for acts of PMSCs violating *ius ad bellum stricto sensu* is subject to very strict conditions. First, a violation of *ius ad bellum* has to be ascertained, which can prove rather difficult in situations where it is claimed to be abiding with the conditions of lawful self-defence operations, peace operations, or humanitarian interventions.

Secondly, the acts violating *ius ad bellum* have to be attributed to a state under one of the alternative criteria set up by Draft Articles 5 and 8 ICL. As we have just demonstrated, the range of states (contracting, home, or territorial) to which the acts can be attributed, as well as the legal characterization of the breaches of *ius ad bellum*, are highly variable according to the concrete situation at hand. It follows from this that state responsibility for acts of PMSCs violating *ius ad bellum* should also be looked at *lato sensu*, from the perspective of the existence of an obligation of due diligence imposed on the state. In such a case the international wrongful act attributable to the state would no longer be a breach of *ius ad bellum* in the sense discussed above, but could rather be characterized as a breach of an extended *ius ad bellum* embracing a positive obligation not to allow PMSCs to commit acts amounting to violations of *ius ad bellum*.

II. State Responsibility for a Breach of Due Diligence and Duty to Regulate

It is argued here that the public international law prohibition on using force in international relations necessarily imposes on states a series of positive obligations. From an international law perspective, this obligation is encompassed in the notion of due diligence (A). From a national perspective, and taking into account the

---

[53] As in the former section, we did only address the issue of the violation of *ius ad bellum*. On violations of human rights, see Francioni (n 33 above), 8–9.
[54] See section I.A.2 above.
[55] See section I.B.1 above.

public international law principle of good faith, it is necessary for the state to take steps in domestic law in order to ensure *ius ad bellum* is respected (B).

A. A Breach of the Due-diligence Obligation

As an illustration, let us assume that a PMSC, X, is contracting with a rebel group operating from state A to participate in hostilities against state B. X participated in an attempted coup against the political leader of state B. The rebel group and X's forces ambushed the presidential convoy during a visit of the leader of state B in a district close to the frontier with state A. The head of state of state B was not killed; however 15 soldiers were killed and 30 wounded. We know Article 2(4) of the Charter of the UN prohibits the threat or use of force against the territorial integrity or political independence of any state.[56] Suppose that the PMSC in question is present on the territory of state A but is incorporated and having its principle place of management in another state. In sum, state A had no direct control or involvement in the activities of X. Then, under which circumstances and on what grounds could the above act constitute a breach of an international norm? Could this breach be attributed to state A? Could the state of incorporation or any other state also be held responsible for the abovementioned private acts? Did those states fail to abide by their duty to protect state B?

1. Identifying the Due-diligence Principle

The International Law Commission has discussed at length the question of state responsibility with regards to the activities of private persons. For instance, in its commentaries on the Draft Articles on State Responsibility, and under the influence of Roberto Ago, the ILC stated in 1975 that:

> The strictly negative conclusion reached regarding the attribution to the State of the acts of private natural and legal persons and of the other persons... does not imply, however, that the State cannot incur international responsibility for such acts on other grounds....A State has often been held internationally responsible on the occasion of acts or omissions whose material perpetrator was a private natural or legal person who, on that occasion, was not acting on the State's behalf.[57]

Depending on the particular facts and circumstances of a case, a 'failed act' or omission of state authorities may constitute a breach of what had been lawfully

---

[56] See section I above.
[57] 'The acts of private persons or of persons acting in a private capacity then constitute...an external event which serves as a catalyst for the wrongfulness of the State's conduct': *Yearbook of the International Law Commission*, 1975, vol II, A/CN4/SERA/1975/Add1, 71, §§4–5. See, inter alia, Arts 11 and 23 of the Draft Articles on State Responsibility adopted in 1996, Report of the International Law Commission on the work of its forty-eighth session, A/51/10, 1996. On the evolution of the Draft Articles, from 1996 to 2001, see J Crawford, *The International Law Commission's Articles on State Responsibility: Introduction, Text and Commentaries* (2002), 422 (introduction). See also P-M Dupuy, 'Reviewing the Difficulties of Codification: Ongo's Classification of Obligations of Means and Obligations of Result in Relation to State Responsibility' (1999) 10(2) EJIL 371–85.

expected of them with regard to the activities of persons or companies over which state organs have regulatory power.[58] In other words, thanks to what is called the due-diligence principle under international law, a state may be held accountable for prima facie private acts that cannot be directly attributed to a state. Simply stated, the due-diligence obligation is then 'the degree of care...expected of a good government'.[59] The principle is based on general international law and can be applied to several facts and circumstances. In our case, however, more specific provisions of international law can also be appropriate when determining the due-diligence obligations regarding PMSCs' activities.

The first main international decision stating the due-diligence principle was taken in the *Island of Palmas* case. In the opinion of the sole arbitrator, Max Huber, territorial sovereignty has as a corollary duty 'the obligation to protect within the territory the rights of other States, in particular their right to integrity and inviolability in peace and in war'.[60] Among several decisions on the issue, the ICJ, in the famous *Corfu Channel* case, also stated 'every State's obligation not to allow knowingly its territory to be used for acts contrary to the rights of other States' as a general and well-recognized principle, linked to 'elementary considerations of humanity, even more exacting in peace than in war'.[61] The protection of the rights of other states does not mean that every state incurs responsibility simply because the rights in question are disregarded. Nonetheless, focusing on the violation of the Convention on the Prevention and Punishment of the Crime of Genocide, the ICJ recalled that 'responsibility is however incurred if the state manifestly failed to take all measures to prevent genocide which were within its power, and which might have contributed to preventing the genocide'.[62] Due to the separation between international and national legal orders, and because the former cannot directly rule the latter, it is necessary to attribute to the state all that happened in the domestic order from the moment that the state in question could have prevented the damage caused to another sovereign.

Nowadays, the due-diligence principle is often invoked with regards to environmental harms and, since 9/11, to the failure to prevent terrorist activities taking

---

[58] See eg RP Barnidge, 'The Due Diligence Principle under International Law', (2006) 8 International Community Law Review 81–121; R Pisillo-Mazzeschi, 'The Due Diligence Rule and the Nature of the International Responsibility of States', (1992) 35 German Yearbook of International Law 9–51 or L Condorelli, 'L'imputation à l'Etat d'un Fait Internationalement Illicite: Solutions Classiques et Nouvelles Tendances' (1984) 189 RCADI 9–221.

[59] H Duffy, *The 'War on Terror' and the Framework of International Law*, quoted by RP Barnidge (n 58 above), 118.

[60] Permanent Court of Arbitration, award of 4 April 1928 (M Huber), *Arbitral award rendered between the United States of America and the Netherlands, relating to the arbitration of differences respecting sovereignty over the island of Palmas (or Miangas)*, RIAA, vol II, 839. See also *Trail Smelter Arbitration (US v Canada)*, 1941, RIAA, vol III, 1905.

[61] *Corfu Channel Case*, ICJ Rep 1949 (9 April 1949), 22. See also *United States Diplomatic and Consular Staff in Tehran* (n 42 above), 32 and *Case Concerning Armed Activities on the Territory of the Congo* (n 50 above), §179.

[62] *Case Concerning the Application of the Convention on the Prevention and Punishment of the Crime of Genocide* (n 51 above), §430.

place within a state's territory.⁶³ Back to our case study, it means that state A may be held accountable for a breach of the due diligence principle because PMSC X had planned to perpetrate a coup from the territory of state A. General international law requires from state a kind of 'obligation de s'efforcer' to prevent any attack from its territory on state B.⁶⁴ As Pierre-Marie Dupuy has stated, 'what counts here is the violation of the best effort obligation, not the end result actually achieved'.⁶⁵ If one can establish, for instance, that state A had the means to regulate activities of PMSC X, the breach would be manifest.⁶⁶

International law may be relevant in certain scenarios involving the use of PMSCs even though a customary prohibition of the use of mercenaries cannot be easily established. It is therefore interesting to explore whether any international agreements contain an obligation to prevent that could be applicable to our case or to other private misconducts. For instance, considering the responsibility of the home state or of the state in which the company operates from, the law of armed conflict could be seen as implicitly prohibiting mercenary activities on the territory of neutral powers.⁶⁷ If a PMSC operates from the territory of a neutral power and participates from this territory in hostilities between belligerents, the responsibility of the neutral power may be engaged for a violation of an obligation to 'not allow any of the acts referred to in Articles 2 to 4 to occur on its territory', based on Article 5 of the 1907 Hague Convention V.⁶⁸ At least two other texts may be helpful in this context: Article 3 of the Convention on the Protection and Punishment of Crimes against Internationally Protected Persons, including Diplomatic Agents; and Article 15 of the International Convention for the Suppression of Terrorist Bombings.⁶⁹ However, there is a lack of relevant jurisprudence that

---

⁶³ See eg RP Barnidge, *Non-State Actors and Terrorism: Applying the Law of State Responsibility and the Due Diligence Principle* (2007), 250.

⁶⁴ See J Combacau, 'Obligations de Résultat et Obligations de Comportement. Quelques Questions et pas de Réponses' in *Mélanges Paul Reuter. Le Droit International: Unité et Diversité* (1981), 582, 181–204. According to R Pisillo Mazzeschi, '*dans les obligations de due diligence, le résultat visé est trop aléatoire pour être pris comme l'objet de l'obligation. Cela explique pourquoi, dans ce cas, on ne peut exiger de l'obligé qu'un comportement particulier, un effort particulier, sans aucune garantie d'atteindre un résultat précis. Et cela explique, par conséquent, pourquoi l'obligé n'est responsable que si l'on démontre qu'il n'a pas usé de la diligence requise pour atteindre le résultat*': 'Responsabilité de l'Etat pour Violation des Obligations Positives Relatives aux Droits de l'Homme' (2008) 333 RCADI 175–506, 285.

⁶⁵ P-M Dupuy (n 57 above), 379.

⁶⁶ See below.

⁶⁷ See the Convention Regarding the Rights and Duties of Neutral Powers and Persons in Case of War on Land, The Hague, 18 October 1907, USTS 540, 2 AJIL Supp 117, and the analysis proposed in Ch 16 by Mancini, Ntoubandi, and Marauhn in this volume.

⁶⁸ See the Convention Regarding the Rights and Duties of Neutral Powers and Persons in Case of War on Land, The Hague, 18 October 1907 (n 67 above).

⁶⁹ Convention on the Protection and Punishment of Crimes against Internationally Protected Persons, including Diplomatic Agents, signed in 1973 and entered into force in 1977. Art 3 states that parties shall take 'all practicable measures to prevent preparations in their respective territories for the commission of those crimes within or outside their territories'. International Convention for the Suppression of Terrorist Bombings was adopted in 1997 (UN Res 52/164) and entered into force in 2001. Art 15 affirms that 'States Parties shall cooperate in the prevention of the offences set forth in article 2, particularly: (a) By taking all practicable measures, including, if necessary, adapting their domestic legislation, to prevent and counter preparations in their respective territories for the commission of those offences within or outside their territories . . .'.

illustrates the practical application of the above provisions. The violation of the obligation of due diligence could be based on particular international laws related to PMSCs or more generally to terrorist activities. Among the rare treaties on the issue, there does not seem to be any relevant Article on the due-diligence principle.[70] The Montreux Document appears more appropriate in this regard, but 'is not a legally binding document'.[71] Therefore, to date, any allegation of a violation of its terms is irrelevant—except when it restates pre-existing human rights and international humanitarian law obligations.[72] The same could be said for two other draft conventions: the Draft International Convention on PMSCs, elaborated in 2008, and the Draft International Convention on the Regulation, Oversight and Monitoring of PMSCs, proposed in 2009.[73]

2. Applying the Due-diligence Principle

The concrete application of the due-diligence principle may not be an easy task, given the relative vagueness of the obligation. Whether the breach is based on general international law or on rare but appropriate treaties, the lack of vigilance of a state remains to be proven. The plaintiff would have to show evidence that a state failed to act with due diligence regarding the activities of a PMSC, and such evidence might be hard to obtain. What is concretely expected from a 'well governed' state with regards to the PMSCs operating on its territory or incorporated under its laws? How does one reveal any failure?

There is a lack of relevant case law regarding due diligence within the *ius ad bellum* or *ius contra bellum* corpus. In any case, the due-diligence principle calls for an assessment in concreto.[74] In the *Corfu Channel* case, the ICJ assessed that even considering the reality of 'exclusive territorial control', the territorial state need not

---

[70] Regarding the Organization of African Unity (the OUA) Convention for the Elimination of Mercenarism in Africa, which entered into force in 1985, the provisions are far too restrictive to be the basis of an obligation to prevent the acts described above. Regarding the UN International Convention against the Recruitment, Use, Financing and Training of Mercenaries which entered into force in 2001, the Convention does not deal with PMSCs as such and the definition of mercenarism it provides is not workable here.

[71] 'Montreux Document' (n 6 above), Preface.

[72] The Montreux Document addresses substantive legal concerns such as the authorities' duty to monitor and screen the actions of PMSCs for potential breaches of international law, even if the text focuses on international humanitarian law and human rights. See eg 'Montreux Document' (n 6 above), §§ 6, 10, 12, 15, 17, 21.

[73] International Convention on Private Military and Security Companies, elaborated by the experts for Regional Consultation for Eastern European Group and Central Asian Region, in Moscow, held 16–18 October 2008 and Draft International Convention on the Regulation, Oversight and Monitoring of Private Military and Security Companies, Working Group on the use of mercenaries as a means of violating human rights and impending the exercise of the rights of peoples to self-determination, 13 July 2009.

[74] *Case Concerning the Application of the Convention on the Prevention and Punishment of the Crime of Genocide* (n 51 above), §430. The ICJ also affirms that it is irrelevant for a state to prove that in any event its actions would not have sufficed to prevent the crime, because 'the possibility remains that the combined efforts of several States, each complying with its obligation to prevent, might have achieved the result' (ibid).

necessarily know that private actors are likely to commit unlawful acts.[75] In sum, the international judge or arbiter would have to assess the facts and circumstances of each allegation. The position would depend upon a precise analysis of which norms apply in each case, and it is clear that there are not many specific norms concerning the relationship between states' policies and PMSCs. One would have to compare the content of the general or particular norm in question with both the wish and the means of a state to act, and take into account—but not decisively— whether the acts occur on the territory of the state in question. There has recently been, for instance, much debate about the Taliban government of Afghanistan's inaction concerning Al-Qaeda training camps or Lebanon's inaction vis-à-vis Hezbollah activities.[76]

In sum, the riskier the situation in which PMSCs are tolerated, the stronger due-diligence obligation for the territorial state is. In our case study, one would probably consider that state A should have known the activities of PMSC X, a fortiori in a troubled area where rebel groups are supposed to be carefully monitored. Any PMSC which aims to participate in hostilities needs to import military equipment, money, or personnel, and it is doubtful that the state whose territory hosts the PMSC and the preparation of an attack could ignore it. In any event, if it cannot act to effectively control the PMSC's activities, it has a duty to inform the other state(s) which may be the target of an attack. The home state should also be aware of any large operation that its PMSCs are dealing with. Moreover, going beyond due diligence *stricto sensu*, the more general principle of the responsibility to protect could also imply, as a corollary, a duty to sanction any abuses actually that would have happened.[77] Suppose, for instance, that the state where the acts occurred had refused to investigate on the facts or refused to prosecute the authors (and on appropriate grounds), the state would also have violated its obligations to prosecute and punish—based upon appropriate personal or territorial jurisdiction, universal jurisdiction or on the *aut dedere aut prosequi* rule.[78] The European Court of Human Rights has found that states can be held responsible for their failure to conduct a proper investigation regarding violence perpetrated by private actors.[79] Therefore, both the home and territorial states should be considered in a position to prosecute PMSCs as such or individuals that would be accused of grave misconducts. After all, general prevention is one of the main objectives of any justice

---

[75] *Corfu Channel Case* (n 61 above), §18. See RP Barnidge (n 58 above), 104–5.
[76] See for instance M Sassoli, 'La "Guerre contre le Terrorisme", Le Droit International Humanitaire et le Statut de Prisonnier de Guerre' (2001) 39 Canadian Yearbook of International Law 211–52; or B Ryan, 'Jus ad Bellum in the Israel–Hezbollah Conflict' [2007] Cork Online Law Review, <http://www.ucclawsociety.com/colr/editions/2007/COLR%202007%20Full.pdf>, accessed on 20 August 2010.
[77] See Francioni (n 33 above), 16. See also Ch 7 by Bakker in this volume.
[78] See C Bassiouni and E Wise, *Aut Dedere Aut Judicare: The Duty to Extradite or Prosecute in International Law* (1995), 340; and Amnesty International, *International Law Commission: The Obligation to Extradite or Prosecute (aut Dedere aut Judicare)*, IOR 40/001/2009 (2009), 98, <http://www.amnesty.org>, accessed on 20 August 2010.
[79] See, inter alia, *Mahmut Kaya v Turkey*, ECHR (28 March 2000), §§ 101, 108–9, (2000) 11 Human Rights Case Digest 125–30.

system and this applies equally when a rebel group or a PMSC plans to commit an armed attack against a state.

To conclude, the due-diligence principle in international law must not be considered an empty legal concept because of its vagueness. Regarding PMSCs' activities and particularly their direct participation in hostilities, the obligation to prevent has a role to play in holding states responsible in relation to private acts that were at least tolerated by the home state or the territorial state. In this field, however, the due-diligence principle is so far mainly based on general international law. Considering the subjectivity of the due-diligence test, it may be appropriate for every state to adopt good practices or precautionary measures vis-à-vis PMSCs that are operating on their territory, with their nationals, or that are incorporated in their jurisdiction. For instance, one would think of a system of ex ante licences for the creation and operations of PMSCs or the creation of authorization and monitoring procedures for exporting any PMSCs services.[80] The good state practices identified by the Swiss Initiative may be helpful but they are not exhaustive.[81] In any case, due diligence should be seen as an appropriate tool to encourage more regulation and lead to less abuse.

B. A Breach of an Obligation to Regulate in the National Legal System

We will now turn to drawing the consequences of the above demonstration in terms of the domestic law of the state. Indeed, we first established the conditions for holding a state responsible for the acts of PMSCs violating *ius ad bellum*. It was then showed how the principle of due diligence in public international law imposes positive obligations on both territorial and home states in order to ensure that the prohibition of the use of force in international law is respected by the PMSCs.

For the sake of consistency, it necessary that a state take the appropriate steps in its internal legal order to ensure the respect of its international obligations. In the context of state responsibility for the acts of PMSCs violating *ius ad bellum*, the state is therefore bound to prohibit, in its domestic order, the perpetration of any violation of *ius ad bellum* by private actors. Such uniform law provisions, accompanied with more precise obligations of the states, could eventually lead to establish state responsibility for the lack of domestic regulation leading to the perpetration of such acts by the PMSCs. It is not the aim of this chapter to address individual criminal liability. Although the natural setting of such a domestic regulation is

---

[80] See Francioni (n 33 above), 11.
[81] 'Montreux Document' (n 6 above). For instance, the territorial state should delimit which types of military services can not be carried out by PMSCs on its territory; require those companies to obtain general operating licenses; ask PMSCs for specific guarantees concerning the possession of certain types of weapons; require references and information from their clients; monitor PMSCs financial, technical, and management capabilities. The home state should eg determine which military services may not be exported; acquire information and references on their PMSCs; introduce and encourage the dissemination of a kind of quality label about the standards adopted by those companies; directly manage contracts between companies and private actors operating in areas of conflict; require PMSCs to notify the home state of certain contracts. All states should ensure that they have the legal capacity to investigate and prosecute PMSCs in instances of misconduct.

1. Prohibiting in the National Legal Order any Violation of Ius ad Bellum by PMSCs

It is held here that as soon as an obligation to prevent and repress crimes of private actors arises in international law, it necessarily implies that the state should enact a criminal law prohibiting this specific activity in its national legal order and providing jurisdiction to its organs, in order to fulfil its international engagements. Although both elements would be provided for in the same national legal instrument, the substantive norm will be distinguished from the competence norm[83] in this exposé.

From the substantive perspective, the national legal order should be compatible with the state's international obligations, and more precisely, with the obligation to prevent and repress international crimes. As the Permanent Court of International Justice (the PCIJ) said in a well-known advisory opinion, a state which has contracted valid international obligations is bound to make in its legislation such modifications as may be necessary to ensure the fulfilment of the obligations undertaken.[84] It certainly does not stem from this, that a state may be held responsible at an early stage, for not bringing his national legal order into conformity with his international obligations. It is however clear that, in some situations, international law requires the state to take positive steps, for example, when the only way to respect the international obligation implies the enactment of a specific norm, or when such an enactment is clearly required by a written instrument such as a uniform law treaty. Therefore, a substantive norm of the domestic legal system prohibiting crimes recognized in international law, participates in the fulfilment of a state's international criminal obligations. Admittedly, this obligation goes beyond a simple obligation to prevent and repress. Uniform law obligations must also be consistent with international criminal law. Indeed, in a legally constituted state, a criminal penalty can never be applied to a subject of domestic law without a specific provision of the law commending it. This derives from the *nullum crimen sine lege* principle, which is also recognized as a general principle of international law.

Furthermore, this obligation to enact a kind of uniform criminal law could arise from the ius cogens nature of the prohibition of certain behaviours. We can easily imagine that if the obligation to prevent and repress private actors' acts were attached to a ius cogens prohibition, this would further result in a positive

---

[82] For a study of individual criminal liability, see contributions in Part V of this volume.
[83] J Combacau, 'Conclusions Générales', in SFDI, Colloque de Rennes, *Les Compétences de l'Etat en Droit International* (2006), 320, 309.
[84] PCIJ, Advisory Opinion of 21 February 1925, *Exchange of Greek and Turkish populations*, Series B, no 10, 3.

obligation for states to put their national legal orders in conformity with it.[85] This appears particularly clearly from the words of the ICTY in the *Furundjiza* case, regarding the prohibition of torture. It was indeed asserted that: 'States are bound to put in place all those measures that may pre-empt the perpetration of torture.'[86] This interpretation undoubtedly derived from the gravity of the crime of torture, and the *ius cogens* nature of its prohibition.

We now turn to apply the above reasoning to the prohibition of the use of armed force. It is clear that states should have enacted a criminal law prohibiting the use of armed force to their nationals and/or residents, in order to be in position to repress such a crime. For instance, armed attack is recognized as a crime in international law, as suggested in UN General Assembly Resolution 3314.[87] Moreover, according to Article 5 ICC Statute, armed attack is a potential crime entering the competence of the Court. In contradistinction with the obligation to prohibit torture, no written rule on the obligation to prohibit the use of force in international relations by private actors is entrenched in a conventional instrument. Approximating rules can nevertheless easily be found in other instruments, as it is the case regarding the prohibition of mercenarism. To give an example, the OUA Convention imposes an obligation on states to prohibit, not only in the civil branch but also in the criminal sector, since: 'Each contracting State shall undertake to make the offence defined Article 1 of this Convention punishable by the severest penalties under its laws including capital punishment.'[88] Similarly, the UN Convention on Mercenarism, reads that states 'shall make the offences set forth in the present Convention punishable by appropriate penalties which take into account the grave nature of those offences'.[89] The obligation to prohibit is, here again, inducted by the importance of the prohibition itself, which is not under discussion regarding the *ius ad bellum* primary rules.

The principal hurdle in our case is the difficulty for states to agree upon a precise definition of armed attack, especially after the 9/11 events. Indeed, how could it be

---

[85] *Mutatis mutandis*, regarding international humanitarian law, see L Condorelli and L Boisson de Chazournes, 'Quelques remarques à propos de l'obligation de "respecter et faire respecter" le droit international humanitaire "en toutes circonstances"', in ICRC, *Mélanges Pictet* (Genève-La Haye, Nijhoff, 1984), p. 25.
[86] *Prosecutor v Anto Furundzija*, IT-95-17/1-T (10 June 1998), §148, 56. Explaining first that 'failure to pass the required implementing legislation has only a potential effect: the wrongful fact occurs only when administrative or judicial measures are taken which, being contrary to international rules due to the lack of implementing legislation, generate State responsibility', the Tribunal immediately afterwards presents the prohibition of torture as an exception, in the case of which 'the requirement that States expeditiously institute national implementing measures is an integral part of the international obligation to prohibit this practice. Consequently, States must immediately set in motion all those procedures and measures that may make it possible, within their municipal legal system, to forestall any act of torture or expeditiously put an end to any torture that is occurring.' Ibid, §149, 57.
[87] UNGA Res 3314(XXIX) (n 30 above). The General Assembly states, as preamble of the definition itself, that 'aggression is the most serious and dangerous form of the illegal use of force, being fraught, in the conditions created by the existence of all types of weapons of mass destruction, with the possible threat of a world conflict and all its catastrophic consequences'.
[88] OUA Convention (n 70 above), Art 7.
[89] Art 5.

possible to press states to put their national legal order into conformity with international law, when international law itself may have appeared unclear? This obstacle may be overcome. First, it cannot be said that there is a total lack of definition of aggression in international law, since the very aim of Resolution 3314 (XXIX) of the UN General Assembly is to attempt to provide one.[90] However, there is no denying the fact that an international tribunal cannot be competent to prosecute a crime until an agreement between states parties on a very precise definition of it has occurred: the international nature of this jurisdiction derives from the will of its states parties. This does not, however, affect the binding effect of the prohibition of the use of armed force on states themselves, or their subsequent duty to prevent violations of *ius ad bellum*—be it in the form of armed attacks against other states by their nationals, and/or from their territory. Simply, the definition of the crime they have to prosecute at a national level is not internationally set, and states—and more precisely their parliaments—are free to provide one of their own, as long as it is compatible with the few existing international guidelines. It is thus only a question of measure, and although it is not possible to identify a real uniform-law obligation binding states to unify their laws on a precise model, it can still be defended that states have to harmonize their national criminal legal orders with the international prohibition of using armed force in international relations. This illustrates the distinction between an obligation to unify and an obligation to harmonize.[91]

Going back to the specific issue of PMSCs, the question arises whether states do need to prohibit the violations of *ius ad bellum* for PMSCs in particular, or whether these private companies would simply fall into the scope of the criminal law that states should already provide for, according to their general duty to implement in their domestic system international law obligations to prosecute and punish breaches of *ius ad bellum*. If states have to prohibit the international illicit use of force in their national legal systems, do PMSCs fall in the scope of these legislations? A difficulty may arise from the possible military status that could be granted by some states to those companies.[92] Indeed, such a qualification would exclude the criminal liability of the companies and their personnel, even in the case of direct participation in an armed attack against another state.[93] State responsibility for the violation of the *ius ad bellum* does not only include the use of force attributable to the state itself. Even if the use of force is attributable to the state, the latter must still

---

[90] See section I above.
[91] See, on these distinctions, M Delmas-Marty. Among others: M Delmas-Marty, 'Le Phénomène de l'harmonisation. L'expérience Contemporaine' in Unité Mixte de Recherche de Droit Comparé de Paris (Université Paris 1/CNRS UMR 8103), *Mireille Delmas-Marty et les années UMR* (Paris: Société de législation comparée, 2005), p. 253.
[92] I Ziemele (Dir), S Zaharova, and I Miluna, 'The Regulatory Context of Private Military and Security Services in Latvia: National Report', *Priv-War Project*, WPVII, 18–19.
[93] O Quirico, 'National Regulatory Models for PMSC's and Implications for Future International Regulation: An Overview', Background Paper for the Priv-War Meeting on National Legislation & Judicial Practice Related to Private Military and Security Companies, EUI, Florence, 13 March 2009, 16.

prosecute among its organs, delegated or controlled entities, those who are personally responsible for the international crime.

To conclude, on the obligation for states to prohibit the use of armed force by PMSCs, no internationally binding instrument specifically refers to those companies, although written obligations to prohibit exist on related matters. One could argue that an international customary rule could gradually arise from the state's domestic prohibition of the use of armed force by PMSCs, since many states actually prohibit such behaviour.[94] However, as already shown, no uniform states practice can be identified at present on this matter. Only international instruments without any binding force are clearly following this path, for example, the Montreux Document[95] and the Draft International Convention on the regulation, oversight and monitoring of PMSCs.[96]

2. Uniform-law Obligations: Going Further

A new question arises at this stage of our study: which is the competent state to prosecute those crimes? And is this issue regulated by international law? After having answered these questions, this chapter will examine whether new obligations related to *ius ad bellum* and regarding the national regulation of PMSCs could be directed to specific states.

On the question of state competence to prosecute the crimes connected to the use of force by PMSCs, no clear-cut solution is possible, since international law only urges states not to let those crimes go unpunished. Some could have accepted their jurisdiction on a universal basis, even without personal or territorial link to the case, as soon as the alleged criminal is found on their territory, as is the case for torture for instance.[97] In any case, usually, the conflicts of competences at stake remain in a latent form. In sum, it is as if the maxim 'the more the merrier' could apply to this issue. One knows that states are often very jealous of their jurisdiction,

---

[94] Ibid.
[95] 'Montreux Document' (n 6 above), Part 1, §5: 'Contracting States have an obligation to enact any legislation necessary to provide effective penal sanctions...'
[96] International Convention on Private Military and Security Companies (n 73 above), Art 3.2: 'Each State Party shall take such legislative and other measures as may be necessary to establish: a) Rules of use of force aimed at ensuring security of the person, society and the state; b) Authorities and responsibilities of state bodies, organizations and officials which have the right to use coercive and combat means and/or carrying out special operations in the framework and in the situations under domestic and international law...' See also Draft International Convention on the Regulation, Oversight and Monitoring of Private Military and Security Companies (n 73 above), Art 19, Regulation of use of force and firearms: '1. Each State Party shall take such legislative, judicial, administrative and other measures as may be necessary to establish rules on the use of force and firearms by the personnel of private military and security companies taking into account that employees may carry firearms in providing military and security services'; and Art 21, Criminalization of offenses in the sphere of military and security services: '2. States parties shall take such measures as are necessary to investigate, prosecute and punish violations of the present Convention, and to ensure effective remedies to victims.'
[97] See eg UN Convention against Torture and other Cruel, Inhuman or Degrading Treatment or Punishment, Art 5.2.

as shown by the affairs involving Belgium and the Congo.[98] We could imagine that international law would forbid states from granting immunity to an alleged criminal but it is improbable that international law could go any further and oblige states to provide for specific competence norms in their national legal order. Needless to say, no uniform-law obligation can be found in those questions of jurisdiction, which are, as part of the constitutional organization of states, left at their total discretion. The obligation to prosecute may give birth to an obligation to prohibit the said crime in the national legal order in a substantive way, but it is difficult to foresee how any obligation to regulate national competence rules could arise from it. International law does not aim at regulating states' competence, but only its exercise.[99]

If no uniform law on competence can be found, are there, nevertheless, specific rules which could solve the problem sketched above? In other words, if international law does not attempt to regulate states' jurisdiction, is there any rule aiming at regulating the legal framework of PMSCs? Until now, we have only showed the existence of a general obligation to prohibit certain behaviour, an obligation which is not directed to any state in particular. Since then, conflicts of jurisdiction between concerned states, or even lack of jurisdiction, are likely to occur. The violations of *ius ad bellum* are not necessarily considered crimes in international law. Nonetheless, states still have to prevent those acts committed by private actors. Then, specific uniform-law norms, going beyond the prohibition of crime of aggression, could be very useful to construe *ius ad bellum* as a whole. Needless to say, nothing of this kind could currently exist in international customary law, since problems arising from the use of PMSCs are too new. Nevertheless, clues could be given by the existing international conventions, even if they do not exactly refer to private companies and focus instead on mercenarism. The aforementioned Montreux Document often confirms these considerations as regards the PMSCs. From these several dispositions, directives for a more precise uniform law instrument could arise. States would still have to agree upon them at a second stage, in order to be bound to put their national legal orders into conformity with them.

Regarding contracting states, it is hard to find any obligation above a general prohibition on using PMSCs in order to violate the *ius ad bellum*. A criterion for the contracting state should be that the PMSC should not be aiming at violating the rules on lawful use of force. The interest of this criterion is that responsibility could arise from the mere fact of concluding a contract with a PMSC in order to violate international law, with no need to wait for any concrete armed attack. Concerning the home state, specific obligations could be put on them when they are neutral, according to the Hague Convention on Neutral Powers.[100] Article 4 of this treaty

---

[98] ICJ, *Arrest Warrant of 11 April 2000 (Democratic Republic of the Congo v Belgium)*, ICJ Rep 2002 (14 February 2002), 3.
[99] P Mayer, 'Droit International Privé et Droit International Public sous l'angle de la Notion de Compétence', Revue critique de droit international privé, 1979-I, 1–29; 1979-II, 350–88; 1979-III, 537–83.
[100] Convention Regarding the Rights and Duties of Neutral Powers and Persons in Case of War on Land (n 67 above).

forbids the formation of combatants and even more precisely the opening of 'recruiting agencies on the territory of a neutral Power to assist the belligerents'. Before any concrete violation of the *ius ad bellum* by a private company, a neutral state should be held responsible for the mere incorporation of a company of this kind in his territory and, even before that, for the mere fact that its national legal order allows such an incorporation. This is also true for states contracting with mercenaries, according to the OUA Convention. In any case, home states should 'harmonise their authorisation system and decisions with those of other States and taking into account regional approaches relating to authorisation systems'.[101] We can easily infer from this that a uniform private law on companies should be adopted by way of an international convention. It should be directed to home states in order to determine which activities a PMSC has the right to propose and the authorizations it must obtain.[102] In the perspective of the prevention of violations of *ius ad bellum*, this uniform-law obligation can be seen as part of the *ius ad bellum* binding upon home states.

Territorial states have also duties deriving from the Hague Convention when they belong to the category of neutral power. Indeed, since belligerents are forbidden by this treaty 'to move troops or convoys of either munitions of war or supplies across the territory of a neutral Power',[103] a neutral state has to prohibit PMSCs from acting from its territory and needs probably to bring its legal order into conformity with this obligation. This does not seem, however, to further the obligation to prohibit the use of force in international relations, that we evidenced above.

III. Conclusions

With the benefit of hindsight, the issue of state responsibility for the acts of PMSCs violating *ius ad bellum* entails a twofold conclusion.

On the one hand, when examining *ius ad bellum stricto sensu*, the main issue rests in attributing to the state PMSC behaviours amounting to violations of *ius ad bellum*. From this perspective, and in concrete terms, we have shown that as far as Article 5 of the ICL Draft Articles on State Responsibility is concerned such acts of a PMSC can only be attributed to the contracting state, provided the PMSC is exercising elements of governmental authority of the contracting state by virtue of its own law. In terms of the legal characterization of the acts of the PMSC, we also stressed that it is only in the situation where a PMSC exercises elements of governmental authority that an act of aggression can with certainty be attributed to the state. From the perspective of attribution to the state of PMSCs' acts

---

[101] 'Montreux Document' (n 6 above), Part II, §56.
[102] The Draft International Convention on the Regulation Oversight and Monitoring of PMSCs (n 73 above), confirms this point of view since it presents in Art 13 several legislative regulations as obligatory for states ('Obligatoriness of special legislative regulation').
[103] Convention on Respecting the Rights and Duties of Neutral Powers and Persons in Case of War on Land (n 67 above), Art 4(1).

violating *ius ad bellum* under Article 8 of the ICL Draft Articles, we concluded that the contracting, the territorial, and the home states may face responsibility in appropriate circumstances. However, the legal characterization of the attributable acts is more restricted in this case; whereas an armed attack would be very hard to attribute to the states under Article 8 criteria, it is more likely that that states could be held responsible for a threat or use of armed force, or a coercive intervention in the internal affairs of a state.

On the other hand, it is suggested here that state responsibility ought to be considered under the prism of *ius ad bellum* defined *lato sensu*—that is, embracing a positive obligation not to allow PMSCs to commit acts amounting to violations of *ius ad bellum*. Building upon the principle of due diligence, as set by general public international law as well as some specific instruments, it has been shown that states should be bound by an obligation to prevent PMSCs from committing acts amounting to violations of *ius ad bellum*, either within or from their territories. It has been acknowledged that the international judge or arbitrator would have to operate his review on an ad hoc basis, according to law applicable to the specific case put before him. It has also been submitted that, because of the subjectivity of the due-diligence test, states should adopt good practices or precautionary measures vis-à-vis PMSCs, in order to prevent acts that could amount to violations of *ius ad bellum*. The second stage of the study of state responsibility under *ius ad bellum lato sensu*, consisted in examining the positive obligation of states to regulate PMSCs in their domestic legal orders. It has indeed been shown that states can be considered bound by an obligation to harmonize their domestic legal orders according to the general prohibition of the use of armed force in international relations, although there is no clear consensus between states on the definition of aggression. From the perspective of the competence of states to enforce such national acts aiming at regulating PMSCs' activities in respect of *ius ad bellum*, no uniform law could be identified. However, drawing from existing specific instruments applicable to either the contracting, territorial, or home state, it has been submitted that such uniform law is likely to be incrementally generated by state practice in the coming years, when the PMSC phenomenon will be better grasped and more comprehensively governed by international law.

PART V

CRIMINAL AND CIVIL LIABILITY OF PRIVATE MILITARY AND SECURITY COMPANIES AND THEIR EMPLOYEES

21

The Criminal Responsibility of Private Military and Security Company Personnel under International Humanitarian Law

Ottavio Quirico

I. Introduction

International humanitarian law (IHL) encompasses rules that bind states, armed groups, and individuals for the purpose of solving humanitarian problems arising from armed conflicts. These rules protect persons affected by armed conflicts and limit the amount of violence in methods and means of warfare.[1] Within this frame, specific substantive and procedural norms establish when and how violations of IHL give rise to individual criminal responsibility, and thus contribute to its implementation.[2] Since private military and security companies (PMSCs) are not 'classical' actors in war contexts, the subjection of their personnel to IHL and their liability for war crimes constitute a complex issue.

PMSCs play an increasingly important global role, specifically by providing support, advice, and security services in hostile environments. Their employees often work alongside state troops in the field through maintenance and operational activities. The complexity of the situation in which private contractors act is perfectly illustrated by the logistic support provided by Blackwater employees in a battle of US Marines protecting the headquarters of the Coalition Provisional Authority (CPA) in Najaf against the Iraqi Militia, where they had to ferry in ammunition supplies and conduct a marine to safety. In this circumstance, the Blackwater crews had to fight their way through, supported by two US Apache combat helicopters helping to repel the Iraqi soldiers.[3] Furthermore, a few PMSCs

---

[1] See M Sassòli, 'Humanitarian Law and International Criminal Law' in A Cassese et al (eds), *The Oxford Companion to International Criminal Justice* (2009), 311; C Emanuelli, *International Humanitarian Law* (2009), 5; C Greenwood, 'Historical Development and Legal Basis: Definition of the Term "Humanitarian Law"' in D Fleck (ed), *The Handbook of International Humanitarian Law*, 2nd edn (2008), 11.

[2] Cf Sassòli (n 1 above), 312.

[3] See D Priest and MP Flaherty, 'Under Fire, Security Firms Form an Alliance', *Washington Post* (8 April 2004), <http://www.washingtonpost.com>, accessed on 15 June 2010.

participate actively in offensive combat operations. The most prominent case is that of Executive Outcomes, whose personnel was contracted directly to engage in hostilities in Angola, Sierra Leone, and the Democratic Republic of the Congo.[4] Sometimes PMSC employees also handle high-tech war systems, as in the case of the Global Hawk surveillance drone operated by Northrop Grumman personnel in Afghanistan.[5] Under these conditions, though PMSCs usually profess their compliance with IHL standards,[6] the possibility cannot be excluded that their personnel get involved in criminal conduct under the law of war. Reported violations range from the shooting at civilians by private contractors in Baghdad during the Iraqi conflict, to the inhuman treatment of Iraqi prisoners in Abu-Ghraib, and the use of warfare methods prohibited under IHL by Executive Outcomes in Sierra Leone and Angola.[7]

Whereas there seems to be no reason why PMSC personnel should be more or less implicated in misconduct than state military forces, empirical evidence shows that they often enjoy immunity in carrying out their tasks. In particular, in the aftermath of the Abu Ghraib incidents, whilst state military officers were subject to court martial, PMSC employees did not face any criminal prosecution. Furthermore, even when prosecution takes place, an effective trial might prove politically unsuitable. Thus, PMSC personnel could be granted immunity justified by procedural rules, in particular under the principle of the due process, according to which legal proceedings must be fair and just in order to preserve the integrity of the judicial system.[8] In this light, the necessity to abide by basic human rights seems a double-edged sword. In fact, the Federal District Court of Columbia in the United States recently decided not to try former Blackwater employees for wilful killing and wounding of civilians in Baghdad by reason of basic violations of procedural law relating to the collection of evidence.[9] The question therefore arises as to what extent PMSC personnel might enjoy exemption from criminal liability because of their unclear formal status under IHL. This chapter explores the problem by focusing on the liability of physical persons operating as agents of the companies, addressing substantive and procedural issues *de lege lata*.

---

[4] Cf N Boldt, 'Outsourcing War: Private Military and Security Companies and International Humanitarian Law' (2004) 47 German Yearbook of International Law 511, 533.
[5] See PW Singer, *Corporate Warriors: The Rise of the Privatized Military Industry* (2003), 12, 15, 17.
[6] Cf eg the IPOA Code of Conduct, <http://ipoaworld.org>, accessed on 15 June 2010.
[7] See D Johnston and JM Broder, 'FBI Says Guards Killed 14 Iraquis without Cause', *New York Times* (7 November 2007), <http://www.nytimes.com>, accessed on 15 June 2010; C Miller, 'Private Security Guards in Iraq Operate with Little Supervision', *Los Angeles Times* (4 December 2005), <http://articles.latimes.com>, accessed on 15 June 2010; MN Schmitt, 'Humanitarian Law and Direct Participation in Hostilities by Private Contractors or Civilian Employees' Chicago Journal of International Law 5(2) (2005) 511, 526; K Nieminen, 'The Rules of Attribution and the Private Military Contractors at Abu Ghraib: Private Acts or Public Wrongs?' (2004) 15 Finnish Yearbook of International Law 289, 289–90.
[8] See JV Orth, *Due Process of Law* (2003).
[9] See section IV.B below.

II. War Crimes

A. International and Non-international Armed Conflicts

1. The Geneva Conventions and Customary Law

Under international law, the regime of war crimes is mainly set up by the Geneva Conventions (GCs) of 1949 and Additional Protocol (AP) I of 1977. Naturally, these provisions do not prevent further national regulation; in fact, states may enact law penalizing every (serious) breach of IHL.[10] In case of armed conflicts of an international character, opposing two or more states, the GCs and AP I establish a list of grave IHL breaches and compel states to provide effective penal sanctions against the perpetrators, so that breaches such as wilful killing, torture, or intensive destruction of property necessarily qualify as war crimes.[11] Jurisdiction over these offences is universal, which means that any state has the faculty to prosecute, regardless of the territory where the breaches occur (*locus commissi delicti*), the nationality of the perpetrator and the nationality of the victim. These crimes are furthermore subject to the principle *aut dedere aut iudicare*, which compels a state either to prosecute the suspect held in its custody or hand him over to the authorities of another state interested in prosecution.[12]

Non-international armed conflicts are not subject to the rules of IHL applying to international armed conflicts, but are only covered by common Article 3 GCs, providing fundamental standards of protection stemming from the right to life and principles of humanity, and AP II. The definition of non-international armed conflicts is a much discussed question and a difficult task.[13] For the purpose of the present analysis it will suffice to outline the basic guidelines of the debate.

According to AP II, non-international armed conflicts, which take place thoroughly within the boundaries of a state, involve 'governmental forces and dissident armed forces or other organized armed groups'.[14] Furthermore, non-international armed conflicts must be distinguished from 'internal disturbances and tensions, such as riots, isolated and sporadic acts of violence or other acts of similar nature', which do not reach the level of intensity necessary to constitute 'armed conflicts'.[15] The International Criminal Tribunal for the Former Yugoslavia (ICTY) specified that non-international armed conflicts require 'protracted

---

[10] See Y Sandoz, 'The Dynamic but Complex Relationship between International Penal Law and International Humanitarian Law' in J Doria et al (eds), *The Legal Regime of the International Criminal Court* (2009), 1049, 1053–4. In the sense that only serious violations of the law of armed conflicts constitue war crimes see Defence Motion for Interlocutory Appeal on Jurisdiction, *Tadić*, IT-94-1, Appeals Chamber (2 October 1995), paras 91–4.
[11] Arts 49–50 GC I, 50–1 GC II, 129–30 GC III, 146–7 GC IV, 85 AP I. See also J-M Henckaerts and L Doswald-Beck, *Customary International Humanitarian Law* (2005), Rules 156, 568 ff; 87, 306.
[12] Ibid, Rules 157–8, 604–11, 157–8, 604–5, 607–8.
[13] See D Fleck, 'The Law of Non-international Armed Conflicts', in Fleck (n 1 above), 605, 605 ff; Emanuelli (n 1 above), 110 ff.
[14] Art 1(1) AP II GCs.
[15] Ibid, Art 1(2).

armed violence' and also include 'situations of conflict between non-governmental organized armed groups'.[16] In the view of the International Criminal Tribunal for Rwanda (ICTR), the existence of non-international armed conflicts must be ascertained in light of the 'intensity and organization of the parties to the conflict',[17] based on a case-by-case evaluation.[18] Traditionally, serious violations of common Article 3 GCs and AP II are considered not to be subject to criminal sanctions.[19]

In order to grant the maximum application of IHL rules, non-international armed conflicts might be 'internationalized'. According to the ICTY, this would be the case when either (a) another state intervenes in the internal conflict through its troops, or alternatively (b) some of the participants in the internal armed conflict act on behalf of another state.[20] The consequences of this approach are nevertheless not fully satisfying. In fact, first, the criteria for establishing the existence of an internationalized armed conflict and the applicable regulation are not clear-cut.[21] Secondly, the same conflict can be characterized at different times and places as either internal, international or internationalized, and thus as a mixed phenomenon, which renders it difficult to establish what type of regulation should apply.[22] An exemplary case is represented by the conflict in the former Yugoslavia,[23] involving private contractors, for instance MPRI, a US military company originally engaged for training purposes in civil–military relations, which ultimately planned and commanded Croatian military operations.[24] Also the qualification of the Iraqi and Afghan conflicts, in which private contractors are heavily implicated, must be carefully evaluated. The Iraqi situation has proved to be complex, at least after the installation of the CPA in 2003 and the subsequent constitution of the Iraqi government in 2004. The Afghan context seems uncertain especially after the settlement of the Karzai Transitional Administration in 2001 and the subsequent installation of the Loya Jirga in 2002.[25] Furthermore, both the Iraqi and Afghan cases raise the issue as to whether terrorist activities could constitute an armed

[16] Defence Motion for Interlocutory Appeal on Jurisdiction, *Tadić* (n 10 above), para 70.
[17] *Akayesu*, ICTR-96-4, Trial Chamber (2 September 1998), para 620.
[18] *Rutaganda*, ICTR-96-3, Trial Chamber (6 December 1999), para 91.
[19] See Sassòli (n 1 above), 115; Sandoz (n 10 above), 1055; L Moir, 'Particular issues regarding war crimes in internal armed conflicts' in Doria et al (n 10 above), 611, 615–17; Emanuelli (n 1 above), 110; G de Beco, 'War crimes in international versus non-international armed conflicts: New wine in old wineskins?', (2008) 8 International Criminal Law Review 319, 321.
[20] *Tadić*, IT-94-1, Appeals Chamber (15 July 1999), para 84. As for the link between the state and the participants in the conflict, the ICTY set out the 'global control' test (ibid, para 115), in opposition to the 'effective control' test established by the ICJ in the *Nicaragua* case (Judgment, *Military and Paramilitary Activities in and against Nicaragua*, Nicaragua/USA, ICJ, 27 June 1986, 64–5, para 115, <http://www.icj-cij.org>, accessed on 15 June 2010).
[21] See JG Stewart, 'Towards a single definition of armed conflict in international humanitarian law: A critique of internationalized armed conflict', (2003) 85 IRRC 313, 323–33.
[22] Ibid, 333–4. See also L Harbom and P Wallensteen, 'armed conflict and its international dimensions, 1946–2004', (2005) 42 Journal of Peace Research 623, 627 ff.
[23] *Tadić* (n 20 above), para 73.
[24] See the University Centre for IHL, Report on Expert Meeting on Private Military Contractors: Status and State Responsibility for their Actions, Section A.3 (a) (iii), 26, <http://www.adh-geneve.ch>, accessed on 15 June 2010.
[25] See H Duffy, *The 'War on Terror' and the Framework of International Law* (2005), 256–7. See also the European Journal of International Law: Talk, 'On the nature of the conflict in Afghanistan', 3

conflict. Though the ICTY distinguished 'organized groups' from 'cases of civil unrest and terrorist activities',[26] the question should be answered in the affirmative insofar as violence perpetrated by terrorists prove at the same time 'protracted' and 'organized'.[27]

Furthermore, the approach that tends neatly to separate the regulation applicable in international and non-international armed conflicts is gradually losing weight. At least since 1948, different proposals to apply the same rules of IHL to all armed conflicts, elaborated especially by the International Committee of the Red Cross (ICRC), were rejected by states, which proves that reaching an all-encompassing definition of war and uniform regulation is a complex problem.[28] For the moment, important steps have been made towards the extension of the regulations applicable in international armed conflicts to non-international armed conflicts.[29] This process has taken place first through national legislation and international treaties. For instance, the 2006 US Department of Defence (DoD) Directive 2311.01E on the Law of War Program provides that 'members of the DoD Components comply with the law of war *during all armed conflicts, however such conflicts are characterized, and in all other military operations*'.[30] In the same vein, many rules of the 1993 Chemical Weapons Convention apply indifferently to both international and non-international armed conflicts. Thus, Article 1(b) provides that states parties '*never and under any circumstance*', develop, produce, acquire, stockpile, retain or transfer 'chemical weapons *to anyone*'.[31] From the penal standpoint, the ICTR was created to prosecute serious violations of common Article 3 GCs and AP II in a purely internal armed conflict.[32] The Statute of the International Criminal Court (ICC) founds jurisdiction to prosecute war crimes in both international and non-international armed conflicts. Moreover, domestic and international courts have tried to outline customary IHL rules indistinctly applicable to both international and non-international armed conflicts. This aim has been achieved by considering that part of the

---

May 2010, <http://www.ejiltalk.org>, accessed on 15 June 2010; European Journal of International Law: Talk, 'What Exactly Internationalizes an Armed Conflict?', 7 May 2010, ibid.

[26] *Delalić*, IT-96-21, Trial Chamber (16 November 1998), para 184. See also *Tadić*, IT-96-21, Trial Chamber (7 May 1997), para 562.

[27] Cf Moir (n 19 above), 617. See also Duffy (n 25 above), 250 ff.

[28] See Stewart (n 21 above), 344 ff.

[29] For an exhaustive exposition of the progressive extension to non-international armed conflicts of the regulation applicable in international armed conflicts see Fleck (n 13 above), 606 ff; Emanuelli (n 1 above), 133–4. See also the International Institute of Humanitarian Law, 'Declaration on the Rules of International Humanitarian Law governing the Conduct of Hostilities in Non-international Armed Conflicts', San Remo, 7 April 1990, <http://www1.umn.edu/humanrts/instree/1990a.htm>, accessed on 15 June 2010.

[30] US Directive 2311.01E on the Department of Defence Law of War Program, 9 May 2006, Section 4.1 (emphasis added), <http://www.dtic.mil/whs/directives/corres/pdf/231101p.pdf>, accessed on 15 June 2010.

[31] See the text of the Convention, <http://www.opcw.org/chemical-weapons-convention>, accessed on 15 June 2010.

[32] Art 4 ICTR Statute. See also *Rutaganda* (n 18 above), para 91.

regulation of international armed conflicts has become a body of general customary law and applies also to non-international armed conflicts. Such a generalization would concern in particular Geneva-type customary law aiming to protect civilians as well as Hague-type customary law that limits the methods and means of warfare.[33] A mechanical transposition must nevertheless be avoided, since only the essence of the rules in issue would be applicable in non-international armed conflicts. Core principles applying to all armed conflicts include the distinction between fighters and civilians, military objectives, and civilian objectives; the prohibition of superfluous injury or unnecessary suffering; and humane treatment without discrimination.[34] For the purpose of our research, it is noteworthy that the way is paved for the acceptance that serious violations of international humanitarian law, especially breaches of common Article 3 GCs—for instance, wilful killing and torture—must be criminally prosecuted in both international and non-international armed conflicts.[35]

2. The Statute of the International Criminal Court

The Statute of the ICC, which entered into force in 2002, provides for a complementary international procedure for judging war crimes, when a state is 'unable or unwilling genuinely to carry out the investigation or prosecution' and the case is of 'sufficient gravity' to justify the action of the Court.[36]

Article 8(2)(a) ICC Statute recalls the grave breaches of the GCs, whilst Article 8(2)(b) ICC Statute provides for criminalization of 'serious violations' of the rules governing international armed conflicts. Concerning non-international armed conflicts, Article 8(2)(c) ICC Statute penalizes 'serious violations' of common Article 3 GCs, against 'persons taking no active part in the hostilities'. This rule is supplemented by Article 8(2)(e) ICC Statute, which further criminalizes 12 serious violations of rules concerning the conduct of hostilities in non-international armed conflicts, figuring also in Article 8(2)(b), when there is a *protracted* armed conflict between governmental authorities and *organized armed groups* or *between*

---

[33] Defence Motion for Interlocutory Appeal on Jurisdiction, *Tadić* (n 10 above), paras 96–127. See also *Strugar*, IT-01-42, Trial Chamber (31 January 2005), paras 261 ff; *Kupreškić and ors*, IT-95-16, Trial Chamber (14 January 2000), para 526 ff. See also *Rutaganda* (n 18 above), paras 87–90; *Akayesu* (n 17 above), para 609.
[34] See Fleck (n 13 above), 613–14.
[35] See *Krstić*, IT-98-33, Trial Chamber (2 August 2001), para 674 ff; *Kunarac*, IT-96-23, Trial Chamber (22 February 2001), para 401 ff; *Delalić*, IT-96-21, Appeals Chamber (20 February 2001), paras 125 and 136; *Furundžija*, IT-95-17/1, Trial Chamber (10 December 1998), para 134 ff; Defence Motion for Interlocutory Appeal on Jurisdiction, *Tadić* (n 10 above), para 128 ff. Cf also *Semanza*, ICTR-97-20, Trial Chamber (15 May 2003), para 353; *Musema*, ICTR-96-13, Trial Chamber (27 January 2000), para 242; *Rutaganda* (n 18 above), para 86; *Akayesu* (n 17 above), paras 608 and 616. For a juristic viewpoint see Moir (n 19 above), 613–14; de Beco (n 19 above), 322; E Crawford, 'Unequal before the Law: The Case for the Elimination of the Distinction between International and Non-international Armed Conflicts' (2007) 20 Leiden Journal of International Law 441, 450–2.
[36] Art 17 ICC Statute.

such groups' (Article 8(2)(f)).[37] Thus, the ICC relies expressly upon the features of non-international armed conflicts defined by the international case law, which are not explicit under AP II. However, important restrictions on the means and methods of warfare, such as the use of prohibited weapons, starvation of civilians, and other war crimes listed under Article 8(2)(b), seem to be missing in Article 8(2)(e).[38]

According to Article 8(1) ICC Statute, the Court exercises jurisdiction over war crimes '*in particular* when committed as part of a plan or a policy' or 'a large-scale commission'.[39] This requirement is in conformity with the Preamble, which submits to the Court 'the most serious crimes of interest to the international community as a whole'. The ICC jurisdiction is nevertheless limited; in fact, it applies only when either the perpetrator of the crime is a citizen of a state party to the founding treaty or commits a crime on the territory of a state party.[40] A non-party state could nevertheless accept the jurisdiction of the ICC over one of its nationals or a crime committed on its territory through a specific declaration lodged with the Registrar.[41] Furthermore, the jurisdictional constraints could be overcome by the Security Council, which has the faculty to refer a crime to the ICC Prosecutor in the exercise of its powers under Chapter VII of the UN Charter, when it regards ICC prosecution as necessary to restore or maintain international peace and security.[42]

B. The Criminal Responsibility of Private Military and Security Personnel

1. The Subjective Scope of Application of the Geneva Conventions and the Statute of the International Criminal Court

Liability for war crimes concerns all subjects without distinction, regardless of their position as civilians or combatants, since the GCs do not provide for any limitation as to their subjective scope of application.[43] This holds true also in light of the ICC Statute, which indifferently addresses 'natural persons'.[44] Thus, for instance, 'wilful killing' of persons protected by the GCs—criminalized under Article 8(2)(a)(i) and (c)(i) ICC Statute—can be perpetrated by both combatants and civilians.[45] Such a

---

[37] Emphasis added.
[38] See Moir (n 19 above), 614–15; de Beco (n 19 above), 324.
[39] Emphasis added.
[40] Art 12(2) ICC Statute.
[41] Ibid, Art 12(3).
[42] Ibid, Art 13(b). In this respect, it is important to notice that the jurisdictional limits set up by Art 12(2) ICC Statute apply only to prosecution under Art 13(a) and (c) ICC Statute, not to the referral by the Security Council under Art 13(b) ICC Statute. In practice, Omar al-Bashir, President of Sudan—a state non-party to the ICC—was indicted based on UN Security Council Res 1593 (2005). For a juristic viewpoint on this issue see N White and R Cryer, 'The International Criminal Court and the Security Council: An Uncomfortable Relationship' in Cassese et al (n 1 above), 459, 460–3.
[43] Common Art 3 and Arts 49–50 GC I, 50–1 GC II, 129–30 GC III, 146–7 GC IV, 85 AP I. See also Henckaerts and Doswald-Beck (n 11 above), Rule 156, 573.
[44] Art 25(1) ICC Statute.
[45] Cf K Kittichaisaree, *International Criminal Law* (2001), 133.

viewpoint is upheld by consistent case law developed in the wake of the Second World War during several trials of agents of the Nazi regime.[46] According to these premises, the unclear position of PMSC personnel under IHL should have no impact on criminal liability, because they could be held responsible for war crimes regardless of their position as either combatants or civilians.[47] In other words, private contractors can be prosecuted in the same way as the state military. However, a further undisputed condition for imputing war crimes to PMSC personnel must be demonstrated, ie the existence of a link between the agent and war, which means that an illicit act might qualify as a war crime only if it is connected to an armed conflict.[48] The nexus cannot be based exclusively on the fact that the conduct takes place in time of war, but must be established factually on a case-by-case basis,[49] either with regard to the objective context in which the conduct takes place or according to the subjective position of the perpetrator of the crime.[50]

2. The Nexus between Criminal Conduct and War

For the purpose of ascertaining the existence of an objective link between criminal conduct and war, the basic principle is that a 'clear nexus' is sufficient, whereas a 'direct connection to actual hostilities' is not necessary.[51] Therefore, when PMSC personnel take part in combat, like the employees of Executive Outcomes in Sierra Leone, Angola, and the Democratic Republic of the Congo, they are responsible for war crimes, but this is not an indispensable requirement for liability.

The ratio of the link is that criminal conduct must be committed because of the conflict.[52] Specifically, according to the jurisprudence of the ICTY in the case *Kunarac*, a war crime does not need to be part of a planned policy, but must be 'shaped by' or 'dependent upon' the armed conflict, which needs to play a 'substantial part' in the action of the perpetrator.[53] Moreover, the nexus exists until the cessation of the combat activities if the crimes 'are committed in furtherance or take advantage of the situation created by the fighting';[54] therefore, the armed conflict must not necessarily occur at the exact time and place of the

---

[46] See UN War Crimes Commission, *Notes on the Case Bruno Tesch and Two Others (Zyklon B Case)*, British Military Court, Hamburg, 1–8 March 1946, *Law Reports of Trials of War Criminals* (1947), I, 93, 103, <http://www.loc.gov>, accessed on 15 June 2010; UN War Crimes Commission, *Notes on the Case Alfons Klein and Six Others (The Hadamar Trial)*, US Military Commission, 8–15 October 1945, ibid, 46, 53–4; UN War Crimes Commission, *Notes on the Case Erich Heyer and Six Others (The Essen Lynching Case)*, British Military Court for the Trial of War Criminals, Essen, 18–19 and 21–22 December 1945, ibid, 88, 88–92.

[47] On the qualification of PMSC employees under IHL see Ch 10 by Sossai in this volume, at section II.

[48] Cf A Cassese, *International Criminal Law*, 2nd edn (2005), 82 ff.

[49] *Kayishema*, ICTR-95-1-T, Trial Chamber (21 May 1999), para 188.

[50] *Tadić* (n 26 above), paras 574–5.

[51] *Delalić* (n 26 above), paras 193–7.

[52] See G Werle, *Principles of International Criminal Law* (2005), 294.

[53] *Kunarac*, IT-96-23, Appeals Chamber (12 June 2002), para 58.

[54] *Kunarac*, IT-96-23 (n 35 above), para 568.

proscribed acts.⁵⁵ Concretely, the link can be determined by having regard to the status of the perpetrator and the victims, the ultimate goal of a military campaign, or the fact that the act is committed in the context of the employee's official duty.⁵⁶

In light of these criteria, torture of prisoners arrested and detained as a result of military operations, like the inhuman treatments perpetrated in Abu Ghraib by members of CACI and International Titan, currently operating as a group of L3-Communications, could be classified as war crimes. Even more blatantly, killing and wounding of civilians by employees of former Blackwater, now rebranded Xe Services LLC, during the Iraqi and Afghan conflicts, could be prosecuted as war crimes.⁵⁷

With regard to the subjective position, it is normally assumed that a link exists between criminal conduct and war whenever the perpetrator is connected, at least de facto, with a party to the conflict.⁵⁸ Along these lines, the link between private contractors and the belligerent party could be demonstrated quite easily when a state directly outsources functions to PMSCs, whereas the proof is rather difficult when functions are subcontracted by a PMSC to another company.⁵⁹

According to the view expressed by the Trial Chamber of the ICTR in the case *Akayesu*, the nexus would be demonstrated for 'members of the armed forces under the military command of either of the belligerent parties' or any 'public official or agent or person otherwise holding public authority or de facto representing the Government'.⁶⁰ PMSC personnel do not necessarily fit in this definition. On the one hand, the first part of the statement is unlikely to apply to many private contractors, who are incorporated in the armed forces of a state only in very specific cases.⁶¹ On the other hand, it is hard to say whether PMSC personnel fulfil the requirements of the second part of the statement. Therefore, a case-by-case evaluation is necessary. For instance, private contractors hired to act as prison guards, who may exercise detention and disciplinary power, could be regarded as personnel exerting public authority.⁶²

In principle, the position of the perpetrator in relation to the belligerent party should not be considered an indispensable condition for war crimes, but only indicative of the nexus between the crime and the armed conflict.⁶³ As a result, PMSC employees should be liable for war crimes whenever a link can be established

---

⁵⁵ *Tadić* (n 26 above), para 573.
⁵⁶ *Kunarac* (n 53 above), para 59.
⁵⁷ See T Lee, 'Military Extraterritorial Jurisdiction Act for Street Crimes, Not War Crimes', (2009) De Paul Rule of Law Journal 1, 4–5, <http://www.law.depaul.edu>, accessed on 15 June 2010.
⁵⁸ *Kayishema* (n 49 above), paras 174 ff. For a juristic viewpoint see Werle (n 52 above), 295–6; BM Yarnold, 'The Doctrinal Basis for the International Criminalization Process' in M-C Bassiouni (ed), *International Criminal Law*, 2nd edn (1999) 127, 148.
⁵⁹ See Boldt (n 4 above), 525–6.
⁶⁰ *Akayesu* (n 17 above), para 640.
⁶¹ See Ch 10 by Sossai in this volume, at section II.A. See also Boldt (n 4 above), 523–5.
⁶² See Nieminen (n 7 above), 299. This condition has anyway been rejected by the Appeals Chamber and thus must be discarded as a general requirement: *Akayesu*, ICTR-IT-96-4, Appeals Chamber (1 June 2001), para 443; see also *Musema* (n 35 above), para 270.
⁶³ *Akayesu* (n 17 above), paras 641–3.

either with a party to the conflict or the war context.[64] The exposed view is nevertheless not uncontroversial. A recent interpretation holds that the position as a member of the armed forces is an indispensable condition for the attributability of war crimes.[65] This approach is based on another passage of the judgment *Akayesu*, where the ICTR stated that 'the duties and responsibilities of the Geneva Conventions and the Additional Protocols will normally apply only to individuals of all ranks affiliated to the armed forces under the military command of either of the belligerent parties'.[66] As a consequence, most PMSC personnel, who do not qualify as military, could not be considered liable for war crimes. Such a restrictive view must nevertheless be rejected, because the ICTR confined itself to state that the category of persons to be held accountable under the law of war 'would *in most cases* be limited to commanders, combatants and other members of the armed forces',[67] which does not exclude the liability for war crimes of non-military personnel.

III. Superior–Subordinate Relationship

A. Command Responsibility

1. Introductory Remarks

In the aftermath of the Second World War the doctrine of command responsibility, first conceived by a USA Military Commission in the *Yamashita* case, was developed together with the progressive criminalization of the most serious IHL violations.[68] According to this doctrine, superiors can be held responsible for failure to exercise due control over international crimes committed by their subordinates. Following the prevailing interpretation of international jurisdictions, this must be regarded as a form of responsibility for omission, ie a 'dereliction of duty' type of liability, unlike indirect participation in the offence, which subsists, for instance, in the case of ordering, instigation, or joint criminal enterprise.[69] The original intent was to cope with the necessity to render military commanders and high-ranking

---

[64] See K Weigelt and F Marker, 'Who is responsible? The Use of PMCs in Armed Conflicts and International Law' in T Jäger and G Kümmel (eds), *Private Military and Security Companies: Chances, Problems, Pitfalls and Prospects* (2007), 377, 380; L Doswald-Beck, 'Private Military Companies under International Humanitarian Law' in S Chesterman and C Lehnardt (eds), *From Mercenaries to Market: The Rise and Regulation of Private Military Companies* (2007) 115, 134; Werle (n 52 above), 295.

[65] See Lehnardt, 'Individual Liability of Private Military Personnel under International Criminal Law' (2008) 19 European Journal of International Law 1015, 1017.

[66] *Akayesu* (n 17 above), para 631.

[67] Ibid, para 630 (emphasis added).

[68] *In re Yamashita* (327 US 1), US Supreme Court, 4 February 1946, (1946) 13 International Law Reports 273, 273–4.

[69] *Orić*, IT-03-68-T, Trial Chamber (30 June 2006), para 293; *Hadžihasanović and Kubura*, IT-01-47-T, Trial Chamber (15 March 2006), para 75; *Halilović*, IT-01-48-T, Trial Chamber (16 November 2005), para 54; *Krnojelac*, IT-97-25-A, Appeals Chamber (17 September 2003), para 171.

officers criminally liable for the widespread commission of serious crimes by their subordinates, but the concept was subsequently extended to civilian officers.[70]

The principle, left almost untouched for many years, has been embodied in Articles 86(2) and 87 AP I, Article 7(3) ICTY Statute, Article 6(3) ICTR Statute. It is finally stated in Article 28 ICC Statute, which, at least to a large extent, relies upon customary international law. In the short space of the present discussion it is not possible to enter into the details of the notion, which are still controversial, especially with respect to the mens rea. It will suffice to outline its main features, which are useful to characterize the position of PMSC personnel.[71]

Basically, three elements must be proved before a person may incur superior responsibility for the crimes committed by subordinates: (1) the existence of a relationship of superiority and subordination between the accused and the perpetrator of the underlying offence; (2) the mental element, or knowledge by the superior that his subordinate had committed or was about to commit the crime; and (3) the failure of the superior to prevent the commission of the crime or to punish the perpetrators.[72]

Current international case law acknowledges that the doctrine of command responsibility applies to both military and civilian personnel.[73] It concerns all international crimes and is based on (gross) negligence; in fact, the ad hoc tribunals require that a superior 'knew' or 'had reason to know' that criminal acts by his/her subordinates were committed or were about to be committed.[74]

For the purpose of our discussion the crucial factor is that superiors must exercise 'effective authority' over their subordinates in order to apply the doctrine of command responsibility.[75] According to the case law, such a condition is not satisfied by the mere influence of the superior over the subordinate.[76] Instead, it subsists whenever the superior has the ability to 'prevent and punish' the commission of the crime and can be ascertained de facto through an analysis of the actual tasks performed.[77] In other words, in order to apply the concept of command

---

[70] See Opinion and Judgment, *Farben*, Nuremberg Military Tribunal VI, 29–30 July 1948, in *Trial of War Criminals before the Nuremberg Military Tribunals under Control Council Law n10* (1952), VIII, 1081 ff, <http://www.loc.gov>, accessed on 15 June 2010; Judgment, *Pohl and ors*, Nuremberg Military Tribunal II, 3 November 1947, ibid, (1950), V, 1052–3; Judgment, *Brandt*, Nuremberg Military Tribunal I, 19–20 August 1947, ibid, (1950), II, 193.

[71] For a complete exposition of the evolution of the doctrine of command responsibility see G Mettraux, *The Law of Command Responsibility* (2009); Cassese (n 48 above), 236–52; Werle (n 52 above), 129.

[72] *Blaškić*, IT-95-14, Appeals Chamber (29 July 2004), para 67; *Kordić and Čerkez*, IT-95-14/2, Trial Chamber (26 February 2001), para 401; *Blaškić*, IT-95-14-T, Trial Chamber (3 March 2000), para 294.

[73] *Kordić and Čerkez* (n 72 above), para 418; *Aleksovski*, IT-95-14/1, Appeals Chamber (24 March 2000), para 76.

[74] *Kordić and Čerkez* (n 72 above), para 427; Judgment, *Delalić* (n 35 above), para 222; *Blaškić*, Trial Chamber (n 72 above), paras 294, 332; *Delalić* (n 27 above), para 383.

[75] *Aleksovski*, IT-95-14, Trial Chamber (25 June 1999), paras 76, 78; *Delalić* (n 26 above), para 370.

[76] *Kordić and Čerkez* (n 72 above), para 415.

[77] *Blaškić*, Appeals Chamber (n 72 above), para 67; *Kordić and Čerkez* (n 72 above), para 421; *Kunarac* (n 35 above), para 396; *Delalić* (n 26 above), paras 377–8. See also J Arnold, 'Responsibility of

responsibility, there is no need to prove a formal superior–subordinate relationship, but it is necessary to prove that the superior had the material capacity to prevent or punish the commission of crimes by his/her subordinates.

2. The Organization of PMSCs and the Application of the Doctrine of Command Responsibility

In light of the above premises, the question arises as to whether the responsibility of PMSCs' superiors can be admitted in case of failure to exercise control over war crimes perpetrated by their subordinates. In other words, PMSCs' superiors might be subject to liability for omission, because of the 'dereliction of the duty' to 'prevent and punish'. Relevant situations in this sense are represented by the battalions of Executive Outcomes deployed in Sierra Leone, which were exclusively directed by internal members,[78] and the inhuman interrogations by CACI's and Titan's contractors in Iraq, which operated according to their own command under the ultimate supervision of state military personnel.[79]

A positive answer is possible only if PMSCs provide an internal organization sufficient to establish 'effective control' of superiors over subordinates. This is questionable, because PMSCs normally do not respond to a continuous system of obedience and control, so that their internal hierarchical structure and superior–subordinate relationships are naturally less tight than that of military organizations.[80] The issue must be addressed in light of two relevant criteria established by the case law of the international tribunals.

First, the standard of organization for applying the doctrine of command responsibility set by the international case law is rather low. In fact, the ICTY is satisfied with command structures that can be 'in disorder and primitive'.[81] Moreover, the temporary nature of a military unit is not, in itself, sufficient to exclude a relationship of subordination between the members of a unit and its commander.[82] In this regard, though sometimes command responsibility seems unclear and chaotic on the ground, especially for many PMSCs operating in Iraq, it must be noted that private contractors tend to be organized according to military lines.[83] Furthermore, they usually incorporate former military commanders in their staff, who are motivated to move to the private sector by the possibility of higher incomes and often run the company

---

Commanders and other Superiors: Article 28' in O Triffterer (ed), *Commentary on the Rome Statute of the International Criminal Court*, 2nd edn (2008), 795, 825–6.

[78] See Singer (n 5 above), 93.
[79] See Boldt (n 4 above), 527.
[80] See Lehnardt (n 65 above), 1026.
[81] *Delalić* (n 35 above), para 193. See also *Kunarac* (n 35 above), para 397.
[82] Ibid, para 399.
[83] See Boldt (n 4 above), 527.

itself.[84] Therefore, based on a case-by-case evaluation, PMSCs could be considered organized enough to apply the doctrine of command responsibility.

Secondly, a crucial factor for applying the doctrine of command responsibility is the possibility of giving orders or exercising powers generally associated with military command.[85] In this regard, unless they are enrolled as state military, which is rarely the case, PMSC personnel could satisfy the requirement only by classifying as 'persons effectively acting as military commanders'. This might be the case when they supervise lower-ranked personnel. In fact, though PMSC personnel do not enjoy equal powers as state military, it can be assumed that they hold similar powers.[86] Such a factor is decisive, because the power of PMSCs' superiors must not be equal, but simply needs to be 'comparable to' or 'as effective as' that of military superiors in order to apply the doctrine of command responsibility.[87]

With regard to the distinction between the 'power to prevent' and the 'power to punish', PMSCs' superiors fully enjoy the former, namely because they can train PMSC personnel, establish a reporting system to inform superiors of IHL violations, and issue orders that ensure the prevention of crimes.[88] By contrast, they normally do not fully enjoy the 'power to punish', since the only faculty they have is to report breaches to public authorities, thus triggering criminal investigations. This must nevertheless be considered enough to regard them as 'persons effectively acting as military commanders'. In fact, though taking steps in the disciplinary process is considered insufficient for the exercise of the power to punish within the military hierarchy,[89] courts normally regard such a faculty as sufficient for establishing effective control with respect to civil authorities.[90]

Concretely, PMSC employees seem to have exerted effective control over the perpetrators of tortures in Abu Ghraib, not only with respect to lower-ranking contractors but also with regard to subordinate state military personnel.[91] Major General Taguba explained to the US Senate Armed Services Committee that military and non-military personnel involved in mistreatment regarded contractors as 'competent authority'.[92] Moreover, PMSC personnel are likely to be held liable for omissions when they are unable to maintain adequate oversight over intelligence operations.[93]

---

[84] Ibid, 534.
[85] *Kunarac* (n 35 above), para 397.
[86] Cf Lehnard (n 65 above), 1026; Doswald-Beck (n 64 above), 135.
[87] *Aleksovski* (n 75 above), para 78.
[88] *Kvočka and ors*, IT-98-30/1, Trial Chamber, 2 November 2001, para 316.
[89] *Kordić and Čerkez* (n 72 above), para 446.
[90] *Aleksovski* (n 75 above), para 78. See also Lehnard (n 65 above), 1026–7.
[91] See J Nyamuya Maogoto and B Sheehy, 'Private Military Companies and International Law: Building New Ladders of Legal Accountability and Responsibility', *Cardozo Journal of Conflict Resolution* 11 (2009) 99, 128–9.
[92] Cf Senate Panel Hearings on Iraq Abuses, Statement of Antonio Taguba (Major General, USA Deputy Commanding General for Support), <http://www.nytimes.com>, accessed on 15 June 2010.
[93] See Nyamuya Maogoto and Sheehy (n 91 above), 129.

3. The Position of the Managers of PMSCs

A specific situation is that of PMSCs' managers, who do not act in the theatre of conflict and have an indirect relationship with lower-ranked personnel liable for war crimes.[94]

In this respect, it must be generally noted that the international case law regards an indirect superior–subordinate relationship as sufficient to satisfy the requirement of effective control and apply the doctrine of command responsibility.[95] Furthermore, similar cases support the application of the doctrine of command responsibility to PMSCs' managers. In fact, in the *Musema* and the *Nahimana* trials before the ICTR civilians holding managerial positions in private entities were sentenced for failure to act with respect to crimes committed by their subordinates. Specifically, Nahimana was the founder and director of a broadcast enterprise, whereas Musema was the director of a tea factory. In *Nahimana*, the ICTR ascertained that the defendant exercised de facto control over subordinate employees, and was empowered to prevent and punish the broadcast of criminal discourse.[96] Musema was convicted by the ICTR, inter alia, according to the doctrine of command responsibility, because he exercised de jure power and de facto control over tea factory employees and the resources of the tea factory, particularly through the faculty to appoint and remove personnel from their positions.[97] The latter decision was nevertheless criticized in that it did not clearly distinguish the authority over crimes committed by subordinates within and outside the exercise of their duty.[98]

The Montreux Document, a common regulatory initiative by the ICRC and the Swiss Federal Department of Foreign Affairs (FDFA) on good practices relating to PMSCs' operations during armed conflicts, explicitly recognizes the application of the doctrine of command responsibility to 'directors or managers of PMSCs'.[99] A case-by-case evaluation is therefore necessary to ascertain whether PMSCs' managers have the faculty to issue instructions that are routinely implemented by employees operating in the field, and thus enjoy a power 'to prevent and punish' equivalent to that of 'persons effectively acting as military commanders', at least with regard to crimes relating to the functions performed by subordinate employees. In particular, according to the Montreux Document, the power to 'prevent and punish' of PMSCs' managers could be satisfied by the faculty to assess the capacity of the personnel to carry out their activity in conformity with IHL as well as to suspend or remove individual suspected members and perpetrators of war

---

[94] Cf M Frulli, 'Exploring the Applicability of Command Responsibility to Private Military Contractors', (2010) Journal of Conflict & Security Law, paras 5 ff; Schmitt (n 7 above), 529–30.
[95] *Delalić* (n 35 above), para 252; *Blaškić*, Trial Chamber (n 72 above), para 301.
[96] *Nahimana*, ICTR-96-11, Appeals Chamber (28 November 2007), paras 803–22.
[97] *Musema* (n 35 above), para 880.
[98] See Zahar, 'Command Responsibility of Civilian Superiors for Genocide', (2001) 14 Leiden Journal of International Law 591, 602.
[99] See ICRC-FDFA, Montreux Document, Part One: Pertinent International Legal Obligations Relating to Private Military and Security Companies, 2009, F-27, 15, <http://www.icrc.org>, accessed on 15 June 2010.

crimes.[100] Furthermore, with specific regard to the power to punish, the 2006 US DoD Directive 2311.01E sets up the duty to report any alleged violation of the laws of war to the competent authorities for '*all* military and U.S. civilian employees, contractor personnel, and subcontractors assigned to or accompanying a DoD Component', without distinguishing between PMSCs' managers and lower-ranked personnel.[101] As to the power to prevent, it is worth mentioning that in January 2009 the US DoD issued a final rule amending the Defense Federal Acquisition Regulation Supplement (DFARS), which requires DoD contractors to 'institute effective programs to *prevent violations of the laws of war by contractor personnel* authorized to accompany U.S. Armed Forces deployed outside the United States', regardless of any further distinction.[102]

B. Superior Orders

1. Introductory Remarks

Since the Second World War a customary rule has emerged according to which superior orders are acknowledged as a crucial factor to mitigate punishment for all international crimes.[103] The basic assumption is that a subordinate may face the dilemma as to whether he should respect the orders given by superiors or comply with the moral duty not to breach the law.

Basically, two conditions need to be satisfied: first, the subordinate must be under an obligation to obey according to a superior–subordinate relationship; secondly, the order involves the perpetration of an international crime. In addition, national courts sometimes require the manifest unlawfulness of the order, so that the subordinate knew or should have known its illegality.[104] For applying the defence of superior orders international law takes into account the liability of the accused person acting 'pursuant to an order of a Government or of a superior', without any further distinction.[105]

The ICC Statute approaches the issue in a different way. In fact, Article 33 does not envisage mitigation of punishment. Instead, it provides that the orders of a

---

[100] Ibid, Part Two: Good Practices Relating to Private Military and Security Companies, 16 ff.
[101] See Directive 2311.01E on the DoD Law of War Program, Section 6.3 (emphasis added).
[102] DoD, Defense Federal Acquisition Regulation Supplement, DoD Law of War Program (DFARS Case 2006–D035), 15 January 2009, <http://edocket.access.gpo.gov/2009/pdf/E9-680.pdf>, accessed on 15 June 2010 (emphasis added).
[103] See Art 8 of the Charter of the Nuremberg Tribunal, Art 6 of the Charter of the Tokyo Tribunal, Art 7(4) ICTY Statute, and Art 6(4) ICTR Statute. On the evolution of the doctrine of superior orders see A Zimmermann, 'Superior Orders' in A Cassese, P Gaeta, and JRWD Jones (eds), *The Rome Statute of the International Criminal Court: A Commentary* (2002), 957, 967; P Gaeta, 'The Defence of Superior Orders: The Statute of the International Criminal Court versus Customary International Law', (1999) 10 European Journal of International Law 172, 188–9; MC Bassiouni and P Manikas, *The Law of the International Criminal Tribunal for the former Yugoslavia* (1996), 384 ff.
[104] *Calley* (22 USCMA 534), United States Court of Military Appeals (21 December 1973), <http://www.law.umkc.edu/faculty/projects/ftrials/mylai/MYL_uscma.htm>, accessed on 15 June 2010.
[105] Cf Art 7(4) ICTY Statute and Art 6(3) ICTR Statute.

government or a superior, whether military or civilian, do not relieve a subordinate of criminal responsibility, unless: (a) the subordinate was under a legal obligation to obey orders; (b) the subordinate did not know that the order was unlawful; (c) the order was not manifestly unlawful.[106] The unlawfulness of genocide and crimes against humanity is presupposed,[107] and thus the relevance of superior orders is generally banned, except in the case of war crimes.[108]

Since war crimes normally consist in serious violations of IHL, it has been suggested that they would obviously be manifestly unlawful, which would automatically exclude the defence of superior orders.[109] Nevertheless, if this holds true for violations such as wilful killing or ill-treatment, the same does not necessarily apply to complex types of war crime, such as, for instance, the improper use of a flag of truce, criminalized under Article 8(2)(b)(vii) ICC Statute. Therefore, the possibility of applying the defence of superior orders to war crimes, though limited, cannot be radically excluded.[110]

2. The Application of the Defence of Superior Orders to Private Military and Security Personnel

From the standpoint of PMSCs, the question arises as to whether superior orders could exclude the responsibility of subordinate employees for war crimes, according to the ICC Statute, or mitigate punishment, according to customary international law. This issue is also problematic in light of the organization of PMSCs. In particular, the defence of superior orders could apply not only to internal superior–subordinate relationships, but also to the relationship between PMSC employees and superiors affiliated to the hiring subject, be it a state, an international organization, or a private entity. In fact, both customary law and the ICC Statute take into account superior orders, regardless of their affiliation and qualification as military or civilians.

The superior–subordinate relationship requires effective control by the authority over the subordinate, which must be ascertained de facto, given that the defence of superior orders is the other side of the coin with respect to command responsibility.[111] In fact, according to the ICTY in the case *Kordić* 'no formal superior–subordinate relationship is required for a finding of "ordering" so long as it is demonstrated that the accused possessed the authority to order'.[112] With specific

---

[106] Art 33(1) ICC Statute.
[107] Ibid, Art 33(2).
[108] For a complete presentation of the defence of superior orders and a critique of the ICC approach see Cassese (n 48 above), 271 ff.
[109] See Gaeta (n 103 above), 185.
[110] See Werle (n 52 above), 155–6.
[111] See *Rutaganda* (n 18 above), para 39; *Akayesu* (n 17 above), para 483. See also Cassese (n 48 above), 271; Doswald-Beck (n 64 above), 136.
[112] *Kordić and Čerkez* (n 72 above), para 388. See also *Blaškić*, Trial Chamber (n 72 above), para 281.

regard to unlawful acts, 'ordering' basically 'entails a person in a position of authority using that position to convince another to commit an offence'.[113]

As to the internal structure of PMSCs, the existence of superior–subordinate relationships has been positively demonstrated within the context of command responsibility.[114] Specifically, with regard to orders issued by PMSCs' managers, it is important to notice that in the case *Blăskić* the ICTY assumed that 'an order does not need to be given by the superior directly to the person(s) who perform(s) the *actus reus* of the offence'.[115] This approach mirrors the view expressed by the ICTY applying the doctrine of command responsibility.[116]

As to PMSCs acting for states, international organizations, or private entities, it is essential to determine whether or not the outsourcing entity might exercise control over PMSCs. Though the legal context varies, the criteria do not change, since the crucial point still consists in establishing whether or not superiors affiliated to entities external to PMSCs exercise 'effective control' over PMSC personnel.

For outlining the relationship between the hiring subject and PMSCs, it must be noted that public rules and contracts normally assign functions to private contractors, set a code of conduct and often define precisely what they have to do, how, and responding to what authorities. For instance, according to the USA Logistics Civil Augmentation Program (LOGCAP), private contractors must abide by the orders given by military commanders and are generally directed by a state Army Procurement Contracting Officer or by different state departments.[117] In this vein, a Memorandum issued by the US Secretary of Defence in March 2008 gives authority to military commanders over civilian contractors in their areas of operation. In particular, the Memorandum makes it clear that state commanders are supposed to exercise control, possess a sufficient degree of authority, and assume precise duties to supervise and report crimes with regard to PMSC personnel contracted by the DoD.[118] With respect to the Iraqi war, the US Secretary of Defence Donald Rumsfeld testified before the Senate Armed Services Committee that civilian contractors in Iraq are 'responsible to military intelligence who hire them'.[119] Thus, even if unclear responsibilities and muddled channels of communication often seem to hinder effective coordination, PMSCs should remain responsible to state organs of the US-led coalition. Moreover, though PMSCs' contracts are generally not made public, under the US Freedom of Information Act the Centre for Public Integrity reported that one contract with a PMSC

---

[113] *Krstić* (n 35 above), para 601.
[114] See section III.A.2 above.
[115] *Blăskić*, Trial Chamber (n 72 above), para 282.
[116] See section III.A.3 and n 95 above.
[117] Army Regulation (AR) 700–137, Logistics Civil Augmentation Program (LOGCAP), <http://www.globalsecurity.org/military/agency/army/logcap.htm>, accessed on 15 June 2010.
[118] Secretary of Defence, Memorandum for Secretaries of the Military Departments, Chairman of the Joint Chiefs of Staff, Undersecretaries of Defense, Commanders of the Combatants Commands, 10 March 2008, <http://www.dtic.mil/whs/directives/corres/pdf/sec080310ucmj.pdf>, accessed on 15 June 2010.
[119] See Senate Panel Hearings on Iraq Abuses, <http://www.nytimes.com>, accessed on 15 June 2010.

involved in the Abu Grahib tortures stipulated that contractors were to be considered 'directed' by military superiors,[120] so that PMSC personnel were supposed to receive orders from the military hierarchy above.[121] According to these premises, the defence of superior orders could hypothetically be invoked for the inhuman acts perpetrated in Abu Ghraib by private contractors, who were expected to operate under the instruction, direction, and control of commanders of the American army, namely Brigade General Karpinski, who was in charge of the whole prison, and Colonel Pappas, commander of the military brigade to which the contractors were assigned.[122] However, in the case of torture, hopefully the defence of superior orders would have little chance of success, given that the manifest unlawfulness of this conduct is usually presumed.[123]

More specifically, the defence of superior orders might apply when PMSC employees can be conceived of as units abiding by a discipline respectful of IHL and are submitted to a command accountable to a state. This should be the case of many PMSC personnel operating in Iraq, whose assimilation to the state military is often very close, also physically, so much that contractors wearing only a different badge on standard US field uniform are practically indistinguishable from US soldiers.[124] The defence might have some chance of success in particular when unlawful orders are given on the battlefield, because in the heat of the battle subordinates do not necessarily have enough time to reflect on the lawfulness of orders.[125] For instance, the defence could be relevant in situations like that of Blackwater employees fighting in Najaf to protect headquarters of the CPA, which showed a very close relationship to the state's military.

Finally, the qualification of PMSC employees under IHL, specifically the distinction between combatants and civilians, should not affect the exercise of effective control. Nevertheless, in case of orders concerning activities directly relating to hostilities the distinction between combatants and civilians must be taken into account. In fact, the defence of superior orders can certainly apply to PMSCs' subordinates qualifying as combatants. By contrast, commands given to civilians, whose direct participation in hostilities is illegal under the GCs, cannot be considered lawful. Therefore, the invocation of the defence of superior orders should be prevented whenever such unlawfulness is manifestly apparent.

---

[120] E McCarthy, 'CACI Defense Contracts Hazy on Civilian Authority: Language Reserves Direction For Military', *Washington Post* (29 July 2004), <http://www.washingtonpost.com>, accessed on 15 June 2010.
[121] See Nyamuya Maogoto and Sheehy (n 91 above), 127, 128.
[122] See Arts 15–6 of the Investigation of the 800th Military Police Brigade in KJ Greenberg and JL Dratel (eds), *The Torture Papers: The Road to Abu Ghraib* (2005), 415, 439.
[123] See eg *The Queen/Private DJ Brocklebank* (CMAC.383), Court Martial Appeal Court of Canada (2 April 1996), 12–13, <http://www.dnd.ca>, accessed on 15 June 2010.
[124] See A Eunjung Cha and R Merle, 'Line Increasingly Blurred between Soldiers and Civilian Contractors', *Washington Post* (13 May 2004), <http://www.washingtonpost.com>, accessed on 15 June 2010.
[125] *Calley* (n 104 above). According to Cassese (n 48 above), 279, the unlawfulness of orders given in the heat of the battle should be taken into account as an extenuating circumstance.

IV. Prosecution

A. Mechanisms of Enforcement

The trial of PMSC employees committing grave breaches of the GCs should be ultimately ensured by the fact that state parties are obliged to criminalize such infringements and to prosecute or extradite their perpetrators.[126] By qualifying as 'civilians', PMSC personnel should normally be tried by criminal courts, whereas their subjection to military courts may vary from state to state. For instance, in the United States, civilian contractors could be prosecuted by criminal courts under the Military Extraterritorial Jurisdiction Act (MEJA)[127] or subject to court-martial via the Uniform Code of Military Justice (UCMJ), recently extended to 'persons serving with or accompanying an armed force in the field'.[128]

Naturally, domestic systems can provide for regulation of war crimes beyond international law, in which case prosecution will be established according to the place where the offence occurs, the nationality of the perpetrator, the nationality of the victim, and the state interest in proceeding. The application of specific principles recognized under international law, such as the doctrine of command responsibility and the defence of superior orders, depends on the internal acceptance of such rules.

In theory, this system ensures the prosecution and punishment of PMSC personnel. In particular, interest in enforcing IHL should be shown by the state on whose behalf the PMSC acts. In fact, it has the strongest connection to the PMSC and ought to ensure that private contractors respect IHL in order to avoid its own liability under the law of state responsibility.[129]

In practice, trying PMSC employees for war crimes could be prevented by several obstacles. First, states show a certain reluctance to try their own troops, both for fear of demoralization and of eroding popular support for military undertakings.[130] Furthermore, not all states have adopted the domestic legislation necessary to prosecute war crimes and many of those which have so done still require a specific link with the state.[131] Rare are the cases of arrest of persons suspected of war crimes by states in application of universal jurisdiction, probably because diplomatic reasons tend to prevail over the independence of the judiciary.[132] In addition, the concepts of war crime and universal jurisdiction are traditionally considered valid

---

[126] See Ch 5 by Francioni in this volume, at section VIII.
[127] See the Military Extraterritorial Jurisdiction Act, Public Law 106–523, 22 November 2000, <http://www.pubklaw.com/hi/pl106-523.pdf>, accessed on 15 June 2010.
[128] Cf Uniform Code of Military Justice, Title 10, s 802(a), para 10, <http://www.au.af.mil/au/awc/awcgate/ucmj.htm>, accessed on 15 June 2010.
[129] See Boldt (n 4 above), 358.
[130] Cf Sandoz (n 10 above), 1054.
[131] For an overview of state legislation and case law concerning the exercise of jurisdiction over war crimes see Henckaerts and Doswald-Beck (n 11 above), 3894–931. See also the ICRC website, <http://www.icrc.org/ihl-nat>, accessed on 15 June 2010.
[132] Cf Sandoz (n 10 above), 1054.

only for international armed conflicts, whereas most conflicts have a non-international character.[133] Finally, the collection of evidence for war crimes might often take place abroad, in which case it would require appropriate international cooperation and could prove particularly complex.[134] As a result, prosecutions, especially based on mandatory universal jurisdiction, are highly selective, largely uncoordinated and, so far, the mechanism has proved unsatisfactory.[135]

B. Problems of Implementation Specifically Relating to Private Military and Security Personnel

With specific regard to PMSC personnel, practical problems, which basically relate either to the host state or the sending state, prevent the implementation of criminal responsibility.

As to the position of the sending state, the will to prosecute could be weakened by the fact that PMSCs are flexible and efficient tools that facilitate low financial and political costs.[136] The problem here is that the state relying on PMSCs' services could be unwilling to challenge the responsibility of their personnel. For instance, in spite of the fact that under the US War Crimes Act PMSC employees holding US citizenship might be subject to criminal prosecution,[137] only tort actions have been undertaken against private contractors before the District Courts of Ohio and Virginia for the facts of Abu Ghraib.[138]

In some cases, criminal prosecution has effectively taken place. For example, six former Blackwater guards active in Iraq recently faced trial for voluntary manslaughter and firearms violations in the United States before the District Court of Columbia because of the shooting and throwing of grenades in Nisoor Square (Baghdad) in 2007, which resulted in the killing of 17 unarmed Iraqi civilians and the wounding of 20 innocent bystanders.[139] Moreover, two employees working for a subsidiary of former Blackwater were recently indicted by a Federal Grand Jury in Norfolk on wilful murder and other charges for shooting and killing two Afghan citizens in

---

[133] Ibid, 1055; Harbom and Wallensteen (n 22 above), 627.
[134] See Ch 5 by Francioni in this volume, at section IX. See also F Jessberger, 'International v National Prosecution of International Crimes', in Cassese et al (n 1 above), 208, 211.
[135] Ibid, 210; Boldt (n 4 above), 544.
[136] Jessberger (n 134 above), 214–15; Boldt (n 4 above), 515.
[137] US Code, Title 18, Part 1, Chapter 118, paras 2441–2.
[138] See Civil Complaint and Jury Demand, *Al Shimari and ors/CACI International Inc, CACI Premier Technology Inc* (Civil Action no 08-cv-0827), USA District Court of Virginia, 15 September 2008, <http://ccrjustice.org/ourcases/current-cases/al-shimari-v-caci-et-al>, accessed on 15 June 2010; Civil Complaint and Jury Demand, *Al Shimari/Dugan, CACI International Inc, CACI Premier Technology Inc, L-3 Services Inc* (Civil Action no 08-cv-637), US District Court of Ohio Columbia Division, 30 June 2008, ibid.
[139] See Memorandum Opinion, Granting the Defendant's Motion to Dismiss the Indictment, *USA/Slaught and ors*, US District of Columbia (Washington), Criminal Action no 08-0360(RMU), 1, <http://documents.nytimes.com/memorandum-of-dismissal-of-charges-against-blackwater-guards#p=1>, accessed on 15 June 2010; C Savage, 'Judge Drops Charges from Blackwater Deaths in Iraq', *New York Times* (31 December 2009), <http://www.nytimes.com>, accessed on 15 June 2010; J Vicini 'US Judge Sets Trial in 2010 for Blackwater Guards', <http://www.reuters.com/article/idUSN06444976>, accessed on 15 June 2010.

Kabul and wounding a third in May 2009.[140] These cases are not isolated and certainly witness accrued sensitivity towards the accountability of private contractors, but still do not demonstrate that PMSC personnel are effectively tried for war crimes.

First and foremost, even when criminal prosecution takes place, PMSC employees are likely to be indicted for 'street crimes', according to domestic penal law, rather than war crimes. For instance, the two employees working for the subsidiary of former Blackwater recently indicted by the Federal Grand Jury in Norfolk were charged with wilful murder, ie an offence unrelated to war, whereas they could face responsibility for grave breaches of the GCs under the War Crimes Act, namely for murder of civilians no longer participating in hostilities.[141] The allegations of the Nisoor Square indictment could also constitute violations within the reach of the War Crimes Act, specifically murder of civilians, mutilation or maiming, and intentionally causing serious bodily injury.[142] By contrast, former Blackwater contractors were charged with the crimes of manslaughter and firearms offences. This might prove inappropriate, because events of war are less clear-cut than ordinary crimes, so that questions of legitimate collateral damage and proportionate response cannot be fairly addressed without using the appropriate standards of the law of armed conflicts.[143] In fact, if charged with war crimes, the defendants would have been enabled to raise the defence of the 'preclusion of intent in case of collateral damage and death, damage, or injury incident to a lawful attack'.[144] By contrast, outside the framework of war crimes, manslaughter must be judged according to the ordinary criterion of the 'sudden quarrel or heat of passion',[145] which is not necessarily the most appropriate standard for a combat environment with alleged exploding bombs and insurgents firing from street corners.

Secondly, the possibility cannot be excluded that PMSC personnel are granted immunity through judicial approaches such as the political-question defence. This doctrine holds that courts might decline claims relating to governmental action when discretion is essential to protect constitutional or political interests.[146] In this respect, it must nevertheless be acknowledged that the political-question doctrine was recently rejected in the course of the civil action brought against CACI's members before the District Court of Virginia with regard to the acts of torture in Abu Ghraib, so that the same attitude can be expected to extend to criminal proceedings.[147]

---

[140] See J Markon, 'Two Defense Contractors Indicted in Shooting of Afghans', *Washington Post* (8 January 2008), <http://www.washingtonpost.com>, accessed on 15 June 2010.
[141] US Code, Title 18, Part 1, Chapter 118, para 2441(d)(1)(D).
[142] US Code, Title 18, Part 1, Chapter 118, para 2441(d)(1)(D), s (d)(1)(E) and s (d)(1)(F).
[143] See Lee (n 57 above), 5–6.
[144] US Code, Title 18, Part 1, Chapter 118, para 2441, s (d)(3).
[145] US Code, Title 18, Part 1, Chapter 51, para 1112(a).
[146] See D Cole, 'Challenging Covert War: The Politics of the Political Question Doctrine' (1985) 26 Harvard International Law Journal 155, 163–4.
[147] See Memorandum Order, *Al Shimari and ors/CACI International Inc, CACI Premier Technology Inc* (Civil Action no 08-cv-0827), US District Court of Virginia, 18 March 2009, 15–19, <http://ccrjustice.org/ourcases/current-cases/al-shimari-v-caci-et-al>, accessed on 15 June 2010.

Thirdly, the principle of due process might be invoked in order to shield private contractors from prosecution. This approach could either respond to the effective requirements of a fair trial or could be a way to cover up political unwillingness to prosecute. The lawsuit against former Blackwater employees for the Nisoor Square incident is exemplary in this respect. In fact, on January 2010, in a 90-page ruling, the judge of the Federal District of Columbia dismissed all charges against the indicted guards from former Blackwater without any comment on the legality of the shooting. The case was dismissed on the grounds that the constitutional rights of the contractors were violated because of the way their confession statements had been collected in the immediate aftermath of the facts and the subsequent investigations. More specifically, the statements were made under threat of job loss in the case of a refusal to cooperate in the investigations and the contractors were promised by the US government that the declarations would have not been used against them in a criminal case. According to the judge, despite this immunity deal the statements have been used in the prosecution of former Blackwater employees, which would taint the investigation and prevent trial against all defendants.[148] The lengthy opinion of the federal district judge appears unlikely to be overturned by an appeals court and new prosecution against the same contractors could be brought only by using untainted evidence. The dismissal cast doubt on the integrity of the US justice system among Iraqis, who complain that local people, victims, and officials who responded to the scene were not called to witness.[149]

As regards the position of the host state, it must be noticed that it is often unable to prosecute in war contexts.[150] For instance, at the time of the intervention of Executive Outcomes the government of Sierra Leone could not control its own capital, and thus would have certainly been unable to monitor and punish private contractors.[151] Furthermore, weak states, where PMSCs usually operate, might be reluctant to exercise jurisdiction. In Afghanistan, for example, security heavily depends on private contractors.

The negative trend can go so far as to grant formal immunity to PMSC personnel, which can be achieved in different ways.[152] First, immunity from local jurisdiction could be granted by way of international agreements (SOFAs—Status of Force Agreements), as the United States and Afghanistan did for conferring exclusive jurisdiction to the sending state over its nationals, including private contractors.[153] Secondly, immunity might be granted by way of internal legislative acts, as in the case of the CPA Order no 17 concerning coalition troops and

---

[148] See Memorandum Opinion, Granting the Defendant's Motion to Dismiss the Indictment, *USA/Slaught and ors* (n 139 above), esp 1–3.
[149] See M Chulov and E Pilkington, 'Iraqui Threatens Action after Blackwater Case Collapses', *The Guardian* (1 January 2010), <http://www.guardian.co.uk>, accessed on 15 June 2010.
[150] See Jessberger (n 134 above), 214.
[151] PW Singer, 'War, Profits, and the Vacuum of Law: Privatized Military Firms and International Law', (2004) 42 Columbia Journal of Transnational Law 521, 535, 537.
[152] On the immunity of PMSC personnel see Chr 22 by Frulli in this volume.
[153] See Treaties and Other International Acts Series, Exchange of notes 26 September and 12 December 2002 and 28 May 2003.

contractors operating in Iraq from 2004 to 2008.[154] Under these circumstances, the US government disallowed Iraqis from prosecuting the Blackwater guards implicated in the killing of civilians in Nisoor Square.[155] In 2009, nevertheless, immunity expired by virtue of the SOFA concluded between the United States and Iraq on the withdrawal of US forces.[156] Thus, following the dismissal of the criminal charges brought against former Blackwater employees in the United States, a spokesman for the Iraqi government stated that criminal prosecution of Xe Services LLC would be pursued through the Iraqi legal system, in order to forbid its private military work in the country.[157]

It must anyway be noticed that immunity should not cover acts performed in abuse of authority, which do not pursue the terms and conditions of the hiring contract, and should not be granted for grave breaches of the GCs, which are protected by a mandatory obligation to investigate or prosecute.

C. The Limits of the International Criminal Court

Technically speaking, the ICC has the means necessary to overcome state sovereignty and investigate war crimes, especially because immunity does not apply by virtue of Article 27 of its statute. More importantly, the lack of state will to prosecute PMSC employees is one of the reasons for triggering the jurisdiction of the Court under Article 17 ICC Statute.

However, besides the jurisdictional constraints established according to Articles 12 and 17 of its statute, immunity from the ICC could be granted by way of international agreements, as envisaged, for instance, by the American Service-Members' Protection Act (ASPA).[158] This Act tends to exclude the ICC jurisdiction over US nationals,[159] and bans military assistance to a 'host' state party to the ICC, except for NATO members or major allies and Taiwan, unless immunity from ICC jurisdiction is granted through bilateral agreements.[160] Though such a policy is questionable in that it clearly threatens the effectiveness of the ICC jurisdiction, it seems admissible under Article 98 ICC Statute and has practically been implemented. In fact, bilateral agreements under the ASPA have been concluded by the United States with many states, both parties and non-parties to the ICC, for

---

[154] CPA, Order no 17: Status of the Coalition Provisional Authority, MNF–Iraq, Certain Missions and Personnel in Iraq, 27 June 2004, <http://www.iraqcoalition.org/regulations>, accessed on 15 June 2010.
[155] See M Apuzzo, 'Judge Dismisses Charges in Blackwater Case', *San Francisco Chronicle* (1 January 2010), <http://www.sfgate.com>, accessed on 15 June 2010.
[156] See the Agreement between the USA and the Republic of Iraq on the Withdrawal of US Forces from Iraq and the Organization of their Activities during their Temporary Presence in Iraq, 17 November 2008, <http://www.globalsecurity.org/military/library/policy/dod/iraq-sofa.htm>, accessed on 15 June 2010.
[157] See Chulov and Pilkington (n 149 above).
[158] See the text of the ASPA, <http://www.state.gov/t/pm/rls/othr/misc/23425.htm>, accessed on 15 June 2010.
[159] See s 2004(d) ASPA.
[160] Cf s 2007 ASPA.

instance Afghanistan and Azerbaijan, in order to exclude the transfer or surrender to the Court of 'persons', be they officials, employees, or nationals, including private contractors, absent the express consent of the party to which they are affiliated.[161]

Furthermore, under Article 16 ICC Statute, a renewable annual deferral of the ICC jurisdiction might be ensured through a resolution of the UN Security Council, acting under Chapter VII of the Charter. This rule has given rise to an important but controversial practice.[162] Security Council Resolution 1422 (2002), relating to the renewal of the mandate of peacekeeping operations in Bosnia-Herzegovina, suspended the exercise of the jurisdiction of the Court over 'officials' or '*personnel*' from states non-parties to the ICC Statute contributing to peace-keeping operations.[163] More radically, Security Council Resolution 1497 (2003), relating to the setting up of a multinational force to support a ceasefire in Liberia, envisaged the exclusive jurisdiction by a state non-party to the ICC Statute contributing to multinational forces over its 'officials' or '*personnel*'.[164] The same approach was adopted in Resolution 1593 (2005), through which the Security Council referred the situation in Darfur to the ICC.[165] The language of these resolutions is broad and could easily include private contractors, which would therefore be granted temporary immunity from the jurisdiction of the Court.[166] In this respect, it is also interesting to notice that the United States insisted on and obtained the withdrawal of any reference to the ICC from Resolution 1502 (2003), which intended to condemn the terrorist attack to the UN headquarters in Baghdad and aimed to ensure protection of peacekeepers and other UN personnel in Iraq.[167]

V. Concluding Remarks

The question as to what extent PMSC personnel can be considered liable for war crimes in spite of their unclear formal status under IHL must be answered differently from the viewpoint of substantive law and procedural law.

With regard to substantive law, PMSC employees can be considered liable regardless of their qualification as civilians or combatants, when a de facto link exists between their conduct and an armed conflict. In fact, the GCs and the ICC

---

[161] See the text of bilateral agreements signed by the United States under Art 98 ICC Statute, <http://www.ll.georgetown.edu/guides/article_98.cfm#countries>, accessed on 15 June 2010.

[162] For a critical exposition of the practice of the UN Security Council under Art 16 ICC Statute see White and Cryer (n 42 above), 466 ff.

[163] SC Res 1422 (2002), para 1 (emphasis added), renewed by Res 1497/2003, <http://www.un.org>, accessed on 20 August 2010.

[164] SC Res 1497 (2003), para 7 (emphasis added), <http://www.un.org>, accessed on 20 August 2010. It must nevertheless be noticed that such an exclusive approach might clash with the principle of compulsory universal jurisdiction.

[165] SC Res 1593 (2005), para 6, <http://www.un.org>, accessed on 20 August 2010.

[166] For a detailed analyis of the resolutions adopted by the Security Council under Art 16 ICC Statute in relation to the situation of private contractors see Ch 22 by Frulli in this volume, at section III.A.

[167] See Coalition for the International Criminal Court, Press Release, 'United States Postpones Adoption of UN Resolution to Protect Humanitarian Personnel over ICC Stance', 25 August 2003, <http://www.iccnow.org/documents/08.25.03USDelaysRes.pdf>, accessed on 15 June 2010.

Statute provide for the accountability of 'natural persons', without referring to any subjective qualification. This regulation, traditionally applying only to international armed conflicts, is gradually extending also to non-international armed conflicts. For the moment, due to the blurring of the distinction between international and non-international armed conflicts, it is not always easy to identify clearly the applicable regulation. Within this frame, the doctrine of command responsibility might concern private contractors insofar as internal superior–subordinate relationships can be de facto envisaged for PMSCs. As to the defence of superior orders, it might be likely to be invoked by private contractors specifically for sophisticated war crimes, such as the improper use of a flag of truce, in the case of unlawful orders received on the battlefield.

With respect to procedural law, prosecution of grave breaches of the GCs should be ensured by national jurisdictions. Under specific circumstances, the ICC enjoys the competence to try war crimes. Thus, theoretically IHL provides the means necessary to prosecute war crimes committed by PMSC personnel. In practice, several criminal prosecutions against private contractors have recently been undertaken, which shows increased sensitivity towards their accountability; nevertheless, to date, the system has not proved particularly efficient. In fact, despite various reported incidents, long after the breakthrough of the private military and security industry on the international scene no private contractor has yet been sentenced for committing war crimes. Besides legitimate procedural obstacles, resulting in particular from the principle of due process, inefficiency depends on the fact that either national implementing regulation lags behind IHL or effective national and international trials might be hindered by extrajudicial factors.

22

Immunity for Private Military Contractors: Legal Hurdles or Political Snags?

Micaela Frulli

I. Introductory Remarks

Private military and security companies (PMSCs) and their employees may, in principle, be subject to the law and jurisdiction of the country in which they are operating. Unlike states and their officials, they are not beneficiaries of customary international rules establishing immunity from jurisdiction. However, as recent practice clearly shows, PMSCs and private individual contractors have been granted different kinds of immunities covering the performance of very sensitive tasks on foreign soil.

In the first place, these subjects have been granted immunity from the jurisdiction of the host state in which they are deployed by special legislative measures or by means of specific agreements between the state that hired them (the hiring/contracting state, which in many cases is their state of nationality, for example, their home state) and the host state.[1] In addition, they have also been granted immunity from the jurisdiction of the hiring/contracting state by virtue of their contract and, more frequently, by the application of judicially created doctrines such as the 'political-question doctrine' or other statutory defences applied, for instance, by national courts in the United States and have, so far, escaped criminal and civil liability in cases of alleged human rights violations.

It is therefore important, as a first step, to set the legal framework by briefly recalling the most important customary and conventional international rules on immunity of state officials and international personnel from jurisdiction, to ascertain whether they may also cover private contractors performing certain functions on behalf of a state. An attempt at critically appraising the application of immunity rules to private contractors against the more general background of jurisdictional immunities accruing to states and their officials is appropriate with a view to see which are the most convincing arguments to overcome the relevant hurdles—at

---

[1] In this chapter 'host state' is the state where the PMSCs are operating, the 'hiring state' is the state which contracted the private employees, and the 'home state' is the state of nationality of the contractors.

least the legal ones—and provide for accountability of PMSCs and their employees. In addition, making reference to the existing case law (which is predominantly US case law), it is important to determine whether immunity was actually granted by virtue of immunity rules or whether a factual immunity stemmed from legal loopholes and lack of political will to proceed against private contractors.

II. Setting the Legal Framework: Different Kinds of Immunities Based on a Variety of Legal Grounds

A. Functional Immunity from Jurisdiction Accruing to State Officials and International Personnel

Under customary international law, state officials are entitled to different types of immunity from foreign jurisdiction. In general, two kinds of immunities are recognized: the so-called functional immunity (or *ratione materiae*), and personal immunities (or *ratione personae*), but the latter kind of immunity is not relevant for PMSCs' personnel.[2]

According to the prevailing position among international lawyers, functional immunity from the jurisdiction of foreign states covers activities performed by every state official in the exercise of his/her official functions and it survives the end of office. The underlying rationale is that official activities are performed by state organs on behalf of their state and, in principle, must be attributed to the state itself.[3] From this perspective, the ultimate *raison d'être* of functional immunity is the protection of the sovereign equality of states enshrined in the Latin dictum '*par in parem non habet iudicium*'.[4] Functional immunity is also granted to international personnel, in particular to the officials of international organizations: for example, this kind of immunity is provided for by the Convention on the Privileges and Immunities of the United Nations of 1946.[5] The rule on functional immunity of UN personnel is considered to have acquired the status of customary international

---

[2] Personal immunities only accrue to a few categories of State organs by virtue of the special relevance of their official positions (diplomatic agents, heads of states, heads of governments and ministers of foreign affairs) and cover every act performed by those who are entitled to enjoy this type of immunity, but they last only until the state organs concerned remain in office. Personal immunities include inviolability, that is to say immunity from arrest and detention, absolute immunity from criminal jurisdiction and immunity from civil jurisdiction (with very limited exceptions).

[3] See H Kelsen, *Principles of International Law* (1952), 235. See also G Dahm, *Völkerrecht* (1958), I, 225, 237, 303, 325; M Bothe, 'Die strafrechliche Immunität fremder Staatsorgane' (1971) 31 ZaÖRV 246 ff; M Akerhust, 'Jurisdiction in International Law', (1972–1973) 46 BYIL 241 ff; H Fox, *The Law of State Immunity* (2002).

[4] See also the position taken by the ICTY Appeals Chamber in *Blaškić*, IT-95-14-AR 108 bis, Appeals Chamber (29 October 1997), paras 41–2.

[5] Convention on the Privileges and Immunities of the United Nations, (New York, 13 February 1946, 1 UNTS 15). The Convention gives a comprehensive picture of privileges and immunities granted to international personnel, and many subsequent agreements are modelled on its provisions. As to functional immunity from jurisdiction, according to Art V, s 18(a) officials of the UN 'shall be immune from legal process in respect of words spoken or written and all acts performed by them in their official capacity'.

law and similar rules may be found in many other conventions and headquarters agreements amongst states and other international organizations.[6]

Most authors affirm that functional immunity accrues, as a general rule, to every organ acting on behalf of a state, the only exception being the commission of serious international crimes entailing individual criminal liability.[7] However, according to other scholars, the scope of functional immunity is more limited: functional immunity from jurisdiction is enjoyed only by some categories of state officials on different legal grounds (customary or conventional)[8] and covers solely activities performed within the limits of the mandate specifically bestowed on these organs.[9] One of the most relevant examples supporting the latter hypothesis is that of consular agents. According to Article 43 of the UN Convention on Consular Immunities, consular agents enjoy immunity from the jurisdiction of the receiving state only for 'acts performed in the exercise of consular functions'.[10] As a consequence, acts allegedly performed in an official capacity, but falling outside the consular functions as defined in the convention itself, are not covered by functional immunity. A number of cases before national courts confirm such a restrictive interpretation of the rule.[11]

The same approach has been adopted by national judges in cases concerning different categories of state officials: several courts have refused to recognize the functional immunity of state organs who exceeded the limits of their mandate, thus acting ultra vires and abusing the powers conferred on them.[12] This trend in the case law of various states seems very important in light of the fact that it developed in the domain of civil jurisdiction; that is to say, in cases where the rules on state immunity might also apply and where there is—according to the prevailing opinion—a substantial overlap between the immunity of the state and the immunity of its officials. In these cases, judges have considered the question of the functional immunity of the state organ as separate from the issue of state immunity and they have decided whether or not to grant functional immunity to the single state official not only taking into account the public or private nature of the activity

---

[6] See eg Art 22 of the Agreement between the Government of the French Republic and the United Nations Educational, Scientific and Cultural Organization regarding the Headquarters of UNESCO and the Privileges and Immunities of the Organization on French Territory (Paris, 1954, entered into force in 1955, available on the website of UNESCO at <http://unesdoc.unesco.org/images/0012/001255/125590e.pdf>, accessed on 20 August 2010).

[7] See eg A Cassese, *International Criminal Law*, 2nd edn (2008), 302 ff.

[8] See extensively P De Sena, *Diritto Internazionale e Immunità Funzionale degli Organi Statali* (1996).

[9] See M Frulli, *Immunità e Crimini Internazionali* (2007), 23–60.

[10] Art 43 (1): 'Consular officers and consular employees shall not be amenable to the jurisdiction of the judicial or administrative authorities of the receiving State in respect of acts performed in the exercise of consular functions.'

[11] See eg the decision of the Supreme Court of New Zealand in *L v The Crown*, repr in (1985) 68 ILR, 175; see also the decision of the Genoa Tribunal (6 May 1970) and of the Italian Court of Cassation (29 February 1972) in *Rissmann* (repr respectively in (1971) 54 Rivista di diritto internazionale 702 and in (1976) 2 IYIL 339). For more detailed references to relevant case law see Frulli, *Immunità e Crimini Internazionali* (n 9).

[12] See eg *Chiudian v The Philippine National Bank and Daza*, 912 F 2d 1095 (9th Circ 1990), part 4, para IV. See also *Jaffe v Miller*, 13 OR (3d) 745, (1993) OJ no 1377. For a comment on these and other relevant cases see Frulli, *Immunità e crimini internazionali* (n 9 above), 50–5.

concerned (as if the respondent was the state itself) but also evaluating whether the state official involved acted within the limits of his/her mandate.

From this viewpoint, it may be contended that the main reason underlying the bestowal of functional immunity on state officials is no longer (or has never been) the protection of state sovereignty, but the necessity of ensuring the accomplishment of activities that are crucial for peaceful and stable relations amongst states, that is to say a 'functional necessity' rationale. There is also no doubt that a restrictive interpretation of the rules on functional immunity would be more consonant with the values protected by the same rules.

The same is true, a fortiori, for functional immunity accruing to officials of international organizations. In this respect, it is interesting to quote the example of the Agreement on the Status of the North Atlantic Treaty Organization, National Representatives and International Staff, which establishes that NATO officials, on missions for the Organization 'shall be immune from legal process in respect of words spoken or written and of acts done by them in their official capacity and *within the limits of their authority*',[13] thus confirming the strictly functional rationale underlying this kind of immunity.

As jurisdictional immunities granted to private contractors may be classed mainly as functional ones, the perspective described above may prove useful for discussing the rationale, content, and application of rules conferring some form of functional immunity to private contractors.

B. Immunities Granted on the Basis of SOFAs to State Officials and Contracted Personnel

State officials, both military and civilian, may enjoy immunity from the host state's criminal, civil, and administrative jurisdiction in cases where an international agreement is concluded. For our purposes it is important to take into account status of forces agreements (SOFAs), which have become one of the most relevant international sources of immunity for private contractors. In fact, at least in recent practice, PMSC employees are often included under the scope of these agreements and must be treated accordingly.

SOFAs may be concluded on a temporary or on a permanent basis to regulate standing military (and in some cases civilian) presence on the soil of a foreign country. They may be negotiated on a bilateral basis or in a multilateral context, such as when regulating the presence of visiting forces standing abroad in the framework of an international organization; this is the case, for instance, of NATO forces stationed in the territory of foreign states.

SOFAs are based on the assumption that the presence of foreign personnel is in the interest of the host state as well as of the sending state. Each SOFA is unique because this kind of agreement is negotiated on a case-by-case basis (except those

---

[13] Emphasis added, see Art XVIII, letter a) of the Agreement on the Status of the North Atlantic Treaty Organization, National Representatives and International Staff (Ottawa, 1951), available on the website of NATO at <http://www.nato.int> (Official Texts Section), accessed on 20 August 2010.

concluded in a multilateral negotiation), but some of their common features may be inferred from current practice. These agreements establish the legal framework pursuant to which armed forces operate within a foreign country and deal with all issues that are necessary to 'ordinary' affairs, such as wearing of uniforms, carrying of weapons, income and sales taxes, labour claims, and so on. More importantly here, SOFAs regulate the exercise of criminal and civil jurisdiction over personnel of the sending state, thus granting some form of immunity from the host state jurisdiction to personnel stationed abroad (more and more frequently including private contractors).[14]

Actually, on careful reading of a variety of SOFAs, the word 'immunity' does not usually appear. Most often other terms are used, making reference to the division of jurisdictional competences between the host and the sending states. Most SOFAs recognize the right of the host government to exercise 'primary jurisdiction'; this means that the host state exercises jurisdiction in all cases in which foreign personnel violate the laws of the host state, with two exceptions generally applying only in criminal cases: according to most agreements, the sending state has primary jurisdiction when the offence is committed by a national of the sending state against another national of the sending state ('*inter se*' cases), and when the offence is committed by the nationals of the sending state in the performance of official duty. Hence, a 'functional' principle—recalling that underlying immunity granted to state officials in different contexts—is used here to grant primacy of jurisdiction to the sending state, and not immunity in a technical sense, although the application of these rules generally entails a de facto immunity from the jurisdiction of the host state for certain categories of offences.[15]

In any case, SOFAs generally provide for concurrent jurisdiction between the sending and the receiving states, apart from exceptional cases where jurisdiction of the host state has been virtually excluded.[16] One relevant example of SOFAs

---

[14] It interesting to note eg that when the Agreement between the Parties to the North Atlantic Treaty regarding the Status of their Forces (London 1951, hereinafter NATO SOFA, available on the website of NATO at <www.nato.int> (Official Texts Section), accessed on 20 August 2010) was signed, there was no mention of contractors as a category of personnel. In some cases, however, supplemental agreements have been concluded (eg between Italy and the United States) and acknowledged the category of 'technical representatives', which include private contractors acting under the supervision of the US Department of Defense who perform work in Italy on more than a temporary basis. This agreement is based on the model of the supplementary agreement to the NATO SOFA regulating the presence of allied forces stationed permanently in the Federal Republic of Germany, signed in 1973, which included contractors. On the agreement between Italy and the United States, see M McCormick, 'Accrediting DoD Contract Technical Representatives in Italy without Reinventing the Wheel', Defense AT&L (March–April 2005), <http://www.per.hqusareur.army.mil/CPD/Doc-Per/Italy/Defense%20AT&L%20Magazine%20Mar-Apr%2005.pdf>, accessed on 20 August 2010.

[15] See eg Art VII of the NATO SOFA, which establishes in detail the sharing of jurisdiction between the sending and the receiving state. Some form of functional immunity stems from Art VII, § 3, letter a).

[16] See eg the controversial extension of wide immunities to all US military and civilian personnel contained in the SOFA concluded between the United States and East Timor in 2002, see Art 1: 'United States military and civilian personnel of the United States Department of Defense who may be present in the Democratic Republic of Timor-Leste in connection with humanitarian and civic assistance, ship visits, military training and exercises and other agreed activities shall be accorded a status equivalent to that accorded to the administrative and technical staff of the Embassy of the United

conferring exclusive criminal jurisdiction to the sending state over its nationals (including over private contractors)[17] is the SOFA concluded between the US and Afghanistan.[18]

The agreements concluded between the UN, the contributing states, and the host state with respect to the deployment of UN peacekeeping operations (PKOs) are also called SOFAs.[19] These agreements usually provide for immunity from legal process in respect of words spoken and acts performed by them in their official capacity for all members of the UN peacekeeping operation,[20] including locally recruited personnel. As to military members of the military component of PKOs, they are subject to the exclusive criminal jurisdiction of the contributing state over any crime committed in the host country—that is to say they enjoy absolute immunity from local criminal courts.[21]

Functional immunity may be granted to private contractors as well, since it is not unusual for the United Nations or other international organizations to hire independent contractors to provide personnel for PKOs or other international

---

States of America under the Vienna Convention on Diplomatic Relations of 18 April 1961' (<http://www.etan.org/news/2002a/11sofa.htm#Full%20text>, accessed on 20 August 2010). Members of the administrative and technical staff of embassies enjoy full immunity from criminal jurisdiction of the receiving state, unless they are nationals of the same state. See Art 37, § 2, of the Convention on Diplomatic Relations (Vienna, 18 April 1961).

[17] With respect to PMSC employees it seems important to underline that immunity may be granted on a contractual basis, but as long as an international agreement exists, the latter must be considered as the proper legal basis for granting immunity from jurisdiction.

[18] Agreement regarding the Status of United States Military and Civilian Personnel of the US Department of Defense Present in Afghanistan in Connection with Cooperative Efforts in Response to Terrorism, Humanitarian and Civic Assistance, Military Training and Exercises and Other Activities (effected by exchange of notes at Kabul September 26 and 12 December 2002 and 28 May 2003, entered into force 28 May 2003. Excerpts from an unofficial copy are available at <http://caaflog.blogspot.com/2008/02/is-that-afghan-sofa-i-see.html>, accessed on 20 August 2010). According to the SOFA: 'The Government of Afghanistan recognizes the particular importance of disciplinary control by United States military authorities over United States personnel and, therefore, Afghanistan authorizes the United States Government to exercise criminal jurisdiction over United States personnel. The Government of Afghanistan and the Government of the United States of America confirm that such personnel may not be surrendered to, or otherwise transferred to, the custody of an international tribunal or any other entity or state without the express consent of the Government of the United States.' 'Personnel' is elsewhere defined as including contractors. See also, for another example, Agreement on Military Exchanges and Visits between the Government of the United States of America and the Government of Mongolia (Ulaan Baator, 26 June 1996), <http://www.state.gov/documents/organization/105696.pdf>, accessed on 20 August 2010.

[19] See the Model Status-of-Forces Agreement for Peacekeeping Operations, UN Doc A/45/594 (9 October 1990).

[20] Art 46: 'All members of the United Nations peace-keeping operation including locally recruited personnel shall be immune from legal process in respect of words spoken or written and all acts performed by them in an official capacity. Such immunity shall continue even after they cease to be members of or employed by the United Nations peace-keeping operation and after the expiration of the other provisions of the present agreement.'

[21] Art 47, b): 'Military members of the military component of the United Nations peace-keeping operation shall be subject to the exclusive jurisdiction of their respective participating States in respect of any criminal offences which may be committed by them in the Host country.'

missions carried out by states under a UN Security Council authorization.[22] This was explicitly the case, for instance, where functional immunity from legal process was granted by UNMIK to KFOR (the NATO Security Force) contractors in Kosovo.[23]

C. Immunities Granted Pursuant to Internal Laws or Judicially Created Doctrines

In addition, immunity of private contractors may be granted ad hoc through the adoption of domestic legislative acts, such as the well-known Coalition Provisional Authority (CPA) Order 17 which conferred immunity to private contractors operating in Iraq from June 2004 to December 2008.[24] Since it was not officially repealed by Iraqi authorities after the transfer of authority it remained in force until 31 December 2008, the date of expiry of the United Nations mandate for the US-led multinational force.

An overview of existing case law suggests that immunities are also invoked by PMSCs and their employees exercising certain functions on foreign soil on behalf of a state on the grounds of internal doctrines crafted by national courts, such as the political-question doctrine, or of other statutory defences, which have actually been applied by US courts to render cases involving private military companies and their employees non-justiciable.[25] In these cases, the lack of accountability of private contractors does not always derive from the application of an immunity rule, but from the decision to give priority to policy considerations.

In other cases, on a more specific level, an internal law has triggered the conclusion of bilateral agreements granting immunity, inter alia, to private contractors from the jurisdiction of the International Criminal Court (ICC). Obviously, the

---

[22] It is important to stress that some PMSCs took the view that the 1946 Convention, in particular Art VI devoted to Experts on Mission for the United Nations, cover contractors hired by a state but sent on a mission within the framework of a UN-authorized operation. This view is not to be shared because it clearly extends privileges and immunities beyond the limits agreed by the states: see DP Oulton and AF Lehman, 'Deployment of US Military, Civilian and Contractor Personnel to Potentially War Hazardous Areas from a Legal Perspective', The DISAM (Defense Institute of Security and Assistance Management) Journal (Summer 2001), 15 ff.

[23] On the Status, Privileges and Immunities of KFOR and UNMIK and their Personnel in Kosovo, UNMIK Reg no 2000/47 (18 August 2000), in particular the following sections: 'Section 4. Contractors. 4.1 UNMIK and KFOR contractors, their employees and sub-contractors shall not be subject to local laws or regulations in matters relating to the terms and conditions of their contracts. UNMIK and KFOR contractors other than local contractors shall not be subject to local laws or regulations in respect of licensing and registration of employees, business and corporations. 4.2 KFOR contractors, their employees and sub-contractors shall be immune from legal process within Kosovo in respect of acts performed by them within their official activities pursuant to the terms and conditions of a contract between them and KFOR.' See also Section 5, Duration of Immunity from Legal Process; and Section 6, Waiver of Immunity.

[24] Coalition Provisional Authority Order 17 (Revised), Status of The Coalition Provisional Authority, MNF–Iraq, Certain Missions and Personnel in Iraq, 27 June 2004, § 4 (3), <http://www.iraqcoalition.org/regulations/20040627_CPAORD_17_Status_of_Coalition_Rev_with_Annex_A.pdf>, accessed on 20 August 2010.

[25] See K Huskey and S Sullivan, 'The American Way: Private Military Contractors and US Law after 9/11', Priv-War, National Report Series, 02/08 (December 2008), <www.priv-war.eu>, accessed on 20 August 2010.

competence of the ICC only operates in cases where serious international crimes have been committed and according to the jurisdictional criteria set forth by its statute.[26] As is well-known, however, the United States tried to oust ICC jurisdiction over their nationals employed on foreign soil (not only state officials, but also US citizens, including private contractors) and adopted the American Service-Members' Protection Act (ASPA)[27] which allows US nationals to participate in peacekeeping or multinational forces only on the condition that they are immune from ICC jurisdiction either through UN Security Council's resolutions or through bilateral agreements signed with the host state.[28] These latter agreements have been concluded with a large number of states (102 states, both parties and non-parties to the ICC Statute)[29] and oblige states not to surrender or transfer to the ICC US officials, employees, personnel, or nationals who are present on the territory of the other party without the express consent of the United States. Regretfully they were concluded, at least with a certain number of states, under the threat of the stemming of US military aid, according to the ASPA, and they jeopardized the possibility of the ICC proceeding against private contractors hired by the United States and employed in 'contingency operations' for the performance of very sensitive tasks (currently an elevated number) when they are suspected of having committed serious international crimes.

III. Immunity of PMSCs Employees from Criminal Jurisdiction

Usually, a crime committed by an individual falls under the laws of the nation where the crime has been committed. However, PMSCs operate with increasing frequency in conflict or crisis situations where special rules are applicable: as recalled above, the immunity of contractors from the criminal jurisdiction of the host state may result from internal law or from a specific agreement (usually a SOFA) between the host state and the hiring/contracting state of the contractors.

The most oft-cited example concerning immunity from jurisdiction of the host state granted to private contractors through a domestic act is the provision inserted in Iraqi CPA Order 17, issued by Paul Bremner in June 2004,[30] just before the

---

[26] As it is well known, the ICC can generally exercise jurisdiction only in cases where the accused is a national of a State party, the alleged crime took place on the territory of a state party, or a situation is referred to the court by the United Nations Security Council.

[27] See 2002 Supplemental Appropriations Act for Further Recovery from and Response to Terrorist Attacks on the United States, §§ 2001–15 (to be codified at 22 USC §§ 7421–32). ASPA was passed as Title II of this legislation and became law on 2 August 2002. The text is available at <http://www.state.gov/t/pm/rls/othr/misc/23425.htm>, accessed on 20 August 2010. The ASPA refers to 'covered United States persons; covered allied persons; and individuals who were covered United States persons or covered allied persons'.

[28] For a detailed analysis see section III below.

[29] For agreements in force as of 1 January 2009 see <http://www.state.gov/documents/treaties/122730.pdf>, accessed on 20 August 2010. For a full account of bilateral agreement see the website of the American Coalition for an International Criminal Court, at <http://www.amicc.org/usinfo/administration_policy_BIAs.html>, accessed on 20 August 2010.

[30] See n 24 above.

transfer of authority to the Iraqi Interim Government. Reference has often been made to this order as granting blanket immunity to contractors operating in Iraq. However, the relevant provisions clearly state that immunity from Iraqi legal process only concerns acts performed by contractors 'pursuant to the terms and conditions of a contract or any sub-contract thereto'.[31]

This wording recalls the formula that is habitually used to describe functional immunity of state officials or international organizations' personnel performing their functions on foreign soil. As we have seen, these organs enjoy immunity from the jurisdiction of the receiving states for acts done in the exercise of their official functions. The interpretation of this rule should be, as argued above, a stringent one: functional immunity should only cover acts performed in the regular course of duty and not when exceeding their powers. A fortiori, this line of reasoning should apply to immunity from legal process provided for private contractors, since the aim of any such provision cannot be the protection of the contractors themselves.

As a consequence, any violation of the laws of the host state apparently committed under an official or contractual cloak, but actually in abuse of authority, shall not be covered by jurisdictional immunity. More specifically, any serious breach of the laws of war, such as the killing of civilians that took place in the notorious incident of 2007 involving Blackwater, should automatically be excluded from the range of acts capable of being performed pursuant to a contract. Other violations amounting to international crimes, such as those occurring at Abu Ghraib, that may be considered acts of torture or inhuman or degrading treatment should not be covered at all by provisions granting jurisdictional immunity to contractors. As recalled above, it is unanimously held that functional immunity can never be invoked as a justification by those individuals suspected of international crimes, not even by high-ranking state officials.[32] It would indeed be contrary to current international law to construe any functional immunity rule (be it provided by an agreement or a fortiori by contract) as impeding the exercise of jurisdiction and thus the prosecution of those suspected of one of these crimes. It must be added that both the Geneva Conventions of 1949 and the 1984 United Nations Convention against Torture—that are very widely ratified—establish an obligation on states to prosecute those responsible for war crimes and torture respectively, through the *aut dedere aut iudicare* mechanism. State parties to these treaties (and arguably even states that are not parties to these agreements since it may be contended that the obligation to prosecute these crimes has acquired a customary nature) may not elude the respect of such an obligation by applying uncertain immunity rules or by construing existing immunity rules in a very broad manner in order to avoid proceeding against those suspected of such serious crimes. In addition, it is worth recalling that both treaties also provide for the universal-jurisdiction principle, which means that third states can also

---

[31] If we compare this section with s 2 of the same Order, relating to immunity from Iraqi legal process granted to MNF, CPA, and Foreign Liaison Mission Personnel and International Consultants, we can see that in the latter case one could speak of blanket immunity. In any case, s 5 of the Order concerns the waiver of immunity, which may be expressly granted, in writing, by the relevant sending state.

[32] See Cassese (n 7 above), 302 ff.

prosecute those suspected of these crimes without having to take into account any functional immunity.

In simple terms, in cases where some form of immunity is provided for contractors, it would be advisable, as a minimum standard, to expressly restate that it does not cover international crimes and to clearly establish which state will exercise criminal jurisdiction over the most serious offences. For lesser offences, a strict interpretation of provisions such as that inserted in CPA Order 17 described above allows for the exercise of criminal jurisdiction of the host government if relevant acts are performed outside the scope of contract/mandate, as happened in certain cases to state officials brought to trial before foreign courts for acts performed outside the scope of their official mandate.[33]

The problem could be—and has been—the readiness of the local state to exercise jurisdiction over these cases. To continue with the same example, only very recently has Iraq tried to repeal the immunity granted to private contractors by CPA Order 17 (namely after the notorious Blackwater scandal) and, as a result of this stance, the SOFA concluded at the end of 2008—that is to say, at the expiry of the United Nations mandate—between the United States and Iraq, which entered into force in January 2009, grants no immunity from Iraqi law to private contractors.[34] The new SOFA specifically grants Iraq 'the primary right to exercise jurisdiction over United States contractors and United States contractor employees'. This means that, beginning in 2009, private contractors hired by the United States and operating in Iraq will be subject to the Iraqi Penal Code and the Iraqi Law on Criminal Proceedings, even when they are performing acts pursuant to the terms of their US government contracts.[35] This recent example sets a very important precedent, taking into account the fact that there is still a considerable presence of PMSCs in Iraq. Hopefully, it will give a strong impetus towards the emergence of a culture of accountability of PMSCs and their employees and could be the first step in inverting a trend that, up to now, has been a trend of averting criminal prosecutions.

---

[33] See section II.A above.

[34] Agreement between the United States of America and the Republic of Iraq on the Withdrawal of United States Forces from Iraq and the Organization of their Activities during their Temporary Presence in Iraq (Baghdad, 17 November 2008). The text of the agreement in its official English version may be found at <http://graphics8.nytimes.com/packages/pdf/world/20081119_SOFA_FINAL_AGREED_TEXT.pdf>, accessed on 20 August 2010.

[35] However, according to the National Report on the UK (N White and K Alexander, 'The Regulatory Context of Private Military and Security Services in the UK', Priv-War, National Report Series, 01/09 (January 2009), <www.priv-war.eu>, accessed on 20 August 2010) it is not clear whether UK contractors in Iraq still benefit from immunity. On the website of the UK Ministry of Defence it is reported that: 'UK forces have the sound legal basis they need to complete their tasks in Iraq in 2009. A Resolution providing the necessary jurisdictional immunities was passed by the Iraqi Council of Representatives and then ratified by the Iraqi Presidency Council on 27 December 2008. A Memorandum of Understanding has since been signed by the Iraqi and British governments, which formally invites UK forces to complete their specific tasks.' This information appears on a facts-sheet available at the following page in the website of the UK Ministry of Defence: <http://www.mod.uk/DefenceInternet/FactSheets/OperationsInIraqAboutTheUkMissionInIraq.htm>, accessed on 20 August 2010. To the best of this author's knowledge, no official version of the Memorandum was publicly released. Therefore it is not clear which kind of immunities accrues to UK officials and contractors operating in Iraq.

458 *Criminal and Civil Liability of Private Military and Security Companies*

In a more general perspective, in cases where a SOFA provides that jurisdiction be shared between the host state and the hiring/contracting state of the contractor and gives primacy to the latter, the hiring/contracting state should exercise criminal jurisdiction, because from a legal point of view there should be no room for the application of any immunity rule based on internal law. In particular, it would be advisable to insert—even in SOFAs—a specific provision dealing with the most serious international crimes and defining the state that is bound to exercise criminal jurisdiction in that respect.

However, in a large number of cases, immunity of contractors from the criminal jurisdiction of the hiring/contracting states seems not to depend on the application of immunity rules but, for a large part, on the combination of a lack of applicable rules to exercise criminal jurisdiction and a lack of political will to proceed. As many of the accurate national reports prepared for the Priv-War project clearly point out, until now most states have only regulated certain aspects of the functioning of PMSCs and their employees and there are still large gaps in existing domestic legislation. The same is true as far as international regulations are concerned.

The US example is again very useful to see how difficult it may prove to fill the legal void in order to permit the exercise of criminal jurisdiction over private military contractors. Traditionally, private contractors could not be brought to trial under the military justice system because the Supreme Court has held that civilians may not be subject to courts-martial absent a declaration of war by Congress.[36] More recently, Congress passed new legislation amending the Uniform Code of Military Justice (UCMJ) in order to place military contractors 'serving with or accompanying an armed force in the field' under the jurisdiction of military courts, not only during a time of declared war but also during 'contingency operations'.[37] The guidelines for the application of the new legislation were only issued in March 2008.[38] The first and only prosecution of a private contractor under the UCMJ ended with a guilty plea in June 2008. An Iraqi working as an interpreter for a contractor supporting the US military in Iraq was sentenced to five months of confinement after pleading guilty in connection with the stabbing of a co-worker.[39]

---

[36] See *Kinsella v United States ex rel Singleton*, 361 US 234, 248 (1960) (prohibiting military jurisdiction over civilian dependents in time of peace, regardless of whether the offense was capital or noncapital); *Grisham v Hagan*, 361 US 278, 280 (1960) (holding civilian employees committing capital offences not amenable to military jurisdiction); *McElroy v United States ex rel Guagliardo*, 361 US 281, 283–4 (1960) (expanding Grisham to include non-capital offenses); *Reid v Covert*, 354 US 1, 40–1 (1957) (holding that civilians in time of peace are not triable by courts-martial for capital offenses). Case law as quoted by L Dickinson, 'Accountability of Private Security Contractors under International and Domestic Law', ASIL Insight 11(31) (2007).

[37] Section 552 of the John Warner National Defense Authorization Act for Fiscal Year 2007 (Pub L 109–364) (FY07 NDAA), amending 10 USC § 802(a)(10).

[38] See Secretary of Defense Memorandum, UCMJ Jurisdiction Over DoD Civilian Employees, DoD Contractor Personnel,and Other Persons Serving with or Accompanying the Armed Forces Overseas during Declared War and in Contingency Operations (10 March, 2008), <http://www.dtic.mil/whs/directives/corres/pdf/sec080310ucmj.pdf>, accessed on 20 August 2010.

[39] Alaa 'Alex' Mohammad Ali, the contractor employed by the United States, was a dual citizen of Iraq and Canada, but the Iraqi and Canadian governments declined to prosecute. The Department of

Federal criminal prosecution may be exercised over private contractors under the Military Extraterritorial Jurisdiction Act (MEJA),[40] which was enacted precisely because private actors could not be brought in front of courts-martial. Under MEJA, US contractors working for the Department of Defense (DoD) or in support of a DoD mission may be charged for offences committed abroad. However, many contractors are employed by other departments[41] or by the CIA, for example, and some commentators argued that the employment of private contractors through departments and agencies other than the DoD was a deliberate option to take advantage of this legal loophole.[42] The US Congress considered expanding the statute to cover contractors working under any federal agency in, or in close proximity to, an area where the armed forces are conducting a contingency operation, but the MEJA Expansion and Enforcement Act of 2007 adopted by the House of Representatives in October 2007 has not become law.[43] Until now there has only been one case of a conviction of a private contractor under MEJA.[44]

Another attempt at closing legal loopholes was made with the US PATRIOT Act of 2001, which expanded the United States' Special Maritime and Territorial jurisdiction (SMTJ) to include US-operated facilities overseas.[45] Through this extension a federal district court convicted a private contractor—hired by the CIA—accused of mistreatment of detainees in a US base in Afghanistan.[46] In cases of serious international crimes, prosecution could be possible, but not likely, under the War Crimes Act of 1996[47] or the Extraterritorial Torture Statute.[48]

Justice also declined to prosecute the case, probably because the individual was not a US citizen. The new UCMJ provision, however, allowed the US military to plug the hole in the system by ensuring that the perpetrator was held accountable. For a report on the case see <http://militarytimes.com/forum/showthread.php?t=1565608>, accessed on 20 August 2010.

[40] Military Extraterritorial Jurisdiction Act of 2000 (MEJA), 18 USC §§ 3261–7 (2004 Supp)
[41] Eg notorious Blackwater contractors were hired by the US Department of State.
[42] See C Bassiouni, 'The Institutionalization of Torture under the Bush Administration', (2006) 37 Case Western Reserve Journal of International Law (2006), 389–425, esp 411–16.
[43] See Dickinson (n 36 above).
[44] Ahmed Hasan Khan, was prosecuted and convicted to 41 months' imprisonment under the *Military Extraterritorial Jurisdiction Act* (MEJA) for possession of child pornography while he was employed as a civilian contractor in the Abu Ghraib prison in Baghdad. United States Attorney's Office, Eastern District of Virginia, 'Military Contractor Sentenced for Possession of Child Pornography in Baghdad', 25 May 2007, <http://www.usdoj.gov/usao/vae/Pressreleases/05-MayPDFArchive/07/20070525khannr.html>, accessed on 20 August 2010.
[45] See USA PATRIOT Act of 2001 § 804 (amending 18 USC § 7 to include 'the premises of United States diplomatic, consular, military or other United States Government missions or entities in foreign States' as well as 'residences in foreign States . . . used for purposes of those missions or entities or used by United States personnel assigned to those missions or entities').
[46] See Department of Justice, United State Attorney, Eastern District of North Carolina, 'David Passaro Sentenced to 100 Months Imprisonment: First American Civilian Convicted of Detainee Abuse during the Wars in Iraq and Afghanistan', 13 February 2007, available at the FBI website, <http://charlotte.fbi.gov/dojpressrel/2007/ce021307.htm>, accessed on 20 August 2010.
[47] 18 USC para 2441 (2000 and Supp II 2002).
[48] 18 USC paras 2340 and 2340A. However, at present only one case has been brought under this statute, the one against Charles 'Chuckie' Taylor, Jr (the son of Liberia's former dictator), for torture committed in Liberia. See Human Rights Watch brief, <http://www.hrw.org/sites/default/files/related_material/HRB_Chuckie_Taylor.pdf>, accessed on 20 August 2010.

Analogous problems (hopefully less so with international crimes than with 'ordinary' crimes) may arise with other states for want of adequate legislation. To give another example, a problem may arise if contractors hired by a certain state are nationals of another state: according to the National Report of the Netherlands, Dutch criminal law applies abroad only to Dutch nationals.[49] In other cases, it may even be more difficult to apply criminal law abroad. As recalled in the UK Report, English criminal law is largely based on the territorial principle meaning that the offence must be committed in the United Kingdom. Only a small number of offences when committed abroad can be prosecuted based on the British nationality of the offender. A British soldier (but apparently not a private contractor hired by the United Kingdom) is subject to military law while abroad and this may include a large element of English criminal law.[50]

In sum, it does not seem that the scant practice of prosecuting private contractors—even those suspected of having committed serious violations of international law—may be imputed to immunity rules. On the contrary, existing rules do not provide any blanket immunity and if correctly interpreted they cannot shield PMSCs' employees from their criminal liability. Immunity rules may of course be improved and crafted in more detail; however it seems that in the first place, attempts should be made at clarifying the rules concerning the exercise of criminal jurisdiction in every situation where PMSCs are widely employed on foreign soil.

A. Private contractors and the International Criminal Court

Unfortunately, recent practice shows that private contractors might be involved in grave human rights violations amounting to serious international crimes and giving rise to individual criminal liability on the international level. As a matter of fact, in cases where an individual private contractor is suspected having committed an international crime under the jurisdiction of the ICC and where the conditions of admissibility apply,[51] the person can be indicted by the ICC. It must be recalled that, according to the ICC Statute, neither international nor internal law rules granting any form of immunity may be invoked before the Court itself.[52]

However, as briefly mentioned above, the United States has adopted specific legislation to bar the jurisdiction of the ICC over its nationals, which triggered both the adoption of UN Security Council resolutions and the conclusion of bilateral immunity agreements amongst the United States and a large number of states with a view to excluding the possibility of surrender of US citizens to the ICC. These developments may lead to a practical impossibility for the ICC of prosecuting individual contractors hired by several states and therefore to a de facto immunity

---

[49] G Den Dekker, 'The Regulatory Context of Private Military and Security Services in the Netherlands', Priv-War, National Report Series, 01/08 (December 2008), <www.priv-war.eu>, accessed on 20 August 2010.
[50] See White and Alexander (n 35 above).
[51] See Art 17 ICC Statute, on issues of admissibility.
[52] See Art 27 ICC Statute, on irrelevance of official capacity.

of private contractors hired by these states or nationals of these states from the jurisdiction of the ICC.[53]

Following the enactment of the ASPA, the US delegation managed to secure the adoption of Resolutions 1422, 1487, 1497, and 1593 by the UN Security Council. Resolution 1422 suspended the exercise of the ICC jurisdiction over officials and personnel from states contributing to a UN peacekeeping operation, but not parties to the ICC Statute, for a 12-month period. The adoption of this resolution was a compromise reached under the US threat of exercising its veto power in order to block the creation or renewal of peacekeeping operations. Resolution 1422, severely criticized by many authors, suspended the ICC jurisdiction but interestingly did not prevent UN member states from prosecuting crimes under the Rome Statute before their national tribunals.[54] As a consequence, whereas a private contractor hired by a state and employed within the framework of a peacekeeping operation, could commit a crime under the ICC jurisdiction in the territory of a state party to the statute, it is the latter state which can and should exercise its criminal jurisdiction. However, even if the territorial state proves unwilling or unable to prosecute the suspects—that is to say if the existence of the conditions of admissibility is verified—the ICC cannot step in and exercise its jurisdiction. The deferral established by Resolution 1422 was renewed for another 12-month period by Resolution 1487.[55]

With Resolutions 1497 and 1593, adopted at a later stage, the Security Council moved a step further. Resolution 1497, which authorized the deployment of a multinational force in Liberia, provided that 'current or former officials or personnel from a contributing state, which is not a party to the Rome Statute of the International Criminal Court, shall be subject to the exclusive jurisdiction of that contributing state for all alleged acts or omissions arising out of or related to the Multinational Force or United Nations stabilization force in Liberia, unless such exclusive jurisdiction has been expressly waived by that contributing state'.[56] It is

---

[53] For a general overview of the US policy aiming at barring the ICC jurisdiction see M Roscini, 'The Efforts to Limit the International Criminal Court's Jurisdiction over Nationals of Non-party States: A Comparative Study', (2006) 5 *The Law and Practice of International Courts and Tribunals* 495–527.

[54] See Res 1422 of 12 July 2002, § 1 of which provided that 'consistent with the provisions of Art 16 of the Rome Statute, . . . the ICC, if a case arises involving current or former officials or personnel from a contributing State not a party to the Rome Statute over acts or omissions relating to a United Nations established or authorized operation, shall for a twelve-month period starting 1 July 2002 not commence or proceed with investigation or prosecution of any such case unless the Security Council decides otherwise.' The deferral of investigations and prosecutions could be renewed for further 12 months under the same conditions on 1 July of each year 'as long as may be necessary' (§ 2). See C Stahn, 'The Ambiguities of Security Council Resolution 1422 (2002)', (2003) 14 EJIL (2003) 85–104.

[55] A proposal for a resolution providing for a further renewal was withdrawn by the United States in June 2004, because of the opposition of the majority of the members of the Security Council and probably due to the Abu Ghraib scandal in Iraq.

[56] Adopted 1 August 2003, para 7. According to some scholars, the term 'exclusive' jurisdiction should be interpreted as meaning 'primary' jurisdiction, according to the *aut dedere aut iudicare* rule. In other words, if the state of nationality of a suspect requests extradition, the *forum deprehensionis* state must meet the request, but if the state of nationality does not investigate or prosecute the case, the jurisdiction of any other competent state would be restored. See S Zappalà, 'Are Some Peacekeepers Better than Others? UN Security Council Res 1497 (2003) and the ICC', (2003) 1 *Journal of International Criminal Justice* 1 676.

interesting to note that this provision concerns both UN peacekeepers and officials or private contractors acting within the framework of a multinational force conducted by states upon a UN Security Council authorization. A similar provision was inserted in paragraph 6 of Resolution 1593 by which the UN Security Council referred the situation of Sudan to the ICC Prosecutor. Through the adoption of these provisions, the Security Council has prevented not only the exercise of the ICC jurisdiction over nationals of states not parties to the statute, but it has also barred the exercise of jurisdiction by both the territorial state and the national state of the victims, not to mention any state which would be entitled to exercise universal jurisdiction. In the latter scenario, had a contractor hired by the United States or by another state not party to the ICC Statute committed a serious international crime in Liberia, for instance, he or she might be tried only by its national courts, with all the limits and pitfalls already shown above. It is worth emphasizing that these resolutions do not provide for the obligation of the national state to investigate or prosecute, thus leaving room for a de facto absolute immunity of officials or employees, including private contractors (and even simple citizens in the case of Resolution 1593) of states not parties to the ICC Statute that are suspected of having committed one of the most serious international crimes.[57]

It has been argued by several commentators that the UN Security Council acted ultra vires, and misinterpreted the powers conferred upon it by Article 16 ICC Statute. Unfortunately, however, many states approved the resolutions thus allowing some room for impunity for state officials and private contractors belonging to states not parties to the ICC Statute and permitting the creation of an inequitable difference amongst peacekeepers. The difference, it is worth underlining, does not relate exclusively to serious crimes falling under the jurisdiction of the ICC. With respect to these crimes, the provisions mentioned here have the effect of barring the ICC jurisdiction, but Resolutions 1497 and 1593 provided for the exclusive jurisdiction of the contributing state with regard to 'ordinary' offences as well, which renders those employed by some states in specific situations almost 'untouchable'.

The resolutions mentioned here prevent ICC jurisdiction only with regard to alleged crimes committed in the framework of or related to UN peacekeeping operations or multinational operations conducted by the states on UN Security Council authorization. At the same time, the US launched a campaign for the conclusion of bilateral immunity agreements (BIAs) to exempt its nationals from ICC jurisdiction in all kinds of different situations. These agreements have been concluded, as mentioned above, both with states parties and non-parties to the ICC Statute. BIAs concluded with states non-parties establish, on a reciprocal basis, the obligation not to surrender or by any means or with any purpose transfer each other's nationals, officials, employees or military personnel to the ICC or to any other entity or third country, or to expel them to a third country, for the purpose of surrender to or transfer to the ICC without the express consent of the state of

---

[57] See the comments of G Gaja, 'Immunità Squilibrate dalla Giurisdizione Penale in Relazione all'intervento Armato in Liberia' (2003) 86 Rivista di diritto internazionale 763.

nationality or of employ. The prohibition to surrender or transfer 'by any means' and 'for any purpose' is very broad and means that it would be impossible to transfer even a person who must be heard as a witness to the ICC. BIAs concluded with states parties to the ICC do not lay down reciprocal obligations but asymmetrically set forth the obligation for these states not to surrender or transfer to the ICC 'Current or former Government officials, employees (including contractors), or military personnel or nationals' belonging to the United States.

According to the US administration, these agreements meet the requirements of Article 98(2) ICC Statute, which provides that the ICC 'may not proceed with a request for surrender which would require the requested state to act inconsistently with its obligations under international agreements pursuant to which the consent of a sending state is required to surrender a person of that state to the Court, unless the Court can first obtain the cooperation of the sending state for the giving of consent for the surrender'. The preparatory works of the ICC Statute, however, indicate that the provision was crafted in order to cover SOFAs or extradition agreements concluded by states parties to the ICC Statute.[58] Both these kinds of agreements may be reconciled with the ICC Statute because—as already shown above—they do not provide for immunities, but they aim at establishing a division of jurisdictional competence between the sending and receiving states.[59] In any case, as we have suggested above, states parties to SOFAs may not elude their obligation to prosecute the most serious international crimes which may never be covered by any kind of functional immunity.

On the contrary, BIAs are too far from these characteristics to be considered as consistent with the ICC Statute. Their aim is to exempt from ICC jurisdiction not only those covered by SOFAs (which in many cases are only military and civilian state officials), but every single citizen, the nationality link being sufficient. What is even more troubling is the fact that BIAs do not provide, as already pointed out with respect to Resolutions 1497 and 1593, for the obligation to prosecute those suspected of international crimes, and that in most of these agreements the United States 'has expressed its intention to investigate and to prosecute *where appropriate* acts within the jurisdiction of the International Criminal Court alleged to have been committed by its officials, employees, military personnel, or other nationals', leaving it at the discretion of the United States to evaluate whether it is appropriate or not to investigate and prosecute, thus creating an unacceptable risk of impunity. In conclusion, the ICC

---

[58] See D Scheffer, 'Article 98(2) of the Rome Statute: America's Original Intent', (2005) 3 Journal of International Criminal Justice 333–53; J Crawford, P Sands, and R Wilde, *In the Matter of the Statute of the International Criminal Court and in the Matter of Bilateral Agreements Sought by the United States Under Article 98(2) of the Statute, Joint Opinion for the Lawyers Committee on Human Rights*, 18, <http://www.iccnow.org/documents/SandsCrawfordBIA14June03.pdf>, accessed on 20 August 2010; Roscini (n 53 above), 513. Some authors suppose that SOFAs are not covered by Art 98 (2) ICC Statute, because they do not provide for the consent by the sending state before the surrender of an accused, but they only define the jurisdiction of the sending and receiving states: see D Fleck, 'Are Foreign Military Personnel Exempt from International Criminal Jurisdiction under Status of Force Agreements?' (2003) 1 Journal of International Criminal Justice 656.

[59] S Wirth, 'Immunities, Related Problems, and Article 98 of the Rome Statute' (2001) 12 *Criminal Law Forum* 455–6.

would not restrain itself when faced with one of these agreements and, should it be the case, it would most likely interpret them as not covered by Article 98.[60] With respect to states parties to the ICC Statute that entered a BIA, they shall incur international responsibility for violating Part 9 of the statute, which contains the obligations for states parties to cooperate with the ICC, including obligations relating to the transfer or surrender of suspects to the ICC.[61] States parties that signed a BIA shall incur international responsibility for assuming conflicting treaty obligations, in violation of the Vienna Convention on the Law of Treaties.[62]

The problem remains, in any case, with states not parties to the ICC Statute that stipulated BIAs with the United States and thus created a high risk of impunity for the most serious crimes allegedly committed by their nationals and by US nationals respectively. Unfortunately, contractors are definitely covered by these agreements and it may prove very difficult to prosecute them even for the most serious international offenses committed in the territory of one of the states who signed a BIA.

IV. Immunity from Civil Jurisdiction

Immunity of private contractors from the civil jurisdiction of the host state may be granted on the same basis as when examining immunity from criminal jurisdiction: it may be provided through a domestic act or, more often, through a SOFA between the host and the sending state, or hiring/contracting state in the case of private contractors. In any case, as we have already seen, in these contexts immunity is not absolute (and actually is usually granted on a more limited basis than immunity from criminal jurisdiction) and in cases where some form of functional immunity is granted, it is based on the assumption that the sending/hiring state shall exercise jurisdiction over its officials or employees where appropriate. Consequently, it often occurs that immunity—based on different legal grounds—is not invoked before a foreign civil tribunal but in front of the courts of the hiring/contracting state of the private individual contractor or PMSCs that are sued for an international or a tort law violation.

Actually, it is worth underlining that, given the fact that PMSCs' employees do not usually have adequate economic resources to compensate the victims, civil proceedings are brought directly against the PMSCs themselves. In fact, in a

---

[60] According to a recent article, the ICC could decide to interpret those BIAs in a restrictive manner as applying only to state officials and not to private actors. Consequently, private contractors would be vulnerable to the ICC jurisdiction. See A Bolletino, 'Crimes against humanity in Colombia: The International Criminal Court's Jurisdiction over the May 2003 attack on the Betoyes Guahibo Indigenous Reserve and Colombian Accountability' (2008) 9 Human Rights Review 508–11. However, this interpretation seems inconsistent with rules on treaty interpretation that do not allow much room for interpretation where the expressions used are literally clear and BIAs do expressly include contractors. It is therefore more appropriate to argue for their inconsistency with the ICC Statute.

[61] H van der Wilt, 'Bilateral Agreements between the United States and States Parties to the Rome Statute: Are They Compatible with the Object and Purpose of the Statute?' (2005) 18 Leiden Journal of International Law 100.

[62] See Roscini (n 53 above), 518.

number of countries—chiefly common law countries—foreign plaintiffs are allowed to bring claims against private actors before the tribunals of the contractors' hiring state, even for tort violations committed abroad.[63] However, in many cases, PMSCs have tried to invoke some form of immunity based on the justification that they acted on behalf of the government that hired them in performing functions that are shielded from sovereign immunity.

Available case law that deals with the issue is again essentially US-based, where claims may be brought mainly under the Alien Tort Statute (ATCA), the Federal Tort Claims Act (FTCA), and the Torture Victims Protection Act (TVPA). Reference can be made to the Priv-War National Report on the USA, which gives an excellent, detailed overview of existing case law pointing also at the 'immunity arguments' presented therein.[64]

Following the line of reasoning developed above, it is interesting to note that the FTCA provides a remedy for torts committed by the government or government employees who are acting within the scope of their employment.[65] A functional rationale may be found here as well, even if framed in a different perspective, since the government must respond when state officials (or individual contractors) acted within their mandate and within their scope of employment. Actually, the FTCA does not expressly address the liability of contractors acting on behalf of the federal government, but it has served as a basis for civil suits against PMSCs. On the other hand, it is also interesting to note that the FTCA provides for two limitations to the immunity's waiver: claims resulting from exercise of the 'discretionary function'[66] and claims 'arising out of the combatant activities of the military or naval forces, or the Coast Guard, during time of war'.[67] Both exceptions have been invoked as justifications for applying immunity to PMSCs and their employees and to pre-empt tort actions against them.[68]

It is not the purpose of this chapter to analyse existing case law in depth. Reference is duly made to the Priv-War National Report on the United States and to relevant legal literature that has carefully examined existing case law and called attention to the immunity exceptions raised therein. It seems instead

---

[63] In these countries, civil proceedings may have some advantages also as a means of redress for criminal offences since they require a less rigorous standard of proof and liability may be easier to prove. However, civil proceedings conducted in a totally separate manner from criminal proceedings may not occur in civil law countries where most systems provide for the adhesion system (*constitution de partie civil*), meaning that the civil proceedings for the claim of damages have to be connected to the criminal proceedings.

[64] See Huskey and Sullivan (n 25 above).

[65] 28 USC, paras 2674 and 2979 (2005).

[66] 28 USC para 2680(a) (2005).

[67] 28 USC para 2680(j) (2005).

[68] The so-called 'government-contractor defence' (GCD) has been judicially crafted and exists as a part of federal common law: its aim is to protect a contractor from tort liability when the latter acted specifically pursuant to government instructions. The doctrine has been applied since 1940, in different forms by different district courts, however its scope was specified by the US Supreme Court in 1988 in *Boyle v United Technologies*, 487 US 500, 512 (1988). Part of its rationale drives from the same concerns underlying the political question doctrine, which as well has been invoked to grant immunity to private contractors. Attempts have been made at expanding the scope of the GCD linking it to the 'combat-activities exception'.

particularly interesting, for our objectives, to focus on the political-question doctrine and on the arguments it raises because the very same arguments could be exported to other systems and successfully employed in order to hinder accountability of PMSCs and their employees.

A. The Political-question Doctrine and Other 'Governmental' Defences

The non-justiciability of 'political acts' or 'governmental acts' is recognized in many legal systems, albeit with some differences in denomination and meaning. Actually, the doctrine was first elaborated in France (*actes de gouvernement*) and later exported to the United Kingdom, under the 'royal prerogative' label, as well as to the US, where it is commonly referred to as the 'political-question doctrine'.[69] By way of this self-restraint doctrine, courts may refuse to consider claims concerning actions taken by their government in circumstances where the exercise of governmental discretion is deemed essential to protect constitutional or political interests.

This doctrine has been invoked in many civil suits against PMSCs and their employees in the United States—hence the choice of labelling this jurisdictional hurdle as the political-question doctrine—and has been accepted by some courts and rejected by others. One of the most recent decisions is the Order issued by a District Court of Virginia which denied CACI's motion to dismiss claims brought by foreign detainees for multiple violations of US and international law, including acts of torture. The Court rejected, at this stage, a variety of justifications brought by CACI, including non-justiciability by virtue of the political-question doctrine. After having carefully reviewed the elements of the Baker test,[70] the Court reversed the 'embarrassment argument' and held that the claims of the plaintiffs 'pose no political question and are therefore justiciable'.[71]

---

[69] For a general overview, see E Lauterpacht (ed), *Individual Rights and the State in Foreign Affairs. An International Compendium* (1977). With regard to the United States, see TM Franck, *Political Questions/Judicial Answers, Does the Rule of Law apply to Foreign Affairs?* (1992); N Mourtada-Sabbah and B Cain (eds), *The Political Question Doctrine and the Supreme Court of the United States* (2007).

[70] The Baker test has been elaborated by the US Supreme Court in *Baker v Carr* and thereafter applied as a standard test in cases where the political question is raised by the defendants. These are the elements of the Baker test: (1) a textually demonstrable constitutional commitment of the issue to a coordinate political department; or (2) a lack of judicially discoverable and manageable standards for resolving it; or (3) the impossibility of deciding without an initial policy determination of a kind clearly for non judicial discretion; or (4) the impossibility of a court's undertaking independent resolution without expressing lack of the respect due coordinate branches of government; or (5) an unusual need for unquestioning adherence to a political decision already made; or (6) the potentiality of embarrassment from multifarious pronouncements by various departments on one question.

[71] *Al Shimari v CACI*, District Court of Virginia, Order denying in part motion to dismiss by CACI, 18 March 2009, <http://ccrjustice.org/ourcases/current-cases/al-shimari-v-caci-et-al>, accessed on 20 August 2010. *Al-Shimari v CACI* is a federal lawsuit brought by four Iraqi torture victims against private US-based contractor, CACI International Inc, and CACI Premier Technology Inc. It asserts that CACI participated directly and through a conspiracy in torture and other illegal conduct while it was providing interrogation services at the notorious Abu Ghraib prison in Iraq. After the decision CACI filed a motion for appeal: see the website of the Center for Constitutional Rights at <http://ccrjustice.org/ourcases/current-cases/al-shimari-v-caci-et-al>, accessed on 20 August 2010.

A short review of existing US case law indicates that a crucial question in evaluating whether the political-question doctrine is applicable to civilian contractors on the battlefield is the specific contractor's relationship to the military and the actual military operation in question. It has been made clear by several courts that the political-question doctrine will not bar judicial scrutiny only because there is some kind of nexus between the contractor and the military. More specifically, the court for the Eleventh Circuit ruling in *McMahon v Presidential Airways* asserted that in order to apply the political-question doctrine to private contractors and their companies, the nexus between the contractor and the military must be linked to 'core military decisions, including [military] communication, training, and drill procedures'.[72] In other cases, such as *Ibrahim v Titan*, the judges made clear that an action for damages against private contractors does not interfere with the conduct of foreign policy or the disposition of military power.[73]

In cases where this argument was accepted, the judges relied on the fact that affirming jurisdiction would have required the court to pronounce on questions to be left to the legislative or executive branches, 'or that the court would have to substitute its judgment for that of the military, and as such would have evinced a lack of respect for the political branches'.[74] It is interesting to note that the US government did not make its position clear with respect to the application of the political-question doctrine to cases involving PMSCs and made no statement of interest in any of these cases. More specifically, it is not clear whether a private actor, albeit performing functions by virtue of a contract with a government, may properly raise a political question to bar judicial examination of his actions.

From a more general perspective, one may not exclude the possibility that non-justiciability arguments could emerge with respect to acts performed by contractors before the courts of different countries, as in the United States.

However, it seems that several factors should limit the application of the political-question doctrine, particularly in cases involving human rights violations. In the first place, the fact that the defendant is not a state actor has not generally been considered as a bar to the application of the doctrine by US Courts, but it could well represent an obstacle before other national courts. In principle, a correct application of this doctrine should be limited to cases potentially involving scrutiny of pivotal political decisions such as, for example, the decision to participate in a military operation on foreign territory, which pertains to the main state organs, namely Parliament or the Executive. It cannot be applied, by default, to all activities undertaken in the framework of a military operation or in combat or war-like situations, but it should be called in question only when the judiciary runs the risk of intruding in crucial political decisions. A fortiori, it should not be applied to acts performed by private actors whose activities cannot automatically be ascribed to the

---

[72] *McMahon v Presidential Airways, Inc*, 502 F3d 1331, 1365 (11th Cir 2007). See see J Addicott, 'Political Question Doctrine and Civil liability for Contracting Companies on the Battlefield' (2008) 28 *The Review of Litigation* 343–64.
[73] *Ibrahim v Titan*, US District Court, District of Columbia, 12 August 2005, 391 F Supp 2d 10.
[74] See Huskey and Sullivan (n 25 above).

state only because they have been performed in a war-like situation, for instance, and excluded as such by judicial review.

In particular, it seems very difficult to raise this argument at least with respect to specific situations or specific incidents, such as those that involved US contractors in Abu Ghraib or in the Blackwater incident. If specific acts, even if undertaken in application of governmental directives (which in the case of torture would be very difficult to demonstrate), violate international humanitarian law or infringe fundamental human rights of individuals, they should be subject to judicial review both in cases where they were performed by state actors and, all the more so, in cases where they were carried out by private contractors. As was proposed by a resolution of the *Institut de Droit International*, adopted in 1993,[75] national courts 'when called upon to adjudicate a question related to the exercise of executive power, should not decline competence on the basis of the political nature of the question if such exercise of power is subject to a rule of international law' (Article 2).[76]

In conclusion, it may be suggested that the judiciary ought to be wary of applying the political-question doctrine to claims based on international law violations, which in many cases result as well in the violation of fundamental rights guaranteed by the constitutions of various countries. Usually, military operations are not constitutionally left to the discretion of political or military organs and national courts should have the possibility of reviewing government actions and determine whether they are consistent with customary international rules or, on the contrary, they have exceeded the authority granted to the executive branch by the constitution or through the constitution.

A survey of US case law, as accurately undertaken in the US Report previously mentioned, indicates that a number of other statutory or common law defences have been raised by private contractors to avoid judicial scrutiny. As already anticipated, it is not the purpose of this chapter to dwell in depth on these specific cases; however, it is interesting to make the following remarks.

In the first place, many of these defences were crafted to protect the exercise of governmental functions and should be narrowly interpreted: the guiding criterion

---

[75] Resolution adopted on 7 September 1993, see (1994) 65 (II) Annuaire de l'Institut de droit international 318–23. The question was addressed in more general terms also in the *Preliminary Report* (Rapporteur, Prof Conforti). In reviewing the political-question doctrine as an obstacle to the application of international law by national judges, the Rapporteur underlined the strong need to establish the conditions under which the exception of the political-question doctrine should be rejected. He indicated precisely two conditions: (i) the existence of a precise and complete international obligation and (ii) the non-existence of an authorization on the part of the legislative branch. See the *Preliminary Report* in (1993) 65 (I) Annuaire de l'Institut de droit international 327–39. In other words, national judges should not be prevented from reviewing their government's action when there is an international obligation to be respected and when the Parliament did not expressly authorize the government's conduct.

[76] The suggestion relating to the role of national judges is reflected in the *Final Report* accompanying the text adopted. It is worth quoting a passage which perfectly suits the matter discussed here: 'It was held in the Commission that if it is "absurd" for a court to stop a war, this does not mean that a court cannot grant compensation...we think one can reasonably propose that the courts have the power to decide on compensation for damages caused to private persons as a consequence of a war or of a use of force contrary to international law.' For the *Final Report*, see 65 (II) Annuaire (n 75 above), 437.

should be that immunity may be applied to the behaviour of a state official or a private contractor only if he/she acted within the scope of his/her mandate. In addition, to strike a proper balance between the protection of political and military interests and the right of victims to seek compensation and redress, PMSCs and their employees should be 'immunized' only when the judiciary risks interfering in crucial political and military decisions and only in cases where private actors acted under complete supervision and control of the military or of a governmental department. In particular, it seems that there should be no bar on judicial review when international human rights violations occur, since the governments themselves are bound to ensure respect for these rules and should foster a culture of accountability for their officials and for private contractors they have decided to hire.

V. Concluding Remarks

The very rare number of criminal convictions of private contractors and the difficulties encountered in adjudicating civil claims against PMSCs and their employees show that there is still much to do in order to render these subjects accountable. Under close examination, it seems that difficulties stem largely from political obstacles. In any case, it is beyond doubt that the impossibility of proceeding against private contractors does not depend predominantly on the application of immunity rules. It derives instead from the combination of a lack of applicable rules for exercising jurisdiction, deference to the executive by judges, and a lack of political will to make proceedings happen. The decision delivered on 11 September 2009 by the Court of Appeals of the District of Columbia in *Saleh v Titan* is a clear example of the prevailing tendency to 'immunize' private contractors through the application of the various available exceptions and controversial arguments.[77]

It is thus timely and appropriate that states fill existing gaps in their domestic legislation and more closely regulate the exercise of criminal and civil jurisdiction with respects to acts committed by PMSCs and their employees sent on field missions to perform very delicate functions on behalf of states and international organizations.

---

[77] On 11 September 2009, in a 2-1 decision, a panel of the Court of Appeals for the District of Columbia affirmed the dismissal of all claims against Titan/L-3, and, reversing to the district court, also dismissed all claims against CACI. Majority (Judges Silberman and Kavanaugh) find claimants' state law claims are preempted under either conflict preemption ('combatant activities exception') or field preemption ('battlefield preemption'). The majority also found that claims of torture and war crimes based on the Alien Tort Statute could not be brought against contractors because they are not 'state actors'. The decision is available on the website of the Center for Constitutional Rights (CCR): <http://www.ccrjustice.org/files/Titan_Decision%209%2011%2009.pdf>, accessed on 20 August 2010. On 26 April 2010, the CCR filed a Petition for Writ of Certiorari in the US Supreme Court on behalf of the claimants and against government contractors CACI International and Titan Corporation.

23
Liability in Tort of Private Military and Security Companies: Jurisdictional Issues and Applicable Law

Andrea Atteritano

I. Introduction

Private military and security companies (PMSCs) are legal entities, subject to legal obligations and rights. The breach of obligations by PMSCs gives rise to liability. This chapter deals with tort liability only, addressing issues regarding both the competent jurisdiction and the applicable law.

Traditionally, national jurisdictions used to be strictly territorial. Technological development and an increase in business exchanges have brought the phenomenon of transnational litigation to the attention of the courts, and the concept of territorial jurisdiction has been shown to have limits. In order to establish jurisdiction, national legal systems shifted their attention from the presence of people and goods on their territory, to the interest of the state in the control and adjudication of disputes of social, commercial, economic, or even political importance. In doing so, legislators and courts have been freed from international ties. Of course, states should avoid forms of exorbitant jurisdiction, but only insofar as the concept of comity requires.[1]

The unilateral delimitation of national jurisdictions has given rise to an absence of a rational division of jurisdictional powers between the courts of different countries. Consequently, there are risks of the practice of forum shopping on the one hand, and a denial of justice on the other hand. An effective solution to these problems may be offered only through recourse to international instruments. States and the European Union (EU) have adopted conventions and regulations on the matter, but their application to the somewhat recent phenomenon of the PMSC is in doubt and the question must therefore be addressed.

Once the jurisdictional rules applicable to the PMSC's tort liability have been analysed, the question of the applicable law will be evaluated. As is evident, PMSCs operate through their employees; therefore their liability for unlawful acts of the

---

[1] See JR Paul, 'Comity in International Law' (1991) 32 Harv Int'l L J 1.

employee may be established only if the applicable rules provide for it. Thus, the issue of the applicable law is a question of great importance, most particularly because it is according to this law that the judge concerned ascertains the existence of an unlawful fact, the quantity of the damages, and the burden of proof.

II. The Jurisdictional Criterion of the Defendant's Domicile

PMSCs are national legal entities and therefore subject to law. Accordingly, the competent jurisdiction is selected on the basis of either ad hoc legislation or ordinary norms of private international law.

In several national legal systems, as well as in the EU, ad hoc legislation regarding PMSCs is still lacking.[2] Only a few states have enacted specific rules on PMSCs,[3] but the competent-jurisdiction issue has never been specifically addressed. Consequently, the general rules of private international law and the ordinary criteria of connection between the dispute and the state's forum must be applied. Among these is the criterion of the place in which the defendant has domicile.

Such a criterion has been adopted within the European Community, first through the conclusion of the Brussels Convention of 1968, and then with the enactment of EC Regulation 44/2001.[4] It has also been accepted under the Lugano Convention of 1988 (and confirmed by the Lugano Convention of 2007),[5] and it is in force in several national legal orders—the Dutch,[6] Spanish,[7]

---

[2] Eg Italy: A Atteritano, *Italian Legislation on Private Military and Security Companies*, Priv-War National Report Series no 02/09, January 2009; Germany: R Everts, *Regulation of Private Military, Security and Surveillance Services in Germany*, Priv-War National Report Series no 16/09, June 2009; France: V Capdevielle, *The Regulation of Private Military and Security Services in France*, Priv-War National Report Series no 11/09, May 2009; Russia: S Novika, *The Regulatory Context of Private Military and Security Services in the Russian Federation*, Priv-War National Report Series no 14/09, May 2009; also Estonia: I Miluna, *The Regulatory Context of Private Military and Security Services in Estonia*, Priv-War National Report Series no 15/09, June 2009, all the above available at <http://www.priv-war.eu>, accessed on 14 June 2010.

[3] US: Huskey-Sullivan, *The American Way: Private military contractors and US Law after 9/11*, Priv-War National Report Series no 02/08 April 2009; UK: Alexander-White, *The Regulatory Context of Private Military and Security Services in the UK*, Priv-War National Report Series no 01/09, June 2009, both available at <http://www.priv-war.eu>, accessed on 14 June 2010.

[4] See Art 2 of both the Brussels Convention on Jurisdiction and the Enforcement of Judgments in Civil and Commercial Matters and the Council Regulation (EC) No 44/2001 of 22 December 2000 on jurisdiction and the recognition and enforcement of judgments in civil and commercial matters.

[5] See Art 2 of the Convention on jurisdiction and the recognition and enforcement of judgments in civil and commercial matters (Lugano, 30 October 2007). The Lugano Convention of 2007, which is a revision of the Lugano Convention of 1998, has entered into force on 1 January, 2010 and has replaced the Lugano Convention of 1988. The jurisdictional rule of the defendant's domicile was provided for also by Art 2 of the Lugano Convention of 1988. Regarding the differences between the two Lugano Conventions, see F Pocar, *Explanatory Report*, OJ EU, 23 December 2009, C-319/1.

[6] Art 2 cpc. See G den Dekker, *The Regulatory Context of Private Military and Security Services in the Netherlands*, Priv-War National Report Series no 01/08 December 2008, <http://www.priv-war.eu>, accessed on 14 June 2010.

[7] Art 22 of the Organic Law of Judicial Power. On this issue see J Abrisketa and F Gómez, *The Regulatory Context of Private Military and Security Services in Spain*, Priv-War National Report Series no 05/09, February 2008, <http://www.priv-war.eu>, accessed on 14 June 2010.

Portuguese,[8] Finnish,[9] and Italian,[10] to quote some examples—but also in many common law countries. One may refer to the US legal system where, in order to seize jurisdiction over the case, the judge must have a specific or a general jurisdiction over the defendant. The test that comes to mind is the one introduced in the *International Shoe Co v State of Washington* case,[11] according to which the national jurisdiction depends on the subsistence of qualified links between the forum and the defendant. In particular, if the defendant carries on a constant and systematic activity in the territory of the forum concerned, the court will have a general jurisdiction over the defendant. But when the defendant's activity in the forum is not continuous, a specific jurisdiction will exist if the claimant's cause of action is based on the activity carried out by the defendant within the forum. Thus, the jurisdiction ratione personae of the US courts can be either specific or general, on the basis of the links existing between the defendant, the forum, and the facts of the dispute: whilst specific jurisdiction is grounded on qualified connections—since links and cause of action are strictly related—general jurisdiction implies the subsistence of connections which are simply continuous and systematic, and not necessarily related to the controversy. Therefore, if the defendant's domicile is in US territory, US courts may recognize their general jurisdiction over the case without difficulty.

In view of the above, PMSCs may be sued before the court of the country where they are incorporated, or where they have their central administration and/or principal place of business. Thus, the claimant's choice on the competent forum is, at least in principle, quite ample. Notwithstanding this, in many cases, the system of justice of the state of incorporation may not be readily available, above all if it has been chosen for fiscal purposes. And if the central administration or principal place of business of the PMSC involved coincide with the place of incorporation, the claimant must look for another forum. Furthermore, corporations are often part of a group of corporations and consequently it may become a complex matter to identify the competent court, because of the problem of the attribution of the unlawful fact to the holding company or to the affiliates. In such cases, the criterion of the defendant's domicile, which is a general jurisdiction criterion, may be replaced by other specific jurisdiction criteria.

III. The Specific Jurisdiction Criteria Related to Liability in Tort: Is EC Regulation 44/2001 Applicable to PMSCs?

Regarding liability in tort, the specific jurisdiction criterion usually available is that of the place where the unlawful fact occurred or that of the place where the

---

[8] Art 65 cpc. See M Kowalski, *The Regulatory of Private Security Services in Portugal*, Priv-War National Report Series no 09/09, May 2009, <http://www.priv-war.eu>, accessed on 14 June 2010.
[9] See K Creutz, *Private Military and Security Services in the Regulatory Context of Finland*, Priv-War National Report Series No 08/09, February 2009, <http://www.priv-war.eu>, accessed on 14 June 2010.
[10] Art 3 L 218/1995.
[11] 326 US 310 (S Ct, 1945).

damages arose. We are dealing here with two different jurisdictional criteria since, although the two places usually coincide (eg in case of extrajudicial killings), sometimes the damage can subsequently arise in a different place. A case in point is—for instance—the unlawful use of white phosphorus during a war, which may cause serious damages to health; the injured party could suffer damages many years after the commission of the unlawful fact, and when the territory of that state has already been abandoned. It therefore becomes important to find a rational combination of these two criteria, a combination that depends on the choices of the national legislators or on the choices expressed in the relevant international instruments.

According to Article 5(3) EC Regulation 44/2001, the national jurisdiction subsists if the 'harmful event occurred' in the territory of the state. Such expression could be interpreted as related to either the place where the unlawful fact occurred or the place where the damage arose. Nevertheless, the jurisprudence of the European Court of Justice (ECJ) has clarified the dual nature of the criterion introduced by the aforementioned regulation: the plaintiff can opt for either the court of the state where the unlawful fact occurred, or that of the state where the damage arose. This trend initially emerged with reference to the Brussels Convention of 1968 (see *Fiona Shevill v Presse Alliance SA*;[12] *Antonio Marinari v Lloyds Bank plc and Zubaidi Trading Co*[13]), and it has been subsequently confirmed in the application of the EC regulation.[14] The Lugano Convention has been interpreted accordingly; in particular, the German Supreme Court[15] expressly stated that the criteria of *locus damni* and *locus commissi delciti* are jointly available under the Convention.

However, both the EC regulation and the Lugano Conventions are applicable only in civil and commercial matters, and it is not clear whether the activity of the PMSCs falls within their scope of application.

In the *Lechouritou* case,[16] the ECJ excluded the *acta jure imperii* of the state from the field of application of the Brussels Convention of 1968 (the same may be said as

---

[12] ECJ, 7 March 1995, Case C-68/93, *Fiona Shevill and ors v Presse Alliance SA* [1995] ECR I-00415. See it also in *Revue critique de droit international privé*, 1996, 495 ff, with comment of P Lagarde. The case was about a claim for damages for libel by newspapers.

[13] ECJ 19 September 1995, Case C-364/93, *Marinari v Lloyds Bank plc and Zubaidi Trading Co* [1995] ECR I-02719. The Court has specified that 'the term "place where the harmful event occurred"...does not, on a proper interpretation, cover the place where the victim claims to have suffered financial damage following upon initial damage arising and suffered by him in another Contracting State'.

[14] ECJ, 4 April 2008, Case C189/08, *Zuid-Chemie v Philippo's Mineralenfabriek*, <http://www.eur-lex.eu>, accessed on 14 June 2010.

[15] Federal Supreme Court of Germany, 6 November 2007 (no 2008/23). See Report no 11 on the application of the Lugano Convention, <http://www.bj.admin.ch>, accessed on 14 June 2010.

[16] ECJ 15 September 2007, Case C-292/05, *Lechouritou and ors v Dimosio tis Omospondiakis Dimokratias tis Germanias* [2007] ECR I-01519. The main proceedings regard the massacre of civilians perpetrated by Nazi soldiers on 13 December 1943. 676 inhabitants of the municipality of Kalavrita (Greece) were victims of the massacre. In 1995, an action for compensation was brought before the Polimeles Protodikio Kalavriton (Court of First Instance, Kalavrita) against the Federal Republic of Germany. In 1998 the Court of First Instance dismissed the case, since Germany was immune from the Greek jurisdiction. In 1999 the decision was appealed before the Court of Appeals of Patras

regards EC Regulation 44/2001). In particular, according to the Court, proceedings taken by 'natural persons in a Contracting State against another Contracting State for compensation in respect of the loss or damage suffered by the successors of the victims of acts perpetrated by armed forces in the course of warfare in the territory of the first State' cannot be considered to fall within 'civil matters'. The Court justified this ruling by citing its previous judgments, according to which some judicial actions or judgments are excluded from the field of application of the Brussels Convention, because of the nature of the elements that characterize the legal relationship between the parties or because of the subject matter of the claim. Since in *Lechouritou* the claim for damages arose from operations conducted by German armed forces, which are a typical expression of state sovereignty (being unilaterally decided and tied up with the state foreign policies), the ECJ excluded the applicability of the Brussels Convention of 1968 to the case. In other words, according to the ECJ, the liability in tort of a state for actions or omissions committed in exercising public powers is not governed by EC norms.[17] Thus, the competent jurisdiction must be selected on the basis of the national rules of private international law.

I would hold that whilst it is one thing to decide to declare war on a state or to participate in a peacekeeping operation—which is undoubtedly an expression of state sovereignty—it is quite another to commit an international crime during a military or peacekeeping operation. The commission of an international crime is not necessarily tied to the state's choices in foreign policy, and may be the result of an action by an individual, not supported by the state. This distinction was not taken into account in the *Lechouritou* case, since the ECJ was dealing with a supposed unlawful fact by a state rather than an individual. However, it could be relevant in cases of international crimes giving rise to liability of the individual and the eventual joint liability of the state: the *Lechouritou* ruling may be applied in proceedings relating to crimes committed on behalf of the state, but not in cases of individual actions unsupported in some manner by the state.

(Greece), which stayed proceedings until the Anotato Idiko Dikastirio (Superior Special Court) had ruled, in a parallel case, on the interpretation of the rules of international law concerning immunity of sovereign states. In 2002 the Anotato Idiko Dikastirio upheld the immunity exception. Later the claimants in the main proceedings pleaded the Brussels Convention, in particular Art 5(3)–(4) which, in their submission, abolished states' right of immunity in all cases of torts committed in the state of the court seized. The Efetio Patron had doubts as to whether the proceedings brought before it fell within the scope of that Convention. Thus the Efetio Patron decided to stay proceedings and to refer a question for a preliminary ruling to the ECJ. Regarding the judgment see L Idot, *Faits de Guerre et Prérogatives de Puissance Publique*, Europe 2007 Avril Comm. 125, 32; O Feraci, 'La Sentenza Lechouritou e l'ambito di Applicazione Ratione Materiae della Convenzione di Bruxelles del 27 Settembre 1968' [2007] RDIPP 657 ff; C Lyons, 'The Persistence of Memory: The Lechouritou Case and History before the European Court of Justice' (2007) 5 Europ L Rev 563; A Leandro, 'Limiti Materiali del regolamento (CE) n. 44/2001 e immunità degli Stati esteri dalla Giurisdizione: Il caso Lechouritou' [2007] RDI 759 ff.

[17] This principle has been expressed also in EC Regulation 805 of 21 April 2004, creating the European enforcement order for uncontested claims and in EC Regulation 1896 of 12 December 2006, creating a European order for payment procedure. This choice has been considered a kind of codification of the ECJ case law regarding the Brussels Convention of 1968. See S Carbone, *Lo Spazio Giuridico Europeo in Materia Civile e Commerciale* (2006), 289 ff.

However, taking into account the ECJ case law, the problem becomes that of understanding whether the *Lechouritou* ruling may also be relevant for PMSCs, and whether EC Regulation 44/2001 governs tort claims instituted against them.

In this regard, it should be highlighted that in *Lechouritou* the ECJ gave great importance to the fact that one of the parties was a state, a public authority exercising sovereign prerogatives. The importance of this fact is further strengthened by the reference made to the *Sonntag* case,[18] where the Court stated that a claim for damage 'falls outside the scope of the Convention only where the author of the damage against whom it is brought must be regarded as a public authority which acted in the exercise of public powers'. Thus, if the parties to the dispute are private entities, the EC regulation may be considered applicable.

PMSCs are undeniably private entities that can be engaged by a state to carry out certain functions. Therefore, if the courts simply look at the juridical nature of PMSCs, EC rules should be applied. Nevertheless, PMSCs could be qualified as de facto public authorities, because of the peculiar type of functions exercised on behalf of the state. The adoption of this 'functional' criterion involves an evaluation of the status of PMSCs and it inevitably leads to diversification in the rules to be applied to them on the basis of the type of activities carried out. In fact, if PMSCs were asked to provide communications support or logistic services, such as billeting or messing, there would be no exercise of sovereign prerogatives and accordingly they could not be qualified as a public authority. On the contrary, if the delegated functions were inherent to public powers, they could be treated as state entities. Consequently, EC Regulation 44/2001 would be applicable to PMSCs in the first case, but not in the second, and the judge should evaluate the type of functions assigned to the PMSC involved at the very beginning of the trial. This means that the court concerned will be obliged to carry out a long and expensive evaluation on the merits of the case, with the exclusive purpose of addressing a mere preliminary issue.

On this basis, as between the criterion of the nature of the parties and that of the type of functions exercised, the former seems to be more acceptable, both for reasons of certainty of law and the costs of the proceedings. Moreover, since the contract concluded between the sending state and PMSCs may be considered a 'contract of service', and since the corporation assigned the contract is not usually considered a public authority, purely on the basis of this assignment, PMSCs should be treated as private entities like any other corporation.

Two matters require clarification at this point. First, the doubts regarding the applicability of EC Regulation 44/2001 concern only unlawful acts committed by PMSCs in the exercise of functions delegated to them by the state. In relation to other kinds of civil crimes, the application of EC rules does not seem open to question.

Secondly, although the jurisdictional rules provided for by EC Regulation 44/2001 may work only if the defendant has domicile within the EU, their

---

[18] ECJ 21 April 1993, Case C-172/91, *Sonntag v Waidmann* [1993] ECR I-1963.

application to PMCSs incorporated in a state which is not member of the EU may be granted by the national legal systems. Just to quote an example, according to Article 3 of Italian Law no 218/1995, the special criteria of jurisdiction contained in the Brussels Convention of 1968 are applicable even when the defendant is not domiciled within the EU, but only if the claim deals with civil or commercial matters. Consequently, in order to establish its own jurisdiction, the Italian court could de facto apply the EC regulation, even beyond its field of application ratione personae. This extension is however not allowed ratione materiae. In fact, the Italian Court of Cassation excluded the application of the EC rules in proceedings for damages stemming from crimes of state armed forces since this issue does not fall within the concept of a civil matter.[19]

In addition, it is important to highlight that the *forum commissi delicti* criterion is provided for by a large number of national legal systems. Thus, even if the EC regulation were considered inapplicable, its effectiveness could be granted by the state legislators. In such case, however, its field of application will be defined by the domestic legal systems. Consequently, the ambivalent nature recognized by the ECJ may be excluded.

IV. The Impact of Jurisdictional Immunities Provided for by National Legislations and International Treaties

The effectiveness of the *locus commissi delicti* criterion could be limited by international treaties, and in particular by the so-called status of forces agreements (SOFAs), which may be concluded on a temporary or permanent basis, at bilateral or multilateral level. SOFAs govern the status of foreign armed forces in the state where they are employed (host state). More and more often they include PMSCs, as well as SOFAs concluded in relation to UN peacekeeping operations.[20]

The content of a SOFA varies, as they are negotiated on a case-by-case basis, but they often provide for the exemption of foreign armed forces and PMSCs employed by the sending state, from the jurisdiction of the host state. This may happen either by providing for their immunity from territorial jurisdiction,[21] or by establishing a rational sharing of the jurisdictional power between the host and the sending state.[22] In the first case, the judges of the territorial state can never exercise their jurisdiction over PMSCs—of course if the dispute falls within those for whom immunity is granted. In the second case, it depends on the modalities in which the organic distribution of jurisdiction has been realized. If the jurisdiction of both the

---

[19] Cass May 6–29, 2000, no 14199, *Federal Republic of Germany v Regional Administration of Vojotia*. This case regarded the execution of a Greek judgment condemning the Federal Republic of Germany to compensate the victims of an international crime committed by Nazi troops, in the Hellenic territory, during the Second World War.
[20] See Ch 22 by Frulli in this volume.
[21] See UNMIK Regulation 2000/47, s 4, which grants immunity also to private contractors.
[22] See Art 47 of the Model SOFA for Peacekeeping operations, UN Doc A/45/594 (9 October 1995).

host and the sending state is established, although the sending state has primacy, territorial jurisdiction may be exercised if the judges of the sending state are inactive; if instead the territorial jurisdiction is excluded a priori, the injured party must claim before the judges of the sending state or before the judges of a third state having jurisdiction over the case. In any case, it must be highlighted that SOFAs are not a source of jurisdiction for national judges. They simply provide for immunity or for an organic division of jurisdiction. Therefore, the court concerned should verify its jurisdiction over PMSCs in the light of the rules in force in its legal system and should eventually dismiss the case, on the grounds of the exemptions provided for by the applicable SOFA. On the other hand, if the jurisdiction of the court is not provided for by the national rules, the application of the SOFA is excluded a priori.

In brief, the application of the *locus commissi delicti* criterion may be barred by an international agreement. The adoption of special national norms may lead to analogous consequences, as happened, for instance, in Iraq. Initially, the Provisional Authority Coalition enacted an order also providing immunity for PMSCs, even though only in relation to acts committed in performing the contract stipulated with the sending state.[23] Subsequently, the order was replaced by a SOFA concluded between the United States and Iraq, which did not establish any form of immunity for PMSCs. Accordingly, if in the past, Iraq was barred from exercising its jurisdiction over PMSCs, today Iraqi courts have a primary jurisdiction over them, although only for facts which occurred after the entry into force of the SOFA. However, it is interesting to note that, whilst the provision of the PAC Order was construed as granting immunity, the SOFA which replaced it established an organic division of jurisdiction. This division grants the Iraqi courts primacy over PMSCs, but not over the regular armed forces, which are still under the primary jurisdiction of the sending state.

In any case, when territorial jurisdiction is precluded or simply suspended by international norms or special national rules, the injured party must look for an alternative forum, which is not necessarily that of the sending state. In fact, since SOFAs are not a source of national jurisdiction, the courts of the sending state could also dismiss the case in light of its jurisdictional national rules. This could happen, for instance, if the PMSC involved is incorporated in a third state.

V. The Availability of Exorbitant Jurisdictions: The Alien Tort Statute

As previously mentioned, if the jurisdiction of the territorial state is excluded by special norms of international or domestic law, then the problem of access to justice arises. The injured party may claim before the judge of the state where the PMSC

---

[23] CPA Order no 17. The Order has been replaced by the SOFA concluded between Iraq and the United States, which does not provide for immunity for PMSCs.

involved is incorporated, but it is also possible to use some forms of exorbitant jurisdiction (although only within the limits in which they are admitted by the national legal systems).

In Italy, for instance, the claimant could avail himself of the jurisdictional norm deriving from the combination of Article 3(2) of Law no 218/1995 and Article 18 of the Code of Civil Procedure. Thus, if the defendant does not have either his residence, his domicile, or his abode in Italy, or if his abode is unknown, the claimant may nonetheless claim before an Italian court, provided his permanent residence is within the Italian boundaries (principle of *forum actoris*). The forum actoris principle works only when EC Regulation 44/2001 does not apply and is available only for Italian residents. Accordingly, the population of the territorial state would not have access to the Italian courts.

Much more meaningful is the Alien Tort Statute (ATS), which confers jurisdiction on US courts in tort claims by foreigners and stemming from the violation of international norms, which are binding on the United States. The place where such violations have been committed does not assume any importance, so a US court can adjudicate violations of international norms wherever they occur. This situation has led some scholars—particularly in the field of constitutional law—to request that the norm be revised as it is accused of being the expression of the so-called principle of universal civil jurisdiction. However, so far this request has not been successful and thus citizens of the territorial (foreign) state, who suffer damage or injury deriving from an international crime, may sue in US courts.

Since the ATS regards the violation of international rules, and since PMSCs are legal entities of domestic law, the ATS would not seem, in principle, to apply to PMSCs. Nevertheless, beginning with the *Kadic* case, the ATS has been considered applicable to non-governmental actors as well,[24] and this principle has been confirmed in many later cases. In *Unocal*,[25] the ATS was used, for the first time, against a multinational corporation and in several subsequent cases[26] the corporations involved have been sued for complicity with government actors in the commission of international crimes. The expansion ratione personae of the ATS field of application has been justified through the juridical concept of the so-called 'aiding and abetting'. This concept is used in criminal international law, especially by the Tribunals for Rwanda and former Yugoslavia, and applied by the US judges,

---

[24] *Kadić v Karadžić*, 70 F3d 232, 239 (2d Cir 1995), which authorized a human rights class action for violations of international norms by Srpska's military forces.
[25] *Doe v Unocal Corp*, 963 F Supp 880 (CD Cal 1997).
[26] Just to quote some examples, see *Doe v Exxon Mobil Corp*, 393 F Supp 2d 20 (DDC 2005), dismissed on the basis of the political-question doctrine; *Abdullahi v Pfizer*, at first dismissed on the grounds of *forum non conveniens* (1 Civ 8118, 2002 US Dist LEXIS 17436—SDNY 2002), and then brought again before the District Court following the annulment of the decision of the lower court by the Court of Appeals (2nd Cir 2003); *Abrams v Société Nationale Des Chemins de fer Français*, 175 F Supp 2d 423 (EDNY 2001), dismissed on the grounds of immunity; *Abu-Zeineh v Federal Laboratories Inc* (not available); *Aguinda v Texaco* 945 F Supp 625 (SDNY 1996), *Aguinda v Texaco* 142 F Supp 2d 534 (SDNY 2001); *Aguinda v Texaco* 303 F 3d 470 (2d 2002), dismissed on the grounds of *forum non conveniens*; *Alomang v Freeport-McMoran* 811 So 2d 98 (La App 2002), dismissed for lack of *personal jurisdiction*. A list of ATS cases against corporations is available at <http://www.law.monash.edu.au>, accessed on 20 August 2010.

sic et simpliciter, in the field of civil liability. The appropriateness of such an analogy, as between criminal and civil liability, is debatable, although it seems sustainable since tort liability may also stem from the commission of a crime. In any case, the fact that private corporations may be sued for damages under the ATS for complicity with government actors is a matter of fact. It must be stressed that they may be sued even without involving the state in the proceedings. Therefore, being private corporations, PMSCs too may be sued on the basis of the ATS[27] as happened for instance in *CACI* and *Titan* cases.[28] Both cases regard acts of torture perpetrated by the employees of both PMSCs against Iraqi people, as well as the cases *Al Shimari v CACI and ors*, still pending before the Court of Appeals for the 4th Circuit,[29] cases *Al-Quraishi and ors v Nakhla and ors* and *Al Janabi v Stefanowicz and ors*,[30] pending before the courts of first instance of Maryland and California. Moreover, proceedings have been started against the PMSC Blackwater for violation of international humanitarian law committed during the massacre of Nisoor square[31] and against the PMSC KBR, accused of international traffic of 70 Nepali citizens forced to work within the US base of Al Asad in Iraq.[32]

Although the ATS confers jurisdiction in the case of violations of international norms, the foreign claimant faces many legal obstacles before arriving at a decision on the merits of the case. US courts do not consider the ATS a norm conferring on them personal jurisdiction over the defendant, which must therefore be evaluated according to the standards established by the *International Shoe* case referred to earlier. In other words, even in ATS proceedings, courts must verify if they have a general or specific jurisdiction over the PMSC involved before resolving the dispute. However, where the violation of the international norm occurred abroad, the concept of specific jurisdiction is manifestly inapplicable. Thus, according to the general jurisdiction standards, the judge can only decide on the case in cases where there exist meaningful links between the PMSC involved and the forum. Of course this 'meaningful links' requirement is met when the PMSC is incorporated

---

[27] On this issue, see T Garmon, 'Domesticating International Corporate Responsibility: Holding Private Military Firms Accountable under the Alien Tort Claims Act', (2003)11 Tul J Int'l & Comp L 325.

[28] *Ibrahim v Titan Corp*, 391 F Supp 2d 10 (DDC 2005); *Saleh v Titan Corp*, 436 F Supp 2d 55 (DDC 2006). Both cases concern acts of torture perpetrated by certain employees of Titan Corp and CACI, operating in Iraq, in Abu Ghraib, on behalf of the United States. Victims of such acts of torture and their relatives sued CACI and Titan before the US courts, on the basis of the ATS, in order to obtain compensation for the damage suffered.

[29] The Court of First Instance (East District of Virginia) rejected the defendant's motion to dismiss the case. The decision, dated 18 March 2009, is available at <http://ccrjustice.org/files/3.18.09%20Al%20Shimari%20decision.pdf>, accessed on 20 August 2010.

[30] For more information see <http://ccrjustice.org/ourcases/current-cases/al-quraishi-et-al-v.-nakhla-et-al> (*Al Quraishi*), and <http://www.contractormisconduct.org/index.cfm/1,73,222,html?CaseID=920> (*Al Janabi*), both accessed on 20 August 2010.

[31] *In Re XE Services Alien Tort Litigation*. With a decision dated 21 October 2009, the Court of First Instance partially accepted the motion to dismiss introduced by the defendant Blackwater (XE Services). The decision is available at <http://ccrjustice.org/files/10.21.09%20Memorandum%20opinion%20re%20defendants'%20motion%20to%20dismiss.pdf>, accessed on 14 June 2010.

[32] For more information, see <http://www.contractormisconduct.org/index.cfm/1,73,222,html?CaseID=1008>, accessed on 14 June 2010.

in the United States, but in this case the ATS overlaps the general criterion of the defendant's domicile. On the other hand, if the PMSC is incorporated abroad, then it will be necessary to carry out complex investigations on factual data, in which the judge enjoys a wide discretion. This broadens if the defendant is the holding corporation, sued for acts of its affiliates. In such circumstances, it will be necessary to investigate the links between the holding corporation and the defendant and to verify whether it is possible to use theories such as 'piercing the corporate veil' or 'agent' (issues that it is not possible to analyse in this chapter).[33]

The most significant limit placed on the ATS stems from the distinction drawn by US judges, and confirmed by the US Supreme Court, between subject-matter jurisdiction and cause of action.

The cause of action may be defined as the ownership of a judicially enforceable right. Thus, if jurisdiction is the power of the judge to grant judicial protection to a certain right, the cause of action represents the possibility of asking the judge for judicial protection of that right, which must be, by its nature, judicially enforceable. Jurisdiction and cause of action are, therefore, distinct concepts and they are not interdependent. Consequently, in some cases the former may exist, but not the latter.

First, judge Bork in *Tel Oren*,[34] then the Supreme Court in *Sosa*,[35] argued that the ATS is only a source of jurisdiction, but does not confer a cause of action on the plaintiff. Thus, the cause of action must be found elsewhere, otherwise the trial cannot proceed.

It could be affirmed that it is for international law to furnish the cause of action in cases involving PMSCs operating abroad. But such reasoning does not convince either the US judges, or the executive branch, or Congress. As regards international treaty law, US courts have affirmed that the rights provided for by a non-self-executing treaty are not enforceable. Applying this principle to the ATS, the claimant will only have a cause of action if the contested violation concerns a self-executing rule. Where this is not the case and the violation regards a non-self-executing norm, the trial cannot proceed. On the other hand, with regard to customary international law, there could be a cause of action for the claimant, only if the violated norm is precise and universally accepted. As specified by the Supreme Court in *Sosa*, in order to verify such precision and acceptance, the judge has to refer to the position adopted by Congress.

In view of the above, several potential cases regarding PMSCs would remain outside US jurisdiction and fall within the scope of the ATS only if we accept the thesis that international norms on human rights are self-executing in nature.[36] This is an interesting thesis but at odds with the traditional freedom of states in choosing

---

[33] Regarding these issues see S Joseph, *Corporations and Transnational Human Rights Litigation* (2004).
[34] *Tel-Oren v Lybia*, 726 F2d 774 (DC Cir 1984).
[35] *Sosa v Alvarez-Machain*, 542 US 692 (S Ct 2004).
[36] R Pavoni, 'Norme non Self-executing in Materia di Diritti Umani e Diritto Umanitario e Violazione del Diritto di Accesso alla Giustizia nella Recente Prassi Statunitense' in F Francioni et al (eds), *Accesso dell'individuo alla Giustizia nel Diritto Internazionale e Dell'Unione Europea* (2008), 305 ff.

the way to execute international norms and would thus appear to be valid in a *de iure condendo* perspective only. Also the European Court of Human Rights—in the *Markovic* case—has affirmed that the individual is not entitled to judicial protection for violations of international humanitarian norms, since they operate only at an interstate level. Thus, it seems unlikely that an American judge would recognize the self-executing nature of the international norms on human rights, especially if they consider that such power belongs to Congress according to the US Constitution.

In light of the above, the field of application of the ATS becomes quite narrow, since it only concerns violations of universally accepted customary rules (*rectius* norms that according to US Congress are universally accepted), and violations of treaty norms declared self-executing by Congress. The appropriateness of this situation may be open to question, but US courts confirmed this view in the aforementioned cases of *CACI* and *Titan*, in which PMSCs operating on behalf of the United States were sued in relation to acts of torture allegedly perpetrated during their mandate. According to Judge Robertson of the District of Columbia[37] the universally accepted notion of torture implies the participation of a state organ in the conduct of the private entity. Thus, a cause of action for the victims exists only if the PMSCs act jointly with or with the support of the state. Since, in the opinion of Judge Robertson, CACI and Titan did not act 'under the color of law', the claimants did not have a cause of action against them. The judgment of the District of Columbia was appealed on various grounds, but was subsequently confirmed in relation to this issue—inter alia—by the Court of Appeals.[38]

Objection may be raised to the ruling by Judge Robertson. In fact, if it is true that according to international law torture is an act by an organ of the state or by an individual acting 'under the color of law', the participation of the state organ is not required if the act of torture is committed in wartime and qualifies therefore as a war crime.[39] In his reasoning, Judge Robertson did not take into account this issue—which has been accepted instead by US jurisprudence both in the *Kadic* case and, with reference to acts of PMSCs, by the District Court of East Virginia.[40]

The point is that in *CACI* and *Titan*, according to the Court of Appeals, the claimants did not present their case as stemming from the commission of a crime of war. Thus, on the basis of the principle according to which a court cannot decide on issues not raised by the parties, the judge did not address the matter. However, it seems to me that, in these cases, the principle of *iura novit curia* could have been applied, and consequently the cause of action of the claimants could have been found in the qualification of the conduct of the PMSCs involved as a war crime, notwithstanding the fact that the claimants omitted to raise this argument.

Furthermore, in speaking of acts of torture, it must be highlighted that courts may rely on the Torture Victims Protection Act (TVPA) to find a cause of action

---

[37] *Ibrahim v Titan Corp*, 391 F Supp 2d 10, 19 (DDC 2005); *Saleh v Titan Corp*, 436 F Supp 2d 55, 57–9 (DDC 2006).
[38] *Saleh and ors v Titan Corp*, 580 F3d 1 (District of Columbia, Appeal, 2009).
[39] *Kadić v Karadžić*, 70 F 3d 232, 239 (2d Cir 1995).
[40] The decision of the District Court is mentioned in n 31 above.

and thus the claimants also referred to this law in the *Titan* and *CACI* cases, to ground their claim. However since the TVPA permits claimants to sue foreign states only, and since CACI and Titan were PMSCs acting on behalf of the US, the referral to the TVPA was quite correctly considered groundless.[41]

Two other questions deserve mention when discussing the ATS and TVPA. Even where US jurisdiction exists and the claimant has a cause of action, the case could be dismissed for *forum non conveniens*, or according to the doctrine of political question or to the so-called 'combatant-activities exception'.

Regarding the forum non conveniens, its application could be barred by the subsistence of forms of immunity from territorial state jurisdiction. When considering Iraq and the immunity provided for PMSCs by the old state legislation, it is evident that the Iraqi forum could not be available to the injured party, who would consequently lack a suitable forum. Accordingly, the application of the forum non conveniens would be impeded a priori and US courts would be barred from dismissing the claim. Such an approach has been accepted by US jurisprudence in a recent case regarding an unlawful act committed in Iraq, although not connected to the activities of PMSCs and armed forces.[42] The Court of Appeals for the 4th Circuit rejected the request of dismissal for forum non conveniens since the defendant, a US citizen sued for actions of defamation completed in Iraq, was immune from Iraqi jurisdiction. Thus, to dismiss the case for forum non conveniens would have implied a denial of justice for the injured party. Applying this principle to PMSCs, it is possible to say that if they enjoy immunity in the natural forum, the US courts cannot bar the trial for reasons of *forum non conveniens*. On the contrary, when immunity cannot be invoked, as happened in Iraq after the entry into force of the relevant SOFA, this principle is inapplicable. However, the statement of the 4th Circuit could be held to be operative in several instances.[43]

With regard to the political question and the combatant activities exception, even though we are dealing with different theories, they can be jointly discussed because of their common ratio and consequences. The ratio is to prevent a court dealing with matters of political relevance, in name of the principle of the separation of powers. The main consequence is that a kind of a de facto immunity is granted to the defendant. Nonetheless, these theories also differ to some degree. The most significant difference is that whilst the doctrine of the political question is general and extremely discretionary, the combatant-activities exception is narrow and becomes relevant when the claim is based on state law rather than on federal law.

---

[41] It must be highlighted that TVPA regards only cases of torture or extrajudicial killings—thus its scope of application ratione materiae is narrower than that of ATS. Besides, it involves the exhaustion of local remedies in the state where the crime occurred.

[42] *Galustian v Peter*, 2010 WL 155456 (4th Cir 2010).

[43] Regarding the forum non conveniens in relation to ATS, see A Atteritano, 'Tutela Giudiziaria dei Diritti dell'uomo e Limiti Processuali nei Procedimenti ATS' (LLM thesis on file at Rome University of Roma Tre).

The combatant-activities exception was discussed in *CACI* and *Titan*. The grounds for the claim by the plaintiff were based on the ATS on the one hand and on state law on the other. With a decision dated 6 November 2007, Judge Robertson allowed the trial against CACI, but not against Titan, applying the Federal Tort Claims Act (FTCA), which excludes the exercise of civil jurisdiction over claims related to 'combatant activities of the military or naval forces, or the Coast Guard, during time of war'.[44] The Court of Appeals considered the combatant-activities exception to also be applicable to CACI.

The reason for the decision resides in the fact that, according to the Court of Appeals, the employees of the two PMSCs were under the control of the military forces and were an integral part of them. On the basis of this, they were considered as combatants for the purposes of the application of the FTCA. Neither the judge of first instance, nor on the judge on appeal used the criteria offered by international humanitarian law on the definition of combatant in verifying the status of the PMSCs involved, nor was the qualification of the PMSCs given by the US Department of State—which defined them as civilians rather than combatants—taken into consideration. It is probable that if the matter had been analysed with greater care, the opposite conclusion would have been reached. Moreover, the judgment handed down by the court is contradictory: it denied the claimants' cause of action since the PMSCs involved were private entities not acting on behalf of the state, whilst at the same time considered them as integrated in the armed forces and therefore qualified as combatants. It is true that the two profiles are different, but it is at the same time strange that the PMSCs are considered independent from the US armed forces, on the one hand, and integrated in them, on the other. It is therefore possible to affirm that the exercise of the forms of exorbitant jurisdiction in the case of PMSCs appears somewhat complicated for several reasons. First of all, there are obstacles at trial level, as in the ATS claims, that can be considered correct and equitable, bearing in mind that we are talking about very wide jurisdiction. Above all, these limits are frequently interpreted in a very broad manner in order to avoid judgment against PMSCs and indirectly against the public administrations on behalf of which they operate. This second kind of obstacle seems to be neither correct nor equitable.

VI. Liability in Tort of PMSCs and the Applicable Law: Is EC Regulation Roma II Applicable to PMSCs?

Since 11 January 2009, EC Regulation Rome II regarding the law applicable to non-contractual obligations, has been effective within the Member States of the EU.[45] Like the Brussels Convention of 1968, EC Regulation 44/2001 and the Lugano Conventions, its scope of application is limited to civil and commercial

---

[44] 28 USC para 1346(b), 2671–80. Cf *Boyle v United Technologies Corp*, 487 US 500 (1992).
[45] Regulation (EC) no 864/2007 of the European Parliament and of the Council, of 11 July 2007, on the law applicable to non-contractual obligations (Rome II), in OJ EU, 31 July 2007, L-199/40.

matters. Accordingly, the same doubts raised in relation to the application of these rules to PMSCs concern also EC Regulation Rome II; and in fact on the basis of the recital: 'The substantive scope and the provisions of this Regulation should be consistent with Council Regulation (EC) No 44/2001 of 22 December 2000 on jurisdiction and the recognition and enforcement of judgments in civil and commercial matters.' Moreover, Article 1 of Regulation Rome II expressly leaves out 'the liability of the State for acts and omissions in the exercise of State authority (acta iure imperii)' from its scope of application.

For the reasons set out above and related to the field of application of EC Regulation 44/2001, it would seem to me appropriate to grant the application of EC Regulation Rome II over PMSCs. Moreover, according to recital number 9, 'Claims arising out of acta iure imperii should include claims against officials who act on behalf of the State and liability for acts of public authorities, including liability of publicly appointed office-holders.' Considering the reference to 'officials', 'public authorities', and 'publicly appointed office-holders', it seems to me that the cases excluded from the scope of Regulation Rome II are exclusively those relating to an organ invested with state powers. It is difficult to imagine that a PMSC could be considered as an officer of the state or a public authority or an entity unilaterally invested with public powers. In fact, practice shows that PMSCs are engaged by states through the execution of private contracts. Nevertheless, on a broad interpretation, the exclusion of the activities *jure imperii* could also concern PMSCs if (a) the activities delegated to them by a state were considered an expression of public authority; (b) the use of the expression 'on behalf' of the state was interpreted as including de facto organs of the state; and (c) the execution of a contract was considered a kind of 'public appointment'. On this point clarification from the ECJ is needed.

When applying Regulation Rome II, the national judge chooses the applicable law using the criterion of the place where damages occurred (lex loci damni). Thus, whilst jurisdictional norms either relate to the place where the crime was committed or the place where the damage occurred, Regulation Rome II provides for the second criterion only. The reasons for this choice are expressed in the Preamble: '(a) connection with the country where the direct damage occurred (lex loci damni) strikes to fair balance between the interests of the person claimed to be liable and the person sustaining the damage, and also reflects the modern approach to civil liability and the development of systems of strict liability.'[46]

The general criterion of lex loci damni is derogated if the author of the crime and the injured party both have their habitual residence in the same state at the time when the damage occurred. In such a case, the law of the country where both parties have their residence will be applied. However, if the unlawful act is more closely connected with a different state, the law of this state will be applied.[47] These are two exceptions to a general rule that, however, seem to be unlikely to apply to unlawful acts involving PMSCs. A limited application of

---

[46] See Preamble, para 16.
[47] Both the exceptions are provided for by Art 4.

these two special criteria may be envisaged in cases other than unlawful acts damaging the population of the states where PMSCs operate, or in cases of unlawful facts of PMSCs resulting in damage or injury to the personnel of allied armed forces.

A further derogation is represented by the will of the parties, who may choose a different law, through the conclusion of an agreement[48] that can be executed either before or after the commission of the unlawful act. However, when speaking about unlawful acts of PMSCs, it is difficult to imagine the execution by the parties of an agreement regarding the applicable law before the unlawful event occurred. In fact, Regulation Rome II links the possibility of agreeing on the applicable law before the commission of the unlawful act to the existence of a commercial relationship between the parties. At the same time it is difficult to imagine that once the unlawful events occurred, the parties would then agree on the applicable law, since it is evident that once the event has occurred, the interests of the parties are directly opposing. Thus, even the application of such criterion seems to be quite unlikely in respect to PMSCs.

In a case in which Regulation Rome II is not applicable, the court will select the law to be applied according to its own norms of international private law. As one may read in the regulation: 'The principle of the lex loci delicti commissi is the basic solution for non-contractual obligations in virtually all the Member States.'[49] One may refer, for instance, to the law of the Netherlands or Italy,[50] although pursuant to Article 62 of Italian Law no 218/1995, the injured party may also unilaterally ask for the application of the lex loci damni. According to most jurists this could be done even at the end of the proceedings.

As will be explained in the next section, norms of this kind affect the principle of the certainty of law and could be particularly oppressive for the defendant.

VII. The Scope of the Applicable Law and the Issue of PMSC Liability for Unlawful Acts of their Employees

In view of the above, if Regulation Rome II found application, the applicable law would be chosen according to the locus damni criterion. On the contrary, should national laws be applied, then the locus commissi delicti criterion would be applied in most cases. Actually, in cases involving PMSCs operating abroad, the two criteria tend to reach the same result even though possible diversifications cannot be excluded.[51]

---

[48] Art 14.
[49] See Preamble, para 15.
[50] Regarding Netherlands, see the Act on the Conflict of Laws Regarding Tort Claims (Wet Conflictenrecht Onrechtmatige Daad), 11 April 2001, Arts 3–6. Regarding Italy, see L 218/1995, Art 62.
[51] See the aforementioned example related to the unlawful use of white phosphorus.

Therefore, the most important question becomes which issues of tort liability of PMSCs will be governed by the applicable law. In this respect, Article 15 of Regulation Rome II comes into consideration.

Certainly, it is according to the applicable law that the subsistence of the crime must be verified. Indeed, in relation to international crimes, the choice of law does not assume a great importance in this respect, since such crimes are directly defined by the relevant international rules. This does not mean that the question of the applicable law is of secondary importance in these cases. In fact, even though the existence of the crime may be verified by applying common norms of international law, it is on the basis of the applicable law that monetary compensation has to be determined, as well as the tort liability of PMSCs for unlawful acts of their employees, the status of limitation, and the burden of proof.

In relation to PMSCs' tort liability for unlawful acts of their employees, the matter is of crucial importance, since the patrimony of the employee, the author of the crime, may be not sufficient to ensure full compensation of the injured party. The involvement of PMSCs is, therefore, a guarantee for effective judicial protection of the victims, but, due to the absence of uniform legislation on these matters, such involvement depends on the choices of the national legislators. This would happen even if Regulation Rome II were applied. And in fact, according to Article 15, the applicable law governs also 'the basis and extent of liability, including the determination of persons who may be held liable for acts performed by them' and the 'liability for the acts of another person'.

In many European countries a form of objective liability of the employer for acts of the employee exists, if certain conditions are fulfilled. Of course, it is not possible to analyse the choices made by each national legal system, but it is necessary to underline two crucial aspects of the matter.

The conditions on the basis of which such joint liability can be established obviously depend on the unilateral choices of legislators. Consequently, given variations in the applicable law, the legal regime and the forms of liability—if any—could diverge. To quote an example, one may take into consideration the Dutch and the Italian norms on the matter. If in Italy Article 2049 of the Italian Civil Code provides for a form of objective liability of the employer for acts of its employees, in the Netherlands the employer's liability is only vicarious. This means, in brief, that the employer is liable towards third parties for damages resulting from acts of its employees only if the employer had control over the employee's conduct.[52] Moreover, in the case of PMSCs operating abroad, and in countries with a young legal system—like Iraq—such forms of liability might not be provided for by the law of that state, where the crime and the consequent damage usually occur. Thus, the liability of PMSCs could be easily avoided, except for in cases of direct participation of PMSCs in the unlawful act. The only way to overcome such a difficult situation would be to provide for a form of objective liability of PMSCs, as has been done in Europe, for instance, in the matter of

---

[52] Dutch Civil Code 6:170. See den Dekker (n 6 above).

investment services. In fact, EC Directive 2004/32 has imposed on Member States the obligation to provide for a kind of objective liability of investment firms for acts of their private bankers. According to Article 24(2): 'Member States shall require that where an investment firm decides to appoint a tied agent it remains fully and unconditionally responsible for any action or omission on the part of the tied agent when acting on behalf of the firm.' Nothing precludes a solution of this kind from being adopted for PMSCs in relation to acts of their employees. Rather, in these cases, the need to protect the victims of violations of fundamental rights is even stronger than the need to protect consumers.

Certainly, even if an EC directive were adopted, where the applicable law is that of a third state, the objective liability of PMSCs could not be invoked if not foreseen by the law of that state. The problem may however be overcome by regarding that norm as a norm of necessary application or public order, or even by providing for a form of objective liability for all PMSCs incorporated in Europe or contracted by European states.

The same thing should be done in relation to the burden of proof that is always governed by the applicable law.[53] In many cases, it is difficult for the injured party to prove the damage suffered and the unlawful acts of PMSCs or their employees, particularly when PMSCs operate in situations of armed conflict or in peacekeeping operations. It would be appropriate to provide for an inversion of the burden of proof, as has been done for investment services. In other words, PMSCs should have the burden of demonstrating the absence of negligence in their activities, whilst the victims would have the burden of proof in relation to the damage suffered and the nexus between the damage and the unlawful act.

The existence of EC legislation in this regard would thus avoid the application of the norms of private international law whilst, in the absence of common European norms, the ordinary criteria regarding the burden of proof would be applied. It must be said that in general, in cases of tort liability, it is the victim who must demonstrate the existence of the damage, the unlawful act, and the nexus between them. It is evident that with this burden of proof, the injured party would have great difficulty in establishing the tort liability of PMSCs.

The law to be applied also governs the limitation period on actions as regards the claim by the injured party. Thus, if the law to be applied were that of Italy, the limitation of actions would be 5 years, whilst if applying Spanish law, it would be 15 years.[54] If the unlawful act generating tort liability is considered a crime under the relevant norms, then the limitation of actions provided for in criminal proceedings will also be applied to the civil claim. Consequently, in relation to international crimes there can be no limitation of actions at all. Obviously, the rules laid down by the applicable law regarding the limitation of actions will be applied also to suspension or interruption of limitation itself.

Finally, the applicable law governs the causes of exclusion of unlawful acts, the transferability (also mortis causa) of the right to compensation, the nature and amount

---

[53] At least, according to the EC Regulation Roma II. According to some authors, the burden of proof should be governed by the lex fori.
[54] See Abrisketa and Gómez (n 7 above).

of damages, and the ways of extinguishing the obligation. According to Regulation Rome II, the type of procedural measures that the judge can adopt in order to grant the right to compensation of the injured party is also defined by the applicable law. However, on the basis of the lex fori principle, this gives rise to debate.

Clearly, according to the applicable law the amount of the damage or the ways in which the obligation may be extinguished can vary, but this is normal when the conflict mechanism of private international law finds application. However, possible differences on these issues do not conclusively preclude the possibility of suing PMSCs before courts. Thus, possible differences between different legal orders on these issues are acceptable.

VIII. Concluding Remarks

The availability of effective judicial protection to address the tort liability of PMSCs is essential in the perspective of the accountability of PMSC and undoubtedly national legal systems are able to offer much more effective tools than those offered by international law or codes of conduct. Of course, PMSCs' accountability is strictly linked to the availability of suitable normative tools, and, considering the novelty of the phenomenon, national laws do not always seem to be adequately equipped. The intervention of state legislators is therefore sometimes required. International law and EU norms can be a propulsionary force for intervention by the states.

Regarding the competent jurisdiction, considering that national laws and international treaties provide for various criteria of jurisdiction, the risk of a denial of justice is probably limited. The injured party has the possibility of involving either the courts of the state where the unlawful act or the damage occurred or the courts of the state where PMSC is incorporated or where they have a secondary seat. Moreover, as already explained, forms of exorbitant jurisdiction, like the ATS, are, in certain conditions, sometimes available.

In light of the above, the risk of forum-shopping practices is manifestly more concrete. Nevertheless, the presence of special national norms or particular international treaties (like SOFAs) may exclude the possibility of involving the courts of the state where the unlawful act or damage occurred. In these cases, the criterion of the defendant's domicile is always available, but it is evident that for the claimant it could be difficult to litigate there, particularly if the state of incorporation has been chosen for fiscal reasons. Moreover, the application of theories like 'Act of State' and 'political question' in the state of incorporation risks granting the PMSC a kind of de facto immunity. In such a case, the principle of the forum necessitatis should be applied, and any state could offer its jurisdiction to the injured party. However, the principle of the forum necessitatis operates only if provided for by the national law of the judge involved and, in any case, its distance from the place where the unlawful act took place could have serious consequences on the effectiveness of the judicial protection and with regard to the execution of the judgment.

This situation could be overcome only through the adoption of SOFAs that prevent the state having primary jurisdiction from dismissing the claim. This may be done only through the adoption of self-executing rules on jurisdiction, but the realization of such a goal is not easy.

Regarding the substantial regulation of PMSCs' tort liability, the conflict mechanism of private international law provided for by national legal systems and EC rules is, indeed, the only possible way to achieve this, notwithstanding the consequent difference of treatment that it involves. Limits may be imposed through an interpretation of Regulation Rome II which permits its application to PMSCs. In this way, at least in European countries, the same conflict norms will be applied. For reasons of clarity, a directive could be adopted, requiring Member States to apply Regulation Rome II in case of unlawful acts of PMSCs. In the same directive the problems previously analysed could be resolved, including those concerning the joint liability of PMSCs for acts of their employees, and the burden of proof.

PMSCs can be considered liable for unlawful acts of their employees subject to the conditions laid down by the applicable national norms. Therefore, according to the applicable law, PMSCs could be jointly liable with their employees or not liable at all (if PMSCs do not directly participate in the crime). Such difference in treatment does not seem justified. The adoption of an EC directive could resolve this situation by adopting uniform material rules excluding the application of the rules of private international law. Such substantive norms should provide for a form of objective and joint liability, as has been done by the EU in relation to other matters.

Finally, if the EC directive also provided for the inversion of the burden of proof, it would be possible to overcome the concrete problems that the ordinary norms in matters of tort liability create for the plaintiff, particularly if the injured party is a human being who has suffered damage caused by a PMSC operating in an armed conflict or in a peace-building operation.

As this book was about to be published, the U.S. Court of Appeals for the 2nd Circuit handed down an important decision on matter of corporate liability and ATS, which may have a significant impact also in relation to the liability in tort of PMSCs. The decision—*Kiobel v. Royal Dutch Petroleum*, September 17, 2010—dismisses an ATS lawsuit against Royal Dutch Shell for allegedly aiding and abetting the Nigerian government in the commission of serious violations of human rights. In brief, according to the Court: (1) International Law governs the scope of liability for violations of international law, hence the question of whether a corporation – such as a PMSCC – is liable for violating international law is itself governed by international law; (2) Under Supreme Court precedent, the ATS requires courts to apply norms of international law, and not domestic law, to the scope of defendants' liabilities. Such norms must be "specific, universal, and obligatory"; (3) Corporations have never been subject to any form of liability (whether civil or cirminal) under customary international law and corporate liability is not a discernable—much less universally recognized—norm of customary international law. Thus, ATS may not be used as a basis for corporate liability and plaintiffs' ATS claims would consequently be dismissed for lack of jurisdiction over the subject matter.

Although the judgment may be still reversed by the US Supreme Court, it raises the possibility to ground tort liability of PMSCs—under the legal category of "adding and abetting"—on the basis of ATS.

Bibliography

Abdel-Fatau, M, and Kayode Fayemi, J (eds), *Mercenaries: An African Security Dilemma* (2000).

Abi-Saab, G, 'Non-international Armed Conflicts' in UNESCO, *International Dimensions of Humanitarian Law* (1988), 217–40.

Abresch, W, 'A Human Rights Law of Internal Armed Conflict: The European Court of Human Rights in Chechnya' (2005) 16 EJIL 741–67.

Acconci, P, 'Accountability of Multinational Enterprises for Human Rights: Is Anything Going Differently?' in MA Moreau and F Francioni (eds), *The Pluridisciplinary Dimension of Corporate Social Responsibility* (2007), 117–54.

Addicott, J, 'Political Question Doctrine and Civil Liability for Contracting Companies on the Battlefield' (2008) 28 The Review of Litigation 343–64.

Addo, M (ed), *Human Rights Standards and the Responsibility of Transnational Corporations* (1999).

Ahmed, T, and De Jésus Butler, I, 'The European Union and Human Rights: An International Law Perspective' (2006) 17 EJIL 779–801.

Akande, D, 'Clearing the Fog of War? The ICRC's Interpretive Guidance on Direct Participation in Hostilities' (2010) 59 ICLQ 180–92.

Akerhust, M, 'Jurisdiction in International Law' (1972–3) 46 BYIL 145–258.

Alexandra, A, Baker, DP, and Caparini, M (eds), *Private Military and Security Companies: Ethics, Policies and Civil–Military Relations* (2008).

Alston, P (ed), *Non-State Actors and Human Rights* (2005).

Ambos, K, 'General Principles of Criminal Law in the Rome Statute' (1999) 10 Criminal LF 1–32.

Amnesty International, *International Law Commission: The Obligation to Extradite or Prosecute (aut Dedere aut Judicare)* (2009).

Arnold, R, 'Responsibility of Commanders and Other Superiors: Article 28' in O Triffterer (ed), *Commentary on the Rome Statute of the International Criminal Court* (2008), 795–848.

Arts, K, and Popovski, V (eds), *International Criminal Accountability and the Rights of Children* (2006).

Avant, D, 'The Privatization of Security and Change in the Control of Force' (2004) 5 International Studies Perspectives 153–7.

——, *The Market for Force: The Consequences of Privatizing Security* (2005).

——, 'The Marketization of Security' in J Kirshner (ed), *Globalization and National Security* (2006), 105–42.

——, 'The Emerging Market for Private Military Service and the Problem of Regulation' in S Chesterman and C Lehnardt (eds), *From Mercenaries to Market: The Rise and Regulation of Private Military Companies* (2007), 181–95.

——, 'Selling Security: Trade-offs in State Regulation of the Private Security Industry' in T Jäger and G Kümmel (eds), *Private Military and Security Companies: Chances, Problems, Pitfalls and Prospects* (2007), 419–42.

Bailes, A, and Holmqvist, C, *The Increasing Role of Private Military and Security Companies* (2007).

Bakker, C, *The Obligation of States to Prosecute Employees of PMSCs for Serious Human Rights Violations* (2009).
Barber, R, 'Facilitating Humanitarian Assistance in International Humanitarian and Human Rights Law' (2009) 91 IRRC 371–97.
Barnidge, R-P, 'The Due Diligence Principle under International Law' (2006) 8 ICLR 81–121.
——, *Non-State Actors and Terrorism: Applying the Law of State Responsibility and the Due Diligence Principle* (2007).
Bartels, L, *Human Rights Conditionality in the EU's International Agreements* (2007).
Bartolini, G, 'The Participation of Civilians in Hostilities' in M Momtaz and J Matheson (eds), *Rules and Institutions of International Humanitarian Law Put to the Test of Recent Armed Conflicts* (forthcoming).
Bassiouni, M-C, and Wise, E, *Aut Dedere aut Judicare: The Duty to Extradite or Prosecute in International Law* (1995).
Bassiouni, M-C (ed), *International Criminal Law* (1999).
——, 'The Institutionalization of Torture under the Bush Administration' (2006) 37 Case Western Reserve Journal of International Law 349–64.
Beapark, A, and Schulz, S, 'The Future of the Market' in S Chesterman and C Lehnardt (eds), *From Mercenaries to Market: The Rise and Regulation of Private Military Companies* (2007), 239–50.
Beco, G, de, 'War Crimes in International versus Non-international Armed Conflicts: New Wine in old Wineskins?' (2008) 8 ICLR 319–30.
Berle, AA, 'Corporate Powers as Powers in Trust' (1931) 44 Harv L Rev 1049–74.
Beveridge, F, and Nott, S, 'A Hard Look at Soft Law' in P Craig and C Harlow (eds), *Lawmaking in the European Union* (1998), 285–309.
Bilukha, OO et al, 'Death and Injury from Landmines and Unexploded Ordnances in Afghanistan' (2003) 290 *Journal of American Medical Association* 650–3.
Blanke, H.-J, 'Protection of Fundamental Rights Afforded by the European Court of Justice in Luxembourg' in H-M Blanke and S Mangiameli (eds), *Governing Europe under a Constitution* (2006), 265–78.
Blockmans, S (ed), *The European Union and Crisis Management – Policy and Legal Aspects* (2008).
Boldt, N, 'Outsourcing War: Private Military Companies and International Humanitarian Law' (2004) 47 GYIL 502–44.
Borelli, S, 'Casting Light on the Legal Black Hole: International Law and Detentions Abroad in the "War on Terror"' (2005) 87 IRRC 39–68.
Born, H, et al, *Regulating Private Security in Europe: Status and Prospects* (2007).
Born, H, and Hänggi, H, *The Double Democratic Deficit: Parliamentary Accountability and the Use of Force under International Auspices* (2004).
Bothe, M, 'Die Strafrechliche Immunität fremder Staatsorgane' (1971) 341 *Zeitschrift für ausländisches öffentliches Recht und Völkerrecht* 246–70.
Boven, T, van, 'Victims' Rights to a Remedy and Reparation' in C Ferstman et al (eds), *Reparations for Victims of Genocide, War Crimes and Crimes against Humanity* (2009), 19–40.
Brayton, S, 'Outsourcing War: Mercenaries and the Privatization of Peacekeeping' (2002) 55 J Int'l Affairs 303–29.
Bronitt, S (ed), *Shooting to Kill: The Law governing Lethal Force in Context* (forthcoming).
Brownlie, I, *International Law and the Use of Force by States* (1963).
Bryden, A, and Caparini, M (eds), *Private Actors and Security Governance* (2006).

Bunch, C, 'Women and Gender' in TG Weiss and S Daws, *The Oxford Handbook on the United Nations* (2007) 496–510.

Búrca, G, de, *The European Court of Justice and the International Legal Order after Kadi* (2009).

Burnham, G, et al, 'Mortality after the 2003 Invasion of Iraq: A Cross-sectional Cluster Sample Survey' (2006) 368 The Lancet 1421–8.

Cabrera, I, and Perret, A, *Colombia: Regulating PMSCs in a 'Territorial State'* (2009).

Callen, J, 'Unlawful Combatants and the Geneva Conventions' (2004) 44 Virginia JIL 1025–72.

Cameron, L, 'Private Military Companies: Their Status under International Humanitarian Law and its Impact on their Regulation' (2006) 88 IRRC 573–98.

——, *International Humanitarian Law and the Regulation of Private Military Companies* (2007).

Caparini, M, 'Regulating Private Military and Security Companies: The U.S. Approach' in D Alexander et al (eds), *Private Military and Security Companies: Ethics, Policies and Civil–Military relations* (2007), 171–88.

Carcano, A, 'End of the Occupation in 2004?' (2006) 11 JC&SL 41–66.

Cassel, D, 'Extraterritorial Application of Inter-American Human Rights Instruments' in F Coomans and MT Kamminga (eds), *Extraterritorial Application of Human Rights Treaties* (2004), 175–82.

Cassese, A, 'Mercenaries: Lawful Combatants or War Criminals?' (1980) 40 *Zeitschrift für ausländisches öffentliches Recht und Völkerrecht* 1–30.

——, 'The Nicaragua and Tadic Tests Revisited in the Light of the ICJ Judgment on Genocide in Bosnia' (2007) 18 EJIL 649–68.

——, *International Criminal Law* (2008/2005).

Cassese, A et al (eds), *The Oxford Companion to International Criminal Justice* (2009).

Cassese, A, Gaeta, P, and Jones, JRWD (eds), *The Rome Statute of the International Criminal Court: A Commentary* (2002).

Chesterman, S, 'We Can't spy . . . If We Can't Buy! The Privatization of Intelligence and the Limits of Outsourcing Inherently Governmental Functions' (2008) 19 EJIL 1055–74.

Chesterman, S, and Fisher, A (eds), *Private Security, Public Order: The Outsourcing of Public Services and its Limits* (2009).

——, 'Private Security, Public Order' in S Chesterman and A Fisher (eds), *Private Security, Public Order: The Outsourcing of Public Services and its Limits* (2009), 222–6.

Chesterman, S, and Lehnardt, C, *From Mercenaries to Market: The Rise and Regulation of Private Military Companies* (2007).

Cilliers, J, and Mason, P (eds), *Peace, Profit or Plunder? The Privatisation of Security in War-torn African Societies* (1999).

Clapham, A, *Human Rights Obligations of Non-State Actors* (2006).

——, 'Extending International Criminal Law beyond the Individual to Corporations and Armed Opposition Groups' (2008) 6 JICJ 899–926.

Cleary, S, 'Angola: A Case Study of Private Military Involvement' in J Cilliers and P Mason (eds), *Peace, Profit or Plunder? The Privatisation of Security in War-torn African Societies* (1999), 141–74.

Cockayne, J, *Commercial Security in Humanitarian and Post-Conflict Settings: An Exploratory Study* (2006).

——, 'The Global Reorganization of Legitimate Violence: Military Entrepreneurs and the Private Face of International Humanitarian Law' (2006) 88 IRRC 459–90.

——, 'Make or Buy? Principal-agent Theory and the Regulation of Private Military Companies' in S Chesterman and C Lehnardt (eds), *From Mercenaries to Market: The Rise and Regulation of Private Military Companies* (2007), 196–216.
——, 'Regulating Private Military and Security Companies: The Content, Negotiation, Weaknesses and Promise of the Montreux Document' (2008) 13 JC&SL 401–28.
Cockayne, J, et al, *Beyond Market Forces* (2009).
Cohen, A, and Shany, Y, 'A Development of Modest Proportions' (2007) 5 JICJ 310–21.
Coker, C, 'Outsourcing War' (1999) 13 Cambridge Review of Intl Affairs 95–113.
Cole, D, 'Challenging Covert War: The Politics of the Political Question Doctrine' (1985) 26 Harv Int'l L J 155–88.
Condorelli, L, and Boisson de Chazournes, L, 'Quelques Remarques à Propos de l'obligation de "Respecter et faire Respecter" le Droit International Humanitaire "en Toutes Circonstances"' in ICRC, *Mélanges Pictet* (1984), 17–36.
Coomans, F, and Kamminga, MT (eds), *Extraterritorial Application of Human Rights Treaties* (2004).
Corten, O, 'The Controversies over the Customary Prohibition of the Use of Force: A Methodological Debate' (2005) 16 EJIL 803–22.
——, *Le Droit contre la Guerre* (2008).
Cowling, MG, 'Outsourcing and the Military: Implications for International Humanitarian Law' (2007) 32 SAfrYIL 312–44.
Crane, A, et al (eds), *The Oxford Handbook of Corporate Social Responsibility* (2008).
Crawford, E, 'Unequal before the Law: The Case for the Elimination of the Distinction between International and Non-international Armed Conflicts' (2007) 20 LJIL 441–65.
Crawford, J, *Supplying War: Logistics from Wallentstein to Patton* (1986).
——, *The International Law Commission's Articles on State Responsibility: Introduction, Text and Commentaries* (2002).
Cullen, P, 'Private Security goes Head-to-head against Pirates: A Practical Answer to Protecting Commercial Shipping' (2008) 4 J of Intl Peace Operations 15–6.
David, E, 'Self-defence and State of Necessity in the Statute of the ICC' in J Doria, H-P Gasser, and M-C Bassiouni (eds), *The Legal Regime of the International Criminal Court: Essays in Honor of Professor Igor Blishenko* (2009), 757–78.
Defeis, E, 'Human Rights and the European Court of Justice: An Appraisal' (2008) 31 Fordham Int'l LJ 1104–17.
Desgagné, R, 'European Union Practice in the Field of International Humanitarian Law: An Overview' in V Kronenberger (ed), *The European Union and the International Legal Order: Discord or Harmony?* (2001), 455–80.
Dickinson, L, 'Accountability of Private Security Contractors under International and Domestic Law' (2007) 11 ASIL Insight (electronic publication).
——, 'Contracts as a Tool for Regulating Private Military Companies' in S Chesterman and C Lehnardt (eds), *From Mercenaries to Market: The Rise and Regulation of Private Military Companies* (2007).
Dinstein, Y, 'Human Rights in Armed Conflict' in T Meron (ed), *Human Rights in International Law: Legal and Policy Issues* (1984), 345–68.
——, *The Conduct of Hostilities under the Law of International Armed Conflict* (2004).
Dodd, D, 'For Whom are Corporate Managers Trustees?' (1932) 45 Harv L Rev 1145–63.
Dominick, D, *After the Bubble: British Private Security Companies after Iraq* (2006).
Donald, D, 'Private Security Companies and Intelligence Provision' in A Alexandra, DP Baker, and M Caparini (eds), *Private Military and Security Companies: Ethics, Policies and Civil–Military Relations* (2008), 131–42.

Doria, J, et al (eds), *The Legal Regime of the International Criminal Court* (2009).
Doria, J, Gasser, H-P, and Bassiouni, M-C (eds), *The Legal Regime of the International Criminal Court: Essays in Honor of Professor Igor Blishenko* (2009).
Dörmann, K, 'The Legal Situation of "Unlawful/Unprivileged Combatants"' (2003) 85 IRRC 45–74.
Dörmann, K, and Colassis, L, 'International Humanitarian Law in the Iraq Conflict' (2004) 47 GYIL 293–314.
Doswald-Beck, L, 'The Legal Validity of Military Intervention by Invitation of the Government' (1985) 56 BYIL 189–252.
——, 'Implementation of International Humanitarian Law in Future Wars' in M Schmitt et al (eds), *The Law of Armed Conflict: Into the Next Millennium* (1998), 39.
——, 'Private Military Companies under International Humanitarian Law' in S Chesterman and C Lehnardt (eds), *From Mercenaries to Market: The Rise and Regulation of Private Military Companies* (2007), 115–38.
Douglas, I, 'Fighting for Diamonds: Private Military Companies in Sierra Leone' in J Cilliers and P Mason (eds), *Peace, Profit or Plunder? The Privatisation of Security in War-torn African Societies* (1999), 175–200.
Drews, I-I, 'Private Military Companies: The New Mercenaries? An International Law Analysis' in T Jäger and G Kümmel (eds), *Private Military and Security Companies* (2007), 331–44.
Droege, C, *Positive Verpflichtungen der Staaten in der Europaeischen Menschenrechtskonvention* (2003).
——, 'The Interplay between International Humanitarian Law and International Human Rights Law in Situations of Armed Conflict' (2007) 40 IsLR 310–55.
Duchêne, F, 'Europe in World Peace' in R Mayne (ed), *Europe Tomorrow* (1972), 32–47.
Duffy, H, *The 'War on Terror' and the Framework of International Law* (2005).
Dumberry, P, 'New State Responsibility for Internationally Wrongful Acts by an Insurrectional Movement' (2006) 17 EJIL 605–21.
Durham, H, 'International Humanitarian Law and the Protection of Women' in H Durham and T Gurd (eds), *Listening to the Silences: Women and War* (2005), 95–108.
Durham, H and Gurd, T (eds), *Listening to the Silences: Women and War* (2005).
Ebbeck, G, 'Mercenaries and the "Sandline Affair"' (1998) 133 *Australian Defence Force Journal* 5–22.
Emanuelli, C, *International Humanitarian Law* (2009).
Erickson, BH, Albanese, P, and Drakulic, S, 'Gender on a Jagged Edge: The Security Industry, Its Clients and the Reproduction and Revision of Gender' (2000) 27 *Work and Occupations* 294–318.
European Defence Agency, *Future Trends from the Capability Development Plan* (2008).
Eyffinger, P, et al (eds), *Self-Defence as a Fundamental Principle* (2009).
Farr, V, and Schnabel, A (eds), *Gender Perspectives on Small Arms and Light Weapons* (2009).
Farrior, S, *State Responsibility for Human Rights Abuses by Non-State Actors: Proceedings of the American Society of International Law* (1998).
Ferraro, T, 'Le Droit International Humanitaire dans la Politique Étrangère et de Sécurité Commune de l'Union Européenne' (2002) 84 IRRC 435–61.
Ferstman, C, et al (eds), *Reparations for Victims of Genocide, War Crimes and Crimes against Humanity* (2009)
Fischer, H (ed), *Crisis Management and Humanitarian Protection: Festschrift für Dieter Fleck* (2004).

Fleck, D, 'Are Foreign Military Personnel Exempt from International Criminal Jurisdiction under Status of Force Agreements?' (2003) 1 JICJ 651–70.
—— (ed), *The Handbook of Humanitarian Law in Armed Conflicts* (2008).
Francioni, F, *Imprese Multinazionali, Protezione Diplomatica e Responsabilità Internazionale* (1979).
——, 'Four Ways of Enforcing the International Responsibility for Human Rights Violations by Multinational Corporations' in MA Moreau and F Francioni (eds), *The Pluridisciplinary Dimension of Corporate Social Responsibility* (2007), 155–74.
——, 'Private Military Contractors and International Law: An Introduction' (2008) 19 EJIL 961–4.
Francioni, F, et al, 'Symposium on Private Military Contractors and International Law' (2008) 19 EJIL 961–1074.
Francis, D, 'Mercenary Intervention in Sierra Leone: Providing National Security or International Exploitation?' (1999) 20 TWQ 319–38.
French, D, Saul, M, and White, ND (eds), *International Law and Dispute Settlement: New Problems and Techniques* (2010).
Frulli, M, *Immunità e Crimini Internazionali* (2007).
——, 'Exploring the Application of Command or Superior Responsibility to PMCs Managers and Contractors' JC&SL (forthcoming).
Gaeta, P, 'The Defence of Superior Orders: The Statute of the International Criminal Court versus Customary International Law' (1999) 10 EJIL 172–91.
Gaja, G, 'Immunità Squilibrate dalla Giurisdizione Penale in Relazione all'intervento Armato in Liberia' (2003) 86 RivDirInt 762–4.
Gardam, JG, 'Women and Armed Conflict: The Response of International Humanitarian Law' in H Durham and T Gurd (eds), *Listening to the Silences: Women and War* (2005), 109–24.
Gardam, JG, and Jarvis, MJ, *Women, Armed Conflict and International Law* (2001).
Garmon, T, 'Domesticating International Corporate Responsibility: Holding Private Military Firms Accountable under the Alien Tort Claims Act' (2003) 11 Tul J Int'l & Comp L 325–54.
Garraway, CHB, 'Combatants: Substance or Semantics?' in MN Schmitt and J Pejic (eds), *International Law and Armed Conflict: Exploring the Faultlines* (2007), 317–34.
Gaston, 'Mercenarism 2.0? The Rise of the Modern Private Security Industry and its Implications for International Humanitarian Law Enforcement' (2008) 49 Harv Int'l L J 221–48.
Gillard, E-C, 'Reparation for Violations of International Humanitarian Law' (2003) 85 IRRC 529–53.
——, 'Business Goes to War: Private Military/Security Companies and International Humanitarian Law' (2006) 88 IRRC 525–72.
Gómez Del Prado, J, 'Private Military and Security Companies and the UN Working Commission on the use of Mercenaries' (2008) 13 JC&SL 429–50.
Gosalbo Bono, R, 'Some Reflections on the CFSP Legal Order' (2006) 43 CML Rev 337–51.
Gossiaux, C, 'Les Règles d'Engagement Norme Juridique Nouvelle?' (2001) 40 RevDrMilDrGuerre 159–79.
Gowlland-Debbas, V, 'The Right to Life and Genocide: The Court and International Public Policy' in L Boisson de Chazournes and P Sands (eds), *International Law, The International Court of Justice and Nuclear Weapons* (1999), 315–17.
Grado, V, *Guerre Civili e Terzi Stati* (1998).

Gray, C, *International Law and the Use of Force* (2008).
Green, L, *The Contemporary Law of Armed Conflict* (2008).
Greenberg, KJ and Dratel, JL (eds), *The Torture Papers: The Road to Abu Ghraib* (2005).
Guilfoyle, D, *Shipping Interdiction and the Law of the Sea* (2009).
——, 'Counter-piracy Law Enforcement and Human Rights' (2010) 59 ICLQ 141–69.
Guillory, M, 'Civilianizing the Force: Is the United States Crossing the Rubicon?' (2001) 51 Air Force L R 111–42.
Hadden, T (ed), *A Responsibility to Assist* (2009).
Haggenmacher, P, 'Self-defense as a General Principle of Law and its Relevance to War' in P Eyffinger et al (eds), *Self-Defence as a Fundamental Principle* (2009), 1–48.
Hagman, C, and Kartas, M, 'International Organisations and the Governance of Private Security' in A Bryden and M Caparini (eds), *Private Actors and Security Governance* (2006), 285–304.
Harbom, L, and Wallensteen, P, 'Armed Conflict and its International Dimensions, 1946–2004' (2005) 42 JPeaceRes 623–35.
Harwell Wells, CA, 'The Cycles of Corporate Social Responsibility: An Historical Perspective for the Twenty-first Century' (2002) 51 U Kan L Rev 77–140.
Hazelzet, H, 'Human Rights Aspects of EU Crisis Management Operations: From Nuisance to Necessity' (2006) 13 *International Law Peacekeeping* 564–81.
Heaton, R, 'Civilians at War: Re-examining the Status of Civilians Accompanying the Armed Forces' (2005) 57 Air Force L R 155–208.
Hegelsom, G-J, van, 'The Relevance of IHL in the Conduct of the Petersberg Tasks' in College of Europe, *The Impact of International Humanitarian Law on Current Security Trends* (2002), 109–20.
——, 'International Humanitarian Law and Operations Conducted by the European Union' in G Beruto (ed), *International Humanitarian Law, Human Rights and Peace Operations* (2009), 107–14.
Heintze, H-J, 'On the Relationship between Human Rights Law Protection and International Humanitarian Law' (2004) 86 IRRC 789–814.
Henckaerts, J-M, and Doswald-Beck, L, *Customary International Humanitarian Law* (2005).
Hoffmeister, F, 'The Contribution of EU Practice to International Law' in M Cremona (ed), *Developments in EU External Relations Law* (2008), 37–127.
Holmqvist, C, *Private Security Companies: The Case for Regulation* (2005).
Hoppe, C, 'Corporate Social Responsibility at the Frontline? The Case of the Private Military Companies' in MA Moreau and F Francioni (eds), *The Pluridisciplinary Dimension of Corporate Social Responsibility* (2007), 61–95.
——, 'Passing the Buck: State Responsibility for Private Military Companies' (2008) 19 EJIL 989–1014.
——, *Passing the Buck: State Responsibility for the Conduct of Private Military Companies* (2009).
ICRC, *Women and War* (1995).
Isenberg, D, 'A Government in Search of Cover' in S Chesterman and C Lehnardt (eds), *From Mercenaries to Market: The Rise and Regulation of Private Military Companies* (2007), 82–93.
——, *Shadow Force: Private Security Contractors in Iraq* (2009).
Jäger, T, and Kümmel, G (eds), *Private Military and Security Companies: Chances, Problems, Pitfalls and Prospects* (2007).
Janowitz, M, *The Professional Soldier* (1960).

Jaques, RB (ed), *Issues in International Law and Military Operations* (2006).
Jonah, OC, 'Foreword' in S Chesterman and C Lehnardt (eds), *From Mercenaries to Market: The Rise and Regulation of Private Military Companies* (2007), I–VII.
Joseph, S, *Corporations and Transnational Human Rights Litigation* (2004).
Kaldor, M, *New and Old Wars* (2006).
Kalshoven, F, and Zegveld, L, *Constraints on the Waging of War* (2001).
Kaufman, W, 'Is there a "right" to Self-defense?' (2004) 23 Criminal Justice Ethics 20–32.
Kegley, CW, and Hermann, MG, 'A Peace Dividend? Democracies' Military Interventions and their External Political Consequences' (1997) 32 *Cooperation and Conflict* 339–68.
Keyuan, Z, 'New Developments in the International Law of Piracy' (2009) 8 Chinese J Intl L 323–45.
Kinsey, C, *Corporate Soldiers and International Security: The Rise of Private Military Companies* (2006).
——, *Contractors and War: The Transformation of United States' Military and Stabilization Operations* (2010).
Kinsey, C, and Franklin, G, 'The Impact of Private Security Companies on Somalia's Governance Networks' (2009) 22 Cambridge Review of Intl Affairs 147–61.
Kirshner, J (ed), *Globalization and National Security* (2006).
Koh, H, 'Bringing International Law Home' (1998) 35 Hous L R 623–81.
——, 'How is International Human Rights Law Enforced?' (1999) 74 Ind L J 1397–417.
Kolb, R, *Ius in bello. Le Droit International des Conflits Armés* (2008).
Kooijmans, P, 'The Security Council and Non-state Entities as Parties to a Conflict' in K Wellens (ed), *International Law: Theory and Practice: Essays in Honour of Eric Suy* (1998), 333–46.
Koopmans, B, 'Developing the European Foreign Security and Defence Policy without the Constitution?' (2006) 59 *Studia Diplomatica* 129–40.
Kopel, DB, Gallant, P, and Eisen, J, 'The Human Right of Self-defense' (2008) 22 BYU Journal of Public Law 43–178.
Koutrakos, P, *EU International Relations Law* (2006).
Krahmann, E, 'Conceptualizing Security Governance' (2003) 38 *Cooperation and Conflict* 5–26.
——, 'Regulating Private Military Companies: What Role for the EU' (2005) 26 *Contemporary Security Policy* 103–25.
——, 'Regulating Military and Security Services in the European Union' in M Caparini and A Brayden (eds), *Private Actors and Security Governance* (2006), 189–212.
——, 'Security: Collective Good or Commodity?' (2006) 14 *European Journal of International Relations* 379–404.
——, 'Transitional States in Search of Support: Private Military Companies and Security Sector Reform' in S Chesterman and C Lehnardt (eds), *From Mercenaries to Market: The Rise and Regulation of Private Military Companies* (2007), 94–112.
——, *States, Citizens and the Privatization of Security* (2010).
Kronenberger, V (ed), *The European Union and the International Legal Order: Discord or Harmony?* (2001).
Ku, C, and Jacobson, H (eds), *Democratic Accountability and the Use of Force in International Law* (2003).
Kufuor, OK, 'The OAU Convention for the Elimination of Mercenarism and Civil Conflicts' in A-F Musah and JK Fayemi (eds), *Mercenaries: An African Security Dilemma* (2000), 198–209.

Kuijper, PJ, 'Customary International Law, Decisions of International Organizations and other Techniques for Ensuring Respect for International Legal Rules in European Community Law' in J Wouters, A Nollkaemper, and E de Wet (eds), *The Europeanisation of International Law* (2008), 87–108.

Larsen, KM, 'Attribution of Conduct in Peace Operations: The Ultimate Authority and Control Test' (2008) 19 EJIL 509–31.

Lauterpacht, E (ed), *Individual Rights and the State in Foreign Affairs: An International Compendium* (1977).

Lawson, R, 'Life after Bankovic: On the Extraterritorial Application of the European Convention on Human Rights' in F Coomans and MT Kamminga (eds), *Extraterritorial Application of Human Rights Treaties* (2004), 83–124.

Layeb, A, 'The Need for an International Convention against Mercenaries and Mercenarism' (1989) 1 AfrJIntl&CompL 466–83.

Leander, A, 'Regulating the Role of Private Military Companies in Shaping Security and Politics' in S Chesterman and C Lehnardt (eds), *From Mercenaries to Market: The Rise and Regulation of Private Military Companies* (2007).

Lee, T, 'Military Extraterritorial Jurisdiction Act for Street Crimes, not War Crimes' (2009) 1 De Paul Rule of Law Journal 1–8.

Lehnardt, C, 'Private Military Companies and State Responsibility' in S Chesterman and C Lenhardt (eds), *From Mercenaries to Market: The Rise and Regulation of Private Military Companies* (2007), 139–57.

——, 'Individual Liability of Private Military Personnel under International Criminal Law' (2008) 19 EJIL 1015–34.

——, 'Peacekeeping' in S Chesterman and A Fisher (eds), *Private Security, Public Order: The Outsourcing of Public Services and its Limits* (2009), 205–21.

Lindsey, C, *Women Facing War: ICRC Study of the Impact of Armed Conflict on Women* (2001).

——, 'The Impact of Armed Conflict on Women' in H Durham and T Gurd (eds), *Listening to the Silences: Women and War* (2005), 21–36.

Lindsey, C, et al, *Addressing the Needs of Women Affected by Armed Conflict: An ICRC Guidance Document* (2004).

Liss, C, *Privatising Anti-Piracy Services in Strategically Important Waterways: Risks, Challenges and Benefits* (2009).

Liubicic, RJ, 'Corporate Codes of Conduct and Product Labelling Schemes' (1998) 30 *Law and Policy in International Business* 111–57.

Lubell, N, 'Challenges in Applying Human Rights Law to Armed Conflict' (2005) 87 IRRC 737–54.

Lynn, JA (ed), *Feeding Mars: Logistic in Western Warfare from the Middle Ages to the Present* (1994).

Lyons, C, 'The Persistence of Memory: The *Lechouritou* Case and History before the European Court of Justice' (2007) 5 ELR 563–81.

McCarthy, C, 'Reparation for Gross Violations of Human Rights Law and International Humanitarian Law at the International Court of Justice' in C Ferstman et al (eds), *Reparations for Victims of Genocide, War Crimes and Crimes against Humanity* (2009), 283–312.

McCormack, T, 'The "Sandline Affair": Papua New Guinea Resorts to Mercenarism to End the Bougainville Conflict' (1998) 1 YIntlHL 292–300.

McDonald, A, 'Some Legal Issues Concerning US Military Contractors in Iraq' in MN Schmitt and J Pejic (eds), *International Law and Armed Conflict: Exploring the Faultness* (2007), 357–402.

McFate, S, 'Outsourcing the Making of Militaries: DynCorp International as Sovereign Agent' (2008) 35 *Review of African Political Economy* 645–54.

McLaughlin, R, 'The Legal Regime Applicable to Use of Lethal Force when Operating under a United Nations Security Council Chapter VII Mandate Authorizing "All Necessary Means"' (2007) 12 JC&SL 389–418.

MacLeod, S, 'Reconciling Regulatory Approaches to Corporate Social Responsibility: The European Union, OECD and United Nations Compared' (2007) 13 EPL 671–702.

——, 'Stuck in the Middle with You? Alternative Approaches to Realising Accountability for Human Rights Violations by Business' in D French, M Saul, and ND White (eds), *International Law and Dispute Settlement: New Problems and Techniques* (2010), 87–107.

Mandel, R, *Armies without States: The Privatization of Security* (2002).

Manners, I, 'Normative Power Europe: A Contradiction in Terms?' (2002) 40 JComMarSt 235–58.

Matheson, MJ, 'The United States Position on the Relation of Customary International Law to the 1949 Geneva Conventions' (1987) 2 AmUJIntlL&Pol 419–27.

Mathieu, B, *The Right to Life in European Constitutional and International Case-law* (2006).

Mazali, R, 'The Gun on the Kitchen Table: The Sexist Subtext on Private Policing in Israel' in V Farr, H Myrttinen, and A Schnabel (eds), *Sexed Pistols: The Gender Perspectives on Small Arms and Light Weapons* (2009), 246–79.

Meessen, K (ed), *International Law of Export Control* (1992).

Melzer, N, *Targeted Killing in International Law* (2008).

——, *Interpretative Guidance on the Notion of Direct Participation in Hostilities under International Humanitarian Law* (2009).

Menefee, PS, 'An Overview of Piracy in the First Decade of the 21st Century' in MH Nordquist et al (eds), *Legal Challenges in Maritime Security* (2008), 441–78.

Meron, T (ed), *Human Rights in International Law: Legal and Policy Issues* (1984).

Mettraux, G, *International Crimes and the ad hoc Tribunals* (2005).

——, *The Law of Command Responsibility* (2009).

Michaels, J, 'Beyond Accountability: The Constitutional, Democratic and Strategic Problems with Privatizing War' (2004) 82 Washington University Law Quarterly 1001–127.

Milliard, TS, 'Overcoming Post-colonial Myopia: A Call to Recognize and Regulate Private Military Companies' (2003) 1 MilLRev 1–95.

Moir, L, 'Particular Issues Regarding War Crimes in Internal Armed Conflicts' in J Doria et al (eds), *The Legal Regime of the International Criminal Court* (2009), 611–8.

Mon, C, Le, 'Unilateral Intervention by Invitation in Civil Wars: The Effective Control Test Tested' (2003) 35 NYUJIntlL&Pol 741–94.

Moraru, M, 'A Critical Survey of Mechanisms for Institutionalizing CSR in Business Organisations' in MA Moreau and F Francioni (eds), *The Pluridisciplinary Dimension of Corporate Social Responsibility* (2007), 201–16.

Moreau, MA, and Francioni, F (eds), *The Pluridisciplinary Dimension of Corporate Social Responsibility* (2007).

Mourning, PW, 'Leashing the Dogs of War: Outlawing the Recruitment and Use of Mercenaries' (1981–2) 22 Va J Int'l L 589–612.

Mourtada-Sabbah, N, and Cain, B (eds), *The Political Question Doctrine and the Supreme Court of the United States* (2007).

Mowbray, A, *The Development of Positive Obligations under the European Convention on Human Rights by the European Court of Human Rights* (2004).
Muchlinski, P, *Multinational Enterprises and the Law* (2007).
Münkler, H, *The New Wars* (2006).
Musah, A, and Fayemi, K, *Mercenaries: An African Security Dilemma* (2000).
Myjer, EPJ, 'Uniform Justice and the Death Penalty' in J Doria, H-P Gasser, and M-C Bassiouni (eds), *The Legal Regime of the International Criminal Court: Essays in Honor of Professor Igor Blishenko* (2009), 927–42.
Naert, F, 'ESDP in Practice: Increasingly Varied and Ambitious EU Security and Defence Operations' in M Trybus and ND White (eds), *European Security Law* (2007), 61–101.
——, 'Accountability for Violations of HRL by EU Forces' in S Blockmans (ed), *The European Union and Crisis Management: Policy and Legal Aspects* (2008), 375–94.
——, 'An EU Perspective' in International Institute of Humanitarian Law (ed), *International Peace Operations and International Humanitarian Law* (2008), 61–4.
Neuwahl, NA, and Rosas, A (eds), *The European Union and Human Rights* (1995).
Nevers, R, de, 'Private Security Companies and the Laws of War' (2009) 40 *Security Dialogue* 169–90.
Nickel, D, and Quille, G, *In the Shadow of the Constitution: Common Foreign and Security Policy/European Security and Defence Policy Adapting to a Changing External Environment* (2007).
Nieminen, K, 'The Rules of Attribution and the Private Military Contractors at Abu Ghraib: Private Acts or Public Wrongs?' (2004) 15 Finnish YBIL 289–319.
Nordquist, MH, et al (eds), *Legal Challenges in Maritime Security* (2008).
Nyamuya Maogoto, J, and Sheehy, B, 'Private Military Companies and International Law: Building New Ladders of Legal Accountability and Responsibility' (2009) 11 *Cardozo Journal of Conflict Resolution* 99–132.
O'Brien, K, 'PMCs, Myths and Mercenaries: The Debate on Private Military Companies' (2000) 145 *Royal United Services Institute Journal* 59–64.
——, 'Private Military Companies and African Security 1990–98' in M Abdel-Fatau and J Kayode Fayemi (eds), *Mercenaries: An African Security Dilemma* (2000), 43–75.
——, 'What Should and What Should Not be Regulated?' in S Chesterman and C Lenhardt (eds), *From Mercenaries to Market: The Rise and Regulation of Private Military Companies* (2007).
O'Connell, ME, 'Defining Armed Conflict' (2008) 13 JC&SL 393–400.
——, 'Unlawful Killing with Combat Drones' in S Bronitt (ed), *Shooting to Kill: The Law Governing Lethal Force in Context* (forthcoming).
Olasolo, H, *Unlawful Attacks in Combat Situations* (2008).
Orakhelashvili, KH, 'The Position of the Individual in International Law' (2000–1) 31 CalWIntlLJ 241–76.
Orth, JV, *Due Process of Law* (2003).
Ortiz, C, 'The Private Military Company: An Entity at the Centre of Overlapping Spheres of Commercial Activity and Responsibility' in T Jäger and G Kümmel (eds), *Private Military and Security Companies: Chances, Problems, Pitfalls and Prospects* (2007), 55–68.
Oulton, DP, and Lehman, AF, 'Deployment of U.S. Military, Civilian and Contractor Personnel to Potentially War Hazardous Areas from a Legal Perspective' (2001) 23(4) The DISAM Journal 15–21.
Palmer, CA, et al, 'The Emerging Policy Agenda for Reproductive Health Services in Conflict Settings' (1999) 49 *Social Science and Medicine* 1689–1703.

Parkinson, J, 'The Socially Responsible Company' in MK Addo (ed), *Human Rights Standards and the Responsibility of Transnational Corporations* (1999), 49–62.
Parks, W, 'Air War and the Law of War' (1990) 32 Air Force L R 1–226.
Patterson, J, 'A Corporate Alternative to United Nations ad hoc Military Deployments' (2008) 13 JC&SL 215–32.
Paul, JR, 'Comity in International Law' (1991) 32 Harv Int'l L J 1–80.
Paulus, A, 'Second Thoughts on the Crime of Aggression' (2009) 20 EJIL 1117–28.
Pejic, J, '"Unlawful/Enemy Combatants": Interpretations and Consequences' in MN Schmitt and J Pejic (eds), *International Law and Armed Conflict: Exploring the faultines* (2007), 335–55.
Percy, S, *Regulating the Private Security Industry* (2006).
——, *Mercenaries: The History of a Norm in International Relations* (2007).
——, 'Private Security Companies and Civil Wars' (2009) 11 *Civil Wars* 57–74.
Petersen, N, 'Life, Right To, International Protection' in *Max Planck Encyclopedia of Public International Law* (2007), <http://www.mpepil.com/>.
Pictet, J, (ed), *Commentaire à la Première Convention de Genève* (1952–9).
——, *The Geneva Conventions of 12 August 1949: Commentary* (1960).
Pictet, J, et al, *Geneva Convention Relative to the Protection of Civilian Persons in Time of War* (1958).
——, *Geneva Convention Relative to the Treatment of Prisoners of War* (1960).
Pilloud, C, and Pictet, JS, 'Article 51' in Y Sandoz et al (eds), *Commentary on the Additional Protocols of 8 June 1977 to the Geneva Conventions of 12 August 1949* (1987), 613–28.
Pinzauti, G, 'The European Court of Human Rights' Incidental Application of International Criminal Law and Humanitarian Law: A Critical Discussion of *Kononov v. Latvia*' (2008) 6 JICJ 1043–60.
Pisillo Mazzeschi, R, 'The Due Diligence Rule and the Nature of the International Responsibility of State' (1992) 35 GYIL 9–51.
——, 'Responsabilité de l'État pour Violation des Obligations Positives Relatives aux Droits de l'Homme' (2008) 333 RCADI 175–506.
Plessis, M, du, and Peté, S (eds), *Repairing the Past? International Perspectives on Reparations for Gross Human Rights Abuses* (2007).
Provost, R, *International Human Rights and Humanitarian Law* (2002).
Quéguiner, J-F, *Direct Participation in Hostilities under International Humanitarian Law* (2003).
Quirico, O, *National Regulatory Models for Private Military and Security Companies and Implications for Future International Regulation* (2009).
Raab, D, '"Armed Attack" after the Oil Platforms Case' (2004) 17 LJIL 719–35.
Ramcharan, B (ed), *The Right to Life in International Law* (1985).
—— 'The Drafting History of Art 6 of the International Covenant on Civil and Political Rights: Note by the Editor' in B Ramcharan (ed), *The Right to Life in International Law* (1985), 42–61.
Randelzhofer, A, 'Article 2.4' in B Simma (ed), *The Charter of the United Nations: A Commentary* (2002), 106–28.
Ratner, S, 'Corporations and Human Rights: A Theory of Legal Responsibility' (2001) 111 Yale LJ 452–545.
Reed, C, and Ryall, D (eds), *The Price of Peace: Just War in the Twenty-first Century* (2007).
Richard, T, 'Reconsidering the Letter of Marque: Utilizing Private Security Providers against Piracy' (2010) 39 Public Contact Law Journal 411–64.

Ridlon, D, 'Contractors or Illegal Combatants? The Status of Armed Contractors in Iraq' (2008) 62 Air Force L R 199–253.
Roberts, A, 'The End of Occupation: Iraq 2004' (2005) 54 ICLQ 27–48.
Roddik Christensen, A-M, *Judicial Accommodation of Human Rights in the European Union* (2007).
Rogers, APV, *Law on the Battlefield* (2004).
——, 'Unequal Combat and the Law of War' (2004) 7 YIntlHL 3–34.
Ronzitti, N, *Le Guerre di Liberazione Nazionale e il Diritto Internazionale* (1974).
——, *Maritime Terrorism and International Law* (1990).
Rosas, A, 'The European Court of Justice and Public International Law' in J Wouters, A Nollkaemper, and E De Wet (eds), *The Europeanisation of International Law* (2008), 71–86.
Roscini, M, 'The Efforts to Limit the International Criminal Court's Jurisdiction over Nationals of Non-party States: A Comparative Study' (2006) 5 LPICT 495–527.
Rosemann, N, *Code of Conduct: Tool for Self-regulation for Private Military and Security Companies* (2008).
Rosenne, S, 'Self-defense and the Non-use of Force: Some Random Thoughts' in P Eyffinger et al (eds), *Self-Defence as a Fundamental Principle* (2009), 49–66.
Roth, J, *The Logistic of the Roman Army at War, 264 BC–AD 235* (1999).
Roucounas, E, 'Peace Agreements as Instruments for the Resolution of Intrastate Conflict' in UNESCO, *Conflict Resolution: New Approaches and Methods* (2000), 113–40.
Rousseau, C, *Le Droit des Conflits Armés* (1983).
Rowe, P, *Control over Armed Forces Exercised by the European Court of Human Rights* (2002).
Roxstrom, E, et al, 'The NATO Bombing Case (*Bankovic et al v Belgium et al*) and the Limits of Western Human Rights Protection' (2005) 23 BostonUIntlLJ 55–136.
Ryan, B, 'Jus ad Bellum in the Israel–Hezbollah Conflict' (2007) 12 Cork Online Law Review 138–51.
Ryngaert, C, 'Litigating Abuses Committed by Private Military Companies' (2008) 19 EJIL 1035–53.
SFDI, *Les Compétences de l'Etat en Droit International* (2006).
Sagafi-nejad, T, and Dunning, JH, *The UN and Transnational Corporations: From Code of Conduct to Global Compact* (2008).
Salzman, Z, 'Private Military Contractors and the Taint of a Mercenary Reputation' (2008) 40 NYUJIntlL&Pol 853–92.
Sandoz, Y, 'The Dynamic but Complex Relationship between International Penal Law and International Humanitarian Law' in J Doria et al (eds), *The Legal Regime of the International Criminal Court* (2009), 1049–70.
Sandoz, Y, et al (eds), *Commentary on the Additional Protocols of 8 June 1977 to the Geneva Conventions of 12 August 1949* (1987).
Sangero, B, *Self-defense in Criminal Law* (2006).
Sari, A, 'Jurisdiction and International Responsibility in Peace Support Operations: The *Behrami* and *Saramati* Cases' (2008) 8 HRL Rev 151–70.
——, 'Status of Forces and Status of Mission Agreements under the ESDP: The EU's Evolving Practice' (2008) 19 EJIL 67–100.
Sarooshi, D, *International Organizations and Their Exercise of Sovereign Powers* (2005).
Sassòli, M, 'La "Guerre contre le Terrorisme," le Droit International Humanitaire et le Statut de Prisonnier de Guerre' (2001) 39 ACDI 211–52.
——, 'Targeting: The Scope and Utility of the Concept of "Military Objectives" for the Protection of Civilians in Contemporary Armed Conflicts' in D Wippman and

M Evangelista (eds), *New Wars, New Laws? Applying the Laws of War in the 21st Century Conflicts* (2005), 181–210.

——, 'Query: Is there a Status of "Unlawful Combatant"?' in RB Jaques (ed), *Issues in International Law and Military Operations* (2006), 57–67.

——, *Transnational Armed Groups and International Humanitarian Law* (2006).

Sassòli, M, and Olson, LM, 'The Judgment of the ICTY Appeals Chamber on the Merits in the *Tadic* Case: New Horizons for International Humanitarian and Criminal Law?' (2000) 82 IRRC 733–69.

——, 'The Relationship between International Humanitarian and Human Rights Law where it Matters: Admissible Killing and Internment of Fighters in Non-international Armed Conflicts' (2008) 871 IRRC 599–627.

Schabas, WA, *An Introduction to the International Criminal Court* (2004).

Scheffer, D, 'Article 98(2) of the Rome Statute: America's Original Intent' (2005) 3 JICJ 333–53.

Scheffler, A, *Piracy–Threat or Nuisance* (2010).

Scheimer, M, 'Separating Private Military Companies from Illegal Mercenaries in International Law: Proposing an International Convention for Legitimate Military and Security Support that Reflects Customary International Law' (2009) 24 AmUIntlLRev 609–46.

Schmidl, M, *The Changing Nature of Self-defense in International Law* (2009).

Schmitt, MN, (ed), *The Law of Armed Conflict: Into the Next Millennium* (1998).

——, 'Direct Participation in Hostilities and 21st Century Armed Conflict' in H Fischer (ed), *Crisis Management and Humanitarian Protection, Festschrift für Dieter Fleck* (2004), 505–29.

——, 'Humanitarian Law and Direct Participation in Hostilities by Private Contractors or Civilian Employees' (2005) 5 Chicago JIL 511–46.

——, 'Precision Attack and International Humanitarian Law' (2005) 87 IRRC 445–66.

——, 'The Interpretative Guidance on the Notion of Direct Participation in Hostilities: A Critical Analysis' (2010) 1 Harvard National Security Journal 5–44.

Schmitt, MN, and Pejic, J (eds), *International Law and Armed Conflict: Exploring the Faultiness* (2007).

Schmitt, MN, Garraway, C, and Dinstein, Y, *The Manual on the Law of Non-International Armed Conflict: With Commentary* (2006).

Schrijver, N, 'Commentaire de l'Article 2§4 de la Charte' in J-P Cot et al, *La Charte des Nations Unies, Commentaire Article par Article* (2005), 437–66.

Schulz, S, and Yeung, C, *Private Military and Security Companies and Gender* (2008).

Schutter, O, de, 'The Accountability of Multinationals for Human Rights Violations in European Law' in P Alston (ed), *Non-State Actors and Human Rights* (2005), 227–314.

——, 'The Responsibility of States' in S Chesterman and A Fisher (eds), *Private Security, Public Order: The Outsourcing of Public Services and its Limits* (2009), 25–45.

Sen, A, 'Human Rights and the Limits of Law' (2006) 27 Cardozo L Rev 2913–27.

Sena, P, De, *Diritto Internazionale e Immunità Funzionale degli Organi Statali* (1996).

——, *La Nozione di Giurisdizione Statale nei Trattati sui Diritti dell'uomo* (2002).

Shearer, D, *Private Armies and Military Intervention* (1998).

Shelton, D, *Remedies in International Human Rights Law* (2005).

——, *Remedies in International Human Rights Law* (2006).

Singer, PW, 'Corporate Warriors: The Rise of the Privatized Military Industry and its Ramifications for International Security' (2001–2) 26 International Security 186–220.

——, *Corporate Warriors: The Rise of the Privatised Military Industry* (2003).

Singer, PW, *The Private Military Industry and Iraq: What Have We Learned and Where to Next* (2004).
——, 'War, Profits, and the Vacuum of Law: Privatized Military Firms and International Law' (2004) 42 ColumJTransnatlL 521–49.
——, *Can't Win With 'Em, Can't Go To War Without 'Em: Private Military Contractors and Counterinsurgency* (2007).
Sivakumaran, S, 'Binding Armed Opposition Groups' (2006) 55 ICLQ 369–94.
Sjursen, H, 'The EU as a "Normative" Power: How can this be?' (2006) 13 *Journal of European Public Policy* 235–51.
Sliedregt, E, van, *The Criminal Responsibility of Individuals for Violations of International Humanitarian Law* (2003).
Smith, A, 'Child Recruitment and the Special Court for Sierra Leone: Some Considerations' (2004) 2 JICJ 1050–69.
Smith, K, 'Beyond the Civilian Power EU Debate' (2005) 17 *Politique européenne* 63–82.
Snyder, F, 'Soft Law and Institutional Practice in the European Community' in S Martin (ed), *The Construction of Europe: Essays in Honour of Emile Noël* (1994), 197–225.
Solis, GD, *The Law of Armed Conflict: International Humanitarian Law in War* (2010).
Sossai, M, 'Accesso alla Corte Europea dei Diritti dell'uomo per Violazioni Compiute dalle Forze Armate degli Stati Contraenti all'estero' in F Francioni et al (eds), *Accesso alla Giustizia Dellindividuo nel Diritto Internazionale e dell'Unione Europea* (2008), 197–232.
——, 'Status of Private Military Companies' Personnel in the Laws of War: The Question of Direct Participation in Hostilities' (2008) 18 *IYIL* 89–115.
Spear, J, *Market Forces: The Political Economy of Private Military and Security* (2005).
Spinedi, M, 'Private Contractors: Tesponsabilité Internationale des Entreprises ou Attribution à l'Etat de la Conduite des Personnes Privées?' (2005) 7 International Law Forum du droit international 273–80.
——, 'La Responsabilità dello Stato per Comportamneti di Private Contractors' in M Spinedi et al (eds), *La Codificazione della Responsabilità Internazionale degli Stati alla Prova dei Fatti* (2006), 67–106.
Stahn, C, 'The Ambiguities of Security Council Resolution 1422 (2002)' (2003) 14 EJIL 85–104.
Stanger, A, *One Nation under Contract* (2009).
Stern, K, 'From the European Convention on Human Rights to the European Charter of Fundamental Rights: The Prospects for the Protection of Human Rights in Europe' in H-M Blanke and S Mangiameli (eds), *Governing Europe under a Constitution* (2006), 169–84.
Stewart, JG, 'Towards a Single Definition of Armed Conflict in International Humanitarian Law: A Critique of Internationalized Armed Conflict' (2003) 85 IRRC 313–50.
Stinnett, N, 'Regulating the Privatization of War' (2005) 28 BCIntl&CompLRev 211–24.
Stober, J, 'Contracting in the Fog of War' in T Jäger and G Kümmel (eds), *Private Military and Security Companies: Chances, Problems, Pitfalls and Prospects* (2007), 121–34.
Stoddard, A, Harmer, A, and DiDomenico, V, *The Use of Private Security Providers and Services in Humanitarian Operations* (2008).
Tanca, A, *Foreign Armed Intervention in Internal Conflict* (1993).
Thomson, J, *Mercenaries, Pirates and Sovereigns* (1996).
Tolbert, D, 'Children and International Criminal law: The Practice of the International Criminal Tribunal for the Former Yugoslavia (ICTY)' in K Arts and V Popovski (eds), *International Criminal Accountability and the Rights of Children* (2006), 147–54.

Tonkin, H, 'Defensive Use of force under the Rome Statute' (2005) 6 Melbourne JIL 86–117.
Torremans, P, 'Extraterritoriality in Human Rights' in NA Neuwahl and A Rosas (eds), *The European Union and Human Rights* (1995), 281–96.
Treacher, A, 'From Civilian Power to Military Actor: The EU's Resistable Transformation' (2004) 9 European Foreign Affairs Review 49–66.
Trybus, M, 'With or Without the EU Constitutional Treaty: Towards a Common Security and Defence Policy?' (2006) 31 ELR 145–66.
Trybus, M, and White, ND (eds), *European Security Law* (2007).
Tsagourias, N, 'EU Peacekeeping Operations: Legal and Theoretical Issues' in M Trybus and ND White (eds), *European Security Law* (2007), 102–33.
Turner, LL, and Norton, LG, 'Civilians at the Top of the Spear' (2001) 51 Air Force L R 1–110.
Tushnet, M, 'The Issue of State Action/Horizontal Effect in Comparative Constitutional Law' (2003) 1 I Con 79–98.
UK Ministry of Defence, *The Manual of the Law of Armed Conflict* (2004).
UNESCO, *International Dimensions of Humanitarian Law* (1988).
——, *Conflict Resolution: New Approaches and Methods* (2000).
UNFPR, *Manual for Reproductive Health Kit in Crisis Situations* (2003).
Unité mixte de recherche de droit comparé de Paris, *Mireille Delmas-Marty et les années UMR* (2005).
Valenius, J, *Gender Mainstreaming in EDSP Missions* (2007).
Vega, C, de la, and Beck, A, *The Role of Military Demand in Trafficking and Sexual Exploitation* (2006).
Virally, M, 'Commentaire de l'Article 2§4 de la Charte' in J-P Cot and A Pellet (eds), *La Charte des Nations Unies, Commentaire Article par Article* (1991), 115–28.
Walker, C, and Whyte, D, 'Contracting out War? Private Military Companies, Law and Regulation in the United Kingdom' (2005) 54 ICLQ 651–89.
Wallace, W, 'Is there a European Approach to War?' in C Reed and D Ryall (eds), *The Price of Peace: Just War in the Twenty-first Century* (2007), 37–54.
Weigelt, T, and Marker, F, 'Who is Responsible? The Use of PMCs in Armed Conflicts and International Law' in T Jäger and G Kümmel (eds), *Private Military and Security Companies: Chances, Problems, Pitfalls and Prospects* (2007), 377–94.
Weiss, TG, and Daws, S, *The Oxford Handbook on the United Nations* (2007).
Werle, G, *Principles of International Criminal Law* (2005).
Wessel, RA, 'Revisiting the International Legal Status of the EU' (2000) 5 European Foreign Affairs Review 507–37.
——, 'The EU as a Black Widow: Devouring the WEU to give Birth to a European Security and Defence policy' in V Kronenberger (ed), *The European Union and the International Legal Order: Discord or Harmony?* (2001), 405–34.
——, 'The State of Affairs in EU Security and Defence Policy: The Breakthrough in the Treaty of Nice' (2003) 8 JC&SL 265–88.
White, ND, and MacLeod, S, 'EU Operations and Private Military Contractors: Issues of Corporate and Institutional Responsibility' (2008) 19 EJIL 965–88.
WHO, *Reproductive Health during Conflict and Displacement: A Guide for Programme Managers* (2000).
Wiesbrock, K, *Internationaler Schutz der Menschenrechte vor Verletzungen durch Private* (1999).
Wijk, R, de, 'The New Piracy: The Global Context' (2010) 52 *Survival* 39–54.

Wilt, H, van der, 'Bilateral Agreements between the United States and States Parties to the Rome Statute: Are they Compatible with the Object and Purpose of the Statute?' (2005) 18 LJIL 93–111.
Wippman, D, and Evangelista, M (eds), *New Wars, New Laws? Applying the Laws of War in the 21st Century Conflicts* (2005).
Wirth, S, 'Immunities, Related Problems, and Article 98 of the Rome Statute' (2001) 12 Criminal LF 429–58.
Wither, JK, 'European Security and Private Military Companies: The Prospects for Privatized "Battlegroups"' (2005) 4 *The Quarterly Journal* 107–26.
Wolfrum, R, 'Fighting Terrorism at Sea: Options and Limitations under International Law' in M Nordquist et al (eds), *Legal Challenges in Maritime Security* (2008), 649–68.
Wouters, J, Nollkaemper, A, and De Wet, E (eds), *The Europeanisation of International Law* (2008).
Wulf, H, *Internationalizing and Privatizing War and Peace* (2005).
Yarnold, B, 'The Doctrinal Basis for the International Criminalization Process' in M-C Bassiouni (ed), *International Criminal Law* (1999), 127–52.
Yihdego, Z, *The Arms Trade and International Law* (2007).
Young, O, *International Cooperation: Building Regimes for Natural Resources and the Environment* (1989).
Zahar, A, 'Command Responsibility of Civilian Superiors for Genocide' (2001) 14 LJIL 591–616.
Zappalà, S, 'Are Some Peacekeepers Better than Others? UN Security Council Resolution 1497 (2003) and the ICC' (2003) 1 JICJ 671–8.
Zarate, JC, 'The Emergence of a New Dog of War: Private International Security Companies, International Law, and the New World Disorder' (1998) 34 StanJIntlL 75–162.
Zegveld, L, *Armed Opposition Groups in International Law: The Quest for Accountability* (2000).
——, *Accountability of Armed Opposition Groups in International Law* (2002).
Ziemele, I, *Issues of Responsibility of Private Persons or Entities for Human Rights Violations: The Case-law of International Human Rights Courts and Monitoring Bodies* (2008).
——, *Human Rights Violations by Private Persons and Entities: The Case-law of International Human Rights Courts and Monitoring Bodies* (2009).
Zimmermann, A, 'Superior Orders' in A Cassese, P Gaeta, and JRWD Jones (eds), *The Rome Statute of the International Criminal Court: A Commentary* (2002), 957–74.
Zwanenburg, MC, *Accountability under International Humanitarian Law for United Nations and North Atlantic Treaty Organization Peace Support Operations* (2004).

Index

Abu Ghraib
  abuses 4, 22, 115
  CACI and Titan 431
  effective control 435
  inhuman treatment 424
  international crimes 456
  legal qualification 211
  political-question doctrine 443
  state responsibility 117
  superior orders 440
  tort action 442
  US contractors 468
  see also **torture**
access to justice
  differential treatment 77
  effective remedies 395
  effectiveness of human rights 77, 98
  indictee 69
  inquiries 395
  jurisdiction 477
  wrongful acts 3
accountability
  2007 Report on Iraq 203
  attribution of acts and omissions 155, 162, 169, 257, 325, 385–386, 389, 391, 393–394, 397, 408, 432–435, 461, 474, 484, 487
  business 350, 356, 358
  children's rights 273, 276, 279
  CoC 373
  contractors 3, 6, 7, 361, 488
  contractual relationship 354
  criminal proceedings 443, 447
  CSR 395
  ECHR 58, 126
  ECtHR 157
  EU 35
  GCs 359
  group 259
  host state's control 104
  human rights 375, 381, 382
  ICC Statute 447
  immunity 449
  incorporation of contractors in armed forces 319
  internal procedures 137
  international initiatives 344
  international organizations 33–34
  IPOA 365, 367
  Iraqi penal law 459
  judicial review 469
  lack of 351, 352, 454, 466
  licensing 29
  mechanisms 354, 356
  multistakeholder regulation 361
  OECD Guidelines 356
  offence 109
  PMSCs 96, 110, 376
  public demand 23
  security operations 17
  Sharp End International 366
  SIP 357
  standards 96
  tort 488
  UN military discipline 388
  use of force 33, 36
  use of PMSCs by international organizations 383, 393, 395
  women 280, 296, 297
Act of State 488
acta iure imperii 484
Aegis
  Afghanistan 331
  major security contract in Iraq 25
  protective security services 207
Afghanistan
  Al-Qaeda 211
  Amnesty International 354
  ASPA agreements 445–446
  business 14
  CIA bases 335
  CIA raids 334
  defensive combat 334
  ECHR (extraterritorial applicability) 161
  Enduring Freedom 253
  enquiries 29
  EUPOL 307, 317
  institutional capacity 104, 137
  legitimate government 220
  military training 332
  Northrop Grumman personnel 424
  operations 13
  PMSCs 277, 331, 337
  reconstruction 21
  recruiting children 266, 272
  security services 95
  SOFAs 444, 453
  Taliban government 412
  US DoD 207, 284
  US Patriot Act 459
  Xe 431

African Charter on Human and Peoples' Rights
    (ACHPR)
  dignity 69
  duty to protect 57
  human rights 59
  jurisdiction 156
  massive human rights breaches 75
  peoples' rights 74, 75
  physical and mental health 65, 66
  right to life 173
African Command, US
  outsourcing 14
African Commission on Human and Peoples'
    Rights (AComHPR)
  acces to justice 69
  collective rights 75
  duty to prevent 141
  family 71
  human rights 59–60
  right to health 65–66
  right to life 62–63
Agent theory
  contracting 22
  market incentives 96
aiding and abetting
  Alien Tort Statute 478
Alien Tort Statute
  cause of action 480–481
  combant-activities exceptions 483
  defendant's domicile 480
  exorbitant jurisdiction 477–478, 483, 488
  forum non conveniens 482
  self-executing rules 480–481
Al-Qaeda
  Blackwater 335
  combat drones 211
  state territory 412
American Convention on Human Rights (ACHR)
  duty to legislate, investigate, prosecute and
      punish 117, 123–125
  duty to prevent 139
  human rights standards 57
  judicial protection 78
  right to life 173
  right to physical and mental health 64
Angola
  criminal conduct and war 431
  Executive Outcomes 246, 424
  military operations 237
  second civil war 239
  special agreements 245
  training 330
applicable law
  EC Regulation Roma II 483–485
  liability in tort 470–471, 489
  scope of 485–488
arbitrary killings
  effective remedy 144
  use of force 191

armed conflict
  AComHPR 141
  armed opposition groups 256
  children 76–77
  children's rights 262–264, 276, 278, 307
  civilians 254
  CoC 362, 370–371
  confrontation of PMSCs with children
      participation in hostilities 272–274
  criminal responsibility 423, 425–431,
      446–447
  damage 487
  displacement 285
  due diligence 410
  duty to legislate, investigate, prosecute and
      punish 117–118
  ECHR 115–117, 126–128
  economic disadvantage 286
  ECtHR 149–151, 154, 161, 164, 169
  effective control 95
  escorting merchant vessels 46
  ESDP/CSDP 304, 306, 315
  EU protection of children 275, 277–279
  governmental authority 101
  health 284
  host state's adequate control 105
  human rights obligations 5, 60
  IACtHR 140
  ICCPR 112
  ICRC 293
  IHL treaties 314
  law of 5
  legal status of captured contractors 233
  liability in tort 489
  managers 436
  mercenaries 321–323, 326–336,
      338, 353
  mercenary activities 28
  Montreux Document 30, 51
  NIACs 5, 235–238, 241, 260
  obligations of the host state 130, 147
  persons belonging to the armed forces of
      legitimate governments 248–249
  persons who accompany the armed
      forces 218, 220, 222, 234
  piracy 50
  POW status 228–229
  prohibition of PMSCs 50
  prosecution 442–443
  protection of private contractors 3
  recruiting children 266–267, 269–272
  remedies 393
  restriction of liberty 255
  right to life and self-defence 171–175,
      178–181, 185–193
  role of women 290
  scope of protection 247
  self-determination of people 242
  sexual violence 292

Index

status of PMSC personnel 197–198, 201–203, 204–209, 216
status of private contractors 2
taking of life 61
torture 63, 65
UN and women 294
violence against women 282–283, 297
vulnerable groups 6
war crimes 289
women 280–281, 287
see also **international humanitarian law**
armed force
  aggression 106
  foreign 237, 241
  illicit use 397
  prohibition of 416–417
  resort to 236, 369–370, 379
  self-defence 201, 309
  training 366
  use of 240, 398, 401, 403, 415, 420
armed forces
  act of the state 99, 153
  affiliation 432
  aggression 402
  allied 485
  attack 253
  chain of command 319
  civilians accompanying 5, 202–203, 207, 215
  combatant privilege 198
  contingency operations 293, 459
  conventional 60
  crimes 283
  dissident 177, 248, 252
  foreign 5, 260
  formal enlistement 254, 261
  hostile act 204
  incorporation into 4, 100, 163, 201, 204, 249, 483
  independent militias 199
  international organizations 190, 386, 392
  irregular 251
  massive human rights breaches 75
  mercenaries, and 323–324, 337
  membership 1, 198–201, 203, 213, 249–250, 338–339, 431–432
  national 1, 4, 5, 17–19, 109, 154
  NIACs 425
  obligation to investigate, prosecute and punish 121
  organized armed group 253–254
  persons belonging to 247–248
  persons who accompany 218–234, 437, 441
  preparatory measures 334
  protection of PMSCs 186, 188
  recruitment of children 76, 262–264, 266–272
  regular 5, 177, 198–200, 202, 216, 250, 382–383, 477
  SOFAs 452, 476
  state organs 17, 176, 184, 190, 261, 382, 476

support to 1, 93, 241
training 212
UCMJ 458
use of force 181–182
victims 474
warship 41
see also **self-defence**
armed guard on private shipping
  coastal states 44
  deterring piracy 39, 50
  IMO policy 44
  reaction 43
  Somalia 43
  supplying armed personnel 43
armed group
  children involved in hostilities 272
  civilians 213, 254
  criminal responsibility 424
  direct participation in hostilities 177–178
  fighting 175
  human rights abuses 140
  ICC Statute 428–429
  IHL 6, 255–256, 269
  insurgency 246
  international criminal responsibility 258
  mercenaries 253
  NIAC 241, 425–426
  opposition groups 251
  PMSCs' members 214, 236, 252
  protection 177, 185, 213
  recruitment of children 271
  right to life 177
  Security Council resolutions 245
  state responsibility 59, 257–258, 450
  violation of IHL obligations 256
armed opposition group
  governmental agreement 242
  liability 6
  NIAC 247, 260–261
  obligation of full reparation 259–260
  obligation of notification 249
  persons belonging to 251–253
  PMSC support 142, 235–236, 239, 246
  PMSCs (acting as) 269
  responsibility 255–256
  SC Resolution 864 (1993) 245
  state responsibility 257–258
  state support (against) 240–241
  third states' assistance 245
arms
  armed security services 365
  carry openly 189
  children 273
  contractors as military objectives 213
  contractual clauses 188–189
  crimes 442–443
  defensive use 182
  export 34–35, 107
  export and brokering 300

arms (cont.)
    governmental authority 404
    illegal 370
    International Traffic in Arms Regulation 28
    neutral individuals 322
    nexus with armed conflict 208
    on board of ships 43, 50
    prohibition 188, 191
    right to carry 15, 94–95, 180, 184, 187, 192–193, 369
    SC Resolutions 244–245
    self-defence 186, 209–210
    small arms attacks 207
    trafficking 28–29, 246, 366, 378
    training 209, 369–370
    use of 172
    violence against women 282
arms to Africa affair
    British government 29

Blackwater
    Afghanistan 331
    breach of the laws of war 456
    CIA raids 334
    civil lawsuit 27
    CPA headquarters 207, 334, 440
    crimes 431
    criminal proceedings 424, 442–443
    dismissal 374
    immunity 457
    Iraq 331
    licensing 138
    logistic support in conflict situations 423
    Maritime Security Services 38
    Nisour Square 202, 265, 350, 444–445, 479
    political-question doctrine 468
British Association of Private Security Companies (BAPSC)
    Charter 364–365
    contracts 367
    CSR 375
    enforcement 24, 373, 379
    self-regulation 24
    trade associations 364
Brussels Convention of 1968
    case law
        Fiona Shevill v Presse Alliance SA 473
        Antonio Marinari v Lloyds Bank plc and Zubaidi Trading Co 473
    claim for damages 474
    compensation 474
    defendant's domicile 471
    jurisdiction 476
    scope of 483
burden of proof
    IACtHR 114
    reversal 125
business and human rights
    accountability 357

regulatory initiatives 343–345, 346–350, 353, 355, 358–361
UN Secretary General's Special Representative 6, 345, 346, 349, 352, 354

cause of action
    ATS 480
    case law
        Saleh and ors v Titan Corp 481
    forum non conveniens 482
    lack of 480–483
    specific jurisdiction 472
    victims 481
Central Intelligence Agency (CIA)
    Blackwater 335
    hiring contractors 459
    offensive operations 334
    weapons system 211
chain of command
    corporate structure 100
    incorporation 200
    military 18, 22, 201, 319, 320
children
    armed conflict 77, 282, 306–307
    ESDP 304
    EU 273–278
    human rights 270–272, 304
    ICL 267–270
    IHL 264, 270
    participation in hostilities 272–273
    PMSCs 6, 265–266
    recruitment 266
    rights 75–76, 262–263
    sexual violence 288
    UN 272
civil-military relations
    MPRI 335, 426
    PMSCs 16
civilian objects 208
civilian operations 299
civilian population 59, 108, 114, 171, 199, 258
civilians
    Afghanistan 13
    accompanying the armed forces 5
    armed opposition group 253
    capture 215, 230–231, 233
    case law
        Blaškic 210
        Ergi v Turkey 62
        Isayeva v Russia 143
        Isayeva, Yusupova and Bazayeva v Russia 143
        Kallis and Androulla Panayi v Turkey 143
        Khashiyev and Akayeva v Russia 143
        Musema 436
        Nahimana 436
        Satabeyeva v Russia 143
        Tadić 210
    combatants 175, 197, 249, 371

command over 439
command responsibility 433
court-martial 458
criminal liability 215
criminal prosecution 441
crisis management 316
direct participation in hostilities 204–205, 222, 224–225, 227–228, 232, 234, 253
effective control 440
EU Guidelines on protection 316
EU SOFA 306
immunity 204
injury 289
intelligence 210
killing 109, 138, 162, 171, 174, 176, 202, 265, 350, 424, 431, 442, 445, 456
murder 443
Nisour Square 4, 7, 27
persons who accompany the armed forces 228
PMSC contractors 176, 178, 192, 201–202, 204, 209, 213–215, 221, 247, 252, 254, 261, 284, 483
political-question doctrine 467
protection 175, 177, 205, 219, 256, 264, 316, 428
security 208
security operations 290
self-defence 180–181, 186–187, 209
sexual violence 284
SOFAs 463
state officials 451
state responsibility 59, 99, 389
superior 438
supporting military force 229
unincorporated agencies 200
use of force 178, 204, 292
victims 6, 162, 280
war crimes 429–430
women 282–284, 287–288, 293, 297–298
see also **combatants**
Coalition Provisional Authority (CPA)
headquarters 423, 440
installation 426
Order 17 27, 444, 454–455, 457
security contracts 25
Coast Guard
activities 37–39, 48–49, 465, 483
codes of conduct
Blue Sky/Guardian Security Consultant 364, 369, 372
classification 363–364, 378–380
CoESS/UniEuropa 366, 367–368, 372
common 363, 368
Control Risks Group 364
Dyncorp 364
enforcement 372, 375–378
G4S 364, 369
IHL 377
IMO 38, 51

IPOA 365, 367–368, 370, 373–374, 379
Law Enforcement Officials 370, 379
PMSCs 439
private regulation 364
PSCAI 365, 368
Sarajevo 363, 366–368, 370
Secopex 364
Sharp End International 364, 367
Swiss Initiative 108
Uni-Europa 365
Xe 364
see also **corporate social responsibility**
coercive services
ACHR 125
armed conflict 117–118, 125, 362
arrest 78
case law
Valle Jaramillo 114
contracting out 59
duty to prevent 112
ECHR 115, 126
governmental authority 163
hiring state 4, 203
human rights 111, 364
internal affairs 420
licensing 106
prohibition of torture 122
right to life 113, 128
security 102
Security Council 245
combat drones
maintenance 211
combatants
armed conflict 446
armed forces 199, 250
armed opposition group 252
arms 187
case law
Akayesu 432
civilians 254
combatant-activities exception 482–483
commander 207
contractors 176, 197, 201, 213, 483
direct participation in hostilities 180, 198, 216, 234
effective control 440
enemy 175–176, 180, 185, 222
GCs 220, 231, 371
Hague Convention on Neutral Powers 418–419
human rights treaties 175
IAC 175
interrogation 211
lawful 71, 250
legitimate 5, 198, 213, 215
mercenary 323–325, 327
military and naval forces 465
NIAC 176, 249
non-combatant 186, 191, 231

combatants (*cont.*)
  personnel supporting armed forces 221
  political-question doctrine 482
  POW 219, 232
  private 396
  Protocol I GCs 204, 208
  rape 292
  right to attack 176, 178
  South African Foreign Military Assistance Act 28
  UN forces 393
  unlawful 189, 233
  war crimes 429–430
  women 280, 283, 286
  command responsible requirement 200
Common Security and Defence Policy (CSDP)
  resort to private contractors 300, 318–320
  case law
    Criminal Proceedings against Maria Pupino 301
    Nold v Commission 301
  fundamental rights 302–305, 307, 318
  IHL 308, 313, 318
  TEU 310
  EU troops in the field 315–316
Complementarity
  ICC 131, 270
  obligations 95
  substantive 5
Congress, USA
  Budget Office 335, 337
  contingency operations 459
  contract 28
  declaration of war 458
  hearing 283–284
  PMSCs operating abroad 480
  PMSCs' regulation 29
  self-executing international norms 481
  UCMJ 458
continuous combat functions
  direct particpation in hostilities 232
  ICRC Interpretative Guidance 201, 214, 221
  organized armed group 253
contract
  ad hoc arrangements 100
  Aegis 25, 207
  Amnesty International 354
  armed forces 269
  armed teams 44
  Blackwater 335
  civilians 261
  coercive functions 59
  collective self-regulation 25
  Congress notification 28
  consent 240–241
  control 29
  CSDP missions 304–305, 319
  direct participation in hostilities 191–192, 213, 224, 424

duress 184
Erinys 208
gender awareness 286
Generic Standards of Behaviour 317
good conduct 23
governmental outsourcing 155, 162
hiring state procurement 94, 111, 115, 131
home government 21
HRL/IHL 320
human rights 23, 163, 343
immunity 27, 448, 451, 456–457, 477
inspection of contractor operations 113
international regulatory body 32
interrogation services 23
international organizations 167, 393
jurisdiction 475, 484
lucrative 22
mercenaries 330, 332
monitoring 23, 31, 35
MPRI 335
NCP 357
non-competitivity 21
objective liability 487
obligations 18, 185
personnel qualification 296
persons who accompany the armed forces 218
PMSCs under a responsible command, and 201
'political and financial support test' 165
POW status 229
preventing and remedying human rights violations 95
private company 162, 167
private military services 16
protection of children 264, 273, 277–279
protective security services 207
public 21–22, 24–25
public functions 164
public power 404
publicity 439–440
regulation 296
Sandline 331, 339
security forces 113
self-regulation 362–363, 367–368, 373, 376–377, 379
services 336
sexual offences 296
sub-contract 203, 266
suspension 202
tasks 201, 203, 439
termination 113, 138, 142, 202
US, UK 137
use of force 172, 187–189, 193, 418
validity 405
VPSHR 25
wartime 29
see also **contractor**
contracting state
  aggression 403
  Al-Saadoon and Mufdhi v UK 58

Issa and ors v Turkey 58
Pad and ors v Turkey 160
children 264, 278–279
direct use of PMSCs 19
duties 85
ECHR 155–156, 159, 162
ECtHR jurisdiction 169
governmental transparency 19
home state, and 22
case law
immunity 168, 448, 455, 458, 464–465, 467
ius ad bellum 418
judicial remedies 90
jurisdiction 58, 133, 155–156, 160, 162, 168, 458, 474
mercenaries 31–33
Montreux Document 30, 397
positive human rights obligations 111, 131, 153–154, 158, 415, 418
proceedings 474
prosecution 140, 297
regulation 26–27, 30–31, 33
responsibility 168, 397, 403, 405, 407–408, 419
state responsibility 85
transnational advocacy networks 27
use of force 16, 20
contractor
Abu-Ghrain 117
armed conflicts 175
armed guards 50
as military objective 213–214
capture 216, 228, 230–233
children's rights 265, 272–273
civil claims 7
command responsibility 434–435, 437
criminal responsibility 215, 423–424, 426, 430–431, 447
direct participation in hostilities 5, 177–180, 204–206, 334
duty to investigate, prosecute and punish 125
duty to legislate 123
ECHR
accountability of hiring states 155
adjudication 152
agents of the state 161–165
jurisdiction 153
positive human rights obligations 166
EU 2, 394
EU crisis mangment 299–300, 305, 318–320
fight against piracy 37
gender-awareness training 286, 296
hiring state
effective prosecution 119–122
human rights obligations 95, 111–112
individuals in custody 114–115
outsourcing 197
right to life 113, 116–117, 122, 128
home state
export of military services 106

governmental authority 101
human rights, and 93
imputability 99
obligation to prevent and remedy 95
prohibition 106
human rights obligations 5, 93–94, 153, 206, 354
IHL obligations 314
immunity 27, 109, 168, 448–449
from civil jurisdiction 464–469
from criminal jurisdiction 454–464
SOFAs 451–454, 469
in foreign conflicts 28–29
intelligence activities 210–212
international organizations 381, 386–388, 392
legal regulation 20
legal status 2, 176, 198–203
liability 3
mercenaries 14, 322, 329, 331, 332, 334–339
military personnel, and 18, 229–230
monitoring 107
motivation 336
nationality 338
residence 338
Obama 17, 29
obligation to protect 186, 188
offshore installations 49
on board 43
oversight 32
persons who accompany the armed forces 218–222
post-traumatic stress disorder 285
private military and security services 1, 12, 111, 222–227
prosecution 441–446
protective services 207–210
recruitment 332
remedies 384
responsibility to protect 102, 104
right to carry arms 184, 187–189, 192–193
right to life 5
self-defence 171–172, 181–184, 193
self-regulation 363, 365
services 15, 17
sexual violence 284, 293, 297
state responsibility 4, 59, 153, 163
superior orders 439–440
supply contractor 224
US in Iraq 13–14
use of force 190
warships 41–42
women 6, 280, 282, 287
see also **Private Military and Security Companies (PMSCs)**
Convention on the Rights of the Child (CRC)
childrens' rights 262–263, 270–272
compliance 287
EU 274
involvement of children in armed conflicts 76

corporate social responsibility
  enforcement 377–378
  ethical codes 363
  EU 349
  human rights 344–345, 350, 354, 358
  NCP 357
  regulatory initiatives 343, 355–356, 359–361, 363, 375, 379–380
  standards 346
  see also **self-regulation**
criminal responsibility
  direct participation in hostilities 233
  enlistment of children 267, 270
  human rights law 132
  ICC 259
  IHL 179, 269, 423
  implementation 442
  individual PMSC employees 6, 369, 429
  individuals 371, 387, 406
  international 258
  PMSCs 369
  superior orders 438
  see also **war crimes**
customary international law
  case law
    Anklagemyndigheden v Peter Michael Poulsen and Diva Navigation Corp 301
    International Fruit Company v Produktschap voor Groenten en Fruit 301
    Opel Austria v Council 301
    Racke v Hauptzollant Mainz 301
  cause of action 480
  command responsibility 433
  conscription, enlistment and use in hostilities of children 267
  EU 301
  government actions 468
  human rights 56, 61
  IHL 233
  immunity 448–449
  accountability of international organizations 386
  mercenaries 327
  piracy 37
  principle of concurrent causation 146
  prohibitions 67
  right to life 173
  self-defence 179, 402
  state responsibility 165
  superior orders 438

democratic control
  over the use of force 2, 29, 382
denial of justice
  competent jurisdiction 488
  division of jurisdictional powers 471
  forum non conveniens 482
Department of Defence (DoD)
  commanders 439
  contractors 13
  human trafficking 285
  IAC/NIAC rules 427
  internal investigation 284
  Iraqi operations 202
  lack of PMSCs' regulation 295
  MEJA 459
  monitoring 23
  persons who accompany the armed forces 218, 223–224
  PMSCs' management 203
  PMSCs' managers 437
  PMSCS' personnel uniforms 200
  POW status 231
  privatization 12
  protective security services 207
  Quadriennal Defence Review 12
  self-defence 209
  sexual assaults 293, 296–297
Department of State
  export of military services 28
  mercenaries 328
  offensive combat operations 334
  status of contractors 483
direct causation
  direct participation in hostilities 204, 333
  ICRC Interpretative Guidance 216, 222
  impact on the enemy 206
direct participation in hostilities
  children 270
  civilians 176
  conduct amounting to 206, 216–217, 254
  contracting for 237
  constitutive elements 204–206
  criminal liability 416
  criminal prosecution for 323
  general prohibition 191
  government consent 237
  IAC/NIAC 177
  ICRC's Interpretative Guidance 201, 204, 221, 253
  intelligence activities 210–211
  isolated acts 213
  loss of protection 227
  membership in armed groups 253
  mercenaries 326, 333–336
  Montreux Document 191
  nexus to armed conflict 205
  operation of weapon systems 211
  outsourcing activities 216
  persons who accompany the armed forces 222–226, 231
  PMSCs 5, 178, 188, 220, 369
  POW status 232–233
  prohibition 209
  rescue operations 212
  right to life 189
  self-defence 180–181, 210
  South African Foreign Military Assistance Act 28

Index

state responsibility 413
status of contractors 197, 204
superior orders 440
targeting PMSC personnel 216
see also **combatants**
discrimination
 anti-discimination clause 82
 Common CoC 368
 NIAC 428
 racial 65, 67–68
 TFEU 311
 VPSHR 379
 women 77, 280, 284–285, 287–288, 294
Draft International Convention on the Regulation, Oversight and Monitoring of Private Military and Security Companies
 armed force 417
 due diligence 411
 mercenaries 31
 PMSCs in armed conflicts (prohibition) 50
 uniform private law 419
Drittwirkung
 direct and indirect 89–90
due diligence
 application 411
 armed opposition groups 6
 arms 184, 188
 case law
  Andronicou and Constantinou v Cyprus 115
  Zimbabwean Human Rights NGO Forum v Zimbabwe 241
 contractor exposing himself to danger 189
 definition 408–411
 export licences 107
 hiring state 172
 home state 104
 home state's responsibility 107–108
 human rights 6, 114, 118, 343, 347–348, 352, 358
 IHL 186, 257–258, 261
 international organizations 392–393
 ius ad bellum 407, 420
 licensing 4
 monitoring PMSCs' activities 107
 obligation to regulate PMSCs 110, 413
 positive duties 106, 108
 duty to prevent, punish, and investigate 56, 114, 122, 125, 141, 153
 duty to protect 186
 principle of 105
 responsibility to protect 108
 right to life 138, 191–193
 state breach 407–408
 state responsibility 59, 102
 state responsibility for private acts 139
 systematic failure 142
 use of force 397
 violence against women 294

duty to investigate and prosecute
 abuse of authority 445
 case law
  Assenov and ors v Bulgaria 115
 Draft International Convention on the Regulation, Oversight and Monitoring of Private Military and Security Companies 417
 ECHR 126–128, 154
 ECtHR 140
 host state 130–131
 human rights violations 111–112, 117, 142–144, 146, 166, 271
 IACHR 122–125
 ICCPR 56, 118–122
 lack of institutional capacity 131–132
 SC Resolutions 462
 UN Declaration on the Elimination of Violence against Women 294
duty to legislate
 ECHR 126, 169
 IACtHR 122–123, 125
 ICCPR 118–119
 PMSCs' violations 111–112, 117
duty to prevent
 abuse of force 94
 ACHPR 59–60
 ACHR 58–59, 113–115
 AComHPR 141–142
 Afrimex 358
 armed attack 412–413
 command responsibility 433–437
 Convention on the Rights of the Child 263, 266, 278
 due diligence 153
 ECHR 115–117, 134
 ECtHR 85, 140
 genocide 385, 409
 host state 130–131
 HRC 137–138
 human rights violations 4, 19, 79, 90, 95, 98, 104–105, 108–110, 111–112, 117, 136, 152, 154, 167, 169, 271
 IACtHR 139, 146
 ICCPR 56, 112–113
 IHL breaches 16, 186
 international organizations 392–393
 PMSCs' activities 27, 94
 PMSCs' crimes 57, 107, 414
 recruitment of children 271–273
 right to life 128, 185
 right to physical and mental health 66
 terrorism 390, 410
 UN Declaration on the Elimination of Violence against Women 294–296
 violations of *ius ad bellum* 416, 418–420
 violence against children 76–77

duty to protect
  case law
    Ergi v Turkey 258
    Island of Palmas 409
    McCann and ors v UK 126
    Osman v UK 141
    Sawhoyamaxa Indigenous Community 124
  children's rights 263–264, 275
  family 71
  freedom from torture 136, 138, 153
  human rights 57–58, 60, 98–99, 104, 108, 139, 142
  individuals 113, 116
  life of private contractors 186, 191, 193
  persons in custody 114, 117
  respect and remedy 348, 349, 351, 360
  right to life 118, 136, 153–154, 166, 181
  victims 487
  women 288
duty to punish
  breach 412
  breach of *ius ad bellum* 416
  coastal states 40
  command responsibility 433–434
  due diligence 294
  ECHR 154
  ECtHR 126–128
  hiring state 111–112, 117–118
  human rights standards 56, 85, 131, 166
  IACtHR 122–125
  ICCPR 118–122
  IHL breaches 16
  immunity 168
  sexual violence 284
  violence against women 294
Dyncorp
  armed services 331
  breach of international law 246
  child prostitution 33
  CoC 365–366
  home state/host state 131
  security sector 364
  sex slavery 283

EC Regulation 44/2001
  applicability to PMSCs 472–475
  defendant's domicile 471
  exorbitant jurisdiction 478
  scope of application 483–484
EC Regulation Rome II
  applicable law 485
  compensation 488
  locus damni 485
  non-contractual obligations 483
  PMSCs' tort liability 489
  scope of 484
  tort liability 486
effective remedy
  business actors 359

Convention on the Rights of the Child 263
ECHR 128
ECtHR 126–127
HRC 144
human rights violations 142–143, 348
IAComHR 124
ICCPR 57, 118, 120
judicial protection 78
positive obligations 117
right to reparation 260
women 293
effective control
  case law
    Nicaragua 102–103, 406
    Tadić 102–103
  contracting state 155
  home state 104, 110
  host state 95, 131
  institutional responsibility 381, 383, 389–393
  jurisdiction 57, 86, 156–158, 162–163
  PMSCs 434, 436, 439–440
  state responsibility 257
  third state 132–135, 146
escorting
  aircrafts 48
  convoys 4, 102, 163
  high ranking officials 60, 207
  merchant vessels 39, 46–48
espace juridique
  case law
    Al-Saadoon and Mufdhi v UK 160
    Bankovic and ors v Belgium and ors 160
    Behrami and Behrami v France and Saramati v France 160
  ECHR 156
  notion 159
EU Charter of Fundamental Rights
  EU human rights regime 80–81
  right to life 173
EU Code of Conduct on Armaments Exports 34
EU common positions
  CFSP 34–35
  implementation of SC Resolutions 87
EU joint actions
  CFSP 34
  civilian mission 319
  CSDP 308
  EUPOL Afghanistan Police Mission 317
  HRL 320, 305
  military assistance 34
EU Navfor Atalanta
  multinational operation 39
European Convention on Human Rights (ECHR)
  armed conflict 5
  children's rights 274

Index

Drittwirkung 90
duty to legislate, investigate, prosecute and punish 117, 126–128
duty to prevent 112, 115, 117, 134
extraterritorial application 58, 85–86, 134–135, 155–156, 158–162, 170
freedom from torture 64, 153
human rights law 57, 81, 83, 88–89, 91, 302–303, 313
infringement by PMSCs 151
obligation to investigate, prosecute, and punish 154
peace operations 391
responsibility of non-state actors 167, 169
right to life 153, 173, 182
right to property 87
self-regulation 368
state responsibility 165–166

European Court of Human Rights (ECtHR)
arbitrary detention 69
duty to prevent 115, 140, 143
duty to protect 58, 117
effective control 133–135, 391
human rights regime 80, 83, 85–88
human rights violations 5, 150–162
IHL 310
immunity 169
judicial remedies 90
non-state actors 167–168
positive obligations 126–127
reparation 145
reporting allegations 129
right to life 62–63
right to private life 72
self-defence 183
state responsibility 164–166

European Court of Justice (ECJ)
acta iure imperii 473–476, 484
anti-discrimination clause 82
customary international law 301, 309
human rights regime 80–81, 83–84, 86–88
IHL 310, 313
judicial remedies 90–91
national jurisdiction 473

European Defence Agency
crisis-management operations 35, 318
use of PMSCs 36

European Parliament
use of PMSCs 36

European Union (EU)
armed forces 190
children's rights 262, 273–279
crisis-managment 6, 299–300
human rights law 300–313
IHL 313–318
defendant's domicile 475–476
escorting merchant vessels 46
fundamental rights 81, 85, 87, 192, 274, 301–302, 312

human rights 4, 80–92, 344–346, 349, 356
jurisdictional power 470–471
multinational operations 39
non-contractual obligations 483
PMSCs' regulation 2, 12, 30, 34–35, 171
responsibility 167–168, 381–383, 393–395
right to life 173
security and defence policy 3
self-regulation 365–366, 368–369
sexual assault 296
tort liability 488–489

Executive Outcomes
armed assistance 239
command responsibility 434
direct participation in hostilities 190, 237, 246, 330, 424, 430
Sierra Leone 444

extraterritoriality
ECtHR 134
PMSCs' conduct 155
prosecution 20, 32

Federal Tort Claims Act (FTCA)
immunity 465
jurisdiction 483
PMSC status 483
remedy 465

fixed oil platforms
jurisdiction 49
protection 49

forced prostitution
AP II GCs 289
GCs 288
ICC 289
ICL 264
rings 280
sexual violence 283
victims of 6
war crime 288
women 77, 282

foreign aid and assistance
non-governmental entities 13
use of force 242

foreign intervention
prohibition of using force 237
request 236

Foreign Military Assistance Act (FMAA)
export of armed services 28

forum actoris
Italian law 478

forum necessitatis
immunity 488

forum non-conveniens
dismissing jurisdiction 482

forum shopping
jurisdictional powers 470
reparation 394
SOFAs 488

functional immunity
civil jurisdiction 464
international crimes 456–457
international personnel 449, 451, 456
organ acting on behalf of the state 450
organizations, of 395
private contractors 453–454
SOFAs 463
state officials 449, 451, 456

Geneva Convention on the Territorial Sea and Contiguous Zone
piracy 37, 40
ships fighting piracy 41–42

gender
awareness training 290, 296–297
children 304, 306–307
crimes 292, 296
CSDP 304
discrimination 77
displacement 285
EU Council 304
EU-led operations 318
Gender Adviser 306
Human Rights Gender Unit 307
ICRC 293
OSCE-UN Instraw Toolkit 295
persecution 286, 289, 291
related issues 6, 280
torture 286
violence 77, 282
violence reporting 297
see also **women**

Geneva Conventions (GCs) of 1949
armed opposition group 251, 253
aut dedere aut iudicare 456
codes of conduct 368–369, 371, 379
combatant status 176, 220–221, 232
direct participation in hostilities 440
EU human rights 312–315
grave breaches 441, 443, 445
legal status of PMSCs in NIACs 247
persons who accompany the armed forces 223, 229–231
POW status 219, 228, 233
power of the adverse party 255
protection of children in armed conflicts 262, 264
self-determination 242
state responsibility 257
universal adherence 328
war crimes 425–429, 432, 446–447
wilful killing 175
women and IHL 287–289, 291, 293

governance
business, and 353
critical areas 101
fragmentation and denationalization 11
global security 26, 36

host state 95
institutional 1
international law 396
PMSCs 3, 12, 93

habitual residence
jurisdiction 484

hiring state
effective control 135, 142
human rights violations 59, 94–95, 110, 137, 152–153, 164–166
immunity 140, 144
jurisdiction 155, 163, 185, 464–465
PMSCs, and 4–6, 55–56
positive human rights obligations 111
  duty to investigate, prosecute and punish 125, 128, 131
  duty to legislate 119, 122–123
  duty to prevent 146
  duty to protect 113, 187–189
  ECHR 117
  IACHR 115
reporting 202
responsibility to protect 106
self-regulation 368
status of PMSC contractors 197
supervision 201

home state
armed intervention 402–403
business 344
contracting state, and 22, 95–96
due diligence 412–413
duty to prevent, investigate and punish 131, 135, 137
duty to protect 186
duty to regulate 410, 413
ECtHR 140
export of armed services 20
foreign policy 22
human rights 93, 153–155, 166–167
judicial remedies 90
licensing 365
Montreux Document 397
neutral 418–419
PMSCs, and 4–5, 18, 56, 96
protection of children 264, 278–279
regulation of PMSCs 26–27
reparation 146
responsibility 66, 98–110, 152
right to life 185
self-regulation 368–369
violation of the *ius ad bellum* 403, 405, 407, 420

host state
business and human rights 354
criminal responsibility 442, 444
CSDP 305, 313
derogation clauses 136
domestic courts 384
duty to legislate 123

duty to prevent, investigate and redress 130–131, 136–147
ECtHR 90, 152–154, 164, 166–169
effective control 95
EU Charter on Fundamental Rights 82
ICC 445
ICCPR 119
immunity 448, 476
  SOFAs 451–453
  internal law and judicial doctrines 455
  from criminal jurisdiction 456–458
  from civil jurisdiction 464
interstate cooperation 108–109
judicial protection 108
lack of institutional capacities 131–132
military occupation 132–133, 135
monitoring 27, 104
PMSCs, and 1, 4–5, 55
positive human rights obligations 111
protection of children 264, 278
PSCAI 365
responsibility to protect 104
self-regulation 368–369
SOFAs 451–455
human rights
arrest and detention 69
business, and 350–360
capture 216
case law
  Application of the Convention on the Prevention and Punishment of the Crime of Genocide 103
  Bankovic and ors v Belgium and ors 134, 156, 158–161
  Behrami and Behrami v France and Saramati v France 87–88
  Erich Stauder v City of Ulm 81
  International Transport Workers' Federation, Finnish Seamen's Union v Viking Line ABP, OÜ Viking Laine Eesti 83
  Internationale Handelsgesellschaft Internationale Handelsgesellschaft mbH v Einfuhr- und Vorratstelle für Getreide und Futtermittel 81
  Kadi and Al Barakaat International Foundation v Council and Commission 394
  Nold v Commission 81
  Rutili v Minister for the Interior 83
children 262–263, 265–266, 271, 273–275, 278
contract 23
CSDP
  human rights law 303–307
  IHL 310–318
customary 301, 395
derogation clauses 136
discrimination 67–68
Drittwirkung 89–90

due diligence 4
duty to legislate, investigate, prosecute and punish 117–120, 122, 124, 142–143
duty to prevent 112–115, 117, 136–137, 139–142
ECJ/ECtHR 83–91, 151–152
EU adjudication 152–159, 161–163
EU regime 80–83, 149–150–151
fight against piracy 51
forcible conditions of work 67
governmental authority 101–102
hiring state 111
home state 4, 96, 98–99, 104–108
host state 4–5, 130–131
IHL, and 5, 258, 299
immunity 168–169, 448, 467–469
international organizations 167–168, 393
lack of institutional capacities 131–132
law 3, 214, 255, 270
massive breach 75
mercenaries, and 325
military occupation 132–135
monitoring bodies 133, 320
obligation to redress 145–147, 260
peoples' rights 74
PMSCs' responsibility 16, 55–60, 64, 192, 382–383, 460
positive obligations 111–112, 153–154, 163–164, 166
privatization of security services 4
proceedings, and 424
promotion 27
regulatory initiatives 97, 343–350, 411
right to life 173–174, 184–185
right to property 73
self-defence 171–172, 179–188
self-executing nature 481
self-regulation 364, 370–372
  hiring contract 367
  activity 368–369
  armed force 369–370
  enforcement 375–378
training 202
use of force 186–187, 189
violations 5, 7, 19, 36, 93–95
vulnerable groups 6
women 77–78, 280–281, 296–297
  IHL 287
  UN 294
human trafficking
PMSCs 284
Human Rights Committee (HRC)
children's rights 76
collective rights 73–74
duty to investigate, prosecute and punish 119, 129
effective control 134–135, 156–157
effective remedy 118, 144–145
espace juridique 159

Human Rights Committee (HRC) (*cont.*)
  human rights 78
  obligation to prevent 137–139
  right to freedom of thought and religion 70
  right to life 61, 112
  right to private life 72
  women's rights 77
humanitarian assistance
  armed protection 209

ICRC Interpretative Guidance on the Notion of Direct Participation in Hostilities
  belligerent nexus 205
  captured personnel 234
  constitutive elements of direct participation in hostilities 204, 216
  defence of military personnel and other military objectives 334
  direct causation 206
  harm 205
  IAC/NIACs 333
  members of armed groups 214
  membership in the armed forces 201, 213
  organized armed group 253
  persons who accompany the armed forces 221–223
  PMSCs' acts 5, 334
  self-defence 210
  specific military operations 226
  use of force in direct attack 214
identity card (GCs)
  POW status 219, 228–229
IMO
  armed guards on board 44
  code of conduct 38, 51
imputability
  home state 99
injured party
  claim 487
  compensation 486, 488
  jurisdiction criteria 473, 477, 482, 484–485, 488–489
  proof of damage 487
innocent transit/passage of escorted vessels
  breach of 48
  territorial sea 47
  warships 48
institutional capacities
  lack of 130–132, 137, 142, 147
  obligation to investigate and prosecute 144
  post-conflict situations 148
insurgents
  armed opposition group 251, 257
  attacks against oil pipelines 208
  control test 391
  high seas 40
  Nisour Square 443
  ONUC 393
  PMSCs' operations against 330

state responsibility 258
status 238
territorial waters 40
third parties 246
UNITA 239
use of force against 18
intelligence
  activities 210–211
  command responsibility 435
  direct participation in hostilities 335
  gathering 93, 153
  governmental authority 101
  high tech 60, 64
  military 66
  on board private ships 39
  outsourcing 15
  privatizing 22
  Sandline 331
  services 1, 15, 19
  superior orders 439
  tactical 216
  US operations in Iraq 335
Inter-American Commission on Human Rights (IAComHR)
  duty to investigate, prosecute and punish 123, 143
  effective control 134, 156–157
  espace juridique 159
Inter-American Court of Human Rights (IACtHR)
  conflict situations 114
  duty to legislate, investigate, prosecute and punish 122–125, 129, 143
  effective control 135
  enforced disappearances 113
  individuals in custody 114
  obligation to prevent 115, 146
  positive obligations 139
  reparation 145
  right to property 73
  state responsibility 58–59, 163
International Covenant on Civil and Political Rights (ICCPR)
  collective rights 74
  effective prosecution 123
  effective remedy 120
  espace juridique 159
  human rights standards 56–57
  positive obligations 112, 117–118, 128, 137
  prohibition of torture 122
  right to health 64
  right to life 61, 122, 173–174, 181
international crime
  ATS 478
  children, and 264, 279
  command responsibility 432–433
  constructive agency 103
  cooperation 109
  damage 478

ICC 455, 462
IHL 269
immunity 450, 456–460, 463
joint liability 474
lack of institutional capacity 131
mercenaries 325
obligation to prevent and repress 414
obligation to prosecute 417
superior orders 437
tort liability 486–487
International Criminal Court (ICC)
  aggression 401
  armed attack 415
  case law
    Germain Katanga and Mathieu Ngudjolo Chui 268
    Lubanga 268
  children 264, 267, 270–272
  command responsibility 433
  complementarity 131, 428
  duress 183
  immunity 454–455, 461–464
  indivudual responsibility 269
  members of an armed group 259
  obligation to investigate and prosecute 132
  private contractors 32, 55, 460
  reparation 259
  self-defence 179–182
  superior orders 437–438
  war crimes 179, 384, 427–430, 445–447
  women 288
international humanitarian law
  armed conflicts 150
  armed forces 248–251, 261, 269
  armed group 269
  armed opposition group 251–253, 255–256, 257–258
  captured contractors 233
  children's rights 262–264, 266, 270–271, 273, 278
  civilians 204
  combat functions 190
  combatant 483
  criminal liability 215, 423–424, 447
    war crimes 424–428, 430, 432
    command responsibility 435–436
    superior orders 438, 440
    prosecution 441, 446
  CSDP 307–310, 313–314
  direct participation hostilities 333–334
  due-diligence obligation 185, 411
  ECtHR 152
  enforcement 32
  EU crisis management 6, 299–307, 318–320
  EU soft-law 314–318
  EU Treaty foundations 310–313
  international organizations 393, 395
  judicial review 468, 479
  lawful killing 174
  legitimate combatants 198–199, 201
  lex specialis 174
  licensing 106
  mercenaries 322, 327–328, 332
  military objectives 214
  NIAC and captured contractors 255
  obligation to prevent, prosecute and punish 16
  persons who accompany the armed forces 218–219, 222, 228
  PMSCs 3, 5, 30, 93–94
  post-conflict situations 220
  responsibility of superiors 186
  right to health 65
  right to life 175–179
  self-defence 5, 172, 179–181, 186, 189, 210
  self-regulation 364, 368, 375–380
  state responsibility 110
  training 137
  use of firearms 171
  use of force 192
  women 280–281, 287, 289–293, 295
international law
  aggression 402
  applicable law 486
  armed conflict 150, 201,209
  armed group 258
  armed opposition group 245, 256
  breach 246
  business and human rights 350
  cause of action 480
  command responsibility 433
  competent jurisdiction 471, 474
  complicity 478
  concurrent causation 146
  direct participation in hostilities 200
  due diligence 409–411, 413
  effective remedy 144
  enlistment of children 267
  EU 35, 84–85, 87, 300, 318
    CSDP 309, 311–314, 316
  forced labour 67
  foreign armed intervention 238, 242
  gender-related violence 280
  governmental authority 190
  home state and hiring state 95, 98
  human rights law 57, 61, 64, 301–302
  immunity 449, 456, 459–460
  inability 131
  institutional responsibility 38–387, 389, 391–392, 395
  ius ad bellum 396, 417–418, 420
  land bases 47
  mercenaries 243, 322, 325–327, 336, 383
  national liberation movements 246
  nationality 96
  obligation to prevent and repress 414
  piracy 37, 39
  PMSCs, and 55, 93–94, 171

international law (cont.)
  political-question doctrine 466, 468
  private 487–489
  regulation of PMSCs 1, 3–4, 7, 19, 23, 26, 30, 33, 108
  reparation 259
  right to life 173
  rights of PMSCs 164
  self-defence 183, 188
  self-regulation, and 367–372, 376
  sexual violence 284, 290, 292
  state responsibility 98–99, 100, 102, 105–106, 152, 161, 165, 397, 400, 404–405, 407–408
  status of contractors 213, 247, 250–251
  subjects of 351
  superior orders 437–438
  torture 481
  use of force 172–173, 179, 235–236, 244, 261, 415–416
  war crimes 425, 441
  women 281, 287
International Peace Operations Association (IPOA)
  account for use of force 370
  Blackwater's withdrawal 360
  compliance procedure 24
  enforcement mechanism 373
  Executive Committee 374
  governmental outsourcing 21
  human rights 368
  IHL 368
  rules of engagement 370
  self-regulation 24–25, 365, 367, 375, 379
  transparency 366
Iraq
  Abu-Ghraib 4, 23, 424, 434
  accountability of contractors 384
  Aegis 25
  armed services 331
  arrest and detention of nationals 157
  ATS 479
  Blackwater 337, 431, 442, 444–445
  blue-to-white fire 18
  command responsibility 435
  contracts 23
  CPA Order No 17 26–27, 445, 454–455, 457, 477
  defensive combat 334
  DoD regulation 202–203
  ECHR extraterritorial application 159–161, 167
  forum non conveniens 482
  Fragmentary Order 09–109 334
  host state's prosecution 444
  human rights standards 354
  human rights violations 138, 151, 133
  IAC/NIAC 326
  immunity 119, 125, 482
  intelligence 335
  interim government 238, 456
  invasion 208, 211, 282
  IPOA 25
  Iran-Iraq war 46
  Iraqi officials 369
  killing of innocent persons 101, 109
  lack of institutional capacities 104, 137
  lethal force 16
  mercenaries 338
  military companies 277
  military occupation 21, 133, 135
  military training 332
  Najaf 207, 334, 423
  Nisour Square incident 27, 141, 265, 376, 380
  objective liability 486
  participation of children in armed conflicts 272
  Party to the conflict 199, 203
  post-traumatic stress disorder 285
  PSCAI 365, 368, 370
  reparation claims 108
  sexual assaults 284
  South-African contractors 28
  superior orders 439–440
  UCMJ 458
  UN personnel 446
  unmanned aerial vehicles 16
  US DoD PMSC personnel 207
  US National Defense Authorization Acts 29
  victims' compensation 128
  war 1, 13–14
iura novit curia
  cause of action 481
ius ad bellum
  case law
    Nicaragua 402–403
  NIACs 5, 235, 237, 260
  state responsibility 396–400, 405–408, 411, 413–420

joint liability
  international crimes (states and individuals) 474
  PMSCs for acts of their employees, of 486, 489
judicial remedies
  EU human rights law 80, 90
  home state 155
jurisdiction
  active/passive nationality 271
  AP I GCs 324
  applicable rules 7, 469
  civil 464–466
  command responsibility 432
  competent 488–489
  criminal 50, 109, 203, 215, 414, 417–418
  defendant's domicile 471–472

due diligence 412–413
EC Regulation 44/2001 472–476
ECJ 81, 84
ECtHR 126, 151, 169–170
exorbitant 477–384
extraterritorial 20, 147
flag state 44
general 472, 489
hiring state 201
home state 98, 104
human rights 95, 105, 186, 271, 350, 353, 371
ICC 32, 55, 264, 270, 445–446, 460–464
immunity 448
  functional 449–451
  internal law and judicial doctrines 454–455, 476–477
  from criminal jurisdiction 455–460
  from civil jurisdiction 464, 466–467
  of organizations 394
international 416
international bodies 150
liability in tort 470
locus commissi delicti 448
MEJA 441
military 29
non-state actors 167–169
personal 479
PMSCs hired by non-state actors 167–168
political-question doctrine 466–467
positive obligation to prevent violations 136, 146, 163–166
Regulation Roma II 484
right to life 173, 184–185
SC Resolutions 244
SOFAs 451–453
specific 472, 479
territorial 26, 85
UN peacekeepers 388
universal 55, 441–442
void of 48–49
war crimes 425, 427, 429, 444
weak states 444
jurisdiction (under human rights conventions)
ACHR 58, 125
case law
  Al-Saadoon and Mufdhi v UK 133–134
  Cyprus v Turkey 135
  Delgado Paez v Colombia 138
ECHR 58, 85–86, 115
ECtHR 85, 154–163
ICCPR 56–57, 112, 118

Kosovo Force (KFOR), NATO
case law
  Behrami 388
ECtHR 87
functional immunity 388

legal status
  armed oppositions groups 251
  auxiliary civilian personnel 319
  captured contractors 233
  case law
    Islamic Republic of Iran Shipping Lines v Turkey 164
    Military and Paramilitary Activities in and against Nicaragua 103
  civilians taking a direct part in hostilities 227
  contractors in NIACs 220, 236, 247
  contractors supporting armed forces 221
  CSDP military operations 313
  PMSCs under IHL 5, 234
  POW 219, 228
  private contractors 2
  Union-led military operations 305
lex fori
  compensation 488
liability in tort
  EC norrms 474
  EC Regulation 44/2001
  EC Regulation Roma II 483
  PMSCs 470
Lieber Code
  IHL codification 219
life (right to)
  ACHR 78, 113–115
  case law
    Pueblo Bello Massacre v Colombia 146
  children 263
  coercive services 59, 113
  common CoC 368
  ECHR 115–117, 126–128
  ECtHR 152–154, 157, 166
  family 71, 158
  HRC 61
  human rights law 61–64, 94, 117–118, 184, 191
  ICCPR 112, 118–119, 122–124
  IHL 173–175, 177, 425
  host state
    obligation to investigate and prosecute 143
    obligation to prevent 136–141
  passengers on a cruise ship 50
  positive obligations of the state 185–188
  private 72–73
  private contractors in armed conflicts 5
  self-defence 61, 171–172, 179, 181–182, 184, 188–189, 191
  state responsibility 258
  see also **self-defence**
Lisbon Treaty
  accession of the EU to the ECHR 167, 302
  fundamental rights 302
  human rights regime 80, 82
  IHL 310–311, 313
  legal personality of the EU 385
  PMSCs' licencing 92

locus commissi delicti
  criminal jurisdiction 425
  effectiveness 476–477
  EU Regulation Rome II 485
  NATO bombing over the Belgrade TV station 151
locus damni
  Lugano Convention 473
  Regulation Rome II 485
logistics
  Blackwater 424
  case law
    Military and Paramilitary Activities in and against Nicaragua 402
  competitive market 21
  duty to assist (host state) 144
  European crisis management 35
  high-risk environment 25
  home state responsibility 102
  Iraq 18
  LOGCAP 439
  outsourcing 14
  sovereign prerogatives 475
  support to armed forces 15, 224
  US military intelligence 210
  US peacekeeping missions 13
  weak states 13
Lubanga case
  active participation in hostilities 208, 268
  enlisting and conscription of children 267
Lugano Convention (1988 and 2007)
  defendant's domicile 471
  harmful event 473
  scope of application 483

market incentives
  consumer demand 21
  home state 96
  international organizations 33
  PMSCs' regulation 12, 20
  unilateral regulation 28
mercenaries
  AP I GCs 324–327
  AP II GCs 322
  armed guards on board 50
  customary law 327–329, 410
  definition of in AP II GCs 322–323
  definition of in customary law 327–329
  direct participation in hostilities 333, 336
  export of military services 106
  IAC 175
  IHL 190, 322–323, 410
  International Convention against the Recruitment, Use, Financing and Training of Mercenaries 324–327, 369
  legal vacuum 31
  membership of the armed forces 338–339
  motivation 336–337
  nationality and residence 337–338

  NIAC 236, 247, 253–254
  ONUC 393
  OUA Convention for the Elimination of Mercenarism in Africa 324–327, 419
  PMSCs' contractors as 2, 5, 14–15–16, 33, 198, 244, 247, 260, 321, 339–340, 369, 382–383
  prohibition of 242–243, 415
  Puntland 49
  recruitment 330–333
  self-determination 243
  Somaliland 49
  South African Foreign Military Assistance Act 28
  state responsibility 396
  treaty law 322, 418
  UN Working Commission on 31
  UN Working Group on the Use of 2, 5, 321, 332, 336–337, 339–340
  UNCHR *Rapporteur* on 31
  UNGA Resolution 3314 (XX) on aggression 106, 402
military crisis-management
  EU in Bosnia and Herzegovina 313
Military Extraterritorial Jurisdiction Act (MEJA)
  federal criminal prosecution 459
  trial of PMSCs' employees 441
military necessity
  act of the state 183
  direct attack 214
  lawful killing 174
  PMSCs' direct participation in hostilities 193
military operation
  acts of violence 206
  armed group 269
  armed opposition group 251
  captured persons accompanying armies 219
  categories 398
  children's rights 276
  civilian casualties 175
  civilian personnel on board 227
  civilians 210
  Croatia 426
  CSDP 310, 313
  direct causation 222
  direct participation in hostilities 226, 333
  DoD Directive 2311.01E 427
  drones attack 211
  enemy's acces to oil 208
  EU 299–300, 305, 307–308, 317–319
  Executive Outcomes 237
  human rights bodies 133
  ICRC Interpretative Guidance 205, 223, 226
  military training 212
  operating weapon systems 212
  peace-enforcement 399
  persons accompanying the armed forces 229
  PMSCs, and 17, 218, 234
  political-question doctrine 467–468

preparatory operations 178
Sandline 237
state agents 158
state responsibility 392
torture, and 431
treshold of harm 224
UN 391
unlawful deprivation of life 62
US 60
use of force 161
military personnel
armed unmanned aerial vehicles 16
BIAs 462–463
command responsibility 434–435
control over 205
CSDP 307–309, 319
DoD Instruction 207, 223
European crisis managment 35
investigation 284
mercenaries 321, 332–333, 335, 337, 339
on board ships 45, 50
PMSC contractors as advisors to 265
privatization 13, 34
provision of violence 22
reduction 220
regulation 19
reporting 297
rescue operations 212
specialization 12
war crimes 432
military training
direct participation in hostilities 212
ESDP/CSDP 304–305
outsourcing 14
PMSC contractors, of 332
women 293
Montreux Document
anti-piracy services 51
armed force 229, 417
attribution of wrongful acts 390
categorization of the relationships between states and PMSCs 396–397
command responsibility 436
contracting out services 191
direct participation in hostilities 335
due diligence 411
guidelines 2
jurisdiction 418
personnel supporting armed forces 221
PMSCs and armed conflict 50
protection of women 293–297
regulatory initiatives 346
signatories 33
soft law 30
state obligations 351
motivation
mercenaries 336
piracy 40
use of force by contractors 187

MPRI
arms trafficking 246
Croatian army 15, 335, 426
Iraq and Afghanistan 331
multinational force
ASPA 455
direct participation in hostilities 334
ICC jurisdiction 446, 461–462
US in Iraq (immunity of) 454

national legislation
abusive use of force 94
criminal responsibility 369
duty to prevent, investigate and punish 294
governmental and non-governmental organizations 164
immunities 476
licensing regime 366
NIACs 427
self-defence 179
third-party claims 7
nationality
children's rights violations, and 265
EU Charter on Fundamental Rights 82
hiring company (of) 167
home state 397, 448
ICCPR 57
ius in bello (application of) 310
jurisdiction 271, 425, 460
mercenaries 322, 337–338
PMSCs (state of) 84, 96
ships 41
special agreements between conflicting parties 145
state of and ICC 463
necessity
compulsory labour 67
functional 451
military 174, 183, 193, 214
self-defence 182–183, 193
Nisour Square
ATS 479
Blackwater 350
children victims 265
CoCs, and 376
criminal prosecution 442–443, 445
duty to prevent 138
IHL and HR violation 380
incident 4, 18
investigation 7, 27, 361, 444
PMSCs' lack of control 202
right to life 141
North Atlantic Treaty Organization (NATO)
accountability 393, 395
Agreement on the Status of 451
Allied Protector and Ocean Shield 39
ASPA 445
bombing over the Belgrade TV station 151
Deputy Supre Allied Commander 375

North Atlantic Treaty Organization (NATO) (*cont.*)
  ECtHR, and 168
  effective control 133
  escorting merchant vessels 46
  hiring PMSCs 157
  IFOR 33
  institutional responsibility 383
  international legal personality 385
  KFOR 388, 454
  SOFAs 451
  use of force 190

objective liability
  employer, of the 486
  IACtHR 59
  investment firms, of 487
  PMSCs, of 487
OECD Guidelines on Multinational Enterprises
  business and human rights 355–356, 360
  due diligence 358
  human rights standards 359
  PMSI 6, 343–344, 352
  state human rights obligations 351
oil
  cargo 37
  gas corporations, and 105, 107
  Ogoni's land 66, 75
  pipelines 208
  platforms 38, 49, 60
  refineries 208
  rigs 39, 49
  Shell Petroleum, National Petroleum Company 63
  tankers 50
ombudsman
  BAPSC 25

Papua New Guinea
  arbitration 405
  Sandline 239, 241, 330, 339
  Special Forces 331
peace-keeping
  ICC jurisdiction 446, 455, 461–462
  injured party 487
  international crimes 474
  international organizations 383–384, 391–393
  Kosovo and Haiti 13
  PMSCs 1, 33
  political control 17
  self-defence 183
  sexual violence 292
  Sharp End International 366
  SOFAs 453, 476
  UN 382
  use of force 397, 399–400, 403
  women 293, 295

piercing the corporate veil 480
piracy
  acts of 38
  crimen iuris gentium 37
  definition 40, 50–51
  escoritng merchant vessels 46–47
  fight against 41–42
  Geneva Convention on the Territorial Sea and the Contiguous Zone 40
  guards on board private ships 39, 43
  high seas 38–39
  land bases 47
  off the coast of Somalia (SC resolutions against) 37, 39, 43–44, 48
  oil rigs and fixed platforms 49
  pirate-hunting 4, 38, 40–42, 45–47
  policing territorial waters 48
  self-defence 42
  UN Convention on the Law of the Sea 40
  vessel protection detachment 45
political-question doctrine
  civilian contractors on the battlefield 467
  dismissal 482
  immunity 443, 454, 466, 482
  state of incorporation 488
  violation of fundamental rights 468
positive obligations
  ACHR 114
  conflict 128
  due diligence 397, 407
  ECHR 85, 126, 158, 162–163, 166
  ECtHR 158
  effective remedy 117
  hiring state 4, 111
  home state 107
  host state 130–133, 135
  human rights 271
  ICCPR 112
  in armed conflicts 185
  military occupation of Iraq 135
  reparation 147
  right to life 184–185
  rights of the children 263
  state responsibility 152–153, 163, 166–167
  states' jurisdiction 147–148
  violation 153
principle of distinction
  combatants/civilians 175, 197–198, 202
Private Military and Security Companies (PMSCs)
  children's rights 262–263
    human rights 363
    ICL 264–265
    IHL 264
    recruiting 266, 269–273
  classifiaction 15
  criminal responsibility 6, 214, 423–424
    command responsibility 432–437
    enforcement 441–445

superior orders 438–440
war crimes 430–432
ECtHR 150–151
  adjudication 154–155, 158, 161–163
  attribution 163–169
  overseeing 151–154
EU
  children's rights 276–278
  crisis management 6, 299–300, 303, 306–307, 314
  discrimination 82–83
  Drittwirkung 90
  ECJ and ECtHR 83–86
  judicial remedies 90–91
hiring state, and 4–5
  duty to legislate, investigate, prosecute and punish 117–119, 122–123, 126–128
  duty to prevent 112–113, 115, 117
home state, and 93–96, 98
  responsibility 98–109
host state, and 120–131
  derogation clauses 136
  lack of institutional capacities 132
  military occupation 135
  obligation to investigate, prosecute and provide reparation 144–147
  obligation to prevent 136–141, 142
international organizations 6, 381–384, 389–394
immunity 7, 448–449, 454, 449, 451, 455, 457–458, 460, 464–467, 469
mercenaries 5, 14, 321–322, 329–332, 334, 336–339
NIACs 5, 235–236
  foreign army intervention 237, 239–245, 247
  legal status 247, 250–255
outsourcing 14, 17
regulation 1, 2, 11, 13, 15, 19–25
  domestic 26–29
  international 29–36
human rights law 3, 5, 16, 55–56
  and business 343–347, 350, 352–355, 359–360
  violations 60–78
IHL 3, 5
  activity 368–370
  enforcement 372, 375–378
  hiring contract 367
  licensing 365–367
self-regulation 6, 362–365, 371–372
piracy
  armed guards on board 43–45
  escorting merchant vessels 47–48
  land bases 47
  maritime domain 39
  oil rigs and fixed platforms 49
  pirate hunting 38, 40–41
  policing territorial waters 49

self-defence 171
state responsibility 396–397
  due diligence 407–413
  ius ad bellum 398, 400, 402–407
  obligation to regulate 414, 416–419
status 5, 197
  combat drones 211
  combatants 198–199, 201–203
  direct paricipation in hostilities 204, 206, 212
  intelligence activities 210
  military objectives 213–214
  protective services 207
use of force 18
tort liability 7, 470–471
  defendant's domicile 471–472
  exorbitant jurisdiction 477–483
  harmful event 473, 475
  immunities 476–477
  non-contractual obligations 484–485
  scope of applicable law 485–488
vulnerable groups 6
  persons who accompany the armed forces 218, 229, 234
  women 280–281
    conflict and post-conflict situations 281–287, 295–297
    IHL 287, 290
    sexual violence 293–294

prisoner of war
camp 198
governmental authority 101
members of the armed forces 99, 249
mercenary 323, 325, 327
NIAC 247, 255
persons who accompany the armed forces 219, 228–234
PMSC members 215
security operations 290
women 288, 293

private actors
case law
  Armed Activities in the Territory of the Congo 185, 257
  Corfu Channel 411–412
  The Social and Economic Rights Action Center and the Center for Economic and Social Rights v Nigeria 63
claims against 465
crimes of 414
human rights 57, 97, 352
ius ad bellum 413, 418
MEJA 459
military and security tasks 3
network of 26
obligation to protect 60
Ogoni, and 75
organs of the state 251
PMSCs 56

private actors *(cont.)*
  PMSCs working for 110
  political-question doctrine 467, 469
  positive obligation to prevent 112, 130
  reparation 145–147
  state responsibility 59
  use of force 415
  violations 141–142, 150
privateering 41
proportionality (principle of)
  attack under IHL 182
  collateral damage 217, 227
  PMSCs' civilian employees 215
  restrictions to the freedom of movement 71
  self-defence 61, 182, 193
Protocol I, Geneva Conventions
  armed forces 248
  armed opposition group 251
  command responsibility 186, 433
  direct participation in hostilities 176–177, 204, 333
  lawful combatant 250
  members of the armed forces 198–199, 201–202
  mercenaries 323–330, 333, 336–339
  persons who accompany the armed forces 220–221
  POW status 231
  prohibition on recruiting mercenaries 243
  recruitment of children 269–270
  self-determination 242
  violence against women 288–290
  war crimes 425
Protocol II, Geneva Conventions
  armed groups 269
  captured contractors 233
  combatant status 177
  direct participation in hostilities 204
  ICC 429
  legal status of PMSCs in NIACs 247–253, 255
  recruitment of children 266, 270
  self-defence 181
  violence against women 289–290
  war crimes 425–427
public demand
  market incentives 20–21, 23
Puntland
  de facto authorities 49
  Hart Security 39
  policing territorial waters 48

recruitment
  armed security services 365
  children 262, 264, 266–267, 269–270–272, 276
  gender issues 292
  mercenaries 244, 260, 326, 329–332, 339
  patterns of 15

PMSCs' personnel, of 296
  women 6
remedies
  Afrimex 358
  case law
    Kadi and Al Barakaat International Foundation v Council and Commission 87
  domestic (exhaustion of) 150
  duty to legislate 118–120
  ECtHR 155
  home countries 27
  home state responsibility 102, 108
  HRC 68
  human rights violations 7, 105, 347–348, 352, 359, 384
  ICCPR 56
  international organizations 393–395
  judicial 80, 90–91
  obligation to protect 60
  women 292, 295
reparation
  AComHPR 141
  armed groups 259–260
  children 263
  host state 130, 144–147
  international organizations 393–394
  judicial protection 108
rescue operations
  direct participation in hostilities 212
residence
  forum actoris 478
  freedom of 68
  lex loci damni 484
  mercenaries 337–339
Revolution in Military Affairs
  high-tech weaponry 12
right to visit on the high seas
  foreign ship 40

Sandline
  military operations 237
  Papua New Guinea 239, 241, 330–331, 339
  SC Resolution 1132 (1997) 245
  Sierra Leone 29, 246
security services
  affected persons 369
  armed 364–365
  civilian companies 286
  conflict situations 208, 330
  displacement of indigenous people 66
  export of 104–105, 109, 155
  fight against terrorism 64
  governmental authority, and 102, 163
  high risk environments 14, 424
  human rights, and 94–95
  international organizations, and 392
  legal responsibility 383

Index

legitimate violence 16
licensing 138, 365
members of the armed forces 269
monitoring procedures 107
non-state entities 58
on board 44
party to a conflict 203
PMSCs 1–4, 15
protective 205, 207
public demand 22
regulation 23
supply 21
self-defence
    active participation in hostilities 334
    armed force 309, 369–370
    carrying of arms 188–189
    case law
        Nicaragua 402
    civilian defence personnel 209
    deprivation of life 61
    firearms 186
    IHL 210
    imminent attack 176
    inherent right of 399
    ius ad bellum 398
    lawful aim 187, 193
    merchant vessels 42–43, 47–48
    personal 5, 172, 179–184, 192–193
    presumption 118
    prohibition of the use of force 190
    protection of high-level individuals 207
    right to life 171, 174, 191
    state responsibility 405, 407
    support for the legitimate government (NIAC) 241
    use of force 176, 400
    see also **use of force**
self-executing treaties
    ATS 480–481
    human rights 481
    rules on jurisditcion 498
self-regulation
    CoC 6, 11–12, 20–21, 23–25, 33, 51, 362–363, 372
    EU 318–319
    sexual offences 296
sending state
    criminal responsibility 442, 444
    immunity 463–464
    jurisdiction 475–477
    SOFAs 451–453
sexual assault
    DoD contractors' training 296
    DoD investigation 284
    DoD reporting 296
    PMSCs' employees harms 285
    PMSCs' women emploees 6, 280
    Sexual Assault Advisory Council 297

UCMJ 294
violence against women 282
sexual harassment
    PMSCs' employees 285
shipping protections
    PMSCs' business 38
Sierra Leone
    children's rights 277
    Executive Outcomes 237, 239, 330, 424, 430, 434, 444
    Revolutionary United Front 246
    Sandline 29, 237
    SC Resolution 1132 (1997) 245
    special agreements 245
    Special Court for 264, 267
Somalia
    Almezaan 44
    EUTM operations 308
    Maersk Alabama 43
    piratical attacks 37–38
    security guard 39
    Somaliland and Puntiland 48
South Africa
    anti-mercenary law 325
    Executive Outcomes 330
    PMSCs 277
spies
    contractors' intelligence activities 210
    protected persons 216
state immunity
    functional immunity 450
state responsibility
    actual knowledge 59
    case law
        Valle Jaramillo 139
    control 5, 6, 79, 84, 142, 389–392, 406–407
    due diligence 407
    ECtHR 85
    home state 98–99, 109
    human rights law 3, 91, 132, 150
    IHL 257, 269
    international organizations, and 387
    mercenaries 325
    prosecution 441
    state agent 62
    victims' protection 58
    violations of *ius ad bellum* 396–398, 403, 413, 416, 419–420
Status of Force(s) Agreements (SOFAs)
    Concordia 313
    EU 305–306, 314, 317, 319
    forum non conveniens 482
    forum shopping 488
    France/Seychelles 45
    hiring/contracting state and host state 458
    ICC Statute, and 463
    immunity from jurisdiction 444, 451, 455, 464, 477

Status of Force(s) Agreements (SOFAs) (*cont.*)
  locus commissi delicti 476
  post-conflict situations 221
  self-executing rules, and 489
  sending state 452
  USA/Afghanistan 453
  USA/Iraq 27, 445, 457
  vessel protection detachment 45
territorial sea
  innocent passage 47
  policing 47–48
territorial state
  armed forces and PMSCs 254
  breach of the law (of) 109
  definition 397
  domestic law 172
  due diligence 411–412
  fight against piracy 47
  forum non conveniens 482
  ICC jurisdiction, and 461–462
  institutional capacity 26–27
  instruction, direction and control 407
  international responsibility 4, 12, 55, 60
  jurisdiction 476–478
  legitimate government (NIAC) 177, 181
  Montreux Document 30, 296–297
  neutral power 419
  obligation to prevent and redress 146, 168
  peacekeeping operations 403
  protection 185–186, 189, 258, 413
  responsibility to protect 105
  right to life 191
  self-defence (NIAC) 180
  self-defence operations 405
  use of force (control over) 20, 79, 172, 181, 187–188
  violations of the *ius ad bellum* 403
torture
  Abu Ghraib 4, 211, 431, 435, 440, 443, 456, 468
  ACtHR 113
  Alien Tort Statute 479, 481
  case law
    Furundžija 415
    Zimbabwean Human Rights NGO Forum v Zimbabwe 62
  children's rights 263–264
  common CoC 368
  counterterrorism 64
  duty to investigate, prosecute and punish 120, 125, 143–144
  duty to legislate 123
  duty to protect 99
  ECHR 115
  ECtHR 126–128, 151
  freedom from 63, 117, 136, 153
  home state responsibility 102
  HRC 118–119, 121–122, 137–138
  human rights violations 55
  ICCPR 112–113, 122
  interstate cooperation 109
  jurisdiction 417
  political-question doctrine 466
  war crimes 425, 428
  women 282, 286, 289, 291–292
Torture Victim Protection Act (TVPA)
  cause of action 481–482
  immunity 465
training
  adequate 6
  Al-Qaeda camps 412
  armed force 369
  armed security contractors in Iraq and Afghanistan 331–332
  armed security services 365
  assistance 243
  children's rights 273, 278
  CoESS/Uni-Europa CoC 366–367
  contract 202
  costs 339
  CSDP missions 320
  direct participation in hostilities 178
  Draft Guidelines on Protection of Civilians in EU-Led Crisis Management Operations 316
  ESDP personnel 318
  ESDP-related training 304–305
  fire-arms 209
  gender-awareness 286, 290, 296, 306
  HRL and IHL 137, 202, 320
  human rights and children 273
  intelligence 210
  International Convention against the Recruitment, Use, Financing and Training of Mercenaries 31, 324, 326, 339, 369
  investigatory and prosecutorial staff 292
  maritime domain 39
  military support 14, 178, 212
  MPRI 15, 335, 426
  OUA Convention for the Elimination of Mercenarism in Africa 324
  political-question doctrine 467
  Russian Criminal Code 329
  Sarajevo CoC 366
  services 1, 15, 19, 60
  sexual assault 296
  Sharp End International 367
  Somaliland and Puntland 48–49
  troops 216
  women 293, 296
transnational advocacy network 27
Treaty on the European Union (TEU)
  children's rights 274
  CSDP 307
  human rights law treaties 302
  IHL 310–313

UN Convention on the Law of the Sea
  armed escorted services 46
  armed guards on board 48
  piracy 37, 40, 41
  ships on government service 42
  training 49
UN Global Compact
  business accountability 356
  CSR 345, 352
  enforcement mechanism 359
  local network 355, 357
UN Security Council
  Afrimex 359
  Chapter VII UN Charter 244
  displacement 285
  ECJ and ECtHR 86, 169
  EU-led crisis managment 316
  functional immunity 453, 455
  ICC jurisdiction 429, 446, 460–462
  intervention 241–242
  KFOR 87
  legitimate authority 238
  maintenance of international peace 399
  non-state actors 245
  peace-enforcement 399
  peacekeeping 183, 399
  piracy 40
  recruitment of children 272
  responsibility of international
    organizations 387–388, 394
  Somali territorial waters 38
  use of force 190
  women 287, 291, 294
Uniform Code of Military Justice (UCMJ)
  court-martial of civilian contractors 203,
    441, 458
  sexual assault 294, 297
uniform law
  criminal law 416
  violations of *ius ad bellum* 413–414, 417,
    419–420
  jurisdiction 418
use of force
  accountability 33
  against civilians 178
  aggression 402–403, 407
  armed opposition groups 245
  control over 16–20, 29, 36
  core state activities 120
  crimes connected to 417–419
  democratic control 2
  direct participation in hostilities 191
  due diligence obligation 408
  ECHR 126
  governmental authority 404
  HRC 137
  IHL 214
  ius ad bellum 235, 370, 397–400

  lawful 187–188
  NIACs 236–237, 260
  outsourcing 173
  PMSC contractors 171–172, 187, 244, 261
  PMSC services 94
  prohibition 6, 413–416
  protection against the threat 184
  right to life 173
  self-defence 176, 180–182, 193
  self-determination 242
  state agents 161
  state monopoly 190, 197
  against children 273

vessel protection detachment
  EU anti-piracy task 46
  innocent transit/passage of escorted merchant
    vessels 47
  practice 44
  WFP 45–46
vetting
  policies 19
  UN-Instraw Report 296
  women 296
**Voluntary Principles on Security and Human
    Rights (VPSHR)**
  CSR 25, 346, 362–363, 371
  defensive services 370
  human rights 379
  law, and 368

war crimes
  Abu-Ghraib 431
  children 264
  command responsibility 434, 436
  duress 184
  enforcement 441
  evidence 442–443
  IAC/NIACs 425
  ICC 384, 427–429, 445
  IHL 179
  immunity 456
  nexus between the crime and the armed
    conflict 431–432
  PMSCs 423, 429–430
  prosecution 215, 297, 446–447
  responsibility of contractors 423, 446–447
  self-defence 180, 193
  sexual violence 291
  state responsibility 295
  superior orders 438
  War Crimes Act 459
  women 288–289
warship
  capture 41
  definition of 41
  escorting merchant vessels 46
  fighting pirates 42–43

warship (*cont.*)
  innocent passage 48
  parent 45
  PMSCs' ships, and 46
  reliance upon 40
  ship on government service 46
  vessel protection detachment 45
welfare services
  persons who accompany the armed forces 218, 223

women
  displacement 285–286
  economic disadvantage 286–287
  health 285
  IHL 281, 287–290
  PMSCs, and 280–281
    employees 6
  racial discrimination 65, 77
  violence against 282–284, 290–297

At the EU level, there is no common regulation of PMSCs and the current code of conduct on the export of weapons does not envisage the export of security services. Yet, given the increasing need for private security services and the expanding field of the EU security and defence policy, the EU Parliament has commissioned a study of the phenomenon[10] with a view to possible regulatory initiatives.

The European Commission, although not directly involved in regulatory initiatives, has recognized the sociopolitical and legal implications of the current outsourcing of military and security tasks to private actors and has provided financial support for study and research on the subject in the context of its 7th Framework Programme. A specific collaborative research project within that Programme was launched in 2008 under the title *Regulating the Privatisation of 'War': The role of the European Union in assuring compliance with international humanitarian law and human rights* (*PRIV-WAR*). This project, carried out with the participation of seven European universities[11] under the general coordination of the European University Institute in Florence, has produced empirical research by collecting data on the state of the security industry throughout the world and by publishing a series of national reports on the domestic legislation on PMSCs in a wide range of relevant countries. At the same time, the project has undertaken a systematic, comprehensive analysis of the role of international law in preventing abuses by private military contractors, in protecting them in situations of armed conflict and in providing a system of accountability of states and private actors in the event of harm caused by such contractors. This book is a product of this research project.

Unlike other books on the subject, the main focus of this volume is the role of international human rights law (HRL) and international humanitarian law (IHL) in the governance of the transnational military and security industry. It examines the applicability *de lege lata* of principles and norms of HRL and IHL to states involved in the provision of private military and security services, to PMSCs and to their employees. Moreover, it addresses questions of state responsibility and of civil and criminal liability of private contractors, and examines issues of access to justice for victims of possible wrongful acts. At the same time, the book provides some policy perspectives, *de lege ferenda*, for improved regulation at the international level.

The volume is divided into five parts. Part I opens with a contribution by Eugenio Cusumano, which explores the nature and sociopolitical implications of the current outsourcing of security tasks and provides a theoretical framework for the analysis of different regulatory options. The chapter concludes with a proposal for a multilayered approach to future regulation. The second chapter, by Natalino Ronzitti, addresses the very timely topic of piracy, and provides an innovative examination of the policy implications of the use of PMSCs in the fight against this renewed plague affecting maritime commerce. The author argues that while

---

[10] See J Bailes and C Holmquist, *The Increasing Role of Private Military and Security Companies* (October 2007).
[11] European University institute (Florence), LUISS 'Guido Carli' (Rome), University of Utrecht, University of Sheffield, Justus Liebig Universitaet (Giessen), Riga Graduate School of Law, Univertsité Panthéon Assas, Centre Thucydide (Paris II).

international law prohibits the arming of private vessels for pirate-hunting, there are no specific prohibitions against the use of security guards for protecting private shipping. Their use should be reconciled with the law of the sea.

Part II examines the human rights dimension of the privatization of military and security services. It opens with a comprehensive survey in Chapter 3, by Federico Lenzerini and Francesco Francioni, of the applicable treaties and customary law, and of the main obligations that derive therefrom, for states involved in the provision or use of private military and security services. The following chapter by Ieva Kalnina and Ugis Zeltins focuses specifically on the role of the EU, especially in light of the Charter of Fundamental Rights and in conjunction with the human rights jurisprudence of the European Court of Human Rights in Strasbourg. More incisive legal analysis follows in the three subsequent chapters focusing on the specific legal obligations of the different states involved in the outsourcing of private military and security services. In Chapter 5, Francesco Francioni addresses the role of the PMSC's 'home state', ie the state where the company was constituted as a legal person or where it has its headquarters or its main place of business. The principal argument developed by the author is that the nature of human rights obligations permits the construction of a general duty of 'due diligence' in the constitution and licensing of the company and of its individual employees, as well as in the licensing of commercial exports of military and security services, as part of the general human rights obligation to prevent and protect against abuses. At the same time, Francioni provides a detailed analysis of the criteria of attribution of a wrongful act to the state, under the general principles of state responsibility, both in the case of private contractors who are integrated in the armed forces of the relevant state and in the (more frequent) case of private contractors who maintain a distinct position from the armed forces.

Chapter 6, by Carsten Hoppe, analyses the human rights obligations of the 'hiring state', ie the state that contractually engages the PMSC for the provision of services, most of the time abroad. The focus of this contribution is on the positive obligations of the hiring state in overseeing what the author calls 'coercive services' by a PMSC. By this expression Hoppe means those services that entail a certain measure of force either in the sense of military force or in connection with activities relating to the running of detention or interrogation centres. To grasp the relevance of this specific focus one need only think of the scandals surrounding the abuses committed by private guards at the Abu Ghraib prison in Iraq, the involvement of private contractors in the practice of secret 'rendition' of suspected terrorists to allow their torture in the receiving country, or the more recent Nisour Square 'incident' in Baghdad where many innocent civilians were killed as a consequence of reckless shooting by private guards escorting a convoy.

In Chapter 7, the issue of human rights obligations is examined by Christine Bakker from the perspective of the 'host state', ie the state in whose territory the private security or military services are performed. Without departing from the basic principle of territorial sovereignty and the international responsibility of the territorial state to ensure that its territory is not used to commit or allow the commission of international wrongful acts, the author cogently argues that the